COLONIALISM IN AFRICA 1870–1960

GENERAL EDITORS

PETER DUIGNAN, *Senior Fellow*
Hoover Institution, Stanford University
L. H. GANN, *Senior Fellow, Hoover Institution*
Stanford University

VOLUME 2

HOOVER INSTITUTION PUBLICATIONS

COLONIALISM IN AFRICA
1870-1960

VOLUME 2
THE HISTORY AND POLITICS OF
COLONIALISM 1914-1960

Edited by

L. H. GANN *and* PETER DUIGNAN

CAMBRIDGE UNIVERSITY PRESS

CAMBRIDGE

LONDON   NEW YORK   NEW ROCHELLE
MELBOURNE   SYDNEY

Published by the Press Syndicate of the University of Cambridge
The Pitt Building, Trumpington Street, Cambridge CB2 IRP
32 East 57th Street, New York, NY 10022, USA
296 Beaconsfield Parade, Middle Park, Melbourne 3206, Australia

First published 1970
First paperback edition 1982

Printed in Great Britain at the
University Press, Cambridge

Library of Congress catalogue card number: 75-77289

British Library Cataloguing in Publication Data

Colonialism in Africa, 1870–1960. –
(Hoover Institution publications)
Vol. 2: The history and politics of colonialism,
1914–1960
1. Africa – Colonization
2. Africa – Politics and government – History
I. Gann, L. H.   II. Duignan, Peter
III. Series
325.6   DT31
ISBN 0 521 07732 X hard covers
ISBN 0 521 28649 2 paperback

CONTENTS

MAPS

TABLES

PREFACE

The first volume of *Colonialism in Africa*, published in 1969 and entitled *The History and Politics of Colonialism, 1870–1914*, was designed to interpret the underlying motivation of what has often been called 'the New Imperialism'. The volume analyses the partition of Africa, along with its consequences, up to the First World War. The present work takes the story forward from the inter-war period to decolonization. Our object in this second volume is the same as that in the first. The literature on Europe's imperial record in Africa is already enormous and continues to proliferate. There is a need to synthesize this material. In addition, a good many new records that merit attention have recently come to light in both European and African archives. Finally, historical perspectives are changing. Today the great majority of Africanists are more interested in the events that took place in Africa itself, in the people on the spot, than in the deliberations of diplomatists and statesmen in Europe.

This volume, like its predecessor, therefore, attempts to strike a balance between the Eurocentric and the Afrocentric approach. Again, we have drawn on experts from several disciplines, representing different schools of thought. The opinions expressed in these essays are therefore the authors' own, and do not necessarily represent those of the editors nor of the Advisory Board. Unavoidably, some gaps remain, partly because of space limitations, partly because the contributors were rightly allowed a good deal of choice.

In putting the second volume together, we have laid more stress on the topical approach than on chronology.

The various contributors deal with subjects as varied as the emerging black élites, the policies of the European powers, the impact of white settlement on selected areas, the military in Africa and decolonization. The majority of our collaborators have, however, approached their respective subjects from a historical point of view, with the result that our project remains essentially a work of history. In a future volume to be entitled *Profiles of change* and to be edited by Professor Victor Turner, emphasis will be placed upon societal aspects of African development.

We have consulted the *Index-gazetteer of the world* of *The Times* of London for the spelling of geographical names. Our guides for linguistic and ethnic terms have been, as in the first volume, Joseph H. Greenberg's *The languages of Africa* and George P. Murdock's *Africa: its peoples and their culture history*. Where authors have expressed special preference for any particular versions, we have tried to respect the writer's wishes. Editorial practices vary a good deal from country to country, and contributors often have a strong preference for their own usage. We have therefore allowed as much freedom as seemed consistent with the standards set by the Cambridge University Press. As editors, we have checked as many facts and bibliographical citations as we could, but we have left to each author the final responsibility for the accuracy of his own statements and citations.

The compilation of the present study has also entailed a good deal of bibliographical work. In fact the relevant literature has now grown to such an extent that we have prepared a separate annex that will supply readers with relevant archival descriptions, citations from finding aids, and selected annotated references, as well as a long list of unclassified entries in various European languages.

We have conformed to the direction of Cambridge University Press in keeping footnotes to the minimum. Footnotes have been provided primarily to supply references to direct quotations used in the text, to cite the main authorities on disputed questions, and to present evidence adduced to substantiate novel or unusual conclusions.

The editors are much indebted for the valuable assistance they have received from the members of the Advisory Board, including Professor P. T. Bauer of the London School of Economics; Professor Gordon A. Craig of Stanford University; and Professor J. D. Fage of Birmingham University, England. Professor Fage especially has given us many detailed suggestions, and has helped us to avoid many errors.

The completion of this book also owes much to the editing of Edna Halperin, to the organizational and administrative skill of Eve Hoffman and Mildred Teruya, and to the various bibliographic checking and typing chores performed by Karen Fung, Liselotte Hofmann and Benedicta Nwaozomudoh Susu.

Once more, we should like to express our gratitude for the kind co-operation extended to us by Dr W. Glenn Campbell, Director of the Hoover Institution, Stanford University. We also owe a great debt to the Relm Foundation of Ann Arbor, Michigan, whose financial generosity has made this project possible.

PETER DUIGNAN, LEWIS H. GANN *General Editors*

INTRODUCTION

During the thirty years between the Berlin Conference and the out-break of World War I, Africa underwent profound and unprecedented changes. Its tribal monarchies, principalities and stateless societies came to be incorporated into the colonies of European powers. By 1914, there were only three sovereign black states in the world; and none of them had much in common with the traditional polities of sub-Saharan Africa. Ethiopia, an Afro-Christian feudal monarchy, had successfully participated in the scramble on her own. Though materially backward, the country had made some initial attempts at modernizing her economy and her government. Liberia, an Afro-American settler oligarchy, main-tained a precarious hold over the 'natives' of the interior, and relied on American support against Anglo-French territorial encroachments. In the New World, Haiti was an object of contempt to both its Anglo-Saxon and its Latin-American neighbours. In fact, Haiti's stormy history was commonly cited as proof of the supposed inability of blacks to rule themselves and as a basis for the evils to be expected from black revolutionary dictatorships. Few challenged European supremacy in Africa itself. Muslim kingdoms such as Morocco or Zanzibar had proved as incapable of preserving their independence as had the 'Black Spartas' founded by Zulu warriors, or the great tribal monarchies set up by peoples like the Ganda and the Lozi.

The colonizers had effectively established their own peace over most of Africa. Slave-trading and slave-raiding had practically disappeared. Islam no longer conquered by the sword. Armed hosts such as those of the Kololo, the Ndebele or the Ngoni could no longer sweep across large parts of the continent. *Völkerwanderungen* by great communities in search of land had ceased; Africa instead had become familiar with labour migration on the part of individual tribesmen anxious to earn cash. All of the once-independent communities of black Africa had been brought, at least nominally, under European control. By 1914 sub-Saharan Africa was divided into something like two dozen colonial territories, all larger than the pre-colonial sovereignties which they had replaced, and capable for the most part of ultimately developing into independent states on a European pattern.

The colonial governments were non-elective. They were also limited

I

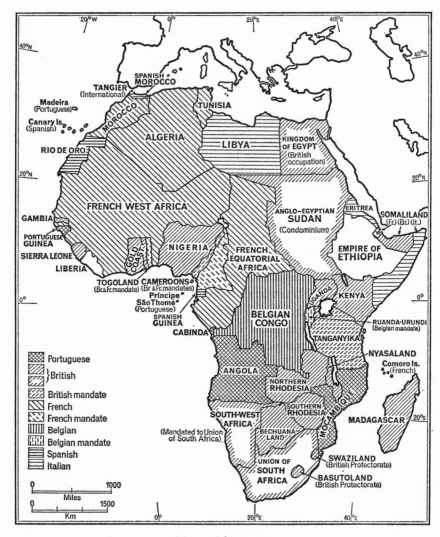

Map 1. Africa, 1919

in their functions. They largely confined their activities to the suppression of tribal warfare and of slave-raiding; in certain instances, they also started to supply transport and a few medical and educational facilities, a difficult task in view of Africa's extreme material backwardness, and the paucity of the resources at the disposal of the colonial governments. The more advanced administrations, such as the British South Africa

Company's government in Southern Rhodesia, were also beginning to shoulder some additional functions. The Southern Rhodesian administration, for instance, had made some progress in enforcing safety regulations in mines, or in insisting on minimum health standards for labour migrants; but even the white workers, by far the most highly privileged segment of the labour force, were not as yet entitled to unemployment pay if they lost their jobs. Southern Rhodesia's first 'Compulsory Education Act' for white children was not passed until 1930, sixty years after the enactment of its prototype in Great Britain.

Humanitarians in the metropolitan countries basically shared the colonizers' underlying attitudes. The most militant radicals were usually perfectly satisfied if the rulers properly carried out their protective functions, if there was no forced labour, if slavery was abolished and oppressive levies were stopped. This attitude is hardly surprising. Most of the colonies were as yet little developed. The colonial powers in Africa were unwilling to pay large-scale subsidies to their possessions.

Governmental services were financed mainly from local revenues, and the colonial governors on the spot lacked the money and the men to provide social services for their subjects. Education and medical help for the indigenous people was therefore left largely—though not entirely—to the private enterprise of the missionary societies with the government providing subsidies. (In 1882, for instance, the Legislative Councils of Sierra Leone, Gambia, the Gold Coast and Lagos had enacted their first Education Ordinances. These provided for the inspection of and the provision of grants to schools. The new departure in time led to a governmental education system.) Educational progress did vary a great deal from region to region. By 1914 the elementary schools in the more favoured parts of Africa had probably reached a level that compared quite well with that existing in a Balkan province such as Bosnia and Herzegovina.[1] A start had also been made in

---

[1] By 1910, Bosnia–Herzegovina, a backward rural region, had an estimated population of 1,900,000. Of this population, only 41,130 children attended elementary schools of a Western type. In addition, there were 64,805 pupils in traditional Muslim schools known as *mektebs* and 7,719 in reformed *mektebs*.

Nyasland, Uganda and Cameroun, to take three colonial examples, had all been placed under European rule after Austria's occupation of Bosnia–Herzegovina in 1878. All three countries had backward economies; indigenous methods of agriculture were a good deal less productive than those obtaining even in a remote Balkan province. Yet by 1910, with an estimated population of just over 1,000,000, Nyasaland had some 25,700 pupils attending elementary schools. In Uganda, the estimated population in 1913 was about 2,900,000, and 32,458 children were attending elementary schools. In

secondary education (first introduced to Sierra Leone in 1845, to Lagos in 1859 and to the Gold Coast in 1876).

African economic development during this period was likewise left mainly—though by no means entirely—to individual entrepreneurs. There were some exceptions. But by and large the most enlightened British administrators in Africa, British businessmen and also anglicized black merchants such as Richard Beale Blaize, a wealthy Sierra Leonian settled in Lagos, would more or less have agreed with Macaulay in holding that governments would

best promote the improvement of the nation by strictly confining themselves to their own legitimate duties, by leaving capital to find its most lucrative course, commodities their fair price...by maintaining peace, by defending property, by diminishing the price of law, and by observing strict economy in every department of state.[1]

Under this policy, only a very small proportion of the capital exported by European investors found its way to tropical Africa. Nevertheless, Africa by 1914 had already experienced a surprisingly large though an extremely uneven degree of development. The present railway system of the continent is largely identical with the network created under colonial auspices before 1914. The economic effects of these lines are of course obvious. Men, merchandise and machinery could move over long distances swiftly and at relatively low cost. Many porters were freed from their labours and released for more productive work. Agricultural goods could be sold; towns could be developed; and men, materials and ideas could spread more readily through the back country. The railways had more intangible consequences, too. Time-scales and distances suddenly contracted. Black villagers and Boer backvelders alike were forced to make mental adjustments unknown to their forebears.

The effects of the railways were enhanced by feeder roads which opened some parts of the interior to wheeled traffic. Cities such as Cape Town, Dakar and Mombasa vastly increased their trade as ocean-going vessels unloaded more goods for shipment by rail inland. South Africa by 1914 had become one of the great mineral producers of the world. European settlers had achieved considerable economic progress

Cameroun, with an estimated population in 1913 of 3,500,000, attendance in the elementary schools was 40,461. As for the number of secondary schools, however, Bosnia–Herzegovina was much better supplied than any African colony.

[1] Thomas Babington, Lord Macaulay, *Critical and historical essays contributed to the Edinburgh Review* (New York, n.d.), p. 121.

in Rhodesia and Kenya. Many black West African communities had gained a firm place for their crops on the world market. Between 1901 and 1914, for instance, the value of cocoa exported from the Gold Coast had increased more than fiftyfold (from £43,000 to £2,194,000), and future progress seemed assured.

From a soldier's point of view, European supremacy in sub-Saharan Africa was maintained with a surprisingly small military outlay. In Northern Rhodesia, for instance, a territory as large as Great Britain, Germany, Denmark, Switzerland and the Low Countries combined, British authority in 1912 rested on just one indifferently equipped African battalion consisting of 750 Africans commanded by nineteen British officers and eight British NCOs. The French kept a much larger number of black soldiers under arms than any other European power, including the supposedly highly militaristic Germans.[1] Even so, the total of African troops scattered throughout the French African Empire numbered no more than 30,742 men. (This was less than the peacetime strength of a small Balkan country such as Serbia, and the black forces of French Africa formed only a very small proportion of the total population.)

Colonial rule was thus upheld in Africa by relatively small forces, supported by metropolitan sea power and, if need be, by the military might of the mother country. The African professional soldier was normally recruited from the so-called warlike tribes, such as the Yao of Nyasaland, who dwelt in a remote mountain country where paid jobs were few, where the people had become habituated to travelling for trade or war, and where many young men looked upon military service as a convenient form of wage employment. The Belgians conscripted some African troops; so did the French, who, from 1912 onward, drafted a limited number of soldiers from West Africa. Unrealistic visionaries such as Colonel Charles Mangin spoke of

---

[1] In 1912 the German colonial forces included 340 white officers and 2,250 white NCOs and men, as well as 3,830 native soldiers. The officers and men were mostly seconded from the home army. The normal strength in South West Africa consisted of, roughly, 150 officers and 2,000 other ranks, all German. The Portuguese colonial forces numbered about 400 officers, drawn mainly from the home army, 3,500 Europeans of other ranks and 9,000 indigenous troops. The armed forces of the Belgian Congo consisted of some 18,000 men commanded by 182 white officers and 259 NCOs. For comparative purposes it might be noted that in 1912, Serbia, with a population of 3,000,000, had a peacetime armed force of 37,000. Its neighbour, Bulgaria, with a population of 4,300,000, kept some 58,000 men under arms in peacetime. And these were much smaller states than the European powers had to control.

recruiting great Negro armies whose prowess would counterbalance Germany's numerical superiority, would make up for the falling French birth-rate and would assure the French military position in a menacing future. In Mangin's view, black soldiers would repay Africa's debt to France by serving under the tricolour. Their exertions would spread throughout the colonies in a more equitable fashion the heavy burden of conscription borne by white Frenchmen; and their training would spread the French language and civilization into the remotest villages of the empire. In fact, however, the enthusiastic slogans such as 'la France: empire de 100 millions d'habitants, les colonies réservoir inépuisable d'hommes', or—to cap them all—'la France de cinq parties du monde', remained nothing but patriotic perorations for after-dinner speeches. The colonizers never succeeded in militarizing their empires, and the colonial forces did not seriously affect the military balance of power of the pre-war world.

Colonial Africa remained largely insulated from the worst disasters of the First World War. The Germans were rightly convinced that the fate of the European empires would be decided on the battlefields of Belgium and northern France. Conscious both of their naval inferiority and of their military weakness in Africa, they would indeed have preferred to neutralize the African colonies altogether. The Western Allies, however, were determined to fight an all-out war. South Africa entered hostilities with the hope of aggrandizing its territory and of eliminating a potential military menace to its security. South African and British troops invaded South West Africa, and the South West African campaign, alone in Africa, was solely a white man's war.

English- and Afrikaans-speaking South Africans, as well as white Rhodesians, now faced a European enemy. This effort involved something like a maximum of 40,000 men employed at any one time. South West Africa was inaccessible because it lacked good harbours and was shut off from the Cape Colony by a difficult belt of waterless country. The result was a foregone conclusion. The open country lent itself to enveloping tactics supported by mechanical transport. The Germans, moreover, could not counter British sea power; and in 1915 the German troops in the country all surrendered.

The Allies attacked Germany's tropical colonies, too. Their object was to deprive enemy raiders of possible bases, to destroy German wireless stations and to seize German territory, either for the purpose of gaining bargaining counters for use during future peace negotiations or to compensate the victors for their wartime losses. Togo, Germany's model colony, was almost undefended and quickly succumbed to Allied attacks in 1914. The Germans put up a much better fight in Cameroun, where they made good use of the difficult terrain, and where their policy had gained them some African friends in the northern part of the territory. Hostilities only ended in 1916, when the last remaining German detachment capitulated to the Allies.

Germany's greatest military feat in Africa, however, was the defence of German East Africa. Here the Allies faced many difficulties because of the great size of the territory, its climatic and topographic obstacles, the often inadequate co-ordination of the Allied multi-national contingents, with their frequently unsatisfactory leadership and staff work. Furthermore, the Allies were pitted against an extraordinarily enterprising and skilful leader, P. von Lettow-Vorbeck. By the end of the war, the Germans had been reduced to 155 European and 1,168 African soldiers. But they continued to fight to the very end, providing an object lesson for the guerrilla potential of well-trained African troops fighting in the bush.

It is difficult to assess the total effect of the war on sub-Saharan Africa. No African community was ever denuded of its manpower to the same extent as were the peoples of Europe. In British Africa, the heaviest blood toll in proportion to the total population was probably borne by the white settlers in Rhodesia and Kenya, who turned out to be excellent fighting men and who gained an unusually high number of commissions.[1] The Europeans in South Africa likewise made a large contribution to the Allied cause; South Africans fought in Europe as well as in German South West and German East Africa. Indeed, twice as many white South Africans put on khaki during World War I as black soldiers from all the British African colonies combined.[2]

[1] In Kenya, the white population totalled something like 3,000. Of these, 1,987 served in the armed forces and 158 lost their lives. In Southern Rhodesia the total white population was 30,000. Of these, 5,577 served in the armed forces, 1,720 received commissions and some 700 lost their lives.

[2] A total of 136,070 white South Africans, of whom 6,928 lost their lives, served in World War I. Some 32,000 Africans from East Africa and Nyasaland served in the King's African Rifles; 24,867 native ranks were recruited into the West African Frontier Force from Nigeria, the Gold Coast, Sierra Leone and Gambia; 6,100 served from the two Rhodesias. In addition the Allies enlisted a large number of African carriers. Their total number is hard to assess. But in East Africa alone, the British conscripted at least 190,000 carriers—possibly even more—for varying periods. Of these, at least 24,000 died in the service.

The French, on the other hand, drew on their black manpower resources to a much greater extent than did any other colonial power; they alone employed black soldiers in Europe on a significant scale.[1] The war brought forth remarkable deeds of bravery on the part of élite troops such as the First Regiment of Senegalese *tirailleurs*. It also bore witness to the apparent solidity of the imperial structure. Admittedly, there was some African, as well as white Afrikaner, resistance to the existing state authorities. Some discontented Boer commandos took up arms in South Africa. A small proto-nationalist insurrection under black clerical leadership broke out in Nyasaland. The Portuguese were forced to crush a great revolt among the Shona-speaking peoples of Portuguese East Africa, who objected to Portuguese maladministration and especially to carrier service in the war against the Germans. The Belgians had minor trouble in the Congo; the French had to cope with unrest among the Saharan Tuareg and other communities. Military service, moreover, was widely resented. Experienced administrators such as Governor-General Clozel thus asserted that the bulk of the indigenous people were profoundly indifferent to the war, that they disliked military service abroad, and that French recruiters all too often had to rely on fear.

Nevertheless, the French, like the British, were able to raise large African forces; they were in a position to denude their colonies of soldiers without fear of revolution. War never seriously challenged the imperial system as a whole. Africans conscripted for military service or for carrier work might curse their fate; but the majority of the black people probably suffered little direct hardship. Prices rose for manufactured goods sold in the stores; but so did prices paid for the peasants' crops. The Gold Coast farmers, for instance, did well out of the war; they understood their dependence on foreign trade and found no reason to rebel. As an official British report put it:

It is generally realized that the existence of the colony, as it is today, depends upon its communications by sea, and this fact, perhaps, more than any other, has brought home to the community their dependence on the crown and their immediate concern in the fortunes of war.[2]

---

[1] Some 215,000 black soldiers enlisted in the French army. Of these, 156,810 were sent outside their respective colonies and 30,000 were killed, nearly all of them in France, in the Near East or in the Gallipoli campaign.

[2] Quoted by Sir Charles Lucas, ed., *The empire at war*, Vol. IV: *Africa* (London, Oxford University Press, n.d.), 25.

European officers, moreover, generally managed to gain the trust and loyalty of the black troops. Lettow-Vorbeck's amazing achievement in East Africa depended on the stamina and fighting spirit of his askaris. British-trained Yao soldiers returned to their villages in Nyasaland proudly displaying their hard-earned decorations and wrote their names and former ranks on signboards outside their huts. Many French-speaking Africans rallied to the tricolour. By an ironic twist of fortune, for instance, all the fourteen sons and grandsons of Samory, the erst-while resistance leader against the French, enlisted in the forces of the Third Republic. Of these, four died in combat and six were wounded or posted missing. Yet, wrote Lieutenant Samory Amadou Touré, 'malgré ces pertes cruelles, nous sommes heureux d'avoir prouvé notre amour pour la France et fiers de compter parmi ses enfants'.[1]

The economic effects of the First World War on Africa may be noted briefly. South African entrepreneurs built many new factories to replace products that could no longer be imported from Great Britain. The First World War thus played an important part in South Africa's industrial revolution. The Germans displayed astonishing ingenuity in building up small-scale *Ersatz* industries in their East African colony, proving thereby that a well-administered European colony, well supplied with technical experts, could stand up to a complete naval blockade.[2] Mineral-producing areas such as Katanga increased their production. In all the more accessible parts of the African continent, white and black farmers alike found more customers for their crops. Admittedly, agricultural countries such as Nigeria, Sierra Leone and Gambia suffered serious initial dislocation as a result of a temporary drop in prices and the feeling of uncertainty induced by the outbreak of war. Between 1915 and 1916, however, prosperity returned to these countries, even though its effects were spread in a very uneven fashion. In Africa, as in Europe, the cost of living rose sharply, and prices of consumer goods, especially of imports, went up.

The hardships of war on the home front were perhaps greatest in backward regions such as north-eastern Rhodesia, where the general

[1] Shelby Cullom Davis, *Reservoirs of men: a history of the black troops of French West Africa* (Chambéry, 1934), pp. 156–7. For additional figures on the African war effort see, for instance: Great Britain, War Office, *Statistics of the military effort of the British empire during the Great War, 1914–1920* (London, 1922); and Lucas, *The empire at war*, Vol. IV: *Africa*.

[2] See, for instance, W. O. Henderson, *Studies in German colonial history* (London, 1962), pp. 87–95.

rise in prices was not compensated for by increased opportunities for earning money. On the contrary, the British impressed large numbers of carriers and thereby artificially deflated wages for this particular form of labour. The war in East Africa and the Cameroun was a war of movement; and since there was little suitable motor transport, the fighting men were forced to depend on porters to transport their supplies. Porters, for their part, needed more porters to carry *their* food, so that even small operations were immensely costly in manpower, and large numbers of carriers lost their lives from sickness or exhaustion.[1] War, on the other hand, helped to mingle people from different tribes and may thereby have served to diminish some existing ethnic prejudice. Africans who before the war had been unaccustomed to wage work became more willing to seek employment. The war certainly helped, therefore, to extend the money economy.

The war frequently brought about subtle changes in the administrative sphere also. A large number of European officials joined the army. A heavy burden was thrown on those European civil servants who stayed behind, and more responsibility was given to the Europeans' African auxiliaries. As Sir Lawrence Wallace, the Administrator of Northern Rhodesia, put it:

the authority of chiefs and headmen had been greatly strengthened, upon them fell much of the onerous work in connexion with the enrolment of the populace for various forms of war work, and, but for their readiness to assist the Administration, such good results could not have been obtained.[2]

War, in other words, may have contributed in an oblique and unintended fashion to the practice of indirect rule which subsequently became part of a rarely challenged political orthodoxy in British colonial Africa.

The war also formed part of the final chapter in the partition of Africa. The Paris peace settlement was the last act of the humanitarian, free-trading ideas that had provided the ideological justification for nineteenth-century colonialism. The German colonies were partitioned between Great Britain, France, Belgium and South Africa. The Allies

[1] For instance, the total of noncombatants raised from Kenya, Uganda, Zanzibar and Nyasaland for the operations against German East Africa numbered 600,000 men, as compared with 34,000 who enlisted in the armed forces. Some 48,000 native noncombatants lost their lives, as compared to 4,500 native soldiers.

[2] Sir Lawrence Wallace, 'Northern Rhodesia and the last phase of the war in Africa', in Lucas, *The empire at war*, Vol. IV: *Africa*, p. 307.

argued that the Germans had betrayed their sacred trust to civilization. (The Allies also had misgivings lest Germany might use her former colonies in the same way as France used hers, as a recruiting ground for black armies in a future war.) On the other hand, the Allies had committed themselves to the ideals of national self-determination; they had declared that they did not aim at the annexation of new territory. Hence, international control seemed the only alternative, for even militant Pan-African nationalists such as Marcus Garvey, a West Indian, had not yet begun to think in terms of setting up independent black republics in backward countries such as Cameroun. Joint administration was condemned as impracticable. Condominiums between different powers had already led to international friction in countries as far afield as Egypt, Samoa and the New Hebrides. The only other course was to charge some European power with the burden of trusteeship.

Individuals had already been appointed as mandatories of the powers. In 1898, for instance, Prince George of Greece had been made governor of Crete under just such an arrangement. Now international trusteeship was, so to speak, nationalized for the benefit of the victorious Western European powers and of South Africa. Germany's tropical colonies were turned into so-called Class B mandates. The mandatory became responsible for the administration and promised to promote the moral and material welfare of the various subject peoples concerned. South West Africa was handed over to South Africa as a Class C mandate, to be administered by the mandatory as an integral part of its own territory, subject to the interests of the indigenous races.

The peacemakers and most of their critics still regarded the moral obligations assumed by the colonial powers in terms of what Germans called the 'Night Watchman's State'. The 'natives' above all were to be protected against abuses. The black parliamentarians, businessmen and intellectuals assembled at a great Pan-African Conference in Paris in 1919 were at one with liberal colonial administrators and negrophilists in the metropolitan countries in calling for safeguards. Africans were not to be deprived of land; forced labour was to be eliminated; blacks should have a bigger say in local and tribal government; they ought to have a chance of ultimately rising to the higher offices of state. The conditions imposed on the mandatory powers differed little from those acceptable to the more progressive colonialists at the time of the Berlin Conference. The Covenant of the League of Nations provided for the prohibition of evils such as the slave-trade, the arms traffic and the commerce in liquor. Africans were to enjoy freedom of conscience and religion, subject only to the maintenance of public order and morality. In addition, the mandatory powers should abstain from building military and naval bases in the mandated territories and from giving military training to Africans, except for police purposes and local defence.

Radical Afro-American thinkers such as W. E. B. Du Bois would have liked to place the Portuguese and Belgian as well as the German colonies under international trusteeship. Du Bois argued, too, that black people should have some say in the disposal of the former German colonies; but no one as yet imagined that the tropical colonies in Africa could conceivably become independent countries within the foreseeable future.

On the face of it, then, the imperial power seemed unshaken; the British, French and Belgian empires in Africa covered a greater area than ever before in history. Patriotic novels of Africa such as *Sanders of the River* found flocks of admirers; untold numbers thronged to Empire Exhibitions; various British government departments made elaborate preparations for settling ex-service men in the Rhodesias and Kenya; some journalists and captains of industry dreamed up elaborate schemes of imperial self-sufficiency. But among intellectuals, imperialism was, on the whole, no longer a fashionable cause. Even the Indian Civil Service, once a plum job for university graduates, was unable to fill all its vacancies. From about the 1920s onward, at least a segment of the British intelligentsia was stricken with a feeling of guilt, not merely with regard to particular aspects of British colonialism but to the British imperial record as a whole. These sentiments commonly went hand in hand with a sense of remorse concerning the Versailles peace settlement and the supposedly unjust treatment meted out to the defeated Germans. There was little enthusiasm in the Allied countries concerning the new territorial responsibilities acquired in Africa in the guise of mandates. The tide of empire began to recede.

In Ireland a widespread rising broke out against the British connexion. For the first time in history a great power, victorious in war and possessed of tremendous industrial and military resources, had become so war-weary that it conceded defeat in 1921 to small partisan formations operating in an isolated island wholly enfolded by British sea power. The Irish rising gained the warm approval of Lenin, and many British conservatives considered the 'Troubles' a milestone on the way to the dissolution of the British Empire. In 1922 the British conceded nominal independence to Egypt. In Southern Africa the British imperial power was unwilling, in 1923, to assume direct responsibility for Southern Rhodesia when the British South Africa Company gave up its administrative responsibilities over the territory. Southern Rhodesia instead became a self-governing colony, and British humanitarians at the time in fact welcomed this step toward imperial devolution.

More significant still perhaps was the Moroccan uprising against the Spaniards and the French. In 1921 the people of the Rif inflicted a crushing defeat on the local Spanish groups, and by 1924 Spaniards had been compelled to abandon all their inland positions. By the end of the year, Abd-el-Krim, the Moroccan leader, became engaged in hostilities against the French, too, and his rebellion was more than just one more tribal affray. The insurgents learned how to use machine-guns and artillery; they manufactured their own hand grenades, combining to some extent modern industrial with more traditional skills. The Rifi forces also contained numerous soldiers with combat experience in the French army. The insurgents became expert at building field telephones, constructing machine-gun posts and camouflaging their positions; and the French were therefore unable to take advantage of their superiority in armour. In a country devoid of towns and factories, bombing from the air had only limited effect against an enemy who could easily reconstruct his simple villages or conceal guns in mountain caves. In the end, the French mobilized a massive force of 160,000 men under Marshal Pétain. New Spanish troops disembarked on the coast; in 1926 Abd-el-Krim, outnumbered and isolated, surrendered. The revolt had failed, but the cost of suppression was high; and to revolutionaries of a subsequent generation, the Irish and Moroccan partisans stood out as pioneers in the techniques of national guerrilla warfare.

Sub-Saharan Africa, on the other hand, experienced no similar outbreaks. Racist philosophers in post-war Germany used to prophesy with anger, not always unmixed with relish, how the French and British-trained black askaris would ultimately wreck Western civilization. The blacks would learn that white men could succumb in battle and white women in bed. Hence, the ex-soldiers would assuredly rise against imperial rule and destroy their white masters. Events did not justify these dire predictions. Contrary to a widespread white stereotype, the black soldiers had never imagined in the first place that white men were gods. Hence the psychological impact of war proved much less severe than had been assumed by armchair philosophers. Most demobilized black soldiers, like their opposite numbers in Europe and America, were usually happy enough to return to civilian life, and the ex-askari rarely gave trouble to the authorities.

There was, however, a good deal of unrest; but none of it was sufficiently important to shake the stability of colonial rule. In Kenya, the Congo and Northern Rhodesia there was much millenarian prophesying. Itinerant preachers called upon the villagers to turn from the white men's ways, and to look to some form of miraculous redemption on earth. But these rural radicals could not set up an effective revolutionary machinery, and rarely looked to seizing power by means of a coup. Militant left-wingers organized a few communist parties; but these remained confined to the geographical periphery of the continent, to South Africa, Algeria and Egypt. None of them was able to acquire a mass membership. The Communist Party of South Africa, set up in 1921 as the first Marxist–Leninist party on the continent, began largely as a white man's party that drew most of its support from English and Jewish intellectuals. The communists were unable to acquire a mass following among the black proletariat. They were equally ineffective in gaining the loyalty of the white South African miners, the only working-class group which ever managed to stage a large-scale armed urban rising in South Africa. The whites protested against the employment of black workers in certain 'European' jobs. In 1922, the Johannesburg miners took to arms, ironically calling upon the workers of the world to unite for a white South Africa; but the rising was smashed, and the European miners in time became part of the white establishment.

After the war, Africans created a fairly extensive network of secular political organizations, many of which combined the functions of social clubs, trade unions, protest organizations and proto-political parties. These bodies ranged from welfare societies, set up on the Northern Rhodesian Copperbelt, to the Industrial and Commercial Workers' Union of Africa (ICW), a large but poorly organized black South African association. None of these bodies, however, had any revolutionary potential; and the colonial powers continued to control their possessions with very modest and relatively inexpensive administrative, military and police establishments.

The present volume does not concern itself specifically with economics and economic history—this field is so important as to merit a volume of its own in this series. Suffice it to say at this point that economic development during the inter-war period proceeded at a very uneven pace. The countries of Africa were hit hard by the recession that followed upon the reconstruction boom after the end of hostilities. The African raw material producers again suffered heavily from the Great Slump. Development moreover, was very uneven in its impact. Katanga, with its huge copper deposits, expanded its wealth at an immensely more rapid pace than the rest of the Belgian Congo. Some colonies, such as Moçambique, advanced very little, despite the efforts of men like General Norton de Matos, who in his capacity as High Commissioner initiated numerous projects during the early 1920s. The colony was unable to pay for Norton de Matos's schemes from its exports, and loans from Portugal or abroad were insufficient to cover the expenditure involved. It was only during the Second World War that Angola, having built up considerable budget surpluses during the Salazar régime, was able to benefit from the world-wide shortage of colonial products and entered into a period of modest prosperity.

Nevertheless, during the inter-war period a large portion of colonial Africa did make substantial and, in certain cases, spectacular advances, as shown by the appended trade figures.[1] Nothing would be more

[1] The following trade figures give some indication of the growth of foreign trade in selected parts of Africa.

(In pounds sterling)

Gold Coast	1913	1938–9
Imports	4,952,494	10,626,284
Exports	5,427,106	16,235,288
Nigeria	1913	1938
Imports	7,201,819	11,567,104
Exports	7,352,377	14,390,700
Kenya	1913–14	1938
Imports	2,147,937	8,004,690
Exports	1,482,876	8,504,650
Tanganyika	1913	1939
Imports	2,667,925	3,039,673
Exports	1,777,552	4,585,658
Northern Rhodesia	1919	1939
Imports	434,354	4,521,082
Exports	454,366	10,220,182
Southern Rhodesia	1910	1939
Imports	2,786,321	9,054,359
Exports	3,199,956	10,168,152

[*Table continued at foot of p. 16*]

mistaken than to view the quarter of a century that elapsed between the outbreak of the First and the Second World Wars as a period of economic neglect and social stagnation for tropical Africa as a whole. In many regions, it was indeed the very speed of development which helped to create so many problems, and which helped also to make both the rulers and the ruled aware of the deficiencies that beset the colonial régimes.

The facts concerning progress in terms of brick and mortar, of tonnages exported, of roads built, of people educated are beyond dispute. New cities appeared on the map. In 1928, for instance, the British opened to maritime traffic the new port of Takoradi on the Gold Coast; in 1935, Lusaka became the new capital of Northern Rhodesia. Aircraft began to be used in Africa for commercial purposes. Cars and motor trucks helped to make many of the continent's more remote areas accessible to commerce and at the same time put an end to the African porters' backbreaking labours. The mineral exports of the Belgian Congo and Northern Rhodesia developed in a dramatic fashion. The trade of Senegal, Kenya and Southern Rhodesia multiplied several times over. The Gold Coast exports of cocoa, gold and other produce grew by leaps and bounds. Detailed commercial statistics speak an eloquent language. In 1899, for instance, the entire cocoa exports of the colony had been valued at no more than £16,000. A quarter of a century later, in 1926, they stood at £9,181,000. There was a rapid growth of Africa's total foreign trade. Some of its benefits percolated down even to the more remote villages in the shape of new consumption goods such as tea, coffee, sugar, salt and matches; new means of transport such as wagons and bicycles; and new forms of capital investment such as cattle dips, ploughs, water pumps or even sewing machines.

The elimination of local wars, the imposition of the European *pax* combined with economic development to create new opportunities of

	(In francs)	
French Equatorial Africa	1913	1936
Imports	21,182,000	178,419,950
Exports	36,865,000	161,761,251
French West Africa	1912	1936
Imports	134,781,892	968,112,000
Exports	118,567,231	978,431,000
Belgian Congo	1912	1938
Imports	61,864,000	1,022,639,930
Exports	83,465,000	1,897,153,811

production for profit. In parts of Africa, land acquired commercial value for those who owned it or who wished to become landowners. The pace of change varied enormously from region to region; all we can do at this point is to refer to a micro-study in a brilliant survey of African problems made during the early 1940s by Sir Keith Hancock.[1] Hancock used the observations made by a British agricultural officer to illustrate African rural development at what was then perhaps its most advanced point. In the 1930s the village of Akokoaso on the Gold Coast comprised some 1,181 inhabitants occupying village lands covering an area of some 38 square miles. The village had 267 independent and 87 dependent farmers whose main crop was cocoa. Some cultivators did other things besides farm work—they hunted, tapped palm-wine, engaged in carpentry, shoemaking and other crafts. Some had abandoned agriculture altogether. According to the figures supplied to Hancock, the little village by the late 1930s already held sixty-six persons whose entire income derived from trade, from a craft or a profession. Participation in the world's business had brought to the people a great increase in wealth. Akokoasoans indeed enjoyed a higher standard of living than most other folk in rural Africa; in fact, their living standards compared favourably with those of many Indian peasants. Hancock surmised that the people of Akokoaso might be better off than the average villager in some parts of eastern Europe.

The village of Akokoaso represented one side of the spectrum. A contemporary observer in the 1930s would have found much less progress in, say, an isolated Lenje or Ila community in Northern Rhodesia. Nevertheless, sub-Saharan Africa as a whole had made impressive advances over the previous generation. Developments in farming and mining, combined with advances in education and health services, had given employment to Africans in many professions unknown to pre-colonial Africa. In order to rule, the colonial powers required black clerks, telegraphists, court interpreters, school-teachers and detectives. An expanding economy could no longer make do with unskilled workmen; there was a need also for foremen in mining and construction jobs, for painters, carpenters and bricklayers. Many Africans became producers of cash crops such as cocoa, cotton, maize and coffee. In addition, some black people began to enter trade. The 'new men'

[1] Sir William Keith Hancock, *Survey of British Commonwealth affairs*, Vol. 2: *Problems of economic policy 1918–1939, Part 2* (London, Oxford University Press, 1942), pp. 273 ff.

played a major role also in the emergent political organizations of Africa, a role that has been emphasized by most of our contributors.

The Second World War put an end to both Germany's dreams of a colonial comeback and to Italy's hopes for enlarging her African empire. Instead Italy became the second great European power to be stripped of its African possessions. British, Indian, white South African and Rhodesian troops, as well as Sudanese, King's African Rifles and soldiers from the Royal West African Frontier Force, invaded Italy's East African possessions. By July 1941 the last Italian forces surrendered in Ethiopia. A great Italian army, composed of some 125,000 white and 200,000 black troops (largely unwilling conscripts) ceased to exist. The British gained a victory which for the speed of operations, the quality of staff work, the leaders' ability to master mechanized warfare, to cover great distances of inhospitable mountain country, to outmanoeuvre a numerically superior enemy, and for skilful co-operation between land and air forces, stood out perhaps as the most remarkable feat in the history of warfare in Africa. The Italian generals, for their part, were obsessed with a fortress psychology, with the perils posed by a recalcitrant native population and by indigenous partisans; and they consistently overestimated British strength. Ethiopia resumed its legal independence after five years of Italian rule. For a brief period the British Empire once more firmly controlled the entire Cape-to-Cairo route that Rhodes had once coveted.

The British Empire thus became the main user of African military manpower, both white and black. White South African and Rhodesian troops fought with distinction in North Africa and in Italy. Black soldiers from East, West and Central Africa upheld their reputation as fighting men in places as far afield as Somaliland and Burma. Fortunately, the casualties suffered by Africans in the Second World War remained much smaller than those sustained between 1914 and 1918. The development of motor transport rendered unnecessary the mass recruitment of carriers and put a stop to the suffering which the porters used to endure. Africans were, however, forced to work on military defence installations and were forced to grow certain crops. The speedy collapse of France prevented large numbers of Franco-African troops from fighting at the front; there was none of the slaughter that had decimated Senegalese ranks in the First World War. A large proportion of black soldiers in Italian employ deserted in preference to becoming prisoners of war. Even the British-African and South African losses remained much smaller than those sustained in the First World War. Hence, for the most part, the peoples of Africa were shielded from the bloodshed borne by the various European nations during the Second World War.[1]

World War II, like the First World War, occasioned many economic hardships, however. The Allied colonies could no longer trade with the German-occupied parts of Europe nor with the regions under the sway of Imperial Japan. Submarines and surface raiders destroyed great numbers of Allied merchantmen; the great industrial powers of the world turned most of their energies to making implements of war. Hence consumer goods became expensive; capital goods were hard to obtain; prices rose. Money kept losing its value. Plant and equipment in French Africa wore down. War, on the other hand, created a great demand for African raw materials, so that even backward colonies like Angola and Moçambique benefited greatly. In Southern Africa, more-over, manufacturing industries expanded at a dramatic pace. Southern Rhodesia, for instance, created an iron and steel industry of its own. Between 1938 and 1946 the colony's gross industrial output increased more than threefold, and the country succeeded in maintaining this momentum in the post-war years. South African enterprises developed at an equally astonishing rate, so that the Union of South Africa developed into the industrial giant of the continent.[2]

At first sight the immediate political effects of this transformation may appear negligible. The British looked upon Africa as a vital strategic bastion and were only inclined to make limited changes while the war was in progress. In 1942, for instance, Governor Sir Alan Burns appointed two Africans to his Executive Council. Burns's decision marked a new constitutional chapter in the colony, but Burns's policy derived from wartime needs and was not intended to initiate the devolution of government to Africans.

The British, of course, also had to meet other challenges. In 1944,

[1] By May 1945, the total number of Africans serving in the regular British military units, combatants as well as ancillary, amounted to about 374,000. British soldiers from all colonies (excluding India and the Dominions) totalled 473,000. South Africa mobilized something like 200,000 white soldiers. Southern Rhodesia raised about 10,000 whites and 14,000 Africans and 76,000 black soldiers in auxiliary services. South Africa lost 8,681 men. The combined losses of the British colonies totalled 21,085.

[2] The gross industrial production of Southern Rhodesia increased from £5,107,000 in 1938 to £17,264,000 in 1946 to £31,316,00 in 1949. The industrial boom continued to the end of the 1950s. The gross value of South Africa's industrial production rose from $559,000,000 to $1,050,000,000 in 1945 and to $2,169,000,000 in 1950.

for instance, Dr Nnamdi Azikiwe joined with some of Nigeria's older leaders to form the country's first modern party, the National Council of Nigeria and the Cameroons (NCNC). But neither the NCNC nor similar bodies were able or willing to make serious trouble for their imperial overlords who, in any case, would not have had the slightest compunction about crushing any attempts to interfere with the conduct of the war. France and Belgium rapidly collapsed before the German onslaught. But even the sudden defeat of these European powers did not lead to corresponding colonial *débâcles*. There were no serious black uprisings in Francophone Africa, and for the time being the colonizers' position seemed secure. In southern Africa, the military planners were so confident about the military position that they practically denuded their respective countries of the best available white troops. (Southern Rhodesia especially made an extraordinary effort in relation to its resources. The colony again mobilized something like fifteen per cent of its white population; about ten per cent of the European population served abroad.)

By the same token, neither South Africa nor Southern Rhodesia was as yet much exposed to the pressure of international humanitarian opinion. The British were grateful to the Smuts government for bringing South Africa into the war, for keeping isolationist or pro-German Afrikaner nationalists out of power, and for making a valuable military contribution to the Allied cause. South Africa commanded the vital Cape route, one of Britain's strategic lifelines, at a time when the Mediterranean was closed to Allied shipping. South Africa's gold resources were of great value to the financial strength of the British Commonwealth; South Africa even acquired increasing importance as an exporter of industrial goods and as a maker of weapons. Southern Rhodesia likewise had a relatively strong bargaining position within the Central African context. Northern Rhodesia became increasingly dependent on its southern neighbour for manufactured goods, for coal and for railway facilities. The Colonial Office successfully resisted the settlers' demand for the amalgamation of the two Rhodesias. In 1941 British Imperial authorities did, however, agree in their own immediate interest to setting up a permanent secretariat at Salisbury to co-ordinate the war effort of the two Rhodesias and Nyasaland. This administrative arrangement was perhaps the first step towards the formation of the ill-fated Central African Federation twelve years later. Many South African whites had even greater ambitions; white politicians began to speak in terms of 'Pan-African' solutions, by which they meant the creation of a white-ruled bloc from the Cape to Kenya.

War likewise contributed to the decentralization of power in Francophone Africa. The Belgian Congo was cut off from the motherland. French Africa became divided in its political allegiance. When the Third Republic went down in military defeat, the French overseas possessions were left temporarily stranded. The Vichy régime, however, lost no time in asserting its power and soon controlled the bulk of the French empire. But a few centres of resistance remained. In Chad Governor Felix Eboué, a black West Indian, decided to back the cause of Free France. In the French Cameroun, the majority of the local French residents and the black élite found submission to Vichy equally distasteful. Capitulation might entail the eventual return of the territory to the German Reich, a prospect as unacceptable to white Frenchmen as to black évolués. With Gabon likewise declaring for Free France, De Gaulle acquired a firm territorial base; and the liberation of France began in Brazzaville, Africa, in 1944. The Gaullists as yet were firmly determined to maintain the French Empire in its full integrity. They were, however, willing to make various social reforms, and as a matter of imperial policy they also accepted a greater degree of administrative decentralization. Most Africans were sympathetic to the Free French and to De Gaulle, but the war did accelerate African political awareness and forced changes in the colonial relationship with France.

As one of our contributors in this volume points out, war also occasioned further social change. Admittedly, the immediate extent of such change should not be overestimated. In the Second as in the First World War, the bulk of black soldiers still served in the ranks as infantrymen. In battle as in industry, the more skilled forms of labour, such as flying aircraft, driving tanks, operating radar equipment, continued to be carried out by better educated and more highly qualified Europeans. The Allies likewise made no attempt to Africanize the officer corps of their colonial forces. Black intellectuals had neither inclination nor incentives to join the army; hence the politically conscious élite remained profoundly civilian in its outlook on life. But even ordinary peasants in uniform now had to handle more complicated weapons than had their predecessors in the First World War. The askaris became proficient in using bazookas, light mortars and Bren guns, as well as rifles. Many also learned new civilian skills as clerks or as truck drivers, and thereby advanced into semi-skilled military occupations. In addition, black soldiers travelled widely, to India, Burma, Palestine and other countries from which they often returned with new ideas and a broader outlook.

In many different ways war affected the African home front as well. In Northern Rhodesia, for instance, the colonial authorities in 1941 set up Lusaka Broadcasting Station to spread news, propaganda, and agricultural and other forms of instruction. Later on, the British even promoted the sale of 'Saucepan Specials', cheap battery-powered radios for Africans. These could be switched on in villages where there were no electrical mains; at a switch of the knob the Saucepan Specials brought the world to the kraal, helping thereby to diminish the sense of rural isolation. Radio stations also broadcast new forms of African music that blended traditional African components with white elements derived from church music and military bands, as well as with Afro-American jazz. In addition, Western machine-made instruments such as the guitar became increasingly popular; so did film shows, especially American cowboy movies. From all this we can see that war and its aftermath occasioned far-reaching changes in popular taste. This important chapter in Africa's cultural history still awaits its historian.

Above all, war in some ways often strengthened the emergent African élites. African cash farmers usually made more money than before. An increasing number of African workmen moved into semi-skilled or even skilled industrial occupations. The emergent administrative bourgeoisie, including government clerks, court interpreters, head messengers and agricultural demonstrators, swelled in numbers. In addition, as large numbers of white civil servants donned uniforms and replacements from home were scarce, the influence of African civil servants who were called upon to relieve the overburdened European officials greatly expanded.

World War II had other significant effects on black Africa, among them an increase in government controls and a power-shift away from Western Europe. Governments stepped in to control trade and to allocate foreign currency. Traders were forced to work through government agencies, which officially determined prices of goods both for export and for the domestic market. Elaborate systems of licensing developed. The British and French also established marketing boards with the sole right to purchase for export the crops under their control, including all the major agricultural exports of British West Africa. These wartime restrictions and boards were not eliminated after the war, but remained as a fateful heritage to African states and to their *étatiste* tradition in economic affairs.

Western Europe was overrun. Part of its empire was neutralized, isolated or even occupied. The USSR and the United States emerged as the world's two great powers, both professing strong anti-colonial and pro-nationalist sentiments. World War II did not in any sense create African nationalism. Global conflict did, however, sharply accelerate existing trends. The new African élites acquired more economic power. They also drew courage from wartime ideals, from wartime documents such as the Atlantic Charter, and from the principles put forward by the founders of the United Nations. Imperialists of the old-fashioned variety became increasingly defensive in their outlook; the colonial powers themselves became convinced that vast changes had become inevitable, and that the rulers themselves should speed up progress. In 1947, for instance, the British Labour government gave the *coup de grâce* to earlier Indirect Rule doctrines by calling for an efficient and democratic system of local government in the colonies. The Labour government also promoted constitutional reforms; the formation of African trade unions and co-operative societies was encouraged. This transformation coincided with a lengthy period of post-war prosperity; some countries indeed developed at a phenomenal rate rarely paralleled in the history of the world. (For instance, during the eight years that elapsed between 1954 and 1961 the gross national product of Northern Rhodesia, Southern Rhodesia and Nyasaland between them rose from £338·3 million to £546·8 million.) Some of these changes benefited educated Africans who stepped into new positions of power.

The complex and often ambiguous roles played by the élites, as well as the changing nature of imperial governance, form one of the main unifying themes in this necessarily somewhat heterogeneous volume. In selecting the contributors, we have drawn from a wide spectrum of opinion, as well as from several disciplines. Hence we find that our collaborators sometimes express divergent views. The editors likewise are not necessarily in accord with all the opinions expressed in this volume. For instance, we should have been inclined to put particular stress on the double-edged nature of the policies pursued in the past by many Westernized black élites. Even by the closing years of the eighteenth century, Sierra Leone had witnessed an early form of revolutionary Africanism on the part of black American veterans settled in the country. But the majority of educated Africans in the eighteenth and nineteenth centuries were convinced advocates of French or of British rule. James Africanus Horton, for example, an educated black African, was the first black commissioned officer in the British Army and a loyal subject of the Queen, as well as a critic of British colonial practices. Historians of African nationalism thus would do well to remember the warning given by E. J. Hobsbawm, a British Marxist, that

Nationalist mythology has often obscured this divorce [between the emergent colonial middle classes and the new intelligentsia on the one hand, and the masses on the other], partly by suppressing the link between colonialism and the early native middle classes, partly by lending to earlier anti-foreign resistance the colours of a later nationalist movement. But in Asia, in the Islamic countries, and even more in Africa, the junction between the *évolués* and nationalism, and between both and the masses, was not made until the twentieth century.[1]

The rupture between the imperialists and the élite occurred at different times and at different stages in the present century. The sense of alienation experienced by so many educated Africans forms one of the main themes of modern African history. The reaction against imperialism should not, however, be predated in an anachronistic fashion. For instance, the Second Pan-African Congress held at Paris in 1919 was still essentially reformist in character. The black participants were as yet demanding no more than an advanced form of European trusteeship for the African colonies rather than freedom now. The decisive break only came later. In this respect the Fifth Pan-African Congress held at Manchester, England, in 1945, was indeed an ideological landmark. That Congress rejected colonialism in all its forms. The participants equated economic with political imperialism, and determined to crush both forms of alleged exploitation alike and to achieve independence.

Many modern African writers strongly uphold this Pan-African tradition. Independence, in their view, has not made it easier for Africans to break the fetters of alien economic control; the African countries remain suppliers of raw materials for the industrialized countries of Europe; their dependence on foreigners persists. The editors see these problems in a different light. The new states, in our opinion, would certainly be at an even greater disadvantage if Western capitalists refused

[1] E. J. Hobsbawm, *The age of revolution, 1789–1848* (Cleveland and New York, 1962), p. 144.

to invest their money abroad. In any case, we do not see the position of the newly independent countries as in any way unique. Throughout the nineteenth century the United States relied to a large extent on British and on other European sources for capital investment. The United States, as well as Canada, Australia and South Africa, started off as raw material producers before embarking on a successful programme of industrialization. Indeed, an exporter of raw material in our view is not necessarily in a greater state of economic dependence than a manufacturing state.

We should be inclined also to place more stress than do some of our contributors on the complexities and internal contradictions of settler society, and on the resultant ambiguities in the European outlook toward African interests. In Northern Rhodesia, for instance, the various white groups were always ready enough to defend their own immediate economic interests; but farmers, miners and merchants often differed on the question of which white interests should predominate. White politicians, on the other hand, were willing to advocate reforms that would not injure their own constituents. During the 1930s, for example, the European Elected Members in the Legislative Council steadfastly called on the colonial government to improve the African reserves by the construction of dips, dams and boreholes. Many argued that Africans were grossly overtaxed and that Lusaka's fiscal policy was unsound. There was also some concern with such civil liberties as did not appear to harm the whites. During the course of African riots on the Northern Rhodesian Copperbelt, for example, the settler-oriented *Livingstone Mail* denounced the government for what its editor considered a detestable 'might is right' philosophy. Later on, during the 1940s, the whites rightly showed that African as well as European workers had benefited from workmen's compensation laws, from health and safety measures that had been placed on the statute book at the white Elected Members' initiative. Likewise, the white Elected Members' willingness to grant funds for African development purposes was frequently acknowledged by government officials. This is not to say that Northern Rhodesian whites were more intelligent and unselfish than any other aspiring ruling class. Neither do these comments suggest that the long-term political interests of the black élites and the settlers coincided, except on certain limited issues such as the royalties paid by the mining companies for the British South Africa Company's mineral rights or the desirability of British financial grants for Northern Rhodesia. We do, however, consider that the relationship between the various local lobbies, black and white, was far more complex than the customary accounts suggest.

The present work does not purport to be the definitive history of colonialism. Hence the editors call attention to certain subjects that require further investigation. The history of the Europeans' contributions to the research into Africa's past remains to be written. Many critics of colonialism have asserted that whites were ethnocentric, that they tended towards self-praise, and that they neglected to study the history and social institutions of traditional Africa. Europeans are accused also of destroying all sense of continuity between the old Africa and the new. In our view, this interpretation is no more justified than the view which holds that Africa between the two world wars was plunged into a morass of economic and social stagnation.

True enough, a great deal of nineteenth- and early twentieth-century writing concerning the African 'natives' was full of generalizations concerning childish savages who would respond only to rule by the mailed fist, who treated their women only as objects of lust and as beasts of burden, and who were devoid of the higher intellectual qualities. Such outbursts sometimes had a racist inspiration. But this was not necessarily so. British historians with the academic reputation of J. A. Froude wrote about Irishmen in terms far more offensive than those later used by Sir Harry Johnston in describing the Bantu of Nyasaland. There was, likewise, a certain stamp of nineteenth-century British traveller who, on returning to his native shores, would regale his audience with the most extraordinary tales concerning the lewd and lazy ways of foreigners. Ethnocentric Britons of this stamp had their opposite numbers in France, in Germany and elsewhere; their outpourings were not essentially different, for example, from the most uncomplimentary accounts sent home by European expatriates concerning the ways of indigenous people in the tropics.[1]

It is true also that a good deal of even the best in European and American scholarship for long remained somewhat provincial in its approach to world problems. But again these parochial predilections did not—as it is now sometimes asserted—necessarily spring from colour prejudice or from colonialist traditions. It was not until the

---

[1] See, for example, James Anthony Froude, *The English in Ireland in the eighteenth century* (New York, 1888), Vol. I; or Henry Mayhew, *The upper Rhine: the scenery of its banks and the manner of its people* (London, 1858), pp. 236, 256, 327, 330–1.

present century that Slavonic studies, to mention only one example, became 'respectable' as an academic discipline in Great Britain. The School of Slavonic and East European Studies was founded as a department of King's College, University of London, in 1915, and not until 1932 was it recognized as a 'Central Activity of the University'. (By comparison, the School of Oriental and African Studies at London University was approved in principle during the years 1908 to 1911; it actually began to operate in 1917.)

But when all is said and done, the European colonizers were the only empire-builders in Africa to take an enlightened and scholarly interest in the history and culture of their subjects. In this respect, the Western invaders were totally unlike any earlier conquerors in Africa. To Western—above all British, French and German—scholarship belongs the credit of pioneering the social sciences in Africa and of re-creating the African past. Missionaries, government officials and academics all had a major share in this cultural endeavour; and the inter-war years were a period of crucial importance in this chapter of Western intellectual history. Anthropologists re-evaluated the social institutions of tribal peoples by means of inquiries based on prolonged periods of field work. Historians and archaeologists such as Gertrude Caton-Thompson (who proved conclusively the Bantu origins of the ancient Zimbabwe culture in Southern Rhodesia) re-evaluated African history.

Specialists also founded a great many new institutions devoted to the study of Africa. In 1925, for instance, Leo Frobenius, a distinguished German cultural historian and African traveller, took over both the Chair in Ethnography and the direction of the Institut für Kulturmorphologie at Frankfurt. In 1926 the International African Institute was established in London. In 1938 the French set up in Dakar the Institut Français d'Afrique Noire (IFAN). The inter-war period also saw a great deal of fruitful research in fields as varied as African geography, tropical disease, African archaeology, agriculture, human ecology and related subjects. Many learned journals were started in Africa, and works about African societies and customs appeared regularly in European scholarly publications.

Our contributors have drawn attention to the international aspects of both colonization and decolonization. But further research still lies ahead in this field. The victorious Allies made history in Africa and also provided their successors with a precedent by confiscating a great deal of German private property after World War I. These seizures of property occurred long before the nationalization of alien economic holdings had become an accepted means of policy in the Third World. The Germans reacted strongly against these measures. They vigorously defended themselves against the charges levelled at German colonial rule by pointing out real and alleged failings in the British, French, Portuguese and Belgian colonies. The dissensions between the European powers therefore contributed to a change of attitude concerning colonialism as a whole, one quite independent of Marxist–Leninist or reformist critiques of the imperial system.

Germany never tired of demanding the return of her lost colonies. By the late 1930s, in fact, some British statesmen were seriously considering territorial concessions to Germany in Africa as a means of appeasing Hitler and his allies. For the Western powers in those days, decolonization meant handing over territories such as Cameroun or Tanganyika—not to the Africans but to the Germans. Scholars can only speculate vaguely concerning the possible result of any such concessions. Decolonization in the modern sense might well have been delayed for many generations. It is ironic, therefore, that imperialist pressure groups such as the European settler lobbies in Northern Rhodesia and East Africa that helped to prevent any appeasement of German claims in Africa, may unknowingly and unwillingly have put the African successor governments of these countries in their debt.

More work remains to be done, also, on what might be called the black expatriates' *internationale*. There were complex relations in the political, the ecclesiastical and the cultural fields between Afro-Americans and Africans; between members of the black diaspora in the United States, the West Indies, Brazil, Great Britain, various European continental countries, the Middle East and black Africa. The full story of this intellectual diaspora merits further attention as does the programme of internationalizing the struggles for African national independence.

The origins of African socialism in its various forms also merit further investigation. In our view, future students will draw attention to its European Marxist and reformist strands. They will also put more stress on ideas that were elaborated in Africa itself by obscure black school-teachers in mission stations or clerks in government offices. Rural radicalism offers a fruitful field of investigation to scholars familiar with similar phenomena in other parts of the world. Future students of African socialism will also emphasize, in all probability, the contribution made by the colonizers' own practices to economic *dirigisme* in Africa. Especially from the Second World War onward, elaborate systems of state marketing boards were set up in various African countries. The colonizers tried to regulate the activities of businessmen through a complex network of regulations. Various kinds of publicly-owned enterprise were established. There were attempts to enlarge the colonial economies through measures such as the British Colonial Development and Welfare Act, 1940. The colonizers began to formulate long-term economic plans; development indeed was often elevated into a new secular Gospel that profoundly influenced the new intellectual climate in Africa.

More might also be made of the various African personalities engaged in the independence struggle. A wide field remains open, for instance, to the political biographer. Future historians may well feel free to emphasize the element of colour, excitement and drama that characterized the politics of African independence. In current political literature concerning the African power struggles, the politics of independence all too often lose their savour. They commonly appear strangely devoid of excitement and life. But commitment in fact was apt to excite the highest and the basest passions alike. Political activism was consonant sometimes with both political sacrifices and cynical peculation of party funds, with selfless 'mission work' among the politically backward, as well as with ruthless extortion rackets. There were serious education campaigns; there were also dark blood-guilt accusations against the whites, reminiscent in certain respects of mediaeval propaganda against the Jews. According to some demagogues at work during the campaign against federation in Northern Rhodesia, for instance, white vampire men would kidnap black children to can their meat; white firms would poison the Africans' sugar to rob black men of their virility. For many Congolese who had retained the traditional picture of the universe in more than vestigial form, national independence in 1960 implied a Messianic revolution. For some it was a dangerous time, when the white men went about to steal souls, when the sun and moon would collide, when chaos would return and only a few would be saved. For others, the ancestors would come back, the ordinary people would fall asleep for a day and then awake as white men, appropriately endowed with all the Europeans' wisdom and unlimited wealth.[1]

[1] Wyatt MacGaffey, 'Kongo and the King of the Americans', *Journal of Modern African Studies*, **6**, no. 2 (August 1968), p. 175.

With the passage of time, more material will also become available concerning the impact of traditional or neo-traditional beliefs on certain African leaders, including charismatic modernizers as well as rural radicals. Nkrumah, for example, paid respect to a renowned sooth-sayer. Kikuyu insurgents developed sado-magical practices that merit further elucidation. All too often, however, these aspects of the African past are inadequately covered. The bright as well as the dark sides of the past emerge in a washed-out grey that merely obscures the outlines of history beneath an academic camouflage.

The pleasant task remains of thanking our contributors. Their combined efforts not only represent much original research, but also open many doors to other students. We trust that their labours will prove of value to scholars currently at work in the field. We hope also that the present project will assist future generations of indigenous African historians who, in times to come, will surely play the most significant role in elucidating the colonial epoch as an integral part of the African past.

BIBLIOGRAPHY

Davis, Shelby Cullom. *Reservoirs of men: a history of the black troops of French West Africa*. Chambéry, 1934.

Froude, James Anthony. *The English in Ireland in the eighteenth century*. 3 vols. New York, 1888.

Great Britain. War Office. *Statistics of the military effort of the British empire during the Great War, 1914–1920*. London, 1922.

Hancock, Sir William Keith. *Survey of British Commonwealth affairs*. 2 vols. in 3. London, Oxford University Press, 1942.

Henderson, W. O. *Studies in German colonial history*. London, 1962.

Hobsbawm, E. J. *The age of revolution, 1789–1848*. Cleveland and New York, 1962.

Lucas, Sir Charles, ed. *The empire at war*. 5 vols. London, Oxford University Press, 1921–6.

Macaulay, Thomas Babington, Lord. *Critical and historical essays contributed to the Edinburgh Review*. New York, n.d.

Mayhew, Henry. *The upper Rhine: the scenery of its banks and the manner of its people*. London, 1858.

Wallace, Sir Lawrence. 'Northern Rhodesia and the last phase of the war in Africa', in *The empire at war*, Vol. IV: *Africa*, Sir Charles Lucas, ed. London, Oxford University Press, 1925.

CHAPTER I

BRITISH POLICY AND REPRESENTATIVE GOVERNMENT IN WEST AFRICA 1920 TO 1951

by K. W. J. POST

Students of colonial rule in West Africa commonly treat the fifteen years from 1945 to 1960 as the most significant period in the history of decolonization. Scholars stress the way in which the British and the French created institutions that they hoped would be sufficiently viable to permit the political disengagement of the metropolitan powers. There is a danger, however, at least in the case of British West Africa, of foreshortening historical perspectives. Such modern nationalist movements as the Convention People's Party or the National Council of Nigeria and the Cameroons must be seen against a background of African social change and of shifting colonial policies going back at least as far as the First World War. Although little work on British West Africa in the 1920s and 1930s has as yet been done by scholars, it is clear that in terms of successive British policies the watershed of the era 1920–60 lies around 1950.

The Second World War did not mark a completely new departure. It may be considered to have accelerated political developments already apparent in the late 1930s, and it delayed rather than hastened the evolution of British policy. In Nigeria and the Gold Coast the British realized by about 1950 that new policies would have to be formulated to accommodate social forces not actually created by the war but strengthened in the course of it. Thus the last years of the colonial period saw an attempt to build up unified, integrated parliamentary political systems that would form the bases for political independence. Most research to date has concentrated on this aspect of British policy; hence the present essay will be concerned with the period 1920–51. Since only a few secondary sources are available to provide guidance, and since access to primary sources for this period is limited, this discussion must be regarded as tentative in nature.[1]

---

[1] Among the few important secondary sources are Martin Wight, *The Gold Coast Legislative Council* (London, 1947); Joan Wheare, *The Nigerian Legislative Council*

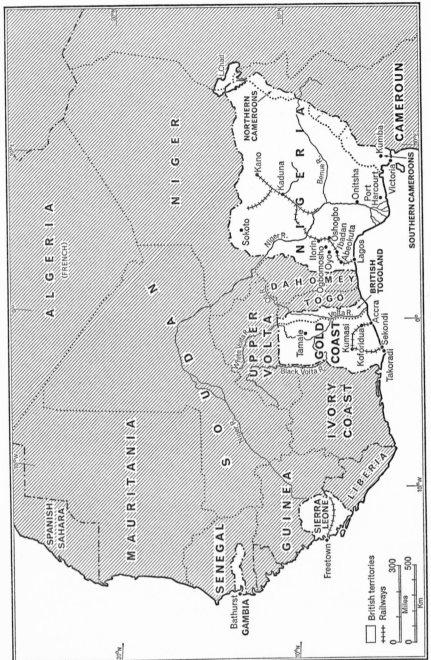

Map 2. British West Africa, 1951

32

Colonial policy between the wars

Professor Kenneth Robinson aptly summarized the general characteristics of British colonial policy when he wrote that the Colonial Office had

> a profound conviction that political development was not to be brought about by social engineering, by elaborate constitutional provisions supported by social planning. Rather, it must be an organic growth, fostered by habits of accommodation, which were taken to be the supreme art in politics. There resulted an assumption that piecemeal concessions of varying degrees of participation in government might be expected somehow to result in the development of political habits which could in the long run be translated into an institutional basis for self-government appropriate to the varying genius of the inhabitants of a given territory.[1]

Colonial policy for at least two decades after 1920 may thus be characterized as one concerned with behavioural manifestations rather than with structural patterns. Institutions were left to evolve pragmatically; they were not created by manipulation consciously directed towards the attainment of political independence. Emphasis was placed upon patience and diversity. As the Parliamentary Under-Secretary of State for the Colonies put it when he spoke to the Gold Coast Legislative Council during a tour in 1926:

> Parliamentary Government such as we have it in the little island in the North Sea has taken many years to evolve. Where there has been precipitancy and where the model has been imitated too closely, without adaptation to

(London, 1950); James S. Coleman, *Nigeria: background to nationalism* (Berkeley and Los Angeles, University of California Press, 1958); David Kimble, *A political history of Ghana: the rise of Gold Coast nationalism, 1850–1928* (Oxford, Clarendon Press, 1963); Tekena N. Tamuno, *Nigeria and elective representation, 1923–1947* (London, 1966); and Martin Kilson, *Political change in a West African state: a study of the modernization process in Sierra Leone* (Cambridge, Harvard University Press, 1966). Primary sources in the Public Record Office in London up to 1937 have now been opened, but distance has precluded their use. The Gambia has not been given a place in the present discussion because of the paucity of material on this territory; see, however, Harry A. Gailey, *A history of the Gambia* (London, 1964). The evolution of this state seems to have followed the pattern outlined below, but more slowly; for instance, it was not until 1946 that an elected representative was given a place on the Gambian Legislative Council—twenty years after such action in the other territories.

[1] Kenneth Robinson, *The dilemmas of trusteeship: aspects of British colonial policy between the wars* (London, Oxford University Press, 1965), p. 89.

local needs, there have been difficulties and reactions. Therefore I say in this matter 'hasten slowly', always realising that progress is not only achievable but is inevitable in the British Empire with its free institutions.[1]

Thirteen years later, however, on the eve of the Second World War, one West African governor, Sir Bernard Bourdillon, began to cast serious doubt on the ability of the system as it had evolved so far to serve as a basis for independence:

The important question which remains for consideration is whether it is possible, under the system, for the Nigerian to attain a greater share not only in responsibility for carrying out a policy imposed on him, but in responsibility for framing policy. In other words, can the system continue to develop and eventually become part of a system of responsible self-government, or does the attainment of responsibility at the centre involve, at some stage or other, the abandonment of the system.[2]

Nevertheless, Bourdillon's basic concern was still with evolution rather than with engineering, with change that would avoid both the 'fossil' and the 'machine'—'The fossil is essentially unadaptable; the machine can only be adapted by spasmodic alterations effected by an external agency; it is the living organism that can change imperceptibly and naturally.'[3] Five years later, when it had been decided that changes must in fact be made, the emphasis was still upon organic growth, pragmatism, and the accommodation of varying interests:

The problem of Nigeria today is how to create a political system which is itself a present advance and contains the living possibility of further orderly advance—a system within which the diverse elements may progress at varying speeds, amicably and smoothly, towards a more closely integrated economic, social and political unity, without sacrificing the principles and ideals inherent in their divergent ways of life.[4]

By 1945 the British were facing the cumulative structural problems of years of pragmatism. Each territory contained a number of quite separate administrative parts. Nigeria consisted of a colony and two protectorates, divided into the Eastern, Western and Northern Provinces;

[1] W. G. A. Ormsby-Gore, reported in the *Gold Coast Leader*, 10 April 1926.
[2] Nigeria, Governor (Sir Bernard Bourdillon), *Memorandum on the future political development of Nigeria* (Lagos, 1939), p. 4.
[3] Bourdillon, *Memorandum*, p. 3.
[4] Nigeria, Governor (Sir Arthur Richards), *Political and constitutional future of Nigeria: Governor of Nigeria's despatch to the Secretary of State for the Colonies December 6, 1944,* Sessional Paper No. 4 of 1945 (Lagos, 1945), p. 1.

Sierra Leone of a colony and a protectorate; and the Gold Coast of two colonies (Gold Coast Colony and Ashanti) and a protectorate (the Northern Territories). Superimposed on these in each of the three territories was a British governor and his subordinate hierarchy of officials, and an executive and a legislative council. Each part of each territory was further divided into a heterogeneous collection of Native Authorities, the product of years of pragmatic evolution. Although all of these were in theory—and often in practice—based upon some traditional authority, Lord Lugard's principle of 'Indirect Rule' through such authority was coherently applied only in Lugard's own Nigeria (and there most successfully in the Islamic states of the north). In Sierra Leone, the Gold Coast and the Gambia, legislation on 'Native Authorities' was not consolidated till the mid-1930s or even later. Local treasuries, regular local tax collection and local courts with clearly defined jurisdictions were only gradually established.

Thus by 1945 the British were facing the consequences of their own policy between the wars. This had envisaged political evolution as occurring almost entirely at the local level where institutions impinged most directly upon the lives of the African subjects. This policy had also required a decision on the part of the Colonial Office as to which African leaders were to be accepted as spokesmen for their people. Throughout their West African possessions the British had preferred to listen to the traditional chiefs, or to those they chose to regard as such. (The exception was the colony area of Sierra Leone, where, for historical reasons, the British could not even pretend that traditional chiefs existed.) This preference had far-reaching effects, because colonialism itself had created a new African élite, 'new men' who in the inter-war period increasingly claimed to speak for the people as a whole.

The new men and the chiefs

Contact with the West inevitably implied social transformation in Africa, for the hand of the European touched nothing without altering it. The dramatic effects of centuries of the West African slave-trade destroyed social and political systems of long standing; but at the same time created new ones based on new economies. Various kingdoms arose on the basis of the traffic in 'black ivory'. After 1809 the switch to legitimate trade, primarily in palm-oil, wrought further changes; and some of the traders who had prospered from the sale of human beings to the Europeans survived the transition while others went under. The legitimate European trader was accompanied and sometimes preceded by the missionary, who in turn brought European education. Direct political control was gradually established over the coast areas. By 1850 the British forts and settlements on the Gold Coast were considered important enough to be separated administratively from Sierra Leone, with their own governor and legislative council, while in 1861 Lagos was annexed by the British Crown. Slowly but inexorably the flag followed trade and the Bible into the interior. In 1896 the Sierra Leone Protectorate was established; and in 1898 the crucial settlement with France gave a huge area of Nigeria to Britain. By 1899 the Northern Territories of the Gold Coast were added to the Colony and Ashanti by agreement with France and Germany. British control over the Gambia had already been confirmed in 1889.

As the work of David Kimble and James Coleman has shown, the main agencies of social change in British West Africa were cash crops and education. The two were of course interlinked, since money earned from trade or agriculture was used to pay for schooling. Together they provided men with new opportunities to achieve higher status through wealth—or at least a regular cash income—and learning. The distribution of both cash crops and modern education was uneven; the Northern Territories of the Gold Coast, for example, remained backward, and the Sierra Leone Protectorate made only limited progress. Nevertheless a new African élite had already emerged in the coastal towns by the time British rule was being consolidated over the interior. As Kimble puts it, 'Gold Coast society in the nineteenth century saw the emergence of a significant educated group, dependent on non-traditional sources of income, who set patterns of social behaviour in the towns, and from time to time exerted a strong political influence on rural chiefs.'[1]

The British administrators thus had to deal with educated Africans, some of them doctors and lawyers. This was true not merely of the Creoles of Freetown, but also in the Gold Coast, where the first barrister of wholly local origin qualified in 1887, and in Lagos, where the first Lagos-born barrister qualified in 1893. These men naturally claimed equality of treatment with Europeans frequently less well educated than themselves. Moreover, they often aided their illiterate brethren who fell foul of the administration. They also acted as advisers to the traditional chiefs, to whom they were often related. Their

---

[1] Kimble, *Political history*, p. 137.

influence thus extended into the hinterland and affected dignitaries whom the British were anxious to employ on their own behalf. Members of the new élite and British officials therefore often clashed, and the administrators frequently regarded the new men as troublemakers.

The British consoled themselves with the thought that their adversaries were not typical of the African population, and, indeed, were quite divorced from their origins.

Europeanised Africans represent no tribe or community, but form a class apart in the principal cities of the West Coast, where they reside in a varying minority among an illiterate population in the tribal stage of development, amid sordid surroundings for men of education and culture...The educated African imitates European dress and customs closely, however ill adapted to his conditions of life, and may be heard to speak of going 'home' to England. He has, as a rule, little in common with the indigenous tribes of Africa, and seldom leaves his native town except to travel by sea or railway. The Europeanised African is indeed separated from the rest of the people by a gulf which no racial affinity can bridge. He must be treated—and seems to desire to be treated—as though he were of a different race.[1]

Such attitudes continued to permeate the administration right up to, and indeed after, the Second World War. From many similar incidents we may choose one from Yorubaland in southern Nigeria, in April 1936. A chieftainship in Egba Division was vacant and in dispute, and a group calling itself the Society of Union and Progress demanded that the new chief should be an educated man. On 2 April the Native Authority Council met, and was addressed by the British Resident:

Now I ask those gentlemen who, in this connection style themselves 'literate' what they mean. A literate person is one who knows how to read and write; he may not be a man of high character, he may be, and often is, the greatest scoundrel imaginable, he may be feeble minded and utterly useless. Anyone can learn to read and write just as they can learn to drive a lorry or a train, there is no special virtue in the mere fact that he can drive a pen, a motor or a train.

---

[1] Frederick John Dealtry Lugard, 1st baron, *The dual mandate in British tropical Africa*, 5th ed. (London, 1965), pp. 80–1. Lugard even suggested that the educated Africans were physically different from the rest: 'The Europeanised African differs not merely in mental outlook from the other groups, but also in physique. Doctors and dentists tell us that he has become less fertile, more susceptible to lung-trouble and to other diseases, and to defective dentition—disabilities which have probably arisen from inbreeding among a very limited class, and to the adoption of European dress, which writers in the native press say is enervating and inimical to the health of the African' (*Dual mandate*, pp. 79–80).

The tone of many of the letters that have been published appears to convey the impression that those who can read and write are a privileged 'caste' which refuses to acknowledge that equal merit may and does exist among those who are unable to read and write. If this is so it is an insult to the large and inarticulate mass of illiterate people...which they may quite justifiably resent. It is a pity that the excellent work and fine example of those who have benefited by the blessings of education should be marred by the snobbery and scurrility of a few who have failed altogether to understand that modesty and courtesy are two of the qualities which a well educated man should possess.[1]

A lapse of rather more than a decade since the publication of Lugard's book had somewhat altered the tone. By 1936 the administrators had come to realize that the new élite were too numerous to be excluded completely from the machinery of government. Hence blanket condemnations of 'the educated African' gave way to careful distinction between those who were 'responsible' and those who were not. Nevertheless, the same allegation recurred: educated people supposedly behaved as a privileged caste and cut themselves off from the people.

The 'new men' indignantly refuted these charges in the columns of local newspapers which, since well before 1900, had served as their mouthpieces. When W. G. A. Ormsby-Gore, in his report on his West African tour in 1926, faithfully reflected the views of his civil servants concerning the new élite, he was answered at length by the *Gold Coast Leader*:

In almost every coast town of the Gold Coast, you have a number of educated men, sons of the soil, who have intimate family connections with well-known houses and families, and these, as above indicated, have been sent to school by their people, taking advantage of the new light in order that they may be a bulwark of strength to their less enlightened brethren in their contact with a higher civilisation. We admit that this is an inconvenient class to the powers that be. It has been the practice persistently from remote times in our relations with Britain for Government authorities to seek to represent this class as antagonistic to Government influence in moulding the local African according to its own ideas and its own convenience. Of course the African also has rights; and when the educated African attempts to assert these rights in the teeth of Governmental forces and opposition, he naturally becomes an inconvenient person, to be specially classed and labelled in order

[1] *Nigerian Daily Times*, 6 April 1936.

that world opinion may regard him as a kind of denationalised bogey, either to be got rid of or to be despised in the consideration of the affairs of the people.[1]

From an early date educated Africans also organized political bodies to bring more effective pressure to bear on the colonial administration. The Gold Coast Aborigines' Rights Protection Society (1897) and the People's Union in Lagos (1908) were only two of a number of such organizations. In March 1920 the National Congress of British West Africa was formed, dominated by men like J. E. Casely Hayford and T. Hutton Mills from the Gold Coast, but with branches in all four territories. The demands of the Congress were moderate. Whatever may have been the personal views of some of its members, it viewed self-government as only a very long-term prospect. More immediately it sought the inclusion of elected representatives on the Legislative Councils of the various territories and control by elected members over finance. It also called for a British West African university, and a British West African Co-operative Association which would enable African businessmen to operate on more equal terms with European banks and trading companies. Similarly, the Nigerian National Democratic Party (NNDP), formed in Lagos by Herbert Macaulay, J. Egerton Shyngle and others in June 1923 (though probably planned since 1919), held that

co-operation of the governed with the governing body is the shortest cut to administrative success, provided the administrative policy of the governing body is inspired by sympathetic liberalism or enlightened statesmanship; and provided true regard is paid to the legitimate and reasonable wishes of the governed when constitutionally expressed or interpreted.[2]

By the time the NNDP was formed, the Colonial Office had already decided to respond to the demands of the new élite. New constitutions

---

[1] *Gold Coast Leader*, editorial, 4 Dec. 1926. A similar comment had been made by the editor of *Sierra Leone Weekly News* on 22 Nov. 1924; 'It may be true that the educated African may not be in the position of sending palm kernels and palm oil to the European markets; it may be true that on account of his training in candour and Christian manliness he may become a more difficult material than his unsophisticated brother to be managed by the class of officials who placed colour as an exclusive right of entrance into privileged and more favourable circles. But it ought to be seen that such a policy is far removed from the realms of consistency, and certainly it is not in harmony with the sage principle of the Golden Rule.'
[2] *Nigerian Daily Times*, 19 Nov. 1940. See also Coleman, *Nigeria*, pp. 197–200; and Tamuno, *Nigeria and elective representation*, pp. 45–9.

introducing the principle of direct election to the legislative councils
were promulgated for Nigeria in 1922, for Sierra Leone in 1924 and
for the Gold Coast in 1925. But the new policy involved only a minimal
amount of structural change. Only four out of forty-six members of
the Nigerian Legislative Council were elected directly, three out of
thirty in the Gold Coast, and three out of twenty-one in Sierra Leone.
The remainder were official members (and thus colonial officials) or
else unofficial members nominated by the governor (or, in the case of
six members in the Gold Coast, chiefs indirectly elected by their fellows).
Only the coastal towns were represented electorally: Lagos and Calabar
in Nigeria; Accra, Cape Coast and Sekondi in the Gold Coast; and
Freetown in Sierra Leone. The franchise was limited: in Nigeria, for
example, there were in 1923 only about 4,000 electors in Lagos and
453 in Calabar.

The Colonial Office had no enthusiasm for its new policy. During
the discussions on the proposed Nigerian constitution, the Secretary
of State had shown considerable reservation. The governor, Sir Hugh
Clifford, had agreed in a dispatch dated 7 July 1922 that in the immediate future there was not much to be hoped for from this innovation,
but pointed out that at least it might improve the political atmosphere
in the coastal towns. In fact, once the principle of direct election had
been admitted, it led to further demands. As the commentator 'Ebo'
put it in his column 'Mixed Pickles' in the *Gold Coast Leader* on 22 May
1926:

It has been held by all right-thinking Africans that the New Constitution
does not advance our status one little bit forward. On the other hand, it
materially sets back the hand of the clock. For while the Government have
been nominating whom they like to the Legislative Council to confer with
them upon important vital matters *seriously* affecting us, and whereas we
have time and time again *asked, knocked* and *beaten* at the door of the said
Legislative Council to be let in by means of electing our own representatives
to the said Legislative Council, and the reasonableness of our request has been
admitted by the said Government, we fail to see why in the New Constitution there should be any more provision for nomination by Government.

The British administration continued to have doubts about the very
limited structural changes it had made. In the case of Sierra Leone, for
example, the railway workers' strike in 1926, which was supported
by some of the educated élite and led to rioting, provoked a suggestion
in official circles that the right of election be withdrawn. In a dispatch

to the Secretary of State the Governor commented that events 'afford unanswerable arguments against any requests for further constitutional development in the present generation'.[1]

By admitting an elected element to the legislative councils the British had in fact admitted the existence of a principle of legitimacy other than that of traditional authority. The new elected members could now claim to have the mandate of 'the people', despite the limited franchise; they thus considered themselves to be representatives rather than merely spokesmen.[2] In these circumstances, conflict between the new men and the chiefs was almost inevitable; and in Sierra Leone and the Gold Coast the administration sought from the beginning to strengthen the hand of the chiefs by giving them a place in the new legislative councils.[3] In the Gold Coast the administration had long been accustomed to lean heavily on the support of educated rulers like Nana Ofori Atta, Omanhene (Paramount Chief) of Akim Abuakwa, nominated to the Legislative Council in 1916 along with two other Paramount Chiefs. The principal author of the Constitution of 1925, the Governor, Sir Gordon Guggisberg, attempted further to associate the colony chiefs with the government of the territory by giving three new provincial councils of chiefs the right to send six members to the Legislative Council. Similarly, in the Sierra Leone Constitution of 1924 the Governor had been given the power to nominate three chiefs from the Protectorate to sit in the Council as spokesmen for that area.

In both territories there were storms of protest from the new élite. On 4 October 1924 the editor of the *Sierra Leone Weekly News* wrote:

The recent awakening in the Protectorate towards the cultivation of western education for their children, accentuated by the marvellous progress [of] the school for the sons and nominees of Chiefs, established by the Government at Bo, has made it possible to make the choice of representatives amongst educated Chiefs, who, the Government is certain, will be able to follow the proceedings of the Council with intelligent interest. But the opinion is held by a large proportion of the people of the Colony, that in view of the relation

---

[1] Quoted in Kilson, *Political change*, p. 121.

[2] This distinction is not in accord with official, or even contemporary, usage; 'representative' was used in official documents and newspapers for either category. The two terms are used here in an attempt to make an analytical distinction between sources of legitimacy.

[3] No similar move was attempted in Nigeria, possibly because of the experience of the abortive Nigerian Council, which existed on paper from 1913 to 1922. The chiefs who were members of this body took no interest in it.

of these chiefs to their Commissioners in whose hands the power of appointing or removing them into or from office largely rests, [this] would render their sitting in council with their Commissioners rather difficult if not altogether a sham, if they are to give free expression of their views.

For their part, the Gold Coast newspapers took a rather different line. 'Ebo' thundered out a rhetorical question:

By pitch-forking six *practically illiterate* Head Chiefs into the Legislative Council and taking advantage of them in debates because of their poor knowledge of the English language, when there are several well-educated Commoners about, who could reason out with the Government on vital questions and thus help to secure the best in a given debate, could the Government be said to be considering the well-being of the society as against the well-being of perhaps one or two Amanhin whom the Government desires to do honour?[1]

In fact, the rivalry between chiefs and new men did not bring about permanent controversy between the two groups in either Sierra Leone or the Gold Coast in the 1920s and 1930s. Nevertheless, conflict was implicit in any future political and constitutional change which further associated elected Africans with the processes of government. If power was to devolve upon African leaders, the chiefs might claim supremacy by reason of their traditional authority. Alternatively the new élite might argue that in a modern democratic state an electoral mandate was the only legitimate form of power. This was the 'fatal dualism' recognized by James Coleman in British policy in Nigeria, the contradiction between indirect rule through the chiefs and the 'vision of ultimate control' held out to the new élite by the promise of eventual self-government.[2]

This contradiction was recognized by the protagonists themselves, though not in these terms. It implied rivalry of two kinds, conflict between ascribed status and achieved status, as well as competition for

---

[1] *Gold Coast Leader*, 22 May 1926; italics in the original. In this context, 'Ebo' made a clear distinction between the sanction of election and that of traditional authority in commenting on the position of Chief Ofori Atta: 'Assuming that Nana Ofori Atta as a Paramount Chief of Akyim Abuakwa is representative of that State, the fact that he was not *elected* by the people of that State or any other, to go to the Legislative Council of the British Government, but that he was *nominated* and appointed to that Council by the British Government itself makes what Nana Ofori Atta says at the said Council reflect his mind *personally* but not the mind of the Akyim Abuakwa State' (*Gold Coast Leader*, 14 Aug. 1926; italics in the original).

[2] Coleman, *Nigeria*, pp. 160–1.

popular support. Before the Second World War, the new men could not hope to equal the chiefs' influence over the people. Politics in the Gold Coast and Nigeria did not become mass politics until the late 1940s; in a sense, it never did so in Sierra Leone. But from the very beginnings of elected representation in British West Africa, all political discussion hinged on the question of what sort of person the British should choose as the mouthpiece of popular demands.

One view of what sort of men the voters should send to the Nigerian Legislative Council was succinctly stated by Dr C. C. Adeniyi Jones, an elected member for one or another of the Lagos wards for fifteen years (1923–38): 'Men who are cultured. Men of prestige who are respected by reason of their character and noble examples not only by their fellow Africans but by the European community as well'.[1] To this qualification might be added some slightly different ones from the *Sierra Leone Weekly News*:

[This candidate] if elected will figure prominently as a sort of oracle in any question of commerce in the Council room; besides which he is a young man of quick parts and high attainments, a typical product of culture, a man of settled life; which makes him a more fit choice to be an Honourable Member of the Colony. Also a liberal man and not tight-fisted, which is a most important and sure passport to be among and to work successfully with the Rural Natives.[2]

This point of view was élitist in nature, typical of the first elections of the 1920s, the product of a small but comparatively highly educated social stratum. Indeed, those who regarded themselves as the real élite, men like Sir Kitoyi Ajasa, who had lived for twelve years in England and was a personal friend of Sir Frederick (later Lord) Lugard, scorned to offer themselves for election at all. An editorial in Sir Kitoyi's newspaper gave a scathing description of the first election to the new Legislative Council in Lagos; it pointed out that according to Lugard's warning, the 'gentlemen' would in such circumstances be 'over-run' by the 'leaders of the noisy element'. 'Time has confirmed the accuracy of Sir Frederick's foresight', the editorial went on.

The noisy element referred to by Sir Frederick on that occasion were, in his day, the water-rate agitators whom, when they essayed to put up a fight in Tinubu Square, the police put to flight so ignominiously; the same lot

---

[1] From an election advertisement in *Nigerian Daily Times*, 19 Nov. 1940.
[2] E. Nichol [Letter to the editor], *Sierra Leone Weekly News*, 4 Oct. 1924.

became the anti-Lemomu element who have made themselves such a nuisance to Government; this same crowd have now blossomed into the Democratic people with Bolshevist proclivities; this 'the Majority' will become the opponents of Law and Order to a greater degree than they have exhibited in the past, unless the authorities see to it that Law and Order are upheld.[1]

By the eve of the Second World War, however, not merely the view typified by Sir Kitoyi Ajasa but also that of Dr Adeniyi Jones was becoming outdated. In August 1939 the *Sierra Leone Weekly News*, by no means a radical journal, wrote concerning the coming elections to the Legislative Council that the electors had become convinced 'of the need of returning a different type of candidate at the next opportunity'.

Sierra Leoneans have been let down so shabbily by those whom their suffrages had sent to the Legislature that there must be a rigid sifting before any claim is supported next November. Of one thing we may be sure none of the common people will ever again vote for a man just because that man is a 'Professional'. Proved honesty of patriotism and a pledge of loyalty to the people's cause through thick and thin should be the main deciding factors in sending our representatives to the Legislature.[2]

A new (and less literate) voice was also now being heard in the land. The following day, the *Weekly News* published a letter on the same subject from an avowed supporter of the new West African Youth League:

Now and again one reads and hear of spasmodic promises to get a walk over to the Legislature or Municipality; a good many of us feels that these promises are forgotten immediately we record our votes, as a sort of a bill of entry into port, for those who we think best to watch our interest in the Council. The next we see our Hon. Member or Councillor finds himself in the most embarrassing position that he ever experience in his life; to speak out, majority votes is against him, to walk out means fine of £25 or £50. Our man ultimately loses heart, and get under the Autocratic Executive, or become an Inferiority Complex of the Legislature and Municipality; thereby notoriously passive and languid in his demeanour. His Constituents on the other hand not having what is required of him, sometimes resort to sporadic

---

[1] *Nigerian Pioneer*, 28 Sept. 1923. The opposition to the proposed Lagos water rate in 1908 led to the formation of the People's Union. The 'Lemomu' issue was a quarrel which split the Lagos Muslim community for a number of years. For more of Sir Kitoyi's views see Coleman, *Nigeria*, p. 453, n. 12.

[2] 'Rambler', in *Sierra Leone Weekly News*, 12 Aug. 1939.

outburst or a continuous hue and cry on him to deliver the goods, conscious that our man has all the knowledge and ability of his responsibility and our limitations.[1]

Such sentiments were not necessarily welcomed by the older generation, even by those who criticized their peers. Thus in its editorial the *Sierra Leone Weekly News* for 26 November 1938 spoke of the National Congress as a 'spent Force', but warned that it might have been succeeded by 'a worthless generation' that had 'turned aside into alien paths' and 'weakened their energies by suicidal practices'. Returning to the same theme the editor commented on the rise of a new Nigerian figure, Nnamdi Azikiwe:

We wish this brimming Pioneer—'Zik'—all success in his effort for the Rebirth of Africa. But if he should leave Religion out of consideration and teach his followers that Age and Experience are mere rubbish, it will not be long before he shall find himself face to face with a stone wall and an impassable one too to prosperity for his Nigeria.[2]

Thus by the late 1930s a conflict of interest was emerging between two generations of the educated élite. The small, tightly-knit older group, represented in Sierra Leone by the leaders of the National Congress, or in Nigeria by men like Dr Adeniyi Jones, permanent residents of the coastal towns if not actually born there, were now being challenged by younger men, many of them significantly from the hinterland, and retaining their interest in local affairs. Economic and social developments during the first few decades of the present century had caused more cash to go into circulation; more schools had opened their doors; more students had acquired an education.[3] The British responded first of all by altering their policy towards local government. Later, on the eve of World War II, they began to give some thought to changes in the political system as a whole. These new themes became dominant after the war.

[1] H. Ade-Morrison [Letter to the editor], *Sierra Leone Weekly News*, 13 Aug. 1939.
[2] *Sierra Leone Weekly News*, 31 Dec. 1938.
[3] Pupils in attendance in southern Nigeria:

	Primary	Secondary
1906	11,872	20
1912	35,716	67
1926	138,249	518
1937	218,610	4,285

(Source: Coleman, *Nigeria*, p. 134.)

45

K. W. J. POST

The evolution of the system

When the British established their rule, they tended to assume that
'government' in effect meant local administration. In all British calculations the position of the traditional chiefs loomed large. By the early
1920s, however, it had already become clear that the educated men,
though few in number, were everywhere eager to participate in local
affairs. Their more affluent brethren who lived in the coastal towns
took some interest in the hinterland; these traders, teachers and clerks
hoped for a more active part. A multitude of organizations sprang up,
through which such men hoped to exert the desired influence. Thus,
to cite an example from the Yoruba people of south-western Nigeria,
when in 1921 an advisory board was set up to work with the Awujale
(king) of Ijebu Ode, an organization called the Ijebu National Brotherhood sought to have the board members elected by itself. Despite the
rivalries occasioned by the establishment of the new legislative councils
in the 1920s, these local organizations were usually much more sympathetic to traditional authority than were the coastal élite. Such was
certainly the case with the Committee of Educated Aborigines, which
in 1922 grouped together most of the educated men from the Sierra
Leone Protectorate. Nevertheless, in Nigeria and the Gold Coast at
least, local conflicts did tend to develop over the years. In the Gold
Coast, the Asante Kotoko Society was active in Ashanti from 1916.
This group usually worked in close alliance with the chiefs; but by
1934 the spread of education had brought into being a group which
could not be so easily accommodated, the Friends of Ashanti Freedom
Society.

The British administration gradually became convinced that
educated men should find a place in the conduct of local affairs.
In Nigeria Sir Donald Cameron's period as governor marked a
fundamental change. Thus in a memorandum written in July 1934 he
commented:

My own growing conviction is that the benefit to the whole of Nigeria
would be almost incalculable if we could—as I believe we could—establish
a more modern form of native constitution (in one of the Yoruba states
as the most suitable in the first instance) modelled for the present on their
own institutions, with a mixed Council in which the educated element of
the people would be more adequately represented, and with the Resident
exercising somewhat the same functions as he does in other British

46

dependencies, i.e. openly as the adviser of the Native Administration and taking a directing interest in its day to day affairs.[1]

Even after the outbreak of the Second World War, however, the British attitude was still one of caution. At a meeting of the Ijebu Ode Town Council late in 1940, for example, when some of the educated non-traditional members attempted to criticize the financial estimates, they were sternly reminded by the British Resident that the Awujale was the Native Authority. Later in the meeting, the Awujale remarked that 'after the war and when things returned to normal, he would put a stop to that sort of thing'; but he expressed a misplaced confidence in the durability of his own authority.

The tendency to incorporate educated men into local government, which became important in southern Nigeria in the 1930s in particular, was also a feature of the Gold Coast and Sierra Leone. The British thus hoped to accomplish two things. Recognizing that the demands of the new men would have to be met to some extent, the administrators sought to give the new men a stake in the established order by getting them to co-operate in the working of local institutions. The British still assumed that the legislative councils—especially their elected members—could be treated as a peripheral part of the system. Traditional authorities, with local educated men as their junior partners if necessary, were still to be the main props of imperial governance. As Sir Gordon Guggisberg had put it in 1927:

I have never concealed my conviction that it is on the native institutions of this country—with the exception of giving certain populous municipalities a voice—that the gradual development of the constitution must be founded. It was at the preservation of native institutions that I aimed when devising what is the outstanding feature of the new constitution—the provincial councils. These provincial councils are really the breakwaters defending our native constitutions, institutions, and customs against the disintegrating waves of Western civilization.[2]

---

[1] A. H. M. Kirk-Greene, ed., *The principles of native administration in Nigeria: selected documents, 1900–1947* (London, Oxford University Press, 1965), p. 202.

[2] Gold Coast, Governor (Sir Frederick Gordon Guggisberg), *The Gold Coast: a review of the events of 1920–1926 and the prospects of 1927–1928* (Accra, 1927), pp. 23–4. A contemporary American academic observer seems to have reflected Guggisberg's views: 'The goal of the Gold Coast should not be an African Legislative Council—which as at present constituted is a European device. Its goal should be a united African nation, governed by institutions of local origin. The Fanti people are a great nation. They attempted to establish a government of their own in 1873—the Fanti Confederation.

Nevertheless, the administration could not avoid some consideration of the system as a whole, particularly in regard to how to link the parts with one another and the localities to the centre. The 1924 Sierra Leone constitution, and that of 1925 for the Gold Coast, had sought to meet the latter problem by securing to chiefs a place on the legislative councils. In the case of Sierra Leone, for the first time this gave a voice in the discussion of policy to spokesmen from the Protectorate. The Gold Coast Legislative Council, on the other hand, included no one who was a native of either Ashanti or the Northern Territories; similarly the Northern Provinces of Nigeria—more than half the country—had only British officials and no African spokesman in the legislature. As the Colonial Secretary put it in the Gold Coast Legislative Council in February 1929, 'The constitution of Ashanti is as separate and distinct from that of the Gold Coast Colony as is, say, the constitution of Sierra Leone'.[1]

The Gold Coast Colony chiefs were thus alone in securing a joint representative organ, known as the Joint Provincial Council, constituted in 1932 from the provincial councils set up by Guggisberg. In suggesting India as a model for Nigeria shortly after the new Legislative Council had come into being, Lord Lugard was concerned with a closer integration for the whole territory, but along two different lines. In the Nigerian equivalent of British India, 'Europeanized Africans' would be admitted to the Legislative Council. The Council's jurisdiction could be 'gradually extended to include the whole of the tribe to which the native councillors belong, whose customary law and language they understand, provided they do in fact represent the tribe and are not in conflict with the legitimate authority of the chiefs'. However, 'it would be unjust to place under their control the interior tribes, who themselves have a right to a measure of self-rule'.[2] We may

It failed because of British opposition. But could not the idea be revived today? Such a Confederation, composed of chiefs and elected representatives, could eventually be given funds of its own with which it could provide for national needs. A development of the Provincial Council idea, such a scheme could apply the Nigerian native treasury system upon a larger scale. Thus a Confederation, which would be subject to European advice, should constitute a supreme court for native affairs to which controversies between stools and those over destoolments [i.e. depositions of chiefs] could be referred. It might wish to have several representatives on the European Legislative Council. But under such an institution, the weight of the government would be gradually and slowly transferred from British to native authority' (Raymond L. Buell, *The native problem in Africa*, 2nd ed. [London, 1965], I, 842–3).

[1] Quoted in Kimble, *Political history*, p. 532.   [2] *Dual Mandate*, pp. 89–90.

assume that Lugard had in mind the traditional states of the north, and intended them to be an equivalent of the Indian Native States, developing entirely along the lines of traditional authority and institutions. Some twelve years later, in the mid-1930s, Margery Perham, one of Lord Lugard's admirers, posed the problem of the integration of Nigeria as a choice between federation or unification by an increasingly powerful central government. Her preference was for federation:

It is probable that the ideal development would be by a gradual increase in the responsibilities of the Native Administrations which should at a later stage be encouraged, though not pressed, to federate. This federation would have to be very loose and mainly financial in its early stages and would be likely to occur first between the more homogeneous groups.[1]

By this time, however, the British throughout British West Africa were faced with the problem of how to accommodate the new men at all levels of government. The position of the legislative councils in the territories remained an anomaly: lacking any real responsibility, they were unable to provide the apex to any system that might ultimately devolve power upon an African leadership. Moreover, by the late 1930s the more perceptive administrators were beginning to realize that this leadership might have to be broadened to include a wider range of the new men than had been admitted to the legislative councils in the 1920s. The new generation of leaders, who had by this time begun to make their mark at the national level, as their counterparts had been doing more modestly for about fifteen years locally, were much more insistent on their rights than those who had found at least partial satisfaction in a limited franchise in a few coastal towns. The declared political objective of the new Nigerian Youth Movement (NYM), for example, was 'a complete taking over of the Government of Nigeria into the hands of the indigenous people of our country' and 'a reversal of the existing condition so that Nigerians will run the Administrative Machinery of their own fatherland'.[2]

The emergence of a new group of leaders at the national level was marked by the founding of a number of such political organizations. They all used the term 'Youth' in their titles, consciously expressing

---

[1] Margery Perham, *Native administration in Nigeria* (London, Oxford University Press, 1937), pp. 356–7.

[2] *Nigerian Daily Times*, 19 Nov. 1940. Quotations are from an interesting article by 'Lasaki', who compares the programmes of the NNDP and the Nigerian Youth Movement.

the fact that they represented a new political generation. As early as 1930 in the Gold Coast, Dr J. B. Danquah held the first of a series of 'Youth Conferences', and the second in 1938. Most activity there, however, centred on I. T. A. Wallace-Johnson's West African Youth League, founded in 1935, and on the *African Morning Post*, edited from 1935 to 1937 by Nnamdi Azikiwe. Having survived a charge of sedition, Azikiwe returned to his native Nigeria, where he joined the NYM, formed late in 1935. Wallace-Johnson, his co-defendant, was found guilty, served his sentence, and then went home to Sierra Leone, where in May 1938 he re-established the Youth League.

The demands of these new organizations were more sweeping, and their leaders had often been exposed to more radical influences than those of the previous generation. Thus H. O. Davies, one of the leaders of the NYM, had been a pupil of Harold Laski at the London School of Economics and Political Science, and Wallace-Johnson had spent some time in Moscow in 1932 and was more overtly Marxist than any of the others. Everywhere the new organizations made a considerable impact. In Nigeria, the NYM gained control of the Lagos political scene in 1938 by winning all three Legislative Council seats in the election of that year, ending the fifteen years' supremacy of the NNDP. The days of men like Dr Adeniyi Jones were over; he lost his seat and never returned to the legislature. More than this, the NYM was the first Nigerian party to make a determined effort to move into the hinterland behind Lagos. In Sierra Leone, too, the Youth League was the first to move out of the Colony into the Protectorate.

By the late 1930s social change in the hinterland was providing opportunities for new leaders, more especially in southern Nigeria and in the Gold Coast Colony. The spread of education and cash-cropping, and the improvement of communications with the increasing popularity of motor transport, had created a large group of people responsive to issues wider than those of the traditional community. West African farmers and traders suffered greatly from the manipulation of produce prices by the expatriate companies during the 1930s. Such movements as the attempted cocoa 'hold-ups' in the Gold Coast, when farmers and traders tried to force up prices by refusing to sell cocoa to foreign buyers, showed that a political sense was spreading rapidly in the more developed parts of the hinterland.

On the eve of the Second World War there were signs that the Colonial Office had begun to respond to these pressures, if only in its customary piecemeal fashion. In Sierra Leone a Standing Finance Committee of the Legislative Council was created in November 1938, securing to African Unofficial Members the dominant voice in supervising government expenditure. In 1939 the Gold Coast Legislative Council (Amendment) Order in Council gave the Joint Provincial Council power to nominate to the legislature commoners as well as chiefs. Had the war not intervened, the British would have found such measures inadequate to satisfy the new leaders. By this date it had become impossible to control the situation by making minor concessions of the kind granted in the 1920s.

One West African governor, Sir Bernard Bourdillon of Nigeria, was keenly aware of this. In a memorandum written in 1939, which is quoted at the beginning of this essay to show the British preference for an evolutionary approach to system-building, he came ultimately to an opposite conclusion:

I fear that, in spite of what I have written on the subject of constitution-mongering, the time has come when we must consider devising something which will not be altogether 'the outcome of slow growth and gradual development'. The fact is that the present Legislative Council is not a natural development of, nor completely in harmony with, the general policy. It is an unnatural excrescence and its removal and replacement cannot be altogether natural processes.[1]

What Bourdillon wanted above all was to find some way to build the Legislative Council more closely into the system; to create more openings for the new élite; and to integrate more effectively the various parts of the system. Thus he suggested the creation of regional councils for the Western, Eastern and Northern Provinces; these were to be advisory, but might later assume legislative powers and even financial control. The council for the North would be based on the Emirs' Conference, which had met regularly since 1930. The council for the West would rest on the Conference of Yoruba Chiefs, introduced by Bourdillon in 1936, with the possible addition of some of the new men. The council for the East would be made up of representatives of the many organizations which the new men had created—the Ibibio Union, the Rivers Conference, the Onitsha Union and the rest. Once these regional councils were set up, the Legislative Council in Lagos might become a Federal Council or a second chamber in a bicameral legislature with three parallel first chambers.[2]

---

[1] Bourdillon, *Memorandum*, p. 9   [2] Bourdillon, *Memorandum*, pp. 9–10.

In these proposals we can clearly see a continuation of Margery Perham's idea of a federation, based now on three different regional structures. Bourdillon's proposals also faced squarely the question of how to link the new institutions with the various local Native Authorities:

If an alien bureaucracy can govern through the agency of indigenous institutions, there appears to be no valid reason why a native central government should not do the same...So long as we do not insist on the 'elected parliament' conforming too closely to some existing model, I see no reason why the native authorities and the elected parliament would not be complementary parts of one harmonious system, nor why the eventual representative Government should not be representative of and function through acknowledged Native Authority.[1]

The advent of the Second World War delayed for a few years all such proposals. When changes of the kind Bourdillon envisaged for Nigeria were made just after the war, they had in fact been outpaced by popular demand.

Post-war developments

By the latter part of 1943 the British government felt certain enough of the eventual victory of the Allied powers to re-examine its West African colonial policy. In September the Secretary of State visited the Gold Coast; Sir Arthur Richards, the Governor of Nigeria, made a trip to London in November. Both took part in talks concerning constitutional change. The discussions and drafting that followed finally resulted in the promulgation of new constitutions for Nigeria and the Gold Coast in 1946 and in the proposal of another for Sierra Leone in 1947. Some changes were made. Unofficial Members obtained a majority over Official Members (that is, the colonial civil servants who sat in the legislature). In Nigeria, Bourdillon's suggestion of advisory regional councils was adopted, and the north for the first time was given the right to send its own men to the Legislative Council in Lagos. Similarly, Ashanti gained a voice in the Gold Coast Legislative Council, though the Northern Territories were still represented only by officials. In both Nigeria and the Gold Coast the central institutions were linked much more closely to local institutions by using the Native Authorities as electoral colleges to choose the majority of the Unofficial

[1] Bourdillon, *Memorandum*, p. 5.

Members of the legislative councils. In the new Sierra Leone constitution this was to be done by the Protectorate Assembly, set up in 1945 and dominated by the chiefs.

Nevertheless, these new constitutions must be regarded as the culmination of the developments of the 1920s and 1930s, rather than as the beginning of a new era. As Lord Hailey put it,

The Constitutions ordained for the Gold Coast and Nigeria in 1946 were the most typical expressions of [the] attempt to effect a reconciliation between the underlying principles of Indirect Rule and that growing body of African opinion in West Africa which saw the attainment of self-government based on parliamentary institutions as the objective of Colonial rule.[1]

In this sense, they came too late. They did not extend the principle of representation, and they made no increase in the number of elected representatives in any of the legislative councils. Even before their promulgation they were political anachronisms; within a few years this had been perceived by the Colonial Office itself. One colonial expert was thus able to write in 1949 of 'the long list of abortive reforms and frustrated legislation which has characterised the past history of the Gold Coast'.[2]

The political effects of the Second World War and its immediate aftermath on British West Africa have been examined in detail for Nigeria and the Gold Coast by scholars such as James Coleman and Dennis Austin. By 1946–7 the new élite had mustered enough popular support in those two territories to make a serious demand for an extension of the elective principle. In Nigeria, Nnamdi Azikiwe's National Council of Nigeria and the Cameroons (NCNC), founded in August 1944, launched an all-out campaign against the Richards Constitution even before this was put into force. In the Gold Coast, J. B. Danquah and other professionals and businessmen organized the United Gold Coast Convention (UGCC) in August 1947, with its slogan of 'Self-government in the shortest possible time'. The UGCC was superseded by Kwame Nkrumah's Convention People's Party (CPP) and 'Self-government NOW' from mid-1949 onward.

In Sierra Leone, political developments took a somewhat different path. By the 1940s social change in the Protectorate had produced a

---

[1] William Malcolm Hailey, 1st baron, *An African survey: a study of problems arising in Africa south of the Sahara* (London, Oxford University Press, 1957), p. 204.

[2] William Malcolm Hailey, 1st baron, *Native administration in the British African territories: Part III, West Africa* (London, 1951), p. 280.

new élite which regarded itself as distinct from, and indeed a rival to, the Creole élite of the Colony.[1] Protectorate politicians such as Milton and Albert Margai and John Karefa-Smart had close links with traditional chiefs; thus they did not emphasize the principle of electing leaders by popular mandate with the same insistence as Azikiwe, Nkrumah, or even Danquah (himself the half-brother of Nana Ofori Atta). The Protectorate élite wanted rather to ensure that the demographic preponderance of their own area should be reflected in the composition of the new Legislative Council. The constitution of 1947 would have ensured this, but it met with such opposition from the Creoles that it was only promulgated in a revised form in 1951. From then onward the Protectorate élite was able to assert its dominance through the new Sierra Leone People's Party (SLPP).

By 1950, the Colonial Office had yielded to pressure from the new nationalist parties in Nigeria and the Gold Coast and was willing to abandon the constitutions placed on the statute book only a few years before. The new constitutions introduced in 1951 marked a fresh departure. For the Gold Coast, the period 1946–51 was 'the great watershed of Ghanaian politics when the "model colony" run by the officials, chiefs, and intelligentsia was tranformed into a national parliamentary system under the control of a People's Party'.[2] This triumph of the CPP represented the emergence of a third political generation in the Gold Coast, Kwame Nkrumah's 'verandah boys'. In Nigeria the change was not as radical. The representatives elected to the new Eastern and Western regional legislatures in 1951 were drawn from the educated élite that had emerged in the hinterland during the 1920s and 1930s, solid and respectable teachers and traders, with a leavening of lawyers. In northern Nigeria, control remained firmly in the hands of relatives and clients of the traditional rulers.

Nevertheless, in Nigeria as in the Gold Coast—and to a lesser extent in Sierra Leone—there existed after 1951 the structural framework for a 'national parliamentary system'. In the Gold Coast, the Northern Territories had at last been brought into the legislature through African representatives. The principle of elected representation as the basis for the majority membership of the legislature had been accepted in Nigeria

[1] Wallace-Johnson's Youth League, which attempted to link the two, failed to survive the detention of its leader by the administration during the war.

[2] Dennis Austin, *Politics in Ghana, 1946–1960* (London, Oxford University Press, 1964), p. 49.

and the Gold Coast. Admittedly, the system still operated subject to certain restrictions. Both countries used indirect elections through electoral colleges, and popular participation existed only at the primary level. But all three countries had adopted the ministerial system, even though in a limited form, and political power began to pass into the hands of the leaders of African parties.

The 1951 constitutions thus marked a decisive break in British policy. Those of the immediate post-war period had represented a final attempt to base territorial political systems on the Native Authorities. The new nationalist parties insisted on attaining power at the centre. They thereby forced the British to give up the idea of working for the 'evolution' from the bottom upward of institutions designed to accommodate 'responsible behaviour'; instead the authorities had to adopt a conscious policy of engineering. The pretence of building the system on the basis of traditional institutions was abandoned, and central control over local government and traditional chieftainship was surrendered to the new men. In eastern and western Nigeria and the Gold Coast the new men then sought to take firm control of the local councils themselves. In northern Nigeria and Sierra Leone the closer social links between new men and chiefs precluded a similar effort. Nevertheless, all three territories had experienced a crucial transformation. Both local and central institutions began to pass under the control of Africans, who now themselves began to play a major part in creating the structural basis of independence.

The British, of course, always retained the ultimate control over this process of what David Apter has termed 'political institutional transfer'.[1] It was they who decided when a sufficient political balance had been struck between forces in each territory to ensure stability in independence, and when enough Africans had been trained to man the senior positions in the administration, the defence forces and the police. Once the British had established the basic political structures, the new African élites had to prove their capacity for controlling the state in a 'responsible' manner; but it was now in the hands of these élites that the country's troubled political future lay.

---

[1] David E. Apter, *Ghana in transition* (New York, 1963), pp. 3–4 and *passim*.

3-2

BIBLIOGRAPHY

Ade-Morrison, H. [Letter to the Editor.] *Sierra Leone Weekly News*, 13 Aug. 1939.

Apter, David E. *Ghana in transition*. New York, 1963.

Austin, Dennis. *Politics in Ghana, 1946–1960*. London, Oxford University Press, 1964.

Awolowo, Obafemi. *Awo: the autobiography of Chief Obafemi Awolowo*. Cambridge University Press, 1960.

Path to Nigerian freedom. London, 1947.

Bourret, F. M. *Ghana: the road to independence, 1919–1957*. 3rd ed. Stanford University Press, 1960.

Bradbury, R. E. 'Continuities and discontinuities in pre-colonial and colonial Benin politics (1897–1951)', in *Proceedings of the 1966 Conference of the Association of Social Anthropologists*, I. M. Lewis, ed. (Association of Social Anthropologists Monograph, No. 7.) London, 1968.

Buell, Raymond L. *The native problem in Africa*. 2nd ed. London, 1965.

Busia, K. *The position of the chief in the modern political system of Ashanti: a study of the influence of contemporary social changes on Ashanti political institutions*. London, Oxford University Press, 1951.

Coleman, James S. *Nigeria: background to nationalism*. Berkeley and Los Angeles, University of California Press, 1958.

Crowder, Michael. 'Indirect rule, French and British style', *Africa*, 1964, **34**.

Deschamps, Hubert. 'Et maintenant, Lord Lugard?' *Africa*, 1963, **33**.

Ezera, Kalu. *Constitutional development in Nigeria: an analytical study of Nigeria's constitution-making developments and the historical and political factors that affected constitutional change*. 2nd ed. Cambridge University Press, 1964.

Gailey, Harry A. *A history of the Gambia*. London, 1964.

Gold Coast. Governor (Sir Frederick Gordon Guggisberg). *The Gold Coast: a review of the events of 1920–1926 and the prospects of 1927–28*. Accra, 1927.

Hailey, William Malcolm, 1st baron. *An African survey: a study of problems arising in Africa south of the Sahara*. London, Oxford University Press, 1957.

Native administration in the British African territories. 5 vols. London, 1950–3.

Hopkins, A. G. 'Economic aspects of political movements in Nigeria and in the Gold Coast, 1918–1939', *Journal of African History*, 1966, **7**, no. 1.

Kilson, Martin. *Political change in a West African state: a study of the modernization process in Sierra Leone*. Cambridge, Harvard University Press, 1966.

Kimble, David. *A political history of Ghana: the rise of Gold Coast nationalism, 1850–1928*. Oxford, Clarendon Press, 1963.

Kirk-Greene, A. H M., ed. *The principles of native administration in Nigeria: selected documents, 1900–1947.* London, Oxford University Press, 1965.

Lloyd, Peter C. 'The impact of local government in the Yoruba towns of Western Nigeria: an analysis of the parts played today by the ọbas and chiefs and by the new groups of traders and literates'. D.Phil. thesis, Oxford University, 1958.

Lugard, Frederick John Dealtry, 1st baron. *The dual mandate in British tropical Africa.* 5th ed. London, 1965.

Mair, Lucy. *Native policies in Africa.* London, 1936.

Nichol, E. [Letter to the editor.] *Sierra Leone Weekly News,* 4 Oct. 1924.

Nigeria. Governor (Sir Bernard Bourdillon). *Memorandum on the future political development of Nigeria.* Lagos, 1939.

Governor (Sir Arthur Richards). *Political and constitutional future of Nigeria: Governor of Nigeria's despatch to the Secretary of State for the Colonies, December 6, 1944.* Sessional Paper No. 4 of 1945. Lagos, 1945.

Odumosu, Oluwole Idowu. *The Nigerian constitution: history and development.* London, 1963.

Perham, Margery. *Colonial sequence, 1930 to 1949: a chronological commentary upon British colonial policy, especially in Africa.* London, 1967.

Lugard. 2 vols. London, 1956–60.

Native administration in Nigeria. London, Oxford University Press, 1937.

Porter, Arthur T. *Creoledom: a study of the development of Freetown society.* London, Oxford University Press, 1963.

'Rambler', *Sierra Leone Weekly News,* 12 Aug. 1939.

Rhodie, Samuel. 'The Gold Coast aborigines abroad', *Journal of African History,* 1965, **6**, no. 3.

Robinson, Kenneth. *The dilemmas of trusteeship: aspects of British colonial policy between the wars.* London, Oxford University Press, 1965.

Sklar, Richard L. *Nigerian political parties.* Princeton University Press, 1963.

Tamuno, Tekena N. *Nigeria and elective representation, 1923–1947.* London, 1966.

Tordoff, William. *Ashanti under the Prempehs, 1888–1935.* London, Oxford University Press, 1965.

Wheare, Joan. *The Nigerian Legislative Council.* London, 1950.

Wight, Martin. *The Gold Coast Legislative Council.* London, 1947.

Wraith, Ronald E. *Guggisberg.* London, Oxford University Press, 1967.

CHAPTER 2

BRITISH SETTLERS NORTH OF THE ZAMBEZI, 1920 TO 1960

by GEORGE BENNETT

The territories of British settlement in tropical Africa were true colonies in every sense of the word. As population-projections of the mother country, they were but the last in a long line that descends from the American colonies through the later settlements that grew during the nineteenth century to become self-governing dominions under the British crown. The twentieth-century colonists in tropical Africa expected to attain in their new lands the same status. As typical frontiersmen, many had come from the older colonies. While in this they followed patterns similar to those in America described by F. J. Turner, it meant in Africa that the immediate source was South Africa. Yet South Africa's emigrants remained within the British Empire, and Britain continued to be responsible for them. Thus the most important discussions concerning their future were always likely to take place in London.

To this general practice there was one exception: Southern Rhodesia. From its inception through the Pioneer Column of 1890, Southern Rhodesia always retained a peculiar status. Whitehall never controlled it either fully or effectively. From being initially part of the personal empire of Cecil Rhodes and his British South Africa Company, it passed in 1923 to the anomalous and contradictory status of 'a self-governing colony'. While the British government retained nominal powers of review over legislation affecting the African population, it was never able to exercise this power openly. The very passage of the Land Apportionment Act in 1930, with a Labour Government in power in Britain, seemed to indicate the weakness, even the powerlessness, of the imperial government in the face of Southern Rhodesian white settler determination.

Thus Kenya was regarded as the real testing ground of imperial policy in regard to African countries with European settlement. Major debates of the 1920s and early 1930s focused upon the Colony. The

Map 3. East Africa, 1960

literature of criticism that developed was enormous. Two books by former Kenya civil servants—*Kenya* (1924) by Norman Leys, a medical officer who was caught up in the Masai move of 1911, and *Kenya from Within* (1927) by the controversial retired Director of Public Works, W. McGregor Ross—were long quarried for argument. It became natural in British humanitarian circles to pay greater attention to activities in Kenya than to those of the other settler colonies. It is thus natural to follow mainly the fortunes of the Kenya settlers until the concept of multi-racial partnership, an idea applied first in Kenya and East Africa, was taken up in the 1950s as imperial policy for Central Africa. In that decade occurred a dual debate about the future of white settlement: over the federation of Rhodesia and Nyasaland and over a Kenya involved in the violence of the Mau Mau Emergency. In the end the multi-racial solution broke down. The territories north of the Zambezi, which remained under Colonial Office control, attained independence in the 1960s under African governments. In these territories the British government retained constitutional power and could act. Their story was different from that of Southern Rhodesia where power, in all senses, remained with the settlers, as it had since 1923.

In many ways Kenya was the most northerly extension of the South African frontier. Boers had trekked overland in 1906 and had settled on the Uasin Gishu plateau around Eldoret in what was then the East African Protectorate. Among English-speaking South Africans who went north in the difficult conditions of the post-Boer War recession were two men from Johannesburg: Robert Chamberlain and A. S. Flemmer. Their obtaining of large land concessions in the Rift Valley was a major factor in the resignation of Sir Charles Eliot as Commissioner of the Protectorate in 1904. Although Chamberlain played a leading role in the politics of the Pastoralists' Association in 1907, the newcomers from South Africa found their main spokesman in an Irishman, a man with colonial experience elsewhere—in New Zealand— Ewart S. Grogan. Although spoken of in the first European election in Kenya in 1920 as 'the people's leader',[1] Grogan was unable to establish himself against the man who was recognized in the 1920s as the Kenya Europeans' spokesman, Lord Delamere.

If the English love a lord, so it appeared did the Kenya settlers, both by accepting Delamere as their first leader, and perhaps even more when they took next, in the 1930s, Lord Francis Scott in this role, for his

[1] *East African Standard*, leading article, 26 Feb. 1920.

aristocratic, and even royal, connexions were impressive. Kenya appeared as the colony with the most aristocratic group of settlers that had ever gone out from Britain. The Europeans of Kenya realized that this might give them strength in their dealings with Britain. They could express themselves in two Houses of Lords: the local, for so was the Norfolk Hotel nicknamed in Nairobi, and, at moments of crisis, its eponymous source in London. They knew also that in the imperial capital the voice of white settlerdom in Africa spoke with more significance after the First World War had raised General Smuts to a position of considerable influence in British political circles. Thus in the battles of the 1920s, appeals from Nairobi's Europeans went both south and north, to Pretoria and Cape Town as well as to London.

However, London was never solidly behind the Kenya settlers. The Colonial Office might be swayed by their pressures, but its sympathetic officials, as well as ministers, did not always find it easy to convince cabinets, who had also India to consider. During the 1920s the British government was increasingly preoccupied with the rising tide of Indian nationalism. While the British and Indian governments did not like Gandhi and the Congress, they did want to hold the support of those whom they regarded as 'the moderates' in India. But these men were no less concerned over the position of the Kenya Indians than was the Congress. Indeed, the powerful Indian business community of Bombay was heavily involved in East Africa, where the predominant Indian group was from Gujarat. Thus Bombay newspapers, and the influential liberal journal of Poona, the *Servant of India*, subjected the government of India to heavy and incessant pressure. Indians were fighting for equal rights as British citizens in the Empire, and Kenya was regarded as the testing ground for this struggle.[1] But the Kenya Europeans could not be persuaded to accept that their interests should yield to imperial considerations. Already in 1919 they had obtained the franchise, then denied to the Indians, just as earlier they had succeeded in shutting the Indians out from land-holding in their White Highlands.

The First World War had given the Kenya settlers the opportunity to establish South African practices in yet another way: through the introduction of a pass-system. While the original legislation for Native

---

[1] For example, see the remarks of Srinivasa Sastri, who visited East Africa for the government of India in 1929, as quoted in Sir William Keith Hancock, *Survey of British Commonwealth affairs* (London, Oxford University Press, 1937), I, 222. Hancock's Ch. 4, sec. 3, in this volume remains the best short account of the Indian controversy in Kenya in the 1920s.

Registration had been passed in 1915, it only became effective in August 1920. From then on, African opposition to this compulsory carrying of the finger-printed *kipande* by adult males provided fuel for the development of African political feeling. Harry Thuku, leading the East African Association, was soon in touch with the Indians. While their immediate interests might be different, they were able to ally in their struggles against settler domination expressing itself in South African methods and terminology. However, it was possible to check the Africans in 1922 with the arrest and deportation of Thuku to the north of Kenya; but the Indians, supported from India, were able to continue the fight.

The significantly named white paper, *Indians in Kenya*,[1] imposed a first check on the aspirations of Kenya's Europeans. They were by this instrument denied their hope of self-government for the foreseeable future in the very same year that internal self-government was granted to the Southern Rhodesian Europeans. Yet to ensure that the Indians would not obtain their demands in the controversy, the Kenya Europeans had been prepared to use violence and even to plot the kidnapping of the governor. The British government did not feel able to reply by force. Possibly they asked themselves whether British officers and British troops would remain loyal if called on to act against white settlers. The Colonial Secretary, the Duke of Devonshire, also told the Cabinet that the use of native troops would, in such an emergency, be 'fatal to British prestige throughout Africa' and, in a more remarkable assertion, that such action would mean that in the whole continent a European would not be safe in any area of native population. Finally, the Duke was sure that such an action would be bitterly condemned in Parliament.[2] The incident, in fact, established a precedent whereby European settlers in British Africa could hold British governments to ransom. In this case the Kenya contestants were summoned to London. Before the governor, Sir Robert Coryndon, left Nairobi, he exacted from the remaining settlers a promise to refrain from 'direct action' during his absence. His remark: 'Gentlemen, you may remember that I am South African born',[3] served to indicate his position in the matter and hence in the coming discussions.

[1] Great Britain, *Parliamentary papers*, Vol. XVIII, Cmd 1922, *Memorandum on Indians in Kenya* (London, 1923).
[2] Duke of Devonshire, secret memorandum for the Cabinet, 14 Feb. 1923 (Copy in India Office, Private Office File No. 300).
[3] Elspeth Huxley, *White man's country: Lord Delamere and the making of Kenya* (London, 1935), II, 156.

After the London discussions Coryndon returned to introduce native policies that had southern African connotations. This was true both with regard to the Local Native Councils (LNCs) and to the Dual Policy. In introducing the former in 1924, Coryndon both obtained Delamere's support and paid tribute to the new Chief Native Commissioner, G. V. Maxwell, who had brought ideas on the subject from Fiji. (From his frequent references to his past, Maxwell soon became known as 'Fijiwe'.) In fact, Maxwell had fitted in with ideas of at least one of the Kenya administrators, the Deputy Chief Native Commissioner, Lieutenant-Colonel Oscar F. Watkins. The settlers, knowing Colonel Watkins's belief in African development, had opposed his becoming Chief Native Commissioner and had asked that the Colonial Office should appoint someone from outside. While they had in mind South Africa, whence other officials had recently arrived, the Colonial Office replied by appointing Maxwell, whom the settlers soon grew to dislike no less then they had Ainsworth, his predecessor, and Watkins. These officials were, in fact, as opposed to settler influence as had been acting governor Frederick Jackson before the war.[1]

There is then a certain irony in Delamere's support for the institution of the LNCs on the grounds that they were patterned on the native councils of South Africa. The other Europeans were more hesitant in the Legislative Council debate.[2] Perhaps they were the more far-sighted; even if the LNCs' development was somewhat slow, they did come to provide more opportunities for democratic debate among Africans than did the chiefs' councils of the indirect rule system in Tanganyika and elsewhere.

Coryndon's Dual Policy, defined as 'the complementary development of non-native and native production',[3] recall the phrases of separate development from farther south.[4] While the East Africa Commission

---

[1] Jackson's feelings about 'nigger-shooters' from South Africa and his communications to the Foreign Office on the matter only became known when the F.O. papers were open to historians (see my *Kenya, a political history: the colonial period* [London, Oxford University Press, 1963], p. 11). In his *Early days in East Africa, etc.* (London, 1930), Jackson was most circumspect in his references to the Kenya settlers.

[2] Kenya Legislative Council, *Minutes of Proceedings*, 20 May 1924, pp. 75-95.

[3] Huxley, *White man's country*, II, 192.

[4] See, for example, discussion of Sir Godfrey Huggins's 'two pyramid policy' in Richard Gray, *Two nations: aspects of the development of race relations in the Rhodesias and Nyasaland, 1918–1953* (London and New York, Oxford University Press, 1960), pp. 151 ff., and of 'parallel development' in Lewis H. Gann and Michael Gelfand, *Huggins of Rhodesia* (London, 1964), pp. 171, 173.

under Ormsby-Gore reported in 1925 in favour of Coryndon's ideas,[1] they did not receive a ready acclaim from the settlers. Indeed, the settlers were no less suspicious of the appointment of the Ormsby-Gore Commission itself, fearing Lancashire cotton interests behind it; and they maintained the same suspicion over the appointment of Coryndon's successor as governor, Sir Edward Grigg (later Lord Altrincham), who came from being Liberal Member of Parliament for Oldham in Lancashire. To the settlers, the Dual Policy seemed likely, through its encouragement of native peasant production, to lead to a decline of their labour supply.

However, they need not have feared. The Dual Policy, as far as native production was concerned, was not prosecuted with any great vigour. The South African Director of Agriculture, Alex Holm, was a convinced believer in European farming and made that his primary concern. Africans who applied for licences to grow coffee under the Coffee Plantation Registration Ordinance of 1918 were refused, unless they were, like the Meru, far distant from areas of European settlement. While the Europeans had fears over disease and the safety of this major crop in the Kenya economy, Africans could note that the Chagga on the slopes of Mount Kilimanjaro were being encouraged by the Tanganyika administration to grow the delicate *arabica*. Certainly the policy of stopping the Kikuyu from growing coffee was but storing up trouble for the future; it added one more grievance to those resulting from the *kipande* and land.

Land, it has been said with some reason, has always been the mainspring of politics in Kenya. The main lines of the division between European and African land were laid down before 1920, the year in which the East Africa Protectorate became Kenya Colony, a status the European settlers had long been calling for. On their side the Africans feared the change, and with good reason as it subsequently turned out; for in 1922 the Chief Justice, Sir Jacob Barth, found, in a famous judgement, that thereby native rights in land in the reserves had 'disappeared, and the natives in occupation of such Crown Lands become tenants at will of the Crown on the land actually occupied'.[2] The Ormsby-Gore Commission pointed in 1925 to the consequent need to reassure Africans by establishing the security of the native reserves,

[1] Great Britain, *Parliamentary papers*, Vol. IX, Cmd 2387, *Report of the East Africa Commission* (London, 1924-5), p. 181.
[2] Cited in W. McGregor Ross, *Kenya from within* (London, 1927), p. 87.

more particularly because a large area of the Nandi reserve had been taken for the Soldier Settlement Scheme of 1919–20. Over this the Colonial Office had been unable to act because it had been informed too late for it to reverse the government's action.[1] Here was but one example in Kenya—of which land questions provided other illustrations—of the impossibility of control from a distance.

However, on his appointment as Governor in 1925, Grigg was instructed by the Colonial Secretary, Leopold S. Amery, to consider devising means to secure the native lands. Grigg put his ideas in a memorandum in March 1927 recommending the permanent establishment of native reserves. At the same time, he rejected the idea of Lord Lugard that the native lands should be divided from the colony and placed under a separate administration. Instead, Grigg and Amery urged that the settlers should be drawn in as 'trustees'. In this they developed a view which Amery put in the House of Commons[2] and which the Conservative Party deployed later in supporting Central African federation, namely, that through the exercise of responsibility white settlers in Africa would learn responsibility and behave accordingly to the African peoples.

Thus in 1928 the Kenya-elected Europeans supported the Native Lands Trust Bill in the Legislative Council, but Canon Leakey, representing African interests, was not so sure: he felt he could not vote for the bill as not providing adequate safeguards. The question of the Indian, A. H. Malik, was more pungent: 'could you set a cat to watch the interest of a mouse?' More striking still, however, was the action of the Senior Commissioners. These officials very rarely contributed to the debates; but on this occasion, led by Colonel Watkins, who was subsequently censured for his action by Grigg, they voiced their criticisms, with Watkins attacking the proposed membership of the Trust Board.[3] At this point the visiting Hilton Young Commission intervened. They requested, and obtained, over the objections of Grigg and the European elected members, a delay in the further progress of the bill until both it and their report had been considered together by the Colonial Office.

The presence in East Africa of the Hilton Young Commission

[1] Great Britain, *Parliamentary papers*, Vol. IX, Cmd 2387, *Report of the East Africa Commission* (London, 1924–5), pp. 28–9.
[2] Great Britain, House of Commons, *Parliamentary debates: official report*, 5th Ser., Vol. CCIX, 34th Parliament, 3rd Sess., 19 July 1927, Vol. VIII, col. 291.
[3] Kenya Legislative Council, *Debates*, 14 June 1928, pp. 320–35.

highlights another element in the European group: the missionaries. One member of the Commission was J. H. Oldham, secretary in London of the International Missionary Council. He had already visited Kenya and had impressed both Grigg and the settler leaders with his sympathy for their position. He appeared to share the view that they were reasonable men and would learn through responsibility. Hence Grigg had pressed for his appointment to the Commission, and it had been both welcomed by the settlers and criticized by the Indians. When the Commission arrived in Kenya from Uganda, the first Kenya missionary of importance to appear before them was that notable critic of the settlers, Archdeacon Owen of Kavirondo. However, he was so handled by the chairman, Sir Edward Hilton Young, that his intervention made little impression. In central Kenya other and more moderate missionaries pressed their criticism, in particular over the Native Lands Trust Bill; but perhaps the missionaries of Nyasaland, both Scottish and Anglican, were more influential in convincing Oldham with their general criticism of European settlers' hindering of African development.[1] Whether this be the reason or not, Oldham drew together with Sir George Schuster on the Commission as they progressed round eastern Africa. Together with Sir Reginald Mant, they concluded in the majority report of the Commission that the power of the European settlers needed answering by a strengthening of the imperial presence to provide greater protection of African interests throughout the area.

The Kenya government later looked back on the coming of the Hilton Young Commission as stirring up African political activity. Certainly after it there was in Kenya an increase of missionary action on behalf of Africans. Canon Leakey and his successors as representatives of African interests in the Legislative Council became steadily more effective in their speaking there. In visiting London in 1931 in order to give evidence to the Parliamentary Joint Select Committee, Leakey was able to consult with the now more informed Oldham, who in the Kikuyu female-circumcision controversy had warned the senior Scottish missionary in Kenya, the Reverend Dr J. W. Arthur, not to make the same mistake in handling nationalism that missionaries had earlier made in India.[2]

[1] Information from Sir George Schuster, member of the Hilton Young Commission. See also the evidence taken in Kenya and Nyasaland (mimeograph in Colonial Office library, London).
[2] Dr J. H. Oldham to Rev Dr J. W. Arthur, 19 Dec. 1929, in papers of Dr Arthur (sometime Scottish missionary in Kenya), Edinburgh University Library, Edinburgh.

However, the Hilton Young report had wider implications. The commissioners had been appointed to examine the question of 'Closer Union' between the British territories of East and Central Africa, and Amery hoped that their report would pave the way for federation in this vast area. He had long been in favour of this and, in appointing Grigg to Kenya in 1925, had instructed him to report again on the matter. Grigg proceeded to convert Delamere to the idea. In October 1925, Delamere called a conference of Europeans from the whole area at Tukuyu in southern Tanganyika, explaining six weeks later in Nairobi that Kenya could not remain 'an isolated island of civilization'; it must 'radiate her civilizing influence southward to meet the same influence filtering northwards from Rhodesia'.[1] Although Delamere organized later conferences in Nairobi and at Livingstone in Northern Rhodesia (now Zambia), the Rhodesians were not convinced; they did not desire to be submerged in 'the Black North'. Such feelings were strengthened in 1930.

The Hilton Young report insisted again upon the paramountcy of African interests—which had been proclaimed for Kenya in the 1923 white paper. Then in June 1930 the Colonial Secretary of the Labour government, Lord Passfield (formerly Sidney Webb), took up the phrase, and in a Memorandum on Native Policy[2] applied it to the whole area that the Hilton Young commissioners had examined. The memorandum was issued without consultation with the governors of the area, who received their copies in sealed packages with orders to open them only on the day of publication.[3] The settler reaction, from Kenya southward, was unanimous, with the Northern Rhodesian whites being, perhaps, the most outspoken:

The British Empire is primarily concerned with the furtherance of the interests of British subjects of British race and only thereafter with other British subjects, protected races, and the nationals of other countries, in that order... To subordinate the interests of civilized Britons to the development of alien races, whose capability of substantial further advancement has not been demonstrated, appears to be contrary to natural law.[4]

---

[1] Huxley, *White man's country*, II, 199 ff. and *East African Standard*, 5 Dec. 1925.

[2] Great Britain, *Parliamentary papers*, Vol. XXVII, Cmd 3573, *Memorandum on native policy in East Africa* (London, 1929–30).

[3] Great Britain, House of Commons, *Parliamentary debates: official report*, 5th Ser., Vol. CCXLVI, 35th Parliament, 2nd Sess., 9 Dec. 1930, Vol. III, cols. 367–8.

[4] Great Britain, *Parliamentary papers*, Vol. XXIII, Cmd 3731, *Correspondence with regard to native policy in Northern Rhodesia* (London, 1930–1), quoted in Gray, *Two nations*, p. 42.

This 'black paper'—as the Kenya Europeans called it—determined the Northern Rhodesians to turn south. Thereafter 'the Black North' was not for them; they would seek safety in union or federation with the self-governing Southern Rhodesia. In so doing, however, they had one tip to pick up from the Hilton Young Commission. Its chairman put forward the idea, in his minority report, that the lands flanking Northern Rhodesia's central 'line of rail' should be linked with Southern Rhodesia, with the rest of the territory separated off as native protectorates under Britain,[1] an idea that in Rhodesian minds was finally laid to rest only with the advent of Zambia's independence.

During the 1920s then, the running was made by the Kenya Europeans. To all this the quietus was applied by the Joint Select Committee of the two Houses of Parliament. The East African question—by which was meant, in effect, the Kenya question—had become of such controversial importance that it had led to an inquiry at the level normally reserved in imperial matters for India. Building on the committee's report, which devised a form of words to satisfy everybody over paramountcy and denied again settler hopes of constitutional advancement, a new Colonial Secretary, Sir Philip Cunliffe-Lister (later Lord Swinton), proceeded on the motto 'action, not words'.

Cunliffe-Lister had, however, to send out to Kenya commissions to investigate finance and land questions. The inquiry of Lord Moyne on finance disappointed the settlers with his comment that they enjoyed 'the amenities of civilization in return for a relatively light scale of contribution'. Moyne considered that the Africans were heavily burdened with taxation and that, as Maxwell and Leakey had urged to the Joint Select Committee, it would be better that African matters should have a statutory revenue freed from supervision by the Legislative Council's Select Committee on the Estimates with its majority of European unofficials. Further, Moyne reopened an old issue by suggesting again the introduction of an income tax.[2] This the settlers had fought off in the 1920s; and this time they managed to delay it until 1937, when they obtained in exchange for 'a light Income Tax' on Rhodesian lines an inquiry into the reconstitution of the Executive Council.

[1] Great Britain, *Parliamentary papers*, Vol. v, Cmd 3234, *Report of the commission on closer union of the dependencies in Eastern and Central Africa* (London, 1928–9), pp. 262–5.
[2] Great Britain, *Parliamentary papers*, Vol. vi, Cmd 4093, *Report by the financial commissioner (Lord Moyne) on certain questions in Kenya* (London, 1931–2).

Having been shut out by the Joint Select Committee from obtaining an unofficial majority in the Legislative Council, the Europeans were seeking power through control of the executive, with the hope that at least some of their number might obtain portfolio responsibility as ministers. In this the lead was increasingly taken by Major (later Sir) F. W. Cavendish-Bentinck, who had attained prominence through organizing the Europeans' demand for greater legal security for their White Highlands. The land commission recommended by the Joint Select Committee was chaired by Sir Morris Carter, who had already carried out the inquiry into Southern Rhodesia's land that lay behind the passing of the Land Apportionment Act there in 1930.[1]

In Southern Rhodesia Carter had accepted the arguments that some measure of segregation between the races was desirable to reduce friction. This principle was now to be applied in Kenya, where the commissioners were to define for the first time the boundaries of the White Highlands. The three fat volumes of evidence that they received record in fascinating form the claims and counter-claims of the various groups in Kenya.[2]

Here is the lively argument over what Europeans and Kikuyu remembered of their transactions at the beginning of the century. The Europeans, under Cavendish-Bentinck's lead, were not satisfied with the final land settlement arising from the Carter report in 1934; they wanted, but did not obtain, the Leroghi plateau of the Samburu. However, they were effective in their pressure for the consolidation of their Highlands by an imperial Order in Council. This they finally obtained in 1939 from a reluctant British government which sought to avoid any discrimination in law on grounds of race or colour. In Kenya's Legislative Council, which had then no African members, only the Indians—though with one European supporter, the member for Mombasa—could in 1939 protest against this strengthening of racial privilege.[3] The lead that Cavendish-Bentinck took in all this lay behind the racial explosion in the Legislative Council in 1945 on his appointment as the first Member for Agriculture. A new governor, Sir Philip

---

[1] Southern Rhodesia, Land Commission, 1925, *Report* (Salisbury, 1926).

[2] Great Britain, Kenya Land Commission, *Report, September 1933* [and *Evidence and memoranda*], Cmd 4556 (London, 1934), 4 vols. (*Evidence and memoranda* issued as Great Britain, Colonial Office, Colonial, No. 91.)

[3] Kenya Legislative Council, *Debates*, 21 April 1939, pp. 256–310. However, one Indian member, Isher Dass, did read into the record, over European protests, the petition to the Colonial Secretary of the African political associations against the Order.

Mitchell, was then introducing a new constitutional system through which local Europeans, but not Asians or Africans, were advanced to positions of authority.

In this new Membership system, the Kenya settlers were again ahead of those in Northern Rhodesia. They were more advanced, too, in their thinking, for in 1947 they devised a phrase, 'merit and ability', which should be the measure for African advance, though with the implied understanding that they, the Kenya Europeans, would decide whether Africans had attained the necessary standards for them to be appointed to positions of responsibility. The Europeans' organization, the Electors' Union, was thus able to express itself with confidence, since Cavendish-Bentinck was not only the Member for Agriculture, but the terms of his appointment included also the encouragement of further white settlement.[1] In the years after the Second World War the European groups of Kenya, Northern and Southern Rhodesia each doubled in size. Many of the new arrivals were seeking to escape from a Britain under a Labour government, believing that in the open spaces of Africa there were opportunities denied them in the heavily taxed welfare state.

Perhaps it was in part through the confidence bred of increased numbers that the European leaders in these British territories began to speak and act with renewed vigour. In Kenya they obtained a modification of the Labour Colonial Secretary's proposals for territorial co-operation in East Africa,[2] while in Central Africa the Southern Rhodesian Prime Minister, Sir Godfrey Huggins (later Lord Malvern), was prepared to look once more at 'the Black North'. On 1 January 1948 the East Africa High Commission came into existence, linking together the common services of Kenya, Tanganyika and Uganda; through it the Kenya Europeans looked for the development of an East African federation. In the following July Huggins instructed his High Commissioner in London to work for an amalgamation with Northern Rhodesia. In pursuit of this the forceful Northern Rhodesian leader Roy (later Sir Roy) Welensky visited London, where he found, however, that neither the Labour government nor the Conservative leaders in opposition would consider anything more than federation.

---

[1] *East African Standard*, 7 March 1947.

[2] Cf. Great Britain, Colonial Office, *Inter-territorial organisation in East Africa, revised proposals* (Colonial, No. 210; London, 1947), with its predecessor Great Britain, Colonial Office, *Inter-territorial organisation in East Africa* (Colonial, No. 191; London, 1945).

To obtain even this there were obstacles to be overcome, and prolonged negotiations proved necessary. However, in the late 1940s, as these negotiations began, a cloud for white settlers was arising in East Africa. As a mandated territory Tanganyika had been largely ignored—even though the Kenya settlers had sometimes been concerned over Sir Donald Cameron's liberalizing policies as its governor in the late 1920s—but the coming of the first United Nations Visiting Mission there in 1948, and still more the Tanganyika governor's idea in 1950 for constitutional development on a basis of parity between the races, aroused fears in Nairobi. A European meeting there, in April 1950, resolved to seek help in the Rhodesias, and even from farther south. Already the Kenya Europeans had fought against, and had obtained a modification of, Sir Philip Mitchell's racial parity ideas for the East Africa High Commission. Mitchell had brought these ideas from Fiji, where he had been governor during the war. Thus he introduced into East African policy-making the concept of multi-racial partnership, and the British government took up the expression as the key to policy throughout East and Central Africa.

Africans, in rejecting partnership, considered it simply as a protection for the Europeans, a device to check their nationalist aspirations. As the federation of Rhodesia and Nyasaland was being negotiated, Africans in Nyasaland asked why there should be two British policies in Africa: one working with African nationalism in West Africa but the other proclaiming partnership in East and Central Africa.

In Kenya the challenge was to be yet more forthright and brutal. There the nationalist leader, Jomo Kenyatta, who had been with the West African Kwame Nkrumah at the Pan-African Congress in Manchester in 1945, had returned to Nairobi in 1946 to a position of considerable difficulty. The constitutional moderates of the Kenya African Union, formed in 1944, were losing control of the situation to those in the Kikuyu tribe, who believed that only through violence could white power be broken. By mid-1952 Kenyatta was a desperately unhappy man. Rejected by the colour-conscious European society of Kenya,

He had no friends...The people who could answer his needs as a western man had erected a barrier of color against him in spite of the fact that the taproots of their culture had become the taproots of his culture too. By denying him access to those things which complete the life of western man,

they had forced him back into the tribalism from which he had so painfully
freed himself over the years...He was the victim both of tribalism and of
westernism gone sick.[1]

This judgement of the South African coloured novelist Peter Abrahams,
visiting Kenyatta just before the Mau Mau Emergency, illustrates most
completely a major failure of settler societies in British tropical Africa:
they had no place for the African who most desired to learn from them
and to take part in their civilization. In Kenya the Kikuyu were the
prime example of a people possessing this desire. Is it an oversimplifica-
tion to believe that the taproot of the violence of Mau Mau was
frustration?[2] How then could partnership be brought about?

In the circumstances of the Mau Mau Emergency, the Colonial
Secretary Oliver Lyttelton (later Lord Chandos) decided to make the
attempt. Arriving in Nairobi shortly after the declaration of the Emergency in October 1952, he told the European leaders 'with brutal
candour' that they could not 'expect to hold all the political power and
to exclude Africans from the legislature and from the Government';
it was necessary for their security to build 'a multi-racial society'.[3]

Even as the Mau Mau violence reached its climax in early 1953, the
final details of the Federation of Rhodesia and Nyasaland were being
settled in London. It came into existence in August of that year with
the objective of partnership written into the preamble of its constitution. There, however, the British government did not insert provisions,
as Lyttelton did in the Kenya constitution of 1954, for non-European
ministers; in the Central African constitution there was a guarantee
only of African membership of the legislature. Perhaps, however, this
was only another reflection of the essential weakness of the British
government in Central Africa.

In Kenya the Mau Mau revolt necessitated for the first time in peace
the coming of British troops to Kenya. Over the years successive
British governments had been, in the traditional manner of British
colonial policy, devolving power into the local situation. The Mau Mau

[1] P. Abrahams, 'The Blacks', in *An African treasury: articles, essays, stories, poems, by
black Africans*, Langston Hughes, ed. (New York, 1960), p. 59. The whole of this
most interesting article will repay study.
[2] At least the Corfield Report (Great Britain, *Parliamentary papers*, Vol. x, Cmnd 1030,
Historical survey of the origins and growth of Mau Mau [London, 1959–60]), p. 26,
appears to support this view.
[3] Oliver Lyttelton Chandos, 1st viscount, *The memoirs of Lord Chandos* (London, 1962),
p. 398.

outbreak was a clear indication that the local people, officials and settlers, had failed to deal with the complex multi-racial problems of Kenya. In the future the effective decisions would be taken in Whitehall. In the multi-racial constitutions of 1954, 1957 and 1960, successive Colonial Secretaries imposed their solutions.

In contrast, it seemed that in the establishment of the Federation of Rhodesia and Nyasaland in August 1953, there was an abdication of power by Britain. Salisbury in Southern Rhodesia became the capital of a state that stretched across the Zambezi to embrace two Colonial Office Protectorates. Even though the constitution was carefully drawn to protect African rights, especially over land, the question was whether through taxation and other fiscal advantages, particularly in the development of the federation's common market, the economic benefits would not flow predominantly to the European interests of Southern Rhodesia. Africans in the two northern protectorates believed that federation would be followed by a tightening of the economic colour bar personified in an influx of Southern Rhodesian settlers. Since neither this nor any immediate changes in administration—such as the feared removal of chiefs and the introduction of white 'direct rule'—took place, their worst fears declined, and with them the strength of the protest movement of the African National Congresses in these two territories. Although propaganda against federation continued, the comparative quiet of the first three years of the Federation did give its rulers a breathing-space in which to prove whether partnership was an effective reality or could be made into one.

Inserted into the constitution was a watchdog for African interests: the African Affairs Board, consisting of members of the Federal Parliament. The Board's chairman from December 1954 was John (later Sir John) Moffat, who appeared to many as the conscience of the Federation. A fourth-generation representative of the great Moffat family, so important in the history of Central Africa as missionaries and officials, Moffat himself had been a government official and was now a farmer. In July 1954 he moved a group of resolutions in the Northern Rhodesian Legislative Council in an attempt to put substance and definition into the concept of partnership.[1] A year later he took the matter on to the Federal Assembly in Salisbury, moving that an 'investigation should be made into the basic principles necessary for a united multi-racial nation' and into the parliamentary and electoral

---

[1] Northern Rhodesia Legislative Council, *Debates*, 29 July 1954, col. 616.

systems to be adopted to that end during the period of transition. Welensky, replying for the federal government, deprecated the application of 'hard and fast rules' in connexion with race relations; the essence of the problem was not primarily political, but economic and social; advances would come gradually and it was a pity to force the pace.[1] While Sir John's original resolutions had been passed in the Northern Rhodesian Legislative Council with only a single dissentient, and though they later formed the basis for proposals for constitutional change there,[2] his ideas were defeated in Salisbury in 1955 by twenty votes to nine.

The crunch for the Federation came over two measures introduced in 1957: the Constitutional Amendment Bill and the Federal Electoral Bill. In both cases the African Affairs Board used its powers to obtain the reservation of the bills for consideration in London as 'differentiating' measures. The British government, despite protests and debate in Parliament, allowed the bills to become law by issuing the necessary Orders in Council. The result was the destruction of what little confidence Africans had ever had in the African Affairs Board as a protective device. A missionary member of the Board, the Reverend Andrew Doig from Nyasaland, resigned from both the Board and the Federal Assembly, commenting: 'In my opinion, further service on the Board is useless. I feel we have got past the "point of no return" as far as an approach to real partnership is concerned.'[3] Sir John Moffat, while feeling bitter at the way the Board had been treated, remained, for he sought to obtain in the Board's place a supra-parliamentary constitutional court. In July 1958 he initiated a debate in the federal assembly on 'co-operation between peoples of the federation'. This the government thrust aside with amendments claiming that the very bills to which the Board had objected formed a basis for the establishment of a political system that could remove 'the main obstacles' to progress, obstacles which the government saw as 'the wide gap between European and African cultural and economic standards' and 'the propagation of misguided African nationalism by certain so-called African leaders'; these obstacles, the government maintained, impeded the creation of a nation working together in partnership 'in which every lawful in-

[1] Rhodesia and Nyasaland, Federal Assembly, *Debates*, 16 Aug. 1955, cols. 1685–724.
[2] Great Britain, *Parliamentary papers*, Vol. xxiv, Cmnd 530, *Proposals for constitutional change in Northern Rhodesia* (London, 1957–8).
[3] Clyde Sanger, *Central African emergency* (London, 1960), p. 170.

habitant shall have the right to progress according to his character, ability and industry'.[1]

The two bills were only part of a larger deal which Welensky had concluded with the British government in April 1957. While White-hall had at that time indicated that they would assist the enactment of the measures, they agreed also that the review of the federal constitution should take place in 1960 (that is, the first opportunity prescribed in 1953), that in the meanwhile considerable responsibility for external affairs would be given to the federal government, and that in the future the British government would not amend or repeal any federal act except at the request of the federal government.

Already, then, in April 1957 Africans were served notice that the federal government was seeking to move forward to dominion-status or independence. The enforcement by Orders in Council of the two bills against which the African Affairs Board had protested confirmed this, especially when a federal general election took place, in August 1958, on the basis of these constitutional amendments. In the elections, the European leaders clearly set out the objective of dominion-status. The trouble always with the communal electorates, both of Kenya and of Central Africa, was that politicians seeking votes necessarily appealed in racial terms and became in consequence steadily more extreme in this way: each was compelled to say that he would best preserve and advance the interests of the community concerned. The reaction was then equal and opposite in the other community.

In this particular case of 1958 the Nyasaland African leader Dr Hastings Banda was already deciding, as a result of the London agreement of April 1957, that he must return to his country 'to break this stupid Federation'. His arrival in July 1958, and the speeches he was soon making, intensified the Europeans' determination to seek security through constitutional change. They believed that Welensky would be best able to obtain this, and so returned his party to power with an overwhelming majority. The Federation was set on a collision course. Welensky and Banda never met.

Moreover, the Europeans of East and Central Africa failed to appreciate the gathering strength of African nationalism, at least as far as it affected colonial territories under metropolitan rule. Among the Europeans of this region one frequently heard it said in the mid-1950s that African nationalism was only something to do with West Africa and that the

---

[1] Rhodesia and Nyasaland, Federal Assembly, *Debates*, 1 July 1958, cols. 149–71.

well-organized and well-administered Belgian Congo would act as a barrier against its spread into this area. However, in April 1957, within a few days of the Gold Coast's independence as Ghana, there took place in Kenya the first African elections to the colony's Legislative Council. As a result, powerful voices were able to express African aspirations in this major political forum.

Looking back on these years, a later Colonial Secretary, Iain MacLeod, has commented of his predecessors that they would not accept the warnings of Sir Charles Arden-Clarke, Governor then of the Gold Coast, that political progress there would prove a marked stimulus to the growth of African nationalism elsewhere in Africa.[1] Not only was this true in Kenya in 1957, but in September 1958 the Tanganyika African National Union (TANU), which had been modelled on Nkrumah's Convention People's Party, won an overwhelming victory in elections in Tanganyika, finding for the European and Asian reserved seats, as well as for the African, candidates whom it could support. Julius Nyerere, TANU's leader, was in the process of convincing the majority of Tanganyika's non-Africans that he was a reasonable man whom they need not fear. His victory in these elections and the ones that followed in February 1959 meant that Kenya's Europeans were isolated from the white south.

January 1959 was a significant month for Central Africa. Then riots occurred in the Belgian Congo's capital of Leopoldville, a month after the All-African Peoples' Conference that Nkrumah had called in Accra in December 1958. The Belgian response to these riots was confusion and loss of morale; during 1959, beset with governmental and political troubles in Belgium itself, the administration lost its grip on the Congo. In January 1959, also, there took place at Chequers, the British Prime Minister's country residence, a conference of the East African Governors and the Colonial Secretary Lennox-Boyd (later Lord Boyd). Sir Richard Turnbull, who had become Governor of Tanganyika in July 1958, had rapidly established good relations with Nyerere and was alleged to be 'forcing the pace' in the belief that political advance in Tanganyika must be accelerated. This, however, would necessarily affect the whole of East Africa. Yet even then the British government was still able to believe that it could control the rate of change. At the Chequers conference 'a tentative time-table was suggested' for Tanganyika's possible independence in 1970, for Uganda's shortly thereafter 'and Kenya much

---

[1] Iain Macleod, 'Blundell's Kenya', *The Spectator*, 20 March 1964, No. 7082, p. 366.

later, probably after 1975'.[1] Hence it was possible for a British minister, Lord Perth, to tell Welensky in Salisbury in March: 'So far as our general colonial policy is concerned, a halt is being called to the rapid advance of colonial territories to independence. For Tanganyika, for example, we are proposing a long-term programme.'[2]

However, Perth had come to Central Africa in the wake of serious disturbances and the proclamation of an Emergency in Nyasaland. There the governor had called for the assistance of the federal government to maintain order, while the Europeans of Central Africa were convinced that there was something more far-reaching behind the Leopoldville riots and the Nyasaland troubles. They looked back to the Pan-African conference in Accra in December 1958 and concluded, though they were unable to produce evidence to substantiate this, that there had been a plot there for common action by the African political parties of Central Africa. Thus, not only the Nyasaland African leaders were arrested, but also those of Southern Rhodesia and of the Zambia Congress led by Kenneth Kaunda in Northern Rhodesia.

On their side the British government appointed a commission under a High Court judge, Mr Justice Devlin, to report on the Nyasaland troubles. But the British government under Harold Macmillan had seen also that the implications of the events in Nyasaland raised even more fundamental questions: concerning the whole working and future of the federation itself. On this, Perth said to Welensky: 'My Government has come to the conclusion that we should appoint a Royal Commission of Inquiry.'[3] The shocked Welensky reacted by a total rejection of the very idea as unacceptable, for he sensed immediately that the commission's appointment would be 'fatal' to his government and to the federation.

But there was more to come. In July the Devlin commission's report was published. This devastating document was the more impressive in its condemnation of the situation in Nyasaland—which it called a 'police state'—because on the commission's appointment all three of Devlin's colleagues had been attacked as known conservatives. Together with Devlin, they produced one of the most important analyses of the colonial position in a British African territory: a civil service paternalistic

[1] Sir Michael Blundell, *So rough a wind* (London, 1964), pp. 261-2.
[2] Sir Roy Welensky, *Welensky's 4000 days: the life and death of the Federation of Rhodesia and Nyasaland* (London, 1964), p. 139.
[3] Welensky, *Welensky's 4000 days*, p. 138.

administration believing that it knew best what was good for the people of Nyasaland faced a political leader who knew, and could work upon, the emotions of the people about federation and their association through it with Southern Rhodesia, regarded as under the control of a colour-bar practising, illiberal and domineering white oligarchy.

The Devlin commissioners saw that the arguments of the two sides never met. It was no use pointing out that Nyasaland was receiving financial benefits from federation when the reply was: 'poverty is better than slavery'.[1] At this fundamental level the commissioners were exposing the emptiness of federation itself. From then on, responsible British opinion came increasingly to the conclusion that Welensky and his European supporters had failed to measure up to the objective of partnership that had been set before them.

While at this level the Europeans of Central Africa were to be in-creasingly bereft of support, a reappraisal of Britain's position in Africa was being carried out in mid-1959 by the hard-headed realists in the Macmillan government. They might protest that they were not accept-ing the criticism of the Devlin report, and the Colonial Secretary, Lennox-Boyd, did not resign. However, after the autumn general election Iain Macleod succeeded in his room.

In Macleod's examination of his new empire, he must have been conscious of the fact that with the ending in 1960 of military conscrip-tion in Britain he had very little power to wield. Moreover, the result of the Devlin report was to make plain the impossibility of maintaining power by acceptable methods in emergency conditions in Nyasaland. British public opinion would not tolerate continued emergencies in Africa, a point which was relevant also to Kenya, where the Mau Mau Emergency still pursued a nominal existence. Macleod has indicated that in his examination of the situation, one factor was his consideration of the worst scandal over Kenya's Emergency prison camps, that of Hola.[2] The Kenya administration had been weighed and found wanting. Macleod concluded that 'swift change was needed in Kenya'.[3] In

[1] Great Britain, *Parliamentary papers*, Vol. x, Cmd 814, *Report of the Nyasaland com-mission of inquiry* (London, 1958–9).

[2] Great Britain, *Parliamentary papers*, Vol. xxv, Cmnd 795, *Record of proceedings and evidence in the inquiry into the deaths of eleven Mau Mau detainees at Hola Camp in Kenya* (London, 1958–9); and Great Britain, *Parliamentary papers*, Vol. xxv, Cmnd 816, *Further documents relating to the deaths of eleven Mau Mau detainees at Hola Camp in Kenya* (London, 1958–9).

[3] Macleod, 'Blundell's Kenya', p. 366.

November he told the House of Commons that the Mau Mau Emergency would end,[1] and in December he visited Kenya in preparation for a constitutional conference. Kenya, the territory under the Colonial Office where settler influence had reached farthest, was to be dealt with first.

Macleod has denied that he approached the Lancaster House conference on Kenya 'with a preconceived plan',[2] but as it met in January 1960 Macmillan, his Prime Minister, was travelling around Africa, noting in speeches from Accra to Cape Town 'the wind of change' blowing across the continent. At a time when it was known that many African colonies would attain independence in 1960, the British government was indicating that it did not intend to be last in the process of decolonization. Sir Michael Blundell, the then Kenya European leader, has recounted the story of Macleod greeting him during the conference with:

Look at this, this is a message to say that the Belgians are giving the Congo independence in June this year—1960—do you know what that means? We are going to be the last in the Colonial sphere instead of the first.[3]

Blundell was later able to look back and acknowledge: 'the decision of the British Government was right though unpleasant. What was wrong was the method and timing of its doing.'[4] Blundell had learned during the 1950s that his position and that of the Kenya settlers depended ultimately on British troops. He therefore had to accept London's decisions.

What of Central Africa? In the end it appeared that the Europeans of Nyasaland and Northern Rhodesia were in the same position. They, too, had no defence—unless through the use or threat of unconstitutional force[5]—against the determination of the Macmillan government to get out of Africa. Britain remained constitutionally responsible for the two northern protectorates, even though they were part of the

---

[1] Great Britain, House of Commons, *Parliamentary debates: official report*, 5th Ser., Vol. DCXIII, 42nd Parliament, 1st Sess., 10 Nov. 1959, Vol. II, cols. 204–6.

[2] Macleod, 'Blundell's Kenya', p. 366.

[3] Blundell, *So rough a wind*, p. 271. Macleod was referring to the announcement from Brussels of the contemporaneous conference there on the Belgian Congo.

[4] Blundell, *So rough a wind*, p. 281.

[5] There has been an allegation that this was tried by the federal government in February–March 1961. See the two accounts in Henry Franklin, *Unholy wedlock: the future of the Central African Federation* (London, 1963), pp. 200–4; and Welensky, *Welensky's 4000 days*, p. 323.

Federation, and the British government was ready to determine their political future. Already in 1958 Welensky had learned that the Northern Rhodesian government, supported by London, would not overlook '*African* aspirations for self-government'.[1] With Macleod's coming to the Colonial Office in 1959, the pressures of African numbers in constitution-making were to be accepted with greater readiness. Moreover, in 1959 Welensky sought to resist the Macmillan government's decision to appoint a commission to report on the federation—but Welensky had to yield. He tried to prolong discussions on the commission's composition, but in November 1959 the membership of the commission under Lord Monckton as chairman was announced. However, Macmillan's evasiveness about the commission's terms of reference suggested to others that there had been some agreement with Welensky. The Labour Party in Britain wanted the possibility of secession by a territory to be specifically mentioned. When they failed to obtain this, they refused to take part; the African members, even though they included the trade union leader Lawrence Katilungu of Northern Rhodesia, were attacked as unrepresentative. However, Welensky on his side received the announcement of the commission in the Commons with 'the gravest concern', for Macmillan had informed Welensky that the commission would be free to hear all points of view 'on whatever subject'; he also explained to Welensky in a secret telegram that 'he had not yielded and would not yield an inch on the Commission's terms of reference'.

Secondly, Welensky was concerned lest evidence presented to the Commission by the African detainees should be published and prove explosive. Nor did Welensky like Macleod, the new Colonial Secretary, taking 'a personal interest' in facilities being provided to help the detainees present their evidence. When Macmillan started on his African tour in January 1960, press reports from Lagos indicated he had said there that there would be a test of popular opinion concerning federation in Nyasaland and Northern Rhodesia. Welensky took this up with Macmillan in Salisbury, along with his two earlier grievances about the Monckton Commission and the 'rumours that Dr Banda is going to be released', on which he asked for prior consultation. However, on 2 February Welensky was simply informed that the British government had decided that Banda must be released, and then the 'subtle and secretive' Macleod—as Welensky thought him—visited Central

---

[1] Welensky, *Welensky's 4000 days*, pp. 91–2. Welensky's italics.

Africa before Banda was released with Welensky's 'very reluctant compliance'.[1]

Soon Macleod was telling Welensky that he proposed to hold a conference on Nyasaland at the end of July and that 'he wanted the Governor of Nyasaland to be driving the train on its next journey'. Welensky, the former railwayman, could only reply that he could not support Macleod's other suggestion of announcing constitutional talks for Northern Rhodesia in 1961 'as this would be interpreted as a concession to a campaign of violence and intimidation by UNIP' (the United National Independence Party led by Kenneth Kaunda). As for Nyasaland, Welensky considered that 'erosion of the European position there' would affect the whole of the Federation. Thus Banda's shout on returning to Nyasaland from the conference, 'Kwacha—to hell with Federation!' was a personal challenge to Welensky. However, he found that he could not prevent the British government from releasing the remaining Nyasaland detainees at the end of September. The power of decision-making had reverted, at least as far as Nyasaland was concerned, to London.

During a visit to Salisbury Duncan Sandys, the new Commonwealth minister, had told Welensky of this, the British government's latest Central African decision. He had come to discuss the recommendations of the Monckton Commission due to be published in mid-October. On reading his preliminary copy, Welensky saw that 'its mere publication will make the continuation of federation virtually impossible'.[2] He was right, for while the commission, with its representation of Europeans from Central Africa, considered that the break-up of the federation was undesirable on economic grounds, it did record the African hostility to federation. The commissioners said that this could not be overcome 'without drastic and fundamental changes both in the structure of the association itself, and in the racial policies of Southern Rhodesia'. Hence they recommended a much higher proportion of seats for Africans in the Federal Assembly, while the majority of commissioners favoured immediate parity between Europeans and Africans there.

Besides, the commissioners wanted a widening of the franchise to make the Assembly 'representative of the broad mass of both African and European opinion'. A bill of rights should be entrenched in the

---

[1] Welensky, *Welensky's 4000 days*, pp. 156–62, 171–3, 181–2, and 187–9.
[2] *Ibid.*, pp. 197–9, 207, and 272–3.

constitutions of both the Federation and the Territories, with Councils of State to prevent the enactment of discriminatory legislation. Any such existing legislation should be removed, and here specific mention was made of Southern Rhodesia's pass laws.

Most striking of all, the commissioners recommended unanimously that the British government should declare that it would 'permit secession by any of the Territories if so requested after a stated time or a particular stage of constitutional development', for this, they said, 'would have a favourable effect and might be decisive in securing a fair trial for the new association'.[1] These judgements of a commission which was widely regarded on its appointment as likely to be biased in favour of the Central African Europeans were damning to their cause in the eyes of responsible British opinion.

Welensky, protesting still that the commission had gone beyond its terms of reference in discussing secession, was faced now with a British government announcing that the Review Conference on the Federation, which was to take place in December, must be free to discuss secession. The federal government had pressed for the conference to meet at the earliest possible opportunity; by so doing it had opened the door to the earliest possible dissolution of the federation.

In the course of his explosions Welensky wrote to Lord Home (later Sir Alec Douglas-Home): 'Perhaps our end will be the same as Kenya's, but, if so, it will not be without a struggle';[2] but this was only his personal protest. The year 1960 closed with an adjourned Review Conference, which was never to reassemble. Two years later the electors of Southern Rhodesia defeated Welensky's United Federal Party and indicated thereby that they had returned to their earlier conviction that 'the Black North' was not for them. Into it they had been temporarily drawn by Huggins (Lord Malvern) and still more by the dynamic Welensky. Yet in reality Welensky was the weaker; he was as a Northern Rhodesian rooted in a territory where the strength of the European position was not truly local, and where the main decisions were still taken by Whitehall and by copper companies based outside the territory.

However, 1960 was the crucial year: it began with the Lancaster House Conference on Kenya whose outcome Cavendish-Bentinck

[1] Great Britain, *Parliamentary papers*, Vol. XI, Cmnd 1148, *Report of the Advisory Commission on the Review of the Constitution of Rhodesia and Nyasaland* (London, 1959–60).
[2] Welensky, *Welensky's 4000 days*, pp. 279–83.

greeted with the justified comment that it was a *volte-face* in which the British government was going back on repeated pledges of support to the Kenya settlers;[1] and it ended with the adjourning of a federal review conference, which meant that the federation had no future. If 1960 was 'the year of decision',[2] the subsequent process that led to African governments in Kenya, Malawi and Zambia took some three to four years to complete and was only carried through in Central Africa under the threat and counter-threat of force. The line of the Zambezi became, as that far-sighted Governor of the Cape, Sir Bartle Frere, had foreseen in the 1870s, the frontier between white power in southern Africa and black power to the north of it.

The political frontier might thus run along the Zambezi and continue the division of the colonial period between territories under Colonial Office rule and those under southern African white settler power. However, patterns antedating Colonial Office control of Northern Rhodesia in 1924 indicated that the line of the Zambezi did not mark economic frontiers. Rhodes's British South Africa Company had straddled the Zambezi. The Company sought for minerals and encouraged European settlement; hence the Company helped to extend the miners' and farmers' frontiers beyond the river. Hilton Young's suggestion, in 1929, of uniting Northern Rhodesia's 'line of rail' with Southern Rhodesia was an acknowledgement of this. Yet Hilton Young was writing before the great development of the Copperbelt as the world, and Northern Rhodesia with it, emerged from the Great Depression. When in 1935 there was rioting on the Copperbelt, Southern Rhodesia sent in police and South Africa offered support to the Northern Rhodesian government. With South African capital, South African labour came also to develop and operate the mines.

Yet the pattern of labour relations was not to be wholly South African. To obtain grants under the Colonial Development and Welfare Act of 1940 and its successors, Northern Rhodesia had to accept the British policy of assisting in the development of African trade unions. Thus while skilled white technicians from the south were necessary and the mining companies were prepared to offer them some of the highest paid jobs and best living conditions of miners in the world,

---

[1] George Bennett and Carl G. Rosberg, *The Kenyatta election: Kenya, 1960–1961* (London, Oxford University Press, 1961), p. 25.

[2] Title of a book on the Federation by Philip Mason (London, Oxford University Press, 1960); a book of importance in British thinking through Mason's connexions with the British 'establishment'.

the principle of African advancement was also introduced. At Zambia's independence, however, Africanization in employment had not equalled the Africanization of politics. This failure of the economic and political frontiers to coincide was bound to cause tension in the future.

In the colonial period the colour bar practices derived from the south caused race relations in Northern Rhodesia to be worse, probably, than those in any other territory under the Colonial Office. The European-owned and managed shops which refused to serve Africans—or would only serve them through side hatches—provided a constant source of grievance for Africans. President Kaunda devotes several pages of his autobiography to detailing incidents arising from this practice. In the 1950s he 'determined to expose this system for what it was, an insult to my race and my people'. However, Kaunda's book has an introduction by a man Kaunda describes as his 'old friend Lieutenant Colonel Sir Stewart Gore-Browne'.[1] Between the European shopkeepers' refusing to serve Africans and Gore-Browne's long representation of African interests in the Northern Rhodesia Legislative Council lay a whole range of white settler attitudes. Perhaps it was that Gore-Browne could afford to be liberal, for the basis of his life was that of an almost feudal existence on his estate of Shiwa Ng'andu.[2]

In an assessment of these settler territories during the colonial period, Kenya is crucial; her Europeans were always the most discussed and the most criticized. While Northern Rhodesia did in the end attain a larger white population than Kenya, this was on account of the Copperbelt. Northern Rhodesia's predominant mining economy meant that the majority of its Europeans, unlike those of Kenya, were not seeking to be rooted in the soil; they were not true settlers. Nor did the Copperbelt's development become significant until after the recovery from the depression of the early 1930s.

Already Kenya had become, as its Governor Sir Robert Coryndon was fond of saying in the early 1920s, 'the power-house of East Africa'.[3] Its influence was felt in Nyasaland, where in the 1920s the Europeans named their political body 'The Convention of Associations', after that of Kenya. The Kenya settlers' presence stimulated developments of all kinds, from agricultural and commercial to political. Nairobi became the commercial capital of East Africa, attracting the later light

---

[1] Kenneth D. Kaunda, *Zambia shall be free* (London, 1962), pp. 31–6 and 20.
[2] For comments on Gore-Browne in relation to the Legislative Council and Welensky, and at Shiwa Ng'andu, see Lewis H. Gann, *A history of Northern Rhodesia: early days to 1953* (London, 1964), pp. 263–4.　　　　[3] Huxley, *White man's country*, II, 195.

industrial development, particularly after the Second World War and possibly at the expense of Kenya's neighbours.

The growing importance of Nairobi business in Kenya's politics was marked by the elevation of Alfred (later Sir Alfred) Vincent in 1944 to the leadership of the Europeans in the Legislative Council. Yet his leadership lasted only a few years before it reverted once more to men who were predominantly farmers. This was fitting, for British business and professional men in the tropics have not usually played a great part in politics. The local managers of expatriate firms were likely to be transients, and in any case their firms did not approve of their overtly engaging in politics. The mores of Kenya's European society were established by the settlers. Indeed, their weight in politics is indicated by the fact that eight of the eleven European constituencies in the years after 1920 were rural; Nairobi had only two seats and Mombasa one, despite the fact that the two towns contained about one half of the European population.

During the Second World War Nairobi was the inevitable centre for the strategic and economic affairs of a wider region. For a while it became the effective capital of East Africa, and the Kenya European leader, Cavendish-Bentinck, entered into a partnership with the military and civil service planners stationed there. The British government hoped to continue the organization then set up, sending in 1944 as Kenya's Governor Sir Philip Mitchell, who had been in charge in Nairobi for a period of this wartime action; he was to bring about 'interterritorial co-operation' in what became, in 1948, the East Africa High Commission.

Thus in the post-war years the fears of the development of a European-dominated federation of East Africa stimulated the growth of African politics throughout East Africa, just as in the 1920s African politics in East Africa had originated in Kenya in opposition to settler influence on the colonial government there. The Kenya settlers were political activists, hoping to take over the colony and even the whole of East Africa in the South African manner. It was then natural that they should provoke a reaction on the part of the other racial groups, first of the Indians and later of the Africans. Even though the Kenya settlers were able, through their influence on the government, to hinder on occasion the development of African politics, it is at least arguable that in the long run their activity has strengthened the Africans through providing a challenge.

There have been other ways, however, in which the existence of the Kenya Europeans during the colonial period has laid the foundations for growth. It was possible for Tanganyika, and perhaps even for Uganda, to stagnate economically between the wars, but not for Kenya. The Europeans were demanding the establishment of an infrastructure. They could speak to the British government and obtain the colony's exemption from the burden of debt occasioned by the construction of the Kenya and Uganda Railway, while later their presence meant that in the transfer of power Kenya received greater financial and economic assistance from the British government than did any other African colonial territory.

While the Europeans' demands for African labour may have hindered agricultural development in the African reserves until after the Second World War, a change was brought about by two governors: Sir Philip Mitchell (1944–52) and Sir Evelyn Baring (later Lord Howick, 1952–60). Playing a major part in the transformation were, however, the European settler leaders, Cavendish-Bentinck and Blundell as successive Ministers of Agriculture. With his able and energetic Permanent Secretary, H. O. Hennings, Cavendish-Bentinck drew up a general strategy for peasant agriculture. Formulated in detail, this appeared in 1954 as the Swynnerton Plan, named after its immediate progenitor, the Deputy Director of Agriculture. To be effective, however, peasant agriculture required land reform: the consolidation of the traditional fragmented and scattered land holdings of the African areas. Security could then be given through land-titles. On this basis, it was felt, Africans might be ready to develop the higher productivity of cash crops. While Kenya administrators had long wanted to bring about such reforms, it was realized that the changes, with the profound social effects inherent in them, would not be easy to bring about.

It was at this point that the Mau Mau Emergency afforded the opportunity. Holding power in the Kikuyu countryside, the administration decided 'to strike while the iron was hot'.[1] A team of forceful and able civil servants carried the measure through in the latter half of the 1950s. In the government they were backed by Blundell as Minister of Agriculture. He told his European supporters in speeches that the best way to protect the White Highlands was by making the Africans contented on their own land. The foundation of this content-

[1] M. P. K. Sorrenson, *Land reform in the Kikuyu country* (Nairobi, Oxford University Press, 1967), p. 7.

ment was to be laid in the creation of a prosperous African middle class based on individual land-tenure.[1] The Kikuyu had certainly been long seeking the European security of 'title-deeds'. Thus the revolution was accepted; and other African peoples in Kenya, seeing the growing prosperity of the Kikuyu through peasant agriculture and land consolidation, began to demand the same for themselves.

Thus when the Europeans were given responsibility as ministers in the 1950s, they did act responsibly; and they have made substantial contributions to Kenya's subsequent development. Perhaps mention might be made also of Wilfred Havelock for his important, though less dramatic, work in developing local government, a ministerial post he held from 1954 to 1962. Then Blundell's successor as Minister of Agriculture, the South African-born Bruce McKenzie, was so appreciated that he was brought back to the same post in the Kenyatta government of 1963.

In 1964 that government obtained a knighthood for Derek Erskine, a man who had stood out as an independent-minded European member of the Legislative Council in the 'finger-printing' controversy of the late 1940s, and whose resignation on the issue in 1950 had not been forgotten. Perhaps Erskine furnishes but another illustration of a fundamental characteristic of the Kenya settlers: their independence, nay, even their aristocratic eccentricity. This fitted strangely with their frontiersman mentality; and of this Delamere, their first leader, had been a striking example, whether in his unconventional hair style and habits or in the way that a visitor to his Rift Valley estate might find an ochre-adorned Masai seated in the drawing-room. Later, the excesses of the social life of the 'Happy Valley' set earned the Kenya Europeans an unsavoury reputation when the sexual mores of this group were displayed in 1941 in the sensational trial of a baronet accused of murdering a peer. This trial naturally received widespread attention in the English-speaking press of the world.[2]

Robert Ruark, an American writer, has used this and other stereotypes of Kenya in a novel (*Something of Value*, New York, 1955). This book contains also European settler ideas, picked up by Ruark, about Mau Mau and provides, therefore, an excellent detailed little example of what has been called 'the myth of Mau Mau'.[3] Of particular interest

---

[1] See Blundell's account in *So rough a wind*, Ch. XII.
[2] *East African Standard*, leading article, 'Kenya's Reputation', 4 July 1941.
[3] Title of a book by Carl G. Rosberg and John Nottingham (New York, 1966).

is his tale that Mau Mau was planned at a conference of an Indian and a Russian with a Kikuyu; this story, current in Nairobi in 1953, indicated well the settler contempt for Africans, the belief that they could do nothing by themselves. Ruark recounts also the life of another group of individuals who seem indeed to be the very creatures of the frontier—the white hunters, who have made, and continue to make, an important contribution to Kenya's economy through the tourist trade. Something of their spirit was found in the counter-guerrilla activities that took place in the Kenya forests during the Mau Mau Emergency. Outstanding in this was the Kenya-born Kikuyu-speaking Ian Henderson, whose courage earned the admiration of a captured Mau Mau 'general'[1] and his continued employment by Prime Minister (later President) Kenyatta himself as head of the Special Branch for some eight months after Kenya's independence.

Another Kenya-born European who has known the Kikuyu intimately is L. S. B. Leakey, son of the missionary Canon Leakey. Unfortunately, because his major anthropological work on the Kikuyu has never been published,[2] his reputation rests instead on the extraordinary archaeological discoveries he has made, which appear to indicate East Africa as the home of the earliest men.

While there have been among the Kenya Europeans such eccentric, and even outstanding, figures, the majority of them would undoubtedly prefer to be judged as men who 'built a country', who carved out farms from the virgin bush of Africa and in so doing believed they were making a contribution to the future. Unfortunately for them, they lived as quasi-aristocratic landlords, aloof from and not understanding the world of the Africans around them.[3] They were caught up and overwhelmed in the African revolution, since most of them had never had either the imagination, nor the desire, to seek to understand the developing forces around them. They were simply contemptuous of what little they knew; they rarely, if ever, met educated men of other races. Blundell has recorded that he did not meet Kenyatta until after his release in 1961, but Blundell's memoirs reveal him as a sensitive man able to sympathize with the more extreme nationalist leader Oginga Odinga, whom he had met and listened to. The comment of Miss Judith

---

[1] Waruhiu Itote (General China), '*Mau Mau*' *general* (Nairobi, 1967), p. 188. See Ian Henderson and Philip Goodhart, *The hunt for Kimathi* (London, 1958).

[2] But see Louis S. B. Leakey, *Mau Mau and the Kikuyu* (London, 1952).

[3] See Bennett and Rosberg, *The Kenyatta election*, esp. pp. 7 and 105–7.

Todd rings true for other European settlers: 'The tragedy of Rhodesia, over and over again, has simply been that the whites have never known those whom they hate, and because of their fear have never made the effort to know those whom they oppose.'[1] White settlement was too often prevented by the blinkers of segregation and separation that it imposed on itself from attaining understanding. Hence ignorance bred fear and even hate, the most unreliable counsellors for men's actions.

BIBLIOGRAPHY

Abrahams, P. 'The blacks', in *An African treasury: articles, essays, stories, poems, by black Africans*, Langston Hughes, ed. New York, 1960.

Altrincham, Edward W. M. Grigg, 1st baron. *Kenya's opportunity: memories, hopes, and ideas*. London, 1955.

Arthur, J. W. The Rev. Dr J. W. Arthur Papers, Edinburgh University Library, Edinburgh.

Bennett, George. 'Imperial paternalism: the representation of African interests in the Kenya Legislative Council', in *Essays in imperial government*, Kenneth Robinson and Frederick Madden, eds. Oxford, 1963.

Kenya, a political history: the colonial period. London, Oxford University Press, 1963.

'Paramountcy to partnership: J. H. Oldham and Africa', *Africa*, Oct. 1960.

Bennett, George, and Carl G. Rosberg. *The Kenyatta election: Kenya, 1960–1961*. London, Oxford University Press, 1961.

Blundell, Sir Michael. *So rough a wind*. London, 1964.

Bunche, Ralph J. 'The land equation in Kenya Colony', *Journal of Negro History*, Jan. 1939, 24, No. 1.

Cameron, Sir Donald. *My Tanganyika service and some Nigeria*. London, 1939.

Chandos, Oliver Lyttelton, 1st viscount. *The memoirs of Lord Chandos*. London, 1962.

Devonshire, Duke of. Secret memorandum for the Cabinet, 14 Feb. 1923 (copy in India Office, Private Office File No. 300).

Franklin, Henry. *Unholy wedlock: the failure of the Central African Federation*. London, 1963.

Gann, Lewis H. *A history of Northern Rhodesia: early days to 1953*. London, 1964.

Gann, Lewis H., and Michael Gelfand. *Huggins of Rhodesia*. London, 1964.

Gray, Richard. *Two nations: aspects of the development of race relations in the Rhodesias and Nyasaland, 1918–1953*. London and New York, Oxford University Press, 1960.

[1] Judith Todd, *Rhodesia* (London, 1966), p. 75.

Great Britain. *Parliamentary papers.* Vol. XVIII. Cmd 1922. *Memorandum on Indians in Kenya.* London, 1923.

Vol. IX. Cmd 2387. *Report of the East Africa Commission.* London, 1924–5.

Vol. V. Cmd 3234. *Report of the commission on closer union of the dependencies in Eastern and Central Africa.* London, 1928–9.

Vol. XXVII. Cmd 3573. *Memorandum on native policy in East Africa.* London, 1929–30.

Vol. XXIII. Cmd 3731. *Correspondence with regard to native policy in Northern Rhodesia.* London, 1930–1.

Vol. VI. Cmd 4093. *Report by the financial commissioner (Lord Moyne) on certain questions in Kenya.* London, 1931–2.

Vol. XXIV. Cmnd 530. *Proposals for constitutional change in Northern Rhodesia.* London, 1957–8.

Vol. XXV. Cmnd 795. *Record of proceedings and evidence in the inquiry into the deaths of eleven Mau Mau detainees at Hola Camp in Kenya.* London, 1958–9.

Vol. X. Cmnd 814. *Report of the Nyasaland commission of inquiry.* London, 1958–9.

Vol. XXV. Cmnd 816. *Further documents relating to the deaths of eleven Mau Mau detainees at Hola Camp in Kenya.* London, 1958–9.

Vol. X. Cmnd 1030. *Historical survey of the origins and growth of Mau Mau.* London, 1959–60.

Vol. XI. Cmnd 1148. *Report of the Advisory Commission on the Review of the Constitution of Rhodesia and Nyasaland.* London, 1959–60.

Great Britain. Colonial Office. *Inter-territorial organisation in East Africa.* (Colonial, No. 191.) London, 1945.

Inter-territorial organisation in East Africa, revised proposals. (Colonial, No. 210.) London, 1947.

Great Britain. House of Commons. *Parliamentary debates: official report.*

Kenya Land Commission. *Report, September 1933* [and *Evidence and memoranda.*] Cmd 4556. 4 vols. London, 1934. (*Evidence and memoranda* issued as Great Britian, Colonial Office, Colonial, No. 91.)

Hancock, Sir William Keith. *Survey of British Commonwealth affairs.* 2 vols. in 3. London, Oxford University Press, 1937–42.

Harlow, Vincent, and E. M. Chilver, eds., assisted by Alison Smith. *History of East Africa,* Vol. II. Oxford, Clarendon Press, 1965.

Hazlewood, Arthur, and P. D. Henderson. *Nyasaland: the economics of federation.* Oxford, 1960.

Henderson, Ian, and Philip Goodhart. *The hunt for Kimathi.* London, 1958.

Hill, Mervyn F. *Permanent way.* 2 vols. Nairobi, 1950–7.

Hughes, Langston, ed. *An African treasury: articles, essays, stories, poems, by black Africans.* New York, 1960.

Huxley, Elspeth. *A new earth: an experiment in colonialism*. London, 1960.
  White man's country: Lord Delamere and the making of Kenya. 2 vols. London,
  1935.
Itote, Waruhiu (General China). *'Mau Mau' general*. Nairobi, 1967.
Jackson, Sir Frederick John. *Early days in East Africa, etc*. London, 1930.
Kaunda, Kenneth D. *Zambia shall be free*. London, 1962.
Kenya. Legislative Council. *Debates*.
  Minutes of Proceedings.
Leakey, Louis S. B. *Mau Mau and the Kikuyu*. London, 1952.
Leys, Colin. *European politics in Southern Rhodesia*. Oxford, Clarendon Press,
  1959.
Leys, Norman. *Kenya*. London, 1924.
Lipscomb, J. F. *We built a country*. London, 1956.
  White Africans. London, 1955.
Macleod, Iain. 'Blundell's Kenya', *The Spectator*, 20 March 1964, no. 7082.
Mason, Philip. *Year of decision: Rhodesia and Nyasaland in 1960*. London and
  New York, Oxford University Press, 1960.
Northern Rhodesia. Legislative Council. *Debates*.
Rhodesia and Nyasaland. Federal Assembly. *Debates*.
Robinson, Kenneth, and Frederick Madden, eds. *Essays in imperial government*.
  Oxford, 1963.
Rosberg, Carl G., and John Nottingham. *The Myth of 'Mau Mau': nationalism
  in Kenya*. New York, 1966.
Ross, W. McGregor, *Kenya from within*. London, 1927.
Ruark, Robert C. *Something of value*. New York, 1955.
Sanger, Clyde. *Central African emergency*. London, 1960.
Sorrenson, M. P. K. *Land reform in the Kikuyu country*. Nairobi, Oxford
  University Press, 1967.
Southern Rhodesia. Land Commission, 1925. *Report*. Salisbury, 1926.
Todd, Judith. *Rhodesia*. London, 1966.
Welensky, Sir Roy. *Welensky's 4000 days: the life and death of the Federation
  of Rhodesia and Nyasaland*. London, 1964.
Whittall, Errol. *Dimbilil: the story of a Kenya farm*. London, 1956.
Wrigley, C. C. 'Kenya: the patterns of economic life, 1902–1945', in *History
  of East Africa*, Vol. II, Vincent Harlow and E. M. Chilver, eds., assisted
  by Alison Smith. Oxford, Clarendon Press, 1965.
Wymer, Norman. *The man from the Cape*. London, 1959.

CHAPTER 3

CHANGING PATTERNS OF A WHITE ELITE: RHODESIAN AND OTHER SETTLERS

by L. H. GANN *and* PETER DUIGNAN

'On the same soil', wrote Macaulay in describing a racially segregated society, 'dwelt two populations, locally intermixed, morally and politically sundered'.

They sprang from different stocks. They spoke different languages...They were in widely different stages of civilization. Between two such populations there could be little sympathy;...calamities and wrongs had generated a strong antipathy...The English settlers seem to have been, in knowledge, energy, and perseverance, rather above than below the average level of the population in the mother country. The aboriginal [inhabitants], on the contrary, were in an almost savage state...They were...of all foreigners...the most hated and despised...for they were our vanquished, enslaved, and despoiled enemies. The Englishman felt proud when he compared...his own dwelling with [their] hovels...and he very complacently inferred that he was naturally a being of a higher order.[1]

Macaulay was not discussing racial attitudes in early North America, New Zealand or the Cape. His 'aborigines' were not Maori, nor Tasmanians nor South African Bantu. His miserable, poverty-stricken 'natives' were white Irish tribesmen subjected to English colonization in the seventeenth century. Similarly, Englishmen and Lowland Scots looked upon the clansfolk of the Scottish Highlands with the same loathing which American colonists felt for the Apaches, or the Boer trekkers for the Hottentots. During the first part of the eighteenth century, the power of the independent Scottish Highland chiefs was destroyed, their people disarmed, and their national garb prohibited. Scarcely had this change been accomplished when public feeling reversed itself. Scottish tribal institutions began to be idealized. Scottish Lowlanders accepted Highland dress as their national costume and started to identify themselves with the very mountaineers whom the

[1] Thomas Babington, Lord Macaulay, *The History of England from the accession of James II* (Chicago, 1888), II, 123, 124, 385.

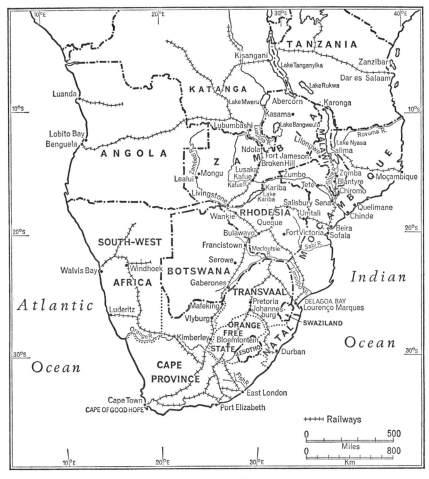

Map 4. Southern Africa, 1965

citizens of early eighteenth-century Edinburgh or London used to regard as barbarous bandits.

Clearly the relations between seventeenth-century English settlers and wild Irish tribesmen or between eighteenth-century Scottish Lowland farmers and wild Highland warriors on the one hand, and between nineteenth-century white colonists and Bantu tribesmen in eastern and southern Africa on the other, had a great deal in common. Indeed, the very phraseology of abuse reserved by the victor for the vanquished was often almost identical. Yet all the inhabitants of the British Isles were drawn from similar stocks. There were no differences of colour between them, and what has loosely been called 'race relations' cannot therefore simply be interpreted in pigmentational terms.

In pre-capitalist and pre-colonial Africa, foreign observers often encountered comparable ethnic tensions. Matabele warriors in what is now Rhodesia, Hutu conquerors in Rwanda and Burundi, Lozi aristo-crats in what is now Zambia likewise treated conquered races with lordly disdain, and ethnic prejudice frequently went hand in hand with status privilege. Indeed as Alan Cairns, a modern historian, puts it:

The ethnocentric attitudes of individual Britons [during Central Africa's early pioneering period] fade into insignificance when contrasted with the attitudes and conduct of African tribes to each other. The appellation 'dogs', used by the Barotse to describe the Mashukulumbwe [Ila] among whom they pillaged and raided, was typical of the attitudes of the haughty powerful tribes...The brutality...of the strong indicated little respect...for the preservation of other tribal cultures.[1]

Race relations are not therefore a unique class of contacts between people. They represent a wide spectrum of human relationships. Race relations are not rooted in prejudice or aversion alone; they are not peculiar to settler-Africa or to black–white contacts. They are subject to change as different ethnic groups clash and compromise. In this essay, we attempt first to outline the impact of various kinds of settler fron-tiers in British Africa. We then discuss what we consider to be some of the most prevalent misconceptions concerning the European colonists in Africa. We concentrate our attention on Rhodesia (formerly known as Southern Rhodesia), but shall take occasion to refer both to East and South African problems where these appear to be particularly relevant.

Economic frontiers in settler Africa

The history of these racial contacts can be written to some extent in terms of colonial frontiers. Historians owe this concept to F. J. Turner, an American historian, who brought to the study of his country's his-tory the illuminating concept of moving frontiers. The American frontier was not to be thought of in his view as a closely administered and well-fortified boundary zone—comparable to a Roman *limes*. It

[1] H. Alan C. Cairns, *Prelude to imperialism: British reactions to Central African society, 1840–1890* (London, 1965), p. 145.

was rather that great expanse of territory to the west of the permanently settled lands of America. Successive waves of hunters, traders, ranchers and pioneer farmers gradually moved into the interior, in turn preparing the way for railwaymen, for intensive farmers and finally for townsmen and industrialists.

Sir Keith Hancock, an Australian scholar, subsequently applied Turner's concept to the history of Africa and discussed European colonization in terms of settler, missionary and trader's frontiers. Hancock's approach in some ways was ethnocentric. He looked upon the history of Africa essentially from the white man's point of view. Yet his methodology remains of great value to the student of racial contacts. For the Europeans in Africa were never a single undifferentiated white mass. White men might all—in Hilda Kuper's phrase—wear the same 'uniform of colour'. But similarities in physical appearance only served to hide a bewildering variety of differences and internal contradictions within the European settler communities, or even to conceal some striking parallels between white and dark-skinned people in comparable social situations. In many parts of southern Africa, European colonization began with what might be called the hunter's and bush-trader's frontier.

The hunter's and the trader's frontier

As the European and Indian luxury industries expanded their production, the demand for elephant tusks rose; and by 1870 Africa supposedly supplied some eighty-five per cent of the world's ivory. The onslaught on the ivory resources of West and Central Africa took the shape of a three-way thrust. Portuguese half-castes and Swahili-speaking hunters from Zanzibar and other cities along the African east coast pushed westward. Egyptian and Sudanese slave-dealers and adventurers cut a path southward from Khartoum. In addition, white and half-caste frontiersmen made their way beyond the Limpopo river from South Africa. Some were hunters, some traders; many of them exercised both professions. The ivory hunter was sometimes a substantial entrepreneur whose capital was invested in wagons and fire-arms. He frequently supervised African 'shooting boys', and thus acted as an employer of skilled labour. These pioneers, however, differed from European immigrants of a later vintage in that, like French Canadian fur traders among the Red Indians, they could operate quite well within the framework of a tribal polity. In some ways these early frontiersmen may sometimes have even helped to strengthen the power of local African potentates who were able to acquire guns and other goods from the strangers in exchange for various local privileges. Some white frontiersmen also played an important part in local politics. George Westbeech, for instance, sat as an adviser on the national council of Barotseland; and during the latter part of the nineteenth century Carl Wiese, a German adventurer, played an equally important role among the Ngoni of what is now Zambia. (Wiese, indeed, became so expert in tribal lore that he became a contributor to the learned German journal *Zeitschrift für Ethnologie*.)

Hunters and traders alike, however, depended on the favour of indigenous potentates. No individual hunter was strong enough to compel obedience to his will from a powerful chief. No trader could oblige tribesmen to become his customers. White men had to deal with black people as equals. Outside the mission stations there were no white women to insist on starched collars and middle-class respectability. The frontiersmen often enough entered into liaisons with one or several black women, and to some extent adjusted to indigenous custom. The strangers commonly enjoyed considerable social prestige. They might even be asked to serve as technical or diplomatic advisers, but they could never enforce obedience simply by force of arms. In their commercial relations, hunters and traders alike depended on African good will. Credit was widely employed on the frontier, and most white pioneers managed to establish a reputation for honesty. The stereotype of the 'low immoral bush trader', one that recurred with considerable frequency in the writings of British 'negrophilists', usually bore little relation to reality.

A Kafir who is owed money by one Englishman, perhaps the wages for a year's work, will take a letter without a murmur, to another Englishman hundreds of miles away, if he is told by his master that, upon delivering the letter, he will receive his payment.[1]

The personal relations between white men and black—certainly those between white men and black leaders—implied at least equality of status. Black potentates usually commanded most or all of the means of coercion available on the spot. White travellers had to conform to African systems of governance. The political relations between white rulers and black can be subsumed during this early period under the

[1] Frederick C. Selous, *A hunter's wanderings in Africa*... 5th ed. (London, 1919), p. 247.

more general heading of foreign policy. The white man's potential technical superiority over the tribes of the interior might be immense. But for many decades, the Europeans' actual military strength at any particular point on the extreme limit of southern Africa's far-flung frontier might be no greater than that of some minor African lord.

During the 1880s an African kingdom like Barotseland could still mobilize an impressive military force. The Lozi monarch dealt with the British South Africa Company's representative as one ruler to another. The indigenous king desired the support of one group of whites, the British, against another group of Europeans, the Portuguese. He required British backing against potential black rivals at home and against the threatening power of another African state, the Matabele monarchy, abroad. From the white strangers he wanted new goods, new skills and new knowledge; but he was a sovereign lord.

This state of affairs, however, was not destined to last. The disparity between white power and black was too great. The passing of the hunter's and the trader's frontier, for instance, marked a stage in a major economic transformation. The early frontiersmen, brown as well as white, made an appreciable contribution to the economy of the interior by selling to the peoples of the interior new goods such as guns, cloth, knives, hatchets, kerosene lamps and beads. But hunting or the trade in ivory and slaves all depended on the export of irreplaceable wealth, and could not provide the basis for lasting prosperity.

Even white Nimrods such as William Finaughty in Rhodesia never acquired great riches. Their occupation depended on metropolitan luxury industries subject to sharp fluctuations in demand. Likewise, the wonderful stories told by European explorers concerning the luxury displayed by east coast Arabs were overdrawn. Gross profits in the ivory business may have been high at times, but entrepreneurs had to balance against these the high cost of transport and the interest on borrowed capital, as well as the risk of total loss. Above all, many regions once rich in elephants were gradually 'shot out', as few indigenous rulers had sufficient foresight to protect the great beasts.

When Selous, the best known of all these early hunters, arrived in what is now Rhodesia, the hunter's occupation was already declining in importance.[1] Selous came too late to share in the ivory boom, and

---

[1] Selous, a Rugby man, came to be regarded as the model of the adventurous upper-class Englishman, and probably served as prototype for Allan Quatermain, the hero of Rider Haggard's famous novel *King Solomon's Mines*.

perforce turned to providing specimens and trophies for museums and to guiding sportsmen, prospectors and immigrants—the characteristic expedient of all professional hunters on a closing frontier. But even at the best of times the hunter and frontier trader played only a very limited part in the development of the interior. With a few inconspicuous exceptions, by the end of the nineteenth century white men from the south had long since ceased to deal in slaves. The 'Far North', however, supplied few trade goods except elephant and rhino tusks. There were no indigenous agricultural exports comparable to the cocoa of the Gold Coast, the ground-nuts (peanuts) of Senegal, or the palm-oil from the Niger Delta. The 'trader's frontier', with its relatively egalitarian race relations, was never anything like as important in southern as in western Africa; this difference in turn had profound consequences for the character of white–black contacts.

Pacification

Once the Europeans had awakened to the potential resources of the regions north of the Limpopo, the white hunters and frontier traders soon became, for the most part, social anachronisms. They alone were able to make their living within the framework of a tribal state—but not so white miners and farmers. No European could profitably sink a mine shaft or plough a field if his life and property might be threatened, if his labourers might be called upon to serve in tribal levies, or if they were abducted or killed in local wars. Lenders could not invest money in land held on traditional African tenures, but only in property held according to Western legal principles. White entrepreneurs could not suffer indigenous 'distributor kings' to enforce rights of royal pre-emption or local trade monopolies, or to insist on apparently capricious levies. White humanitarians objected to the brutalities of indigenous customs and of internecine African conflicts. White soldiers sought for military security from raids and counter-raids. Tribal and Western societies were bound sooner or later to come into conflict, though the clashes were resolved in many different ways. Some favoured indigenous ruling groups managed to conclude treaties with the whites, thus obtaining more or less tenuous privileges from their new overlords. Other Africans, such as the Lala in Northern Rhodesia, accepted European rule in a more or less passive fashion, and white occupation came about gradually and peaceably. Still other African communities that took to arms suffered the consequences.

We cannot here discuss the details of the resultant pacification campaigns; we can only point to certain features. First of all, the combatants were rarely divided solely on lines of skin colour. The Portuguese had always relied to a very considerable extent on African allies. The British imperial forces in Nyasaland at war with Yao and Swahili slave-traders obtained a good deal of support from the indigenous Nyanja-speaking people. The British South Africa Company in Southern Rhodesia employed 'Cape Boys' as well as indigenous troops to supplement white forces operating against the Matabele.

The initial white impact on the various African communities differed enormously from region to region. A military society like the Ngoni of what later became North Eastern Rhodesia was shaken to its very foundations. The Ngoni depended for part of their subsistence on raiding their neighbours for cattle and for crops. They also brought back from their forays many captives who were gradually assimilated within the Ngoni social structure. According to John Barnes, the results of this policy were beginning to make themselves felt even before the British conquered the country. Given the primitive methods of Ngoni agriculture, the Ngoni country became overpopulated in relation to its carrying capacity. There was probably not much land in reserve; and the Ngoni, with their large villages, were exhausting the wealth of their own soil as well as that of their neighbours.[1] Ngoni society may well have already suffered from insoluble internal contradictions from within before it was overthrown from without.

But the British victory over the Mpeseni Ngoni in 1898 completely disrupted traditional Ngoni society. 'Pacification', which is still remembered by the local people, profoundly changed the local pattern of race relations. Most African communities, on the other hand, did not experience European penetration in anything like this form. The Lovale of North Western Rhodesia were certainly unaware, at the time, of the agreement between the British and the Barotse which placed the entire region under British protection; and subsequent British penetration was undertaken slowly and cautiously. Indigenous folk traditions in many parts of Africa do not therefore record the coming of the white man as a sudden traumatic experience. Local folklore frequently records almost nothing of the pacification period other than the eccentricities of some early district commissioner.

[1] John A. Barnes, *Politics in a changing society: a political history of the Fort Jameson Ngoni* (Oxford University Press, 1954), pp. 104–5.

The British impact on the various peoples of South Eastern Africa was thus very uneven. But speaking in general terms, the indigenous people were never liquidated, as were the Tasmanians in Australia or many Red Indian communities in North America. For one thing, a great change had come over the European climate of opinion. By the end of the last century, the outright extermination of coloured people was no longer acceptable to the white public. In addition, the Bantu never experienced the same pressure of white numbers to which Australian or North American aborigines were exposed during the nineteenth century. The Bantu were physically and mentally resilient and they were usually more resistant to tropical diseases than were immigrants from Europe. They were used to drinking beer in large quantities, and did not suffer from the ravages of imported liquor as many South Sea island communities and many North American Indian tribes had done in the past. (Some black communities may indeed have benefited from imperial attempts to control the importation of liquor and fire-arms into tropical Africa in the interests of humanity.)

Above all, the Bantu were technically far more advanced than the Australian 'black fellows' or than most North American redskins. The Australian aborigines and many North American Indians traditionally made their living as nomadic hunters and food-gatherers. They might be useful to selected groups of Europeans as suppliers of fur, as trackers or as cattlemen, but they could not easily be turned into farm labourers or mine workers. The Bantu, on the other hand, were Iron Age agriculturists. Their farming techniques were advanced for the times and capable of sustaining a substantial population. They could be trained with relative ease to work on white-owned farms and mines, especially at a time when the methods of production employed by the colonists were themselves not complicated. The Bantu thus adapted themselves to rapid changes with remarkable facility and as a people they rarely faced the peril of physical extinction.

Early settler Africa did, however, experience many varieties of local terrorism. During the first years of white occupation in Rhodesia, for instance, white ruffians, and also blacks in European employ, inflicted all manner of outrages on the indigenous people. The Germans in South West Africa (and Tanganyika) went even farther. During the first decade of the present century, the Germans, after heavy fighting, liquidated a large portion of the Herero people, a warlike pastoral race. But even the Germans never destroyed the entire Herero nation. Indeed, the worst instances of colonial brutality in sub-Saharan Africa took place not in settler Africa but in the Congo Free State, in the tropical forest zone. The excesses in the Congo owed their origin not to white colonists in search of land, but to concessionary companies in quest of wild rubber. The Congo brutalities were a characteristic of early *Raubwirtschaft* (robber economy), not of an agricultural or a mining economy of the kind created by the first settlers. To contemporary humanitarians like E. D. Morel or J. A. Hobson, or to present-day communist critics of colonialism, the real enemy of the African was not therefore the European workman or farmer in Africa, but the European capitalist.

Far more important was the silent and more unspectacular pressure exerted by the invaders on the indigenous people. The impact of the Austro-Hungarian occupation on the backward white peasant peoples of Bosnia and Herzegovina (1878) has been brilliantly described by Ivo Andrić, a modern Yugoslav writer. His description is of equal relevance to many parts of colonial Africa:

The newcomers were never at peace; and they allowed no one else to live in peace. It seemed that they were resolved with their impalpable yet ever more noticeable web of laws, regulations and orders to embrace all forms of life, men, beasts and things, and to change and alter everything, both the outward appearance of the town and the customs and habits of men from the cradle to the grave...Every task that they began seemed useless and even silly. They measured out the waste land, numbered the trees in the forest, inspected lavatories and drains, looked at the teeth of horses and cows, asked about the illnesses of the people, noted the number and types of fruit-trees and of different kinds of sheep and poultry. (It seemed that they were playing games, so incomprehensible, unreal and futile all these tasks of theirs appeared to the people.)...But a few months later, sometimes even a year later, when the whole thing had been completely forgotten by the people... [t]he *mukhatars* of the individual quarters would be summoned to the *konak* (the administrative centre) and told of a new regulation against forest felling, or of the fight against typhus, or the manner of sale of fruit and sweetmeats, or of permits for the movement of cattle. Every day a fresh regulation. With each regulation men saw their individual liberties curtailed or their obligations increased, but the life of the town and villages...became wider and fuller.[1]

---

[1] *The bridge on the Drina* (New York, 1960), p. 178. We are grateful to the Macmillan Company for permission to use this excerpt.

The planter's and the farmer's frontiers

The history of British settlement in Africa does not contain long periods of lawlessness. Once the first white settlers had begun to arrive, the British set about establishing effective police and administrative control with reasonable dispatch. The settler usually came either at the same time as, or followed in the footsteps of, the missionary, the police officer and the civil servant. In this way possessions such as Kenya or the Rhodesias differed sharply from many white settlement areas in other parts of the world. In many sections of the American West, for instance, the first settlers arrived long before the permanent administrator. A number of Western townships passed from the 'first state of mule-stealing and monte' through a second period of vigilance committees, lynch mobs and hanging trees, until at last they entered the third stage, that of churches and 'city officers' or police. A similar position obtained in early Johannesburg, where the original Boer administration was weak, where lawlessness was rife among the cosmopolitan crowd of miners who flocked to the Rand, and where a tradition of violence became entrenched almost from the start.

In Kenya, in the Rhodesias and in Tanganyika, on the other hand, crime was comparatively rare, or at least did not go unpunished, once the machinery of law and order had been established. The constabulary functions of government were soon entrusted to professionals, who exercised them with a considerable degree of efficiency. White Rhodesia never experienced mail robberies or ambushes on stage coaches of the Wild Western kind. Even subsequent urbanization and the rapid influx of African workmen did not seriously disturb this pattern. Rhodesian cities thus had few race riots of the American kind, or white disturbances such as that experienced by Chicago in the 1850s, when a full-scale riot launched by foreign-born whites required a show of artillery to crush it.[1] On the contrary, settlers of all nationalities took pride in being a law-abiding people.

Settler representatives in the local legislatures were normally men of cast-iron respectability—farmers, former military officers and civil servants, trade unionists in the craft tradition. There were few of the colourful or contemptible rogues who won their political reputations on many early American and on some early Australian state legislatures.

[1] St Clair Drake and Horace R. Cayton, *Black metropolis: a study of Negro life in a northern city* (New York, 1962), I, 20.

The Europeans' commitment to legality in turn affected race relations. The white colonists did impose certain legal disabilities on Africans. But generally speaking, discrimination was exercised within rather than without the framework of British-imposed law. Lynchings were unknown on the Rhodesian or Kenyan frontier. There was little violence as between one member of the white ruling caste and another. Personal abuse of Africans, on the other hand, was common throughout the pioneering days; and little personal stigma was attached to employers or to native commissioners who, for all practical purposes, exercised their own private jurisdiction over 'their' Africans.

Early European penetration into the highland areas of the interior took many different economic forms. Some regions, like the Northern Rhodesian railway belt, formed part of a wider mining frontier. Others, such as Kenya, owed their prosperity solely to agricultural enterprise. Patterns of farming again differed a great deal. Some pioneers came as ranchers; others pursued mainly arable farming. Much depended on the nature and location of markets, on transport facilities, and above all, on the characteristics of climate and soil. Historians must therefore differentiate, for instance, between what might be called the planter's and the farmer's frontier, though the two often overlapped. White farming settlement in Rhodesia and on the Zambian railway belt was in many ways the northernmost extension of the South African frontier. The early Rhodesian settlers bred cattle and planted maize in order to supply local markets; and usually came to stay in the country of their adoption.

Nyasaland and Tanganyika, on the other hand, lacked local markets. These territories attracted men who were more like British expatriate planters in Ceylon and India, individual entrepreneurs or managers of big companies, who grew coffee, tea, sisal or some other specialized crop for export overseas and who considered themselves to be temporary exiles in the tropics. Much depended in turn on the presence or absence of local mineral wealth. In many parts of Southern Rhodesia and along the Zambian railway belt, for instance, the pattern of white settlement was originally determined above all by the miners' needs. The railways were largely constructed to transport fuel and equipment to the mines, and to carry ores from the mining centres to the ports. Farmers subsequently settled along the line of rail to supply the compounds with food.

In the Kenyan Highlands, on the other hand, white settlement was shaped in the first place by the exigencies of an apparently uneconomic railway line. In 1895 the British began to construct a railway from Mombasa up to the shores of Lake Victoria for the purpose of wiping out the slave-trade, to advance British influence inland, and to open a strategic back door to the Nile Valley. But because the railway required a great outlay of money, the British Imperial authorities endorsed a recommendation by Sir Charles Eliot, Her Majesty's Commissioner in East Africa, that Kenya's vast and half-empty highlands, favoured alike by climate and geography, should be occupied by white farmers. The traffic derived from land settlement would make the railway a profitable undertaking. The early settlers in the highlands therefore began to raise stock, and also to grow coffee, sisal, maize, barley, flax, vegetables and other crops. Settlers in the lowlands started sisal, cocoa-nut and other plantations. The pioneers, including both newcomers from Great Britain and Afrikaners from South Africa, as well as a great many ex-servicemen after the First World War, encountered tremendous difficulties. Gradually, however, they mastered their problems; and by the early 1920s the white agricultural economy had become firmly established and the typical settler was an estate owner, employing large numbers of Africans. In addition, many whites worked in commerce, in administration and in the liberal professions.

There was, however, no European working class corresponding to that in Southern Rhodesia or in South Africa. Many of the intermediate positions that went to white men south of the Zambezi were taken up by Indian immigrants. Settlers from Asia made their living in occupations such as clerks, mechanics, telegraphists, and building foremen. Above all, they opened up large numbers of back-country stores (*dukas*) that often provided a scanty living for the trader's many relatives as well as for himself. Indian shopkeepers, working on very low profit margins, thus pioneered rural commerce in many parts of East Africa, and their presence became indispensable for the functioning of the country's cash economy.[1] Some Indians also made their way to the Rhodesias, where they often came to compete with small European traders, many of them of Scottish, Jewish or Greek origin. Competition between white men and brown would, however, also entail co-operation. Many European storekeepers moved out of the 'native' trade to become wholesalers. White wholesale merchants or bankers in turn

[1] By 1911, Kenya already contained 11,886 Asians, as compared to only 3,175 Europeans. Ten years later, the Indians numbered over 23,000 and the whites 9,600.

supplied Indian dealers with credit, and Indians—who were always credit-hungry—in their turn climbed up the economic ladder.

Despite all these differences in the nature and origin of European colonization, some generalizations seem in order. The Europeans were fortunate in that for the most part they made their way into the interior at a time when a great revolution in tropical medicine was already under way. Contrary to a widespread assumption, many parts of Southern and Northern Rhodesia were originally as dangerous to white new-comers as the lands adjoining the Gulf of Benin. Malaria was rife on the early frontier; at the beginning of this century, for instance, many of the pioneer Boer trekkers examined by British medical officers in North Western Rhodesia were found to suffer badly from malaria and to be in poor physical shape. Soon, however, the whites learned how to protect themselves against the malaria mosquito, and the white death rate rapidly dropped. In time, life in the two Rhodesias became almost as suitable for white families as in England.

European settlement, moreover, was usually extensive rather than intensive. In this respect there were indeed certain parallels between white and black farming. The European peasant, used to tilling small acreages by his own labour and that of his family, never made his appearance in Africa. An early attempt was made in Kenya to attract settlers by offering them farms of up to 600 acres on the Canadian home-stead principle under stringent development clauses. But settlers were unwilling to acquire land under such conditions in a country whose agricultural possibilities were little understood, where transport costs were high, where there were no local markets and where the amenities of Western culture could not yet be secured. In any case, the great age of northern European peasant emigration was already closing at the end of the nineteenth century. Scandinavian, British or German farmers who still thought of farming abroad preferred North America, Aus-tralia or New Zealand, rather than the little known Black Continent. In any case small European farmers without much capital could hardly compete with black cultivators; the Europeans' costs were too high. The nearest approximation to the European peasant was the Afrikaner *bywoner*, who made his home on a relatively small number of Afrikaner-owned farms in the two Rhodesias. The *bywoner* was a poor man, usually an indigent relative of the farmer, who was unable or often unwilling to acquire land of his own. He worked for the landowner as a foreman or as a sharecropper, obliged in some cases to give a third of his crops and of his trading profits to the *baas*. *Bywoners*, however, only arrived in scanty numbers, and white farmers usually came to the lands beyond the Limpopo as rural entrepreneurs.

White immigrants confined their land purchases largely to the cooler highland regions, especially those areas easily accessible from the lines of rail. They occupied but a tiny proportion of the enormous belt that stretched from the Limpopo northward to the borders of Ethiopia. Even within the plateau regions they tended to cluster in certain territories. The pressure on land claimed for actual or potential African use was heaviest by far in Southern Rhodesia, where, by the early 1920s the local administration had already alienated to white colonists something like 32 per cent of all the land. In Northern Rhodesia European colonization was largely confined to strips along the railway and to some enclaves in the south and north-east. In Nyasaland white plantations were restricted to the southern highland zone. In Kenya, on the other hand, land was reserved to Europeans in what became known as the White Highlands.

The European settlers in Rhodesia took over a much larger proportion of the available land. Nevertheless, Rhodesian Africans, not to speak of those in Kenya, Tanganyika or Nyasaland, retained a vastly larger share of their country's acreage than did the black people in South Africa. Throughout the history of white settlement in Rhodesia, the indigenous people never suffered from anything like the mass displacement that had largely cleared indigenous people such as the Maori of New Zealand, the Araucanians of Chile and the Indians of North America from their ancestral acres.[1]

Farmers and Africans

The early white pioneers were sometimes idealized by imperial propagandists as the very embodiment of their country's national honour, perhaps unconsciously so, as representatives of the British public school virtues in the wilds of Africa:

[1] By the end of the First World War something like 20,000,000 acres were reserved to Africans, who had about 50 acres of land *per capita* of the total population. By 1961, the African agricultural areas amounted to just over 40,000,000 acres. Of this land, about 30,000,000 acres—slightly less than the total area of England—was suitable for ploughing or grazing. On the other hand, the African population had probably increased threefold or more during this period. (Exact figures cannot be given, as official population statistics seem consistently to have underestimated African numbers.)

Jimmy...is big and broad, and tanned to such an extent that...you might almost imagine him to be coloured...[On his farm he] reigns supreme and unquestioned...When necessary, he deals out justice, generously tempered with mercy...and for miles around, far beyond his lawful domain, law and order prevail, and his name is loved almost as greatly as it is feared.

The Jimmy of the storybook falls in love with a nice British girl, a 'sporting little devil [who] walked up to that lion and, as cool as a cucumber shot him dead.' The hero proposes marriage to his lady-love while the two are perched in a tree and the dead lion's mate angrily prowls around below. Jimmy wins his fiancée's favours by promising her to make a success of his farm.[1]

But the real Jimmies were usually a mixed and a less romantic lot. They comprised a great variety: South Africans wise to the ways of the veld and apt to avoid the mistakes made by the 'home-born', retired army officers willing to risk their pensions on a farm in the bush, labour recruiters, ex-policemen, an occasional Jewish cattle trader turned rancher, or younger sons of gentlemen with an itch for adventure. A few English noblemen, such as Lord Delamere in Kenya, turned to pioneering. Other high-born landowners, such as the Duke of Westminster, Lord Winterton and Lord Wolverton, acquired African estates which they ran with hired managers. Some agricultural development work was done by large mining and mine companies, but most European agriculturists worked for themselves.

Whatever the settler's social origins, he usually led a harsh life. All too often the Rhodesian pioneer farmer lived in conditions that resembled those of Australian rural slums, in a cramped little house covered with a galvanized iron roof, painted dull red, the best conceivable material for transmitting heat. He often experimented under unknown conditions; he commonly suffered from lack of markets and from high transport charges. He might have to cope with sharply fluctuating prices for his produce or to face the ravages occasioned by locusts or by unfamiliar plant or animal diseases. Schools and hospitals were few and far between; scientific services hardly existed. There was little opportunity for the use of machinery on the farms. Farmers therefore depended very largely on unskilled African labour. Workmen hired from the villages might come cheap, but they required constant supervision; and the farmers usually tried to substitute quantity

[1] Sheila Macdonald, *Martie and others in Rhodesia* (London, 1927), pp. 25, 26, 100, 242, 243 and *passim*.

for quality of labour. In the early days of colonial rule, the labour problem thus appeared to the whites always in the light of a perennial shortage; the problems of African unemployment were always those of a more highly developed and at least partly urbanized economy. The white farmer's outlook was producer-oriented rather than consumer-oriented.

Not surprisingly, the frontier farmer's racial outlook was usually of the harshest. His own life was tough, and all too often his interests seemed to clash with those of black people. The farmer's cash economy competed with tribal economies for unskilled labour and often also for land, the basic means of production on which they both depended. As employers, the immigrant farmers came into actual or potential conflict with their workmen over wages and living conditions. The white farmers were rarely able to pay wages comparable to those which a mining company could offer its workmen. Rhodesian employers not only competed with one another on the labour market; they also faced competition from rivals in South Africa who tempted African migrant workers to the Rand mines by offering still more money. The black labourer was thus able to benefit to some extent from competition between various sectors of white society. He derived a certain degree of protection also from governmental paternalism.

Nevertheless, there can be no doubt that early white colonization in Rhodesia rested on an elaborate structure of coercion. The pioneering period saw a great deal of cruelty, for on the farms and in the mining camps the white boss was usually a law unto himself. Insults and beatings went unpunished; manslaughter or even murder earned derisory penalties. White juries were notoriously unwilling to convict whites for crimes committed against blacks. Formal justice in interracial cases only improved in 1927, when the new 'Responsible Government' administration put a new law on the statute book permitting accused persons to opt for trial by a judge and two assessors, both of whom had to be Native Commissioners of long standing, and who were not so dependent on the goodwill of their white fellow citizens as European merchants or craftsmen selected as jurors.

Physical cruelty of the overt variety slowly diminished as the country became more settled, as the state machinery became more effective, as the private jurisdiction exercised *de facto* by white farmers and housewives over their workmen gave way to a more impersonal system of administering justice. But Africans instead found themselves enmeshed in an elaborate legal network that consistently favoured white over black, master over man. From 1892 onward, for instance, the Rhodesian administration issued a complicated series of pass laws. Africans who migrated to the cities were required to carry a variety of identification papers.

The pass laws, like many other discriminatory measures, were not devoid of a paternalistic element. Identification documents enabled workmen to claim wages from dishonest white employers who would otherwise have insisted that the black applicant had never been near his place of work. These documents also had certain administrative advantages. Indeed many interterritorial agreements designed to protect labour migrants relied for their efficacy on the operation of a pass system. But passes at the same time developed into an oppressive means of police control. For instance, no African was allowed to seek work without a pass; residence permits were required for black workmen living in urban locations. Migrants were liable to be harried, intimidated or imprisoned if they could not show the required piece of paper to the European in authority. Pass legislation became a means, albeit a crude and only half-effective one, of controlling the influx of workers into the city. Moreover, such legislation may have prevented workmen from selling their labour to best advantage. The measure also benefited white farmers, who wanted a plentiful labour supply, as against urban employers, whose access to employable manpower was thereby restricted.

Above all, the pass laws, like many others of their kind, formed part of a whole array of white-made offences unintelligible to blacks, unknown to traditional society, edicts whose violations the Europeans then proceeded to punish through the machinery of their own courts. Even the best-intentioned of these measures often had a strange Janus-like quality. All negrophilist lobbies in Europe, for example, agreed as part of their faith that 'low-bred' white merchants should not ruin innocent savages by selling guns and liquor to the aborigines. But when these humanitarian principles were applied in practice, they all became embodied into race legislation of one kind or another. The sale of hard spirits to Africans was prohibited. The white employer could get drunk; the black workers, on the other hand, were supposed to stay sober. The ruling race owned rifles; the subordinate black strata were largely though not entirely deprived of fire-arms.

In the field of labour legislation, the employer likewise acquired the whip hand. The 'Masters and Servants' legislation, put into force during the first decade of the present century, in many ways resembled the disciplinary code of an army. Desertion and other kinds of mis-demeanour became criminal offences. Racial discrimination extended into many other spheres of legislation as well. Indeed, the classic work on the Rhodesian administrative system, written by a distinguished Belgian lawyer and labour expert just before the outbreak of the First World War, might be described almost as a compendium of race-caste legislation.[1]

But even more important than the labour problem and the pass-system was the land question. Only a limited proportion of Africans laboured for Europeans at any one time. Nearly all Africans, on the other hand, depended on land. The European farmer in many cases naturally competed with his African neighbour for this most essential means of production, and in Southern Rhodesia especially, the white cultivator was in a strong position to assert his claims.

During the earlier period of European settlement, the European farmers were the most numerous occupational group among the European settlers, not only in Kenya, but also in the two Rhodesias. (In 1921, out of 2,110 gainfully employed whites in Northern Rho-desia, 714 were farmers. In 1926, agriculture and forestry accounted for 3,995 out of 17,449 gainfully employed whites in Southern Rhodesia.) Farmers dominated European society; they were well organized and powerfully represented in the Southern Rhodesian legislature. Farmers also had numerous allies in other white social strata, for many business-men, civil servants, professional people or even ordinary workmen would invest their savings in land as a speculation, allowing the investor to benefit from rising real estate values, or as a saving for eventual retirement.

Despite their apparent strength, the early white farmers, however, were never a single undifferentiated bloc, not even within the borders of a single country such as Rhodesia. The large maize growers, working with more capital, competed on the market against the smaller culti-vators. All European employers competed with one another for African labour. European farmers might toast the future of a 'White Rhodesia' at their sundowner party; but they were perfectly willing to employ black rather than white artisans to build and make repairs on the farm and thereby to save on their bill. European farming also gave a stimulus to African production. White Rhodesian maize growers might look

---

[1] Henri Rolin, *Les lois et l'administration de la Rhodésie* (Brussels, 1913).

askance at black competition. But white tobacco farmers or dairymen, dependent on more specialized products, were quite willing to buy African-grown grain to feed their labourers. European farmers introduced new crops, new types of breeding stock, new methods and new implements. Many Rhodesian Africans began to learn from their white employers and neighbours. 'All the irrigation [on my farm]', wrote an unusually progressive European farmer in the early years of the present century,

is done by natives; the binders and reapers are also worked by them. The ploughing with disc and mould-board ploughs, double and treble furrow, is done by them. The separating and churning work is also done by them. The majority of these boys have been with me from four to eight years, and...take a keen interest in their work, and are proud of excelling in any one department.[1]

Some African cultivators thus began to use new methods on their own land, to hire or purchase a better class of bull from white farmers and to improve their herds with superior breeding stock. By the beginning of the present century, many Rhodesian Africans had learned how to use the bullock as a beast of burden. Other cultivators began to use ploughs instead of the traditional hoes. The more progressive or more enterprising African farmers also began to use bullocks to draw wagons, carts or sledges. The pacification of the countryside also prevented warlike people such as the Matabele in Southern Rhodesia or the Masai in Kenya from raiding their neighbours' cattle. The weaker African communities were enabled to use their land more effectively, for villages no longer had to be located in inaccessible terrain with an eye to their tactical defence possibilities. From the turn of the present century, Rhodesia accordingly witnessed a very striking expansion of the acreages under African cultivation. The number of African-owned cattle increased rapidly, especially as the more intelligent whites came to realize that the battle against infectious stock diseases and the struggle against soil erosion could not be confined to the white-owned areas. White farming settlement was accordingly contradictory in its result, and Africans therefore gained as well as lost from the white cultivator's enterprise.

European pioneers, for their part, were never quite certain whether to welcome or to deplore African economic advance. The white employer

[1] Percy F. Hone, *Southern Rhodesia* (London, 1909), pp. 60 ff.

soon became aware of the advantages of having a more efficient, a more ambitious and a better-trained labour force. Some Europeans, traders as well as farmers, also began to acquire a stake in the local African market. Yet the African's economic progress and his slowly rising standard of living also upset the pattern of social subordination desired by most Europeans. The white 'kaffir trader' accordingly came in for a special share of the blame. As a Rhodesian official complained in 1909:

[The itinerant merchant comes] with his wagon full of cloth, ornaments and European food, barters his wares for the grain and meal of the natives; he encourages their vanity and their taste for luxury, and the Mashona who a few years before thought it sufficient clothing to have two or three jackals' tails from his loins, to-day requires a tall hat or a second-hand frock coat, and will add now and again to his daily supply of meal a tin of salmon or sardines. Vanity and desire for luxury increase every year; the children who are growing into young men take their parents' luxuries as necessities and require to gratify their tastes still further.[1]

The miner's frontier

The impact of the miner's frontier on race relations was equally complex. In Southern Rhodesia in the early days the advanced guard of white mining enterprise was usually composed of scattered prospectors working on their own account. The typical explorer of fiction wore a bush-hat and galloped across the veld on a magnificent stallion. The real prospector more likely wore a battered old khaki helmet, a crumpled shirt and a pair of slacks tied under the knee with string. He rode bare backed on a donkey, and lying in front of him, across his animal's back, was his canvas bag containing samples. He knew the Africans; indeed much of his information was often obtained from African informants in exchange for trade goods. Like the farmer, he had rough and ready, though often garbled, knowledge of the African villagers' ways, a knowledge of the kind inaccessible to white townsmen. He had in many cases tested his fortune in several different countries—England, South Africa or sometimes even Australia or California. He had generally tried his hand at many occupations—farming, transport riding, running a pub—for occupational like geographical mobility was as characteristic of the Rhodesian frontier as of any other.

[1] Hone, *Southern Rhodesia*, p. 63.

Some of these prospectors became mining entrepreneurs on their own account. Southern Rhodesia, unlike Northern Rhodesia or the Transvaal, contained widely disseminated bodies of low-grade gold ore that could be profitably worked by individuals or syndicates composed of small capitalists with just enough money in the bank to buy the required machinery. Mining remained a chancy business: the names of many early Rhodesian mines—'Cross Your Luck', 'Last Chance', 'Stony Broke'—read like aliases on lottery tickets.

The 'small workers' nevertheless played an important part in building up the country's early gold industry. They were self-reliant men, with plenty of initiative; but they were themselves subject to harsh economic conditions. They were unable to provide social services for their African workmen. They had to deal for the most part with unskilled labour migrants who wished only to earn their tax money or to buy a few manufactured goods before returning to their villages. The bulk of the African workers had no time to pick up skills, and the majority had neither interest in nor understanding of their work. Their white foremen could not get to know them, and were thus faced with the unenviable task of handling men whom they regarded as inferior, whose linquistic and whose technical ignorance might even cause serious mine accidents. All too often the whites responded by imposing a ruthless discipline; beatings and abuses were commonplace. (This state of affairs, one might add, also had parallels in the 'white' parts of the world. German skilled workers in Bohemia, for instance, often used to look down with fear and contempt on Czech unskilled labourers. The liberties taken by English and Welsh supervisors, the earliest arrivals, against Irish miners—usually newcomers—in the early Pennsylvania coal mining industry contributed to the bloody 'Molly Maguire' outbreaks in the 1870s.)

The outlook of the white foremen and the white 'small workers', a backveld mining bourgeoisie who employed Africans on only a relatively small scale, exerted a considerable influence in shaping Rhodesia's early race attitudes. But the future lay with the bigger companies, those with enough capital and technical knowledge to work at great depths, to tide themselves over bad times and long periods of development work, and with sufficient cash reserves to pay better wages for a better-trained and healthier workman. Many of the smaller firms were bought up or amalgamated. (As early as 1914, fifteen producers accounted for fifty-five per cent of Southern Rhodesia's gold output.) The extraction of base minerals such as copper, zinc and coal was a task even more beyond the financial strength of 'small workers'. Large-scale mining enterprise received an additional impetus from the discovery of vast coal deposits at Wankie in Southern Rhodesia, which did much to solve the country's fuel problems.

At the same time, living conditions on the mines rapidly began to change for the better. For all their assumed romance, the early compounds were backveld slums where white and black workers alike died in large numbers from disease. Improvements in mining techniques and in the scale of mining coincided, however, with striking improvements in working conditions. From the beginning of the present century, moreover, Southern Rhodesian civil servants came under heavy pressure not only from their own superiors and from the Imperial government, but also, in some instances, from local white notables, to do something about the social evils in the bush. In some cases the London head offices of the larger concerns pressed for improvements. The Rhodesian administration thus began to enforce measures for bettering the treatment of both African and European labourers; and during the second decade of the present century the African death-rate for the Southern Rhodesian mine dropped dramatically.[1] In time the Southern Rhodesian administration acquired a good reputation for its labour legislation and its care of migrant workers. The labour laws compared favourably with those enforced in British East Africa or in the French and Portuguese colonies on the African continent.

The Rhodesian African, though harshly treated at first, thus benefited from entering industrial employment under the aegis of colonial paternalism at a time when medical science had already made considerable progress and when an established metropolitan tradition of social welfare legislation had come into existence. In this respect, the African miner was often better off than the farm-hand; and because the larger mines usually provided better conditions than did landowners, mining as an occupation became increasingly popular among Africans. In general terms, not many black workers in Central Africa paid the same price for the Industrial Revolution that many British workmen in Europe had been forced to pay a century and a half ago. Black women, for instance, never had to work modern Rhodesian mineshafts, as they had in eighteenth-century England, or indeed in

[1] The mortality figure dropped from 75·94 per thousand in 1906 to 21·68 in 1917, and to 15·39 in 1925.

the mines of early pre-colonial Rhodesia under the sway of the Monomotapas.

The colonizers also effected far-reaching improvements in urban health. The early Rhodesian townships usually began as ill-managed, unsanitary settlements where malaria and other diseases were rife. The Europeans gradually introduced the urban techniques developed overseas under the impact of the Industrial Revolution. Town-builders made provision for clean water, for the disposal of sewage, for electrical illumination. The colonial cities thereby acquired advantages of a kind unknown either to mediaeval European cities, to traditional African agro-towns or to centres of handicraft industries, commerce and administration of the Sudanic kind. Life became safer; the European urban death-rate gradually declined, and so did that of the Africans.

At the same time there was a shift in the larger European employers' attitudes towards African labourers. The pioneers, working with relatively unsophisticated methods, had looked upon African tribesmen in their kraals in much the same way as English landlords had looked upon the 'vicious and idle poor' who preferred to work on their own account rather than to work for wages. Many early pioneers had relied on forced labour. Later white entrepreneurs frequently depended on the indirect pressure of native taxation (the hut tax) which forced tribesmen to seek employment in order to pay their imposts in cash. Soon, however, the colonial economy became more productive. Employers were able to offer more incentives, and the pressure of taxation became progressively less important as a means of mobilizing unskilled labour. The Europeans instead relied increasingly upon what early settlers had stigmatized 'the natives' insensate desire for luxuries'. As large-scale mining and similar enterprises required more complicated techniques, employers gradually abandoned the moralistic terminology of the pioneering period. They became more willing to look upon black people as 'economic men' rather than as filthy heathen who ought to be 'civilized' by wage work.

Large companies also came to dominate the mining industry of Northern Rhodesia. A major economic revolution was initiated north of the Zambezi when, in 1925, technologists found a profitable way of working the low-grade copper deposits of the Copperbelt. During the late 1920s and the 1930s a vast amount of British, South African and American capital was invested in Northern Rhodesia. The companies began development work on a tremendous scale, with new townships springing out of the bush in short order. Northern Rhodesia became one of the world's greatest copper producers and a land of giant mining concerns *par excellence*.

The mining companies even became city-builders on their own account, and the lay-out of the Copperbelt townships reflected the social composition of these new communities. Large mining enterprises, of course, are like armies, requiring a strict chain of command from management downward. The rough egalitarianism of the malaria-ridden white pioneer settlements soon gave way, therefore, to the differences in wealth characterizing a well-run garden city. There was not only residential segregation between white and black, but also between white and white. By 1930 white workers were already making angry complaints at the undemocratic structure of the new townships. 'A' houses for heads of departments contained ten rooms and cost £10,000, while 'F' houses, for ordinary white workmen, were put up for a mere £800. Worse still, the white miners said, houses of different types were grouped into separate areas with rigid class divisions between them, so that even African servants took their social status from their masters; and 'A' house-boys presumed to give orders to 'F' boys and refused to mix with them socially!

The white Copperbelt miners soon became by far the most numerous occupational group among Europeans in Northern Rhodesia. The European mine-hands never attained anything like the same importance in Southern Rhodesia, with its smaller and more scattered mineral deposits; but Southern Rhodesia attracted growing numbers of technicians, artisans and foremen heretofore employed in other industries. Within less than one generation, the typical settler in Northern and Southern Rhodesia had become a skilled urban worker, foreman or supervisor rather than a farmer.[1]

The European worker in South East Central Africa performed many different tasks, such as driving railway engines, repairing machinery,

---

[1] The number of Northern Rhodesian whites in gainful employment rose from 2,110 in 1921 to 16,694 in 1951. During this same period, the number of white miners increased from 714 to only 4,608. Industrial workers taken as a whole, including whites employed in manufacturing, building, mining and transport, increased from 553 to 9,309. The number of persons employed in farming and agriculture rose from 714 to 1,338. In Southern Rhodesia, the number of gainfully employed whites stood at 17,449 in 1926 and at 60,494 in 1951. The number of white miners increased from 2,034 to only 2,709 during this period. Industrial workers, taken as a whole, increased from 6,470 to 26,348. In farming and forestry the number rose from 3,995 to 7,129.

supervising African mine-workers; but all these workers had certain problems in common. They, or their parents, had come to Rhodesia from South Africa, from Great Britain or from the Continent in order to get a better job with higher wages. They brought new skills to the land of their temporary or permanent adoption. Immigration thus represented a transfer of trained personnel whose technical and general education had been paid for by the 'exporting' country at no expense to the 'importer'. As long as his skills were rare, the immigrant was in a relatively favourable position. But he lacked security. Unlike the unskilled African labourer recruited from the native reserves, the European worker had no foothold left in the countryside. He was a townsman; if he lost his job, he could not return to an ancestral plot. In some ways, therefore, the European artisan, though far more highly paid, was far less crisis-resistant than his unskilled African workmates who still had links to the land.

The early white Rhodesian workers faced other difficulties, too. Rhodesia was initially deficient in social services. There was no unemployment insurance, and 'distressed British subjects' were expected to return to their respective countries of origin rather than burden the local economy with their presence. Wages might be relatively high, but there was a considerable spread between the pay received by the most highly and the most poorly paid white workmen.[1] The cost of living was high on the Rhodesian frontier. In fact, some white miners might have done better by emigrating to Australia or Canada. Employment opportunities, moreover, were naturally limited in a backward country, and once a man lost his job he was often hard put to find another.

The European workers, most of them familiar with British traditions, reacted by forming trade unions similar to those at home in order to defend their living standard—one comparable, roughly, to that of an Australian workman—to extract better working conditions and more pay from their employers, and to protect themselves against the 'dilution of labour' by poorly paid Africans who were gradually acquiring more skills and who were starting to take over certain defined occupations like truck-driving.

[1] The myth of the pampered white worker on the mine able to subsist in idle luxury dies as hard as its counterpart, the myth of the happy savage in the bush. In actual fact, in 1951, for instance, 871 whites employed in the Northern Rhodesian mining industry earned less than £500 a year, 496 took home between £500 and £900, 930 made between £1,000 and £1,250, 413 earned between £1,250 and £2,000, and only 52 had salaries exceeding £2,000 a year.

In organizing themselves, Rhodesian workmen, like South Africans, were not necessarily motivated by race prejudice. The first trade unions in southern Africa were set up by skilled British immigrants at the Cape during the early 1880s. The first non-Europeans encountered by these newcomers were skilled coloured workmen used to urban ways, and the white trade-union pioneers made no attempt to exclude the mulattos from the benefits of industrial organization. On the diamond fields of Kimberley, however, British miners came into contact with non-Europeans of a very different kind, with 'raw native' unskilled gang workers with whom they had nothing in common. Kimberley soon developed a rigid industrial colour bar that was carried to the gold-mines of the Transvaal by English-speaking workers. The colour bar was enthusiastically accepted by Afrikaans-speaking workers who gradually replaced British-born foremen and artisans on the South African mines. Many white Rhodesian mine-workers were of South African origin or had obtained their training south of the Limpopo. Rhodesian trade unionism and labour laws likewise were profoundly influenced by South African precedents.[1]

The white workers in southern Africa enjoyed a relatively strong bargaining position, especially from the First World War onward, when European labour became scarce and when the unions' bargaining power increased. The white workers had the vote and were able to make their power effective through the ballot. On the Rand mines in the Transvaal they showed themselves equally ready to use bullets. The Rand Rebellion of 1922 was the only urban rising of the 'classical' variety that had ever occurred in Africa. The rising was smashed, but it shook the country to its foundations, for the whites fought hard, and

[1] In Southern Rhodesia economic discrimination with regard to trade-union matters was embodied in the Industrial Conciliation Act, 1934, which was designed to protect white trade unionists from competition by cheaper black labour, as well as from competition by non-unionized whites willing to work at lower wages than those acceptable to the unions. African trade unions were denied official recognition, though in practice some unions operated. It was not until 1959 that there was a major departure in principle. The Industrial Conciliation Act, 1959, was for the first time made applicable to all races, though it nevertheless still tended to benefit the skilled (that is to say, mostly European) as against the unskilled workmen. Rhodesian trade-union affairs bore certain similarities to those of South Africa. From the early 1960s onward, the leaders of the Trade Union Council of South Africa (TUCSA) argued that Africans should join unions of their own. From 1962, South Africa witnessed the unusual sight of white artisans, traditionally among the most conservative members of the white community, sitting down with Africans at TUCSA's congresses, a shift which reflected the changing social position of the white community.

the South African army reservists (many of them poor farmers from the backveld) often wavered in their loyalty to the government. The rising thus convinced both employers and the state that it was cheaper to conciliate than to fight the unions. In 1924 the South African Parliament passed the Industrial Conciliation Act, which helped to consolidate the white workers' privileges.

Southern Rhodesian trade-union legislation, designed likewise to protect white workmen against black competition, owed a great deal to the South African example. The Rhodesian workers' resentment at the way in which their comrades had been treated on the Rand helped, moreover, to keep Southern Rhodesia politically separate from South Africa at a crucial period in its history. In Northern Rhodesia the Imperial authorities similarly acquired a healthy respect for the white workers' ability to make trouble. They were initially far more frightened of trouble from white than from black workers. As late as 1942, for example, white Southern Rhodesian troops were rushed to the Copperbelt in order to prevent a possible outbreak on the part of white miners led by a strange coalition of militant Afrikaner nationalists and a militant British left-winger.

But the white workers never formed a monolithic bloc. There was always a considerable difference in outlook between a semi-skilled bricklayer or a house-painter afraid of ultimately losing his livelihood to a lower-paid African, and a highly trained technician, say a Volkswagen mechanic sent out from Germany, able to earn an excellent salary and unconcerned about potential competition from an African. Even the most restrictionist white worker's position had many internal contradictions. From the early days onward many European artisans would employ African assistants in order to get more work done. But in doing so, the European could not help passing on to black people some of his jealously guarded skills. More ambitiously minded whites sought promotion; and once they had obtained it, they might end up as technical instructors teaching Africans. White men might employ the strike weapon in their own interest, but the strike technique was adopted in turn by black workers. Europeans agitated for shorter hours, for improved safety regulations and for other reforms that could not help but benefit African as well as white workers. By the early 1950s, for instance, few Northern Rhodesian employers were asking for more than a forty-eight hour week, while some contented themselves with forty.

African mine-workers thus found themselves in a highly ambivalent position. While they encountered economic and social discrimination from their white workmates, they also derived indirect benefits from European trade-union activity. Black as well as white workmen benefited from the shorter hours of labour extorted from their employers by European workers. Africans as well as Europeans gained from improved safety facilities in mines and workshops, from factory inspection and from other innovations that derived in part from the white workers' agitation.

The manufacturer's frontier

The socio-economic structure of settler Africa became even more complex as the manufacturer's frontier began to move northward from the Limpopo. From the First World War onward, the South African secondary industries began to expand with dramatic speed, and South Africa in time became the industrial giant on the continent. Contrary to the pessimists' predictions at the time, the net value of South Africa's industrial output grew by 110 per cent between 1933 and 1939. South Africa thus found itself in the extraordinary position of experiencing swift economic growth at a time when most other countries were still suffering from serious economic difficulties occasioned by the Great Depression.

In Southern Rhodesia industrialization followed after a slight time-lag, and owed a great deal to South African capital and entrepreneurial skill. (Manufacturing in Rhodesia started—as in so many other colonial territories—with railway workshops, cement works, agricultural processing industries and similar small-scale enterprises designed to serve the primary sector of the economy.) During the Second World War the country's infant industries received a further impetus. Few manufactures could be imported from overseas. Customers from Southern Rhodesia as well as from Northern Rhodesia and Nyasaland looked to Rhodesian factories to supply many of their consumer as well as some of their military needs. Rhodesia developed a substantial secondary industry, and also began to manufacture a whole range of other products. The colony's industrial output continued to grow swiftly during the two decades following the Second World War. (Indeed the international trade boycott imposed on Rhodesia in 1965 as a result of her unilateral declaration of independence (UDI) further forced the Rhodesians to diversify their industrial production.)

The economic development of southern Africa disproved the pessimistic forecasts current in the 1930s that the social and industrial colour bar, by restricting skills and purchasing power, would always prevent economic progress on a large scale, and that southern Africa would only win prosperity by a root-and-branch change in politics. Industrialization affected every stratum of society. In 1911 more than one-third of the European children in Southern Rhodesia between seven and fourteen had received no formal education. A generation later the Europeans were a well-educated group. Trucks and motor cars had done away with the traditional isolation of the backveld, and the level of industrial skills had vastly increased. The white farmer became increasingly a highly skilled entrepreneur, often a man with a diploma in agriculture or even a degree in engineering, who commonly operated with a great deal of capital and with the most advanced methods. The Rhodesian development was part of a wider economic revolution that affected European agricultural enterprise in most parts of South Africa, and also in Kenya, where farming in the 'White Highlands' became a highly skilled and heavily capitalized affair. The poor backveld farmer largely disappeared. White workers in the towns were no longer subject to prolonged bouts of unemployment, as during the Great Slump. In Rhodesia, as in South Africa, the 'poor white', whom Establishment Rhodesians used to castigate as 'something considerably lower than a decent native',[1] was absorbed by the expanding economy.

In southern Africa, the process of white urbanization created special problems of its own. Poor Afrikaners streamed into the cities from the backveld looking for jobs. They used their voting power to gain protected employment on the railways and in other state enterprises where they remained immune from black competition. In the short run, urbanization helped to worsen race relations as white trade unionists called for more colour-bar legislation to safeguard their position against black competitors. But as southern African entrepreneurs put up more and more factories, there simply were not enough skilled workers to fill all the jobs. Many European workers gained industrial promotion, and some Africans slowly filtered into more advanced positions. Hence the industrial colour bar began to give way.

In Rhodesia, industrialization produced problems of similar complexity. For many years Southern Rhodesia's rate of industrialization was

[1] Godfrey Martin Huggins, *Southern Rhodesia: recent progress and development* (London, 1934), p. 12.

one of the fastest attained by any backward country in the twentieth century. The country ceased to be solely dependent on primary production, and became Africa's second manufacturing country, following in the wake of South Africa. Rhodesia, though poor by world standards, became a relatively favoured country by African standards.[1]

The rapid growth of the secondary sector in the country's economy completely changed its social structure. Industry, which in the 1920s had provided jobs for only a small proportion of the European settlers, became the largest employer of white labour. Rhodesia also provided new opportunities for a large number of white people in the professions, in management, in commerce, in insurance and in other areas.[2] Between 1954 and 1965 the country's gross domestic product more than doubled. Figures for this period are shown in Table 2.[3] Domestically generated capital provided an increasingly important share of the funds for local investment. Rhodesia developed a substantial local bourgeosie that gradually became less dependent on foreign lenders for its capital.

Rhodesian immigration, though large by local standards, never remotely approached the dimensions of countries such as New Zealand or Australia, not to speak of the United States. Rhodesian governments of whatever complexion used to insist that the whites must form an élite population. In 1965 an official Rhodesian pamphlet thus warned intending immigrants in terms almost identical to those used from the country's very beginnings: 'Rhodesia...needs a considerable number of skilled men and immigrants with money to invest. There is no shortage of unskilled labour in Rhodesia.'[4]

The Rhodesian newcomers' social composition, coupled with a high birth-rate and a low death-rate, considerably affected the settlers' outlook on life. White Rhodesian society reflected a much greater degree of self-confidence than its British counterpart, and the settlers' psychological attitude was probably influenced both by the country's long

[1] The *per capita* share of the gross domestic product in Rhodesia was estimated at $240 in 1964, as compared with $177 in Zambia, $86 in Kenya, $59 in Tanzania, $58 in Nigeria [1963] and $30 in Malawi [1963].

[2] In 1926, manufacturing, construction, water and electricity services employed between them 2,437 people out of a total of 17,449 in employment. The corresponding figures stood at an estimated 33,180 out of 88,620 in 1960.

[3] In 1954, the Gross National Product stood at £168,500,000. In 1965 it had risen to £353,600,000. Details are shown in Table 1, p. 147.

[4] Rhodesia, Rhodesia Information Service, *Rhodesia in brief, 1965: a brief summary of the basic facts about Rhodesia* (Salisbury, n.d.), p. 26.

spurts of economic growth and by its demographic structure. White Rhodesia more or less lacked an indigenous intelligentsia of the kind found in South Africa. Traditionally, the role of the intelligentsia had largely been taken by missionaries, whose contacts with the settlers were naturally limited. Rhodesia was too small to attract large numbers of university professors, artists, journalists, television producers and other immigrants in highly specialized service occupations. Those academics who did come to the country usually came as labour migrants, and few established permanent links in the new country. White Rhodesian society in some ways retained a curiously archaic quality; the values of Edwardian England survived as in a kind of sociological museum. The economic opportunities created by industrialization caused additional immigrants to come to southern Africa. In fact, in post-war Rhodesia the tide of European newcomers was so great as to swamp the pre-war generation of settlers.[1]

The new Rhodesian was usually a young person, for older people do not often go overseas. Since a youthful population has more children than an ageing one, and since Rhodesia had developed excellent health services, white Rhodesia had one of the highest reproduction rates in the world.[2] It was a land where babies abounded and grandmothers were few. The demographic structure of the white population thus bore certain resemblances to that of the African townsmen, whose communities were likewise lacking in aged folk. The European immigrant, however, differed greatly from the bulk of African newcomers to the cities, or for that matter from the bulk of Polish, Slovak or Irish immigrants who flocked to the United States during the last century. The Africans and the nineteenth-century migrants whom we have mentioned were countrymen who moved to the towns. The great majority of new Rhodesians were townsmen who moved from city to city. The new Rhodesians, unlike so many of the foreign immigrants who made

---

[1] The European population rose from 55,408 in 1936 to 82,386 in 1946, to 175,800 in 1956, and to about 225,000 in 1966. (In 1951, 42,617, that is to say, 31 per cent of the total population, had been born in Rhodesia, 41,252 in South Africa, and 39,075 in the United Kingdom and Ireland. The remainder came mostly from various European countries, especially Holland, Italy, Portugal and Greece.) The increase in the European population in other 'white settler' countries was equally striking during the 1940s and the 1950s. In Tanganyika, the white population went up from 11,300 to 22,300 between 1948 and 1960; in Kenya the corresponding figures were 30,800 and 67,000; in Zambia, the white population rose from 21,907 in 1946 to 76,000 in 1960.

[2] Between 1956 and 1958, for instance, the rate of natural increase for whites fluctuated between 2·1 and 2·3 per cent per annum.

their homes in America a century or so ago, were not necessarily poorer or less well educated than the people on the spot. Most white immigrants to Rhodesia, since they came from English-speaking countries, had no language problem to hold them back, and men with ability could rapidly rise to the top.

White Rhodesian society, not to speak of European society in Zambia or Kenya, remained small in scale, smaller even than Afrikaner society south of the Limpopo, sharing most of the virtues and vices of provincial towns. Many factors combined to produce a strong sense of community cohesion. These included a sharp sense of ethnic differentiation from Indians and Africans alike, a strong conviction of the European's cultural superiority, pride in the settlers' own economic achievements and the country's swift progress, as well as a lingering sense of imperial destiny that sharply distinguished Rhodesia from Great Britain. By the early 1960s, the crime rate of Rhodesia had sharply declined since the country's pioneering days, and compared favourably with that of its neighbour, South Africa or the United States.[1] The white community had developed a proto-nationalism of its own, a sense of community that often indeed took some comfort from the growing estrangement from the mother country and its ways. Political isolation solidified rather than dissolved the sense of white community.

Industrialization in southern Africa also helped to unify white society in other respects. Before the First World War, the typical Afrikaner both in Rhodesia and in South Africa, for instance, was a countryman. The skilled mineworkers came mainly from Great Britain. Most senior government officials, as well as city merchants and managers, spoke English as their native tongue. For the most part, the settled population in South African and Rhodesian towns sprang from British stock. When country-born Afrikaners began to drift into the cities because their fathers' farms would no longer support a huge family, they often faced grim problems. They lacked the training, the capital and the aptitudes to compete with skilled English or even coloured artisans. They had to contend with more experienced Jewish competitors in trade and with better educated British rivals in the race for government jobs. The more fortunate Afrikaners became teachers and clergymen. Some made a name for themselves in the civil service, in law or in politics. But few

[1] F. Y. St Leger, 'Crime in Southern Rhodesia, *Rhodes–Livingstone Journal*, 1966, **38**, 11–41.

Afrikaners were to be found in the country's most highly paid jobs in banking or in business. In many respects the Afrikaners' social position in the first decade of the twentieth century resembled that of the Africans a generation later.[1]

At the same time there were sharp regional distinctions within southern Africa. Natal and Rhodesia were the strongholds of the English, while the Orange Free State and the rural parts of the Transvaal were bastions of Afrikanerdom. The Cape was rightly regarded as the oldest and most civilized European colony in Africa, the only country in sub-Saharan Africa where—for all theories to the contrary—a large group of non-Europeans had to some extent been culturally assimilated by the whites. The coloured people of the Cape, a mulatto group, had abandoned Hottentot, Malay and other tongues in favour of Afrikaans, an Indo-European language. Together with the tongue, they had absorbed many other Afrikaner ways. The Cape had a 'colour-blind', property-weighted franchise; and Cape administrative practices, Cape native policies and a Cape-type franchise had found acceptance in Rhodesia. The Transvaal, on the other hand, had been shaped in the image of the Boer voortrekker and later also of the English-speaking mine-worker. It contained no substantial coloured element, and the franchise was rigidly confined to white men alone.

Industrialization brought about other profound changes. The Afrikaners became primarily an urban people. Unskilled Afrikaner workmen moved into semi-skilled and skilled jobs, while skilled workmen in turn moved up the social ladder. Afrikaners made their name in trade, in industry and in banking, which ceased to be English and Jewish preserves. English- and Afrikaans-speaking South Africans and Rhodesians came to resemble one another more and more. Similarly, many of the old political cleavages became less important. In the late 1940s and the 1950s, the Afrikaner Nationalist Party (which obtained power in 1948) ceased to be what it had been in the 1930s, a militant Afrikaner organization backed mainly by poor farmers, mine-workers and salaried intellectuals. Instead the party tried to appeal to white men of whatever ancestry. Having displayed many characteristics of an anti-semitic, anti-capitalist Eastern European peasant organization,

[1] There are interesting parallels also between the social evolution of the Afrikaners and the black Americans. The First World War enabled American Negroes to move into semi-skilled employment in factories. During the Second World War, American Negroes moved into skilled industrial jobs on a much larger scale than before.

the Nationalist Party developed into a complex class alliance with a strong urban and bourgeois component.

In Rhodesia, Afrikaners had never accounted for more than fifteen per cent of the white population. Hence the whites had never been split along national lines to the same extent as in South Africa. Nevertheless, the Anglo-Afrikaner *rapprochement* in South Africa affected Rhodesia in an indirect fashion. In the 1940s, the majority of British Rhodesians had looked upon the Afrikaners of South Africa as the main threat to their own state. Anti-Afrikaner sentiments, provoked by the victory of the Nationalist Party in South Africa, had played a considerable part in the Rhodesian general election of 1948. The Federation of Rhodesia and Nyasaland (which existed from 1953 to 1963) was intended by its makers to defend British Rhodesians from the Afrikaner nationalist, as much as from the African nationalist, peril. By the later 1950s, however, Rhodesian politics ceased to revolve around inter-white relations. The 'Native Question' or—as the Africans saw it—the European question came to dominate public controversy.

In Kenya a different but nevertheless related process was at work. In the 1920s Kenyan politics represented a struggle for political power between the two main immigrant races. The Europeans, mainly farmers and their allies, stood arrayed against the Indians, most of them small traders and artisans, led by a handful of wealthier merchants and professional men. Although there was much bitterness, the desirability of white settlement and of European political rights was never challenged. Even a militant advocate of African rights and of 'Indirect Rule' like Lord Lugard believed that Kenya's problem consisted in

defining the area to be appropriated to British settlement, and granting to the settlers within that area representative government leading up eventually to that complete self-government which a virile and progressive British colony may rightly claim.[1]

By the 1950s, sentiments such as Lugard's had become unacceptable in most circles in Great Britain, except among a small group of right-wing conservatives. In the economic field, the settlers had made immense progress. European farming had become a highly capitalized and efficient undertaking, and local industries were beginning to develop on a small scale. The Indian community had become wealthier

[1] Frederick John Dealtry Lugard, 1st baron, *The dual mandate in British tropical Africa*, 5th ed. (London, 1965), pp. 321–2.

than ever before. But neither group was capable of facing the African challenge, and the old struggles between white men and brown had become irrelevant to Kenya's political future. What was now at stake was the permanence of alien settlement itself, for Indians and Europeans both constituted small minorities and the future of both communities was being called in question by the political awakening of the Africans.

Industry and the African

The effect of industrialization on the African was equally far-reaching. The African social structure changed beyond recognition. In the first decade of this century, the African top stratum in Rhodesia consisted of a few chiefs who were substantial stock-owners, who had benefited from the growth of urban markets and who had managed to put some bore-holes (wells) and other improvements on their land. There were also a handful of prosperous African kulaks, mostly immigrants from the Cape, who farmed their land on individual tenure and—like many white backveld farmers—often eked out their living with the sale of firewood, transport riding and other subsidiary occupations. The mission stations and the administration employed a small African staff composed of teachers, evangelists, clerks and interpreters. Finally, there was a small aristocracy of labour, including 'boss boys' on mines or cooks, the only workers whose incomes approached those of the most poorly paid whites.[1] The great majority of tribesmen made their living by tilling the land with traditional methods, or they worked as un-skilled labourers in white employment. By the 1930s the mining and agricultural revolution had had some effect. African farmers were com-peting with white men on a larger scale; industrial skills had become more widespread; and something like 3,000 Africans were working in such independent occupations as builders, carpenters and traders.

From the late 1940s, and to an even greater extent from the late 1950s, the number of economic choices open to Africans increased sharply. Industrialization also gave impetus to social differentiation within the African community. Africans, like the Afrikaners before

---

[1] In 1909, the best-paid African domestic worker could earn up to £2 a month, together with board and lodging. European domestic servants and children's nurses (numerically an insignificant group, but the only white group in civilian employment that also obtained the bulk of its wages in kind) received £3 a month to start with (figures obtained from British South Africa Company, *A land of sunshine: Southern Rhodesia*, London, 1910, p. 15).

them, moved in increasing numbers from the countryside into the towns, from unskilled into semi-skilled or even skilled professions. There was a real rise in wages paid to Africans and in the income of African rural households—even though the benefits of industrialization continued to be divided in a very uneven fashion and though Europeans, Indians and coloureds continued to enjoy a much larger *per capita* income than their African fellow citizens.[1] (The details on national income in Rhodesia from 1954 to 1965, the year of UDI, are shown in Table 2, p. 162.) Within the African community, townsmen usually profited more than villagers. All the same, a fair number of Africans managed to rise into the ranks of an emergent bourgeoisie. This was composed of bus-owners, building contractors, well-to-do farmers, traders with a chain of village stores, and professional people (as yet mostly teachers, clergymen, a sprinkling of journalists and a few doctors). In addition, government policy and the rising demand for food helped to produce a substantial class of 'master farmers', comprising something like 25,000 black smallholders, farming their land with modern methods in special 'Native Purchase Areas' where they could acquire plots on individual tenure. Reforms, initiated to a considerable extent by the government's agricultural department, also helped to improve the yields of ordinary farmers, with the result that rural Africans became substantial food producers. Rhodesia also acquired a fairly substantial 'administrative bourgeoisie', holding such posts as clerks, court interpreters, village postmasters. From 1961, Africans at long last were admitted to the permanent civil service, and by 1967, black people filled something like sixteen per cent of the more senior posts.

At the same time, the country's expanding industries required a better educated labour force. The demands of employers combined with administrative interests, centring especially on the African Education Department, with the local variety of settler paternalism and with missionary pressure to promote further educational expansion. Whatever the political complexion of the Rhodesian authorities, they continued to build more schools.[2] Africans in Rhodesia had better educa-

---

[1] We must, however, distinguish between contrived and natural scarcities of skill. It is evident that even without restrictionist legislation, there would have been sharp differences of income among the various groups.

[2] School enrolment thus continued to expand at considerable speed even during the most recent and most controversial period of Rhodesian history, that is to say, after

tional chances than those in Liberia or in Ethiopia. Nevertheless, only a small proportion of students were able to go on from primary to secondary schools. From the scholastic point of view, however, Rhodesian Africans by the 1960s were better off than the great majority of indigenous people in most independent African states. By the mid-1960s Rhodesia had largely achieved universal education of some kind for the great majority of its black youngsters at a time when such an accomplishment was still a remote objective for the less industrialized countries of independent Africa.[1]

1962, after the Rhodesian Front had assumed power. The following are enrolment figures for schools of all types:

	Primary	Secondary
1963	590,795	6,954
1965	627,806	11,329
1967	664,706	15,337

[1] By the mid-1960s Rhodesian primary education had by far outstripped the targets set by UNESCO for Africa as a whole; in 1961, a conference held at Addis Ababa had expressed the hope that universal primary education might be attained by 1980. A correspondent for the liberal-minded London Institute of Race Relations reported as follows: 'Towards the end of April [1966], the [Rhodesian] Minister of Education announced an imaginative plan for African education, which compares favourably with the best anywhere else in Africa. This envisages achieving full primary (seven years) education from 1969 (at present only the urban areas provide full primary (eight years) education for their children), thereafter 12½ per cent will be able to go on with normal secondary education, mostly four years, with provision for the brighter students going to form VI and thence to University. Another 25 per cent, rising by 1974 to 37½ per cent, will have vocational training, those in the towns being orientated to industry and in the country to agriculture and 'other activities suited to the area'. Between 1960 and 1962 (December) when the Rhodesian Front came into power, 18 new secondary schools were established. Since then 45 new ones have been built, increasing the intake of children to Form I to 6,000 per annum. It is now planned to establish at least 300 junior secondary schools in the next 10 years. From 1970, two new senior secondary schools per annum will be provided. To finance all this, a budget equal to 2 per cent of the gross national income has been promised, in the expectation that this will expand rapidly enough to cover the steadily increasing expenditure. This might not be as much as some might wish, but seeing that it is being financed entirely from Rhodesian sources without external aid, it is a significant and real step forward.' 'Rhodesia', London Institute of Race Relations, *Newsletter*, June 1966, p. 31. This record compares favourably with that of earlier Negro education in the United States, a far older and far richer country. According to St Clair Drake and Horace R. Clayton, *Black metropolis*, pp. 515–16, even black Chicago in the early 1940s was still 'essentially a community of sixth graders'.

Race relations in settler Africa: an appraisal

The successive advance of the trader's, the farmer's, the miner's and the manufacturer's frontiers across the Limpopo into Rhodesia brought about profound changes in the field of race relations. In the early days of white settlement, Rhodesia—as we have seen—was a poor country, producing but a small range of primary products for the world market. The great majority of white men met black people in two capacities only: as unskilled labourers or, more rarely, as tribesmen in the villages. Europeans in those days saw the 'native problem' in very simple terms: Africans ought to be pried out of their traditional economies and tribesmen should be turned into proletarians. At the same time, the government ought to secure the settlers' physical safety. But within less than the life span of one aged person, the country had altered beyond recognition: a substantial portion of Rhodesian society had passed from the Early Iron Age to the Industrial Revolution. There was no longer one 'Native Question'; there were a whole array of social problems that sprang from the tensions occasioned by rapid industrial-ization, by urbanization, by the clash of competing colour groups, by culture clashes, and by class struggles that were often superimposed, but that also sometimes cut across the more traditional cleavages within African society.

Economic progress not only led to increased productivity; it also brought about changes in what might be styled 'group prestige'. The rise of social groups to a position of greater prestige is, however, always a difficult undertaking. The new men not only have to overcome economic and social difficulties; they may have to cope with entrenched privileges designed to protect specific economic and political interests. In the psychological field they also have to surmount prejudice.

Prejudice, in our view, cannot for the most part be explained in terms of psychological maladjustment on the part of the prejudiced, though such maladjustment may play its part in individual cases. Preju-dice more often is based on the 'frozen' race attitudes that prevailed a generation or two ago. The European stereotype of the impassive Englishman used to be based on impressions received from upper-middle-class travellers to the continent in the nineteenth century. Stereo-types of the Jewish cloth pedlar or of the fighting drunk Irishman were based on impressions produced by immigrants, Jewish hawkers and textile workers, and by Irish labourers who settled in New York or in

London during the last century. (To this day, Jewish secondary-school students in Johannesburg are much less favourably disposed towards Germans than towards Africans or Coloureds.[1])

The European settlers in Africa worked out similar stereotypes about Africans. A long tradition of border clashes, cattle thefts and prolonged periods of drought earned the Bantu peoples a reputation for treachery, violence and idleness. These stereotypes continued even after great changes had occurred in African society. They were intensified not only by social segregation, but also by work-day experiences with African workmen. All too often the white man's opinion of Africans tended to be based on his contacts with unskilled and poorly educated labourers and on distorted versions of history. These were commonly exacerbated by the fears of whites concerning their political and economic status. The European strata most exposed to black competition usually displayed greater prejudice than the more highly qualified. Admittedly, the social roles and the prescribed behaviour between whites and blacks were not immutably fixed; they varied with the period of contact. Moreover, not all whites reacted in the same way. There were many gradations, ranging from outspoken and sometimes unbalanced negrophilists to the 'pukka sahib' variety of military ruler, or the authoritarian personality who went out of his way to keep the 'kaffir' down. (Overt behaviour and an abusive terminology would not, of course, always mean the same thing to members of different social classes. Rough language used by a white mine-worker commonly meant a great deal less than the same kind of speech employed by an educated white mine-manager.) Nevertheless, there was personal abuse in plenty, and insults and colour bars only contributed to worsening the racial atmosphere.

Indian settlers in Africa as well built up their own set of stereotypes about Africans. Indians rarely accepted Africans as business associates. They argued—usually quite correctly—that Africans lacked the required skill and capital, that Africans were unwilling to save like Indian shopkeepers, that partnerships with strangers would interfere with the kinship obligations of the Indian extended family. In this respect Indians were not 'prejudiced'; they simply acted in what they considered to be a rational fashion, in a manner that corresponded to their economic interests. But many Indian storekeepers would also treat

---

[1] H. Lever and O. M. J. Wagner, 'Ethnic preferences of Jewish youth in Johannesburg', *Jewish Journal of Sociology*, June 1967, **9**, no. 1, pp. 34–47.

their clientele in an unnecessarily rude fashion. Indians, to a greater extent than Europeans, consider a fair skin to be a mark of physical beauty. Indians might talk of integration, but they objected to inter-marriage with Africans more rigidly than did white people. Some Indians did indeed, keep African concubines; but Indians are as resent-ful of African approaches to their own women as Europeans.

Observers who wish to understand the racial problems of Rhodesia and of other settler territories in Africa must therefore rid themselves of the tendency to look upon the ethnic clashes simply in terms of black and white. They should also avoid a number of misleading com-parisons. For instance, some scholars excessively preoccupied with problems of colour alone have become fond of referring to Rhodesia as 'Britain's Deep South'. But despite the clash of black men and white, and despite the presence of similar colour bars and racial stereotypes, there has not been much similarity between southern Africa and the American South. The Deep South was on the whole the most economically back-ward portion of the United States. Southern Africa, including Rhodesia, was economically by far the most advanced part of Africa. Many Southerners, including both white and black Americans, were leaving the South to find work in other parts of the United States, whereas Rhodesia, a relatively industrialized state, was attracting black newcomers on a large scale. (By the mid-1960s more than a quarter of a million Africans had come into Rhodesia from beyond its borders. The number of black people strangely referred to in settler terminology as 'alien natives' in fact exceeded the total number of European residents in the country.)

But the bulk of Africans in Rhodesia, like those in South Africa, had never been anglicized. Black people continued to speak Zezuru, Sinde-bele or some other indigenous tongue learned in childhood. In this respect, they were quiet unlike Afro-Americans, who talked in English, sang in English and prayed in English and who —irrespective of their political views—had been assimilated into the culture of North America. Rhodesian Africans continued to form separate national groups. Rho-desia continued to be divided into four distinct communities—Euro-peans, Africans, Coloureds and Indians, each of them further subdivided into several social and linguistic sub-groups.[1] The country's varied

[1] In 1966 the estimated population of Rhodesia amounted to 4,210,000 Africans, 225,000 Europeans and 22,000 Coloureds and Asians. The Coloured and Indian people formed the most highly urbanized segments. In 1966 the percentage of urban popula-tion to total population was 13·8 for Africans, 76·0 for Europeans and 77·3 for Coloureds and Asians.

ethnic composition was rendered even more complex by differences in social habits, by sharp contrasts in religious convictions and even in marriage customs. In addition, Rhodesian society was rent by class struggles that sometimes cut across ethnic divisions.

Socially, however, the various races had little in common. Inter-marriages between, say, Indians and Africans were as rare as legitimate unions between Europeans and Africans. The vast majority of Rho-desians mingled with people of different colours only at work. But the productive process had itself become so intricate that by the 1960s relations between members of different races had become far more fre-quent and also far more complex than ever before in the country's history, involving, as they did, contacts in a multitude of economic enterprises: factories, workshops, farms, warehouses.

In so far as historical parallels are at all admissible, the Rhodesian development in many respects resembled the evolution of society in many countries of nineteenth-century Europe, rather than that of the American South in the twentieth century. The old empires of Eastern Europe, like the new colonial empires in Africa, were artificial aggre-gates; their boundaries took no more notice of ethnic divisions than did those of colonial Africa. Some Eastern European towns, like the cities of southern Africa, had originally been created by foreign immi-grants who settled among the indigenous peasantry. (Lodz, for instance, owed its creation to German and Jewish pioneers, permanent towns-men without roots in the local countryside, dependent solely on wages, urban pioneers who had certain features in common with the early British immigrants who built a city like Bulawayo.)

In some growing towns of Eastern Europe, the class struggles often became intensified by national and religious differences. The employers, and sometimes also a substantial proportion of the aristocracy of labour or of workers in specific industries, were often Germans or Jews, while the unskilled proletariat was usually composed of peasants' sons speak-ing some Slavonic tongue. This position had much in common with the Rhodesian situation, where employers and the highly skilled workmen were mostly Europeans, where Indian traders and entrepreneurs occu-pied an intermediate position comparable in some ways to that of Jewish dealers in Eastern Europe, and where the unskilled and semi-skilled labourers were Africans. As time went on, Eastern European towns such as Lodz or Poznań, increasingly assumed the 'national' character of the surrounding areas. Similarly, Salisbury in Rhodesia was founded as a European city by white immigrants (1890). In 1921, Salisbury still had a white majority. By the mid-1960s, however, the European component had dropped to about one-third of the city's total population, and the great majority of the population consisted of Africans.

In settler Africa, the leadership of the African nationalist opposition owed a great deal to African clerks, to school-teachers and, later on, to African university graduates. African socialism, an ill-defined but widely accepted ideology among these new strata, had much in common with the nationalism of the 'unhistorical' nations of Eastern Europe. Black Rhodesian nationalism is thus a very real thing. However exaggerated and crude black protests may sometimes be, they do represent the efforts of African leaders to improve the condition of their countrymen. African grievances are obvious and genuine; and the nationalism in which they find expression is itself the inevitable product of Western conquest, which provided the essential framework of a unified state, improved communications, a common language, widespread literacy, and which was responsible in the first place for breaking down the tribal barriers of old.

African nationalism also stands for something more than merely economic aspirations, which whites keep pointing to as justification for continued white domination. For Africans now insist that they be treated with greater respect. They want the parity of esteem which all too often is denied to them, not only by the negrophobe's open abuse but also by the painful conviviality and genteel condescension that sometimes prevail at 'advanced' interracial tea-parties. The mystique of *négritude* and the talk of an 'African personality' symbolize the efforts of Africans to restore their inner dignity, even if the means adopted are often ill-chosen. To counter the white man's pride of race, many Africans adopt a similar stance. They are suffering from a 'colonial mentality' and seek to compensate for self-doubt by aggressive assertions of African virtues and settler evils.

The justification of African nationalism is morally the same as that of its Polish, Afrikaner or Irish equivalent. Racial discrimination and the imposition of contrived disabilities do not necessarily interfere with the economic progress of certain minorities—be they dissenters in eighteenth-century England, Jews in nineteenth-century Germany or Chinese in twentieth-century Malaya. But in terms of Western egalitarian values, alien rule and social privileges are both indefensible.

Africans must not be artificially restricted from access to Western culture; there must be no selective giving. Africans argue, moreover, that they must have a chance to acquire the arts of government, even if they make mistakes. Furthermore, they feel, the denial of economic as well as of political opportunities is both morally wrong and economically inefficient. For a society that arbitrarily denies to itself the talents possessed by many of its members will certainly not progress as fast as it would with full use of its potential. Even if society should avoid stagnation, growth would obviously be impeded if the positions of power are confined to a small white oligarchy.

Settlers certainly developed any African country in which they established themselves. In Rhodesia their achievements were outstanding. And whether they intended it or not, the advances they pioneered also spilled over to Africans. What is harder to judge or to weigh is the personal humiliation, the sense of inferiority that many Africans suffered at the hands of Europeans. The Africans were made to feel inferior, the laws treated them as inferior, and enforced their subordination. Person-to-person relationships, colour bars, segregation, all were indignities which the African had to bear. To be called 'boy', to have to stand in queues and let any white person go ahead, signs 'for whites only', these things scarred and angered Africans, especially the educated ones.

For these reasons settlers have to be judged not only by their economic achievements but also by their moral and human values. Humanitarians argued that, if the settlers' economic development of Kenya or Rhodesia were outstanding achievements, their efforts to achieve the ideals of Christianity and democracy fell far short. In Malinowski's phrase, white men have been guilty of 'selective giving'. They attempted to withhold from Africans the full patrimony of Western civilization. Many tried (and failed) to give only things that would make the African more useful to them, but not to develop him technically or to give him the rights of a political and social being. Black men were advanced as long as their advancement did not conflict with powerful white interest groups. Still the whites were divided; some white people did, in fact, continue to work for African advancement, and Africans did improve their land and their stock and received increased schooling and more medical and welfare services and job opportunities.

The political history of Rhodesia, although it forms no part of this essay, cannot, in our view, be written simply in terms of vice arrayed against virtue, of reaction against progress, of right against left, of racial obscurantism against enlightenment. White colonization in Rhodesia made not only for a swift economic transformation, but also for sharp changes along political, social and ethnic lines. White farming policies created the black master farmer. White land policies restricted the master farmer from buying land freely on the open market. Europeans established constitutional rule but resisted majority government, and ignored many of the ideals set forth in their own constitutions. The most successful African economic pioneers, the small emergent group of well-to-do farmers and contractors, were not those who were most dedicated to the aim of national liberation; nor were the advocates of African majority those most enamoured with the rights of minorities.

Throughout the modern history of Rhodesia, or for that matter of Zambia or Kenya, no ethnic group ever moved with the cohesion of a solidly drilled phalanx. There were political divisions; there were also conflicting economic aims within each race. The Europeans arrived at all kinds of policy formulae designed to defend their interests, but the slogans chosen only faintly reflect the complexities of social change. Even apparently straightforward demands for 'segregation' embodied a great variety of aims. In truth, there were almost as many different forms of segregation as there were European pressure groups, and one variety of segregation would commonly run counter to the next.

The white farmer's segregation, for instance, for long represented the interests of the more advanced European agriculturist as against the more backward landowners. The old-style white Rhodesian pioneer, who was often content to grow a few patches of maize and to keep some native cattle, was in fact rather pleased to have an African village or two near his homestead so as to be able to engage labour more easily. Optimistic white planners moreover often had high hopes for the future of white settlement, and accordingly resented what they considered to be the arbitrary delimitation of native reserves. Hence, in the early 1920s plans for staking out native reserves still met with a good deal of opposition from many Kenyan and Northern Rhodesian settlers.

But once the farmer had begun to improve his methods and to farm on more intensive lines, his attitude gradually changed. He did not want African neighbours whose 'slash and burn' methods of agriculture were liable to start uncontrolled bush fires, and who could not fence their land. A backward system of tribal agriculture could not easily coexist next to a more developed capitalist one, even if there had not been added the difficulties occasioned by sharp differences in race, language and custom.

The farmer's version of segregation sometimes conflicted with, and sometimes worked hand in hand with, the forms of apartheid that used to be advocated by paternalistically-minded British administrators, by missionaries, by secular humanitarians and social planners. In the 1920s and 1930s, British supporters of Native Trusteeship were determined to protect African tribesmen from European spoliation and from the immorality and irresponsibility that supposedly emanated from the white men's towns. Provided the areas reserved to Africans were sufficiently large, segregation was the best policy as far as humanitarians were concerned. European missionaries, including militant Christian socialists like the Reverend Arthur Shearley Cripps, author of *An Africa for Africans: a plea on behalf of territorial segregation areas and their freedom in a South African colony* (London, 1927), shared this view. So did the Southern Rhodesian Missionary Conference, which, in 1928, congratulated the Southern Rhodesian Government and Legislative Council for accepting the principle of land segregation, and which rejoiced that the principle would be embodied in law.[1]

Finally, segregation appealed to humanitarian conservatives such as Howard Unwin Moffat, the premier responsible for placing the Land Apportionment Act, 1930, on the Rhodesian statute book. Moffat meant to avoid the mistakes previously made in the Cape. He saw that on an open land market, the wealthier and better connected European purchasers were bound to get the better of the Africans, and he feared the emergence of a landless African proletariat with revolutionary proclivities.[2] He therefore considered that the delimitation of separate areas would serve the interests of both races. Nor were these convictions confined to settler Africa. They formed part of a wider imperial tradition which placed severe restrictions on free-land purchases on Jews in mandatory Palestine or on Chinese settlers in Malaya, all in the real or supposed interests of the indigenous population.

[1] *Proceedings of the Southern Rhodesian Missionary Conference held at Salisbury, Southern Rhodesia, 26th to 29th March 1928* (Salisbury, 1928), pp. 5–6.

[2] See Lewis H. Gann, 'The Southern Rhodesian Land Apportionment Act, 1930: an essay in trusteeship', *Occasional Papers of the National Archives of Rhodesia and Nyasaland*, No. 1 (Salisbury, 1963), pp. 71–91.

The African in settler society

As African farming advanced, as African master-farmers accumulated more capital and looked for more land to buy, their perspective began to change. Land apportionment came to be seen as both a grievance and an anachronism, designed as a means of racial oppression. And indeed, the law sometimes operated in precisely this fashion. In Rhodesia as well as in South Africa, possessory segregation was also used to allay the fears of white landowners lest Africans joined into syndicates might by combination buy their way back into European areas. The fact remains that the Rhodesian law of 1930 as well as subsequent South African legislation in 1936 contained protective as well as repressive elements; both acts actually added to the areas made available to Africans; both attempted to meet previous engagements assumed by the white community; both formed part of a wider attempt to grapple with the problems of soil erosion and with advances in African agriculture, which Rhodesia in particular tackled with unusual success.[1]

Land apportionment in the countryside affected none but the farmers. Possessory segregation in the cities, however, was a matter of keen interest to the entire white community. Urban, like rural land, segregation, was for a time oddly linked to economic progress rather than to regression.

In the early days of Salisbury, for instance, there was no segregation. Both poor whites and poor blacks put up their shacks wherever they liked, and African slums grew cheek by jowl with European *bidonvilles*. In the 1900s, however, disease struck the shanty-towns and convinced the white citizens that something must be done. They hastily cleared the infected area and shifted the Africans into a 'location'. In 1905 the ad-

[1] Sir William Keith Hancock thus subsequently wrote of the South African legislation: 'It is now abundantly plain that the land legislation of 1936, and the administration of that legislation in subsequent years, do honestly fulfill the engagement which the European community assumed in 1913 and evaded throughout the two following decades. The new land policy, indeed represents something far more positive...a work of salvage, an attempt to grapple with the problems of congestion and soil destruction, which...menace the future' (*Survey of British Commonwealth affairs*, Vol. II: *Problems of economic policy, 1918–32*, London, Oxford University Press, 1942, p. 87). On pp. 107–8, the author gives a very complimentary account of the Rhodesian Agricultural Department which, in his view, was bringing about 'an agricultural revolution...[based on] a middle way between the excessive individualism which was the price of progress in eighteenth-century England, and the excessive collectivism which has been its price in twentieth-century Russia'.

ministration then passed the Urban Location Ordinance. The government was not thinking in terms of sophisticated theories of segregation; they certainly had not conceived the idea at that time that Africans should 'develop on their own lines'. The spasmodic efforts of civic councils, however, could not cope with the problems occasioned by the increase in the urban African population. The town authorities moreover lacked both the money and the men to provide adequate sanitation and to combat disease among the black people effectively. As the country's economy advanced and as employers came to require a healthier and more efficient labour force, this state of affairs became intolerable.

The Rhodesian legislature therefore intervened in the 1920s with a double purpose, protective and repressive at the same time. Urban segregation was to be strictly enforced. The towns belonged to the white man, the 'native' areas in the countryside to the blacks. The influx of Africans into the cities was rigidly controlled; but at the same time minimum standards of health and efficiency had to be maintained. Separate development in the end became orthodox policy. It was enforced by measures that did not differ greatly from those put into practice by the Colonial Office administration north of the Zambezi during the same period. The immigration of Africans into the cities, however, could not be stemmed; and public authorities were compelled to provide subsidized housing on an ever-increasing scale. Hence, in a roundabout way the general taxpayer helped to subsidize the needs of urban industry.

European policy was therefore double-edged in its effects. During the late eighteenth and the nineteenth centuries, Europeans had developed new ways of applying industrial, scientific and managerial techniques to the art of urban administration. Plumbing, water purification, canalization and similar innovations revolutionized health conditions. These techniques were gradually applied to the emergent towns of Africa, with the result that plagues were largely wiped out and that the industrial city ceased to be a killer. Medical improvements, of course, could not be confined to the white sections of a town. Disease knew no boundaries, and public health pioneers also began to ameliorate conditions to some extent in the African 'locations'. In many ways, Africans thus benefited from urbanization. Even the most shoddily constructed brick building was more sturdily built and less of a fire hazard than a traditional wood and mud hut. However poor, an

African housewife was better off when she could draw water from a tap in the wall instead of having to obtain water from a bilharzia-ridden, crocodile-infested river.

Urban segregation was not such a hardship as long as African labourers were poor, as long as no African could think of investing his savings in real estate, as long as land values remained relatively undifferentiated, so that it did not matter much where a man chose to put up his house. As time went on, some African traders even acquired a vested interest in residential segregation, which reduced commercial competition from other races within the black areas.

White settlement and residential segregation did not by themselves occasion African urban poverty, the instability of African labour and lack of African family cohesion in the towns. Studies such as A. W. Southall and P. C. W. Gutkind's treatise on Kampala and its suburbs in Uganda give a great deal of information on the impact of labour migration, on the lack of urban stability, on the deficiencies of African family life in a country where there are no white settlers, no segregation and no Land Apportionment Act. Living conditions in Harari, an African quarter in Salisbury, Rhodesia, do in fact compare quite favourably with, say, the *bidonvilles* of Dakar in Senegal. The fact remains that segregation as practised in Rhodesia rendered adaptation to city life even more difficult. Police raids for pass and liquor offences were a constant grievance to Africans, and even at their best, municipal services for Africans left much to be desired.

Urban segregation became a major grievance, however, not so much to the poor as to the better-off and educated African, who was limited in his human relations and who found severe restrictions in his social life and in his opportunities for investing money in real estate. On a more imponderable plane, urban segregation symbolized the inability or unwillingness of European society to absorb even the most educated African, the man who had made the greatest effort to Westernize his way of life. In the end he found himself socially rebuffed, psychologically often humiliated and politically largely without a voice. Colour bars and high voting qualifications limited his mobility and his power to change the political order.

In some of these respects, there was of course nothing peculiar about white Rhodesians. In Uganda, by the late 1950s, there were no laws to prevent or even hinder informal social relations between the races. Though the hotels had all abandoned the colour bar and social restrictions had ceased, yet there was little mixing. Apart from clergymen and college teachers, Europeans had little in common with black people. Africans, being used to different housing, lower income levels and a different style of life, rarely entertained Europeans. Race relations ended when the workers went home.[1]

Traditionally the integration of differing ethnic communities has met with great difficulties even where the colour factor has not been involved. Historians of nineteenth-century Russia, for instance, have pointed out the difficulties produced by nineteenth-century attempts to Russify part of the Jewish population in the Tsarist empire. For a time, the government of Alexander II (1855–81) attempted a policy of vigorous assimilation. But the Russification of Jewish intellectuals all too often produced alienated men with university degrees who, at the end of their studies, found acceptance neither in the traditional society of the *shtetel* nor in gentile society.[2]

Yet the Russians' task was infinitely easier than the white Rhodesians'. The Russians formed the vast majority who might have been expected to assimilate small minorities with relative ease. The Europeans in Rhodesia were a small minority. A policy of large-scale absorption would have entailed the disruption of the white community. The indigenous Africans differed both in their cultural traditions and in their physical appearance to a much greater extent from the Europeans than Jews did from Russians. Hence, the whites' failure to absorb Europeanized Africans is hardly surprising.

Even had the Europeans succeeded in assimilating a small African or Coloured minority within their ranks, wholesale amalgamation of the two races would in any case have been out of the question. The British never succeeded in 'anglifying' the Afrikaners of the Cape, nor the Frenchmen of Quebec. Arabs and Africans lived apart and voted differently in Zanzibar. The French-speaking Walloons never managed to gallicize the Flemings in Belgium; Greeks and Turks have remained apart in Cyprus, even though all these varying races had a long history in common.

[1] Michael Banton, *Race relations* (London, 1967), p. 245.
[2] Louis Greenberg, *The Jews in Russia*, Vol. I: *The struggle for emancipation* (New Haven, Yale University Press, 1944), p. 85.

Settler ideologies: some explanations and counterexplanations

The fact remains that assimilation in Rhodesia was never even attempted. White men and black remained separate in their institutions, in culture, in law, in living standards and in outlook.[1] The Rhodesian laws, for instance, contain many discriminatory provisions. Twenty-four acts apply only to Africans. There is the Land Apportionment Act, the Municipal Act, the Criminal Procedure and Evidence Act (Africans may not be tried by juries), the Industrial Conciliation Act (this law hurts the growth of African trade unions and the training of skilled African workers). The Firearms Act is discriminatory in that it prevents most Coloureds and Africans from having fire-arms. Service in the military is discriminatory too; there are wide differentials in terms and conditions of service. The African Education Act is by name discriminatory; in practice it maintains segregated schools except at the university level. School is not compulsory for Africans. The amount spent on European pupils in 1965 was £99 per head, but for African pupils only £9. 9s. (Nevertheless, by standards of African nations Rhodesia has achieved an outstanding educational system and the main tax burden is now borne by the whites.)

Other acts while not discriminatory in language are discriminatory in fact: the Electoral Act, the Municipal and Town Management Act, the Law and Order (Maintenance) Act, the Unlawful Organizations Act, the Emergency Powers Act and the Masters and Servants Act—all had as their primary aim the control of Africans. The consequences: political power remains firmly in European hands, and discriminatory laws or practices are hard to displace. Discrimination continues on many different levels. While peaceful coexistence between the races might be regarded as an ideal, cultural amalgamation of the kind effected by the ancient Romans in many of their provinces has proved beyond the ability of modern Rhodesians.

The total impact of the European settler on Africa remains a difficult subject to assess. Each generation of historians naturally reinterprets the past in the light of its own preconceptions. But as they try to avoid

[1] As regards the legal framework of segregation and discriminatory legislation, the most comprehensive work for Southern Rhodesia is Claire Palley, *The constitutional history and law of Southern Rhodesia, 1888–1965, with special reference to imperial control* (Oxford, Clarendon Press, 1966), *passim*.

the mistakes of their predecessors, scholars often go too far in the other direction. The image of the white settlers in Africa, like that of many other ruling strata, has thus undergone a profound change over the past seventy years. At the turn of the century, academic and popular literature alike tended to idealize the European expatriate as a clean-cut empire-builder, the representative of imperial power, of middle-class values and of private enterprise. This interpretation was in fact wide of the mark. It concealed the complexities of European colonization, though it accorded well with the self-congratulatory mood of late-Victorian imperialism. Two generations later, the prevailing climate of opinion had become unrecognizable.[1] The settler's past identification with the British ruling strata now turned out to his discredit. All too often the European became identified with the so-called 'Guilty Men' of British Labour mythology in the 1930s, a hardened group of conscienceless reactionaries, of functionless, obtuse and prejudiced parasites. The adventurers of old had become the 'New Bourbons' of Africa,[2] unreasoning reactionaries, who changed only to move as yet farther to the right.

In the earlier pages we have tried to show that the Europeans were never a single, undifferentiated mass; that their class interests often diverged; that their race attitudes were not all of a piece, and that their social composition and economic functions have undergone major changes during the past two generations.[3] We have argued also against

[1] See Lewis H. Gann, 'The white settler: a changing image', *Race*, May 1961, **2**, no. 2, pp. 28–40.

[2] The phrase derives from Patrick Keatley, *The politics of partnership: the federation of Rhodesia and Nyasaland* (Harmondsworth, Middlesex, 1963), p. 219.

[3] Rogers and Frantz, in a major inquiry concerning white race attitudes in present-day Rhodesia, have found, among other factors, that both occupation and length of residence in Rhodesia affect race attitudes. Immigrants who have been in Rhodesia for less than five years are the least conservative, until they subsequently level out. These findings might be compared with changes in attitudes among American police investigated by Arthur Niederhoffer. Niederhoffer found that what he called 'cynicism' with regard to the ideals learned at police training institutions will increase with length of service, and tends to reach its maximum between five and ten years of service. Thereafter cynicism will tend to level off. Both policemen and many settlers, of course, find themselves exposed to what might be called the tensions of authority. For the Rhodesian study, an important pioneering work in race attitudes, see Cyril A. Rogers and C. Frantz, *Racial themes in Southern Rhodesia: the attitudes and behavior of the white population* (New Haven, Yale University Press, 1962). The book is too substantial to be summarized in brief. For a study of American police attitudes see the excellent study by Arthur Niederhoffer, an American police officer turned professional sociologist, entitled *Behind the shield: the police in urban society* (Garden City, N.Y.,

what Marxists used to call 'South African exceptionalism'. The social structure of South Africa, Rhodesia or Kenya was nothing unusual in history. It could only appear extraordinary to those who took for granted the social patterns prevailing in the highly industrialized and nationally more homogeneous societies of Western Europe.

We disagree with those who view the pride and prejudice of settler Africa as a social phenomenon peculiar to the New Imperialism which supposedly represents the last stage of capitalism. An influential school of Marxist or quasi-Marxist writers believes that the big capitalists have a vested interest in stigmatizing tribal people as inferior. The dissemination of race prejudice—according to this argument—serves the capitalist in two ways. The capitalists acquire a specious argument to exploit coloured workmen with an even greater degree of impunity than white proletarians. Worse still, white and black workers are set at loggerheads, and thereby become incapable of uniting against their common oppressors. In some areas, such as Southern Rhodesia, the argument continues, the immigration of European workers with few skills is indeed subsidized by artificial means, so as to provide the capitalists with a reliable reservoir of supervisors and soldiers.

These arguments are insubstantial at best. Race prejudice is much older than capitalism; race prejudice moreover transcends colour. This, for instance, is the way in which a mediaeval English chronicler described the Welshmen of the thirteenth century: as

a Trojan debris swept into the wooded savagery of Cambria under the guidance of the devil. Their sexual promiscuity played havoc with the laws of God and the principles of hereditary succession. Their lives were spent in theft and rapine or in slothful ease; only a few villeins, who tilled the lands for them as best they could, were exceptions to their depraved way of existence. If it were asked why the English had not long ago blotted out the memory of this disagreeable people from the earth, the answer should be sought in the mild forbearance of the English kings who on frequent expeditions had too often allowed themselves to be affected by a show of Welsh penitence.[1]

As regards white–black contacts, all students of race relations in South and Central Africa, as well as in Britain and the United States,

---

1967). Dominique O. Mannoni's book has been translated into English as *Prospero and Caliban: the psychology of colonization*, trans. by Pamela Powesland (London, 1956).

[1] Quoted by Sir Maurice Powicke, *The thirteenth century, 1216–1307* (Oxford, Clarendon Press, 1953), pp. 383–4.

agree that the wealthier and better educated whites on the whole display less prejudice against black people than do European workers. In Kenya, it is now the black trade unionists who are among the racial minded, and who oppose concessions to the non-black citizens.[1]

The immigration policies adopted in multi-racial countries are also much more complex than would appear from the generalization we have previously discussed. Ever since Rhodesia obtained Responsible Government in 1923, nearly all white Rhodesians of whatever social class agreed that unskilled Europeans should be excluded from the country. The present Rhodesian Front government is as keen on selective immigration as its predecessors. White immigrants without marketable skills or capital are excluded from the country. Ironically enough, the young Cecil Rhodes himself might not be admitted to present-day Rhodesia on the grounds that his schooling, his cash and his health did not meet the requisite standards!

We take issue also with those who interpret the problems of white race attitudes primarily in terms of irrational or psychological factors. We cannot, for instance, agree with D. O. Mannoni, who believes that settlers go to Africa because they are already psychologically disposed towards ruling others. Theories such as Mannoni's take inadequate account of the economic factor, of variations occasioned by changes in occupational status, or of changes in race attitudes that occur in time from one generation to the next. Neither do such interpretations explain changes in racial outlook that may occur within the life-span of a single person.

Some scholars as well as novelists have approached the problem of inter-ethnic contacts in other psychological terms. According to their interpretation, white settlers in Africa, irrespective of their class background, are more authoritarian in character than the 'stay-at-homes'. We do not agree with this point of view. In Great Britain, H. J. Eysenck, a student of psychology, found that British voters could be divided into two types, the 'tough-minded' and the 'tender-minded'. The tough-minded praised all the virtues of the fighting man and favoured flogging or hanging as a form of punishment. The tender-minded stood for permissive attitudes in education and penology; they defended the toleration of conscientious objectors, pacifism and similar

[1] Yash P. Ghai, 'Prospects for Asians in East Africa', in *Racial and Communal Tensions in East Africa*, East African Institute of Social and Cultural Affairs, Contemporary African Monographs, No. 3 (Nairobi, 1966), p. 23.

causes. In terms of party affiliation, British fascists were the most tough-minded of the lot. British conservatives stood at about the middle of the scale. British socialists were slightly more tender-minded than the Tories. British liberals were the most tender-minded of all. In the 1950s Cyril Roger subsequently applied Eysenck's method to the study of white Rhodesian voters. He discovered that Rhodesian voters were far from conforming to either the fascist or the communist pattern. Supporters of the Dominion Party, which at the time stood on the extreme right of the Rhodesian political spectrum, stood very close to British conservatives. Rhodesian backers of the United Federal Party, the party of the Rhodesian Establishment during the 1950s, were similar to British socialists; whereas the United Rhodesia Party, a liberal opposition group, resembled British liberals.[1]

We likewise disagree with those who interpret the power structure of Rhodesia or of South Africa purely in terms of military coercion, who regard these countries as nothing but 'White Spartas'. Contrary to public belief, neither South Africa nor Rhodesia spends an unduly high percentage of its national income or of its budget on the armed forces, as is apparent from Table 1, showing defence expenditures.

We are equally sceptical of explanations that link race attitudes or associated forms of economic behaviour primarily to religious observances. Clearly, a man's faith does affect his general outlook on life. But the influence of any particular religious affiliation on a man's conduct in the market-place should not be overestimated. Mercantile groups such as Indians in East Africa, Lebanese in West Africa or Armenians in the Levant commonly display the virtues associated with the Protestant ethos to a particular degree. Yet none of them adhere to the doctrines of Calvin or Melanchthon. Their aptitude for business seems to derive from more general factors. Lebanese and Indians, at any rate, are ethnic minorities who are excluded from the more lucrative and prestigious jobs in government and administration. If they want power and prestige, they need to make money. Their social traditions, however, give them many advantages. Indians are willing not only to save, but also to take commercial risks. Unlike the Coloureds, they have a strong sense of ethnic identity, of cultural pride, of loyalty to an extended family. They benefit in business from a tightly-knit kinship system, whose existence may well be essential in the development of early

---

[1] Cyril A. Rogers, 'The organization of political attitudes in Southern Rhodesia', *Rhodes–Livingstone Journal*, 1959, no. 25, pp. 1–19.

Table 1. *Defence expenditures of selected African countries in relation to national income and budget, January 1966*

Country	Defence budget as percentage of estimated GNP (%)	As percentage of total government expenditure (%)
Congo (Brazzaville)	10·9	8·9
Kenya	9·8	6·9
United Arab Republic	8·6	17·4
Senegal	7·6	11·6
Algeria	4·2	11·1
South Africa	3·5	19·9
Mali	3·2	21·2
Zambia	2·5	5·7
Rhodesia	1·9	6·6
Uganda	1·5	10·2

Source: David Wood, *The armed forces of African states* (Adelphi Papers, No. 27, London, 1966), p. 29. Wood provides much more detailed figures than those here cited. Nevertheless, military expenditure has gone up in a striking degree. Between 1961 and 1967, for instance, South Africa's military budget estimates increased from 43,591,000 to 255,850,000 rand. The expenditure on the manufacture of weapons and ammunition rose from 368,000 to 51,102,000 rand between 1960 and 1966.

capitalism and whose characteristics still offer a fertile field of inquiry to sociologists and economic historians. Kinsmen usually prove more reliable as assistants, as agents or as partners than do strangers in a foreign land. Kinship ties may help to spread economic risks; they may help to make a man more credit-worthy, or may help to bring about new capital accumulations by the bonds of marriage. (Such ties serve similar functions, no matter whether among Jews in nineteenth-century Poland, among Indians in twentieth-century Kenya or among Chinese in present-day Java.)

Historians, in our view, have also overstressed the importance of religion, in this case of the Protestant tradition, in the formation of Afrikaner racial attitudes. Many have argued that the Afrikaners' outlook derives at least partly from seventeenth-century Calvinism, with its puritan and predestinarian doctrines. Calvinism, according to this theory, helped to persuade the Afrikaners to look upon themselves as a race apart, a people chosen by God to rule the sons of Ham. Other religious interpretations assume that Catholic peoples, such as the Portuguese or the French, have traditionally had fewer racial prejudices than Protestants, and that Catholic cultures have greater assimilative powers than Protestant cultures.

We regard such views as dangerous oversimplifications. The Dutch Reformed Church, for example, used to be far from restrictive in the racial sphere. During the first two centuries of Dutch settlement at the Cape, the Dutch Reformed Church consistently tried to maintain common worship for white and Coloured believers alike. The decisive break came only in the middle of the last century, when under pressure from white frontier congregations, the church agreed to separate ministration for white and non-white members. The clerical authorities sanctioned this policy at the time not as a matter of principle, but as a concession to the 'weakness of some' and as a device for giving more responsibility in church government to non-Europeans.[1] In any case, the relevance of seventeenth-century Calvinist doctrines to modern race attitudes in South Africa or Rhodesia is limited. Few Afrikaners nowadays regard the black people as the sons of Ham, destined by God to be hewers of wood and drawers of water. They defend their position by arguments essentially secular in character. So do white Rhodesians, many of whom are militantly anticlerical, and whose religious outlook generally differs profoundly from that of Bible-reading backwoodsmen in the American South.[2]

In any case, Protestants do not necessarily discriminate more harshly against persons of colour than do Catholics, or indeed than members of non-Christian religions. The Hindu settlers in Africa have traditionally abstained from mixing socially with, let alone marrying, black people. French Catholics in eighteenth-century Haiti, for example, enforced colour legislation harsher than any that obtained at the Cape.

Admittedly, generalizations in this field are always dangerous. Race attitudes in Catholic Brazil were traditionally more fluid and somewhat more permissive than in the Protestant American South, where the white element was generally larger, and where the American settlers lacked the traditions of legal and religious restraints on the abuses of slavery which had long since existed in Mediterranean countries. Nevertheless, Brazilian slave-owners could be quite as ruthless as North

---

[1] Susan Rennie Ritner, 'The Dutch Reformed Church and apartheid', *Journal of Contemporary History*, 1967, **2**, no. 4, pp. 23–7.

[2] According to published census figures, by 1921 already 53·2 per cent of white Rhodesians had no church affiliation; only 9·7 per cent regularly attended religious worship.

Americans. Seventeenth- and eighteenth-century settlers in Brazil were prone to discriminate not only against black people and against mulattoes, but also against Catholics of Jewish origin, the so-called New Christians. Recent research seems to show that racial prejudice in eighteenth-century Bahia, as in twentieth-century Salisbury, may well have been strongest among white working men, the people most obviously threatened by competition from below.[1] In eighteenth-century Bahia, these ethno-economic clashes found expression in racially separate religious brotherhoods. Their ceremonies and terminology were more picturesque than those of a present-day trade union, but their social functions and the outlook of their members had certain points in common.

The European settlers in Africa are likewise very different from the self-indulgent parasites depicted in literary productions such as Doris Lessing's *Going home*, or in sociological analyses such as Boris Gussman's *Out in the mid-day sun*.[2] Works of this kind ignore the settler's economic function, and assume that African poverty largely derives from the white oppressor's ill-gotten privileges. The points of attack differ. Sometimes it is the white farmer who emerges as the main culprit, sometimes the urban capitalist. More often than not, it is the *petits blancs*, the skilled workers and their dependents, who are regarded as the most worthless and the most dispensable members of the community. The charge of parasitism, however, constantly recurs; it is commonly associated with oddly puritanical denunciations of colonists who supposedly take their ease in a sinful life compounded in equal measure of languid self-indulgence and energetic repression.

These charges have little substance and are not supported by more serious studies. An interesting micro-analysis of the Greek community at Moshi in Tanzania, for instance, shows how a handful of coffee-planters have revolutionized the economy of an entire district by pioneering a new form of enterprise, by technological innovation, by

---

[1] A. J. R. Russell-Wood, 'Class, creed and colour in colonial Bahia: a study in prejudice', *Race*, Oct. 1967, **9**, pp. 133–57.

[2] See, for instance, Boris Gussman, 'Problems of adjustment in British Central Africa', *Civilisations*, 1959, **9**, no. 4, pp. 445–56; and Boris Gussman, *Out in the mid-day sun* (New York, Oxford University Press, 1963). The conventional view asserts that the white Rhodesian population is 'hardly noted for its intellect' (John Hatch, 'Wilson's gift-horse', *New Statesman*, 18 Oct. 1968), a characteristic assessment on the part of an intellectual journal, which in the past has consistently underestimated the settlers' ingenuity in countering both the effects of sanctions and the impact of world opinion at large.

providing local employment on a large scale and by an extraordinarily high *per capita* rate of local investment.[1] Micro-studies of European farming enterprise in Kenya, Rhodesia, Zambia or Tanzania would, in our own experience, yield comparable results. European agriculture has made an equally impressive contribution to the economy of entire territories. In Zambia, for instance, the European farming community embraces no more than some 700 agricultural entrepreneurs who occupy but three per cent of the total cultivable area and who nevertheless produce a large portion of all marketed maize and virtually all the country's Virginia tobacco.

European entrepreneurs in mining and industry have similarly provided a great deal of managerial skill, capital and economic initiative. The skill of European foremen and technicians similarly represents an important form of wealth for the countries of their temporary or permanent adoption. In so far as they come as immigrants, they bring in a technical training paid for by the country of their birth—not by the country where they make their living. If the *petits blancs* were truly as parasitic a group of residents as assumed by the more biased propagandists, Algeria should have experienced an economic boon from the departure of something like 800,000 whites. Algeria in fact has sustained a very considerable economic set-back from the loss of so many productive people. Large-scale European emigration from Kenya, Zambia or Rhodesia would, in our opinion, have equally serious consequences.[2]

There is equally little merit in analyses that interpret, say, the politics of white Rhodesia in terms of an unswerving swing towards the right, or that exaggerate past differences in outlook between the imperialhumanitarian school on the one hand, and leading settler groups on the other. There were, of course, many divergencies between London and Salisbury, but until the late 1950s, at any rate, their extent was strictly limited. In many cases the white Rhodesian Establishment simply took over the imperial orthodoxy of a decade or two ago. In some instances, Rhodesian ministers were actually in advance of imperial administrators in fields such as the care of migrant workers or the enforcement of industrial safety measures.

[1] Nikos Georgulas, 'Minority assimilation in Africa: the Greeks in Moshi—an example', Syracuse University, Maxwell Graduate School of Citizenship and Public Affairs, Program of East African Studies, *Occasional paper*, No. 22 (Syracuse, N.Y., n.d.), pp. 25–31.

[2] See recent report issued by economists at University College, Nairobi, warning of economic danger of too rapid Africanization.

To give some specific examples, the outlook of a militant late nineteenth-century 'negrophilist' such as the Reverend John Mackenzie, a missionary statesman and a convinced advocate of direct imperial rule in Southern Rhodesia, in many ways corresponded to that of Sir Charles Coghlan, Southern Rhodesia's first premier a generation later. (Coghlan was premier from 1923 to 1927.) Mackenzie wanted imperial trusteeship for native territories as yet unoccupied. But like Coghlan, he also believed in self-government for European states in Africa. Mackenzie, like Coghlan, wished to promote white land settlement; he merely insisted that the colonists should be 'solid' farmers from the Cape rather than 'shiftless' Boer trekkers. Mackenzie and Coghlan alike advocated European mining and prospecting enterprise; both were equally anxious that small men should have their chance and that development should not be solely entrusted to monopolistic concerns. Alike they insisted that Africans were 'teachable', that they should be habituated gradually to the Christian faith, to individual tenure and to English as opposed to tribal law. Both had much regard for the interests of the small white entrepreneurs; both were profoundly influenced by the conditions that prevailed at a time when southern Africa's economy hinged on the production of primary products for export.

Coghlan's doctrines found an echo north of the Zambezi. In Northern Rhodesia, the imperial authorities, during the 1920s and 1930s, gave active encouragement to European land settlement, on the assumption that only white farming enterprise would create a food surplus sufficiently large and reliable to feed the expanding townships of the Copperbelt. Colonial administrators in Northern Rhodesia, like their opposite numbers in the south, for long insisted also that African workers should come to the mines for only limited periods, and that the assumed perils of urbanization, detribalization and potential unemployment in the cities must be avoided at all costs.

In the field of urban policy, as well as in the provision of social services for black people, Southern Rhodesia did in fact for a time move ahead of Northern Rhodesia. During most of the 1930s Sir Godfrey Huggins (later Lord Malvern, Prime Minister of Southern Rhodesia, 1933–53, and then of the Federation of Rhodesia and Nyasaland, 1953–6), thus advocated rigid territorial segregation, which he likened to the construction of two separate pyramids, one white, one black. As industrialization proceeded in Southern Rhodesia, however, Huggins became reconciled to a cautious policy of African urbanization. In 1941 he issued a statement that while parallel development would have to continue for the time being, the two lines of parallel development would ultimately have to converge. Huggins's statement not only left many of his white voters aghast; it was also well in advance of the views expressed by white colonial administrators in Northern Rhodesia at a time when the northern Protectorate as yet depended largely on mining, and when the imperial authorities on the spot were as yet reluctant to accept the stabilization of African labour on the Copperbelt.

No Rhodesian government, whatever its racial outlook, was in fact able to return fully to the segregationist position of the 1920s. The negrophobe terminology of the early days has become dated. (In this respect there is a good deal of similarity between the white Rhodesian and the South African experience. The South African right-wing Republican Party is now unable to make headway against the ruling Nationalist Party by using traditional racist slogans such as *swarte gevaar* or *kaffir op sy plek* ('black peril' or 'the nigger in his place') which had been the staple of Afrikaner propaganda less than a decade earlier.[1]

In Rhodesia—as in South Africa—the change owes much to the socio-economic development of the subcontinent as a whole, to the material advances experienced by most of its white and by many of its brown and black peoples. Rhodesia in 1962 was no longer the backveld colony that had striven for Responsible Government forty years earlier. The Rhodesian farmer was no longer a backwoodsman, but more often a highly trained agricultural entrepreneur. The white artisan was a skilled technician, not a semi-skilled painter or a taxi-driver. The Rhodesian administration had become a complex and efficient mechanism. The average Rhodesian parliamentarian was better educated and more sophisticated than the members of the local legislative councils a generation earlier.[2] (In 1965, when Rhodesia openly

[1] See Edwin S. Munger, *Afrikaner and African nationalism: South African parallels and parameters* (London, Oxford University Press, 1967), p. 66.

[2] In 1968, something like two-thirds of the Europeans representing Upper Roll seats in the Rhodesian legislatures held university degrees or equivalent professional qualifications. The figures are not quite complete, as full details concerning the relevant educational qualifications were not always available. At least 7, however, had qualified in various branches of engineering; 7 were trained as Chartered Accountants, in business management or civil administration, including the Prime Minister, who held a B.Comm. from Rhodes University, Grahamstown; 4 had qualified in medicine or dentistry and 4 in law; 4 had graduated from the Royal Military Academy, from Sandhurst or from the Royal Air Force Staff College; 3 held degrees or equivalent

clashed with Great Britain over the issue of independence, both the British authorities and world opinion at large widely assumed that white Rhodesia would be incapable of coping with sanctions and other forms of pressure, and that the Rhodesian régime was bound therefore to end in rapid collapse. This miscalculation may have derived partly from an out-of-date estimate about the Rhodesian leadership. Some politicians erroneously assumed that the country was still run by naïve backwoodsmen, by a 'cowboy cabinet'. This assessment, widely shared by many academics and by the more opportunistic type of British colonial civil servant, may in fact have had the ironic effect of strengthening the Rhodesian position by causing the British to mis-apprehend their difficulties.)

In fact the Rhodesian public services, including their technical depart-ments, were extremely efficient—more so in many cases than the British colonial services with their expatriate personnel. White planners assessed the immediate local power realities with a considerable degree of sophistication. When, in 1965, white Rhodesians declared UDI, they did not have to carry out a *putsch* against a foreign administration. From 1890 to 1923 the country had been ruled by a chartered company with only vague imperial supervision. In 1923 Southern Rhodesia ob-tained effective local autonomy, including effective control over its own

higher diplomas in agriculture and 3 held other unspecified degrees; 1 had qualified in journalism.

The professional affiliation of these men is not always easy to determine. Some changed their jobs while others had retired before they entered Parliament and some held several jobs. For instance, a Chartered Accountant might also list himself as a director of companies, or a landowner might manage agricultural companies. The following tabulation gives an approximate breakdown. It shows that the white working class had almost been eliminated from Parliament, and that the legislators were com-posed primarily of businessmen and of farmers with higher educational qualifications.

Civilian status of Members of Parliament

Directors of companies or businessmen	17
Farmers or ranchers	14
Doctors or dentists	4
Lawyers	4
Mine managers or owners	3
Armed forces or public administration personnel	4
Railway officials	1
Other professions	3

A comparatively high percentage had risen to the rank of lieutenant-colonel or above, or to the equivalent of these positions in the Royal Navy and Royal Air Force. These former soldiers included two brigadier generals.

public services and defence forces. The Rhodesians did not make the mistake of Rhodesianizing the service by using it for political patronage. Their administrative machine remained small, efficient and cohesive. Ministerial decisions were made on the spot and the administration was not beset by the delays that tend to plague larger administrative structures.

The Rhodesians managed to employ technical experts of high quality —a policy that came to stand white politicians in good stead. Long before UDI, senior Rhodesian civil servants and members of public commissions had studied the difficulties involved and the countermeasures to be taken to defend UDI. White Rhodesians relied on the ineffectiveness of so-called world opinion, on the likelihood of a long-range swing to the right in the major Western countries, on growing disillusionment with global philanthropy and with African commitments in the West, on increasing disunity between the newly independent states as well as on ethnic dissensions within them, and on the inability of black Africa to unite effectively in its own defence.

The whites were convinced that their country would be able to evade the worst effects of sanctions by diversifying its industrial and agricultural production, by developing clandestine trade channels, by ending their accustomed dependence on the British market and by various financial countermeasures. The white Rhodesians discounted major threats from Zambia. They assumed they could strangle the Zambian economy by denying railway facilities, coal and electricity supplies to the Copperbelt, and thereby paralyse Great Britain's chief source of sterling copper. The Rhodesians placed much faith also in South African economic export. Rhodesian like South African gold producers also received an unintended dividend as a result of the British decision to devalue the pound sterling.

Rhodesian planners relied too on the high quality of their armed services, combining, as they did, highly trained professional cadres with mobile professional troops and a mainly white conscript force. The Rhodesians, so to speak, drew on the white electorate in arms; hence they had an army which, unlike many forces in independent Black Africa, would never develop Praetorian pretensions. In addition, they enjoyed the advantages of a small but highly efficient police force, of a far-flung intelligence network with ramifications beyond their own borders, of military and economic co-operation with Portugal and South Africa, of thorough familiarity with the local terrain and modern counter-insurgency techniques, as well as a tight physical grip on the segregated 'native' townships.

Besides all this, the Rhodesian military authorities felt convinced that the British would never interfere with force, that the enormous logistic difficulties in moving an airborne army from Great Britain to southern Africa, in creating staging, refuelling, supply and repair points all the way, would never be solved, and that the weakness of the British strategic reserve, the limitations of the RAF Transport Command, as well as the political climate in Britain, would prevent the most militant British Labour government from armed intervention. The British imperial authorities were thus placed in the unenviable position of having to conquer positions which they had never held in the past, of assuming physical control over a far-off country at a time when they were seeking world-wide disengagement. Great Britain's difficulties had been compounded by British unwillingness to risk a confrontation with South Africa at a time when the British economic position was shaky, when the British greatly valued their trade and investment with southern Africa as a whole, and when the temporary closure of the Suez Canal through the Arab-Israeli war made them more dependent on South African ports than ever before.

The object of this analysis is not to indulge in speculations concerning an uncertain future. By the time of writing, the calculations of the Rhodesian Establishment seem to have made fairly good sense, far more sense in fact than those of the academic intelligentsia which, on the whole, seriously underestimated the quality and determination of European leadership. Rhodesia did suffer from sanctions. In particular, the highly vulnerable tobacco industry, which has many foreign competitors, is unlikely to return to its former prosperity even if sanctions should be lifted. The Rhodesians also had to forgo that economic expansion which would almost certainly have been theirs if sanctions had never been imposed. They face a dangerous long-term problem of black unemployment, especially as more and more African school-leavers come onto the labour market. But the whites have kept their economy afloat; their state machinery remains unimpaired and they are not in a mood for major political concessions.

At the same time, however, the Africans' social 'water level' has also risen appreciably. The Rhodesian Front, for all its militant oratory, now in fact depends on the passive co-operation of a new African sub-élite of African detectives and police sergeants, court interpreters, telegraphists, postmasters, agricultural instructors and other similar métiers to an extent that would have appeared incredible (and also extremely unsafe) to Sir Charles Coghlan. This state of affairs found expression, for instance, in the country's public service regulations. When the Rhodesian Front assumed office in 1962, it would no longer go back on the decision of its immediate predecessors to admit Africans to the civil service. On the contrary, more black people were appointed to higher posts—a policy unthinkable under a so-called right-wing government a decade earlier.[1]

Southern Africa's ultimate political destiny remains uncertain. To the African nationalist of whatever persuasion, however, there can be only one outcome. Africans—in the view of the nationalist—form the great majority of the population in every part of southern Africa; in nearly every portion of the subcontinent they also enjoy the right of prior occupation. Justice, social progress and the standards of democratic morality alike demand that power should pass into African hands. Some African critics of the present white establishments may grant that much of the Africans' earlier optimism concerning independence has been unwarranted, that many post-colonial black ruling strata in other parts of Africa also have serious deficiencies. But decolonization is nevertheless seen as an essential instrument of social revolution. It is also regarded as an indispensable means of restoring African dignity. The import of this psychological factor, the intense desire to assert one's inner worth against the real or assumed slights received at the hands of white foreigners, is hard to overestimate. It plays a much greater role in the thinking of educated Africans, men who are in frequent touch with Europeans and who have acquired European standards, than of peasants who have much less contact with white men and who therefore see less reason to emulate the strangers.

The Europeans, for their part, rarely identify themselves with such attitudes. Their cultural confidence remains unshaken. The main exceptions are to be found in the ranks of university lecturers and clergymen, who do not form a significant element. The settlers, moreover,

---

[1] By July 1967, the total number of permanent Rhodesian civil servants had reached 10,457. Of these, 8,482 were Europeans, while 636 Africans were employed on permanent conditions of service and were eligible for promotion to the most senior posts. There were 1,091 Africans employed on permanent conditions of service who were deemed ineligible for further advancement because of lack of qualifications. The service also employed 248 Coloured, Asian and Chinese officials eligible for promotion to the most senior posts.

never tire of pointing out that intellectuals can easily moralize and assume an unwarranted position of ethical superiority, because intellectuals would stand to lose nothing from the expropriation of white farms or the Africanization of white-owned enterprises under a black régime. Nevertheless, there have been some overall changes in the white position—changes corresponding to modifications in the European social structure. In South Africa, for example, the Afrikaner nationalists have abandoned the crude frontier beliefs of old. They have taken over instead some of the legacy bequeathed to them by paternalistic British imperialists and by segregationist-minded missionaries of an earlier vintage. They are experimenting with a limited kind of accommodation based on a restricted form of autonomy for selected African areas. At the same time, South Africa is consolidating its economic and military strength to an extent that would have appeared improbable to liberals of an earlier era. But no European in southern Africa now thinks in terms of solving his country's race problems by forcing black people to emigrate. Even the most ardent advocates of apartheid agree that Afrikaners will have to coexist with Africans within the confines of the same subcontinent.

On the other hand, Rhodesian politics still have certain principles in common with those of the Progressive Party in South Africa, a mildly liberal body by South African standards. At the time of writing, the Rhodesian electors have not abolished African voting rights. A majority of white voters now remain willing to concede eventual parity to Africans in the legislature in exchange for an end to sanctions and for British recognition of Rhodesian independence. But the future is hard to chart, and the whites may yet seek further entrenchment of their political power.[1] When the Federation of Rhodesia and Nyasaland

---

[1] The history of the Rhodesian franchise is complicated, and we can only briefly allude to it here. The constitution promulgated in 1923 provided for a non-racial franchise. The imperial authorities retained certain veto powers; and even though the veto was never used, it may have acted as a theoretical restraint in certain cases. The franchise qualifications were, however, so high that in practice the suffrage remained largely confined to the Europeans and also to the small Indian minority and the wealthier Coloureds. Only a handful of Africans were able to vote. In 1950, for instance, only 419 Africans were on the voters' roll. More well-off Africans might perhaps have registered, except for fear of exciting the unwelcome attention of the income tax authorities. White income tax officers in turn did not look too closely into the financial affairs of potential African voters, many of whom of course did not keep records of their affairs because they were ignorant about book-keeping.

In 1961 the largely white Rhodesian electorate approved of a somewhat more liberal

collapsed, and with it the last attempt to create a British bastion in Central Africa, Rhodesia necessarily came to depend on South African support. Hence Rhodesia is likely to remain within South Africa's orbit as an English-speaking ally. The verdict of the Boer War has been set aside in a way that would have appeared incredible to the most militant Transvaaler two generations ago.

We do not profess to prophesy. Neither do we consider that academics are better qualified than other students of world affairs to make policy decisions. Intellectuals do, however, have an obligation to use their intellect, to think in a clear and consistent fashion. We are therefore opposed to the curious double standards that are widely, though

constitution, largely, perhaps, in order to preserve the Federation of Rhodesia and Nyasaland. There were some concessions, but again power remained firmly in European hands. The 1961 constitution was used as the basis for the 1965 constitution which came into force after Rhodesia's Unilateral Declaration of Independence. The initial independence constitution removed various existing safeguards but retained the 'dual roll' system introduced by its predecessors. Of a parliament consisting of 65 members, 50 were elected to represent constituencies by the more highly qualified electors—in practice largely whites; and 15 were elected by voters of lower property and educational qualifications—in practice largely Africans. Owing to a complex system of 'cross voting' 'B' roll voters could exercise some influence on 'A' roll seats, and vice versa. Under this system, thirteen Africans and one Euro-African were able to take their seats in Parliament. Africans might even gain eventual majority rule, but for a long time power would remain in white hands. By 1967 8,925 Africans had registered as voters.

By this time, however, the whole system of a property-weighted franchise had become unacceptable to African nationalists. The Africans had at first accepted the 1961 constitution as an initial instalment of reform. Later they rejected it and demanded 'one man—one vote' on the grounds that no other system would represent the black masses at large. The European authorities crushed all opposition groups of a more militant kind, and only a small group of Africans continued to participate in the electoral process. But many Europeans took fright; and present plans (at the time of writing in 1968) offer Africans ultimate parity at best or a *de facto* system of modified *apartheid* at worst. Basically, the Europeans are divided on whether they want a system of merit (which would permit of an ultimate African majority in the more distant future) or whether they desire to maintain their own ethnic predominance at any price, with only token representation for black people. Hence no African nationalist and no European liberal would disagree with the following statement in the *Bulletin of the International Commission of Jurists*: 'the Constitution of Southern Rhodesia is a striking example of the futility of laying down human rights in the Constitution and thereafter subjecting those same human rights to the sway of a legislature which does not adequately represent the people of the country; an examination of Southern Rhodesian legislation in relation to the human rights proclaimed in the Constitution makes one wonder why the trouble was ever taken to put those human rights in the Constitution'. See 'Southern Rhodesia—Human Rights and the Constitution', *Bulletin of the International Commission of Jurists*, No. 18, March 1964, quoted in Palley, *Constitutional history and law of Southern Rhodesia*, p. 628.

not universally, held in present-day academia on the subject of southern Africa. Many intellectuals call for peaceful coexistence between opposing socio-economic systems in Europe, often on the grounds that the result of war would be too terrible to contemplate. Yet at the same time they vehemently object to pleas for this same peaceful coexistence when applied to southern Africa, and instead put their trust in the sword. Many scholars assert, on what we consider dubious grounds, that industrialization in communist countries must excuse the cruelties of the régime, that industrialization in the communist world must ultimately bring about a liberalization of the various communist régimes and occasion a long-term convergence between East and West. Yet many intellectuals protest, often with highly charged moral overtones, when a similar analysis is applied to southern Africa. In the same way many academics object to racial segregation in southern Africa. But they find sociological or historical excuses when white communist or non-white post-colonial countries solve their ethnic minority problems by mass expulsions, which in themselves enforce ethnic segregation in an infinitely more radical fashion.

We can share neither the excessive short-term pessimism nor the undue long-term optimism that now affects so many students of southern African affairs. The economic future for the subcontinent as a whole looks bright. The Europeans' ideological position in white-ruled Africa has undergone some modifications and may be subject to still further changes in the future. Yet the interests that divide society are real enough. A statesman will attempt to reconcile them as far as he can. But society—by the very nature of man—is incapable of achieving perfect harmony. Neither will a revolutionary dictatorship necessarily effect progress. The term 'progress' itself has many different and often contrary connotations. Progress may stand for advance towards greater economic productivity, towards greater social equality or political stability, towards greater aesthetic creativity or a more philanthropic outlook on life, or towards any number of other worthy objectives. But these desiderata do not necessarily go hand in hand. A country may attain high productivity without producing artists. It may be famed for its painters and rightly despised for its political morality. Above all, revolutionary dictatorships do not necessarily find the answers to the problems of society. The Stalinist terror has not created a new man in the twentieth century. The black one-party states founded since the 1960s have not, on the whole, proved particularly apt at solving the ills that beset their respective countries. Many enthusiasts now talk of a 'second independence'. They take up the old-fashioned district commissioner's argument that the black intelligentsia does not truly represent the masses, and that educated black people are only out for the spoils of office. The new radicals instead extol revolutionary violence as a cure for Africa's ills. But history does not lend much support to their optimism. Haiti, for instance, did achieve its independence through a genuinely revolutionary black dictatorship. But the successors of Toussaint L'Ouverture were unable to achieve either stability or substantial progress in their strife-torn country.

No matter whether we agree or disagree with the white settler's political outlook, we should try to understand his view. Stripped of its imperial terminology and civilizational verbiage, the European case in Rhodesia now rests essentially on the settlers' social usefulness and on their collective group interests, which are identified with economic progress as well as with security of person and property for all. According to the spokesmen of European interests, minority rule is inevitable in the new Africa. As many African nationalists now agree, the rules of habeas corpus or of Western parliamentary traditions have little or no future in Africa. Preventive detention laws are applied in Tanzania just as much as in India or in many other countries considered progressive. It is not therefore legitimate to blame the whites for not practising the principles of Western democracy. Indeed, the struggle for the vote is important in Rhodesia only because the franchise still has a real meaning unknown in military states or in single-party dictatorships. The alternative to settler rule is not governance by the majority; the alternative is domination either by a new élite of black state functionaries who exercise power within the framework of a single-party dictatorship, or —more likely—government by black army officers.

Judged by the standards that prevail in the new Africa, the European élites are better qualified from the technological point of view for positions of power than their African rivals. They have also demonstrated much entrepreneurial skill, notably in their efforts to circumvent the effects of sanctions. Rhodesia, in fact, is more highly endowed with this ability than is Zambia, which suffers from a relative lack of entrepreneurial resources despite the fact that she has at her disposal a good deal of capital. The whites have built up an efficient administration. There is no huge, top-heavy party bureaucracy of the kind found, say, in Guinea. The permanent civil service accounts for only a negligible proportion of the country's total labour force. The whites do not use government as an instrument of political patronage. They do not engage in that peculiar form of exploitation which consists in maintaining functionless members of the ruling oligarchy in public employment at the taxpayer's expense (a practice that is widespread in many backward countries of the world).

White (as well as Asian) income levels certainly, though not invariably, contrast in a striking fashion. But so do the living standards between the rich and the poor, the skilled and the unskilled, in every underdeveloped country—regardless of the skin colour or the political phraseology of the élite. The rise in European incomes has not prevented a corresponding increase in African incomes—in fact, the two appear to be economically interdependent (see Table 2).

The white ruling stratum, moreover, is not much concerned with ideological history of a more theoretical kind, partly perhaps because the settlers lack either a solidly-based intelligentsia of their own or a linguistic nationalism such as that developed by the Afrikaners in the south. The colonists have plenty of prejudices; but they have no desire as a group to impose any metaphysical beliefs on their subjects—be they Christian, pagan or atheist. Provided life and property are secure, the colonists do not worry about such issues as the general will, the march of history or the mythical past. There is no academic *Gleichschaltung* of the totalitarian variety. On the contrary, public bodies such as the National Museum of Rhodesia or the National Monuments Commission have acquired a good reputation for the high quality and the objectivity of their work on African history and archaeology. Rhodesia is the unusual example of a so-called police state where the ruling party does not command a single daily newspaper, and is openly opposed by a parliamentary opposition, by the bulk of the clergy and by the academic intelligentsia.

The Europeans moreover can rightly plead that they are not a functionless class of absentee landlords; neither can they be regarded as parasitic tribute-raising conquerors of the pre-colonial kind. Unlike many ruling groups in Latin America or south-east Asia, they fully shoulder the burden of taxation. Should power fall into African hands in Rhodesia, settlers fear the new rulers would insist on the expropriation of white farms in the name of land reform, on the replacement of white by black officials in the name of Africanization, on the take-over of the larger enterprises by Africans in the name of African socialism. Such a transfer of power would hurt many Africans as well as Europeans,

Table 2. *Gross domestic product, gross national income and other income per head in Rhodesia, 1954 to 1965*

	1954	1955	1956	1957	1958	1959	1960	1961	1962	1963	1964	1965
1. Gross domestic product (at factor cost) (£ million)	168·5	186·5	211·6	238·0	249·1	264·6	281·2	297·0	302·6	312·5	329·7	353·6
2. Total population (*thousand*)	2,990	3,090	3,190	3,330	3,410	3,520	3,640	3,760	3,880	4,010	4,140	4,260
3. Gross national income (£ *million*)	170·5	183·8	202·3	215·5	219·5	231·2	242·9	249·5	249·2	251·1	258·3	270·0
4. Gross domestic product per head (current prices) (£)	56·4	60·4	66·3	72·1	73·0	75·2	77·3	79·0	78·0	77·9	79·6	83·0
5. Gross national income per head (in real terms) 1954 prices (£)	57·0	59·5	63·4	65·3	64·4	65·7	66·7	66·4	64·2	62·6	62·4	65·1
6. Europeans, Asians and Coloureds in employment:												
(i) Total earnings (£ *million*)	56·9	63·8	71·8	84·1	93·3	96·8	101·3	102·0	104·9	107·5	107·7	114·4
(ii) Number in employment (*thousands*)	64·4	69·0	72·6	79·7	85·6	87·8	89·4	88·4	88·5	88·2	86·6	89·0
(iii) Average earnings (£)	884	925	988	1,056	1,091	1,103	1,134	1,154	1,186	1,219	1,243	1,285
7. Africans in employment												
(i) Total earnings (£ *million*)	35·8	40·2	45·1	50·6	55·1	57·4	60·2	64·3	67·6	71·1	75·8	80·6
(ii) Number in employment (*thousands*)	555·0	574·0	602·0	620·0	628·0	628·0	640·0	628·0	616·0	608·0	621·0	629·0
(iii) Average earnings (£)	65	70	75	82	88	91	94	102	110	117	122	128
8. Rural household income (£ *million*)	17·1	17·9	20·3	20·0	19·5	19·8	18·9	21·3	22·5	23·5	25·5	24·6
9. Rural household population[a] (*thousand*)	1,415	1,452	1,469	1,518	1,597	1,704	1,782	1,930	2,082	2,236	2,327	2,443

NOTE: In arriving at the national income aggregate for the years 1954 to 1963, the figures of net income paid abroad do not take account of corporate income transactions between Rhodesia and Zambia and Malawi. This series and the resulting *per capita* figures are accordingly approximate and are at best an indication of long-term trends. No reliance can be placed on the year-to-year changes.

[a] Defined as total *de facto* African population less all Africans living in urban areas, all Africans and dependents working on mines, all Africans living on European-occupied farming land and all male employees living in tribal areas other than those working for African employers.

Source: *Economic Survey of Rhodesia for 1965*, Salisbury, Government Printer, July 1966, p. 50.

the settlers argue, because it would result in lowered efficiency both in the administrative and the economic spheres. It might easily lead also to the increased use of coercion as the new rulers might attempt to make up for their deficiencies by national mobilization.

Some may object that the settlers ought to throw in their lot completely with the new Africa. But Europeans in fact cannot become Tanzanians or Zimbabwians—there are as yet no Tanzanian or Zimbabwian nations with which foreigners can seek identification. No African country has as yet managed to replace ethnic by national loyalties. Indians in Kenya are not regarded as Kenyans, whether they take out citizenship papers or not. Lunda and Luba are not Congolese. Ibo and Yoruba are not Nigerians. There are as yet no emergent African nations. Hence the whites feel that a European's loyalty, like that of every other community, ought to be directed in the first place to his own in-group, his own ethnic community, the only group from whom he can derive support in times of pressure. In any case, cultural differences between white and black men are of a basic kind, not only those that exist between Europeans and African subsistence farmers, but also those that obtain between Europeans and the new Africans. Such differences derive not solely from race; indeed, the racial component may be of only secondary importance. The cleavages between the Europeans and their African fellow-citizens have their origin also in divergent concepts of family life, in deep-seated differences in language and custom, as well as in a different sense of the national past and the national destiny.

A comfortably optimistic doctrine concerning race prejudice to which we have already referred sees discriminatory practices as being rooted primarily in white prejudice. But in fact Arabs in Zanzibar, Ibo in Nigeria, Chinese in Indonesia, Indians in Burma—all of them wealthy and privileged traders from the host country's point of view— have received infinitely harsher treatment than, say, Asians in Rhodesia. Indians may not like all aspects of the existing order in Rhodesia. But their lives, their property, their citizenship and their voting rights are secure. Ian Smith's government represents 'stability' to Indians who are keenly aware of the disabilities suffered by their compatriots in newly independent Burma, Ceylon, Zanzibar, and Tanzania. Indians are sceptical of their future in Africa; they remember that Ghana and Nigeria were once hailed as model African states.[1]

[1] Floyd and Lillian O. Dotson, *The Indian minority of Zambia, Rhodesia and Malawi* (New Haven, Yale University Press, 1968), pp. 361–73. The Indian population in

Indians likewise do not emigrate from South Africa, where they are subject to racial discrimination. They are, however, being squeezed out of Kenya, Zambia and Tanzania, where the African-dominated governments are determined to replace them by Africans in government, in commerce and in semi-skilled jobs. Indians now plead despairingly that such a policy will injure the host countries' respective economies, that many Indians had in fact identified themselves with the Africans' liberation struggle against the British. Such protests are not, however, likely to modify seriously the policy of Africanization. Neither can they undo personal tragedies such as those of Ambu Patel, an Asian businessman who, after having completely identified himself with Kenyatta and the cause of African independence, was physically thrown out of a bus that carried African nationalists to their first *uhuru* celebration. There is, of course nothing peculiarly African about the predicament facing men like Patel. His difficulty was no greater, for instance, than that faced by assimilated Polish Jews who supported Polish freedom during World War I, only to be rejected by the new *Staatsvolk* when Poland became a sovereign state. The Indian's future, moreover, may not be universally bleak. Some Indians have indeed moved into manufacturing and are doing well. But again, the Indians' future will depend on political factors beyond their control, and their condition is not enviable.

Ironically enough, the outlook for the European settlers in the independent states north of the Zambezi seems somewhat brighter than that of the Indians. Zambia, for instance, suffers from a severe shortage of specialized labour; she thus continues to employ on the Copperbelt European skilled workers, technicians and managers. Europeans are still at work in Kenya and Tanzania. They do not arouse the same hostility as Asians, for highly qualified white labour migrants generally do not compete with Africans to the same extent as do Indian commercial employees, semi-skilled workers or clerks.

Nevertheless, the chances for a *permanent* European presence in East

Central Africa represents, of course, only a small number. In 1961 there were only 7,253 Indians in Southern Rhodesia, 7,790 in Northern Rhodesia and 10,063 in Nyasaland. Kenya's estimated Asian population in 1960 was 175,000, Tanganyika's about 117,000, Uganda's 72,000. At the same time the occupational composition of the East African Indians was more diversified than those of the three Central African territories. They are likewise ethnically more variegated than the Indians in Central Africa, most of whom speak Gujurati as their native tongue. See also A. Bharati, 'Political pressures and reactions in the Asian minority in East Africa', Syracuse University, Maxwell Graduate School of Citizenship and Public Affairs, Program of East African Studies, *Occasional paper* No. 12 (Syracuse, N.Y., 1964), pp. 1-9.

Africa are not good. In the palmy days of early decolonization, Tanzania, for instance, used to be regarded as a model in the field of race, the kind of country often held up to recalcitrant white Rhodesians as an example to follow if they wished to live in Africa in permanence and peace. Now the prospect seems very different, and the chances of an enduring white presence in Tanzania seem only slightly better than those of an Indian presence. As a recent investigator put the matter:

the present and future role of the European in Tanganyika is small indeed. It is probable that his temporary presence will be required in technical posts for some time to come, but only until such time as Africans can fill his place. He may be needed for some years in education, particularly at the higher and technical levels. In the commercial world he will be gradually squeezed out by the government controlled cooperative organizations. In farming he may retain his independence for a few more years, but after that his land will almost certainly be nationalised. If he is willing to stay and work as a manager he may be allowed to do so—but only if he becomes a citizen. In other words, he must integrate or disappear. And if he does integrate he will, of course, disappear.[1]

Whites in Rhodesia were faced with an enormously difficult racial situation. There are at least two distinct nations or societies in Rhodesia: one is white, Western and supports in general the principles of parliamentary democracy; the second society is African, tribal, tradition-oriented and hierarchical. In between—in a no-man's land—restlessly moves the Westernized African. He wants power; so do the whites, even though some Europeans would ally themselves with this emerging African middle class and rule somewhat the way the British aristocracy allied with the middle class in 1832 to share control of government in Great Britain.

There is a tremendous disparity between the races in wealth, in social position, in skills, in occupations, in power—all of these based on colour —or so it seems to the African. And it is on these grounds that Europeans fear African politicians will use racism to destroy whites by appealing to the black masses. Given the present climate of opinion,

[1] James L. Brain, 'The changing role of the European in East Africa', Syracuse University, Maxwell Graduate School of Citizenship and Public Affairs, Program of East African Studies, *Occasional paper* No. 12 (Syracuse, N.Y., 1964), p. 14. Donald Rothschild, 'Kenya's minorities and the African crisis over citizenship', *Race*, 1968, **9**, 421-37, esp. p. 433, gives a valuable insight into African race attitudes in Kenya. There is a good deal of ambivalence in these attitudes. Rothschild nevertheless finds that '73 per cent of the [African] responses disagreed with the proposition that Europeans and Asians who have become Kenya citizens should have equal chances with Africans now', though African attitudes were more favourable towards whites than towards Asians.

politics will remain racial and Africans will fear whites because they lack the skills and the capital of the Europeans. This situation is not peculiar to Africa nor to black–white relations; it is common throughout the world where one people have technological and cultural advantages over another.

But in Africa we have had an analogous racial situation—that of Zanzibar—which Britain tried to solve by constitutional means and failed. In spite of efforts of the Arabs to gain African co-operation and to foster multi-racial concepts, politics here remained racial. Africans had racial fears about their inferiority in education, in technical skills, in capital. They feared a slow rise of Arab power and felt the Arabs would dominate the country for generations. Africans also had racial hatred for Arabs as the island's social, economic and political élite. From the beginning of their drive for self-government Africans waged an anti-Arab campaign. Massive African enfranchisement (one man-one vote) without social and economic improvement did not save the Arabs. It led instead to the Zanzibar revolution. Efforts of Great Britain to guarantee minority rights, to ensure peaceful change, to mediate between the races, to change slowly political institutions and to ensure stability all failed.

Whites in Rhodesia face similar problems of African racial hatred and racial fears stemming from the imbalance of power and skills between whites and blacks. Hence Rhodesian whites see in UDI the only way to control the force of political change and hence to secure their safety.

White Rhodesians, not to speak of white South Africans or Angolans, are therefore reluctant to accept black majority rule; so to some extent are many Indians and Coloured people. There is universal distrust of minority agreements of the kind concluded in Eastern Europe after the First World War, of minority guarantees such as those made in the Franco–Algerian Evian agreement and of British promises to protect Arab minorities in Zanzibar. The Europeans at the same time are optimistic concerning their chances of resisting either revolution from within or invasion from abroad. Up to the present, their own forecasts have proved quite realistic; the South African revolution prophesied by liberal academics and clergymen for the past twenty years seems as remote as ever. White Rhodesians have consolidated their *de facto* independence. Even a firm opponent of the present Rhodesian régime such as the London *Economist* concludes that Ian Smith, the Rhodesian Prime Minister, is in control:

Britain can do precious little now. It cannot invade Rhodesia, even if British public opinion wanted to do so. It would be wrong to encourage black Africa to embark on a war of liberation, one still beyond black Africa's powers...the fewer the promises that cannot be fulfilled, the fewer the hopes that are raised in vain, the better for Britain itself.[1]

Whatever one's personal value judgements, it is therefore quite unrealistic to interpret the settlers' motives and actions simply in terms of deep-seated irrational factors. The whites have shown a considerable degree of tenacity and foresight. Their expectations and their fears do have some rational basis in the historical experience of other minorities.

If there is any merit in this analysis, critics of the whites may adopt any one of the following arguments. First, the revolution has not yet come, but it is bound to come in the future. In any case, the maintenance of the *status quo* requires too many sacrifices from the whites as well as from the blacks. The Europeans should therefore come to terms with history while they can still do so with advantage. The effectiveness of this argument has, however, suffered greatly from the disunity among the independent African states themselves, from their inability to mount a co-ordinated military assault, from the instability that plagues so many of these countries, and from the large number of mistaken estimates made of the settlers' strength and resilience in the past. The treatment accorded minorities since the granting of independence has not been reassuring to the white settlers.

Alternatively, the settler's critic may argue that there are no lessons of history. The experiences of other plural societies are not therefore of concern to southern Africa. White Rhodesians should therefore stop concerning themselves with the fate of the Ibo in Nigeria, the Arabs in Zanzibar, the Indians in Kenya, the Tamils in Ceylon and other distinct ethnic groups subject to political pressure, persecution or expulsion, for every historical event is unique. This point of view is philosophically perfectly defensible. But if it is true, much of the work done by present-day sociologists and political scientists becomes irrelevant to scholarship. Hence, this argument is not likely to meet with acceptance in academia today.

On the other hand, one might argue that while lessons can indeed be learned from experiences elsewhere, the lessons from abroad are not applicable to southern Africa. This point of view would require a thorough analysis showing how and why the fate of a powerless white

[1] *Economist*, 9 March 1968, p. 11.

minority in Rhodesia or South Africa would be different from that of similarly placed minorities elsewhere. Such an investigation might well draw on the experiences of Zambia; but it would carry conviction only if Zambia should indeed prove an exceptional case in the long run as well as in the more immediate future.

Again, one might argue that on moral grounds it is incumbent on the settlers to make concessions. But this reasoning remains fraught with difficulty even for those who are willing to suffer for their convictions. Surrender at this juncture might have serious consequences for others or for generations yet unborn. Moral argument, moreover, cannot fairly be used by foreigners, whose moralizing, made at a safe distance in London or Washington, does not entail any personal sacrifice. We conclude that the settlers' fate must ultimately be decided by those who have made their home in the subcontinent.

BIBLIOGRAPHY

Andrié, Ivo. *The bridge on the Drina*, trans. by Lovett F. Edwards. New York, 1959.

Banton, Michael. *Race relations*. London, 1967.

Barnes, J. A. *Politics in a changing society: a political history of the Fort Jameson Ngoni*. London, Oxford University Press, 1954.

Bharati, A. 'Political pressures and reactions in the Asian minority in East Africa', Syracuse University, Maxwell Graduate School of Citizenship and Public Affairs, Program of East African Studies, *Occasional paper* No. 12. Syracuse, N.Y., 1964.

Brain, James L. 'The changing role of the European in East Africa', Syracuse University, Maxwell Graduate School of Citizenship and Public Affairs, Program of East African Studies, *Occasional paper* No. 12. Syracuse, N.Y., 1964.

British South Africa Company. *A land of sunshine: Southern Rhodesia*. London, 1910.

Cairns, H. Alan C. *Prelude to imperialism: British reactions to Central African society, 1840–1890*. London, 1965.

Dotson, Floy and Lillian O. *The Indian minority of Zambia, Rhodesia and Malawi*. New Haven, Yale University Press, 1968.

Drake, St Clair, and Horace R. Cayton. *Black metropolis: a study of Negro life in a northern city*. New York, 1962.

Fanon, Frantz. *The wretched of the earth*, trans. by Constance Farrington. New York, 1963.

[Gann, Lewis H.] 'Behind the treason trial', *Central African Examiner*, 2 Aug. 1958.

Gann, Lewis H. 'The Southern Rhodesian Land Apportionment Act, 1930: an essay in trusteeship', *Occasional Papers of the National Archives of Rhodesia and Nyasaland*, No. 1. Salisbury, 1963.

'The white settler: a changing image', *Race*, May 1961, **2**, no. 2.

Georgulas, Nikos. 'Minority assimilation in Africa: the Greeks in Moshi—an example', Syracuse University, Maxwell Graduate School of Citizenship and Public Affairs, Program of East African Studies, *Occasional paper* No. 22. Syracuse, N.Y., n.d.

Ghai, Yash P. 'Prospects for Asians in East Africa', in *Racial and communal tensions in East Africa*. East African Institute of Social and Cultural Affairs, Contemporary African Monographs, No. 3. Nairobi, 1966.

Gray, Richard. *The two nations: aspects of the development of race relations in the Rhodesias and Nyasaland*. (Institute of Race Relations.) London, Oxford University Press, 1960.

Greenberg, Louis. *The Jews in Russia*. 2 vols. New Haven, Yale University Press, 1944–51.

Gussman, Boris. *Out in the mid-day sun*. New York, Oxford University Press, 1963.

'Problems of adjustment in British Central Africa', *Civilisations*, 1959, **9**, no. 4.

Hancock, Sir William Keith. *Survey of British Commonwealth affairs*. 2 vols. in 3. London, Oxford University Press, 1937–42.

Hatch, John. 'Wilson's gift-horse', *New Statesman*, 18 Oct. 1968.

Hone, Percy F. *Southern Rhodesia*. London, 1909.

Huggins, Godfrey Martin. *Southern Rhodesia: recent progress and development*. London, 1934.

Huxley, Elspeth, and Margery Perham. *Race and politics in Kenya: a correspondence between Elspeth Huxley and Margery Perham*. 2nd rev. ed. London, 1956.

Keatley, Patrick. *The politics of partnership: the federation of Rhodesia and Nyasaland*. Harmondsworth, Middlesex, 1963.

Lever, H., and O. M. J. Wagner. 'Ethnic preferences of Jewish youth in Johannesburg', *Jewish Journal of Sociology*, June 1967, **9**, no. 1.

Leys, Colin. *European politics in Southern Rhodesia*. Oxford, Clarendon Press, 1959.

Lugard, Frederick John Dealtry, 1st baron. *The dual mandate in British tropical Africa*. 5th ed. London, 1965.

Macaulay, Thomas Babington, Lord. *The history of England from the accession of James II*. 5 vols. Chicago, 1888.

Macdonald, Sheila. *Martie and others in Rhodesia.* London, 1927.

Mannoni, Dominique O. *Prospero and Caliban: the psychology of colonization,* trans. by Pamela Powesland. London, 1956.

Mnyanda, B. J. *In search of truth: a commentary on certain aspects of Southern Rhodesia's native policy.* Bombay, 1954.

Munger, Edwin S. *Afrikaner and African nationalism: South African parallels and parameters.* London, Oxford University Press, 1967.

Niederhoffer, Arthur. *Behind the shield: the police in urban society.* Garden City, N.Y., 1967.

Palley, Claire. *The constitutional history and law of Southern Rhodesia, 1888–1965,* with special reference to Imperial control. Oxford, Clarendon Press, 1966.

Powicke, Sir Maurice. *The thirteenth century, 1216–1307.* Oxford, Clarendon Press, 1953.

Proceedings of the Southern Rhodesian Missionary Conference, held at Salisbury Southern Rhodesia, 26th to 29th March, 1928. Salisbury, 1928.

Quarles, Benjamin. *Lincoln and the Negro.* New York, Oxford University Press, 1962.

Rhodesia. *Rhodesia: economic survey of Rhodesia for 1965.* Salisbury, 1966.

Rhodesia Information Service. *Rhodesia in brief, 1965: a brief summary of the basic facts about Rhodesia.* Salisbury, n.d.

'Rhodesia', London Institute of Race Relations, *Newsletter,* June 1966.

Ritner, Susan Rennie. 'The Dutch Reformed Church and Apartheid', *Journal of Contemporary History,* 1967, **2**, no. 4.

Rogers, Cyril A. 'The organization of political attitudes in Southern Rhodesia', *Rhodes–Livingstone Journal,* 1959, no. 25.

Rogers, Cyril A., and C. Frantz. *Racial themes in Southern Rhodesia: the attitudes and behavior of the white population.* New Haven, Yale University Press, 1962.

Rolin, Henri. *Les lois et l'administration de la Rhodésie.* Brussels, 1913.

Rothschild, Donald. 'Kenya's minorities and the African crisis over citizenship', *Race,* April 1968, **9**.

Russell-Wood, A. J. R. 'Class, creed and colour in colonial Bahia: a study in prejudice', *Race,* Oct. 1967, **8**.

St Leger, F. Y. 'Crime in Southern Rhodesia', *Rhodes–Livingstone Journal,* 1966, **38**.

Sampson, Anthony. *The treason cage: the opposition on trial in South Africa.* London, 1958.

Selous, Frederick C. *A hunter's wanderings in Africa.* 5th ed. London, 1919.

Sithole, Ndabaningi. *African nationalism.* 2nd ed. London, Oxford University Press, 1968.

Wood, David. *The armed forces of African states.* London, Institute for Strategic Studies, 1966.

CHAPTER 4

PORTUGUESE AFRICA, 1930 TO 1960

by JAMES DUFFY

By 1930 Portugal's colonial momentum had come to a halt. Fifty years of dreaming, planning and building (on a small scale) had ended in exhaustion, frustration and indifference. The benefits from the raw materials sold during World War I and during the reconstruction boom of the 1920s had been dissipated, and the world slump had ended the transient prosperity in Portuguese Africa. For the Portuguese government now in power, the neo-dictatorship of Dr António de Oliveira Salazar, there were more important problems at home, problems in which the African colonies had but small share. The cautious finance minister into whose hands Portugal's destiny had been placed had but one programme for the African territories: a balanced budget. Until the years after World War II, this was the programme for Angola, Moçambique and Guinea that superseded all other plans for African development. Portuguese Africa entered a period of restraint and, in the eyes of critics, of stagnation.

For centuries before, in good times and bad, the African possessions had created in the Portuguese imagination curious compensating visions. The new government was following a historical pattern when, in place of achievement, it was obliged to talk in terms of spiritual and cultural progress. Such dreams and speculations grew out of national pride and the knowledge that the administration and development of the enormous African estates was a task beyond the human and financial resources of the poverty-stricken metropolis. Thus, abstractions such as 'Honour', 'Duty' and 'Lusitanian Spirit' were the ideals to which African policy could aspire.

The Colonial Act of 1930, partly the work of Dr Salazar himself, who served briefly as Minister for Colonies in that year, was a piece of retrospective and theoretic legislation—retrospective because it contained a vision held in earlier centuries, theoretic because of its image of the years to come. It was an attempt by the new Portuguese government to bridge an unsuccessful past with an uncertain future.

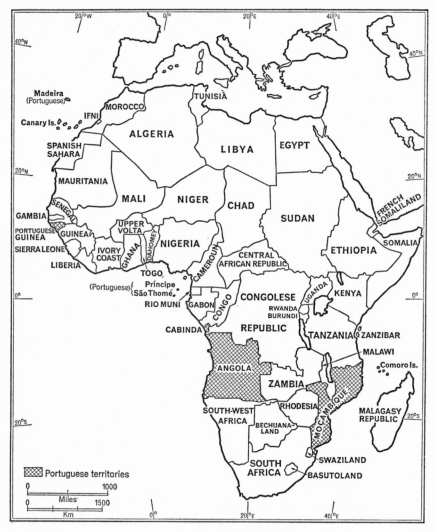

Map 5. Portuguese Africa, 1965

The act reworked and recapitulated previous colonial legislation. Although the government's view of colonial responsibilities and freedoms differed sharply, for example, from that of the Portuguese Republic (1910–26), the differences were administrative, not truly political; and the Colonial Act was a decisive document precisely because it acknowledged a Portuguese tradition in Africa and sought to give it a kind of legislative reality.

What was the origin of this tradition that permeated and at times replaced the practical and administrative purpose? What was the source of a sentiment and a literature that colonial publicists could elaborate into a semi-mythical African policy? What was, really, the 'imperial vocation'? It proceeded, more than from any other source, from a sense of geographic expanse and a sense of Christian responsibility. From the beginning of the Portuguese voyages along the African coast early in the fifteenth century, Portuguese poets, historians and statesmen were awed by the geographical extent of their country's enterprise. Garcia de Resende, for example, and the court dramatist Gil Vicente celebrated the glories of the Portuguese discoveries. The great historians of the sixteenth century and the epic poet Camões, whose *Lusiads* stands out as the treasured monument of patriotic exultation, were the major literary architects of the myth. By the middle of the sixteenth century, when Portugal ruled over many territorial fragments scattered all over the globe, the idea of small Portugal, conquering, trading and colonizing in a distant and exotic world was fixed in the national consciousness. The dimension of Portugal had increased ten times over and with it the notion of the nation's importance. But expansion was a provincial ethnocentric effort, viewed always from within. It was the idea of Portugal in the world, never the idea of Portugal and the world. The small country never lost the purity and innocence of this view.

The expansion of Portugal into the world entailed, in the national view, the responsibility for carrying Christianity and civilization to distant shores. From the beginning there was present a sense of historic vocation: small Portugal spreading the values of Christian Europe in ignorant and hostile lands. This idealism served to buttress the national pride. It provided the basis, where trade and conquest did not, for a relationship between Portugal and the peoples of Africa, Asia and America. The concept of extending the outposts of civilization was recognized early in the sixteenth century and had been exalted into a sense of national myth before the century was out.

The imperial rhetoric and purpose, as part of Portugal's self-recognition, survived the collapse of the imperial design. In a sense, the mystique not only was beyond the vicissitudes of historical change but also afforded compensation for national misfortunes. The mystique was invulnerable to the despair and violence of Portuguese critics of expansion and of the so-called empire, who dedicated themselves to attacking

Portugal's policies and failures overseas but who seldom attacked the ideas that allegedly determined these policies. Diogo do Couto and Faria e Sousa in the sixteenth and seventeenth centuries and Oliveira Martins in the nineteenth century never really questioned the essential rightness of overseas enterprise. The pride in Portugal's geographic and spiritual accomplishments came to be almost an inherent national characteristic, even though many Portuguese neither knew nor cared about fragments of a past called Angola, Moçambique, Goa and Timor.

The Salazar government set about to mould these ethnocentric sentiments into an African policy. There were perhaps practical lessons to be learned from the past, but Portugal's resources in 1930 did not permit this experience to be applied. It was easier and cheaper to theorize and synthesize the colonial tradition. 'We are the legitimate heirs', Colonial Minister Armindo Monteiro wrote in the early 1930s, 'of a great tradition that the generation of today is entitled to invoke ...as a source of inspiration for the future.'[1] The sacred impulse of the past, seen in epic proportion, was to be the spirit of the present and the hope for the future. In the words of a colonial prophet, Jorge Ameal: 'The task of civilizing must have, above all else, a spiritual content. The Portuguese, like no other people, made their enterprises of exploration and conquest a transcendent campaign, a sharing of spiritual values.'[2]

From the efforts of the Portuguese missionary and colonist there had evolved, it was believed, a spiritual unity between the African possessions and the mother country, a community of cultural interests to which Portugal's 'New State' was to give administrative cohesion. Language, race, religion and history were to cement the scattered territories of what the government's publicists called the 'Third Empire'. The African colonies were an extension of Portugal, a projection of Portugal separated only by distance. 'Angola or Moçambique or India', wrote Dr Salazar, 'are under the single authority of the state. We are a political and juridical unity, and we desire to go along the road to economic unity.'[3] In the 1930s this sentiment was for a *white* Portuguese community.

The words of Dr Salazar and his theories were more than voices in

[1] Armindo Monteiro, 'Portugal in Africa', *African Affairs*, 1939, **38**, 259.
[2] João Ameal, 'Mostruário do Império', *O mundo português*, March 1934, **1**, 100.
[3] Quoted in João Ameal, 'Os três chefes do Império', *O mundo português*, May 1934, **1**, 164-5.

the wind; they were meant to convince and educate a nation and her colonies. School-children were instructed in the glories of their country's overseas achievements. Street names, postage stamps, posters carried the same reminder. Various publicity campaigns sought to reinforce colonial awareness in the nation. An official nationalism was formed out of Portugal's genuine pride in the overseas expansion—and out of the simulated historical values of that expansion. The significance of the effort is not that it failed, as far as such things can be measured, to create a new colonial mentality, but that by dint of repetition it made its way into the official mind, from there into the official word, thence into the official act. At that point, the New State's nationalism became policy in Africa.

In real terms this policy had very little to do with Africa and practically nothing to do with Africans in the Portuguese territories. In its plainest terms it meant the perpetuation of Portugal in Africa—the prolonged presence of a culturally superior Christian community in a backward, if not barbaric, land. The first decade of the New State's leadership in African policy saw an extraordinary intensification of this ethnocentric illusion.

Certainly the African population had no place in the practical policies Lisbon wanted to implement in Africa. First thoughts were for the Portuguese, or urban, populations of Angola and Moçambique. Since the early days of African discovery, the Portuguese presence had centered in several small cities or towns or in several interior fortresses. Since the end of the slave-trade, most of the development of Angola and Moçambique had resulted from external influences and the development of lands on Portuguese African frontiers—the Congo, the Rhodesias and South Africa. Portuguese capital had always been reluctant to invest in Africa, even under monopolistic conditions. Under the Salazar government, the weak existing economic base was slowly broadened over a period of some twenty years; the port facilities at Lourenço Marques, Beira, Lobito and Luanda were enlarged; rail routes were gradually extended; ancient settlements were improved, and new white towns came into existence.

Economic control over Portuguese Africa from Lisbon grew more intense. Trade discriminations in favour of Portugal were maintained; the artificial barriers between the territories and their natural foreign markets remained high. The banking and currency system came again under the control of the metropolitan government, much to the annoyance of Portuguese settlers in Angola and Moçambique. Gradually government economists evolved long-term plans for the creation of a so-called *escudo* area; there was to be more political than economic advantage in such a scheme. Thanks to Lisbon's attention to the colonies' economic details, budgets were balanced in Portuguese Africa in the 1930s and 1940s; but stringent control prevented what might have been the natural development of the two territories. Many critics thought that Salazar's economic nationalism worked to the severe disadvantage of colonial interests.

World War II brought something of a release from the restraint. Financial resources had been built up, the provincial economies seemed sound and there was optimism in the air. The Portuguese state was solvent, the fears of external pressures on the colonies had disappeared and the future for metropolis and colony looked very bright. Now tariffs on goods, raw materials and tools for development began to be lowered. New overseas ports were planned; a large-scale transportation and communication complex began to link the isolated centres of Portuguese interest and to provide for their expansion. Immigration increased. After centuries of failure and despair, Angola and Moçambique felt assured of a genuine economic success.

To bring direction and coherence to the development of the African territories, the metropolitan government inaugurated an Overseas Development Plan, the first phase for 1953 to 1958 and the second for 1958 to 1964. Rather than being programmes for economic development, the plans were really a schedule of priorities and an allocation of funds. The first plan concentrated on primary problems: the expansion of white settlement, rail construction (45 per cent of all funds spent in Angola and Moçambique), hydroelectric projects (about 16 per cent of the funds) and port development (about 11 per cent). Whatever the results of the first plan—which aroused controversy in the colonies—it provided visible evidence of an awakened interest in Portugal on behalf of the African possessions.

Partly as a result of these programmes and partly as a consequence of recent prosperity, the physical face of Angola and Moçambique began to be transformed. Nowhere was this more evident than in the cities and towns, which took on new life. Trade increased; agriculture and local industry flourished as they had not in the past; air and land communication with the interior began to break the patterns of isolation. A new economic optimism thus began to reinforce Portugal's concept of its mission in Africa. Where previously the idea of promoting and perpetuating a Portuguese culture in Africa had been an abstraction, it now became, if not a reality, at least an economically viable possibility. The Portuguese world in Africa was visibly expanding at a measurable pace. And it was largely Portuguese: cities and towns, small industries, new farms and estates, the colonial apparatus. As these investments increased, so did the consciousness that Portuguese Africa was Portuguese, not African.

A staggering increase in Portuguese migration served to strengthen in certain ways the economic expansion. From 1830 to 1930 Portuguese governments had made repeated attempts—with very little success—to plant a white population in Angola. Only as penal colonies did the two territories receive any continuing influx of people from Portugal. Between 1930 and 1945 the colonial ministry had no better luck in its intensive campaigns to stimulate a migration to Africa. Statistics for the period are not entirely accurate; but the number of white inhabitants in Angola rose from about 30,000 in 1930 to about 44,000 in 1940, to 78,000 in 1950, to about 170,000 in 1960. Moçambique's white population rose less spectacularly, from about 18,000 in 1930 to 27,500 in 1940, to 48,000 in 1950, to about 85,000 in 1960. Overpopulation and poverty in Portugal, the promise of financial success in Africa, and the government's subsidies had their effect at last. In the 1950s Angola and Moçambique took on more and more the aspect of white colonies. A significant aspect of the immigration was that it included larger numbers of Portuguese women who came to make their homes in Africa.

At the same time, Portugal's social structure was to some extent rebuilt in Africa. Under the quick and heavy influx of Portuguese immigrants, the cultural and economic life of the white communities in Africa became more intensely Portuguese. The occasional blending of African and Portuguese worlds was now less frequent. The homesickness and the insecurity of the new arrivals led them to re-create their cultural patterns and to assert their presence on the basis of the colour of their skin. In years and centuries before, the Portuguese colonist had been a trader, an estate owner, a member of the administrative class. His interests and his needs had led to a fairly intimate association with at least a small part of the African population. The new Portuguese, however, were mostly, on their arrival at least, labourers, poor workers or peasants, unskilled workers from Portugal's proletarian society, psychologically unequipped to do more in the new world than to cling together in a Portuguese community.

But there was a design to the migration to Africa. Colonial sociologists, taking their lead from Dr Salazar, foresaw the creation in Africa of a modern peasant society. In their view, it would be madness to make the Africans pass right away from tribal to modern industrial ways of life. (Even in Portugal itself, the transition from a peasant to an industrial society had not yet been accomplished.) A new agrarian society was to be built through Portuguese settlements on the land; the white cultural nuclei of the towns in the interior were to be expanded. The policy envisioned the creation in Africa of a semi-literate population of Portuguese—and ultimately of Africans—who were to be hand-workers, devoted to family and church and non-political in outlook. White colonization was the only way to the future stability of Portuguese Africa. Africa was to have a Portuguese motherland, and all the people there, black and white, were to be Portuguese. In the words of the preamble to the second Overseas Development Plan: 'We must people Africa with Europeans who can assure the stability of sovereignty and promote the "Portuguesation" of the native population.'

Final success was admittedly distant. Colonial planners spoke of one hundred, two hundred years before the projects would be completed. The assimilation of the great African majority into a prosperous and stable Portuguese community was a task for centuries. In the meantime one had to strengthen the white structure in preparation for the day. Particularly this meant the *colonato*, the independent peasant colony, a model Portuguese colony in the middle of Angola and Moçambique. In Angola two *colonatos* were set up in the 1950s, one at Cela in the Cuanza Sul district and the other in the Cunene Valley; in Moçambique at Guijá along the Limpopo a third *colonato* was established. Each colonist received a house, a tract of land and livestock, and he shared in the use of heavy farm equipment. The government was to be repaid through a long-term mortgage. The difficulties in the *colonato* system were many, and it did not achieve the success or growth that had been anticipated.

Africans in the Portuguese possessions were regarded mostly as an administrative problem.[1] They could hardly be anything else, given

---

[1] Not a single item, for example, in the budgets for the development plans had direct relevance to African interests or necessities, although it was argued that Africans were bound to share with Portuguese in the general good.

the avowed purposes of Portugal's policies. To achieve equal rights and privileges (uncertain prospects under Salazar's rule), Africans had to forsake their own identity. This cultural confidence was the bedrock of Portugal's policy of assimilation. Portugal's historic role—that of civilizing barbaric peoples—was spoken of with renewed fervour, and exotic plans were concocted for the evolution of Portuguese Africans. 'Our whole policy', wrote Morais Cabral in 1939,

> has been and continues to be to raise the cultural, economic, and social level of the Negro, to give him opportunities and to drag him from his ignorance and backwardness, to try to make of him a rational and honorable individual, worthy of the Lusitanian community.[1]

Success was slow. Only in the Cape Verdes and the cocoa isles of São Tomé and Príncipe was the goal of assimilation considered accomplished by the 1950s. In the large continental possessions, the mission had barely begun. By 1950 there were allegedly 14,000 *assimilados* (a very doubtful figure) in Portuguese Guinea and about half a million 'uncivilized' Africans; about 30,000 were assimilated from Angola's African population of over 4 million; and from Moçambique's nearly 6 million, some 5,000 Africans were legally assimilated. The figures did not increase substantially over the next decade. Such statistics were justified by the government as resulting from a careful process of selective assimilation.

For an African to become a Portuguese citizen was difficult, and in some cases the benefits were not great. The candidate for Portuguese citizenship had to demonstrate that he no longer lived in an indigenous manner, that he could read, write and speak the Portuguese language, that he had sufficient means to support himself and his family, and that he was of good character and possessed the qualities necessary for the exercise of the public and private rights of the Portuguese citizen. *Assimilados* were conscripted into the army, like white Portuguese. Stringent requirements were even more stringently applied by Portuguese administrators. Certain of the African élite, those who had a secondary-school education, those who served in the colonial administration, and African merchants and businessmen were issued a *bilhete de identidade* gratuitously. The number of these men and women was not large.

[1] Morais Cabral, 'A vitória do nosso espírito colonizador', O *mundo português*, May 1939, 6, 216.

For thirty years, until the Angolan rebellion of 1961 made it clear that the African revolution had reached Portuguese Africa, Portugal's policies remained virtually unchanged. The obligation of the state, defined in every serious piece of colonial legislation, was to protect the African ward in his 'primitive' condition, to protect his property, to supervise his labour relations and commercial dealings with Europeans, to educate him slowly in the Portuguese language and customs and in the Christian way of life. The remote and mystical goal of the spiritual, or cultural, assimilation of the African mass was perhaps a compensation and excuse for the impossibilities of the present.

As a distraction from the cultural racism and inequality so evident in a policy that divided the population of Portuguese Africa into categories of indigenous and nonindigenous (white, mulatto and assimilated Africans), the Portuguese government began to publicize a philosophy of racial tolerance. Historical antecedents—an African bishop here and an African governor-general there (only one of each) —the acceptance of miscegenation, and the lack of racial tension in the colonies were cited as proof of Portugal's ancient acceptance of any man of any colour as a brother.[1] It was questionable whether a long history of casual intermarriage and an easy-going association between Africans and Portuguese on the margins of colonial society necessarily made for a colonial society free from racial prejudice. There was indeed abundant historical evidence to demonstrate that this had not been the case, though there was an element of truth in the assertion.

But whatever might have been true in the past and whatever might have been the ideals of the government for a multiracial society in Portuguese Africa, the realities of the 1940s and the 1950s were different. The sharp edge of colour discrimination began to cut Angola and Moçambique into what policy had already declared them to be, separate provincial societies, one white and one black. Signs in shops and restaurants restricting entrance, separate facilities in hospitals, theatres and even gaols, the creation of white towns, and a growing sense of racial superiority in the Portuguese population were serious indications that an ideal of racial tolerance could

---

[1] 'Negroes will fight to the last drop of blood for the liberty of being Portuguese, for the greatest pride of the Negro is to belong to a country of men who are brothers' (Eduardo de Azevedo, *Terra da esperança: romance duma viagem a Angola* [Lisbon, 1954], pp. 114–15).

not exist side by side with a policy that stressed cultural and racial inequality.

The African peoples of Angola, Moçambique and Guinea were governed under the *regime do indigenato*, an administrative policy having its origin earlier in the century; the 'civilized' population of the territories was ruled by Portuguese law. The theoreticians of the New State believed that the *regime* would gradually wither away as the process of assimilation expanded; ultimately all of Portuguese Africa would come under the law and civil administration of metropolitan Portugal. But until then the *regime* was to protect the African peoples; it was an extension of Portugal's traditional policy of paternalism. Each colony was divided and subdivided into administrative units, into districts and circumscriptions and posts. The circumscription was the basic, if not the smallest, unit of government, and the administrator of the circumscription was envisioned, and frequently became, the white father figure. He and the *chefe de posto* were the officials in immediate contact with the governed peoples. They were registry officers, judges, tax collectors, agricultural directors and labour overseers. These officials possessed considerable authority over the lives of Africans. Their power reached deep into the villages, where local leaders and African auxiliaries were made directly responsible to them.

The purpose of the *regime do indigenato* was fundamentally neither to encourage nor to suppress: it was to maintain. The African world in Angola and Moçambique was to exist in a kind of limbo while the Portuguese got on with their job of making a success of white colonial development. Behind the rhetoric and the legislation lay the desire to do nothing (in material fact, very little could have been done); they would improvise as the situation demanded, they would continue in Africa as Portugal had for centuries past. There was a repressive, if not destructive, quality in such a practice that was consistent with the view that Africans were all children—in this case, children who were never to be allowed to grow up.

Under the *regime* Africans had few rights but many responsibilities, the most important being to pay taxes, to farm as directed, and to supply Portuguese private and state enterprises with cheap labour. The only law recognized in the colonies was Portuguese common law, although this could not be applied to an African, who was described in successive pieces of legislation as 'an individual of the Negro race...

who is still not sufficiently enlightened and does not possess the individual and social customs to permit the integral application of the
public and private rights of the Portuguese citizen'.[1] Through most of
each territory, then, a makeshift arrangement prevailed; the administrator or chief of post adjudicated on the basis of a modified tribal law
as given to him by an African adviser. The makeshift legal apparatus—
which had, however, a permanence of its own—was an evasion of
the purpose, even the remote purpose, of assimilation; it was typical of
the New State's basically undetermined policy. Confusion created
confusion and nothing changed where nothing was really meant to
change. The preamble to a decree of 1954, having to do with organization of municipal courts in Angola and Moçambique, revealed an
indecision which had become purposeful and which had found its own
language of ambiguity:

The peculiar circumstances of the overseas provinces do not permit, or even
recommend, that the administration of justice be handled exclusively by
regular magistrates. On the one hand, it is necessary to give special heed to
native questions, submitted for the most part to the traditional laws of the
indígenas, the knowledge of which implies an intimacy, as profound as
possible, with local life. Only the direct representative of the Administration, protector of the natives and constant agent of Portuguese culture, is
the appropriate person to resolve, in principle, native questions, using the
prestige of his authority, which thus appears indivisible, to obtain the peaceful
fulfilment of all decisions.

And even when problems arising from the conflict between Portuguese
law and native law demand adherence to the former and justify in such a
case the intervention of common tribunals [i.e. a Portuguese court] the
process must be kept uniform, as simple as possible, because the obligation
to protect the native justifies the elimination of complex legal processes, since
these would be incomprehensible to the indígena...

On the other hand, the judicial occupation of the whole territory cannot prescind the intervention of the administrators in the preparation and
judgment of questions completely subject to common law. Since, however,
the complexity and multiplicity of tasks assigned to the administrators do
not permit them to handle involved judicial problems, which only specialists
can solve, the system has been evolved of assigning to his competence only
the most simple and urgent cases; otherwise he acts as a delegate of the

[1] Article 2, Ch. 3, of Decreto-Lei No. 39,666, 'Promulga o estatuto dos indígenas
portugueses das províncias da Guiné, Angola e Moçambique', in *Nova legislaçao
ultramarina* (Lisbon, 1953), II, 203.

common court, receiving for each case the orientation necessary. It is believed that in this manner the judicial occupation of the territory and the respect for legality will be simultaneously assured.[1]

Where it mattered, the colonial administration could be efficient, that is, in the supervision of the indigenous population. If the Salazar dictatorship did not export its secret police apparatus to the African colonies until the late 1950s, it did strengthen Portuguese control there. Through an administration that penetrated every African village, through labour laws, through the pass-book system, through the segregation of living areas, the governments in Angola and Moçambique maintained the measure of supervision and control necessary. Exile, gaol, torture, beatings, and disappearance were the fate awaiting political dissidents—black or white. Beyond these restraints, isolation and ignorance were powerful forces working for the same effect. Portugal took public pride in the safety and surface order of Angola and Moçambique, attributing it entirely to the success of humane policies and to Portugal's traditional racial tolerance.

In another direction tradition continued to assert itself—in the use of African labour. Consistent with the idea that Africans were wards of the state and with the ideal that they should become some day genuine Portuguese citizens was the concept that Africans had to work to deserve that distinction. Much of the long history of Portuguese enterprise in Africa has been told in terms of the slave-trade, slavery, forced labour, and contract labour, and the New State did nothing to alter tradition. The cornerstone of Portugal's policy for Africans was the obligation to labour. In 1943 Colonial Minister Vieira Machado wrote:

It is necessary to inspire in the black the idea of work and of abandoning his laziness and depravity if we want to exercise a colonizing action and protect him...If we want to civilize the native we must make him adopt as an elementary moral precept the notion that he has no right to live without working. A productive society is based on painful hard work...The policy of assimilation which I conceive of must be complete...It is to be an unenlightened Negrophile not to infuse the African with the absolute necessity for work.[2]

[1] Preamble to Decreto-Lei, 39,817, 'Promulga a organização dos julgados municipais nas comarcas judiciais da Guiné, Angola e Moçambique...', in *ibid.*, II, 223–4.

[2] Quoted in 'A estadia do sr. Ministro das Colónias nas terras africanas do Império', *O mundo português*, 1934, 10, 554.

The Native Labor Code of 1928 (not the work of the Salazar government) remained the basic labour law for Angola and Moçambique. Philosophically of a piece with earlier legislation, the 1928 code tried to achieve twin goals that had never been attained before in Portuguese Africa: to develop the colonies economically and to protect the rights of the African workers. The code tried to put African labour on a semi-voluntary basis and to make working conditions, payment and social care indispensable parts of all contractual agreements. The Colonial Act of 1930 stated that 'the system of native contract labor rests on individual liberty and the native's right to a just wage and assistance, public authority intervening only for purposes of inspection'. Articles 32, 33 and 34 of the 1954 *Estatuto dos indígenas das províncias de Guiné, Angola, e Moçambique* declared: 'The State will try to make the native recognize that work consitutes an indispensable element for progress, but the authorities can only impose work upon him in cases specifically covered by law' (article 32); 'The natives may freely choose the work they want to carry out, either on their own account or for another' (article 33); 'The use of native labor by *não-indígenas* rests on freedom of contract and the [worker's] right to a just wage and assistance, and must be inspected by the State through its appropriate organs' (article 34).

To the extent that all African adult men were obliged by law to work productively six months every year, either for themselves or for someone else, all African labour in the Portuguese colonies was obligatory, but various distinctions could be made to soften the appearance of such a labour code. Forced labour was penal labour—punishment for minor crimes or tax delinquency—and all other labour was free labour. A worker who contracted his services directly was perhaps more 'free' than the worker who was rounded up, contracted, and shipped hundreds of miles away to a road gang or a sugar estate; but within the general pattern of labour abuse in Angola and Moçambique the distinction was not great. The colonial government was in the labour business, as it had always been in the labour business, directly and indirectly. So long as the government demanded that Africans work and so long as the government expedited and supervised the recruitment and treatment of that labour, it remained responsible for the unhealthy result of its policies.

Irregularities abounded, the most persistent being in the recruitment of the workers. Private employers, particularly estate managers in need of large numbers of workers, had to skirt the law in order to acquire them. Local officials, notably chiefs of post, were bribed to supply the men, either so-called tax delinquents or men the village chief was forced to round up. The period of the contract (usually six months, although some companies, such as Diamang, and the Angolan fisheries were allowed to recruit for periods up to eighteen months) was often illegally extended. Child labour, inadequate wages, bad treatment and corporal punishment of workers, theft of withheld pay, unsatisfactory accommodations and services—conditions the labour laws specifically prohibited—were common abuses. The arrest and conviction of colonial officers and repeated instructions from Lisbon did little to correct a corrupt practice, the most visible and lasting example of Portugal's racial discrimination and the point around which controversy was to build and explode.

Portuguese administration in the colonies suffered also from the same bureaucratic complexity found in the mother country. White planters and businessmen often faced difficulties in getting a permit for this, an authorization for that, and a licence for something else. Successful entrepreneurs might have to become experts in circumventing regulations that involved long and apparently useless trips from their place of work to the nearest administrative centres; they might have to become skilled diplomatists able to take advantage of the quirks and foibles of local officeholders. Some planters, especially those of foreign origin, complained of the seeming unpredictability of administrative decisions, of having to live in an atmosphere of semi-legality where an administrator might or might not 'pick' on them for some technical offence. Foreign enterprise was particularly subject to rigid supervision designed to safeguard the interests of Portuguese subjects. Slow-motion control, exercised by an overstaffed and underpaid bureaucracy, was frequently accused of restricting economic development, while bureaucratic paternalism—even at its best—often stultified its own objects.

But nothing could really be changed so long as the New State was committed to a particular development programme in Africa. Labour was a chronic scarcity in Angola and Moçambique and could only be obtained, it seemed, by coercion. An editorial in a 1956 issue of O século, the foremost Lisbon newspaper, stated the prevailing official attitude:

For all the effective resources of the overseas soil and subsoil to be exploited and developed...much work, much perseverance, much human effort is absolutely necessary. Translated into everyday speech, this means that an abundant, permanent, and very reliable *mão-de-obra* [work force] becomes fundamentally indispensable. Now, this labouring force can only be supplied by the native.[1]

To escape the requirement and to earn higher wages, large numbers of African workers migrated to neighbouring territories. The flow of migratory labour, up to 250,000 workers a year, was controlled, and restricted, by conventions between Moçambique and the governments of the Union of South Africa and the Rhodesias; in return for the grant of recruiting privileges in the colony, Moçambique received certain economic guarantees. The outflow of clandestine or irregular migration to the Congo and the Rhodesias reached equal proportions. It was estimated in 1950 that up to a million and a half Portuguese Africans were living outside the colonies in any given year.[2]

The positive aspects of the *regime do indigenato* scarcely compensated for the harm done in the name of contract labour. The New State had no more money at first to spend on social advancement in Africa than previous Portuguese governments, and had less desire to spend it. A government that exalted the right to be poor as a civic virtue in Portugal was not likely to act any differently in a distant African province. Plans and projects for the gradual revolution—or evolution, not revolution, as some Portuguese maintained—filled the air for twenty-five years, from 1930 to 1954; during the six subsequent years there were cautious attempts to put some of them into practice.

An early project was the formation of new villages, African *colonatos*, to draw people out of their isolation into a peripheral contact with the Portuguese world. Village settlements, each with its school, infirmary, and co-operative farm services, were envisioned; but several attempts made in the 1930s were failures (partly because the *colonatos* acquired the reputation of being work camps). For the next fifteen years the subject was given over to serious study. In 1940 the colonial ministry prepared a draft for the organization of African *colonatos*; after considerable revision this was to be the basis for the farm colonies established in the middle 1950s. Villages of twenty families or more were to be set up, each with common ground and farm buildings. Places in the villages were to go to family men between the ages of

[1] *O século de Lisboa*, 4 Aug. 1956, p. 1.
[2] For a synthesis of Portuguese African labour laws, see Joaquim Moreira da Silva Cunha, *O trabalho indígena: estudo de direito colonial*, 2nd ed. (Lisbon, 1955).

twenty-five and forty who had fulfilled their military service or had experience in agricultural work. The colonial administration and the Catholic missions were to provide for the village's social, spiritual and educational needs. Self-supporting African men in the villages were to be exempt from the labour draft.

The first attempts, varying somewhat from locale to locale, came in the 1950s—at Inhamissa in Moçambique's Gaza district and at Caconda in Angola's Cunene Valley. Elsewhere in Angola, at Damba, Bembe and Loge, co-operative colonies appeared; and in Moçambique's Zavala area a more truly co-operative scheme enjoyed some success (about a thousand members reportedly had an income of a thousand dollars a year). By 1960 about seven hundred families were living at Caconda, where 600,000 acres had been set aside. Caconda, like the all-white Portuguese settlement at Cela, had become the model. A paternalistic little society regimented by colonial officials, Caconda was hailed as the example for the future. The number of Africans who lived in these admittedly expensive colonies was small; even had they proved entirely successful, it was difficult to foresee how Portugal could expand the *colonato* programme to any significant degree over the following critical decades.

In other directions the New States made few efforts to encourage African commerce and industry, these areas of economic interest being increasingly reserved for Portuguese colonists. Lisbon's efforts to get white emigrants into Portuguese Africa eliminated most of the channels of economic advancement for Africans. Increasingly, technical positions, jobs for skilled or semi-skilled workers were taken over in the 1950s by Portuguese immigrants; the economic expansion of the decade brought no particular advantage to African artisans. The economic stratification had by 1960 become an additional barrier to assimilation.

A more important goal than material advancement was spiritual assimilation. The New State's position on the Church in Portuguese Africa was made clear in the Colonial Act: 'Portuguese Catholic missions overseas and those establishments preparing personnel for that service...shall be protected and aided by the State as institutions of instruction and assistance and instruments of civilization.' After more than a hundred years of bickering and uncertainty Church and State were joined again in the task of making Portuguese Africa Portuguese. The Catholic missionary programme in the colonies, 'to Christianize and educate, to nationalize and civilize', was acknowledged by the Portuguese constitution, the Concordat of 7 May 1940, between Portugal and the Vatican, and the Missionary Statute of 1941. Catholic missionary work was in part supported by the state. By the mid-1950s the number of missionaries, many of them foreigners, had reached about 400 in Angola and 300 in Moçambique. At the same time, there were an estimated million and a half African Catholics in Angola (an overblown figure) and about 200,000 in Moçambique.

After 1941 the Catholic missions were given the responsibility for directing the basic education programme for African students, and another former role of the Church in Africa was reaffirmed. Not until ten years later, however, had the semblance of an educational system for young African students been established. Consistent with the idea of two cultures, Portuguese education in the colonies was based on two systems: the state duplicated that of metropolitan Portugal; the other hinged on the so-called basic programme for African students, *ensino rudimentar* (*ensino de adaptação* after 1956), an aspect of the 'indigenous régime'. State schools were to be found in cities and towns and in other areas where the population was predominantly Portuguese.

Ensino rudimentar was a vague attempt at assimilation. The three-year programme offered the rudiments of reading and writing Portuguese (all instruction was supposed to be in the Portuguese language), some arithmetic and perhaps the elements of hygiene. Instructors were Africans trained for the most part at Catholic mission normal schools. At the end of the basic course, students were given an examination made up in Lisbon. Students passing the examination were allowed to go into the third year of the national elementary school.

But education for African students in Angola and Moçambique was a selective process. To continue his education, the African student had to be under fourteen years old—a considerable disadvantage since his progress through the *ensino* programme was usually delayed. And for the overwhelming majority of African students there were no elementary schools in the vicinity. Where such schools were found, they existed only for Portuguese, mulatto and assimilated African students, with the result that an African had to attend missionary schools, Catholic or Protestant, usually as a boarder. Fees for a year's education could take a third of his family's annual cash income. The labour draft was another interruption in the continuation of study.

For the few African students who succeeded in surmounting these obstacles, there was the final possibility of attending one of the several high schools in each territory. To fulfil the seven-year programme was a virtual impossibility, and the number of Africans who were able to go to a university in Portugal or abroad was negligible. In 1955 in Moçambique 240,000 students were enrolled in *ensino rudimentar*, 3,729 in state or church elementary schools, and 10 in high schools. Four years later, the number in the *ensino* programme was 390,000 (but only 9,500 passed the third-year examinations in that year), 5,400 in elementary schools, and 41 enrolled in high schools. The estimated illiteracy rate in Portuguese Africa in 1960 was between 92 and 95 per cent.

Technical schools, seminaries and private schools made their small contribution; but where there was not enough money, not enough schools, and not enough teachers, the work of education was difficult and slow. Besides, there was not sufficient official interest in education. The Salazar government did not want the African majority to become more politically conscious than the rural majority in Portugal. For the semi-literate peasant class envisaged by the Salazarian sociology, an *ensino rudimentar* was enough, a kind of basic psychological assimilation. For the few students who struggled on, an intensive Portuguese education could be expected to produce an assimilated Portuguese citizen.

Government health programmes were no more adequate. A programme of establishing small infirmaries and maternity hospitals in the interior of Angola and Moçambique was undertaken in the 1950s. But again, progress was slow, the training of personnel uncertain, and the contribution of the medical outposts insignificant. Most of the medical personnel and facilities in the colonies served the white population. Occasional campaigns of inoculation reached the countryside, and teams of dedicated public health men made a contribution to the welfare of Portuguese Africans; but the effects were sporadic and limited.

Could Portugal succeed in Africa? While Angola and Moçambique were making economic progress, and while the various programmes for the assimilation of the African population made a modest start, voices of protest began to be heard. By 1960 Portuguese Africa had become an important international issue and the African battle-line had moved to the frontiers of the territories. What were the practical hopes for maintaining white nationalist colonies in Africa? Could there be an accommodation with African aspirations?

The answer was clear and prompt. In April 1960, for instance, Dr Castro Fernandes, President of the Executive Committee of the National Union, said:

We are in Africa and it is our duty to stay there, for ourselves, for the West to which we belong, for the peoples which have been entrusted to us and which have mingled with us in the same moral unity.[1]

A year before, Dr Salazar had spoken on the African emergence (or 'conflagration', as he put it) and Portugal's position:

there is a work of human understanding and sympathy which from generation to generation builds up interracial contact that is invaluable. This is the basis for the solution of the problems of Africa, for without it they can have no lasting solution. This is more than our conviction: it is our way of being.[2]

Portugal would not go under. Unity and integration were the policies to be stressed and continued. As early as 1951 the government, with a cautious eye to the future, realized that now was not the time for talk of colonies and empires, and by a legislative declaration the colonies had become overseas provinces, a term that had more significance in legislation than in reality.

Gradually, with considerable caution, the Portuguese government, sensitive if not responsive to changing sentiments on European rule in Africa, began to strengthen its bulwarks. By the Organic Law of 1955, the establishment of *concelhos*, or units of local government, was provided for in what were almost totally African areas, the change from post or circumscription to *concelho* to take place when a region was deemed sufficiently indoctrinated. The responsibilities of the Legislative Council (a white advisory board) were increased. The *regime do indigenato* was abolished in São Tomé and Príncipe in 1953. In the countryside the token powers of village leaders were slightly increased and instructions urged administrators and chiefs of post to harmonize relations between the races. Attempts were made to correct the serious abuses in the contract labour system, which was now openly criticized in Portugal as well as in the rest of the world.

[1] 'The presence of Portugal in Africa', *Portugal: An Informative Review*, July–Aug. 1960, **4**, no. 4, p. 262.
[2] António de Oliveira Salazar, 'Portugal's position with reference to Europe, America and Africa: speech delivered by the Prime Minister, Professor Oliveira Salazar, before the chairmen of the district committees of the National Union on May 23 1959', *Portugal: An Informative Review*, May–June 1959, **3**, no. 3, p. 133.

The distinction in Portuguese colonial administration between *indígena* and *não-indígena* came under official scrutiny, and a sort of middle ground was defined for Africans emerging from one culture into another. To these people in transit, it was argued, the rights of Portuguese citizenship could be extended. The high standards of formal assimilation would hardly serve Portugal in critical times ahead, and the official way was cleared for a kind of bestowal of Portuguese citizenship on great numbers of inhabitants of Angola and Moçambique—to strengthen the argument that these were indeed Portuguese provinces.

Fanciful though the discussions and tentative plans seemed at the moment, they were the beginnings of Portugal's preparation for troubled days to come; in their twisted remoteness they were perhaps an unrealized acknowledgement that some final accommodation would have to be made.

An extension of this policy of integration was the attempt made in the late 1950s to join with Brazil in the formation of an amorphous commonwealth of Portuguese-speaking nations. Treaties of friendship and consultation were signed between the two countries, and a sustained flurry of visits and cultural exchanges served to strengthen the public ties between the two countries. Brazil stood to gain nothing in particular from the proposals, but for Portugal the formation of a commonwealth was seen as a resounding demonstration of the unity of the Lusitanian world. Brazil, with its Negro, mulatto and Portuguese population, was in every sense a multiracial community (such as Angola and Moçambique were supposed to be) that would offer convincing proof of the non-racial quality of Portuguese policies. Essentially the commonwealth was a propaganda creation, a fantasy to counter the rising attack on Portuguese rule in Africa. But the men in Lisbon probably had the notion in the back of their minds that if the moment came when Portugal could not hold on in Africa, the commonwealth could provide the framework for colonial independence. By 1960, however, the plans for such a Lusitanian community had foundered.

In Africa itself Portugal worked to consolidate its relations with the governments of the Congo, of Southern Rhodesia, and of South Africa. A good feeling between the various states of southern Africa arose. Their common military, economic and geographic interests grew stronger during the 1950s. With the departure of Belgium from the Congo, the Portuguese territories, Southern Rhodesia and

South Africa became the last redoubts of white government in black Africa.

In Europe, Salazar's diplomacy had been discretely skilful. After a decade of sympathy with Germany and Italy and a cautious neutrality during World War II, Portugal moved into the Western Alliance, becoming a member of NATO in 1949. Her relations with France, Great Britain and the United States, based on a variety of interests, economic, cultural and military, were cordial throughout the 1950s. Now Portugal began to put forth the argument that, just as NATO was the bulwark against communist expansion in Europe, so Christian Portuguese Africa was the bulwark against the potential communist threat in Africa, one of the last outposts of the Western world. Until 1960 Portugal's position in Africa found fairly uncritical acceptance in London, Paris and Washington, and during the harsh debates in the United Nations in the last years of the decade, Portugal could count on the substantial, though sometimes silent, support of her powerful allies. Military assistance to Portugal through NATO permitted Portugal to strengthen her defences in Africa.

Thus, by 1960 Portugal was, in a sense, prepared, and the course of Portuguese policy in Africa was set. Echoing the words of President Thomaz, Dr Salazar addressed the National Assembly in November:

Surely they [the Portuguese people] are not going to suppose that the fate of millions of men, the order and peace of their way of life, the fruit of their work, the principles of civilization they have adopted, can be handed over to the emptiness of speeches at meetings and the anarchy of the so-called movements of liberation...

A multiracial society is therefore possible, whether of Luso-American stock as in Brazil...or Luso-African stock, as we see in Angola and Moçambique ...It would be most unwise for us now to innovate with practices, feelings, and concepts different from those which have been the secret of the work we have achieved and which are still the best safeguard for the future.

I do not see that we can rest in our labours nor can we have any other care than to hold with one hand our plough and with the other our sword... Great sacrifice will be called for, as well as the most absolute devotion, and, if necessary, also the blood from our veins.[1]

[1] António de Oliveira Salazar, *Portugal and the anti-colonialist compaign: speech delivered by H.E. the Prime Minister Professor Oliveira Salazar, before the National Assembly at the session held on November 30th 1960* (Lisbon, 1960), pp. 11–12.

BIBLIOGRAPHY

Ameal, João. 'Os três chefes do Império', *O mundo português*, May 1934, **1**.
'Mostruário do Império', *O mundo português*, March 1934, **1**.
Azevedo, Eduardo de. *Terra da esperança: romance duma viagem a Angola*. Lisbon, 1954.
Boxer, Charles R. *Race relations in the Portuguese colonial empire, 1415–1825*. Oxford, Clarendon Press, 1963.
Cabral, Morais. 'A vitória do nosso espírito colonizador', *O mundo português*, May 1939, **6**.
Cunha, Joaquim Moreira da Silva. *O trabalho indígena: estudo de direito colonial*. 2nd ed. Lisbon, 1955.
'A estadia do sr. Ministro das Colónias nas terras africanas do Império', *O mundo português*, 1943, **10**.
Hammond, Richard J. *Portugal's African problem: some economic facets*. New York, 1962.
Monteiro, Armindo. 'Portugal in Africa', *African Affairs*, 1939, **38**.
Portugal. Laws, statutes, etc. *Nova legislação ultramarina*. 2 vols. Lisbon, 1953.
'The presence of Portugal in Africa', *Portugal: An Informative Review*, July–Aug. 1960, **4**, no. 4.
Salazar, António de Oliveira. *Portugal and the anti-colonialist campaign: speech delivered by H.E. the Prime Minister Professor Oliveira Salazar, before the National Assembly at the session held on November 30th 1960*. Lisbon, 1960.
'Portugal's position with reference to Europe, America and Africa: speech delivered by the Prime Minister, Professor Oliveira Salazar, before the chairmen of the district committees of the National Union on May 23rd 1959', *Portugal: An Informative Review*, May–June 1959, **3**, no. 3.

CHAPTER 5

BELGIAN RULE IN THE CONGO AND THE ASPIRATIONS OF THE 'EVOLUE' CLASS

by ROGER ANSTEY

By the end of the Second World War a number of observers of the Congo scene had come to see the position of the Congolese *évolué* as one of the colony's major problems. The veteran Jesuit, Father J. van Wing, drew attention to it;[1] it was a subject of debate in the columns of the Elisabethville newspaper, *L'Essor du Congo*, when that journal, in open forum, was conducting an inquiry into the shortcomings of colonial policy. A plea of the Luluabourg *évolués* for consideration of their situation, written in the aftermath of the Luluabourg Force Publique mutiny of 1944, likewise received considerable publicity.

The purpose of this essay is to consider the nature and aspirations of this *évolué* class, the policies and attitudes which particularly affected it, and the *évolué* reaction to European culture, to colonial rule and colonial attitudes. The focus of attention is the period from the Second World War onward.[2]

What precisely is meant by the term *évolué*? Crawford Young has pointed out that the term is imprecise, but suggests that in the period after the Second World War 'anyone with some post-primary education could probably be considered a reasonable candidate'. Young adds, however, that 'any form of successful entry into the new world created

[1] See esp. J. van Wing, 'La situation actuelle des populations congolaises', Institut Royal Colonial Belge, *Bulletin des Séances*, 1945, **16**, no. 3, pp. 584–605; J. van Wing, 'La formation d'une élite noire au Congo belge', Centre d'Etude des Problèmes Sociaux Indigènes, *Bulletin* (superseded by *Problèmes Sociaux Congolais*), 1947–8, no. 5, pp. 8–22.

[2] This essay must borrow somewhat from my *King Leopold's legacy: the Congo under Belgian rule, 1908–1960* (London, Oxford University Press, 1966); see esp. Chs. 10, 11 and 12. But I have attempted to examine the development of *évolué* feeling in much more detail, and have devoted greater attention to the unfolding of the *immatriculation* policy, the highwater mark of measures aimed at benefiting the *évolués*. Moreover, certain sources have been used which were not available to me when *King Leopold's legacy* was being written, whilst other sources have been used more intensively. But it would be idle to disguise that I have not worked systematically over the periodical and other material likely to shed light on *évolué* thought and action in post-war Congo.

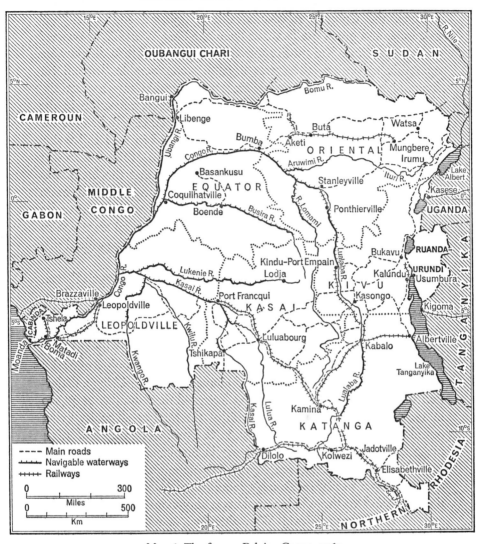

Map 6. The former Belgian Congo, 1960

by the arrival of the colonizer, be it commercial or intellectual, would be relevant', whilst 'subjective self-identification would need to be included as well as objective attainment':[1] a man might truly be an *évolué* if he thought himself one. Representative figures were the clerk, the male nurse, the teacher.

[1] *Politics in the Congo: decolonization and independence* (Princeton University Press, 1965), pp. 196–7.

Given the Congo's relative wealth of mineral and agricultural resources, and given the fact that from the First World War onward market conditions had much more often encouraged than discouraged economic expansion, there was usually a considerable demand for African labour. In addition, there was an appreciable 'non-market' demand for Congolese to serve in such capacities as conscripts in the Force Publique. Whilst the original demand could clearly be only for completely untrained men, some of these learned to read and write, and even became clerks. More important, the sons of those who first forsook traditional society (this is not to imply that the break was complete, or never able to be reversed) frequently acquired more education and were less likely to return to their villages, other than for visits. The extent of this movement away from the rural areas was so marked in some regions as to lead, from 1924 onward, to official disquiet and measures designed to restrict emigration.

But such was the relative intensity of economic development that an increasing proportion of men came to live outside the sway of custom. By 1939, 441,634 men, or about 14 per cent of the adult male population, were officially regarded as living outside the village. By 1947 the figure had risen to 637,878 and the percentage to 20·6;[1] by 1958 the figure was 956,615 and the percentage 26·8.[2] Evidently only a minority of these men were *évolués*, as defined above by Young. Using a definition very broadly similar, van Wing hazarded their number as 40,000 in 1947,[3] that is, about one-sixteenth of the total of all males living outside the sway of custom, whilst V. G. Pons, in a sample of 1,894 males of sixteen years and over living in Stanleyville in 1952–3, discerned 176 white-collar employees. His definition of 'white-collar employee' was similar to Young's definition of *évolué*, and the proportion of *évolués* to the whole sample was about one-eleventh.[4] By the end of the Second World War, therefore, a sufficient number of *évolués* had emerged for them properly to be termed a class. What

[1] Léopold Mottoulle, *et al.*, 'Rapport sur l'hygiène et la démographie', in Belgium, Congrès Colonial National, 6th Sess. (Sénat de Belgique, 4–5 Oct. 1947), *Comptes rendus des séances et rapports préparatoires* (Brussels, 1948), p. 97.

[2] Belgium, Parlement, Chambre des Représentants, *Rapport annuel sur l'administration de la colonie du Congo belge pendant l'année 1958* (Brussels, 1959), p. 69.

[3] Van Wing, 'La formation d'une élite noire,' p. 9.

[4] V. G. Pons, 'The growth of Stanleyville and the composition of its African population', in *Social implications of urbanization and industrialization in Africa south of the Sahara*, Daryll Forde, ed. (Paris, 1956), p. 267.

kind of life did they lead in the town, and how did urban life generate new aspirations?

The life of the urban Congolese, even the illiterate labourer, was vitally different from that of his brother in the village. The basis of this difference was that the family, the clan, the village community no longer provided the context and the sanctions for work, for recreation, for morality, for religious observances, for human relationships, for authority—though they still had an influence. But the departure from tradition was most marked in the case of the *évolué*. This can be seen in several, specific, areas of his life. For instance, the most intimate of all relations, marriage, was, under customary law, 'a combination of a contract between two persons of different sex, creating between them a common life, with reciprocal rights and duties, and a contract between groups of relatives which makes the union valid for them, assures their support of it and legitimizes the children'.[1] But in the town the institution underwent major change—especially amongst *évolués*. Pierre Clément who, with Pons and Mme Xydias, undertook a study of the social effects of urbanization in Stanleyville in 1952–3, showed that in marriages contracted in the town the bond was usually much less 'a contract between groups of relatives' and was 'tending to become simply a union of two persons'.[2] Evidence from Elisabethville in 1957–8 corroborates the spread of this new conception of marriage by spelling out a changing attitude to the disposal of a deceased's estate. In a test given to a sample of 254 *évolués*, Marc Richelle found that only 16 per cent approved simple obedience to custom, whereby the deceased's possessions should go to his brother, whereas 49 per cent favoured a division between brother and wife, and 35 per cent approved the inheritance of everything by the wife.[3]

Again, whereas in traditional society marriage outside the tribe was rare, Clément found, in a sample of seventy-seven case histories in Stanleyville, that as many as 32·5 per cent were intertribal unions. The percentage was markedly higher in that part of the sample situated in the more advanced, more *évolué* of the two districts from which the overall sample was taken—45·9 per cent as opposed to 27·1 per cent. Richelle, for his part, found that only 29 per cent of his sample of 254

---

[1] Albert Sohier, quoted in Pierre Clément, 'Social patterns of urban life (Stanleyville survey)', in *Social implications of industrialization and urbanization*, p. 383.
[2] *Ibid.*, pp. 422–3.
[3] Marc Richelle, *Aspects psychologiques de l'acculturation* (Elisabethville, 1960), p. 163.

évolués in Katanga approved marriage to a simple village girl of the same tribe. Thirty per cent approved of marriage to an educated girl, regardless of her tribe, whilst 41 per cent favoured marriage to a girl of the same tribe, but one who was accustomed to modern life. Moreover, choice of an uneducated, customary wife was rarely approved by the youngest age-group in the sample.[1]

Though the evidence is less precise, there are a number of indications that moral and material factors discouraged polygamy amongst town dwellers, and especially amongst the more educated. But lest one suppose that the towns of the Congo in the 1940s and 1950s were witnessing a smooth transition to a Western type of marriage, one should notice that divorce was easy and frequently resorted to, that concubinage and prostitution were sometimes widespread, and that the matrilineal system, where it existed—in Stanleyville most of the tribes represented were patrilineal—seems for obvious reasons to have offered more serious obstacles to a Western type of marriage.

For the town-dwelling *évolué*, the pattern of friendships was also changing. Clément asked nineteen persons (admittedly a small sample, in which one respondent was not even an *évolué*) to name those whom they would choose as next-door neighbours, and also to indicate their best friends and the friends of their respective wives, all in order of preference. The respondents as a whole chose 52 per cent of their preferred neighbours from their own tribe and indicated that 41 per cent of their friends and 39 per cent of their wives' friends belonged likewise to the respondents' tribes and the wives' tribes, respectively. When the desired neighbours, and friends, were categorized by socio-professional class, however, a more telling picture emerged, for 79 per cent of the chosen neighbours, 82 per cent of the friends and 77 per cent of the wives' friends were from the respondents' own class. Residence patterns in Stanleyville told a similar story. The *évolués* were less likely than their more backward brethren to cluster together in adjoining lots with others of the same tribe.[2]

In the post-war years, too, the non-tribal *évolué* association came to play an increasing part in the life of some of the educated. Some of these groups were alumni societies, such as the Association des Anciens

---

[1] Richelle, *Aspects psychologiques de l'acculturation*, pp. 161, 164–5.
[2] V. G. Pons, 'The changing significance of ethnic affiliation and of Westernization in the African settlement patterns in Stanleyville (Belgian Congo)', in *Social implications of urbanization and industrialization*, pp. 638–66.

Elèves des Pères de Scheut (ADAPES). For many years—ADAPES was founded in 1925—these bodies had little more life than Old Boys associations commonly have elsewhere; but from the end of the war onward they concerned themselves more self-consciously with the needs and problems of the *évolué* class and seem often to have had a substantial active membership, with branches and local committees in the major towns. Although in practice a man could become an 'old boy' even if he had not gone to 'the old school', some of these associations were formally open to all *évolués*—for example, the Association des Evolués de Stanleyville, formed in 1944.

Apart from Protestant or Roman Catholic societies, of which the *évolué*, amongst others, might be a member, tribal associations were also bodies in which he played a part. In these most important of all urban associations the *évolués* always had a significant role—their skills were necessary for the running of the association—and sometimes, as with the Leopoldville Bakongo, amongst whom traditional leadership had much declined in prestige, the major directing role. Membership of a tribal association by a clerk or male nurse was in no sense incompatible with membership of an *évolué* association.

A further new relationship into which the town-dwelling Congolese man normally entered was with an employer or firm, usually European. Thus urban life involved a whole new series of relationships, relationships which in some ways had a more disturbing effect on the educated than on the uneducated. The horizons of the simple labourer being limited, the boundary of his concern was drawn closer. Reasonable treatment by his employer, satisfactory living conditions—matters such as these are likely to have been his main preoccupation. For his children, perhaps, he nurtured the hope that they might one day enter the world of the European—meanwhile he would seek in membership of his tribal association the closest approximation available to the enveloping comfort of the traditional group. For the educated—or partly educated— man it was different. Though to an extent he shared the experience of the uneducated, he had by his training and work become more directly aware of European ways and culture, and had been drawn more closely towards the new way of life. For this very reason, and whilst he was a member of the Congolese urban community as a whole, and usually, indeed, had a continuing link with his ancestral village as well, these affiliations were not in themselves sufficient to satisfy him.

Two important questions therefore arise. What were the *évolué*'s aspirations in this situation; and how far did Belgian policies, and the general European comportment towards him, satisfy them? It is clear that the *évolué* in the immediate post-war years was conscious of belonging to a different category from the mass of Congolese, that he felt acutely the failure of Belgian policy to distinguish between the ordinary person and himself, that he wanted a separate status and that he wanted closer relations with Europeans.

The consciousness of belonging to a separate group could sometimes be painful. 'Cruelle équivoque' was the title of a contribution to the *évolué* monthly, *La Voix du Congolais*, in which the author describes the situation of his fellows. 'Challenged on all sides, sniped at in every sense, they feel themselves like weathercocks pirouetting on unsteady pivots'.[1] Even the more restrained 1944 petition of the Luluabourg *évolués*, which attained some publicity in the heart-searching which followed the mutiny of the Force Publique in that town, had as its first grievance that the administration would not recognize that a separate social class of *évolués* existed.[2] Whilst M. Mondjeni-Mobe, in *La Voix du Congolais*, dwelt on the psychological and cultural tensions of the *évolué*, the Luluabourg petition had earlier pleaded for separate treatment in specific ways, all stemming from the premise that *évolués* did not wish to be lumped with 'an ignorant and backward mass', as the petitioners termed it. They should have periodic right of access to the provincial governor, a separate, weekly, hearing of their disputes by the local administrator, better houses and separate accommodation in public transport—and in prison.

[1] J. Mondjeni-Mobe, 'Cruelle équivoque', *La Voix du Congolais*, 1950, no. 6, pp. 599–601. Citation of this journal inevitably raises the question of the value, as evidence of *évolué* thinking, of a periodical created by the Information Service, whose officials continued to exercise oversight of the Congolese editor, A. R. Bolamba. Doubts certainly increase when one discovers only limited mention in the issues of the late 1950s of the hectic party political activity of that time. Clearly what went into *La Voix du Congolais* was controlled—though a well-informed Congolese has told me that this censorship was much eased from 1955–6 onward. As against this it should be remembered that the journal was founded—in 1945—precisely in order to give *évolués* a forum and that there was an influential section in the administration which wanted the *évolués* to have a better deal and so would welcome the pleas for better treatment and the complaints at abuses, which constantly recur in the journal. Whether it reflected *all* that *évolués* were thinking is more open to doubt.
[2] Belgium, Parlement, Chambre des Représentants, *Projet de loi contenant le budget ordinaire du Congo belge pour l'exercice 1948. Rapport fait au nom de la Commission des Colonies*, by M. Housiaux, 1947–8 Sess. (Documents parlementaires, No. 662; Brussels, 1948), pp. 31–5; Antoine Rubbens, 'La solution de "l'intégration des élites": plaidoyer pour le sauvage', in *Dettes de guerre*, Antoine Rubbens, ed. (Elisabethville, 1945), p. 128, f.n.

It would not be fair to dismiss the Luluabourg petitioners, nor Congolese *évolués* generally, as wanting simply an improved material position. Just as the Luluabourg petition contained, as negative protest, strong resentment at being publicly insulted by being termed 'macaque',[1] for example, so there is abundant evidence of resentment at being so used by Europeans.[2] 'Sale nègre', 'sale imbécile' and 'espèce de singe' were linked with 'macaque' as terms which were, understandably, particularly resented.[3] 'How many readers of this journal have not experienced a thousand vexations in the course of the various interrogations to which they are subjected?' asked M. Kashamura (a future leader of the Centre de Regroupement Africain [CEREA] party) in the columns of *La Voix du Congolais*.[4] In the same journal the editor criticized the climate of discrimination that was the context of vexation and abuse:

Certainly racial discrimination is legally prohibited in the Belgian Congo. It nonetheless exists in fact. In cinemas, hotels, boats, trains, churches and other public places all the Africans are either excluded or clearly separated from the Europeans.[5]

The intense resentment at insults seems to have been directly proportional to the *évolué* yearning to be initiated into European ways and techniques and to be accepted by Europeans. Certainly the literature has considerable evidence of such yearning. Note, for example, Bolamba's editorial plea in *La Voix du Congolais*:

And as the white man in fact enjoys a superior education to ours, is it not up to him to incline towards us to read what is in our hearts and to learn better how to know us? What difficulties would be flattened out and suppressed if our civilizers knew us better, and tried to understand us more.[6]

The *évolué* feeling of having been deceived, said *Le Congo Pratique*, was not 'dictated by ambition to be above his brothers [a charge frequently made]; the Congolese (*évolué*) desires above all meaningful relations between white and black'.[7] J. Franki, writing in the same number of the

---

[1] *Ibid.*
[2] See, for instance, Belgium, Sénat, 'Procès-verbal de la visite au cercle des évolués à Paulis', appendix to *Rapport de la mission sénatoriale au Congo* (Brussels, 1947), p. 268.
[3] *Le Congo Pratique*, Nov. 1953. This was apparently a privately run *évolué* journal which appeared somewhat intermittently during the 1950s.
[4] *La Voix du Congolais*, Dec. 1952, p. 745.
[5] *Ibid.*, Oct. 1952, p. 587.   [6] *Ibid.*, Feb. 1948, p. 54.
[7] *Le Congo Pratique*, March 1953.

same journal, makes a direct plea to Belgians to reach out to his fellow *évolués*:

Make contact with them and they will open their heart to you. Delusions will be dissipated and relations will become quite different...A young child believes unquestioningly what his father says...But when he has become a young man he has the right to express his wishes to his begetter without being regarded as rebellious...

I conclude...Belgians, give us your hand; we shall trust you like brothers and you will find in us collaborators whom you will appreciate.[1]

Or again, in the words of a contributor to *La Voix du Congolais*:

We must seek to love each other, and to love each other we must know each other; to know each other we must come closer to each other, and speak to each other. It is only by knowing each other, in loving each other, that we can make relations develop harmoniously.[2]

Behind all these pleas of the post-war years is the assertion that Belgian policies in the Congo had taken no account of the fact that a class was emerging significantly different from the untutored mass. The assertion is largely justified. For instance, it *was* the case that there was no separate provision for *évolués* in public transport, hospitals, etc.; there was no separate quarter of the town for them, and they were forbidden to live in the European quarter; they were subject to the sanctions of the *contrat de travail*, which bound Congolese wage earners generally, and which was increasingly resented as being less favourable than the *contrat d'emploi* governing a European's employment; they were rarely given any significant part in the government of the *centres extra-coutumiers* which had been created from 1931 onward as the unit of urban administration. Separate treatment was thus denied to the *évolués*—and this despite the fact that, in principle, there had been provision since a decree of 1892 for the emergent African to secure 'immatriculation aux régistres de la population civilisée', which would bring him under the civil law applying to Europeans. But far from this provision's broadening into a fuller assimilation, this early measure fell into disuse.

At a more everyday level, European attitudes toward *évolués* often more than reflected legislation founded on a simple distinction between natives and non-natives. For this there is not only the evidence of bitter *évolué* feeling in their periodicals, but the testimony of officials

[1] *Le Congo Pratique*, March 1953.   [2] *La Voix du Congolais*, March 1952, pp. 128–31.

and of other Europeans. Thus, the colonial laywer, M. Piron, in a paper submitted to the 1947 Colonial Congress, wrote of the *évolués*: 'although they daily apply themselves to drawing nearer to the European, the latter often snubs them, pokes fun at their efforts or at the very least, is unaware of them'.[1] The full commission of the Congress on the *évolué* question 'was unanimous in establishing that too many Europeans in Africa do not show towards *évolués* the consideration to which they have a right'.[2] A telling indication of what *évolués* might experience from Europeans when they sought 'to raise themselves' is in some chance words in *La Voix du Congolais*. Warmly approving the action of M. Dumont, the Procureur-Général of the colony, in taking four *évolués* to the theatre as his guests, the editor felt impelled to add that the European audience 'showed themselves correct and courteous towards them'.[3]

The result of ardent aspirations' being snubbed, as they often were, is not far to seek. M. Met den Anxt, a Kivu settler leader, found in 1950 (to his surprise) that a group of *évolués* was strongly critical 'of the mass of the European population in the sense that they think this mass has done very little to civilize the natives and that only the missions have accomplished this task'.[4] (Certainly it would appear that it was the missions who showed the most active concern for the *évolués*—it was a natural part of their pastoral and educational activity.) M. Piron, before the 1947 Colonial Congress, put it that 'rejected by the Europeans, ill at ease in the bosom of native society with which the law persists in identifying him, *évolués* constitute from a social point of view what refugees represent at the national level'.[5] Albert Sohier put it more graphically: 'At the moment when, responding to the appeal: "Civilize yourselves", some have replied: "Here we are", they have found themselves before a closed door'. This, he added succinctly, was 'in reality what one calls the problem of the *évolués*'.[6]

[1] Pierre Piron, 'L'évolution des populations détribalisées', Belgium, Congrès Colonial National, 6th Sess. (Sénat de Belgique, 4–5 Oct. 1947), *Comptes rendus des séances et rapports préparatoires* (Brussels, 1948), p. 453.

[2] 'Les évolués' (Report of Eighth Commission), in Belgium, Congrès Colonial National, 6th Sess. (Sénat de Belgique, 4–5 Oct. 1947), *Comptes rendus des séances et rapports préparatoires* (Brussels, 1948), p. 424.

[3] *La Voix du Congolais*, Oct. 1950, p. 622.

[4] *L'Echo de Kivu*, 29 Sept. 1950.

[5] Piron, 'L'évolution des populations détribaliseés', p. 453.

[6] Albert Sohier, 'Le problème des indigènes évolués et la commission du statut des Congolaises civilisés', *Zaïre*, Oct. 1949, 3, no. 8, p. 844.

This rebuff took place at various levels, and Father Placide Tempels, the author of *Bantu Philosophy*,[1] offers an interpretation at the most profound level of all.

The African considers the white man as possessing a life higher than his own. He considers him as possessing a life which he communicates to him, which he 'brings to birth' in him. He is not only loyal towards the white man who has proved his strength and power, a mysterious and external power, but he esteems in us the inmost capacity of being, a dominant existence, the ontological quality itself. He expresses himself by saying ingenuously, according to the logic of his traditional thought, that the white man is his father and mother.

Some, Tempels went on, thought that by 'adoption' by a particular European they had acquired a new affiliation; others remained convinced that the Europeans brought only harm.

But those who have really experienced disillusion are the young. They have rejected the counsel of their elders. They have rallied to the whites who have become their father and mother. They have thought themselves able, under the influence of the white, and with every certainty and assurance, to dispense with the institutions of the clan, to reject their traditional ontology which we call magic, and to become participants in the vital power of the white man.

But in recent years the colonizer

leaves him [the African] to himself for the ideas, in all the immense work of adaptation of his ancient civilisation to our modern civilisation. This very complex process of development, which is so difficult that no white man can even manage to describe it in writing, still less to live it, is imperiously demanded of this new native society. Formerly there was a semblance of direction of native life by the State and by the generality of whites; now the *évolué* sees that this task of direction has not been continued; his thought is neglected; his soul does not receive nourishment any more; he will be as a beast, although he formerly believed himself a free man, a thinking man, organised in the clan, possessed even of a metaphysic, possessing a will to prosper, for fertility, for the progress of the clan. Today he sees how much the opportunism of government has lacked a principle of native policy. He sees that we have an opportunity to degrade him into a mere member of the masses instead of raising him up by a system of thought and an élite...

He had thrown in his lot with us in order to become one of us; instead of being accepted as a son of the family, he only becomes a wage earner. He

[1] Trans. Colin King (Paris, 1959).

now knows himself to be definitely rejected, disowned as a son, classed as unassimilable...

And so everywhere, in place of a frank adaptation, of an assimilation of hearts and of ideas, of an acquisition of the citizenship and of the law of the fatherland and of nationality, and of this profound [sense of] community which the native locates in the metaphysical domain, there is no other bond for him than payment, than pennies if not halfpennies which, from one devaluation to the rest, he himself learns to throw away...

In place of friendly relations one offers him, in return for all that he and his have to offer, a new domination, harder than that which his ancestors knew.[1]

With the ending of the Second World War, official Belgian attitudes began to change. The provisions of the United Nations charter on dependent territories jolted official thinking in Belgium, as elsewhere. It was decided that something must be done for the *évolués*. Young, indeed, asserts: 'that élite satisfaction was the central issue in colonial society'.[2] Indications of this new concern included the foundation in 1945 of the journal from which we have already quoted— *La Voix du Congolais*—and official encouragement of the establishment of *Cercles d'Evolués* in centres up and down the colony. At the end of 1946 there were 113. From 1947 eight persons were appointed to the Conseil du Gouvernement to represent African interests; all of them, from 1951, were Africans, and some were *évolués*. Then, in 1948, a new status was created—not so much for men who might be termed *évolués* as for those who might more justly be described as *évoluants*. Any African who was literate, who was not a polygamist, and who had not within the previous five years been convicted of certain specified offences, together with certain illiterates of distinction, could apply for the *carte du mérite civique*. This entitled the holder, notably, to be judged in the *tribunal de territoire*, which was presided over by a European, and to a special position in regard to the acquisition of real property. Moreover, the administration was clearly feeling some sense of urgency about the whole matter, for the normal laborious legislative process was bypassed by the device of an *ordonnance législative* of the governor-general.

But the really radical proposal was to create a new status for the *évolué*. In theory the basis for a separate legal status had existed since

[1] Placide Tempels, 'La philosophie de la rébellion', in *Dettes de guerre*, Antoine Rubbens, ed. (Elisabethville, 1945), pp. 17–23 *passim*.
[2] Young, *Politics in the Congo*, p. 74.

1892, when provision was made for the registration, or *immatriculation*, of Africans who were prepared to be regulated by the terms of the Belgian civil code. But this first attempt towards creating a new status for detribalized Africans, though enshrined in Article 4 of the *Charte Coloniale* of 1908, conferred no worth-while privileges and the procedure fell into disuse. Nor did anything come of a proposal in 1923 to reform *immatriculation*, nor of another attempt in the 1930s, when it was sought to create through *immatriculation* a new, intermediate category, distinct both from Europeans and from the mass of Africans. Now, in 1948, Colonial Minister Pierre Wigny appointed a commission '"charged with the study in all its aspects of the problem of the status of the civilised Congolese population..."'[1] The leading spirit on the commission was Antoine Sohier, who had been a magistrate in the Congo before becoming a magistrate in Belgium and who was very much in the tradition of the colonial magistracy, which saw itself as the protector of the Congolese—over against the administration if necessary. He was also a member of the Conseil Colonial, the body to which all major colonial legislation had to be referred. Sohier clearly was convinced of the importance of the question, and perhaps because of his influence the commission went quickly to work. The basic principle underlying its recommendations was succinctly summarized by Sohier in one of the number of articles in which he publicized the *immatriculation* question and the work of the commission:

The Congolese who has acquired European civilisation will be placed, integrally, by *immatriculation*, under the régime [governing] non-natives to whom he is in actual fact assimilated. The other *évolués* will receive, from the different legal and social points of view, special intermediate treatment adapted to their development, to their capacity and to their particular interests.[2]

This second category of *évolués* was, then, to advance in status by piecemeal alteration to existing laws which, as Sohier reminded his readers, were 'founded on the distinction between natives and non-natives'.[3] The most radical proposal, however, was undoubtedly the one about *immatriculation* with its explicit corollary of full assimilation. Quite specific was a simple, draft *article unique*: 'Congolese *immatriculés* are governed by the legal and statutory dispositions of the Colony

[1] Sohier, 'Le problème des indigènes évolués', p. 854.
[2] Albert Sohier, 'Le statut des Congolais civilisés', *Zaïre*, Oct. 1950, **4**, no. 10, p. 816.
[3] Sohier, 'Le problème des indigènes évolués', p. 844.

applicable to non-natives of metropolitan status'.[1] At a touch, *immatriculés* would acquire the status of Europeans in any field covered by legislation distinguishing between European and native—and these included housing, type of employment contract and schooling.

But the *article unique* never saw the light of day. When the draft decree was submitted to the Conseil de Gouvernement in July 1950, it met with hostile comments from some of the non-official Europeans. No decision was taken at that session of the council. On the grounds that the papers had only been made available to the council a few days before it assembled, its members resolved that, though they agreed with the principle of the proposed changes—and it is difficult not to feel that this 'agreement in principle' had the usual connotation of disagreement with every particular, concrete expression of the principle—the papers should be referred to the detailed examination of the Députation Permanente, or standing committee of the council. This body in turn would convene special meetings of provincial councils to assist them in making their recommendations. According to the *Courrier d'Afrique*, the Leopoldville Catholic daily, the provincial councils gave 'contradictory and often passionate' opinions concerning the draft decree. The extraordinary session of the Kivu council, for example, took place on 6 September. An influential settler, M. Met den Anxt, took a distinctly moderate line, but another settler, M. Castadet, expressed the more general settler view that the *évolués* were not ready for *immatriculation*. (Interestingly it seems to have been assumed that all *évolués* would enjoy the new status.) The one Congolese who spoke was himself an *évolué*. He gave a reasoned advocacy of the draft decree; but his assertion that the Congolese élite 'ardently desires to escape from ancestral customs' can only have given support to those who opposed *immatriculation* on the grounds that it would create a separate, rootless caste. The most constructively liberal speech came from Father Guy Mosmans, future author of the perceptive and challenging *L'Eglise à l'heure de l'Afrique*.

In reports of the debate in the colony generally (and remember that the means of expression open to Congolese were very limited), it seems to have been the European settler view which predominated. The view of Ucol (Union pour la Colonisation) may not be untypical. No one refuses to admit the African to the great Belgian family; but warm though the welcome may be, the Congolese 'is not yet able to

---

[1] Belgian Congo, Conseil de Gouvernement, *Compte rendu...* (Leopoldville, 1950).

penetrate intimately and completely into the personality of his civiliser' because 'the personality of the civilised person...is still not open to the understanding of the black man'. Certainly there is equality of intelligence but there is a real difference in moral values. Those of the European tend to the constructive, to achievement and to edification, whilst from European society springs the capacity for civic virtue, philosophy, altruism, investment and saving. The Congolese is cour-ageous and loyal, willingly follows a good example; but he has inheri-ted no spiritual or material heritage from his ancestors. It is the mission of the Belgians to elevate the African, but the work of developing his qualities and aptitudes is gradual, and assimilation must, therefore, come by stages.[1]

It does not appear that views such as these were strongly combated in the Députation Permanente, and Professor Guy Malengreau believes that it was there that the real damage to the *article unique* was done. One can only conclude that the liberal Governor-General Jungers either did not attach enough importance to the moral effect of the recommenda-tions of the Députation, or that he was unable to generate much liberal enthusiasm amongst its official members. Nor is this wholly surprising, for the attitudes of civil servants do not seem to have been very much more liberal than those of the settler population. The ranks of both included many devoted paternalists and, I am persuaded, a fair number of coarse and brutal men at the lower levels. The former were not necessarily more likely to approve the offer of *equality* of status than the latter. Amongst many specific examples of a basic illiberalism towards the *évolué* one might instance an observation of a lecturer addressing students on the preparatory course in Belgium which intending non-Belgian missionaries to the Congo commonly attended. In a period *after* the *immatriculation* debate, this lecturer could point, figuratively, to Brazzaville in the then French Congo and tell his audience that there a black man could not only become a fully qualified judge but could actually sentence Europeans who might appear in his court! But, the lecture audience was reassured, 'that will never happen in the Belgian Congo'.[2]

Whilst the opposition to an *immatriculation* based on the *article unique* was important, there is also evidence, from some who knew Sohier,

[1] Union pour la Colonisation, 'Toujours le projet de l'immatriculation' (communiqué), *L'Echo du Kivu*, 13 Oct. 1950.
[2] Personal information.

that he had swung away from the *article unique* himself. He seems to have been particularly impressed by the argument that complete assimilation, by subjecting *immatriculés* to the *contrat d'emploi*, a more favourable employment contract than the *contrat de travail*, and one hitherto enjoyed exclusively by Europeans, would, paradoxically, seriously harm the interests of *immatriculés*.[1] This was because the *contrat d'emploi* and the status thereby implied, were very expensive for the employer, and, where private employers were concerned, they would be likely to favour the employ of a European candidate over a Congolese, in the belief that the former would be more efficient if both were going to be equally costly. The outcome was rejection of the clause promising full assimilation to *immatriculés*—inevitably, though no doubt in the honest conviction of men like Sohier—'in the interests of the *immatriculés* themselves'. Assimilation should rather be realized by a series of specific decrees in various fields. A new draft decree should be prepared which 'would permit the progressive extension to *immatriculés* of the legal and statutory dispositions applicable to non-natives of metropolitan status'.[2]

The matter was now reconsidered in Brussels; but, although there were lengthy debates in the Conseil Colonial in the early part of 1952, the recommendation of the Conseil du Gouvernement proved decisive. When the *immatriculation* decree was finally promulgated later in 1952, the only sense in which the *immatriculé* was assimilated to European society was in being given legal equality. He was subject to the European and not to the customary courts, had all rights under the civil code and similar treatment with Europeans in public transport. The important right which he did *not* have was automatic exemption from all laws and regulations applying to Africans, whilst acquisition of the new status involved a complicated process of application, and searching inquiry into his way of life.

The debate on *immatriculation* also covered a good deal of other ground. How precisely should the qualifications for the new status be defined? What was to be the status of an *immatriculé*'s wife? and children? Should any other specific benefits be included in the decree? and so on. But the details of this protracted debate are not as important as the different misunderstandings of what the debate was about, and,

[1] *Ibid.*
[2] Belgian Congo, Conseil de Gouvernement, Proceedings of Commission No. 3, Question No. 18 (Leopoldville, 1950).

more especially, misunderstanding of the implications of *immatricula-tion*, as originally conceived. The original Sohier plan foresaw the full assimilation of a very few, and piecemeal, improvements in the con-dition of the broad mass of *évolués*. Sohier himself, in a discussion of the question in 1950, suggested that a mere half-dozen individuals were currently eligible, apart from the some hundreds of Congolese priests —who had certainly had a long and rigorous education. Yet the *évolués*, like many opponents of *immatriculation*, seem to have sup-posed that what was under examination was a measure affecting at least a considerable proportion of their number. A settler leader, A. Maus, rightly argued that the *évolués* would not have been so interested in the question if they had realized that it would apply only to a handful. As early as 1945 the possibility of a new status for *évolués* was discussed and desired by Bolamba in *La Voix du Congolais*, whilst the anti-assimilationist stand of Ucol, which we have already noticed, and of settler leader A. Defauwe in the Députation Permanente, aroused sometimes violent feelings in the correspondents of the journal. 'Courtesy forbids us to publish the whole of these articles', commented the editor. It is also significant that the hostile conclusions of the Députation Permanente were leaked to the press, doubtless in order to arouse feeling against the whittling away of the original proposal and probably by an *évolué* member of the Députation.

Confronted with the radical modifications proposed by the Conseil de Gouvernement, Sohier still believed that his cherished aim of assimilation would be achieved, albeit by stages and more slowly. Only a change of tactics was involved.

The legislation on *immatriculation* is the affirmation of a policy. It says solemnly to the Congolese: 'All racial discrimination is excluded from our régime. No part of that which is accorded in the colony to Belgians of metropolitan status is henceforth denied you. The door is open, it depends on you to pass through it.'[1]

When the decree had taken its final form, the Minister of the Colonies, M. Dequae, asserted that '*Immatriculation* constitutes the antithesis of every tendency based on racial segregation'.[2] No such pious reactions could conceal the fact that the whole operation had, at best, potential

---

[1] Albert Sohier, 'La politique d'intégration', *Zaïre*, Nov. 1951, 5, no. 11, pp. 905–6.

[2] Belgium, Conseil Colonial, *Compte rendu analytique des séances, publié en exécution de l'article 17 du règlement d'ordre intérieur* (Brussels, 1952), I, 854.

value. As Professor Malengreau pointed out in a perceptive commentary on the decree, the measure simply was not what it was puffed up to be, whilst Young makes the equally important comment that gestation had been insufferably long.[1] Intended to have shock value, to be a striking example of Belgian goodwill, discussion had in the event taken four years—and longer if its beginning is dated from the revival of interest in the subject in 1945. There was also an apparent lack of drive in the Colonial Ministry, perhaps related to the departure from office of Wigny, who had set up the commission in 1948, and to the absence of any weight of informed, liberal opinion in Belgium strong enough to counter anti-assimilationist European opinion in the Congo. One must also reckon with the quite extraordinarily slow and cumbersome process of consultation and modification involved in Congo legislation.

From the *évolué* point of view, juridical assimilation was probably the least interesting of any form of equality. The comment of *Le Congo Pratique* reveals a keen disappointment and, in reproducing the words of two Belgian administrative officers in Leopoldville when asked to explain to *évolués* the significance of *immatriculation*, underlines what a mouse of a measure it was. Said MM. Tordeur and Lafontaine:

'For the moment the decree brings you nothing new in the social domain: your salary will remain what it is, just as your access to European cinemas and hotels will not be allowed by the proprietors of these establishments.' It is there that Congolese lovers of *immatriculation* were deceived.[2]

The damp squib that *immatriculation* was might have had its potential restored if further, more appealing, measures of assimilation had succeeded it without delay. In fact, with the belated exception of such limited measures as the conferring in 1955 on both *immatriculés* and holders of the *carte du mérite civique* of the right freely to buy alcoholic drinks in restaurants—a right which was effectively a precondition of the patronage of European restaurants—nothing was done. According to Patrice Lumumba, a Congolese member of the Députation Permanente sought in 1953 to introduce a motion recommending total assimilation of all *immatriculés*, only to elicit no more favourable response than that body had shown three years previously.[3]

---

[1] Guy Malengreau, 'Chronique de politique indigène', *Zaïre*, Nov. 1952, **6**, no. 11, p. 960; Young, *Politics in the Congo*, p. 87.

[2] *Le Congo Pratique*, March 1953.

[3] Patrice Lumumba, *Le Congo, terre d'avenir, est-il menacé?* (Brussels, 1961), p. 73.

Belgian policy had gone on to another tack. No longer did it concern itself with the question of a separate status for *évolués*, or for some of them, but rather addressed itself to the general removal of racial discrimination in successive areas of the colony's life, and the encouragement of Congolese participation in government 'from the ground up', within the context of Belgo-Congolese community. This notion of a Belgo-Congolese community, born in 1952, aroused for four years or more a good deal of emotional support in Belgians and Congolese alike, partly because, the doctrine never having been precisely defined, both were able to read their own hopes into it. But whatever its inadequacies, 'to an extent it provided the liberal with a framework within which to urge change and adaptation, and the conservative a way of accepting it'.[1]

Though not directed solely at them, the new policy of ending discrimination and encouraging Congolese participation in local government would have brought particular satisfaction to the *évolués* if it had been more vigorously pursued. In the period up to January 1959, when serious rioting in Leopoldville ushered in a new era, important progress was made in the removal of racial discrimination in education, notably in the creation, in 1955, of interracial *athénées* (high schools), and in the foundation of the Catholic University of Lovanium in the same year and of a State University at Elisabethville in 1956, both being likewise interracial.

The year 1957 saw the beginnings of African participation in urban government. Unification of the two-tiered civil service—Africans were excluded from the higher branch—was slower. From 1953 there was an increasing number of Congolese who had the necessary professional standing for admission to the higher branch, but integration was debated acrimoniously, and was long in gestation, the decision to integrate being taken only in the spring of 1958. Not until February 1959, after the January riots, was discrimination in housing ended, whilst a decree of December 1957 laying down penalties against anyone who showed racial or ethnic hatred does not seem to have been much used against Europeans.

The everyday attitudes of Europeans towards *évolués* were at least as important as legislation on the subject. Patrice Lumumba, when he accidentally bumped into a European woman in the European residential area of Leopoldville, received the humiliating 'Can't you take care,

[1] Young, *Politics in the Congo*, p. 53.

sale macaque (dirty ape)',[1] whilst both Governor-General Jungers in 1952 and Governor-General Petillon in 1955 were attacked by sections of the European press in the Congo for their moderately liberal policies. Moreover it was Richelle's experience, gained in parts of Katanga in 1957–8, that Europeans who attempted to establish with Africans social relations similar to those they maintained with other Europeans ran the risk of ostracism.[2] As late as 1959 an *évolué* could complain that, when two European and one Congolese broadcasting official called at a business concern, the European subordinate could telephone to his principal that *two* gentlemen had called.[3] Another *évolué* reported how three European doctors in succession had recently refused to treat his sick wife, despite his readiness to pay.[4] When, during the same year, a quite high Belgian official invited some Leopoldville *evolués* to his house, socially, the governor-general received a positive shoal of protesting letters.[5]

Almost as hurtful must have been the patronizing tone of some of the remarks publicly addressed to *évolués* or likely to be read by them. Thus the provincial commissioner of Equateur when he addressed a *cercle des évolués* at the end of 1949:

Have no illusions; it is not you who will profit from the true civilization... Your children will attain a higher degree of civilization than you, but will still not profit integrally from it. Only your children's children will be (truly) civilized.[6]

As to *évolué* abilities, a M. Emile Dehoux could write in *L'Avenir Congo Belge* in 1953 that

the better elements [amongst the clerks] are only wretched copyists, men of whom one can only ask routine work. But such is the magic of a diploma that these young Africans have incommensurate pretensions and imagine themselves to be the equal of whites, which, alas, is manifestly false.[7]

M. Dehoux's scathing assessment of *évolué* clerical ability might often be valid. The slow, unsystematic and uncomprehending way in which a clerk would sometimes make out a railway ticket, or conduct a customer's business in a bank, could defy belief, whilst *évolué* characteristics were often such as to alienate sympathy. He could be arrogant,

---

[1] Pierre de Vos, *Vie et mort de Lumumba* (Paris, 1961), pp. 30–1.
[2] Richelle, *Aspects psychologiques de l'acculturation*, p. 84.
[3] *La Voix du Congolais*, July 1959, p. 383.   [4] *Ibid.*, June 1959, pp. 326–7.
[5] Personal information.   [6] *La Voix du Congolais*, Jan. 1950, pp. 47–8.
[7] Quoted in *Le Congo Pratique*, Nov. 1953.

treating his compatriots much more harshly than would a European;
he could indeed be avid for the certificate but ignorant of real learning;
how ardent might be his professions of civilization, how real the actual
grip of sorcery and witchcraft; how moral might be his professions,
how immoral his conduct. Another factor in determining European
attitudes to *évolués* was that, the special case of the highly educated
Congolese priests excluded, *évolué* ranks included only a few men who
could be seen by their attainments to have entered thoroughly into
European culture. Paule Bouvier has pointed out that it was easier for
a Frenchman to recognize the quality of a Senghor, for an Englishman to accept a Nkrumah, an Awolowo, a Nyerere. They were men
who had obtained formal academic qualifications, and not to recognize
them would in some sense be to deny one's own culture.[1]

The fact remains that the action and inaction of the Congo's rulers
might have done much to bring about the *évolués'* condition, whilst
what has just been said does not relate to, or limit, the traumatic shock
of rebuff. Moreover it was often a gratuitous rebuff of a harshness that
a wise parent would hesitate to use when dealing with even a difficult
adolescent—to use an idiom which Belgians were disposed to apply to
their relations with the more advanced Congolese, just as they were
wont to regard ordinary Congolese as children.

Of course, there were a number of Europeans who went out of their
way to help aspiring *évolués*, Patrice Lumumba being a notable example
of one whose early career owed much to such assistance.[2] But whether
the individual *évolué* experience was of rebuff or encouragement it is
noteworthy that, given a general anti-assimilationist comportment on
the part of Belgium and Belgians, *évolués* continued to cherish the hope
of acceptance or even of integration long after the crushing disappointment of 1952. Certainly by the mid-1950s there was profound disillusion with *immatriculation*, especially by the *immatriculés* themselves,
who had come fully to realize its partial nature and the fact that it
involved onerous obligations in return for limited advantages.[3] But
the attraction of the Belgo-Congolese community still held: on the
occasion of King Baudouin's tour of the Congo in 1955, for example,
the idea of the community was enthusiastically hailed by the editor of

[1] Paule Bouvier, *L'accession du Congo belge à l'indépendance: essai d'analyse sociologique*
(Brussels, 1965), p. 58.
[2] De Vos, *Vie et mort de Lumumba*; Pierre Clément, 'Patrice Lumumba', *Présence Africaine*,
English ed., 1st Quarter 1962, **2**, no. 40, p. 79.
[3] Lumumba, *Le Congo, terre d'avenir*, pp. 66–8.

Le Congo Pratique, whilst the caption beneath one of the pictures of the royal progress read, revealingly, 'Ah, our Congolese have welcomed their young king with all their heart'.[1] But because of his later career as the most colourful and skilled nationalist leader, the attitudes of Patrice Lumumba are perhaps the most valuable pointers of all.

These attitudes are clearly spelt out in *Le Congo, terre d'avenir, est-il menacé?*[2] probably begun in the second half of 1956 and completed by early January 1957. Lumumba's starting-point was twofold—a real thirst for European culture and a desire to be accepted by Europeans. The voracity of his reading[3] is one testimony to the former

---

[1] *Le Congo Pratique*, May 1955.

[2] The book was not published until 1961, after Lumumba's death. Some have doubted that the views expressed in it were genuinely held, citing such reasons as censorship and the possibility of being victimized as grounds for the view that Lumumba was at that time, as later, really a militant nationalist. Such a view takes too little account of the fact that in the pages of the book biting criticism of Belgium is interspersed with adulation, and is perhaps not uninformed by the difficulty which some on the left feel in recognizing that Africa's archetypal nationalist leader could ever have harboured some less conventional—by their criteria—thoughts. Critics of this type must also reckon with Pierre Clément's memoir of Lumumba, based on close friendship with Lumumba in 1952–3. As well as testifying to Lumumba's love of books and avid intellectual curiosity, to his integrated personality and his aptitude for hard work, Clément's assessment of his friend's attitude to racial and political issues entirely coheres with the views expressed in *Le Congo, terre d'avenir*. Thus, 'Patrice reacted intensely to everything which touched him or his brothers ("the evolved" Negro Congolese) in their dignity as men...He bitterly deplored the fact that many among them [Europeans] (especially the authorities) failed to treat him in accordance with his position on the social level, and according to his education, aspirations and degree of "civilization"...he rebelled against the fact that those Congolese, whose professional competence he judged equal or superior to that of certain Europeans, remained, nonetheless, the subordinates of the latter...In spite of this, and because he was convinced that the "civilizing" and material work of the colonizer (even when he called him a usurper) was inestimable, and further, because of the immensity of that latter's past and future roles, he did not imagine that the Congo and the "mother country" could ever be other than indissolubly linked together...His knowledge of Marxism was barely nominal, and in his eyes, Communism was a frightful scarecrow...Patrice wanted to succeed, this much is certain. But if he aspired to accede to a social, cultural, intellectual and responsible level, it was not only to satisfy a strong individual need, but was also, and especially, to be better able to aid in the perfectionment [*sic*] of the élites and the realization of their juridical and economic assimilation, and even more to have them socially accepted by the Europeans' (Clément, 'Patrice Lumumba'). See also Roger Anstey, 'Patrice Lumumba: the myth of savagery', *The Listener*, 12 Aug. 1965, **74**, no. 1,898, pp. 221–3.

[3] See, e.g., de Vos, *Vie et mort de Lumumba*, p. 17; Lumumba to van Lierde, 24 Dec. 1959 and 13 Jan. 1960, in *La pensée politique de Patrice Lumumba*, Jean van Lierde, ed. (Paris, 1963), pp. 81, 100; and Clément, 'Patrice Lumumba', pp. 74–5.

quality, whilst he was quite unfeigned in his concern for closer relations:

How can we profit from the qualities of the whites, learn their knowledge of the world, their abilities, their manners and ways of thinking, how can we know their customs, if we have no means of coming into close contact with the better type of European?

The real answer, Lumumba continues, should

consist in personal relationships and it follows that every Congolese who has aspirations towards a certain ideal should make a serious effort to draw much closer to every European with whom he comes in contact. This European should be both friend and guide, or 'godfather' to him. This sort of contact is much better than meetings of groups in cafes, or meetings for propaganda.[1]

It follows that, in Lumumba's view, 'the essential wish of the Congolese élite...is...to be "Belgians" and to have the right to the same freedom and to the same rights, taking into account, evidently, the merits of each (individual)'.[2] Understandably Lumumba is much preoccupied with the *immatriculation* question, and the similar privilege of the *carte du mérite civique*. Reading the three chapters which Lumumba devotes to various aspects of integration, one becomes aware both of the author's disillusion with the practice of integration so far, and of his continuing yearning for complete integration:

For our part we believe that by virtue of the principle of non-discrimination, the act of *immatriculation* ought to have the same juridical effect as an act of recognition or adoption, and that Congolese *immatriculés* and...mulattos ought consequently to be treated on a perfect footing of equality [with Europeans] on the social and economic plane as well as the juridical.[3]

The link which he most desires for the *évolués* is in an important sense with Europeans rather than with the mass of Congolese. It would be wrong 'to introduce prematurely...the ferment of political life amongst the ignorant and irresponsible mass':[4] what should be done quite soon is, rather, 'to give...political rights to the Congolese élite and to Belgians [resident] in the Congo, according to certain criteria which will be laid down by the Government'.[5] Of these two groups, the Congolese élite should have the natural function of serving as 'the intermediary between his people and the colonizer'.[6] Early in 1957,

[1] Lumumba, *Le Congo, terre d'avenir*, p. 126.
[2] *Ibid.*, p. 29.
[3] *Ibid.*, p. 71.
[4] *Ibid.*, p. 40.
[5] *Ibid.*, p. 41.
[6] *Ibid.*, p. 73.

then, it is integration—a term which Lumumba uses in specific distinction from assimilation with its overtone of absorption—and the proper realization of the Belgo-Congolese community, which is the goal of the man who is shortly to become the most dynamic of nationalist leaders. The only indication that Lumumba saw conflict as an alternative to integration is contained in his comment on the formation of an association of *immatriculés* for the purpose of claiming their full rights. If policy did not change in certain respects, the formation of this association would be, 'whether one wishes it or not, the prelude of...nationalism, of this unfortunate white–black dualism'.[1]

Patrice Lumumba, and others, might cherish their hopes, but from 1956 onward the aspirations of the *évolués* are expressed in major *évolué* participation in nationalist politics. The politics of this final period of Belgian rule have been studied, from different perspectives and in some detail, by various scholars, mostly political scientists; what will be attempted here is a tentative explanation, in the broadest lines, of *évolué* motives and the *évolué* role.

The dominant role of *évolués* is attested by such evidence as the composition of the first Congolese government. Drawing primarily on Pierre Artigue's *Qui sont les leaders congolais?*[2], Young shows that most of the twenty-three ministers were, or had at some time been, clerks, whilst the occupations of medical assistant, teacher, salesman, research assistant, journalist and planter had been either the occupations of the remainder of the twenty-three, or were additional employments of those categorized as clerks.[3] But does anyone really require to be persuaded that *évolués* played the dominant role? And to assert this is not to deny that chiefs and elders played an important part in the rural organization of many small tribal parties, as well as in the much more substantial Parti National du Progrès (PNP).

Until 1956 the *évolués* did not turn to even rudimentary forms of political action. Perhaps the signs of movement in Belgian policy (see pp. 211–12 above) took the edge off their disappointment at the *immatriculation* decree. The negative reasons for quiescence were probably stronger. In a territory in which political activity simply was not allowed, and when the administration possessed considerable repressive powers, it would have been no light matter for any Congolese to resort to agitation. It is probably significant that the first proposal for radical

[1] *Ibid.*, p. 72.　　　　　　　　　　　　　　[2] Brussels, 1961.
[3] Young, *Politics in the Congo*, p. 198.

217

change came from a European, whilst the second came from an *évolué* group which perhaps could claim some immunity in that its members included a leading Congolese *abbé* and certainly enjoyed the support of two professors at the recently established Université Lovanium.[1]

The European proposal came at the end of 1955 from a Belgian professor of colonial legislation, A. A. J. van Bilsen. It was a plan for political emancipation, envisaging self-government at the end of a period which van Bilsen felt that he could not publicly avow as less than thirty years, as the consummation of a positive process of training for independence and of the gradual transfer of powers within a federal framework.

It was the ferment produced in Leopoldville *évolué* circles by the van Bilsen plan that led to the appearance of the first *évolué* plea for radical change. Since 1953 a group organized by the Abbé Joseph Malula had met to discuss social, economic and cultural questions and had published some of their proceedings in an occasional periodical, *Conscience Africaine*. It was in the July–August 1956 issue of this journal that the so-called *Conscience Africaine* manifesto saw the light of day. Interestingly, because it clearly stemmed from the *évolué* concern for acceptance, the manifesto stated as its central principle that 'the colour of the skin confers no privilege. Without this principle, union is impossible.' Accepting the van Bilsen plan in broad outline, the manifesto was a moderate document, but did demand a progressive increase in political power for Congolese and 'total emancipation' at the term of the stated thirty years.

Widely read by *évolués* in the main centres throughout the colony, the manifesto was the immediate cause of the publication of a much more impatient document, the counter-manifesto of ABAKO. 'Immediate cause' is used advisedly, since it is the contention of Joseph Kasavubu's biographer, the only person who has so far published an assessment of that enigmatic man, that Kasavubu, the president of ABAKO, had long awaited the opportunity to express his opposition to the colonial world. Kasavubu had in 1954 become president of what had originally been a cultural association of the Bakongo. The decisive experience of his life had come much earlier in 1939, when he had not

---

[1] René Lemarchand, *Political awakening in the Belgian Congo* (Berkeley and Los Angeles, University of California Press, 1964), pp. 156–7. It was Lumumba's view that every time a Congolese publicly attacked authority he was supported by a European (Lumumba, *Le Congo, terre d'avenir*, p. 189).

been allowed to proceed from the three years' seminary training in philosophy when he had successfully completed it, to the five years of theology which would have culminated in his ordination as a priest. On ordination he had set his heart. This experience, in Gilis's view, was fundamental, 'for it explains how he became aware, personally and painfully, of an opposition between himself and the colonial world, an opposition which...came to be placed gradually on the political plane'.[1] If this was indeed Kasavubu's traumatic experience, he had to wait the seventeen years from 1939 to 1956 to begin his protest. With the way paved by van Bilsen and the *Conscience Africaine* group—and publication of these two programmes having been allowed—it would have been difficult for the administration to stop publication of the ABAKO counter-manifesto.

The impatience of the counter-manifesto was shown in its unequivocal assertion of the need for political action—the *Conscience Africaine* group being chided for their failure properly to face up to this—and in its rejection of the thirty-year time-table. 'Our patience is already exhausted. Since the hour has come, emancipation should be granted us this very day rather than delayed for another thirty years.' Another notable characteristic of the counter-manifesto was its premise that political action should be based on ethnically based parties as opposed to the simple Mouvement National Populaire which the manifesto had proposed. The serious reservations which the *Conscience Africaine* group had registered about the Belgo-Congolese community were spelt out in more detail by ABAKO. Such a community could only come if 'freely chosen and accepted'.

The two manifestos were *évolué* reactions of first-class importance, and their publication marked an important stage in the conversion of ABAKO into a political party, and a lesser stage in the emergence of the Mouvement National Congolais. *Evolués*, though aided by others and whilst still treasuring the ideal of the conversion of the Congo into a racially equal society, had broken new ground in contemplating political action—and independence. Further development of Congolese political activity came as a result of new movement in Belgian policy when in March 1957 the Belgians promulgated the *statut des villes*. Its provisions included the grant to Africans of the means of taking part in urban administration; and, in practice, though it was not laid down

[1] Charles André Gilis, *Kasa-Vubu au coeur du drame congolais* (Brussels, 1964), pp. 31 ff. and esp. p. 34.

in the decree, elections were held to appoint communal councillors. At first the decree applied only to Leopoldville, Elisabethville and Jadotville; but in December 1958 it was extended to Bukavu, Stanleyville, Luluabourg and Coquilhatville. The significance of this measure is that in creating an electoral process, it stimulated the growth of parties. Lemarchand makes the further interesting claim that in the absence of a specific right to organize parties lay at least part of the reason why competition in the elections was mostly on a tribal basis[1] —the pre-existing tribal union was the obvious vehicle for electoral activity. From this initial ethnic root Congolese political parties for the most part never got away.

The whole process is tellingly portrayed by Lemarchand. In Leopoldville, for example, the resounding victory of ABAKO at the polls in the communal elections led to the foundation of the Interfédérale in an attempt to mobilize against the Bakongo numerous other tribes represented in Leopoldville. Similarly, the success of Kasai Baluba in the Elisabethville communal elections led to the foundation of a federation of 'authentic Katangan' tribes, the Confédération des Associations Tribales du Katanga, better known as Conakat. In a broad sense the process repeated itself in Luluabourg, with the transposition into political party warfare of the deep-rooted Lulua–Baluba tension, and in Equateur province as well.[2]

Successive concessions by Belgium, each acceleration of the timetable of Independence, brought a new flurry of new tribal parties or new federations of existing ones. Only Lumumba's Mouvement National Congolais made any sort of real attempt to become a national party—and this, paradoxically, at the cost of a division which effectively prevented the MNC proper from gaining much support from the tribes of leaders of the break-away group.

In contrast with the évolué role in those early protests in 1956, in this period of tribal politics the évolués were for the most part, it may be hazarded, simply carried along by the tide. This is not to say that they did not play a vital role in party organization and propaganda, for they did, as has been documented in the case of ABAKO and the Parti Solidaire Africain.[3] But as the tempo quickened, many of the

---

[1] Lemarchand, *Political awakening*, pp. 72–3.   [2] *Ibid.*, pp. 192–7.

[3] Herbert Weiss and Benoît Verhaegen, eds., *Parti Solidaire Africain (P.S.A.): documents 1959–1960* (Brussels, Centre de Recherche et d'Information Socio-politiques, 1963); Benoît Verhaegen, ed., *A.B.A.K.O., 1950–1960: documents* (Brussels, Centre de Recherche et d'Information Socio-politiques, 1962).

évolués engaged in politics increasingly abandoned the moderate aspirations of an earlier period and allowed themselves to be swept away in a whirlwind of phrenetic activity. There was fear that, unless one exerted oneself to the utmost, one's own tribe would be unrepresented or under-represented at the new seats of provincial and national power. There was fear that one's own claim to rule would appear unconvincing if not sustained by onslaughts upon Belgian authority. Independence was commonly presented to the man in the bush in an almost millenial fashion. 'Freedom' would bring freedom from all restraints; independence would usher in the golden age or perhaps even the apocalypse.

Everyone who has worked on Congo politics during this period has had his authentic stories of mudhuts that would be changed for skyscrapers, of taxes that would no longer have to be paid, of European possessions which would fall to the Congolese.[1] And many of the *évolué* politicians, in the excitement of it all, must have come to suppose that their political activity corresponded to the real world just as Plato portrayed men as supposing that the shadows dancing on the walls of the cave were real persons. For the *évolué* political activist, as for Plato's chained humans in the cave, 'the truth would be literally nothing but the shadows of the images'.

Of course the increasingly hectic political activity of 1957 onward was in a real sense the further development of the protest, first made in 1956, into revolt, in accord with an almost classical pattern. But it is at the very least interesting to see the continuing existence of earlier *évolué* ideas. Thus, for instance, in the autumn of 1958 the Groupe de Travail, the Belgian parliamentary commission appointed to recommend a programme of political advance for the Congo, found that a great number of Congolese who gave evidence wanted immediate independence. But what was the content of that independence?

Invited to explain what they meant by that, they declared that they wished, without delay, for the accession of the indigenous inhabitants to equality of rights and duties with Europeans at all levels of administration, public and private, as well as the complete suppression of racial discrimination. The Groupe de Travail had concluded from these declarations that its witnesses meant by immediate independence the immediate liberation of the individual.[2]

---

[1] See, e.g., Bouvier, *L'accession du Congo belge à l'indépendance*, p. 143; Anstey, *King Leopold's legacy*, pp. 249–50.

[2] Belgium, Parlement, Chambre des Représentants, *Rapport du groupe de travail pour l'étude du problème politique au Congo belge*, 1958–9 Sess. (Brussels, 1959), p. 10.

And elsewhere in their report the commission expressed the view that for many Congolese, Africanization constituted 'the essential content of the autonomy or the independence to which they professed to aspire'.[1]

Noteworthy, as coming at a time when tension was high as the Round Table Conference was in session in Brussels, were the views of 'Philpos', a *Présence Congolaise* correspondent. The Congo could no longer remain dependent upon another nation; nonetheless for the more discerning Congolese

the vision evoked by the ex-Minister of the Congo...M. Petillon, is nothing else than the ideal of which every Congolese dreams for the nation of tomorrow: human brotherhood based on the fundamental equality of men without distinction of race.[2]

This essay has been concerned to focus attention on *évolué* aspirations and on the unsuccessful attempts of Belgium to meet them. In doing this we have sought to suggest that in the Congo the general pattern whereby the *évolué* class, after first seeking special treatment, and assimilation by the colonizer, turns to revolt when it cannot cross the threshold, was complex rather than simple. In particular there is much evidence that *évolués* continued to desire association with Belgium, with Europe and Europeans, with European culture, and out of genuine attachment rather than expediency, after they had passed over to political action. This truth is sometimes disguised by the militancy of their political activity which, though it was genuine revolt against the colonizer, was also in part self-generating and escalatory, and in that sense artificial.

Clément wrote of the Lumumba he knew in 1952–3:

From the very beginning, he told me of his pride in being black, in being a 'Negro' in the fullest meaning of the term...Nevertheless, when Patrice was in contact with a white person who evinced no more satisfaction in being white than he would have were he yellow or black, once he understood that his interlocutor addressed himself only to the man and was blind to one's

---

[1] *Rapport du groupe de travail*, pp. 13–14. There was sometimes a real element of the banal in the protests against discrimination, protests which sought now a remedy only in independence. Thus in January 1960 the journal *Présence Congolaise*, in a column headed 'Why Congolese claim their independence', cited the exclusion of Congolese hunter's meat from the markets in Boma and Matadi in order to protect European butchers. 'Is it surprising', commented the editor, 'that Congolese are claiming their independence, that is their own direction of the country's affairs?' (*Présence Congolaise*, 23 Jan. 1960.)   [2] *Présence Congolaise*, 30 Jan. 1960.

colour, when he found himself outside a situation which provoked him to affirm himself a black man, then this chromatic claim, this exaltation of 'negritude' evaporated into thin air, lost all meaning and *raison d'être*. There remained the infinite distress of being immured in a black skin.[1]

The evidence about Lumumba's later career suggests, in my view, that these words could equally well have been written about the Lumumba of 1958–60, the Lumumba who was then the most dynamic nationalist leader in the Congo. For the mass of the *évolués*, too, there was the same tension between the assertion of *négritude* and the constraint of being black.

BIBLIOGRAPHY

Anstey, Roger. *King Leopold's legacy: the Congo under Belgian rule, 1908–1960.* London, Oxford University Press, 1966.

'Patrice Lumumba: the myth of savagery', *The Listener*, 12 Aug. 1965, **74**, no. 1,898.

Artigue, Pierre. *Qui sont les leaders congolais?* Brussels, 1961.

Belgium. Congrès Colonial National, 6th Sess. (Sénat de Belgique, 4–5 Oct. 1947), *Comptes rendus des séances et rapports préparatoires.* Brussels, 1948.

Belgium. Conseil Colonial. *Compte rendu analytique des séances, publié en exécution de l'article 17 du règlement d'ordre intérieur,* Vol. I. Brussels, 1952.

Belgium. Parlement. Chambre des Représentants. *Projet de loi contenant le budget ordinaire du Congo belge pour l'exercice 1948. Rapport fait au nom de la Commission des Colonies,* by M. Housiaux. 1947–8 Sess. Documents parlementaires, No. 662. Brussels, 1948.

Rapport annuel sur l'administration de la colonie du Congo belge pendant l'année 1958. Brussels, 1959.

Rapport du groupe de travail pour l'étude du problème politique au Congo belge. 1958–9 Sess. Brussels, 1959.

Belgium. Sénat. 'Procès-verbal de la visite au cercle des évolués à Paulis', appendix to *Rapport de la mission sénatoriale au Congo.* Brussels, 1947.

Bouvier, Paule. *L'accession du Congo belge a l'indépendance: essai d'analyse sociologique.* Brussels, 1965.

Brausch, Georges E. J. B. *Belgian administration in the Congo.* London, Oxford University Press, 1961.

Clément, Pierre. 'Patrice Lumumba', *Présence Africaine*, 1st Quarter 1962, **12**, no. 40.

'Social patterns of urban life (Stanleyville survey)', in *Social implications of industrialization and urbanization in Africa south of the Sahara,* Daryll Forde, ed. Paris, 1956.

[1] Clément, 'Patrice Lumumba', p. 81.

Comhaire-Sylvain, Suzanne. 'Food and leisure among the African youth of Leopoldville', summary in *Social implications of industrialization and urbanization in Africa south of the Sahara*, Daryll Forde, ed. Paris, 1956.

Congo, Belgian. Conseil de Gouvernement. *Compte rendu...* Leopoldville, 1950.

Proceedings of Commission No. 3, Questions 17 and 18. Leopoldville, 1950.

Davier, Joseph. 'Méditation', *La Voix du Congolais*, March 1952, no. 72.

De Backer, M. C. C. *Notes pour servir à l'étude des 'Groupements Politiques' à Leopoldville*. Brussels, 1959, stencilled.

De Vos, Pierre, *Vie et mort de Lumumba*. Paris, 1961.

Devaux, V. 'Rapport sur un projet de décret sur l'immatriculation des indigènes, *Zaïre*, Feb. 1949, **3**, no. 2.

Gérard-Libois, Jules, ed. *Congo 1959, documents belges et africains*. Brussels, Centre de Recherche et d'Information Socio-politiques, 1960.

Gérard-Libois, Jules, and Benoît Verhaegen. *Congo 1960*. 2 vols. Brussels, Centre de Recherche et d'Information Socio-politiques, 1961.

Gilis, Charles André. *Kasa-Vubu au coeur du drame congolais*. Brussels, 1964.

Hailey, William Malcolm, 1st baron. *An African survey: a study of problems arising in Africa south of the Sahara*. London, Oxford University Press, 1938.

Hoskyns, Catherine. *The Congo since independence, January 1960–December 1961*. London, Oxford University Press, 1965.

Lemarchand, René. *Political awakening in the Belgian Congo*. Berkeley and Los Angeles, University of California Press, 1964.

Lumumba, Patrice. *Le Congo, terre d'avenir, est-il menacé?* Brussels, 1961.

Malengreau, Guy, 'Chronique de politique indigène', *Zaïre*, Nov. 1952, **6**, no. 11.

Merlier, Michel. *Le Congo de la colonisation belge à l'indépendance*. Paris, 1962.

Merriam, Alan P. *Congo: background of conflict*. Evanston, Northwestern University Press, 1961.

Mondjeni-Mobe, J. 'Cruelle équivoque', *La Voix du Congolais*, 1950, no. 6.

Mosmans, Guy, *L'église à l'heure de l'Afrique*. Brussels, 1961.

Mottoulle, Léopold, *et al.* 'Rapport sur l'hygiène et la démographie', Belgium, Congrès Colonial National, 6th Sess. (Sénat de Belgique, 4–5 Oct. 1947), *Comptes rendus des séances et rapports préparatoires*. Brussels, 1948.

Piron, Pierre. 'L'évolution des populations détribalisées', Belgium, Congrès Colonial National, 6th Sess. (Sénat de Belgique, 4–5 Oct. 1947), *Comptes rendus des séances et rapports préparatoires*. Brussels, 1948.

Pons, V. G. 'The changing significance of ethnic affiliation and of westernization in the African settlement patterns in Stanleyville (Belgian Congo)', in *Social implications of urbanization and industrialization in Africa south of the Sahara*, Daryll Forde, ed. Paris, 1956.

'The growth of Stanleyville and the composition of its African population', in *Social implications of urbanization and industrialization in Africa south of the Sahara*, Daryll Forde, ed. Paris, 1956.

Richelle, Marc. *Aspects psychologiques de l'acculturation*. Elisabethville, 1960.

Rubbens, Antoine, ed. *Dettes de guerre*. Elisabethville, 1945.

'La solution de "l'intégration des élites": plaidoyer pour le sauvage', in *Dettes de guerre*, Antoine Rubbens, ed. Elisabethville, 1945.

Slade, Ruth M. *The Belgian Congo*, 2nd ed. London, Oxford University Press, 1961.

Sohier, Albert. 'En marge du décret sur l'immatriculation', *Journal des Tribunaux d'Outre-Mer*, 15 June 1952, **3**, no. 2.

'Le problème des indigènes évolués et la commission du statut des Congolaises civilisés', *Zaïre*, Oct. 1949, **3**, no. 8.

'Le statut des Congolais civilisés', *Zaïre*, Oct. 1950, **4**, no. 10.

Tempels, Placide. *Bantu philosophy*, trans. by Colin King. Paris, 1959. [French ed.: *La philosophie bantoe*, trans. from Dutch by A. Rubbens. Paris, 1949.]

'La philosophie de la rébellion', in *Dettes de guerre*, Antoine Rubbens, ed. Elisabethville, 1945.

Union pour la Colonisation. 'Toujours le projet de l'immatriculation' (communiqué), *L'Echo du Kivu*, 13 Oct. 1950.

Van Lierde, Jean, ed. *La pensée politique de Patrice Lumumba*. Paris, 1963.

Van Wing, J. 'La formation d'une élite noire au Congo Belge', Centre d'Etude des Problèmes Sociaux Indigènes, *Bulletin* (superseded by *Problèmes Sociaux Congolais*), 1947–8, no. 5.

'La situation actuelle des populations congolaises', Institut Royal Colonial Belge, *Bulletin des Séances*, 1945, **16**, no. 3.

Verhaegen, Benoît, ed. *A.B.A.K.O., 1950–1960: documents*. Brussels, Centre de Recherches et d'Information Socio-politiques, 1962.

Weiss, Herbert, and Benoît Verhaegen, eds. *Parti Solidaire Africain (P.S.A.): documents 1959–1960*. Brussels, Centre de Recherche et d'Information Socio-politiques, 1963.

'Why Congolese claim their independence', *Présence Congolaise*, 23 Jan. 1960.

Young, Crawford, *Politics in the Congo: decolonization and independence*. Princeton University Press, 1965.

CHAPTER 6

FRANCE IN BLACK AFRICA AND MADAGASCAR BETWEEN 1920 AND 1945

by HUBERT DESCHAMPS

The French colonial empire reached its zenith at the Treaty of Versailles. From the ruin of the Turkish and German empires, it inherited mandates in the Levant and over Togo and Cameroun. Its stations in India, Indo-China, the Pacific Islands, the West Indies and French Guiana encircled the world. But it was in Africa that it occupied the greatest expanse of territory: North Africa (Algeria, Tunis, Morocco), protruding into the Sahara; in Black Africa, the two huge federations of French West Africa and French Equatorial Africa; in the Indian Ocean, the great island of Madagascar surrounded by various satellites.

In 1920 *French West Africa* comprised an area of some 4,600,000 sq.km, nine times the area of France. It is true that all the northern part consisted of the Sahara desert, that the thorny steppe that bordered it was traversed only by a few black nomads (Moors and Tuareg), and that the great forest of the Ivory Coast, only recently explored, was still for the most part uninhabited. The red bush of the Sudan and the green savannahs in the south alone were fairly densely populated; but because of wretched soil (laterite), tsetse fly or past wars, vast expanses were unoccupied. In 1920 there were not more than twelve million inhabitants over all, the great majority of them black, divided into numerous tribes speaking different languages. The frontiers of French West Africa resulted from the chance effects of European occupation towards the end of the nineteenth century; they cut across ethnic boundaries (Hausa, Ewe, Malinke, for example), separating peoples who had not previously been united politically. The French West African Federation was divided into eight colonies: Senegal, the oldest, the mother colony, where the capital of French West Africa, Dakar, was situated; Mauritania, French Sudan, the Upper Volta, Niger in the Sudanian and Sahelian zone; Guinea, the Ivory Coast and Dahomey in the humid zone of the Gulf of Guinea. To these were added the recent mandate of *Togo* (56,000 sq.km and 800,000 inhabitants).

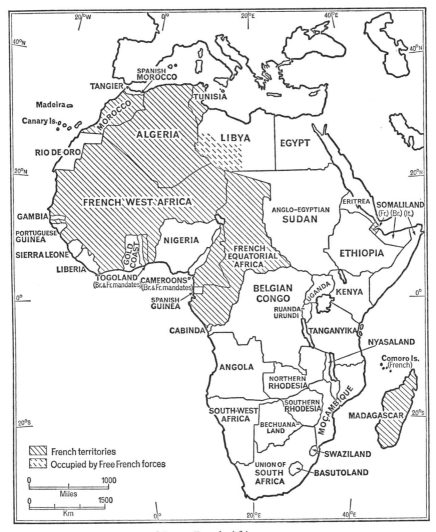

Map 7. French Africa, 1945

Ethnic and linguistic dispersion was matched by economic diversity: the camel in the Sahara, cattle in the Sahel, millet in Sudan, yams and maize in the savannah. Life was based on a subsistence economy: each family (and we use the word in its broadest sense) produced what it needed—food, clothing and shelter. Only the countries on the periphery had begun to engage in foreign trade: ground-nuts in Senegal, palm-oil in Dahomey, timber in the Ivory Coast. This was the outcome, on a modest scale, of the commercial economy practiced by the free traders of the nineteenth century. The colonizing power had up till then established no more than a governmental system whose factitious unity resulted from a foreign domination that was still recent, and whose purpose was uncertain.

The impression of something thrown together by chance is even more striking when one considers *French Equatorial Africa*. Starting out from Gabon, De Brazza reached the Congo. His efforts, and those of his team as well as their successors, extended the frontiers to Bahr-el-Ghazal, to Chad and to Tibesti, improvising a monstrously unbalanced edifice, spread over geographical zones, forests, marshes, desert, devoid of all historic tradition and of all economic sense. It was divided into four colonies—Gabon, Middle Congo, Oubangui-Chari, Chad—with its capital, Brazzaville, at the outer extremity.

The French, however, were completely at a loss as to what to do with it. They had gone there in the first place only to keep others out, rather than with any preconceived plans for colonization. The area had been handed over in 1899 to great companies whose abuses De Brazza himself denounced. It was hard to see how this 'Cinderella of the Colonies' could acquire a dowry. Its territory, covering two and a half million square kilometres, had fewer than four million inhabitants. In the south, there was a mere sprinkling of black tribes, completely innocent of previous contacts with the outside world except for those occasioned by the slave-trade (Europeans on the coast, Sudanese Arabs in Oubangui); in the Chad, Moslem populations, black or white, were formed into kingdoms based on the spoils of wars and pillage. There was no outlet, for the Congo was barred by rapids. The burden of having to provide carriers weighed heavily on the inhabitants—the only noteworthy effect of colonization up to that time.

After the Treaty of Versailles, the bulk of *Cameroun* (with 430,000 sq.km and two million inhabitants) was attached to French Equatorial Africa as a mandate. Cameroun, too, had its disparities; but it was better organized and had been endowed by the Germans with the beginning of a railway network. It might have been possible to unite the two countries and make the coast of Cameroun an outlet for the interior of French Equatorial Africa; but the scruples of the government vis-à-vis the League of Nations prevented any such solution.

The situation of *Madagascar* was quite different by reason of its island situation, its smaller size (only slightly larger than France), its mixed population derived from two continents, the unity of its language and its customs, its political unity largely begun by the Merina kings and completed by Gallieni, the conversion of a large part of its people to Christianity. A railroad linked the capital, Tananarive, with the coast. During World War I the island had supplied France with rice, meat and manioc. The volume of exports attained a new level in 1924, and the future of the island appeared assured.

French Somaliland, on the route to Madagascar and to Indochina, was a desert where the French had built Djibouti. The harbour and the town were still unimportant; but their founder, Léonce Lagarde, had made them the outlet of Ethiopia, to which they were linked by railroad. On each side of the Great Island (Madagascar), there was an archipelago. To the west, the *Comores*, small volcanic islands inhabited by Moslems, were attached to Madagascar for administrative purposes; on the east, of the three Mascarenes, *Réunion* was all that was left to France. In spite of having a governor, this ancient colony had municipalities and sent deputies to the French parliament. Its status was analogous to that of a French department, and it will not be included in the account of the colonial system that follows.

Politics and administration

THE METROPOLITAN COUNTRY. There was, in effect, no French colonial system as such, only a way of political life distinct from that of the metropolis. The 'France with 100 millions of inhabitants' envisioned by General Charles Marie Mangin, father of the black French army, was no more than an ideal inspired by the Roman Empire and the former European assimilation. 'Overseas France', a term which the radical minister Albert Sarraut substituted for the expressions 'colonies' and 'empire' (the latter was never official under the Republic), stood at the same time for a vague assimilatory label and a practical separation. The colonial exhibition of 1931, organized by Louis-Hubert Lyautey, represented the apogee of the system. The French derived from it both the pleasure of exoticism and the pride of a resurgent nationalism. The businessman, Octave Homberg, spoke of 'la France des cinq parties du monde'. Like the Austrian Empire of Charles V, France never saw the sun set on its possessions. After 1919, Waterloo and Sedan had finally been avenged.

Apart from this, people thought no more about the subject. Since the Senatus-Consulte of 3 May 1854, the colonies had become a matter for specialists. Parliament, where Black Africa had only one deputy, elected by the four communes of Senegal, did not legislate for the Empire, and concerned itself for the most part only with matters connected with loans or scandals. All colonial legislation was in the form of decrees of the President of the Republic, prepared by the Ministry of Colonies, a ministry considered of secondary importance since it had only limited funds at its disposal. The same men tended to return to the ministry in different governments, notably two radicals, Léon Perrier and especially Albert Sarraut, a politician but also a former governor of Indo-China. The deputy for Senegal, Blaise Diagne, a black man, was also at one time Under-Secretary of State for the colonies; thus, the very political chiefs tended to be specialists. Their subordinates belonged to the corps of specialized civil servants: directors and clerks in the Central Administration, colonial inspectors, colonial governors and district officers, members of the Colonial Health Service and the colonial technical services.

There was less and less exchange of personnel between the cadres of the mother country and those of the colonies largely because the latter were recruited through specialized schools or by competition. Officials of the Central Administration rarely went overseas, and inspectors were occupied mainly with financial control. Decisions were usually proposed, and indeed prepared, by the governors and their staff; the ministry did no more than make modifications of detail. It refrained from giving general instructions both for fear of becoming involved and from a sense of its own incompetence. This was the era of the proconsuls.

There was no counterweight to the omnipotence of the men on the spot. The Africans were 'French subjects', except for the citizens of the four Senegalese communes, who had political representation but no political interests beyond Senegal. The other colonies elected only delegates to the Conseil Supérieur des Colonies, a consultative body placed under the minister and in fact stripped of all influence. Its delegates were regarded in Paris as the representatives of the interests of their electors, the French citizens, that is, for the most part, the European colonists. The press sometimes intervened to draw attention to scandals, as in the articles of Albert Londres, collected in his book *Terre d'Ebène*. André Gide, in his *Voyage au Congo*, denounced the evils of porterage, certain administrative abuses and the sacrifices of human life resulting from the construction of the Congo railway. But these campaigns at best had only a feeble and ephemeral effect on public opinion. Lasting, on the contrary, was the activity of pressure groups representing economic interests with overseas investments: commercial banks, trading companies, great plantations. Their directors, often supported by members of parliament, intervened with ministers to discuss economic measures or perhaps to have a governor deposed whom they disliked. Ministers resisted or acquiesced on the basis of political expediency or according to their connexions or their personal character.

The weak position of colonial ministers, menaced ceaselessly by parliamentary intrigues and economic pressures, ill-informed besides and often not very interested in a job they hoped was transitory, explains why no overall direction of colonial policy emerged from the rue Oudinot (offices of the ministry). Ministers dealt with matters from day to day, coped with problems that were brought to their notice and counted themselves lucky if there were no news stories. The great controversies of principle that had marked the growth of the second colonial empire had ended. *Assimilation* was a relic of the classic notion of a humanity that was all alike. This concept had inspired the texts of the two first Republics, but had now been definitely rejected as out of date and *simpliste*. The social sciences—history, geography, sociology—had revealed the diversity of men and of their civilizations; it would be foolish to upset them by seeking to impose a uniform status on all.

During the early part of the twentieth century the doctrine of *association* had first made its appearance: let us give these countries good administration, with a considerable delegation of power, and let us take care of their economic and social progress under the aegis of France. Lyautey and Sarraut, influenced by the protectorates that they had administered in Morocco and Indo-China, respectively, came to advocate evolution towards self-government for a distant future. But these were exceptions. There was to be none of that for Black Africa. 'Association' was in fact but a negative formula: a tacit refusal of assimilation, the desire to perpetuate the *status quo* by governing in the light of circumstances. In official speeches, 'the civilizing mission of France' was evoked in ringing terms: the practical effects of this vague patriotic and humanitarian idealism were not negligible either on the colonial civil servants whose task it exalted, or on the native élites who tended to think of themselves as French. But no long-term view emerged. This period of stability was a period lacking in constructive imagination and in sense of evolution: one can see in it the contentment of the man in possession who prefers not to think about questions of the future.

The political parties themselves offered no positive programme. The opposition of the radicals to colonialism had long since ceased, and the party had become bourgeois. The communists proclaimed the catch-words of Lenin against 'imperialism' and 'colonialism', without having followed Stalin in his constructive system for changing the Russian Empire. The Socialist Party preserved, in a confused way, the ideal of egalitarian assimilation of the old republicans, but contented itself on the whole with negative criticisms. In the midst of the celebrations of the 1931 Colonial Exposition, the present author denounced as reactionary the British doctrine, defined by Lord Lugard, of consolidating traditional kings and chiefs: the future, he said, rested upon the new educated and westernized élites; assimilation was the way suggested by history. But colonial doctrines interested no one at that time. It was only after the great shock of World War II, in which France was cast out of France, that the idea of assimilation would be resuscitated and written into the constitution, at a moment when the world was already condemning it.

The victory of the Popular Front in 1936 brought no general change of policy. The diverging views of the three left-wing parties of the coalition, as well as their lack of any positive programme and the vagueness of their good intentions, made collective action difficult; and political stability was lacking for a continuous and durable policy. However, Léon Blum had entrusted the Ministry of Colonies to his friend Marius Moutet, a lawyer known as the defender of native interests. With the help of Robert Delavignette (one of the contributors to this volume), at that time a district officer who had written a good novel about the life of the 'Black Peasants', Moutet elaborated a 'big programme of little works' (dams, cultivation of swamps, provision of watercourses, etc.) to ameliorate the conditions of life in the villages. Native trade unions were authorized for urban workers. A Commission of Inquiry into the Colonies began to collect the material for far-reaching reforms. Among its numerous members was André Gide. But all the proposals of the socialist-led Popular Front were defeated in the Senate and all efforts were stymied. The hopes aroused among the native *évolués* turned to rancour. The only socialist governor-general, Marcel de Coppet, was faced with a strike on the Dakar railroad, the first strike in the country; and this event was exploited by the right-wing press. The opportunity to bring the Africans into the French system had passed.

Even during this brief interlude, political influence had not triumphed over colonial specialism. The incumbent governors retained their jobs. Parliament had formed the habit of disregarding the colonies. The financial law of 1900, an expression of the mistrust of the average Frenchman, peasant or *petit bourgeois*, for far-off adventures, had refused any subsidy to the colonies, thus compelling them to look after their own interests and to pay all their officials, including the French whose salaries were increased by 'colonial allowances'. Thus, governors and district officers found themselves, for lack of money, obliged to resort to all sorts of expedients in order to promote the country's development. The authorities imposed taxes that were often too heavy for a poverty-stricken population; 'prestations' (a tax in labour of ten days per year working on the roads) and requisitions of labour which often degenerated into abuses. Even so, there was not enough man-power for large-scale public works. Albert Sarraut, who had experienced these tragic difficulties on the spot, proposed in 1921 a colonial development plan for which he was successful in securing loans placed by the colonies in the metropolis and guaranteed by the metropolitan government. Major roads, railroads, and harbours could thus be undertaken. Successive devaluations of the franc afterwards reduced very considerably the interest charge on these loans.

Thus, aside from a few ministerial initiatives and whims, political intervention was not often apparent in this period. The minister relied on his local officers to administer and develop the distant possessions. The average Frenchman was vaguely proud of these useless jewels without giving them any thought except when it suited his convenience. He remained a countryman in his world outlook; by tradition and necessity, he was interested in European questions; the colonies had been given to him out of vanity. They interested only a small specialized minority, 'the colonials'—soldiers, civil servants, traders and missionaries—all with their headquarters in France: the ministry, the commercial banks and the trading companies and the missionary societies. It was a world apart, virtually limited to Paris and certain large towns like Lyon, Bordeaux and Marseille. Its importance in national life was less than that of the colonial interests in 1789 when the overseas domain of France was limited almost to a few islands in the West Indies.

LOCAL ASPECTS. The driving force of the system was the colonial administration. Civil servants who had succeeded the soldiers of the conquest had taken over certain of their predecessors' characteristics. The African native called the district officer *mon commandant* and saluted him in military fashion; all the officials were provided with uniforms with gold and silver braid, which was the mark of rank. At the outset, the army had trained a number of administrators; but their number had diminished considerably, except in the *services civils*, a subordinate cadre where alongside newcomers were to be found a number of old non-commissioned officers. The administrators, a superior cadre, passed through the Ecole Coloniale, which has since become the Ecole Nationale de la France d'Outre-mer (ENFOM): half of them were students recruited by competition and had done three years at the Ecole; the other half were selected from the *services civils* and had put in only a year at the Ecole. Some professors belonged to the University of Paris; others were specialists, former colonial servants like Maurice Delafosse, who was then the greatest savant of African languages and civilizations in France. On emerging from the school, the students were incorporated in the cadre of 'colonial administrators' and sent overseas.

The governor was chosen from among the senior officials; he was no longer as in former times a politician or soldier, but a career colonial. 'The depositary of the Republic's powers', he alone had the right to promulgate decrees, to issue instructions, to correspond with the minister. He was the head of all the civil servants and had a general staff of administrators and technicians. Next to him was a secretary-general to whom certain powers were delegated, and a 'privy council' or 'government council' made up of certain high officials and nominated leaders, which had a consultative role in certain decisions. But neither the secretary-general nor the privy council constituted a counterbalance to his authority. Two colonies alone had an assembly: Senegal, which had a 'colonial council' composed of members elected by the citizens of the four communes and of representatives of the chiefs in the interior; and Madagascar, where economic and financial delegations had been created on the Algerian model, with a section of citizens and a native section. These assemblies met but rarely, and exercised no real power.

The governor of Madagascar had the title of governor-general, although the colony was a unitary one. The governors-general of French West Africa and French Equatorial Africa had under their orders the governors of the colonies within the groups, who for a long time had the title of lieutenant-governor. But the governor-general alone reported to the minister. He had at his disposal large staffs who sought more and more to centralize all decisions; hence, there was some conflict with rich colonies like the Ivory Coast, which objected to being subordinated to Dakar. Poverty-stricken French Equatorial Africa, for reasons of economy, was made a unitary colony in 1934, but the absence of internal communications made it necessary to return to the former régime. The French mania for centralization could not triumph entirely over the realities of an enormous and diverse continent.

Thus the governor reigned supreme, from a distance and through his staff, showing himself only in the course of rare and hasty tours. The real commanders, the 'kings of the bush' (according to Delavignette, 'the true rulers of the Empire'), were his subordinates, the district officers (*administrateurs*). Each colony was divided into circumscriptions (called circles, provinces or departments), divided themselves into sub-divisions (districts, *arrondissements*) and sometimes grouped in regions. At the head of each of these units was placed an *administrateur* of higher or lower rank. The *administrateur* was in charge of everything: administration, police, justice, taxes, roads, building, development of the economy and social progress. With him rested all the initiative and all the responsibility. Supreme over the natives, he was also the first among the Europeans, the representative of the governor and therefore of France. The development of technical services had not yet deprived him of more than a few of his functions, and he remained the co-ordinator in the circumscription. What he made of 'his' area largely depended on his conscience, on his work, on his 'wangling', on the interest he took in this or that aspect of his work and on his knowledge of the country and of the people. This produced a certain competition of which the governors were able to take advantage, a sense of belonging and of pride which often expressed itself in naïve possessive pronouns: 'my circle', 'my roads', 'my policy', 'my natives'. The district officers tended to identify themselves with the territory; but governors-general were mindful of this, and the system of rotating appointments gave them a new posting on each return after their six months' furlough in France, or even more often. Thus, there was no risk of feudalism, for no one was king in the same place for more than two or three years, in accordance with the rule of centralizing democracy. It was, however, rare for a man to leave the group of colonies where he served: French West Africa, French Equatorial Africa, Madagascar, or even Cameroun and Togo saw the same administrators return time and again. The system thus tended to develop not only specialists, but also a certain routine.

To the administrators and other classes of civil servants such as the *services civils*, public works, economic services, doctors, etc., was added another European element: the *settlers* and the traders. The former were not numerous except in certain plantation colonies, such as the Ivory Coast, Guinea, Cameroun, and Madagascar. The traders were mainly settled in the towns. *Administratifs* and settlers frequently were in lively opposition, the former defending general interests and regulations, the latter their own interests above all. But their relations in general were more or less friendly. There was a European society which, once the coming of white women had put an end to the first period of celibacy and miscegenation, tended to dwell apart. The Frenchman had an easy manner in the company of blacks, and genuine friendship between the two races was not uncommon. But, except for the mayors and councillors of the four communes, the Africans were not received in private homes. This was true also of the Asiatic traders (Syrians and Lebanese in French West Africa, Indians and Chinese in Madagascar). This situation came about not because of any doctrinaire racism as such, but rather from diverging patterns of life that progressively widened the gap between the races. Even within European society itself, there were subtle hierarchical nuances. The numerous *petits blancs* (low-grade officials, poverty-stricken settlers and commercial travellers, and 'pauvres réunionnais' in Madagascar), did not fraternize much with their superiors save in the bush. This again was not a caste question— for most of the administrators sprang from the *petite bourgeoisie*—but a matter of disparate education and background.

The administrators had under their orders native guards employed for police work, African personnel such as school-trained secretaries and the traditional chiefs. In Madagascar, where the colonization by the Merina had preceded that by the French, the chiefs had gradually been replaced by officials—'governors' and 'chefs de canton'. In Africa, the former systems were more or less retained under French control. According to the region, one might find stateless societies (without any authority above the level of the clan), chieftainships (with a *chief* of a more or less religious character but limited to a single district), states (more extensive with a social hierarchy and an army). The chieftainship tended to become the subordinate organ of government. The stateless societies forced the administrator to attempt the virtually impossible and burdensome task of establishing direct contact with his subjects. The states were either broken up, as in Dahomey; or, as in Mossi, the sovereign was left the title of superior chief without defined powers, but with his ministers and his vassals retained. The French succeeded more or less effectively in achieving a kind of administrative uniformity, with cantons each run by a chief—a traditional chief if there was one, an appointed one if there was not. The chiefs were the direct agents of the administrator for census taking, for recruiting, for the collection of taxes, for labour services, for the maintenance of order, for public works, for the proper management of agriculture and of villages, etc. The village headmen served as the chiefs' auxiliaries.

Although chieftainship thus survived, its character gradually changed. In former times, the chief had been a sovereign, with warriors and resources of his own, such as slaves, taxes in kind, customary presents, the free upkeep of his crops and his houses. All this was abolished in principle and replaced by a straight salary, made up of percentages out of taxes, the total far too small to permit customary practices. Thus, the prestige of the chief diminished before that of the new men: old soldiers, planters, and traders who had become rich and educated. The government, which formerly had fought against the power of the chiefs, now felt the need to support them, for they had become its auxiliaries. A ministerial circular of 1929 saw in them 'the basis of a policy which tends to allow the evolution of the groups under our control on the lines of their traditional social organization'. One may see in this an echo of the doctrine of Lugard, replacing assimilation. In fact, traditional chieftainship continued to be enfeebled: its prestige was transferred to those who had effective control, that is, to the administrators. They tended to become native chiefs of a new type unless they were frequently replaced; at any rate, their authority had taken on the paternalistic style of their predecessors.

This multiplicity of temporary kingships did not operate in the four communes of Senegal, which had an elected mayor and a municipal council, and whose inhabitants were French citizens. Furthermore, certain categories of persons might acquire citizenship by following a complicated legal procedure. In Madagascar, which was the most advanced in this regard, there were in 1940 almost 8,000 citizens out of 4,000,000 inhabitants. All the other natives, African or Madagascan, were French *subjects*. They were subject to 'native justice', in which the tribunal was presided over by the administrator, assisted by two native assessors and passed judgement in accordance with local custom. They were subjected, furthermore, to the *indigénat*, that is, sanctions enforced by the police, up to as much as five days in prison and fifteen francs fine, for a variety of misdemeanors, such as nonpayment of taxes, failure to perform the *prestation* (ten days of public work), failure to grow enough crops, etc. These systems of summary justice were more reminiscent of former local practice than of the principles of the mother country; they were thus readily accepted by the masses, but less and less willingly by the *évolués*. Moreover, the organization of the 'black army' had brought conscription along with it: Africans were subject theoretically to three years of military service. Only a small minority of them was in fact recruited; in Madagascar, however, a second group of those liable to serve was mobilized for major public works. In certain frontier regions of Africa, conscription often led to the flight of young men into the adjoining British colonies.

THE ECONOMY. The idea, descended from antiquity, that a 'colony' presupposed colonists from the mother country had prevailed among the French for a long time. It was now abandoned, at any rate for tropical countries. Madagascar, where colonists were most numerous, had only 40,000 Frenchmen—most of them from Réunion. Everywhere the colonist might obtain a 'concession' of land, on a provisional basis, which would become his freehold if he developed it. Plantations worked by colonists constituted pilot enterprises for coffee and vanilla in Madagascar, for plants for the extraction of essential perfumery oils in the Comores, for cocoa and coffee in the Ivory Coast, for bananas in Guinea, for coffee and bananas in Cameroun. The natives came to work on these plantations and learned the processes of cultivation, which they then took back to their villages. There rapidly developed a shortage of labour; the colonists had recourse to the administrative machine in order to obtain manpower. But except for certain crops requiring a specialized organization and considerable capital, such as bananas and cultivated rubber, production by Europeans was, as late as 1939, swamped by native production of the so-called *cultures riches*, which accounted for more than eighty per cent of the total.

The commercial banks were interested in certain plantations, and in the exploitation of forests and of mines, which were still few in number. But the greater part of private capital was employed in large-scale import–export business. The commercial companies, which were family affairs to begin with, tended to group themselves into powerful organizations like SCOA, Unilever and the Bordeaux group in West Africa, or the Compagnie Lyonnaise and the Compagnie Marseillaise in Madagascar. Each group had its stores in town, and its depots, which also functioned as buying posts for local products, in the bush. They were headed by Europeans, assisted by numerous natives, acting as travelling salesmen or buyers. Many small and medium-sized traders in French West Africa were Syrians and Lebanese; in Madagascar, Indians and Chinese. The native stores and markets dealt only in the smallest kind of retail trade. Big business was a power with which the government had to reckon.

The administration played a vital part in the organization of agricultural production. It forced the African to abandon his traditional economy, which had been limited to his village and to his own needs. The poll tax compelled him, in order to get money, to grow cash crops or to seek employment at a distance. The habit of migration was sometimes brought about by forced labour: a corvée of ten days in the year for public works, called 'prestations', along with recruitment for the needs of public services and sometimes even for private employers. Voluntary recruitment for far-off work became a tradition in some areas: Malagasy from the south-east went to seek cattle in exchange for work; Malagasy from the extreme south were driven northward by hunger; Navétanes from the Sudan came to grow ground-nuts in Senegal; Mossi from the Upper Volta laboured on the plantations of the Ivory Coast or in the mines of the Gold Coast. One of the administrator's jobs was to spread the cultivation of cash crops—sometimes by the setting up of nurseries and the distribution of plants, as for instance, coffee in Madagascar and in Cameroun; sometimes even by force, for cocoa in the Ivory Coast, at least at first, and for cotton in the whole interior zone of French Equatorial Africa.

The administration created an infra-structure. Railroads, begun in the preceding period, were built rather slowly; motor roads, on the other hand, developed more quickly, in spite of the administrators' shortage of funds, and largely because of the *prestations*. Certain essential arteries were built from the proceeds of local budgets; and loans made possible the completion of harbours and railroads. Economic service departments, such as those of public works, agriculture, stock raising, forests, began to expand. The government regulated prices and the periods for buying the crops, and created *Sociétés de Prévoyance* to maintain stocks of seed and to regulate sales.

The crisis of 1929–30 led to protective measures. France gave premiums to the colonial products threatened with depression, and these were henceforth sold on the metropolitan market at prices higher than world prices. A protectionist system was thus set up in which the metropolitan country took more and more of the output of the colonial economy.

The results of colonial policy

ECONOMIC DEVELOPMENT. Improvements were made in the layout of certain existing railroads. Some were extended, such as that of the Ivory Coast towards Upper Volta and that of Cameroun up to Yaoundé. Two new lines were opened: the Congo-to-ocean railroad, completed in 1934, joined Brazzaville to the coast, but by using forced labour, caused thousands of deaths; the southern Madagascar railroad, finished in 1936, employed the second group of military conscripts with excellent results. Roads, a great novelty for the time, joined the administrative centres one with another and ended the isolation of the bush; human porterage, the scourge of earlier periods, largely disappeared. Ports were created where ships could tie up at the quay; Tamatave, Djibouti, Douala, Pointe Noire, Conakry, and above all, Dakar. Work began on turning the lagoon at Abidjan into a port. The Sahara was crossed by automobiles, and from 1930 onward airlines were developed. It still took three days to reach Dakar from Paris, six to Tananarive, but this was an improvement on sea voyages, which required from ten to thirty days. At the same time as the means of communication with the metropolitan country were becoming more rapid, a number of interior airlines were organized.

The Africans continued to rely mainly on a subsistence economy. Each group produced all it needed with more or less elaborate methods, ranging from the 'slash-and-burn' of the brush and the jungle to the irrigated rice field, but with archaic tools and without much selectivity in the choice of crops. However, the introduction of money and the development of communications in certain favoured regions, mainly along the coast, led to the creation of an exchange economy based on export crops. From 1920 to 1939 Senegal's export of ground-nuts rose from 220,000 metric tons to 600,000 metric tons, the export of bananas from Guinea from 100 metric tons to 53,000, the export of cocoa from the Ivory Coast from 2,000 metric tons to 53,000. Exports of coffee, starting from zero, reached 45,000 metric tons in Madagascar, 18,000 in the Ivory Coast. Wild rubber had disappeared from exports, but other crops made progress: palm-oil and palm-kernels in Togo and Dahomey, okoumé wood in Gabon. Certain areas like the Ivory Coast and Cameroun, thanks to the variety of their resources—cocoa, coffee, wood—were able to achieve financial prosperity. Madagascar could boast of a wide range of products—rice, manioc, cattle, coffee, vanilla, etc.—which gave it a certain economic stability. The dry interior regions of Africa were less favoured: the crops that were encouraged there by the administration, cotton and ground-nuts, were *produits pauvres*, and their purchase price was depressed by heavy transport costs to seaboard.

Taken together, these changes amounted to an economic revolution. The regions of the interior—Sudan in French West Africa, the interior plateau of Madagascar, the north of Cameroun, and Chad—which in former times had been the most politically lively and commercially active regions, were overtaken by the coastal regions, formerly of marginal importance, which had the advantage of greater humidity and shorter communications. Some of these were no longer self-sustaining: Senegal, concentrating on ground-nuts, did not produce enough millet and had to import rice from Indo-China.

The more or less protectionist customs system, the bounties, the direction of production toward the crops needed by the mother country, the domination of trade by French houses, all had increased the French share in the trade of the colonies. France sold them manufactured goods and bought their foods and raw materials: a system which, without going to the lengths of the 'Exclusif' of the *Ancien Régime*, led to almost the same degree of subordination and monopoly. In 1938, the 'franc area' accounted for 82 per cent of the exports and 69 per cent of the imports of French West Africa; for Madagascar, the proportion was a little more equal as between imports and exports, roughly 75 per cent for each. The share of the colonies in French trade reached a fourth or a fifth. It was a form of assimilation for which autarchic notions, born of the crisis, were responsible; it benefited the trading houses and French industry, but was not so advantageous for the metropolitan consumer, who had to pay a higher price.

SOCIAL AND CULTURAL EFFECTS. In former times, the severity of the tropical climate, the prevalence of disease-carrying insects, the want of hygiene, the primitive and harmful character of witch doctors' medicine, had both made the colonies dangerous for white men and maintained the native population in a state of demographic stagnation. The soldiers of the conquest had been accompanied by doctors, and this 'Colonial Health Corps' afterwards provided the essential personnel for the Assistance Médicale Indigène (AMI). This body, set up at the beginning of the century in Madagascar, then in French West Africa, and subsequently extended everywhere, administered free treatment and medicine in town hospitals and dispensaries in the bush. The Africans gradually became accustomed to using these facilities. European doctors, very few in number, had to be assisted by native doctors; these were trained in special schools at Tananarive and at Dakar that had a four-year course. Midwives and nurses were also trained. But the hospitals and the clinics served only the administrative centres and some other localities: for the whole of French West Africa in 1946 there were 152 medical centres and 253 dispensaries with 170 European and 335 African doctors. For lack of funds, the buildings were often in very precarious condition—a situation that could not be compensated for by the dedication of the staff.

In addition, the French began to wage war on the great epidemic diseases. In 1933 the Institut Pasteur of Tananarive produced a vaccine for the plague; in 1938, that of Dakar began to distribute a vaccine for yellow fever. These two mortal scourges disappeared within a few years, once vaccination, as for smallpox, was made obligatory. The battle against sleeping-sickness was vigorously led by Doctor Jamot, beginning in 1921 in Cameroun and after 1935 in French West Africa; great regions menaced with depopulation could begin to live again.

These medical activities, along with the improvement in roads that put an end to great famines—the last of these were in 1931 in the Niger area and the south of Madagascar—brought about a falling death-rate, notably in infant mortality. In consequence, the population began to grow during the inter-war period: from 12 millions to 15½ millions in

French West Africa, from 3 to 4 millions in Madagascar. However, certain thinly populated areas like the borders of Sahara, the jungle of the interior of Gabon, and the marshes of the Oubangui, tended to lose still more people in favour of the more active economic regions of the coast and of the towns. The administrative centres or harbour towns began to increase in population: Tananarive, from 70,000 to 140,000 inhabitants; Dakar from 20,000 to 120,000; Abidjan was founded in a clearing on its lagoon and became the capital of the Ivory Coast. Everywhere the ports grew and the administrative centres became genuinely urban centres with some semblance of town planning. In short, a new civilization was being born.

In the towns, the economy was mainly monetary and rested on wage-earning employment: officials, clerks in stores, labourers, mechanics, were for the most part detribalized persons, maintaining only tenuous links to their district of origin; others were temporary immigrants. Those who settled permanently gradually adopted European ways in matters of dress, diet, and housing. In the bush, changes were less marked. However, thanks to migration, to improved communication and to the spread of trading posts, the self-sufficient societies of former times did begin to change; the products of local craftsmen, such as cloth and iron work, gave place to imported wares; the prestige of the old men declined before the newly-found freedom of the young; the monetary economy boosted the price of dowries; and the areas of *cultures riches* gave rise to a planter bourgeoisie.

Modifications of traditional ways of life were also taking place. Labourers on the plantations, workers in the towns, old soldiers, had all been taken for at least a time out of their traditional milieu, and their contacts with the outside world had made some impression. The townspeople were even further removed from tradition. The hold of paganism was broken in the towns and was considerably weakened in the countryside, for the young men simply did not put in an appearance at local ceremonies. Islam made inroads in the Sudan, Christianity on the coast; in Madagascar, the whole central plateau was Christianized; south-west Cameroun underwent a wave of spontaneous conversions to Christianity. Most of the faithful were recruited by French Catholic missions; but there were also French, English, American and Norwegian Protestant missions. The practice of Christianity contributed towards separating the faithful from their cultural milieu and to making them question the wisdom of their ancestors.

The first schools had been set up by the missions. But the French state, even though no longer as anti-clerical as before, developed alongside the mission schools an official system of secular instruction. Its ends were not clearly defined. Perhaps it would be more fitting to speak of its general direction. The system stressed the belief in the civilizing mission of France, in the desirability of spreading the French tongue, in the need for clerks for commerce and officials for the administration. The spirit of assimilation was manifest throughout: the programmes of instruction were virtually those of the metropolitan country, and the teachers, at least those in the larger schools, were French. In the villages the primary schools had native teachers, trained in the normal schools of Dakar or Tananarive, or monitors with much less training. The regional schools and the superior primary schools made up the system. Most people did not get beyond the primary stage, and the proportion of pupils, at the end of our period, was still small: 20 per cent in Madagascar, 15 per cent in Cameroun (a relatively high proportion owing to the mission schools), 7 per cent in Dahomey, 6 per cent in French Equatorial Africa, 4 per cent in Senegal, less than 1 per cent in Niger. Here, too, as in the economic field, the Moslem countries of the interior fell behind the colonies of the south.

Access to secondary education was extremely limited. There were two *lycées* in Tananarive and two for the whole of French Africa (one at St Louis and one at Dakar), and the majority of their pupils were Europeans. The pursuit of higher education involved a costly journey to France. This had not yet become common except for a few brilliant exceptions that could still be counted on the fingers of both hands: Senegalese like Senghor, a university graduate, and Lamine Gueye, a magistrate; and a sprinkling of doctors and dentists from the assimilated upper strata of Madagascan society. All these were French citizens. In contrast to what happened in the British colonies, cultural assimilation had occurred at the primary level, not at the university level.

POLITICAL DEVELOPMENTS. The educational system reflects the political stagnation of the period, the disregard for republican principles, the preponderance of material interests, the fear of forming an élite of *déclassés*, that is, of people whom one did not want to recognize socially. The native cadres remained inferior, while the régime remained one of white domination in both the bureaucratic and economic spheres.

Its leaders had no thought of changing it; any tendency in that direction appeared revolutionary and was therefore opposed.

But the régime did not, in fact, appear to be menaced. Between the flow of conquest and the ebb of decolonization, the period between the two world wars appears to have been, politically, one of slack water, of a more or less stagnant peace. However, the two tides, one of the past, the other of the future, did make themselves felt, however feebly.

Pacification was accomplished in the only region that had not been already subdued—in Mauritania, adjoining Spanish Rio de Oro, which, since it was unoccupied, offered a refuge to the Regueibat. In 1934 the last great raiding expeditions were put down, and in the following year a link was forged between the French troops of Mauritania and those of Morocco. In 1929 a rebellion had broken out in the Baya country in the west of Oubangui in connexion with the recruitment of forced labour for the Congo–Ocean railroad; this was suppressed the following year. These were the last echoes of the past.

On the other hand, the influence of French republican ideas began to make itself felt among the *évolués* who had received a certain degree of education: teachers, African doctors, clerks, some old soldiers who had been in contact with left-wing elements in France. In Senegal, in opposition to the deputies who were considered too moderate, Lamine Gueye created the Senegalese Socialist Party, which affiliated with the French Socialist Party (SFIO). In the Congo, at the instigation of an old soldier, André Matsoua, a 'friendly society' collected funds and demanded French citizenship. It achieved great success. Matsoua was arrested in Brazzaville in 1930; but he escaped and returned to Paris, only to be called up in 1939, to be arrested afresh at Brazzaville and to die a short time afterwards. He was subsequently put on a pedestal by his followers.

In Madagascar, a movement curiously similar to that of Matsoua was launched by a teacher, Ralaimongo, a former slave, an enthusiast for 'France the emancipator' and a soldier of World War I. On returning home, he started a journal, *L'Opinion*, in which he demanded that the Malagasy should become French citizens and that their country should be made a French *département*. He denounced the malpractices of certain administrators and settlers, but was protected by the freedom of the press (in French, for the press in the Malagasy tongue was censored). In 1929, however, he was banished to a remote part of the interior after his supporters had demonstrated in front of the office of the governor-general. The Malagasy *évolués* were disconcerted and reduced to silence; the more ardent among them turned to a nationalism which evoked the days of the ancient Malagasy kingdom rather than republican sentiment. The short period of the Popular Front in France led to a certain reaction in favour of assimilatory socialism; but when the hopes of this movement faded, a moderate nationalism reappeared—the cause had not yet acquired a mass following. Ralaimongo died shortly afterwards, almost forgotten.

Thus, it was under the banner of French revolutionary ideas, which were still alive among the teaching profession, that political movements awakened. The *évolués* considered themselves French Africans and demanded French citizenship. But French officialdom made no great effort to seize the opportunity; the 'France of a hundred million inhabitants' was no more. It was only later, at the moment of decolonization, that the profound influence of the colonial period on political evolution in Africa could be measured.

The formation of a small Frenchified élite, even though it could not boast an education above the level of the secondary school, provided cadres for the political parties and afterwards for the republics. Their leaders were mindful of the inferior status which had made them wish for emancipation, but at the same time for identification with the French intellectual élite. This fact, along with the established relations with the French and a long attachment to the metropolitan economy partly explains the duration of the 'Union Française' and the maintenance of close relations with France after independence.

Furthermore, the administrative structure had been transformed through the decline or the disappearance of older forms of government based on war and religion. The earlier small units—clans, cantons, kingdoms of limited extent—had been replaced by far larger colonies with a centralized and hierarchical administration. This change of scale would be irreversible. Despite the survival of tribal tendencies, representing former loyalties, it was the colonies that served as a base for the new succession states.

World War II and the French African colonies

SCISSION (1940–3). Before these new developments occurred, World War II had shown the firmness of the structure. Even the defeat of France in 1940 failed to evoke any native political reaction except one of sympathy and concern. Decisions were taken by the governors. Although at first favourable to a continuation of the fight, the governors were impressed by the personality of Pétain and did not dare to break with the metropolitan country in her days of misfortune. The destruction of the French fleet at Mers el Kébir on 3 July 1940, ordered by Churchill, was a rude blow to pro-British sentiment; and the appeal of De Gaulle, a personality little known or discussed at the time, was not heeded. During the course of July 1940, the chief colonial governors rallied to Vichy, but latent opposition persisted among a number of Europeans.

The emissaries of De Gaulle profited from this to win over French Equatorial Africa to their cause. On 26 August 1940, Governor Félix Eboué of Chad, a black man from Guiana, announced that the colony would support De Gaulle. On 27 August Colonel J. P. Leclerc reached Douala and rallied Cameroun. On the 28th, the physician-general, Sicé, seized the government of Brazzaville in the name of Free France. These were the 'Three Days of Glory'. On the 30th the movement was joined by the governor of Oubangui. The governor of Gabon hesitated, changed his mind, was conquered and imprisoned by the Gaullists, and finally committed suicide. French Equatorial Africa and Cameroun helped to defeat the Germans and Italians in Libya and provided landing fields for British aircraft bound for the Middle East. The products of the territory were bought by the British: their orders revived the wild rubber industry; the local budgets had never been in better shape. Eboué, appointed governor-general, worked out a native policy based on the chiefs.

In French West Africa, Governor-General Boisson remained firmly loyal to Vichy. From 23 to 25 September 1940 the British fleet, after an abortive attempted rising by Gaullist emissaries, bombarded Dakar but suffered damage and was forced to retire. This attack confirmed the political *status quo*. A cult of Marshal Pétain developed, backed by the Légion des Anciens Combattants and police reinforcements. Clandestine resistance groups were formed, made up of diverse elements in which the extreme right and the extreme left mingled. Their effectiveness was limited to exchanging messages with Gaullist missions in neighbouring countries, to the dissemination of leaflets, and to the organization of some flights to the British colonies; but when they were caught, they were court-martialled, and the penalties were heavy. Boisson, a former teacher who had been severely wounded in the

1914–18 war, jealously preserved his territory against the efforts on the part of Laval and the Germans to seize it. He secretly rested his hopes on the United States, but his hostility to Gaullism was only equalled by his Breton faith in Pétain. Life in the territory was difficult and the subsistence economy was revived. Shortages caused the first industries —oil-seed crushing plants and soapworks—to be established. An effort was made to develop production to meet the needs of the starving metropolis, and the demands on labour were increased.

The Anglo-American landing in North Africa, at the beginning of November 1942, brought the long-awaited opportunity. Boisson went to Algiers to confer with Darlan. On the 22nd he proclaimed his adherence to the Allies. The last followers of the Marshal were brought into line without difficulty, and Boisson collaborated actively with the Americans. But there was no reconciliation with the Gaullists; and when De Gaulle seized power in Algiers in 1943, Boisson was deposed and imprisoned. He died before he could be brought to trial.

Madagascar had lived through some very bitter experiences. On the basis of charges that the island might render assistance to Japanese submarines, Churchill on 5 May 1942 ordered a bombardment of the French ships and aircraft at Diego Suarez; and the base was subsequently occupied. The invasion of the island, begun on 14 September, was completed in a few days. The island was handed over to Free France, that is, to authorities designated by De Gaulle. These officials set about mobilizing an economy that was in bad shape, not, however, without generating a certain amount of discontent.

Soon afterward, Réunion rallied to the Gaullist cause, to be followed in short order by French Somaliland, which was starving on account of the British blockade.

PLANS FOR THE FUTURE (1943–5). The Provisional Government at Algiers, feeling the need to legitimize its power, convoked a Consultative Assembly in which, alongside delegates from the French Resistance, sat delegates from the colonies, most of them Europeans. This was no more than a preview of future institutions.

René Pleven, the 'Commissaire des Colonies', prepared the way for the examination of a new policy that would take account of changing opinion, of the Atlantic Charter and of the American presence, and that had as its aim the union of the Empire and of restored France in one institutional framework. In December 1943, he summoned at Tananarive a 'mixed Franco-Malagasy Commission'. At the end of January 1944, he called together the Brazzaville Conference, which was inaugurated by General de Gaulle himself and which, thanks to long preparations, managed in the course of a single week to reach some definitions of principle.

The conference was not a parliament, but apart from certain members of the consultative assembly, it was a conference of governors, better fitted to deal with practical questions than to define a long-range policy. Their chief concern was the preservation of the Empire, but assimilation seemed to them to pose certain threats. Hence the conference produced decisions of varied and sometimes of contradictory import, based on a wish to innovate freely without giving up anything. Thus the members espoused an extension of gubernatorial powers, fiscal decentralization, the creation of industries, the consolidation of the powers possessed by the chiefs, a special status for outstanding *évolués*, the suppression of the *indigénat*, the extension of education (to be given exclusively in French), the freedom of labour (subject to the registration of workers), and the employment of Africans in the administration. Politically, however, France must remain indivisible. 'The aims of France's civilizing mission in her colonies preclude any thought of autonomy or any possibility of development outside the French empire. Self-government must be rejected—even in the more distant future.'

However, this policy was not entirely negative. The conference favoured the creation of general councils, composed partly by Europeans and partly by Africans for each colony. The colonies were to advance gradually 'from administrative decentralization to political personality'. The conference finally urged that the colonies should be represented in the future Constituent Assembly.

These were the essential recommendations whose consequences, though scarcely envisioned by the members of the conference at the time, were to play a decisive role. The Constituent Assembly, convoked in September 1945 after the return to Paris, included more than a tenth of the representatives of the overseas territories of whom half were Africans. These, particularly Senghor and Lamine Gueye, were to play a decisive part in the elaboration and discussion of the new constitutions; all Africans were to be proclaimed citizens of the French Republic. The issue of assimilation seemed to have carried the day. In fact, however, the existence of local assemblies and the evolution of the neighbouring British territories caused the system to lead, within fifteen years, to the break-up of the Union and to the formation of independent states. The Brazzaville Conference, despite its naïve contradictions and its authoritarian manner, thus served to abolish the colonial *status quo*, put an end to political stagnation, and opened the way toward the future. Emancipation, thus made possible, would follow and would be essentially the work of Africans.

BIBLIOGRAPHY

Conférence Africaine de Brazzaville, *Compte-rendu*. Paris, 1945.

Delavignette, Robert L. *Freedom and authority in French West Africa*. London and New York, Oxford University Press, 1950.

Deschamps, Hubert. *Les Méthodes et les doctrines coloniales de la France du XVIe siècle à nos jours*. Paris, 1953.

   L'Union française: histoire, institutions, réalités. Paris, 1952.

Ganiage, Jean, Hubert Deschamps and Odette Guitard. *L'Afrique au XXe siècle*. Paris, 1966.

Olivier, Marcel. *Six ans de politique sociale à Madagascar*. Paris, 1931.

Sarraut, Albert. *Grandeur et servitude coloniales*. Paris, 1931.

   La mise en valeur des colonies françaises. Paris, 1923.

CHAPTER 7

FRENCH COLONIAL POLICY IN BLACK AFRICA, 1945 TO 1960

by ROBERT L. DELAVIGNETTE

How will future textbooks on universal history summarize in a few lines the events that took place in French Black Africa between 1945 and 1960, and that resulted in the creation of fourteen republics? Perhaps for our purposes it would suffice to point out that during this period all the colonial empires were approaching the end, and that the French Empire shared their lot. The political problems presented to France by her Black African dominions were dominated by two opposing trends: the drive towards independence and the desire to maintain French sovereignty in a new form. We know now, of course, that it was the first drive that succeeded; but we know less about the conditions of its success. The achievement of independence resulted not only from a world-wide movement, but also from a phenomenon peculiar to French Africa. From 1945 onward, French Africa had begun to disengage itself from the colonial régime under which it had been ruled since its founding in the second half of the preceding century. It had taken part in the elaboration of the French constitution of October 1946. French Africa entered into the French Republic on the same terms as those enjoyed by the metropolitan country. After having existed for a certain period as an integral part of the French Republic, it seceded peacefully in 1958–60 and formed itself into fourteen independent republics. It is this phase, by and large, that we shall analyse.

In 1945, French Black Africa comprised two territories ruled by governors-general, French West Africa and French Equatorial Africa; and two mandated territories from the League of Nations, Togo and Cameroun. French West Africa (which, for convenience, we shall refer to as AOF) was a group of eight colonies which, running from west to east along the Atlantic coast, were: Mauritania, Senegal, Guinea, the Ivory Coast, Dahomey; and in the interior along the sub-Saharan Sahel, Sudan, Upper Volta and Niger. French Equatorial Africa (AEF) joined four colonies: Gabon, and—from south to north—

Congo, Oubangui-Chari and Chad. In December 1946, Togo and Cameroun became subject to the trusteeship agreements by which France administered them under the control of the United Nations. It should be noted that the fourteen republics of 1958–60 corresponded to these colonies and territories. Only two have since changed their names: the Sudan became Mali; Oubangui-Chari, the Central African Republic. To distinguish the former French Congo from the former Belgian Congo, the French Congo is now called Congo-Brazzaville. What was novel in 1960 was that the governor-generalships of AOF and AEF had ceased to exist.

In our brief analysis of these changes, we shall stress the administrative and political factors. But it goes without saying that these changes must be considered in the context of the economic and social background of the times. In Black Africa, this framework is particularly hard to define; and we must limit ourselves to pointing out the facts in a general way. The economy had a dual character: it was based in part on commercial production, in which the export of agricultural products was of prime importance, and in part on agriculture for home consumption. Social patterns were deep-rooted in African tradition, with its infinite variety and its unsuspected depths. This diversity was expressed on the political level by many different kinds of chieftainship. The Moorish emirates, the Nigerian sultanates, the Cameroun lamidates, for instance, were not the same institutions as those of the Mossi Nabas and the Bambara kingdoms; the Dahomean throne was not the same as the Baoulé stool. The depths are difficult to sound, because ancient customs blend with new ways of life. Black Africa was colonized before it was understood, and it was emancipated as soon as Frenchmen thought they understood it. This is another way of saying that politics preceded scientific research, especially in ethno-sociological matters. The Negro-African societies studied during the colonial period were already in the melting-pot. When independence arrived, they had neither the same structures nor the same jurisdictions that they had at the time, recent though it was, at which they had been explored. 'To write about Africa', says Professor Bustin, 'is to write upon the sand; it is to describe a momentary reality which is not that of yesterday and which tomorrow will overturn.' Although I do not share this opinion entirely, I feel strongly that it contains a valuable element of truth. The chief difficulty in studying African politics is to discern the forces at work, which are often obscured by ideology and phrase-making.

The Brazzaville Conference (1944)

The textbooks of the future to which we referred in the opening paragraph may well ascribe to the Brazzaville Conference (January and February 1944) an importance not borne out by the relevant documents. The conference was a meeting, not of elected Africans but of higher European officials, except for Governor-General Eboué, a black West Indian. The conference is reputed to have brought about the independence of the French colonies, whereas in fact it proclaimed the very contrary. Let us recall its recommendations:

[whereas] the aims of the civilizational work accomplished by France in her colonies rule out all idea of autonomy and all possibility of development outside the French Empire; [therefore] the eventual constitution, even in a far-off future, of self-government in the colonies is out of the question.

That is clear enough. What follows is no less explicit:

It is desirable that the political authority of France be exercised with precision and rigour over all parts of the Empire. It is desirable also that these colonies enjoy considerable administrative and economic freedom. It is desirable, furthermore, that the colonial peoples experience this liberty themselves, and that their responsibilities be gradually created and increased until they become associated with the conduct of public affairs in their countries.

Try as one may, it is impossible to extract anything further from these documents than a promise of eventual 'great administrative and economic freedom'. The texts left unquestioned the matter of French sovereignty, which was to be exercised 'with precision and rigour'. The only hope they held out for the colonies—for all the colonies of the French Empire—depended on a kind of political pedagogy that was to create and enlarge, 'little by little', the political responsibility of the colonial peoples. They would be allowed, in due course, to participate increasingly in the conduct of public affairs, but only on the local level.

The Brazzaville Conference is nevertheless interesting on more than one count. In the first place, it bears witness to a state of mind that was to persist long afterward. This spirit dominated the promoter of the conference, General de Gaulle, the chief of Free France; its president, René Pleven, the commissary of colonies; and above all, Félix Eboué, one of its originators, who had been made governor-general of French Equatorial Africa by De Gaulle on 12 November 1940, and who, being a black man, was the most significant of the three.

General de Gaulle did not play a merely routine role at Brazzaville. Beginning on 18 June 1940, when France fell, he boldly took on heavy responsibilities. However, the Brazzaville recommendations inspired by him had nothing revolutionary about them; they appeared rather to be dictated by loyalty to the concept of empire. De Gaulle did not wish Vichy to be able to boast of having saved the empire. He himself had need of it, as he had said on 18 June 1940: 'For France is not alone! She is not alone! She has behind her a vast empire'.

René Pleven, one of the first associates of General de Gaulle, had lived in the United States, in the world of great industrial and commercial companies. His sense of purpose was not tied to administrative strings, French-style. He was well aware that the United States intended to promote throughout the world the policy of colonial independence which it had applied to the Philippines and of which Roosevelt had said in 1942: 'This is a model that men of good will ought to follow in the future'. The third principle of the Atlantic Charter, to which France had adhered, was very explicit: it respected the right of all peoples to choose the form of government under which they would live; it looked to the restoration of sovereign rights and self-government for all those who had been deprived of them. The founders of the United Nations equally hoped to assist the colonial peoples in acquiring home rule. The fate of the colonial peoples should no longer lie solely with the mother country, but ought to be the concern of an international organization. The United Nations took the position that independence was the inevitable and the only morally desirable goal of colonization. However, René Pleven, himself faithful to the Empire, made his own the words of General de Gaulle, who in opening the Brazzaville Conference had declared without equivocation:

It is the business of the French nation—and it is its business alone—to proceed at the appropriate time to reforms in the structure of the Empire which she in her sovereignty will decide.

It was well understood that these reforms would be 'imperial'. We have seen that they were opposed to autonomy, even in the distant future, and to self-government.

In the Brazzaville Conference, composed mainly of officials, Félix Eboué was unlike any of the other governors. He was a black man, born in Guiana of an African family transported to America in the slave-trade. He had been a district officer in Africa, and he was made a governor, in 1936, in spite of racist clamour, by Maurice Viollette, deputizing for Marius Moutet, the Socialist minister of colonies in the Popular Front government led by Léon Blum. As governor of Chad, he rallied to De Gaulle on 26 August 1940, and he soon led the whole of French Equatorial Africa into the Free French camp.

One fact ought not to escape historians: there were, in 1940, two juridical types of French colony, those that were called *à législature* and those that were called *à décrets*. The first had democratic institutions, were represented in the French Parliament, had a general council and municipalities. The second were ruled in an authoritarian fashion by executive decree, and with the exception of four Senegalese communes had no share in legislation, no municipalities, no general council. It was the first type of colony that submitted immediately to Vichy without bringing into play the democratic resources at its disposal. It was French Equatorial Africa—an authoritarian government-general, the archetype of the colony *à décrets*—that, under Eboué's leadership, pronounced in 1940 in favour of the democratic ideals symbolized by Free France and General de Gaulle. This did not prevent Eboué from affirming his loyalty to the Empire in 1944. It is true that he was equally faithful to an African policy which was supported by numerous administrators in the bush.[1] He defined it in a circular of 8 November 1941 and he afterwards put it into effect. It was a 'native' policy of an experimental character founded on ethno-sociological inquiry, inspired by district officers who worked in constant contact with the people. Eboué had faith in the worth of an enlightened administration that would respect African societies, and that would work in co-operation with them to recruit an élite and to extract from their traditions all that might serve the purposes of modern Africa. For Eboué, to colonize was to start with the African himself, to have a sense of Africa. In opening the Brazzaville Conference, General de Gaulle praised Eboué as 'having his feet firmly planted in African soil; hence, he would not lose the sense of what was realizable and consequently practicable'. Devoted to the Empire—an Empire which he did not distinguish from his vocation of *'broussard'*—Eboué died, worn out, on 17 May 1944. His practical ideas lived on in the colonial service until 1960. But they were not properly understood, for they were detached from the

---

[1] I refer to my book, *Les vrais chefs de l'empire* (Paris, 1939), reprinted in 1946 under the title, *Service Africain*, and translated into English as *Freedom and authority in French West Africa* (Oxford University Press, 1950; reprint, London, 1968).

context in which they had been formulated and in which they had alone been fruitful and communicable.

The three principal protagonists of the Brazzaville Conference were thus determined to maintain the Empire. Their personalities, diverse and exceptional, might have led them to turn audaciously towards the path of innovation. But instead, they were tied to a policy in which fear for the future paralysed initiative. Was this policy adopted because they were confronted with a particularly delicate colonial situation, if not in Black Africa, at any rate in North Africa and above all in Indo-China? Or did they wish to counteract the Atlantic Charter (14 August 1941), the Declaration of the United Nations (1 January 1942), and the inter-allied conferences of Moscow (1 November 1943) and of Teheran (December 1943), whose proceedings seemed to menace the integrity of the Empire? For ourselves we cannot do more than ask these questions.

But these questions give rise to another: how did the Brazzaville Conference come to be regarded as a signpost towards independence? How did it acquire a significance that it did not really possess? Whence came this powerful myth? It was as a result of the Conference that African political parties sprang into existence and set their course on seas as yet uncharted. The Conference now appears to us as an instrument of timid reform; it aimed solely at the salvation of the Empire. Yet it was the first indication that something new was stirring in French Africa. It would be as mistaken to regard the Conference as the cradle of independence as to deny the importance that Africans attributed to it. Africans were not represented directly at Brazzaville. Even Eboué had not asked any to attend, and they took no part in the proceedings. But though the proceedings of the conference became the subject of a myth, it was the Africans who created this myth. For a clear understanding of the transformation in the relations between France and Black Africa between 1945 and 1960, the importance of this element must be grasped at the outset.

Black Africa under the Fourth French Republic

On 8 May 1945 Germany surrendered. The liberated French were no longer rationed, subject to requisitions, prisoners in their own country and in their own homes. They were no longer in that state of siege-fever in which the Empire seemed their last hope of refuge. They had not been really acquainted with the Empire before the war; they were proud of owning it without knowing what it was really like. It was so vast, so heterogeneous that they could not grasp the elements of it clearly, but it was indeed the Empire! An empire that covered Asia and Africa with the national flag and that had caused to shine on captive France the glory of Bir-Hakeim (1942) and the glimmerings of a miraculous salvation. Moreover, the salvation had actually come. The Empire had taken part in it. A French army raised in the Congo had taken off from Africa, had reached the Rhine and the Danube. The Brazzaville Conference, whose echoes had been vaguely heard in France in 1944, would itself suffice to bring about the minor reforms that were necessary to the smooth working of the Empire. Once republican legality was re-established, matters would work themselves out. Thus, in the public mind the Brazzaville myth was linked to the myth of the Empire.

Be that as it may, innovations came about under cover of a truly republican tradition—the tradition of 1848. When the government of General de Gaulle, set up in Paris in August 1944, convened the Constituent Assembly of the Fourth Republic, it apparently drew its inspiration from the decree of 27 April 1848. By means of this instrument, the provisional government of the Second Republic had proclaimed that 'the colonies, freed of servitude, shall be represented in the National Assembly'. The servitude referred to in 1848 had been brought about not by French sovereignty but by the earlier enslavement of black people in the colonies. The Second Republic freed the slaves by making them French citizens. A century after 1848, the ordinances of 21 August, 13 September, and 21 September 1945 set up two electoral colleges in the colonies, one for citizens, the other for African non-citizens. These two colleges would send to the Constituent Assembly a total of sixty-three representatives. Indo-China was excepted, for the clouds of war were already gathering in south-east Asia.

It would be beyond the scope of the present essay to analyse the work of the Constitutional Commission, whose outstanding member was Léopold Senghor, a Senegalese deputy. The proposals of the commission, in March 1945, were marked by a compromise between the federal position, which would have given the colonies autonomy within a system of union freely agreed upon with the metropolis, and the Jacobin position, which held that the Republic should remain one and indivisible in the colonies just as in the metropolis. The first Constitution of 1946 was rejected by referendum on 5 May. This still-born constitution, however, produced new principles and a new terminology. The Africans ceased to be French subjects and became French citizens. Local assemblies were to be created in every overseas territory, the name 'territory' being substituted for the old word 'colony', to which a certain stigma had already been attached. The term 'Union Française' became fashionable, though its meaning had not become clear.

A number of fundamental laws were voted which were validated by the constitution of October 1946:

1. A law dated 19 March 1946 turning the old colonies of French West Indies, Guiana and Réunion into departments.

2. A law dated 30 April 1946 setting up FIDES (Fonds d'Investissements pour le Développement Economique et Social). Up until this time, the colonies had lived under a régime laid down by a simple article in the financial law (article 33 of the law of 13 April 1900).[1] They were obliged to finance their development out of their own resources. The law of 30 April 1946 allowed them to obtain help from the metropolis. They would henceforth participate in the national revenues, which would be distributed to them in a given proportion by FIDES, in the light of their development plans. (As early as 1936, the government of Léon Blum had proposed a colonial fund of this type, but the senate had rejected it.)

With the law of 30 April 1946 we may associate the abolition of forced labour. The government of Léon Blum had prepared for this also by the law of 17 June 1937 ratifying the Geneva Convention of June 1930, and by the decree of 12 August 1937 ordering all governors to suppress forced labour both for public and private purposes. The best way of making this legal provision effective was to provide for the development of the colonies through FIDES. Without FIDES, the Labour Code promulgated in 1952 could not have been implemented.

3. A law of 7 May 1946, the most important from both the political and the juridical points of view, made all the inhabitants of the Overseas Territories French citizens *without distinction of personal civil status*. We shall have occasion to refer to this matter later, for it is the key to the development of the relations between French Black Africa and France up to the granting of independence in 1960.

[1] The financial law in France is the law by which the annual budget is voted

After the fundamental laws of the first Constituent Assembly had been enacted, a new constitution was drawn up. Title 8 converted the Empire into the French Union. The French Union comprised, on the one hand, the Associated States (Indo-China), and on the other, the French Republic, which embraced the metropolitan country and the Overseas Departments and Territories. The Overseas Departments were the French West Indies, Guiana and Réunion. The Overseas Territories were essentially Black Africa and Madagascar. Passed enthusiastically by the Constituent Assembly on 29 September 1946, the constitution was approved by referendum on 13 October 1946. Henceforth the Black African colonies enjoyed the status of Territories constituting an integral part of the Republic, with the right to intervene in French political affairs.

THE LAW OF 7 MAY 1946: BLACK AFRICA IN FRENCH POLITICS. Without going back as far as the Revolution of 1789,[1] we may take 1848 as the reference point for the genesis of the law of 7 May 1946. In 1848 the French Republic abolished slavery and by decree conferred citizenship on all the inhabitants of the colonies. At that period the colonies meant mainly the French West Indies and Réunion. For the republican legislator nothing seemed more normal than to enfranchise the blacks in these areas by conferring on them the same status as that of their masters, in public as well as in private law. Liberation for the black slave consisted of entering on equal terms, juridically speaking, into the family of his master; not of recovering his own rights as an African, rights that he had had before his deportation as a slave. At any rate, in 1848 there were few who were conversant with African law and few to sing the praises of *négritude* or to go in search of African civilizations. The enfranchisement of the black slaves represented, therefore, a complete separation from the Africa of their origins. The freed man was not returned to his mother country, but became a new citizen in the city of his master. In the French Senegal of 1848—which consisted merely of a few trading posts—the granting of French citizenship applied to a small African population in which there were, besides free Negroes, only some 10,000 slaves. In the French West Indies and in Réunion, the 242,000 black slaves became French citizens governed by the French civil code. In Senegal, the black people were

---

[1] The bourgeois of St Louis of Senegal (a tiny town at this time) sent a list of grievances to the States-General.

at the same time French citizens in public law and Africans in terms of private law. This meant applying in Senegal a different principle from that in the West Indies. This was tantamount to admitting that French citizenship was not linked with the civil code and that it stood above personal civil status. Thus, one could be a French citizen in Senegal without renouncing the Law of the Koran or animist beliefs. France was, in fact, embracing in the same citizenship men whose family and social background were very different from that of the metropolis.

French constitutional lawyers considered this situation illogical. They saw in it an irrational privilege, best limited to the four small Senegalese communes where it had been allowed. Later, when French West Africa and French Equatorial Africa came into existence, the black citizens of the four Senegalese communes played an important role in the development of these French territories. But no new communes were created, and the four communes of Senegal remained an exception. During the First World War, Blaise Diagne, the black deputy from Senegal, the only black representative from all French Africa, inspired the laws of 19 October 1915 and 24 September 1916, which confirmed the French citizenship of the black natives of the four communes. Lamine Gueye, a Senegalese, wrote his doctoral thesis in 1922 on the subject of these laws of 1915 and 1916. By 1946 he was sitting in the French chamber as a deputy from Senegal, and it was he who promoted the law of 7 May 1946. This law, which was based on the principles that had given rise to the four Senegalese communes, represented a great leap forward. Between them, the law of 7 May 1946 and the subsequent constitution of October 1946 resurrected the traditions of 1848. The exception originally made for the four communes became the rule for millions of Africans. Muslims and animists, Christians and atheists, tribesmen subject to special native courts and Africans answerable to French tribunals, all acquired the right to vote. All were enabled to exercise civic rights in the political life of France itself.

In 1946, the African electorate was at first limited to certain categories of persons, but these limitations soon disappeared. In the elections to the National Assembly of 1946, French West Africa had 803,000 registered electors of whom 519,000 voted; French Equatorial Africa, 110,000 registered and 72,000 voting; Togo, 9,600 registered and 6,500 voting; Cameroun, 41,000 registered and 22,500 voting. In the election of 1951, the number of electors had markedly increased. In the elections of 1956, French West Africa had 6,054,300 registered and 3,305,000 voting; French Equatorial Africa, 1,195,000 registered and 905,000 voting; Togo, 213,400 registered and 185,700 voting; Cameroun, 833,600 registered and 484,500 voting. From 1946 to 1956, within a single decade, the electorate of French Black Africa had increased ninefold. In 1956, two years before independence, it equalled almost one-third of the metropolitan electorate.[1] A wave from Black Africa had broken upon the French political scene, which in the course of its long history had never seen such an irruption of new citizens.

These new electors presented startling novelty: Moorish and Tuareg camel-drivers, Fulani cattlemen, peasants from the savannah, planters from the coast. How different they were from the people of the metropolis! Polygamous, whereas in the mother country bigamy was a crime, they were members of agrarian communities which had nothing in common with the metropolitan society. Yet, they were all integrated into a French Republic of which they knew little, and which in turn had scarcely any knowledge as to what manner of people they were.

It has been said that this extension of French citizenship derived from a policy of assimilation, as in 1848. This was not the case, however, for the blacks were not assimilated; they retained their African status in civil law. They entered into the Republic while at the same time preserving their African customs. This was an important fact, for within the body of the Republic any man, whatever his race, colour, religion, juridical status or worldly wealth, might act as a member of a sovereign people.

Was this move an afterthought in response to pressure from the United Nations? In thus enlarging the African electorate, not only in French West Africa and in French Equatorial Africa, but also in the trusteeship territories of Togo and Cameroun, France—it might be claimed—showed that Africans were using their right of self-determination in favour of the mother country. The French African territories were no longer colonies, depending on an external ruler; they were represented within the framework of French sovereignty. France affirmed her national independence together with the overseas territories,

---

[1] In the AEF the two-college system still operated for elections to the National Assembly (as it did in both AOF and AEF for the territorial assemblies). The abolition (1956) of the two-college system, which gave a premium to European votes, was as important as the widening of the franchise.

mingling empire and democracy. She pursued a policy that was dear to her, a policy of high principles, of grandeur throughout a domain extending from Dunkirk to Brazzaville. After 1960, when this realm had shrunk like a piece of dry leather, the slogan 'from Dunkirk to Tamanrasset', used by the defenders of French Algeria, still expressed nostalgia for a Eurafrican France.

The French Republic had never been as vast as it was between 1945 and 1960. But by its very vastness did it not risk being overextended? Would France not be diluted in the African mass? A close examination of the situation reveals its weaknesses.

THE AFRICAN DEPUTIES REPRESENT THE ENTIRE FRENCH PEOPLE. The number of African representatives did not increase in the same proportion as that of the electors. In 1946, Black Africa sent to Paris 23 deputies, of whom 3 were chosen by the European electoral college. In 1956, there were only 10 more, a total of 33. It might be charged that France was afraid of letting her policy follow its logical course. Certainly, Africans were present in the three parliamentary assemblies: the Conseil de la République, in 1956, had 20 senators from French West Africa, 8 from French Equatorial Africa, 2 from Togo and 3 from Cameroun. The Assembly of the French Union, a creation of the Fourth Republic, had 27 councillors from French West Africa, 7 from French Equatorial Africa, 1 from Togo and 5 from Cameroun. But the Assembly of the French Union did not play a very active role; the Conseil de la République did not have the prerogatives of the National Assembly.

But in each of these three assemblies, Africans made up a minority which knew how to manoeuvre. There were 114 of them in all; and whatever their party affiliations, they were linked by a natural affinity. They soon had a party of their own: the 'Rassemblement Démocratique Africain' (RDA), which was run by a group of fighters for independence, an ideal which had been proclaimed in 1946 at the Constitutional Congress of Bamako. The leaders of the RDA, Félix Houphouët-Boigny, Modibo Keïta, Diori Hamani, Léopold Sédar Senghor, Sekou Touré, would be the presidents of the future independent African states. We shall return to the RDA: the important point to grasp about the role of African deputies to the National Assembly is not so much that their numbers were small, but that according to French public law they were the representatives of the whole French people. They did not speak for Africa alone. They also legislated for the metropolitan country. Though they might be Muslims, their vote counted no less in debates in which the traditional policy of nonsectarian education opposed subsidies to Catholic schools. They exerted influence on the formation or fall of ministries. In 1957, the French government had four Africans as ministers or secretaries of state. And right up to 1960 there would always be at least one African minister in each successive government in Paris.

THE ESTABLISHMENT OF ELECTED ASSEMBLIES. In 1946, the Fourth Republic established in Black Africa a fundamental institution. In each territory there was an elected assembly; in each government-general a grand council of 40 members elected by the territorial assemblies.

The number of those elected to each territorial assembly varied from 34 to 70 for the territories of French West Africa, from 40 to 65 in French Equatorial Africa; there were 30 in Togo and 70 in Cameroun, a grand total of 774. The African members of parliament in Paris took part, by law, in these territorial assemblies and in the grand councils of French West and French Equatorial Africa, respectively, where they dominated the proceedings. It was in these assemblies that independence was to have its legal home and from them it would take its initial impetus. From being consultative in 1946, the territorial assemblies soon became deliberative, and by 1958 had turned into legislative bodies. Between 1946 and 1958, they had profoundly modified the workings of the colonial administration and had steadily reduced the authority of the governor. We shall have occasion later to trace this development.

The social composition of these assemblies is noteworthy. In French West Africa and in Togo, the members were elected from a single roll; in French Equatorial Africa and in Cameroun, from a double roll, one for Europeans and assimilated Africans, the other for Africans having indigenous status. In 1951, those elected from the second roll for the territories of French Equatorial Africa and Cameroun included a total of 293 members, of whom 165 were African civil servants. Among these 165 officials, 53 were teachers, 49 employees of the administration, compared with 24 commercial employees and only 8 planters. Along with these 165 functionaries one might count 65 customary chiefs who, in a way, were a kind of quasi-official because they were subject to dismissal by the colonial administration and might appeal to the highest level of administrative tribunals, the Conseil d'Etat in Paris.[1] Where Europeans and Africans were elected on a single roll in French West Africa and Togo, it is more difficult to ascertain the number of African officials, but it was not fewer than those elected by the second roll in French Equatorial Africa and Cameroun. On the whole, these assemblies were composed largely of civil servants.

We may make three observations concerning African representatives: (1) Although French Africa is 80 per cent rural, its assemblies were not comprised of country dwellers. (2) The Africans in the parliamentary assemblies in Paris were also for the most part officials, and were linked with the members of the territorial assemblies by the solidarity that comes from the same education and the same professional status in the original administrative cadres. (3) On the political plane, in Paris as well as in Africa, the administration represented the indigenous cadres of the colonial administration. The Parisian members of parliament and the councillors of the territorial assemblies were the very functionaries who before 1946 had been subordinated to Europeans in the colonial administration, and who between 1946 and 1958–60 would first control their former superiors and finally replace them.

THE PROBLEM OF THE MUNICIPALITIES. Another important facet of African life—one worthy of future research—is the problem of the municipalities. The political awakening of French Black Africa predated the development of municipalities. For half a century, the only municipalities had been the well-known Four Communes of Senegal. Although towns and cities had sprung up and flourished in French West Africa, Equatorial Africa, Togo and Cameroun, these new communities did not at first attain municipal status. It was not until 1955 that a French type of municipal law—providing for an elective *maire* and town council—made its appearance in the larger towns. These were known as 'communes with full powers', and by 1957 there were thirty-eight of them. The smaller towns had mixed communes where the *maire* was a colonial administrator. The great mass of African villages remained under the colonial régime represented by the traditional chiefs, the *commandant du cercle* and his subordinates. The *collectivités*

[1] Togo became a republic in 1956, and gained its independence in 1960. Nevertheless, in 1965 the Conseil d'Etat re-established in his functions a customary Togolese chief who had been dismissed in 1959, and who had appealed to the French courts.

rurales, which had been tried since 1950, were groups of villages on the level of the former subdivision. It appears that the Republic had set up high political authorities in Africa at a single leap without attempting to base them solidly on communal foundations in Africa. What was the reason for this delay in establishing the municipalities? Was it that the African town posed new problems?[1] True, it was often an aggregation of separate quarters each belonging to a separate ethnic group; it was not yet a city.

From the foregoing, it is clear that from 1946 onward a paradoxical situation had arisen: Africans enjoyed representative government on the national plane, while on the local level, they continued to be administered under their customary institutions, subject to the authority of colonial functionaries. This authority was no longer exactly the same as it had been before 1946, but there was now clearly an imbalance between politics and administration.

THE SYSTEM PERSISTS UNDER NEW CONDITIONS. The French colonial régime in Black Africa had rested on an authoritarian principle to which the four Senegalese communes formed a solitary exception. French rule had its juridical source in a *sénatus-consulte* of the Second Empire dated May 1854. This measure provided that certain colonies would be ruled by decrees of the emperor until such times as they should be organized by specific laws. The Third Republic replaced the emperor, but did not promulgate new organic laws peculiar to the Republic. French territorial expansion in Africa merely extended the territory subject to the decree. Traditions going back to the First French Republic, when it was 'one and indivisible', laid down that the colonies were an integral part of the national territory. They admitted, however, that special laws should be applied to them, on account of their peculiar character. No such legislation had been passed, either during the Restoration or the July Monarchy, except with regard to the most important colonies of that time, the islands. The Second Empire rested on its oars; the Third Republic did the same. The French preferred to rule by decree over the mass of humanity that had been brought under their sway in Black Africa.

Few people in France questioned the extraordinary power possessed

---

[1] An exhaustive analysis of the role of the European society, concentrated as it was in the towns and more cut off from the African world than the old colonial society of unmarried *broussards*, will have to await a future study.

by the minister of colonies. In theory, he was the only republican minister who combined executive powers and legislative powers over a collection of African Negro countries which before 1914 had claimed 14 million souls in French West Africa, 4 million in French Equatorial Africa, and after 1919, a million in Togo and 3 million in Cameroun. Thus, we may observe, from the Second Empire to the Third Republic, the permanence of administrative institutions in the face of political changes. Certainly, legislation by decree was flexible and expeditious. It also seemed more appropriate than legislation proper to deal with the problems presented by colonies still immature and far distant from the metropolitan country. True also, these African countries had their own peculiar character. But it was a character that the French legislator did not choose to analyse; until 1946 he handed over the problem of dealing with it to specialized functionaries who could struggle with it on the spot. Scientific research—a field in which the colonials were often the self-taught pioneers—had made progress, but it had not dissipated the conformism dear to the heart of the metropolitan country.

In 1946, for the first time in the history of French constitutions, a special article—Title VIII—was applied to Overseas France. French Black Africa had its members of parliament, its assemblies. Its period of rule by decree was ended. And still the colonial administration remained on the spot. How can this be explained?

In the first place, the French could not change from one moment to the next the administrative machinery to which the mass of the African population had become accustomed. In the capital city of each colony, the governor or lieutenant-governor still resided in his palace. He remained the kingpin of the public services. In the bush, the villagers still recognized the authority of the *commandant* and of his subdivisional chiefs. The administration continued to carry responsibility for the maintenance of order, for the smooth working of the multiple tasks of the state, and for the proper execution of budgetary provisions. If the administration broke down or ceased to function, who would collect taxes, who would pay the civil servants, who would look after general security?[1]

In the second place, there were the characteristics peculiar to the separate countries. All Africans were now citizens, but the Moor was

[1] Nothing could be more significant than an examination of the small numbers of police in the circles and subdivisions. French peace rested on the moral authority of the *broussards*.

nonetheless completely different from the Bambara or the Baoulé. Moreover, there was the question of the chiefs: the Mogho Naba of the Mossi in Upper Volta was not the same sort of dignitary as the sultan in Niger or in Chad. The traditional chief was now a French citizen just like his subjects. But he still retained his long-accustomed dignity and a majesty that the African had not yet taken away from him, and that the colonial administration had made use of from the beginning.

African chieftainship was in fact one of the essential resources of administrative authority. Without the chiefs, the governor-general, the eight lieutenant-governors of French West Africa and the three hundred district officers in the bush would have been helpless. For it was the chief who represented his community in its dealings with the administration, and, even more importantly, the administration vis-à-vis his community. In French West Africa there were some 2,000 *chefs de canton* and around 50,000 *chefs de village*. In French Equatorial Africa, in Togo, in Cameroun, the administration and the chiefs were similarly linked. If this network had been destroyed at one stroke, chaos would surely have followed.

Nevertheless—and this is the important point—the administration was no longer master as it had been before, but it was still the servant, without whom a state of utter confusion—a confusion fatal to the gropings towards independence—would have set in. The colonial administration had to face obligations and problems for which it had not been prepared and for which it was ill-equipped. It had the same responsibilities, sometimes heavier than before; but it had not the same powers and had to work in a new climate.

It had to organize elections in districts where civilian authority was still in the embryonic stage. It had to deal with the new authorities created by the elections. It had to apply a policy derived from Paris and from the local assemblies, not inspired—as Eboué would have had it—by knowledge drawn from the African milieu. Eboué was dead and the era of the district officers was coming to a close. They were men of wide knowledge, having worked as jacks-of-all-trades in the day-to-day administration of their particular bailiwicks. They had a fierce pride in Africa. But their native policy was now suspect. The individuality of the African States was now personified by elected Africans who intended to be the only ones to make use of it, the only ones to pay homage to *négritude*. The colonial administration, moreover, no longer exercised exclusive jurisdiction over African problems. The colonies now attracted numerous heads of missions, quickly promoted to their new posts, and technicians sent out from the metropolitan country, often ill-suited to work in a rural African environment without modern comforts.

Two conflicting movements were now intertwined. On the one hand, the colonial administration continued to play its role while trimming its sails with the wind. On the other hand, a new African policy had come into being, and under the Fourth Republic the Negroes were to be French citizens. But the hour was already at hand when these same people would be African citizens in their own republics. In the end, it appeared that French citizenship had been no more than a half-way house towards complete independence. When in 1958 De Gaulle offered Africans the choice between immediate independence and the 'Community', few remembered the imperial recommendations of Brazzaville in 1944. The Community was to bear an ephemeral character. The African states would see in it no more than a formal association that did not prevent them from treating with France on equal terms. In 1958, only Guinea chose independence, but the other states did not take long to follow in its footsteps.[1] The tradition of 1848 had in 1946 taken on a new complexion, brilliantly suited to the formation of African states and to the birth of African nationalism.

Basic structure of the major African political units

Between 1945 and 1960 the process of decolonization led to two apparently contradictory consequences. On the one hand, it dethroned the colonial system at its summit; on the other hand, it maintained the base on which that system rested. After making use of their organization, it destroyed the governments-general, which for more than half a century had constituted the highest political and administrative entities of French Black Africa. But at the same time it left in existence territories that had been created out of bits and pieces in the colonial epoch

[1] An objective scrutiny of the Community of 1958 reveals that two of its major institutions never functioned. The Senate met only twice before dissolving. The Supreme Court, which had a magnificent opportunity to inaugurate its authority by arbitrating the conflict that provoked the break-up of the Mali Federation in 1960, never made its presence felt and, like the Senate, ceased to exist. As for the presidency of the Community, the activities of this office remain hidden in sources not yet accessible for historical research.

and that were now to become each, in its turn, the cradles of new states. The newly independent states retained the old administrative organization, the circumscriptions which the colonial period had founded—the circle and the subdivision.

Let us examine these two phenomena one by one.

THE GOVERNMENTS-GENERAL: ASSOCIATION OF COASTAL AND HINTERLAND COLONIES. It is doubtful, as some have asserted, that the creation of governments-general in Black Africa was inspired by the Indo-Chinese example. As a matter of fact, the governments-general in both French West Africa and Equatorial Africa derived from needs that were essentially African, and from a colonial mythology that was peculiar to nineteenth-century Africa. The French sought to join within the same political and administrative framework countries that were still little known. Some of these territories lacked any pre-colonial tradition of territorial unity; others had been included in larger African states even before colonization.

Initially, the government-general of French West Africa resulted from Senegalese expansion eastward towards the distant Nigerian savannahs. The first governor-general of French West Africa in 1902 was also governor of Senegal. In 1854, to persuade Faidherbe to become head of their trading posts, the traders of St Louis had said in substance the following: 'Our Senegal has nothing in common with the West Indies and Réunion; it looks out onto a vast continent'. As a student in the Ecole Polytechnique, Faidherbe had had his mind fixed on this continental horizon, looking towards the Niger river; and he had been the first to sketch out the traces of a Senegambian–Niger colony.

In 1904, the governor-general of French West Africa was relieved of the local administration of Senegal so that he might concentrate on the co-ordination of all the five colonies in the group. The first and most extensive was called Upper Senegal–Niger and was subsequently broken into three, the Sudan, Upper Volta and Niger. Essentially, the offspring of Senegal, it was flanked by two military regions, Mauritania and Niger, and was, so to speak, the Sudanic core of the three coast colonies, Guinea, Ivory Coast, and Dahomey, which were separated one from another by British colonies. The policy that was the legacy of Faidherbe was the precise opposite of that of his adversary, al-Hajj 'Umar. The natural course of expansion of the Sudanese empire, of which al-Hajj 'Umar was one of the last protagonists, was from the Niger river towards the Atlantic Coast; while the natural path for French West Africa was from the western point of Senegal towards the Niger. The Niger, moreover, had about it an air of Oriental mysticism; it symbolized regions that were reputed to be rich. In 1904, the governor-general of French West Africa, Ernest Roume, a graduate of the Ecole Polytechnique and a *maître des requêtes* before the Conseil d'état, was the reverse of a dreamer. However, like Faidherbe, he dreamt of the future cotton manufactures of the Niger; and he pushed the railway up to the Niger in order to provide an outlet for its new cotton.

In French Equatorial Africa, the myth bore a political rather than an economic significance. It was not based on a river, but on a lake— Lake Chad. The government-general of French Equatorial Africa extended from Congo to Chad, the central point of French colonization in French Africa. It linked North Africa with French West Africa and French Equatorial Africa. It was the keystone of the enormous and bizarre edifice from which the French mind would fashion an empire.

In both French West Africa and French Equatorial Africa, but with more success in the former than in the latter, the government-general linked the coast with the interior: a coast abundant in plantation products that were exportable, profitable, and *productive of customs receipts;* a hinterland believed to be populous and potentially prosperous. The inland colonies would have access to the sea through a railway network that would make their fortune. Had not America proved that the railroad was a civilizing force? At a time when the economic and social development of Africa depended on foreign loans, the association of colonies into larger units offered prospective lenders wider opportunities than those furnished by individual territories. By joining the littoral with the hinterland, the French hoped to make available to the interior a part of the customs receipts levied in the ports, to supplement budgets by loans, and to use these for great harbour and railway projects. The governments-general accordingly obtained political and administrative authority over their constituent territories. These in turn were run by lieutenant-governors subordinate to the governor-general. French West Africa was governed more along federal, French Equatorial Africa on unitary principles. But both formed great territorial aggregations that gave to the separate colonies a common interest and led to a new form of inter-African co-operation.

AFRICAN CIVIL SERVANTS AND THE FIGHT FOR INDEPENDENCE. Before 1945, the governments-general in both French West Africa and French Equatorial Africa had begun to carry out tasks not foreseen when these bodies had been set up. The governments-general had established new standards of public service. From the Atlantic coast to the Sahara not only had they built up a uniform type of administration but they had also imparted a federal character to the native administrative cadres. Post office employees, public works foremen, clerks, the medical doctors employed by the public health authorities, schoolteachers, railwaymen—all these *indigènes* whose work was indispensable to the colonial administration—were federal civil servants. They might be employed in any colony within their government-general. They all had a common affiliation to the government-general schools that had recruited them. They were united by the solidarity that comes from a common administrative status, and thus acquired a certain *esprit de corps*. Independence was put into effect by African functionaries who had found part of their common loyalty through having worked within the *cadres communs* of the same government-general. Independence would not perhaps have worked as it did had it not been based on the common administrative machinery that the government-general had everywhere installed. The William Ponty School in Senegal was a melting-pot for people of very different ethnic origins. Drawn from all the colonies of French West Africa, its graduates were united by a *camaraderie* that persisted throughout their careers.

THE RASSEMBLEMENT DÉMOCRATIQUE AFRICAIN. Beginning about 1945 to 1946, numerous political parties sprouted in all parts of French Black Africa. These may be divided into two categories: first, those that derived from the three principal metropolitan parties—the Socialist Party, the Section Française de l'Internationale Ouvrière (SFIO), the Mouvement Républicain Populaire (MRP) and the Communist Party; and second, those that had purely local African origins. In Upper Volta, for instance, there were the Union Voltaïque—which in 1955 became the Parti Social et d'Education des Masses Africaines—the Indépendants d'Union Française and the Mouvement d'Évolution de la Population Africaine. It was the Rassemblement Démocratique Africain (RDA) which, under various names in different colonies, led the independence movement to success. Independence was its sole aim. It was the only party to have a solid doctrine, the only one to constitute hierarchies of its own, paralleling those of the administration both in the towns and in the bush. The RDA was the only party to turn against the colonial system, the administrative organization that the government-general had set up all over Black Africa and had made familiar to the African mind. The RDA was to suffer electoral defeat and to incur the hostility of a socialist governor-general between 1949 and 1950. Its militant members nevertheless remained strategically placed—in government offices, in the capital cities, in the great inter-colonial public services and in the posts of the bush—and were thus enabled to lead the African masses.

One of the unquestioned leaders of the RDA, Félix Houphouët-Boigny, stands out as truly representative of the French West Africa that the government-general at Dakar had created. As a doctor in the Assistance Médicale Indigène, he was an official belonging to the common cadres. He had studied at Dakar in the educational institutions that brought together Africans of all origins. As a native of the Ivory Coast, from the Baoulé country, he was a planter and a traditional chief. He knew what the Ivory Coast plantations—cocoa trees, coffee trees, banana trees—were worth to a modern Africa. And he was not unaware that the Ivory Coast disputed pre-eminence in French West Africa with Senegal. He was opposed, certainly, to the colonialist and Senegalese outlook of the government-general, and he supported African independence; but in his struggle the government-general served him as both target and tool. If there had been no government-general, Houphouët-Boigny would have had more difficulty in communicating with his followers. Nevertheless, he was a traditional Baoulé chief and for this very reason perhaps more deeply rooted in the African soil than many other African functionaries. But although a chief, he could see at close hand the limitations of the former tribal community and the restrictions of his ancestral customs. He was proud to be a chief by birth, but he was too much of a realist to believe that independence would ever bring back the Africa of old-time chieftainships, which the governments-general had converted to administrative organs.

From 1946 to 1951, the RDA was to be the militant wing in Black Africa of the French Communist Party, the most anti-colonial of French parties and the one most favourable to independence. From 1949 to 1950, a trial of strength took place between the RDA and the government, represented at Dakar by a Socialist High Commissioner.

In 1951 the RDA, ever on the alert for the most prudent means to independence, suddenly changed course. It left the orbit of the Communist Party and joined with a metropolitan party, the Union Démocratique et Socialiste de la Résistance (UDSR), whose leaders were François Mitterand, then minister for Overseas France, and René Pleven. Houphouët-Boigny in 1957 was to be Minister of Health and Population in Paris. In 1960 he became the president of the Republic of the Ivory Coast and the moving spirit behind the Entente Africaine, which, in an attempt at a larger unity, associated Ivory Coast with Niger, Dahomey and the Upper Volta.

French West Africa was dead, though the newly independent states, to some of which she had given birth, attempted to regroup themselves. The Federation of Mali with Senegal in 1960 was still-born. But the states bordering the River Senegal—Mauritania, Senegal, Mali (the former French Sudan) and Guinea—then made an attempt along the same lines. French Equatorial Africa now ceased to exist. However, Gabon, Congo-Brazzaville, the Central African Republic (formerly Oubangui), and Chad were linked with Cameroun to form a customs union.

NÉGRITUDE. Not only did the governments-general impart to the former colonies the solidarity that derives from a common administrative system, but they also served as a vehicle for developing the concept of *négritude*. We shall consider this phenomenon only from the political point of view. In this light it is inseparable from the independence movement. The Africans of the RDA particularly conceived of African emancipation as having a cultural impetus. In order to emerge into the post-colonial Golden Age, Africa must make a pilgrimage to the pre-colonial Golden Age. She must replenish her strength by returning to her origins. Not only would she become aware of her own civilization, but she would enrich other world civilizations by her philosophy. Through their own conception of human existence, Africans would lead the whole of humanity towards a better life.

Let us consider a man who symbolizes *négritude*, Léopold Sédar Senghor, the president of the Republic of Senegal. Born in Senegal of a Catholic family, he studied at Dakar and at Paris. He is a graduate of the French University. He is a poet. His *négritude* is expressed in French verse. And in a general way, from the West Indies of Aimé Césaire to the Senegal of Senghor and to the Cameroun of Mongo Bati, the advocates of *négritude* are French-speaking. Africans accuse France of having forced them to wear alien garb. A Frenchman has gone even further and has accused France of intellectual genocide. But in what tongue did the real Africa speak? In the Ivory Coast alone, more than seventy dialects. The African language is not one, but a mosaic of languages. There are many Africas. Hence, for Africans, French was the linguistic infra-structure on which *négritude* was built. Without the government-general with its schools, its academic inspections, its university disciplines, how could the French infra-structure of multi-lingual Africa have been so readily set up? For that matter, would *négritude* have been communicable? In April 1965, while receiving a number of African presidents at Dakar, Senghor said, 'Let us admit that we all have a nostalgia for that great council of French West Africa where we used to meet to discuss our common interests together.' If this poet of *négritude* had not written in French his 'Hosties Noires', his 'Ethiopiques', his 'Chants d'Ombre', if he had not had at his disposal, in France and Africa, a kind of grand common market for the diffusion of thought, it is probable that the link between culture and politics would not have had the same strength. In that case, the African leaders would not have been able to discuss jointly the best political and cultural tactics to deploy to attain their common end—independence.

BALKANIZATION. Let us now consider why the great African terri-torial aggregations were broken up by the independence movement that had used them to such advantage. There was, of course, one exception to the general tendency towards disintegration—the Camer-oun. By colonial terminology, the Cameroun, a country first under a League of Nations mandate, then under United Nations trusteeship, was not a government-general. But it nevertheless constituted a great territorial unit. Regions of great diversity and varied races, from south to north, from dense jungles to open savannahs, were placed under the same authority and put on the road towards the same general develop-ment. With the granting of independence in 1960, none of these regions or races demanded autonomy. Yaoundé and Douala remained the administrative and commercial capitals for the north and south, respec-tively. The Bamileké traders continued to traverse the Cameroun roads, far from their native mountains. The Fulani and the Moslems from the plateaus of Adamawa and the banks of the Benue did not seek to ally themselves with their brother in race and religion, the emir of Yola in Northern Nigeria. It was Ahidjo, a man of the north, a Fulani, a Musulman, who was to be president of the Cameroun Republic whose capitals, Yaoundé and Douala, were Christian cities. Furthermore, in 1961, the Cameroun recovered those provinces which, since 1919, had been administered from Nigeria under a British mandate. It became a Federal Republic with the restoration of the former German Kamerun to its pre-1919 frontiers. It put a seal on its independence by taking possession of all the territorial heritage that German colonization had accumulated during the scramble.

But with the exception of the Cameroun, all the other great associations of French-speaking Black Africa were broken up by independence as if there were no further need for them. French West Africa split into eight states, and French Equatorial Africa into four. How do we account for this?

It is certain that the definitive law of June 1956[1] and the decrees of March 1957 helped to open the way to scission. From March 1957 onward, in the words of the documents just cited, the two pillars of an independent state—the legislative power and the executive power— were set up in every territory of French West Africa and French Equatorial Africa. Each territory was provided with its own sovereign assembly and its own national government. The governments-general appeared only as surviving traces of the Empire, and their significance as great entities was overshadowed by the new glow of young nationalities.

This process of Balkanization offered immediate advantages to France as well as to the African élites. On the international plane, notably at the United Nations, French-speaking Africa had a much larger number of votes. The African élites found, in their respective republics, plenty of jobs. Each state would have its own president, its deputies, its ministers, its ambassadors, its consuls, its directors of ministries, its prefects, its military chiefs. Surely the newly-created sovereign states could not be expected to give up the advantages which Balkanization had drawn from independence!

RETENTION OF THE FORMER UNITS OF AUTHORITY. While independence sounded the death-knell of the governments-general, it did not touch the local administrative units.

---

[1] An important step on the way towards the defining law of 1956 had been taken by the law of 15 April 1955 concerning Togo, which gave this territory a measure of executive power.

The new African republics were built in place of the colonial territories, without modifying the shape or content of each territory. The
Senegalese Republic retained the frontiers of the old colony of Senegal;
the same was true of all the French republics except Cameroun. That
situation might change, but no territorial transformation had been
written into the programme of the independence movement. The
African ethnic entities broken up by the partition of Africa did not
recover their former cohesion. The Hausa of the Niger Republic did
not unite with their brothers in Nigeria. The Ewe of Ghana did not
rally to those of Togo. French Africa and British Africa remained
under independence what they had been during the colonial period.
And in the interior of French-speaking Africa the republics clung
faithfully to the relics of the colonial bequest they had taken over.
Contrary to current opinion, they had never existed in the form of
territorial states before being colonized. They had been given birth
after the colonial period and, in large measure, by the colonial government, which had bequeathed to them their present national boundaries.

None of them re-established native dynasties. The independence
movement had not revived the power of the great chiefs of pre-colonial
Africa. In the Niger Republic, a former teacher was the chief who gave
orders to the sultans. In Guinea, the Fulani diarchy of Fouta Djallon
was put down by President Sekou Touré (who, however, claimed to
be descended from the former chief, Samory).

Lastly, at the very base of each republic, the independence movement maintained the same administrative core as had existed during
the colonial epoch. Only the names were changed: the circle was now
called the department, and the *commandant de cercle*, the prefect. But the
same principles, the same organization remained. On the eve of independence, French Black Africa had 500-odd basic administrative
circumscriptions consisting of circles and subdivisions. The independent
republics in 1960 had 576 in all. The colonial administrative engine had
not been consigned to the scrap-heap; it had merely been painted in
African colours. The machinery had changed hands but not the parts.

The pressure of outside events

During the greater part of the colonial epoch, French Black Africa
had existed on the fringe of international events. The rivalry between
France and Britain had ended with the partition of Africa. The First

World War, however, brought about a new situation. African riflemen were recruited by the thousand for both the European and the Eastern fronts. This recruitment precipitated the migration of Mossi workers from Upper Volta to the Gold Coast (Ghana). World War II was to have even more extensive and more profound effects. On the Asiatic and African continents, as in the Indonesian archipelago, the war sounded the knell of colonialist Europe.

LACK OF EUROPEAN PLANNING FOR REFORM. Between 1945 and 1960 there was no collaboration between the interested European powers such as might have allowed them to seek a common solution to African problems. There was a certain amount of technical co-operation to the south of the Sahara, between Great Britain, France, Belgium and Portugal; but it was limited to subjects which did not call for their taking up a concerted political position. At the end of the nineteenth century, African colonization had been supervised by the great congresses of Berlin and Brussels. The colonial empires dissolved, between 1945 and 1960, in a series of clashes in which each metropolitan country fought alone. Decolonization in the British, Belgian and French territories was not synchronized. A comparison of this process, though it would be of interest, is outside the scope of the present essay.

THE BANDUNG CONFERENCE. One very important congress did take place. Europe and the world of the whites not only did not attend, but stood accused before the assemblage. This was the Afro-Asian Conference at Bandung, held in 1955 on the slope of a Javanese volcano as if to symbolize the eruption of subterranean forces. There began the trial of Western civilization, which had believed itself universal. The metropolitan countries up to that time had been able to flatter themselves that they were above reproach, except for isolated abuses or lapses in their colonial activity. But at Bandung, the very spirit of their civilization was torn to shreds.

COLONIAL WARS AND ANTI-COLONIALISM. From 1945 onward, France was forced to give a dramatic priority to her own Asiatic problems. The war had begun in Indo-China. The Fourth Republic seemed to be obsessed by a kind of linear strategy. Because it was trying to hold on everywhere, its position became so attenuated that it was not truly powerful anywhere. It assumed that if it did not win a victory on behalf of the Associated States of Indo-China, it would not be able to hang onto the African territories. Public opinion had never grasped the juridical distinction between the Associated States and Overseas Territories. The Union Française was not, for the man in the street, anything other than a new name for the Empire! And if the Empire was in peril in Asia, it was equally in peril everywhere else.

In these circumstances, any innovation appeared as a dangerous retreat. For instance, to admit that the inhabitants of the French stations in India might have a double nationality, French and Indian—India having been independent since 1947—would give Algerians, in their turn, a pretext to claim a double nationality. In fact, the French of France knew little about their empire; they had no clear understanding of the different parts of it, much less of its myriad difficulties.

Furthermore, they fell victim to a curious argument in which anti-colonialism and colonialism were paradoxically joined. If the empire no longer represented a single entity, it ought to be rejected *in toto*. A superiority complex was succeeded by a guilt complex. To colonize had been criminal; to decolonize was to wipe out the stain. To liberate Asia and Africa was to liberate one's conscience. This Afro-Asiatic concept certainly served to accelerate the independence movement in Black Africa. The political situation of the mother country also had its effect. In 1954, French Indo-China expired at Dien Bien Phu. In the same year, a no less atrocious war began in the Algerian Aurès.(Its turning-point was 1956, after the failure of the Suez expedition.) France was certainly not about to wage a third war in Black Africa! Certain African nationalists regretted this. They would have liked to win their independence in blood; instead, independence was plucked like a ripe fruit by the expert hands of the RDA, after the *loi-cadre* of Gaston Defferre (1956-7) and the presidential tour of Africa by General de Gaulle in 1958.

It is certain that Ho Chi Minh and the Viet Minh in Indo-China, and the National Liberation Front in Algeria, indirectly but surely prepared the way for the independence of Black Africa. The time had come when, from Asia to Africa, no obstacle would hinder the propagation of this faith in themselves that aroused all peoples under all forms of colonialism, whether it was a well-intentioned tutelage or a yoke. The African mind was being influenced more and more by the slogans of the emancipation put out by the RDA. Even the black troops, long famous for their loyalty to France, had changed: the young men repatriated from Indo-China were not the same as the survivors of 1914–18.

Up to 1919, just after the First World War, the lot of the colonial territories was still being decided in Europe. The possessions of the defeated European countries were passing into the hands of the victors, who were Europeans too. Under the influence of the United States, the League of Nations, with its colonial mandates, had already applied the first corrective to a situation that went back for centuries. Generally speaking, however, the redistribution of colonies after European wars had not been the concern of the colonized people. Heretofore, the separation of colonies from their metropolitan country, as had occurred in North America in the eighteenth century and in South America in the nineteenth century, had always implied the emancipation of colonists of European origin. Professor Gaston Berger, whose mother was Senegalese, observes that the American rebels had a cultural and economic life at least on a par with that of Great Britain, and that their independence followed their economic development, instead of preceding it, as in Black Africa.

After World War II, a new phenomenon appeared: Asia and Africa liberated themselves as a result of wars which they won by their own efforts, with their own masses, on their own territory, by imposing their guerrilla tactics and their revolutionary strategy on the enemy. Asia and Africa succeeded in rending the colonial ranks asunder in a political earthquake whose repercussions are still to be felt. The two great victors in the Second World War, the United States and the Soviet Union, favoured the rise of the Third World, which was to modify international relations on every level, including the psychological. Humanity had entered into an era in which ideologies might operate from a distance on peoples whose lives had formerly been steeped in their own traditions, even while they were under colonial rule.

One would hardly have thought, at the beginning of this century, that an African country could, under the influence of Chinese preaching, be converted to a German doctrine put into operation by the Russians.[1]

But this is what actually happened.

---

[1] Pierre Quevremont, *Dieu et l'homme créateur* (Paris, 1965).

The effects of the independence movement on Africa's future

The dates 1945–60 serve to delimit a field of observation and of reflection that overlaps both the initial and the terminal dates. In Africa, as everywhere else, history does not divide itself into scholarly slabs. It is made of overlapping strata in which the distant past becomes admixed with more recent events. Within the confines of this brief study we should like to point out that French-speaking Black Africa attained independence carrying the weight of all its past, pre-colonial as well as colonial, in order to meet head on the true problems of its future.

In 1960 French Black Africa gave way to fourteen independent republics which had previously not existed and which now figure in the international scheme of things. *Each has its own life, its own face, its own personality.* But all have certain common traits which we shall try to distinguish.

THE WEIGHT OF THE COLONIAL HERITAGE. In the first place, all the new republics energed from an immediate colonial past[1] whose importance must be emphasized and whose interpretation has often been inaccurate. To believe that they had only to proclaim their independence to recover *ipso facto* an identity obliterated during the colonial period is to commit an error in history; and it is also to misjudge their difficulties and the efforts they are making to become nations in the true sense of the word. They are, as Professor François Perroux has said, nations in the course of making themselves; for myself I would add, nations in the course of making themselves states. These young republics have already succeeded in organizing themselves into states. They have not yet had the time to instil in their people a civic awareness. Their national conscience is comparable to young plants whose growth requires a prop. This prop is the state.

Each of the republics must assume the heritage of its colonial past. This does not consist solely in the territorial frontiers, even though these have taken on a very great significance. At the Conference of the International African Institute, held at Ibadan in April 1965, someone said that 'the African natives did not feel any link with the colonial territorial units'. That may have been true at the outset; but as the process of colonization went on, a bond was forged. The political map

---

[1] This recent past evidently does not stand for the same thing in Senegal, colonized for at least 150 years, as in Chad, colonized for no more than fifty.

of each republic may be superimposed exactly on the map of the former colony. But the heritage of the colonial period is also made up of other elements that raise serious problems: means of communication that are the same as in the colonial times, towns of which the majority date from the colonial period. They are growing rapidly; they project their tall buildings and strong lines over the old rural Africa of huts and cabins. They are at the same time the centre of attraction for the young and the centre of gravity of politics.

No one can say whether all fourteen of the present republics will remain content with the boundaries of the former colonial territorial units. It is impossible to foresee the regroupings and the fusions that the French-speaking republics may be led to bring about, not only among themselves, but also with their English-speaking neighbours. But as they were set up in 1960, they were obliged to make do with the nerve centres and the network of communications that they found already established. The towns, the harbours, the airports, the railroads and the roads are not merely the material goods of which the republics have become the owners. All these go hand in hand with the economic and social activities, the professional organizations and trade unions that are essential to their smooth functioning. These make up a whole that the republics must in their turn keep going and to which they owe much.

THE DEAD WEIGHT OF TRIBALISM. The resources from the immediate colonial past are combined and penetrated by the revival of a more distant past, the most profound influence of any, that of tribalism.

It is often asked why all the republics, without exception, are characterized by a single or dominant party underlying the state, claiming to represent the mass of the people, and controlling the administration. African democracy in some ways resembles a pyramid of which the base is the party and the president of the republic the apex. In our view, this structure is explained by the necessity to master centrifugal tribal forces that would menace the republic were they given free play. By being supported on a single or dominant party, the power of the state is armed against anarchy, can gather together all the various ethnic groups and lead them from tribalism towards nationhood. With dedicated personnel and a sense of purpose the party provides the means to build the civic infrastructure that is essential to the growth of a national consciousness.

In such circumstances, the president plays a leading role; but he may not be wholly free from the insidious influences of tribalism. In 1946, with General de Gaulle in mind, a leader of the RDA said: 'It is absolutely necessary that Africans give their support to sincere democrats in order to bar the way to personal power exercised by a presidential form of government.' Twelve years afterward, that very African democrat would be the president of an African republic. He directs it in the manner of a strong man who allows no one to contest his highly presidential régime and his personal power. Does he then contradict himself? Yes and no. Beneath this contradiction, frequent among politicians of yesterday and today, we may find the older African mingled with the new. In the Africa of former times, power was sanctified. In modern Africa, it is far from being secularized, and it excommunicates its opponents as anti-social. The chief, although he may be the president of an atheistic republic, is the Word of his nation, which recognizes itself in him. He is not the Lord's anointed, but his power is merged with his personality in a whole which still retains a sacred essence, because he personifies the vital sap of the original trunk.

ADMINISTRATION AND THE SACRED QUALITY OF POWER. If this analysis is correct, we shall understand better the nature of the civil service in these young republics. It, too, to the extent that it shares in the exercise of power, has taken on a sacrosanct quality. We have already noted how great a part African officials played in the march to independence. They were naturally in the front ranks to gather the fruits of victory to which they had so largely contributed. Independence, without innovating at all in administrative matters, created many new jobs. In each republic, the administration developed according to the principles common to all modern states.[1]

Economic planning produces a multitude of companies that are wholly or partly state-owned, whose employees are virtually civil servants. But the apparatus of the state bears heavily on the budgets of Africa, with its poor soils and its embryonic industry. Officials are paid at a much higher rate than the average annual income of the population. From this results an imbalance that acts as a brake on economic and social development. The heads of state admonish their functionaries

---

[1] The burden of colonial administration had already been increased between 1945 and 1960 by the development of technical services, but it was the French budget that supported these.

publicly—in Senegal in 1964 there were 42,000—and preach austerity to them. But the administration is as deeply rooted in the humus of the tribal past as in the volcanic ashes of the colonial past. An African who becomes a government official not merely gains improved social status, reaping the prestige and profit that redound to all his extensive family connexions; he also obtains a share in the sacred quality that goes with power.

The African republic, even when it professes Marxism, exudes a kind of administrative clericalism that tends to become cloistered and to impede the growth of the nation. All this may change. The present-day officials are still for the most part very close to their rural origins and to the spirit of the traditional chieftainships. Their sons will no doubt have a different attitude. What direction will it take? This is one of the innumerable questions posed by the African sphinx.

THE PROBLEM OF THE MIDDLE RANKS OF ADMINISTRATION. The most lofty democratic conceptions, the best prepared reforms, are doomed to defeat if they are not served by an administration capable of realizing them in the field, in contact with the people. Such an administration cannot be limited to an élite of brilliant technicians; it is characterized by the quality of what we call the middle ranks. What is meant exactly by this term? In the industrial civilization in which Africa, together with the whole world, is caught up, they are the fore-men and the skilled artisans without whom no economic and social development can take place. They make up the connective tissue of the social body. These people are chosen from the so-called middle classes, who possess a social mobility that constantly renews their ranks and which puts them in direct touch with the mass of the people. Independent Africa, faced as it is with innumerable problems to solve all at once and with the need for a solid administration, has not yet created enough of these intermediate cadres.

It may seem that we place too much emphasis on a comparatively minor question. But in probing somewhat deeper into the adminis-trative problem, we find it a useful measuring-stick for judging the real situation. Let us consider, for example, the case of Mauritania. This country is still the land of great numbers of nomadic peoples, but it also has untold mineral wealth. The Moslem republic requires administra-tors who know how to communicate with camel drivers as well as with workers and engineers. All the republics have, in different degrees, similar difficulties to solve. French-speaking Black Africa, in its local and regional organization, as well as in its relations with other African states, will be in great measure what the public services make of it.

One cannot but think of countries, perhaps more favoured by nature than Africa, that after more than a century of decolonization are prey to successive *pronunciamentos* and to endemic disorder simply because they lack a middle class, the great nursery of the middle ranks of administrators. In French-speaking Black Africa, the movement towards independence has accelerated the confrontation of its rulers with a fundamental problem—the problem of the middle class.

We are familiar with the role played by the Third Estate in France, and we ought certainly not to reason by analogy. But to the extent to which democracy is intimately associated with social structure, it is safe to say that the future of the African Third World rests upon the social formation of a Third Estate.

In this process the role of the African woman will be decisive. A young high-school girl from Brazzaville noted this recently. She did not hesitate to criticize her tight-trousered male contemporaries who still treated girls as inferiors. 'If they will only let us work,' she wrote, 'and give us time, we shall be the true Congolese of whom the Congo will one day have need.' These words convey to us the expectation of an awakening national consciousness and also the atmosphere of awakening Africa.[1]

BIBLIOGRAPHY

Alexandre, Pierre. *Langues et langage en Afrique noire*. Paris, 1967.

Angsthelm, André. 'Le service public africain'. Thèse de doctorat, Faculté de Droit de l'Université de Grenoble, 1965.

Blanchet, André. *L'itinéraire des partis africains depuis Bamako*. Paris, 1958.

Brunschwig, Henri. *L'avènement de l'Afrique noire du XIXe siècle à nos jours*. Paris, 1963.

Mythes et réalités de l'impérialisme colonial français, 1871–1914. Paris, 1960.

Cornevin, Robert. *Histoire de l'Afrique*. Paris, 1964.

Histoire des peuples de l'Afrique noire. Paris, 1960.

Coste, Jean. 'Problèmes et perspectives de l'administration du Sénégal'. Thèse de doctorat, Faculté de Droit de l'Université de Bordeaux, 1965.

---

[1] From the third portion of my book, *Christianity and colonialism*, trans. by J. R. Foster (New York, 1964).

Decraene, Philippe. *Le panafricanisme*. Paris, Presses Universitaires de France, 1958.

Delafosse, Maurice. *Negroes of Africa*, trans. by F. Fligelman. Washington, D.C., 1931.

Delavignette, Robert L. *L'Afrique noire française et son destin*. Paris, 1962.
Christianity and colonialism, trans. by J. R. Foster. New York, 1964.
Du bon usage de la décolonisation. Paris, 1968.
Les vrais chefs de l'empire. Paris, 1939. [1946 edition entitled *Service africain*. English ed., *Freedom and authority in French West Africa*. London, Oxford University Press, 1950; reprint, London, 1968.]

Delavignette, Robert L., and Charles-André Julien, eds. *Les constructeurs de la France d'outre-mer*. Paris, 1946.

Deschamps, Hubert. *Les institutions politiques de l'Afrique noire*. Paris, Presses Universitaires de France, 1962.
Les méthodes et les doctrines coloniales de la France du XVIe siècle à nos jours. Paris, 1953.

Favrod, Charles-Henri. *L'Afrique seule*. Paris, 1961.

Froelich, Jean-Claude. *Les musulmans d'Afrique noire*. Paris, 1962.

Gonidec, P. F. *Droit d'outre-mer*. Paris, 1959–60.

Grimal, Henri. *La décolonisation, 1919–1963*. Paris, 1965.

Julien, Charles-André. *Histoire de l'Afrique*. Paris, Presses Universitaires de France, 1955.

Merle, Marcel. *L'Afrique noire contemporaine*. Paris, 1968.

Paulme, Denise. *Les civilisations africaines*. Paris, Presses Universitaires de France, 1959.

Quevremont, Pierre. *Dieu et l'homme créateur*. Paris, 1965.

Richard-Molard, Jacques. *Hommage à Jacques Richard-Molard*. Paris, 1953.

Senghor, Léopold Sédar. *Liberté*. Vol. 1: *Négritude et humanisme*. Paris, 1964.
Nation et voie africaine du socialisme. Paris, 1961.

Suret-Canale, Jean. *Afrique noire, occidentale et centrale*. 2 vols. Paris, 1958–64.

Thompson, Virginia, and Richard Adloff. *French West Africa*. Stanford University Press, 1957.

CHAPTER 8

MILITARY AND POLICE FORCES IN
COLONIAL AFRICA

by WILLIAM F. GUTTERIDGE

The development of police and military forces was an essential con-
comitant of the extension of European imperial rule in Africa. Contingents of African troops and police were raised *ad hoc* to meet particular
needs. Much of French West Africa was acquired in the last twenty
years of the nineteenth century by the deployment of relatively small
numbers of African soldiers under French officers: tribal chiefs were
employed as recruiting officers, and in many areas there were adequate
numbers of willing recruits. In the early stages of the assumption of
political control, though the British tended to rely less heavily on
indigenous troops than did the French, Lugard's efforts at establishing
law and order in Northern Nigeria led directly to the creation of the
local military establishment. It was from this organization that the
national armies of English-speaking West Africa in due course derived.

Throughout British and French colonial Africa, it was difficult at the
beginning of the twentieth century to draw a sharp distinction between
military and civil administration. Military officers governed provinces,
administered justice and engaged in road construction and public
works, while civilian officials sometimes directed military expeditions.
In French Equatorial Africa the more remote areas of Chad were
under military administration until after the First World War, and
even in Gabon three Fang districts continued under military rule until
1910. It was not until law and order had been established nor until in
British Central Africa, for instance, slave-raiding had been suppressed,
that any clear-cut distinction between military and police personnel and
functions became possible. Most military operations were concerned
essentially with internal security, and might, therefore, be classified as
policing. Only occasionally did local military arrangements in Africa
before 1914 have any serious international significance: Uganda in the
1890s was an exception at the time when the control of the Nile
waters and the reconquest of the Sudan were both urgent issues. During

this period, in response to demanding situations, spontaneous, apparently insignificant decisions were taken that were to have far-reaching consequences. Some of these actions tended not only to establish policy precedents, but to create habits of mind on the part of expatriate officers and officials with regard to the very nature and functions of security forces.

Origins of African military forces under British rule

The armies of Ghana, Nigeria and Sierra Leone are the descendants of the West African Frontier Force (later the RWAFF) whose formation was ordered in 1897 by Joseph Chamberlain, then Secretary of State for the Colonies in the British government. The force in its early stages was essentially an amalgamation of the Lagos Constabulary, founded in 1865, the Oil Rivers Constabulary and the Royal Niger Constabulary; and the first Commander was Captain F. D. Lugard. Parallel constabulary units had existed for some time in Sierra Leone and more recently in the Gold Coast. The fact that the new force was based initially in Nigeria rather than farther up the coast was the fortuitous result of Sir George Taubman Goldie's urgent reaction to French rivalry in that part of West Africa.

From the first the force was a regional rather than a territorial one; the Lagos Constabulary had, in fact, previously served in the Ashanti War of 1873–4 under the leadership of Captain John Glover, R.N. Henceforward the imperial government's dependence in West Africa on the West India Regiment and British troops was at an end. Until the disbandment of Headquarters West Africa Command at Accra in 1956, as a preliminary to Ghanaian independence, British strategic thinking treated the area from the Gambia to Nigeria and the Cameroun as a whole. The regional approach to defence arrangements was an important feature of British practice in Africa generally, and encouraged recruitment and other policies that were specifically imperial in outlook rather than concerned in any way with the preparation of colonies for nationhood.

Apart from the Gold Coast experience of the Lagos Constabulary, the Royal Niger Constabulary had played a useful role in the Bida and Ilorin expeditions of 1897. The Oil Rivers Constabulary originating in the delta had been responsible primarily for the protection of commercial traffic on the Niger. These units with their counterparts from the Gold Coast and Sierra Leone were all involved in the consolidation of the WAFF in 1900 after the final Ashanti War, and formed the basis for local regiments. The Southern Nigeria Regiment, for instance, was compounded of the Lagos and Niger Coast constabularies and a proportion of the Royal Niger Company's force; the Gold Coast Constabulary became the Gold Coast Regiment, and a similar development took place in Sierra Leone.

In an assessment of the British military legacy in modern Nigeria, the prominent part played by WAFF regiments in the expeditions against Bida, Kontagora, Yola, Bornu and Zaria and, of course, Kano and Sokoto in the first five years of this century deserves some emphasis. Local populations, especially in remote areas, tend to have long memories of military misdemeanour that are sometimes reflected in later attitudes to the army as a profession and in reactions to military leadership. When there is also historical association with earlier slave armies, as in Northern Nigeria, the resulting prejudices are not easily eradicated even sixty years later and after independence.

As it happened, the amalgamation of the two Nigerian protectorates and of the Northern and Southern Nigeria Regiments in 1914 was followed almost immediately by prolonged service outside Nigeria. Common service and fresh experience abroad not only stimulated the political consciousness of the British West African soldiers, but allowed time for the memories of punitive expeditions in their own countries to fade. This was important for the Ashanti region of the Gold Coast as well as for the areas in Nigeria already mentioned. Unfortunately the Egba rising dramatically revived such memories in Western Nigeria in 1918. Even when independence was achieved in 1960, the prejudice against the army there remained: it had incurred the odium which ought rightly to have attached to those responsible for the policies that led to riot and disorder and affected the recruitment from the area to the new Nigerian army of officers and other ranks as well.

Operations against the Germans in the Cameroun and Togoland brought WAFF units into contact with French overseas troops, mainly from Senegal. There and in East Africa they were mercenaries, as it were, in the service of a foreign power serving against people of their own race and sometimes of their own tribe; but there is no firm evidence of any adverse reaction to this situation. There seems to have been no feeling of guilt experienced, for instance, in killing 'fellow Africans' such as that sometimes apparent in the United Nations force in the Congo more than forty years later. The RWAFF, which between the wars acquired the designation 'Royal', was reorganized in such a way as to emphasize the territorial origin of regiments and sub-units. This structure remained substantially the same until independence.

A feature of the early development of the WAFF was Lugard's heavy reliance on his Indian experience. 'He was', as A. H. M. Kirk-Greene has said, 'always sensitive to the possibility of calling in personnel from India',[1] and gave Northern Nigeria a capital, Kaduna, avowedly laid out on the lines of an Indian military cantonment. In parts of East Africa,[2] especially Nyasaland, the nucleus of army units was actually formed by Sikh volunteers from the Indian army, who in some cases remained in Africa until 1911; and the original 5th Battalion, the King's African Rifles, was an Indian unit sent from India to help quell the mutiny in September 1897 of Sudanese troops in Uganda. After 1904 there was for a time a mixed African–Indian unit in British East Africa. As in West Africa, levies had been raised to meet local needs, and were constituted units of the King's African Rifles in 1901; contingents from East and Central Africa served in the Gambia and in the Ashanti war of 1900 as well as in Somaliland.

The policy of reliance on Indian assistance having proved expensive and unpopular with the government of India, military forces in East Africa developed much as in British West Africa: the forces were organized regionally but recruited territorially, though the identification of units with Uganda, Kenya and eventually Tanganyika was less clear-cut, at any rate until the 1950s, than was the case on the other side of the continent. This was a result primarily of the contiguity of the three territories and of the fact that pockets of certain tribes inhabited areas without regard for the tidiness of colonial boundaries.

The decisions taken in 1901 with regard to both the WAFF and KAR—that men should be recruited voluntarily on a long-term engagement with an obligation to serve abroad while retaining an essentially regional allegiance—were of fundamental importance. Though in East African villages there were occasional fears of forcible recruitment, apparently solely because of language difficulties, there was no basis for panic measures to escape military service such as

---

[1] A. H. M. Kirk-Greene, 'Indian troops with the West African Frontier Force, 1898–1900', *Journal of the Society for Army Historical Research*, 1964, **42**, pp. 17–20.

[2] Hubert Moyse-Bartlett, *The King's African Rifles: a study of the military history of East and Central Africa* (Aldershot, Eng., 1956), pp. 123–31.

occasionally occurred in French Africa. As a result, the forces that were organized not only had good morale and were singularly free from disaffection, but were willing to fight in strange lands, even as mercenaries. In this way at least the colonial power provided a measure of experience and stability on which new nations could build. Inevitably, however, the fact that independence was for the greater part of the period not seriously predicted meant that opportunities for detailed preparation for the new circumstances were missed.

The importance of overseas experience in India and Burma in the Second World War by both East and West African troops can scarcely be overestimated: more than any other single factor this exposure helped to bring the colonies politically into the modern world. The specific contacts that took place with the Indian Congress party have not yet been properly examined or assessed; but the total effects of Asian service were to open the eyes of African soldiers to developments in other territories under imperial rule, to dispel the notion of European invincibility and to develop personal maturity. The respect which ex-servicemen afterwards commanded both in urban and rural areas gave them an important status in subsequent political, social and economic development.

The nature of the white settlement of Southern Rhodesia in the 1890s gave rise to a form of military establishment unlike that to be found anywhere else in British-dominated areas of Africa. The initial pioneer force dispatched from South Africa was accompanied by a strong contingent of the British South Africa Company's Police. The specifically military role was, however, soon in the hands of citizen volunteers in the shape of the Mashonaland Force and a small troop of artillery.[1] This pattern has in general been maintained through Southern Rhodesia's several changes in constitutional status. The Matabeleland Rebellion of 1896, however, led to the establishment of a police force known as the British South Africa Police. This body was organized on a military basis, and became henceforth the senior element in the Rhodesian defence system, continuously laying claim, on ceremonial occasions, to the position on 'the right of the line'. Until UDI in 1965 this force relied heavily on white officers and on non-commissioned officers recruited in Britain; it has, almost from the beginning, included African constables. In 1914 white settlers were enlisted for the

[1] See Lewis H. Gann, *The development of Southern Rhodesia's military system, 1890–1953* (National Archives of Rhodesia, Occasional Papers, No. 1, Salisbury, 1965), pp. 60–79.

Rhodesia Regiment and served in the East African campaign. The Rhodesia Native Regiment was raised also, only to be disbanded at the end of the war.

In 1926 Sir Charles Coghlan's newly constituted government instituted compulsory training of a very limited nature for the white territorial force with a small regular cadre. This force along with the Rhodesia African Rifles, raised in 1940, has since formed the core of Rhodesian defences along with the post-1945 Royal Rhodesian Air Force. These forces were absorbed in the Federal Defence Forces from 1953 to 1963, and in 1959–60 were reinforced by the new wholly European and regular Rhodesian Light Infantry and Special Air Service Squadron. Since 1963, when all these elements reverted to Southern Rhodesian control, the compulsory period of Territorial Force training for all young whites has been extended to nine months. (In addition, Indians and Coloureds are drafted for noncombatant services.) Events have thus produced a degree of continuity in Rhodesian military development that has effectively identified the European-manned units with the administration by a conscription procedure. African military experience and tradition, though not wholly inhibited as in South Africa, have been very carefully limited and controlled.

The French African experience

Like the British in Africa, the French developed the concept of defence on a regional basis; but their distinctive approach to the problem of empire in the wider sense led to armed forces of an entirely different nature. The first modern colonial force raised in French black Africa was a unit of the *tirailleurs sénégalais* recruited by General Louis Faidherbe from the late 1850s onward. The *tirailleurs sénégalais* played an essential part in Faidherbe's forward imperial strategy; they did valiant service against the Muslims of the interior, and enlisted under conditions which permitted the creation of a stable and efficient colonial army.

Though for many years metropolitan and overseas troops had different conditions of service, they belonged essentially to the same army; and while an overseas unit was necessarily recruited in a specific territory, it was not always clearly identified with that territory or stationed within its borders. The French system differed fundamentally from the British in that it relied predominantly on conscripts rather than on volunteers. In French West Africa conscription was instituted in 1912, and almost from the first the abolition of conscription and restriction on the use of volunteers were keystones of the arguments of African nationalist politicians: France's reliance on African troops was continually used to secure from her concessions with regard to citizenship and the franchise.

The net political effect of the policy pursued is, however, not easy to assess. While in 1956 the Rassemblement Démocratique Africain (RDA) was strong in its opposition to the use of French West African troops in North Africa and for the Suez operation, there had been genuine loyalty to France in her hour of defeat in 1940. There was, at that time, particularly in French Equatorial Africa (AEF), strong support for Free France, and many Africans volunteered for service with De Gaulle's forces. Indeed, AEF has been called 'the cradle of the French resistance movement'.[1] By 1942 there were 10,000 men from AEF alone serving with General Leclerc's Free French Army, and many took part in his trans-Saharan march from Chad to Bir Hakeim.

During the First World War it was the French need for large-scale recruitment which enabled Blaise Diagne, Senegal's first African deputy, to secure legal confirmation of the citizenship rights of Africans while preserving their personal civil status. This was achieved by the law of 29 September 1916 'at the price of cooperating with the French government in the recruitment of 181,000 French West African soldiers to fight on the Western front'.[2] Again in 1939, in West Africa the drive for intensified recruitment was coupled with the grant to those who had completed their military service of the right to vote for colonial councillors. By 1948 in Dahomey, fifty-eight per cent of the 54,000 electorate were ex-servicemen or serving soldiers. It was not, however, until 1946 that the franchise in AEF was extended to soldiers and veterans. Equatorial Africa was, however, different from other French overseas territories in not being expected in the inter-war period to make a contribution to the expenses of the imperial military establishment. Nor had conscription been operative in AEF until 1919, seven years after it had been adopted in French West Africa.

There is abundant evidence of a sympathetic understanding of

---

[1] Virginia Thompson and Richard Adloff, *The emerging states of French Equatorial Africa* (Stanford University Press, 1960), p. 21.

[2] Virginia Thompson and Richard Adloff, *French West Africa* (Stanford University Press, 1957), p. 109.

France's international difficulties and of the link between military service and political progress. Yet conscription and the intensive searches for volunteers carried on in many areas helped to put the armed forces in a bad light and contributed to the development of a long-lasting distaste for things military. The numerous punitive expeditions and the behaviour of 'brutal and licentious soldiery' attributed to the British in some areas had had a similar tendency to create an unfavourable image. In the Ivory Coast, especially in that part which eventually became Upper Volta, there was occasionally disaffection amongst isolated tribes because the activities of recruiting officers were equated with those of slavers—in their preference for the strongest physically and the best human specimens. In spite of these fears, warrior tribesmen from the north, attracted apparently by the lure of possible loot, volunteered in overwhelming numbers; but in 1917, in the forest zone of the Ivory Coast, some of the Agni of Assinie fled to the Gold Coast rather than be put under pressure to enlist. At a later period the Fouta of Djallon in Guinea were strongly opposed to conscription on the grounds that they were warriors, not *tirailleurs*, and Nigeria was regarded as the natural refuge for those escaping from military conscription in Dahomey.

The combination of strong martial traditions with resentment of compulsion and foreign interference created a curious ambivalence in outlook on the part of African troops towards French authority, which itself was not far-sighted in its understanding of the implications of the African armed forces that it was in the process of creating. Between the world wars, in spite of an overall dearth of able-bodied youth, about ten thousand soldiers were recruited annually in French West Africa alone. Accelerated recruitment in the wars was not matched by an added awareness of the subsequent problems of demobilization. There was ill-considered discrimination between French metropolitan and overseas soldiers and veterans in conditions of service and treatment on discharge. Soldiers from areas with strong martial traditions, however, had a high respect for their French officers, whom they regarded in the same light as their traditional chiefs. In spite of an inadequate system of compensation and pensions, they generally remained loyal to France and refused to desert her in 1940. This spirit was matched by a strong sense of paternalistic responsibility on the part of their European officers that led at one stage to an impassioned crusade on behalf of the veterans by French residents in West Africa, notably Robert Delwas and Michel Dorange. Proper arrangements for demobilization were not made, however, and the morale of the remaining forces was adversely affected.

But in 1948, as a preliminary to redressing grievances and removing legal inequities, a mission was sent out under Commandant Henri Ligier to take a census of veterans of the two world wars. Territorial offices were established to deal with veterans' affairs, and veterans' club-houses were built. In certain services of the overseas administration twenty per cent of jobs were reserved for discharged soldiers, who were granted such privileges as low-cost housing. There had also been strong objections to secondary service—'deuxième contingent'—for labour on public works; this was abolished by decree in 1950. Gradually the problems stemming from conscription and heavy voluntary enlistment were reduced—they had been severe enough to cause some migration to British West African territories—only to be revived by service in North Africa, at Suez, or in Indo-China.

In French West Africa more than in French Equatorial Africa the residual problems stemmed not only from conscription, which though regarded in some quarters as a 'tax in blood'[1] was also seen in others as providing opportunities for travel and for acquiring relative wealth: many of the difficulties in the army and amongst veterans arose from the existence of three separate categories of fighting men in the same army. There were metropolitan soldiers and those assimilated to them, soldiers born in the four full communes of French West Africa, and *tirailleurs* from other parts of Senegal, Morocco, Madagascar, Tunisia and elsewhere. Of these the third category did not necessarily enjoy all the privileges of the others.

The reasons why the French administration allowed the continuance of such a potentially dangerous policy are not altogether clear. It is, however, a fair assumption that they were primarily economic. In 1948 metropolitan soldiers serving in French West Africa cost a total of 111 francs a day each to maintain, while African soldiers cost only 57 francs. Only a proportion of the margin was properly accounted for by differences in clothing, diet and the scale of amenities necessary to Europeans in the tropics. There were other signs of discriminatory attitudes not only on the part of officials whose outlook had become outmoded. Metropolitan soldiers did not always regard it as obligatory to salute African NCOs, but expected to be saluted by African soldiers

---

[1] Thompson and Adloff, *French West Africa*, p. 230.

of the same rank as themselves. African NCOs were rarely admitted to NCO messes but sometimes were allowed to eat with metropolitan soldiers. The use of 'pidgin' French (*petit nègre*) by white officers was resented by Africans. The government was accused of putting deliberate obstacles in the way of Africanization, especially of the officer ranks.

From 1950, after the establishment of the Military Defence Committee of Central Africa, there was a marked change in the French attitude to military problems in the area. Africa was now seen as important strategically in relation to NATO and to the security of the Western powers generally. The situation in which in 1948 only 2 per cent of officers in French West African units were Africans, and in AEF a total of 6 out of 321 commissioned officers, was changed. By 1955 the first African parachutists had been produced by the training school at Dakar, and five hundred African students were attending four preparatory military schools in French West Africa. In 1956 a training school (l'Ecole Général Leclerc) for African officers was established in Chad. In both West and Equatorial Africa there was talk of changing to wholly volunteer forces, and there was some difficulty in relating the proportion of volunteers to conscripts. Some were encouraged to transfer to the gendarmerie, and there was an excess of Sara volunteers from northern Chad for the Indo-China war.

The modification of French policy with regard to the overseas forces, however, occurred at a time when African political activity was beginning to intensify. The employment of African soldiers in North Africa and at Suez was bitterly opposed by many organizations, including Catholic and student bodies. In AEF the Gaullist Rassemblement du Peuple Français (RPF) endeavoured to make use of veterans' organizations for propaganda purposes, and indeed sometimes actually held party meetings in territorial offices of the 'Office des Anciens Combattants'. The authorities countered in the Sara country, from which a majority of soldiers came, with the establishment in the Logone region of 'villages de 15 ans' in which were grouped long-serving veterans in a semi-military environment. Perhaps for this reason and because they were non-Muslim, Arab propaganda about events in North Africa had little effect on Sara soldiers. Wounded war veterans were exempted from the poll-tax.

On the whole, in spite of political agitation, the loyalty of soldiers and veterans to France was maintained by these and other means at a remarkable level. In Moyen-Congo in 1948, communist attacks on the RPF deputy had been badly received by African veterans at political meetings at Brazzaville and Pointe Noire, and this mood was maintained right up to independence. This exceptionally close identification of the military element with the imperial power was not, however, psychologically the best preparation for political freedom; and it may account in some measure for the role played by the army since 1960 in such territories as Dahomey, the Central African Republic and Upper Volta.

In this connexion the very gradual approach to the creation of national military establishments in French-speaking Africa generally is of some significance. In the Ivory Coast, a typical example, the French did not hand over to the local administration military units raised in the area until the first anniversary of independence: in sharp contrast with the 'instant' British transfer of colonial forces to indigenous control, this policy was calculated to slow down the acculturation of these important institutions. In some senses, however, this is a controversial issue from which definitive conclusions cannot be drawn. What are less controversial are the social and economic effects of conscription and large-scale recruitment generally, especially in French Equatorial Africa. There is little doubt that food production was seriously affected in the less densely populated areas of central Africa by the withdrawal of a high proportion of the young able-bodied men and that on their return they spread forms of disease new to the area. In Chad, in particular, the large volume of military pay and veterans' pensions has been a cause of inflation leading to chronic economic instability in the successor state.

Much more comprehensively than was the case in British Africa, the French allowed the military to provide the framework for civil administration and services. Army doctors at an early stage laid the foundation of medical provision. Educationally and technically, however, military service was not used to its full advantage; the whole emphasis was on obedience to simple military commands. At one stage twenty-eight days was held to be sufficient for basic recruit training whereas in British West Africa six months was regarded as the minimum. The scale of the operation in French territories seems to have limited its importance for the development of technical skills. Both the British and French authorities, however, seem to have preferred for reliability Muslim recruits from the hinterland if they could get them. There was even a tendency on the part of French officers to give an impetus to Islam on the anthropologically curious grounds that it was a superior and more advanced religion and, therefore, likely to provide a promising basis for total absorption by Gallic culture. In this and almost every respect, the incidental, indeed accidental, daily decisions relating to the administration of imperial defence policies had implications for the long-term development of the eventual successor states.

Military arrangements in the Belgian Congo: 'La Force Publique'

The early history of the army which the Belgians raised in the Congo was not dissimilar to that of the forces recruited by the British in Africa. The 'Force Publique' was first officially mentioned in the decree of 30 October 1885, which defined the structure of government in the Congo Free State; and its first official commander, Léon Roget, appears to have been appointed in August of the following year.[1] Previously a number of *ad hoc* forces had been raised for particular expeditions and for policing. The decree of October 1885 prescribed the task of the force as being

to assure the occupation and defence of the colony, to maintain peace and public order, to prevent insurrection, and to overlook and assure...the execution of laws, decrees, ordinances and rules, especially those which are relative to the police and general security.

Initially, and probably inevitably, soldiers for the force were recruited locally from the coast round the mouth of the Congo, but contingents included men from as far afield as West Africa proper and Zanzibar. As the exploration of the Congo proceeded, recruitment was extended to the Bangala and eventually in 1891 spread over all the districts then under the control of the Free State.

This delegation of recruitment to district administrations was consonant with the policy of attaching to each district a contingent of the force and distributing sub-unit posts widely over the whole area. This policy differed markedly from those of the British and French, and the Force Publique expanded from eight companies in 1888 to sixteen in 1893 and twenty-seven in 1907.[2] It is worth recording that, perhaps

[1] See Robert Cornevin, 'De la Force Publique à l'armée nationale congolaise', *Le Mois en Afrique*, Feb. 1967, 14, 74–112.
[2] *Ibid.*

because of recent memories of the slave-trade, recruitment was not always easy and bounties had to be paid to chiefs for raising fit and suitable men. The fact that the Force Publique was expected to play a dual role, combining strictly military functions with responsibility for the collection of the rubber production, which constituted a high proportion of the revenue of the government, was an exceptional complication.

The bulk of officers in the Force Publique were regular officers from the Belgian army, but there were a number of Italians and Scandinavians serving on contract. The officer corps in the first twenty-three years of its existence suffered losses from operational casualties and disease amounting to twenty-nine per cent of the total. Evidence suggests that the majority of officers volunteered out of a sense of idealism to combat slavery and promote civilization, though a few were strictly mercenaries. Certainly there was amongst many of them a continual effort to improve the conditions of the soldiers and their families and generally to lift their condition above that of the bulk of the population. Nevertheless between 1895 and 1899 a series of mutinies in the Luluabourg district that may be ascribed to the severe discipline and bad conditions prevailing at the camp there, left its mark on the Force Publique. Considering that by 1900 there were 15,000 men in the Force Publique, its involvement in the economic exploitation of the resources of the Congo had an adverse effect on morale that was important for the stability of the Free State. During the 1914–18 war, however, the 18,000 men in the force were invaluable in maintaining the integrity of the Congo in the face of the German threat from Tanganyika.

After the war the Force Publique was reorganized into two sections, one of which was strictly military and the other virtually a *gendarmerie*. Recruitment remained difficult; there was, in fact, a decline in strength leading to revised terms of service based on a seven-year engagement and the requirement of a quota of recruits from tribal areas. The whole force was again reorganized in 1932–3 and assumed considerable strategic importance, serving in Ethiopia and elsewhere in the Second World War. An important by-product of the intense recruitment of this period and of the nature of the foreign service of the Force Publique was the resulting pool of mechanics, technicians and craftsmen in many different trades which was thus generated for the future development of the Congo.

From time to time also the Force Publique was called upon to quell internal unrest. In 1915 alone there were twenty-one police and nine military operations against tribes who were in open revolt.[1] In 1941 at the Union Minière installation at Elisabethville sixteen strikers were killed when the Force Publique opened fire. More significantly, in 1944 there was a mutiny of a contingent of the force itself at Luluabourg, allegedly over confusion about the nature of a 'battle inoculation' exercise: ten mutineers were, in fact, subsequently executed.

The development of tribal politics in the Congo in the late 1950s and the emergence of popular political leaders put strains upon the Force Publique unlike those experienced in French and British-administered territories. The disorders between Baluba and Lulua in the Luluabourg area in 1959 are a case in point. The unease created by the general political climate was magnified by the complete failure of the Belgian authorities to develop and train a competent Congolese African officer-cadre. Though technically there were channels by which commissioned status could be achieved, in practice they had not been open to Congolese: by independence just nine sergeant-majors had achieved the intermediate grade of adjutant.

It was not surprising that the African soldiers felt left out when the alleged material advantages of approaching independence were taken into account. This was a precarious situation in an army which numbered about 1,100 Belgian personnel, half of them officers, out of a total of 24,000. Moreover, the force was tribally representative of the whole Congo and almost entirely literate. Such a force was almost bound to react to a situation in which it saw its civil counterparts elevated to positions of power and authority. The signs of revolt, already present before independence, required only its actual realization together with a few ill-chosen words by General Janssens, the Belgian commander, to bring on a disastrous mutiny of an apparently well trained and certainly well armed colonial force. The fact that the Force Publique mutinied against its white officers almost at the moment of independence distinguishes it from those forces in Malawi and Zambia where preparation for independence in terms of African officers was almost as inadequate.

[1] Cornevin, 'De la Force Publique'.

Portuguese policy

In contrast with the Belgians, the Portuguese have relied more heavily on metropolitan soldiers. In the early days of Portuguese colonization, the Portuguese did indeed employ tribal levies on a considerable scale. By and large, however, white troops have played a more significant role in Angola, in Moçambique and in Portuguese Guinea, than European soldiers did in any French or British colonial possession (except Southern Rhodesia). Between 1880 and 1916 the administration in Portuguese Africa faced widespread unrest. The Portuguese used black mercenaries, sometimes even white convicts or patriotic student volunteers of the kind who enlisted to defend Angola against the assumed British menace in the early 1890s. But in addition, conscripts had to be brought out from Portugal. Only in this fashion were the Portuguese able to deal with incidents such as the Bakongo rising of 1913, or the much more serious German menace during the First World War. Portuguese willingness to recruit black soldiers on a large scale was limited by the political unreliability or indiscipline of so many tribal levies, by financial considerations, and by the ready availability of low-paid white conscripts from the motherland.

By the end of the First World War, however, the German threat had disappeared. White Rhodesians had become reconciled to the fact that Beira would not become a Rhodesian port. The empire seemed effectively pacified, and the colonial army was stabilized. By the late 1920s, the service numbered some 12,500 men, including a small air unit of its own. The colonial forces formed an integral part of the Portuguese army. Colonial soldiers spent ten years with the colours and five in the territorial reserve. Soldiers of the Home Army who joined colonial units had to serve four years overseas. The Portuguese colonial forces thus came to share the character of other colonial armies. By the early 1950s, between 70 and 85 per cent of its effective strength consisted of black professional soldiers, led by Europeans. (Before the outbreak of the African rising in Angola in 1961, the Portuguese maintained only some 9,000 soldiers in the country; of these, between 2,000 to 3,000 were whites.) The task of these forces was purely military—to defend the empire against assaults from abroad and to put down minor uprisings.

The outbreak of guerrilla war in Angola in 1961 found the Portuguese army completely unprepared. Black partisans scored significant initial successes in Angola; large parts of Portuguese Guinea were later taken over by African guerrillas; in addition, black partisans subsequently staged incursions into Moçambique. The Portuguese reacted by sending out white troops in large numbers from the motherland. By the end of 1965 Portugal had an army of more than 100,000 men overseas, something like 50,000 in Angola, 30,000 in Moçambique and 20,000 in Portuguese Guinea. The percentage of Africans in the Portuguese army, including conscripted *assimilados* thus declined sharply, though the civil police (numbering something like 10,000 men in 1965) remained largely African with Portuguese officers.

The Portuguese now faced a novel military task. They had to battle against guerrillas, often supplied with foreign weapons, trained abroad, and frequently able to rely on bases beyond Portugal's colonial boundaries. The Portuguese tried to solve their problems by adopting modern counter-insurgency techniques, by employing helicopters and small, mobile combat groups and by creating a supporting body, the Organição Províncial de Voluntários e Defesa Civil (OPVDC), which served as an auxiliary to the regular forces, to protect life and property against the partisans, and to carry out civil defence.

Above all, the Portuguese attempted to use their army for the purpose of carrying out a 'psycho-social programme' designed to integrate the Africans more closely into the colonial framework and to maintain more efficient control. The Portuguese army was used to improve communications, build schools, carry out engineering projects, teach various skills, and also to prevent the activities of white vigilantes anxious to avenge themselves on Africans. The military schools, the officer corps and the technical services had in the past often served as a means of providing professional and social advancement to poor but gifted Portuguese boys. (For instance, specially qualified staff sergeants and sergeants are able to acquire commissions, though no African has as yet ever attained a rank higher than captain.)

The successes and failures of the 'psycho-social' programme, as well as speculations concerning the ultimate outcome of the military struggles in the Portuguese colonies, lie beyond the scope of this essay. But the Portuguese army in Africa has experienced a complete and perhaps irreversible change in character. Living standards remain low in the motherland; hence garrison duty is not usually regarded as anything like the same hardship for a Portuguese peasant lad as it used to be for a French conscript in Algeria. Portuguese colonial chauvinism remains a potent psychological force. But imperial defence has become an expensive proposition. By the end of 1965 the Portuguese army in Africa contained nearly as many soldiers as the combined forces of the black states in sub-Saharan Africa. Portugal had become unique among the countries of Europe (except for France during the Algerian rebellion) in that its centre of military gravity had moved to Africa. The leisurely days of the 1920s will not return, and Portugal's colonial commitments may well inhibit economic development at home. They render Portugal militarily powerless in Europe. The 'psycho-social' programme, whereby non-commissioned officers, for instance, teach black children in primary schools, may have unintended effects on the army's ethos, with unexpected effects for the motherland itself. But Africa is the land of the unpredictable, and the verdict of the future remains open.

Army and people in British Africa

POPULAR ATTITUDES. The ability successfully to convert colonial defence forces into national military institutions depends to some extent, as already suggested, on the image of the military created and modified over a period of years. At the beginning of the century, when Africans were first recruited in Gold Coast Colony, a poor relationship between the army and the public prevailed for some time. This resulted from the employment of soldiers in the police function of attempting to control petty thieving from European houses. But service by the Gold Coast Regiment under General Smuts in East Africa during the First World War changed the situation: praise from the commander and a general impression of success ensured the troops a tumultuous reception throughout the country on their return home.

Even in Ashanti, where the series of wars had left lasting resentment, the people's ingrained dislike of the regiment was temporarily over-come. This was not, however, sufficient to reconcile Ashantis to the loss of military prestige and sovereignty which they had suffered at the hands of British-raised forces. For them even more than for other West Africans the army remained for long a symbol of foreign rule, though in Ghana the role of ex-servicemen in the political upsurge of 1946–51 helped to blur the adverse recollections. In northern Nigeria the army was a good enough career for the Hausa but beneath the dignity of the Fulani aristocrat. In Sierra Leone, the contempt of Freetown's Creole population for the Protectorate Africans affected the army's status; nowhere else has the soldier been so emphatically categorized as an 'ignorant illiterate', though here again the tide began to turn after he displayed his usefulness in the Freetown riots of 1955. In so far as the tribal composition of the forces in East Africa was concerned, the Kikuyu in Kenya and the Baganda in Uganda maintained a detachment from things military that combined with the prejudice of the British in favour of the remoter tribes to produce a difficult situation at the time of independence.

Though popular attitudes towards the defence services were clearly of considerable importance, these could be outweighed by political opinion. Few African politicians, even in the 1950s, however, had been so far-sighted as to think through a fully integrated plan for the creation of all national institutions, including those concerned with security. It is true, as has been suggested, that French-speaking leaders used military problems to achieve political ends and that one or two individuals in British Africa were alert to the potentialities of armed forces. Nevertheless there was no awareness of the subject comparable to that exhibited by a number of the non-violent leaders in India twenty years before independence there. Julius Nyerere, for instance, even though contemplating the possibility of dispensing with an army altogether, did take the trouble to become acquainted with its ways; but in Kenya, because of the closeness in time of the Mau Mau emergency, the King's African Rifles remained firmly identified with the imperial establishment. On the west coast Kwame Nkrumah, though wary of the dangers of the rapid Africanization of the officer corps, only recognized them after independence; but in Nigeria, significantly, the political potentiality of the army had been given some thought. Dr Azikiwe occasionally referred in speeches to 'the martial glories of the Ibo race' and was reputed to have wanted to establish an Institute of Military Science at the University of Nigeria at Nsukka. Chief Awolowo, on the other hand, is on record in his autobiography[1] as opposed to military expansion for political reasons. The Sardauna of Sokoto and the Northern Emirs came to realize rather late—that is, by about 1958 —the dangers which might arise from allowing the leadership of the army to fall into other hands.

Generally in Africa political recognition of the inherited armies as national institutions has overcome popular prejudices against them.

[1] Obafemi Awolowo, *Awo: the autobiography of Chief Obafemi Awolowo* (Cambridge University Press, 1960), p. 307.

Such recognition has been accorded partly for the conventional reasons of prestige, of internal security and of frontier defence; and partly because it has been generally felt that all the relevant trappings were essential to the achievement of statehood. There is little evidence that colonial rule developed a strong interest in military matters: in fact, though African armies have become active in politics, there are few signs of an unhealthy trend to military aggrandizement.

THE NON-COMMISSIONED RANKS. Throughout the period of British rule in East and West Africa, recruitment was seen primarily in terms of the imperial situation. Loyalty was the prime requisite and warrior qualities came to be identified with it. As times changed and some emphasis had to be placed on literacy and education generally, if only to fill the basic technical requirements of an infantry battalion, so the axiom came to be accepted that it was more effective to educate a fighting man than to militarize a soft ex-schoolboy. This was the theme, and from territory to territory it varied in its application only marginally to meet the local tribal and political situation. Much the same attitude had indeed prevailed in British India: nor was this surprising in view of the large-scale interchange of personnel between the two continents. The preference for warrior tribesmen from remote areas was understandable and in the imperial situation completely justifiable: such fighters were likely to be detached from and even hostile to the urban African when internal security problems arose.

But like their French counterparts, the British generally preferred the Muslim to the animist, the pagan or the Christian convert. Whether this approach derived from Indian experience, reinforced by Lord Lugard's doctrines or those later enunciated by Lawrence of Arabia, is hard to say. Admittedly, the British were by no means doctrinaire about their recruitment policy. For instance, many pagans from the Middle Belt, including numerous Tiv, enlisted as ordinary infantrymen. But the British preference for Muslims, or at any rate for Hausa-speakers, can be accepted as a fact that has had profound bearing upon the situation, both civilian and military, in Nigeria today. For the cult of the Muslim led to support for men and institutions that were despotic and corrupt. Islamic resistance to Western education was accepted, and the encouragement in the armed forces and elsewhere of Hausa—as of Swahili in East Africa—also tended to discourage educational and technological development. In the end, however, when the situation demanded educated men for officers and for positions requiring more elaborate technical skills, those who had pursued a European-type progress in this respect were inevitably accepted. This chain of events heightened tribal tensions and substantially contributed to the explosive fission of the Nigerian army during 1966.

Until after the Second World War the Nigerian battalions of the RWAFF were recruited primarily from Hausa-speakers both from inside Nigeria and from French territories as far away as the shores of Lake Chad. As recently as 1961 the Regimental Sergeant Major of one battalion came from that area. In the early 1950s, between seventy and eighty per cent of the fighting force was drawn from north of the Niger and the Benue; but almost all the clerks, drivers, educational personnel and other specialists came from the south and were mainly Ibos.

The notion of a federal Nigeria as it developed led to a definite rationale with regard to the composition of the public services, and the army was no exception. The principle of an ethnic balance was accepted and a procedure developed for its maintenance. It is, however, important to record that both within the army and outside it, it was the northern element which actively promoted proportional regional representation because imbalance would almost inevitably follow a premium on educational or other specific qualifications. Ironsi,[1] as a comparatively junior officer, used to argue at conferences that this was not in the interests of a sound federal force. The quota system established before independence provided for recruitment from the Northern Region of fifty per cent of the total intake at any time and twenty-five per cent each from the east and the west. There were also built-in safeguards aimed at preventing southern Nigerians resident in the north from representing that region: recruits or their fathers were supposed to be native to the region whose quota they helped to fill. The realization that Middle Belt residents might deprive those from the 'true north' of their opportunity led to a trend to provincial allocations, but this does not seem to have been particularly successful in confining Tiv recruitment to its strictly appropriate proportion.

The safeguarding of the regional balance tended to protect the interests of the north while at the same time serving the imperial purpose. The policy was readily open to the twofold criticism that an artificial

[1] To Major-General J. T. Aguiyi-Ironsi, later Supreme Commander in the Military Government of Nigeria, killed in army disorders July 1966.

ethnic balance was not appropriate to a modern state, which ought to select for the federal public services strictly on merit; and that in any case there was still a Hausa predominance in the army as a result of earlier bias in recruitment. A minimum standard of education, it was argued, would save time taken up with the basic education of illiterates, but this was countered by the view that restriction to a short-term engagement of fifty per cent of soldiers would in practice serve the social purpose of spreading literacy in Nigeria. In the event, the Nigerian army at the time of independence reflected in its ranks on the whole regional aspirations and characteristics: the bulk of the infantry soldiers were from the north and Middle Belt, while the technical, administrative and clerical appointments were often filled by Ibos. Yorubas from the Western Region were on the whole under-represented, probably because of a lack of enthusiasm for military service.

Traditionally in the Gold Coast also the northern illiterate, often a Muslim—sometimes one from a French-administered tribal area—had been preferred by recruiting officers. As late as 1960, three years after independence, the Armed Forces Training Centre at Kumasi made provision for the absorption of those who had a smattering of French rather than of English as a second language. While even in 1961 about sixty per cent of Ghana soldiers were drawn from the Northern and Upper regions in spite of the sparse population of these areas, the pattern of recruitment to the non-commissioned ranks was never a political issue. It was the practice rather than the policy in Gold Coast Colony for general infantry recruitment to be concentrated at Kumasi, with occasional recruiting safaris to the north, and for technical specialists to be enlisted in Accra. The pendulum swung from hinterland to coast and back again.

Until well after independence the procedure was deliberately kept in the hands of expatriates who, unlike their counterparts in Nigeria, developed no particular regional commitment; and politicians, in so far as they had any views on the matter, seemed more interested in a neutral army than in one which might take sides. Thus politicians from the coast seemed almost to have the expatriate's strong preference for the remote tribesman for the same reason: that such a person was likely to be detached and efficient in the event of urban disorder. This distinction between the armies that Nigeria and Ghana inherited from the British accounts as much as any single factor for the recent differences in the political behaviour of the two armies. The two different behaviour patterns might be attributed simply to the existence of intertribal enmity in one country as contrasted with comparative tribal harmony in the other; but imperial policy with regard to education and other matters certainly played its part.

The situation in Sierra Leone bore some resemblance to that prevailing in Nigeria before independence: it was not only the relationship between the Creole population of the capital and the Africans of the Protectorate but the rivalry between the Mende and Temne tribal groups in the hinterland that created problems within the Sierra Leone Regiment.

There was also the question of the illiterate, predominantly Muslim, people from such tribes as the Fula, Limbe, Korankos and Mandingos. As early as the Karene War of 1897, Lord Wolseley, with memories of Mende men serving under his command in the Ashanti Campaign of 1873-4, had appointed an experienced staff officer to raise Mende recruits. His purpose was to obviate extensive use of the West India Regiment, which was just as dependent upon carriers as a European unit. His interest in developing a strong indigenous foundation for a Sierra Leone force was no doubt sparked by the strategic importance attached to Freetown in Carnarvon's Royal Commission report on the defences of the empire in 1879. Once the immediate effects of the Mende rising of 1898 had worn off, the military manpower pattern was established, especially as Creoles were discouraged from enlisting by a rule against the wearing of boots by soldiers and by the general lack of educational opportunities.

By the 1950s a local force strength of about a thousand men required recruitment of up to two hundred a year. The declared objective was a tribal balance, but there was no fixed quota. Though the easiest area in which to recruit was in Mende country, on either side of the railway line to Bo, it was policy to try to keep Mende strength down to about forty per cent of the total. However, this ratio was occasionally exceeded. More important was the fact that almost all Mende recruits had some education, generally up to secondary school level. As a result, while the colonial administration's policy was to avoid recruiting too many sophisticated individuals into the security services, those who were recruited almost inevitably had the advantage when promotion or key specialist posts were in question. The unwillingness of Creoles to enlist except as potential officers and intense Mende–Temne rivalry also contributed to an unhealthy situation even in sub-units.

In Kenya, Uganda and Tanganyika a policy was adopted in the King's African Rifles (KAR) that was in some ways more discriminatory than those pursued in West Africa. The tribal balance was not considered in relation to the population as a whole: it was normal practice to enlist men from designated areas on the basis of the 'worthwhileness as soldiers' of particular tribes and language groups. This was, in effect, a quota system restricted to an approved range of peoples, from which for one reason or another there were tacit exclusions at different times. This was another form of application of the concept of 'martial races' that had been transferred from India; but in East Africa it was actually possible for the largest tribal groups to be almost totally unrepresented in the army, and those omitted turned out to be the groups which most quickly absorbed Western education and became politically active.

Figures given by the Kenya Ministry of Defence at the end of 1961 reflected the culmination of this long-term policy; of nearly six thousand Africans serving in the KAR, thirty-four per cent were Kamba, thirty-four per cent from the Nandi group, and other tribes including Somali, Rendille, Samburu, Masai and Luo amounted to thirty-two per cent. The total allowed from unspecified tribes was five per cent, and the Kikuyu were not even mentioned. Their negligible representation was due only in part to the prohibition on their recruitment imposed during the Mau Mau emergency.

In Tanganyika, with its large number of small tribes, the policy of tribal selection had little apparent effect; and it seems to have had no bearing at all on Tanzania's military difficulties. In Uganda, however, a preference for Acholi soldiers was established early in the century. This has not only helped to create the divisions from which the Uganda army has suffered since independence, but has intensified the hostility between Obote's government and the Baganda. In short, the composition of colonial defence forces in accordance with criteria used in the colonial period, and the professional ethos and preferences of expatriates seconded from an imperial army, left a difficult legacy to a number of new states. The new political leaders still have in most cases to solve the problem of finding the appropriate way in which to identify the army with the state. It may be that some new solution of a kind that would be anathema to developed Western countries may provide a temporary means to stability.

THE OFFICER CORPS. Though African soldiers had rendered distinguished service to the Commonwealth in the Second World War, little consideration was given at that stage to the possibility of commissioning officers from the ranks. A few of the Africans became non-commissioned platoon commanders, but only one, from the Gold Coast, achieved officer status. As in India, the problem of localization came to the fore as political demands for independence accelerated; but in Africa the initiative came from expatriates rather than from political leaders who, as has been indicated, showed little concern for the armed forces. One reason for this, as well as for the initially slow progress in finding officer material, was that to the local communities the staffing of the civil service and the foreign service seemed a more urgent problem.

In these circumstances, with many job opportunities offering, it was not surprising that British officer selection boards found it difficult to discover many Africans sufficiently in their own image to be acceptable successors. This vain search as much as any other single factor reduced the possible rate of Africanization of the officer corps. However, in order to avoid the possibility of dilution at the Royal Military Academy, Sandhurst, admissions of overseas cadets were restricted to a figure of around twelve per cent of the total enrolment. Besides, there were some African politicians who were not themselves anxious to hasten the process of Africanization. It may be that a more positive approach during the inter-war period to members of the Gold Coast élite, for example, such as encouragement to join University Officer Training Corps during higher education in Britain, would have resulted in some improvement in the situation; but it is unlikely that the benefit could have been more than marginal.

The provision of African officers for the RWAFF became a serious issue in 1949–50 as the prospect of self-government for the Gold Coast loomed. The future commanders of the Ghana armed forces, such as S. J. A. Otu, J. A. Ankrah, N. A. Aferi, D. A. Hansen, as well as J. Michel, who was to die in an air crash in 1961, were commissioned at this time mainly from the ranks of the education service, the one source of experienced, literate soldiers. These were men educated at established secondary schools like Achimota and whose background was similar to that of the civil élite. From that time onward the process of Africanization gradually gained momentum. From 1953 Ghanaians were admitted freely to Sandhurst and to the two officer cadet schools,

Mons at Aldershot and Eaton Hall near Chester, which offered the shorter training courses for British short-service commissions. Major-General C. M. Barwah, who was killed in the coup of 24 February 1966, had attended Sandhurst, and Major-General E. K. Kotoka, the principal architect of that coup, Eaton Hall. In this way the foundations of a Ghana army officer corps were laid. Though the process was a gradual one, it did move with enough speed so that the complete Africanization of the executive ranks by the end of 1961 was accomplished with an acceptable degree of efficiency. In this process, expatriate advisers did as much to maintain the momentum as did political leaders; and by the time independence had been gained, senior Ghanaian officers were, as planned, attending staff college courses and the like.

Much the same policy was adopted in Nigeria, which achieved independence three and a half years later than Ghana. The initial search for officer material in 1949–50 proceeded as it had in Ghana. At this time the future Major-General Ironsi was commissioned. In 1952 the first Nigerian to attend Sandhurst was Brigadier Z. Maimalari, who was later killed in the army rising on 15 January 1966. He was a Kanuri from the north and as such an exception to the early rule, for four-fifths of those Nigerians commissioned by independence were Ibos. Many of them came from a comparatively small homeland round Onitsha on the east bank of the Niger. This faithfully reflected the uneven distribution of educational facilities in the Federation and the lack of enthusiasm in the West, on historical grounds, for the army as a career. The area bounded by Onitsha, Umuahia, Owerri and Afikpo is not only an Ibo heartland but contained in the 1950s more secondary schools than the whole of the vast northern region.

No attempt was made by the British command to accept candidates for officer training on grounds other than merit, which meant substantially academic qualifications. A quota system was introduced only after independence. Thus in the colonial period, as far as officers were concerned, the 'martial races' notion was submerged by the evident need to appoint as officers Africans who were as close as possible educationally to the European expatriates whom they were to succeed.

There was, therefore, in the British approach to the composition of Nigerian defence forces, an inherent inconsistency. In so far as it was consciously considered, it was rationalized as a realistic acceptance of the facts; but the policy has had serious consequences. The optimism of those who assumed that officer and other rank bodies of essentially different tribal composition would simply neutralize politically the army of the new Nigeria has been proved to be disastrously misplaced. The response of the northern leaders, especially of the Sardauna of Sokoto, to the emergence of an Ibo officer corps was such as to pave the way for the subsequent suspicion that the northerners intended by whatever means to reverse the process. At first they set about encouraging officer candidature among the sons of emirs. Of these, however, only Hassan, second son of the Emir of Katsina, was commissioned at an early stage—in 1959. The fact was that the earlier resistance to Western education had loaded the dice against the achievement of a balance by normal legitimate means, and the northerners then reproached Lugard for not having imposed the schools upon them in the 1920s. The combination of a tribally biased group of senior officers with a federal administration and, in particular, with a minister of defence who were essentially affiliated to the north inhibited the Africanization of senior posts, shortened the available time for the development of a professional ethos and generally contributed to the eventual break-up of Nigeria in 1967.

In Ghana and Nigeria the substantial bases of officer corps were laid well before independence, though with different results. In East Africa, however, events conspired effectively to prevent any such preparations. The fact that until 1961 the King's African Rifles was regionally organized under Headquarters East Africa Command was not particularly important in this respect: its responsibility to the British War Office only tended to delay somewhat reforms and improvements in conditions of service. The important factors were the backwardness of educational provision and, particularly in Kenya, misplaced optimism about the possibility of a multi-racial state. African officer candidates fulfilling the required standards of education were just not forthcoming from the ranks of school-leavers. By the end of 1960, apart from a handful of young European officers commissioned directly into the Kenya battalions of the KAR after 1956, Tanganyika had one Asian and one African officer and Kenya one Asian and one Goan. In the ensuing twelve months another Tanganyika African, one more Goan from Kenya and an African from Uganda passed out of Sandhurst. This trickle constituted a desperate situation that could only be met by massive direct commissioning from the ranks of men with long service and experience, but with no particular level of educational attainment.

The commissioning of Europeans and Asians reflects what now seems the naïve assumption of earlier years that Kenya and Tanganyika were on the road to real multi-racialism. Kenya nevertheless had achieved an African lieutenant-colonel as battalion commander by the time independence was celebrated; and perhaps because of this and the generally greater sense of urgency generated, they were in a stronger position than either Tanganyika or Uganda to ride out the mutinies of January 1964. The British policy for officer provision in African forces is open to criticism, but in some ways it is surprising that the rapid acceleration to independence did not find it even more wanting. At least the fear of a Congo situation that in 1961 haunted black and white alike in Kenya has not been realized, and for this the belated appreciation of the dangers of an essentially officer-less army must be substantially responsible. The lesson of the Force Publique had been learnt.

The police

In the early stages of colonial rule the distinction between police and army was hard to draw, but in the more settled conditions which followed the establishment of law and order the two forces soon drew apart in both composition and function. In British West Africa, as has been seen, irregular constabulary forces actually formed the nucleus of the RWAFF; but in East Africa the historical connexion was less clear. Moreover, there was soon apparent the subtle difference in role of which perhaps the best short description is 'Policemen are soldiers who act alone; soldiers are policemen who act in unison'.[1] In distinguishing between the police and the army in the developing countries in Africa, no facts are more important than the obvious ones that the police are distributed around the countryside in sub-units generally of fewer than twenty men under a sub-inspector, while the army is usually located in battalion groups in perhaps five or six main centres. So the police are inevitably closely integrated with the population and speak the local language, while the army is detached in its barracks with its own social nexus and, in many parts of a large country like Nigeria, probably known to the people only by vague repute. Thus the army, because of its isolation, concentration and exclusiveness, is the reserve line in maintenance of internal security, with infinitely greater political potential than the police. Nevertheless its effectiveness

---

[1] William Robert Foran, *The Kenya police, 1887–1960* (London, 1962), p. 6, quoting Herbert Spencer, *Social Statistics*.

politically may well be enhanced by good relations with the police. In this regard a great deal depends on the tradition of co-operation developed during the colonial period. No better instance of the political importance of a close military–police connexion may be cited than that of Ghana; but the development of the police force in Kenya during the colonial period illustrates perhaps more clearly the inherent problems.

In British East Africa Baluch sepoys from India were initially used as police to guard stores in Mombasa and generally to deal with petty crime. Even the laws invoked, including the Penal Code, were Indian. However, in 1896 an officer, R. M. Ewart, was appointed to raise a police force for the Protectorate; and in the following year the Uganda Railway began to enrol its own force, which by 1902 had detachments stationed at intervals along the line of rail as far as Kisumu. Though British army drill instructors were employed, for many years the Indian influence remained dominant, with the result that Urdu and some Swahili were used but little English. The character of the police was essentially determined by its Indian inspectors. Even after an official report in 1909 on the improvement of selection and training, military rather than police procedures tended to predominate; and in the First World War the formation of infantry units from police personnel reinforced this tendency. It was not until 1925 that the situation was radically changed and some effort made to provide education for African ranks who might be promoted. At that time only sixteen African policemen were literate in English and 246 in Swahili. In the following year for the first time four African sub-inspectors were appointed.

The employment of the police in Kenya in secondary military roles in the Northern Frontier Province was re-emphasized in the Second World War when the KAR were needed for overseas campaigns. It was, therefore, a natural development that in 1948 there should be established a special mobile police emergency company equipped with armoured cars and Bren gun tracked carriers. This became a permanent feature of the Kenya Police in 1953 when it was redesignated the General Service Unit (GSU) with a total establishment of about 1,100 men. This unit saw frequent active service in other areas besides the troubled Northern Frontier Province. By the end of the Mau Mau emergency a detachment equipped with Land Rovers and automatic weapons was normally at the disposal of each of the five provincial administrations.

Men for the GSU, generally from the remote minority tribes, were specially recruited for their toughness and dedication. Their co-operation with the Police Air Wing, founded in 1949, was and has remained since independence a formidable factor in the ability of the Kenya government to check local disorder.

The pattern was repeated with success in Northern Rhodesia (now Zambia) and to a limited extent in the other two East African territories. The Kenya General Service Unit indicated a possible means of economizing on armed forces in that it could be argued that such an organization obviated the need for an army. Of all the new African states, only Gambia, however, has decided to dispense with a conventional military establishment and to rely on mobile police.

Like other territories in British Africa, Kenya was able to make a timely effort to Africanize the senior ranks of the police force, and thus to avoid more than marginal discontent. Though in 1961 only nine per cent of the police were Kikuyus as opposed to seventeen per cent Kamba, this was a margin which was fairly easily redressed. There was generally in the colonies a greater local concern for the police force than for the army. This was due largely to the fact that from the first the police were a territorial responsibility, with the result that the machinery to deal with grievances on the spot already existed. By contrast, the regional organization of the colonial defence forces and the part played by the British War Office meant that there was less immediate sensitivity to problems and consequent delay in handling them even when they were recognized. The East African army mutinies in 1964, while the police remained loyal, suggested that even then the adjustment had not fully taken place; the police, on the other hand, had always been in effect national institutions.

The importance of control of the police as a means of assuaging the fears of ethnic and other minorities was appreciated, however, during the colonial period. Considerable thought was given to this problem, especially in Nigeria in the 1950s and in Kenya. In Nigeria, for instance, a situation was actually permitted to exist in which a federal police force operated alongside local government police in the western region and native authority police in the north. The east was content with detachments of the national force, perhaps because of the ascendancy of Ibos in that force.

The federal force was controlled by a complex system of consultation with regional premiers subject to a veto by the Federal Prime

Minister. This was seen by the British administration as an essential check on local misuse of a federal force. It is worthy of note that since independence all the states formerly under British rule have found a large-scale expansion of the police force essential. In Ghana the force was increased from 4,000 in 1957 to 7,000 in 1960, a ratio that is by no means untypical. Generally these forces have adopted to a surprising degree British police practices modified by the influence of expatriate officers with experience in Palestine, Malaya and elsewhere. The result has been one of the strongest stabilizing elements in otherwise delicately balanced states. The widely praised conduct of the Nigerian and Ghanaian police contingents in the Congo in 1960–1, for example, was a genuine reflection of a real achievement by the imperial power in transplanting its own codes of conduct and procedures. Though, as has happened in Ghana, the police are not likely to remain totally detached politically, for the time being their inherited tradition of moderation will probably be an asset to Africa.

In French colonial Africa the *gendarmerie*, especially after the Second World War, had a reputation for brutality and inefficiency which was so widespread that it could not be ignored. Attention was focused on imperial military needs and on the satisfaction of these needs by large conscript forces. Occasionally, as in the early 1950s, an embarrassingly rich flow of volunteers for the army was partially diverted to the *gendarmerie*; and this helped to blur the already vague distinction in the popular mind between the two forces. As in the overseas army, so in the *gendarmerie*, Africanization was a slow process. In 1953 in Equatorial Africa, for instance, there was not a single African commissioner or inspector, nor, for that matter, a deputy inspector; but three years later forty-seven per cent of deputy inspectors were Africans. Feared and disliked, the *gendarmerie* inherited from the French is unlikely in the new era to become a social institution of influence comparable with that of the military with its network of veterans' organizations.

Conclusion

Colonial administrations bore the responsibility for maintaining law and order over vast areas at minimum cost and with only cadres of experienced military manpower. They sought the most efficient and expedient means of achieving this end.

The main result is that in general they cannot be accused of having left to their successors unwieldy or overlarge defence forces. This was particularly the case in British-administered Africa. In Northern Rhodesia, for instance, up to 1953 there was never more than one weak infantry battalion available to support the police over the whole vast area. In Sierra Leone, even at independence in 1961, there were only about a thousand men under arms; and in the much larger state of Tanganyika the figure was only twelve hundred spread over a wider area and responsible for a population of nine and a half million. Proportions of soldiers to civilians varied from country to country but one man in a thousand under arms was considered, during the colonial period, a high figure, although it contrasts sharply with one in a hundred in Britain and other developed countries. At least these colonial forces involved no great drain on the local economies. Nor were small armies compensated for by large police forces. The Sierra Leone police force had to be increased in strength from 700 at the time of the Freetown riots in 1955 to 2,000 at independence. Even in Ghana, which had a generally more adequate security framework, the force of 4,000 at independence was deemed wholly inadequate for its responsibilities and had to be expanded.

The situation in French Africa was a little different in view of the extent of recruitment for the overseas army and its deployment outside the region. But one would be completely justified in asserting that with the possible exception of the two world wars, the colonial administrations did not indulge in military exploitation of the financial or human resources of their colonial territories. Indeed the figures suggest their willingness to operate locally on a very narrow margin of safety in relation to any security crisis. Their plans were based in varying degrees on their ability to deploy European troops, and perhaps contingents from other dependent territories, in times of acute need. And such occasions were, in fact, rare. The British were able to operate at the lowest level locally because of their continuing command of the seas until after 1939. The European powers in Africa raised local colonial military forces to fit their world-wide strategic needs; and their criteria, therefore, rested inevitably on imperial rather than on local policy, partly because there was no incentive to do otherwise: for most of the time self-government and independence were remote possibilities. They therefore took decisions of policy and apparently trivial detail without, for the most part, regard for a political situation which could at the time barely be imagined. It was therefore not surprising that difficulties were created for the successor states which in some circumstances have proved very serious. We have seen, however, that there was not always a divergence of interest between the imperial power and its legatees: on the whole, both wanted security forces that would be capable of escaping emotional involvement in a domestic emergency and that would be loyal to the territorial government. It would not be profitable to speculate about the possible results of military decisions that might have been taken: more important are the real consequences of those that actually were taken.

The imperial powers, notably Britain and France, have left to Africa security forces organized like their own, with the same kind of command-structure and training. The basis of African armies is the Second World War infantry battalion, often still armed in the same way. The powers have also handed on traditions and an ethos which may or may not be suitable to the conditions of independence. The most important aspect, at any rate in the case of Britain, is the notion of an allegedly apolitical army. It is true that since the revolution of 1688 the British army has eschewed overt support for a particular political group and that with the possible exception of the Curragh incident in Ireland in 1914, it has effectively remained detached, confining the expression of its views on defence policy very largely to the constitutional channels, with the occasional organization of pressure groups when it has felt itself in some way threatened as an institution. But it is doubtful whether the young African—or Asian—officer training with the British forces and living in an officers' mess during the 1950s, particularly at the time of Suez, would appreciate this detachment in that the expressions of personal view that he heard would be likely to have been partisan. What has been handed on is a respect for constitutional procedures, as Colonel A. A. Afrifa's book clearly shows.[1]

At the same time, it is likely that the study of government and Commonwealth affairs undertaken at Sandhurst reinforced in the young Africans a respect for the 'liberal' point of view. Taking the sum of individual experience, it is probably not unfair to say that African military personnel trained by the British or the French, while not to be described contemptuously as Anglo- or Franco-Africans, are nevertheless closer to their imperial counterparts than the élite in other sectors of their society. Living as they did in closed communities, their absorption rate of foreign traditions was inevitably higher than for

[1] Akwasi A. Afrifa, *The Ghana coup, 24th February 1966* (London, 1966).

those outside and so, correspondingly, was the degree of profession-alism acquired. A compensatory factor is the greater relative importance of the military leadership in the élite of developing countries: its rela-tionship with the civil service and the police is likely to be closer and more influential than in the complex society of an advanced industrial community. Most significantly, the armed forces and the police in African countries developed in one tradition have a vested interest in maintaining it, and are likely to be resistant to the consequences of seeking military training assistance from another source.

In more mundane ways armies have assisted the development and modernization of new states because of the skills acquired under colo-nial auspices. In any armed force recruited since 1945 there has been an opportunity to acquire minor technical skills connected with the maintenance of mechanical transport and telecommunications, bridge building and demolition. Men from the Sara country of Central Africa, Yao from the mountains of Malawi and Tanzania, Ibos from eastern Nigeria and Ewes from the Volta region of Ghana and the Togo Republic have developed particular aptitudes. Soldiers on leave and on discharge have brought back to their tribal areas standards of hygiene that have gradually percolated through society. The role of the colonial armies and the police forces in effecting social and political change has been considerable. By independence, personnel in one or two countries had begun to acquire the ability to pilot aircraft, and in many more they were poised to do so. Technical skills, however, have proved politically less significant than the administrative, educational and organizational techniques with which officers have been imbued during their experiences in Western military training establishments. These, combined with the professional ethos, have made possible the succession of coups since independence.

BIBLIOGRAPHY

Afrifa, Akwasi A. *The Ghana coup, 24th February 1966*. London, 1966.

American University, Washington, D.C. Foreign Area Studies. *Area hand-book for Angola*, Allison Butler Herrick *et al*. Washington, D.C., 1967.

Awolowo, Obafemi. *Awo: the autobiography of Chief Obafemi Awolowo*. Cambridge University Press, 1960.

Cornevin, Robert. 'De la Force Publique à l'armée nationale congolaise', *Le Mois en Afrique*, Feb. 1967, no. 14.

Finer, Samuel Edward. *The man on horseback: the role of the military in politics.* New York, 1963.

Foran, William Robert. *The Kenya police, 1887–1960.* London, 1962.

Fyfe, Christopher A. *A history of Sierra Leone.* London, Oxford University Press, 1962.

Gann, Lewis H. *The development of Southern Rhodesia's military system, 1890–1953.* (National Archives of Rhodesia, Occasional Papers, No. 1), Salisbury, 1965.

Gutteridge, William F. *Armed forces in new states.* London and New York, Oxford University Press, 1962.

'Education of military leadership in emergent states', in *Education and political development,* James S. Coleman, ed. Princeton University Press, 1965.

Military institutions and power in the new states. New York, 1965.

Janowitz, Morris. *The military in the political development of new nations: an essay in comparative analysis.* University of Chicago Press, 1964.

Johnson, John James, ed. *The role of the military in underdeveloped countries.* Princeton University Press, 1962.

Kirk-Greene, A. H. M. 'Indian troops with the West African Frontier Force, 1898–1900', *Journal of the Society for Army Historical Research,* 1964, **42**.

'Preliminary note on new sources for Nigerian military history', *Journal of the Historical Society of Nigeria,* 1964, **3**, no. 1.

Moyse-Bartlett, Hubert. *The King's African Rifles: a study in the military history of East and Central Africa.* Aldershot, Eng., 1956.

Okonkwo, Cyprian O. *The police and the public in Nigeria.* London and Lagos, African Universities Press, 1966.

Stacpool, H. A. J. W. *Regimental Museum, Nigerian military forces: a short historical background to some of the exhibits in the Regimental Museum Nigerian military forces.* Lagos, c. 1959–60.

Thompson, Virginia, and Richard Adloff. *The emerging states of French Equatorial Africa.* Stanford University Press, 1960.

French West Africa. Stanford University Press, 1957.

Wood, David. *The armed forces of African states.* London, Institute for Strategic Studies, 1966.

CHAPTER 9

THE WHITE CHIEFS OF
TROPICAL AFRICA

by MICHAEL CROWDER

For the kings and chiefs of tropical Africa, colonial rule meant the alienation of their sovereignty to a new group of chiefs, the European 'bush' administrators. However much power chiefs may have retained under colonial rule—and some retained a great deal—one fact was clear to them as well as to their subjects: ultimate authority now lay with the white man. This authority was represented immediately in the person of the bush administrator, who arrogated powers that had hitherto been the exclusive preserve of the African chief. To these powers he added those delegated to him by his central government as its local agent. However, the extent and manner to which the administrator usurped powers from the chiefs depended both on the colonial power he served and on the particular territory in which he was serving. So too did his functions as agent of the central government.

The aim of the present essay is to study the role of this new white chief under five different colonial systems during the years between World War I and World War II: France in West Africa; Britain in Nigeria, where there were no settlers; Britain in Kenya, where settlers exerted great influence on the administration; Portugal in Angola; and Belgium in the Congo. This period represented the hey-day of European colonial rule in tropical Africa. The work of occupation, or 'pacification', as it was euphemistically called by Europeans, had been for the most part completed; and the colonial powers were unmoved by criticism of their policies either from non-colonial powers or from Africans themselves. It is during this period that the true nature of the differences in the administrative systems of the colonial powers in tropical Africa can best be seen—in particular the contrasts in the role and function under these systems of the new white chiefs of tropical Africa.

The African context

For the vast mass of Africans the advent of colonial rule made very little difference in their lives. Few found that their economic position had changed for the better. Most of them lived too far from the colonial railway lines and roads to sell cash crops to the European traders. Few produced cash crops that brought high enough prices or sold in sufficient quantity to make any appreciable difference in the economic status of the growers after they had paid the taxes levied on them by the colonial governments. There were exceptions, as in the case of the cocoa-farmers of southern Ghana, who enjoyed great prosperity because of the high prices obtained for this crop. Tonga farmers in Northern Rhodesia began to sell grain and cattle to the Copperbelt. Shona cultivators in Southern Rhodesia started to compete with white farmers on the local grain market to such an extent that the whites called for protected quotas for themselves. In Tanganyika the government fostered the cultivation of cotton and *arabica* coffee by Africans. But the total effect of these innovations remained limited. In many cases, the few crops that did bring high prices were produced by Europeans. In numerous other instances, only Europeans with adequate capital were in a position to grow low-price crops profitably on a large scale. Moreover, both white and black cultivators suffered from sharp price fluctuations for their produce on the world market, with the result that cash farming remained an economically hazardous undertaking.

During the inter-war period, educational facilities for Africans in sub-Saharan Africa as a whole remained minuscule. Admittedly, there was some expansion. Between 1924 and 1939, for example, the number of African children at school in Northern Rhodesia went up from something like 40,000 to 120,000. But educational standards were usually low. Only a small number of Africans were able to go to schools of any sort, fewer still to secondary schools. The position during the 1930s of four of the colonies under consideration is shown in Table 3.

Sub-Saharan Africa did not therefore produce a substantial black westernized élite, though the impact of westernization was, of course, uneven, and there were marked differences between the various African territories. Not many Africans were drawn into the non-agricultural sectors of the economy. The demand for clerks on the part of commercial houses and government offices remained small. Few processing industries were established on the spot. Only the railways, the

Table 3. *Children attending school during the* 1930s

Colony	Estimated population	Year	Attendance in primary school	Attendance in secondary school
Belgian Congo	11,000,000 (1935, part enumerated, part census)	1938	716,857	7,540[a] (1946)
Angola	2,600,000 (1930–1, estimated)	1930–1	6,537	[b]
Nigeria (northern provinces)	11,500,000 (1931 census)	1939	25,067	[c]
Nigeria (southern provinces)	8,630,359 (1931 census)	1938	267,788	[d]
French West Africa	14,575,973 (1931 census)	1935	c. 60,000	c. 600[e]

[a] In this year there were no secondary schools as such, but some post-primary education was given at a few of the primary schools. Two-thirds of the pupils at primary schools attended mission schools, which received no subsidies from government. (Source: Lord Hailey, *An African survey: Revised 1956*, London, 1957, p. 1207. Source for 1946 figures for secondary school pupils: Georges Brausch, *Belgian administration in the Congo*, London, 1961.)

[b] There was, for instance, an advanced *lycée* at Luanda to which assimilated Africans and *métis* were admitted. (Source: Lord Hailey, *An African survey*, London, 1938, p. 1278.)

[c] Michael Crowder, *West Africa under colonial rule* (London, 1968), p. 376.

[d] The figure given does not differentiate between students in different types of schools.

[e] Source: W. Bryant Mumford and G. St. J. Orde-Brown, *Africans learn to be French: a review of educational activities in the seven federated colonies of French West Africa based on a tour of French West Africa and Algiers undertaken in 1935* (London, 1937).

plantations and the mining enterprises offered large-scale opportunities for wage labour. During the period, the wage-earning class as a whole remained tiny in comparison with the mass of peasants. Thus in Nigeria in 1936, out of a population of some 20 million there were only 227,451 wage-earners; in Kenya in the same year only 182,858 out of a population of 3,084,351; in French West Africa in 1935, only 178,908 out of a population of 14½ million; and in the Belgian Congo in 1936, only 409,274 out of a population of 11 million.[1]

[1] Lord Hailey, *An African survey: a study of problems arising in Africa south of the Sahara* (London, 1938), p. 607.

Black peasants thus constituted the mass of Europe's subjects in Africa. For them, the main feature of colonial rule was the maintenance of 'law and order', which was only rarely disturbed during the inter-war years. The agent of law and order was the European administrative officer, the only white man with whom the average African ever came into contact. For the African, he alone represented the new European government, based in a far-off capital, and ultimately responsible to a European metropolis of which most Africans had little or no conception. It is true that during the 1930s, the number of technical services began to increase in the more highly developed colonies. The administration began to assume new functions, which might range all the way from the collection of meteorological data to the compilation of ecological surveys, or to a more systematic provision of agricultural services. Generalizations in this respect are of course hard to make because there were significant differences, not only as between one territory and another, but also as between different regions of the same colony. The gradual invasion of the expert created various new problems for the district administrator, who often lost some of his accustomed powers, and sometimes tended to become more 'chair-borne' than in the olden days. But up to the 1930s, this process had not in most cases made much headway. In so far as colonial rule was brought home to the ordinary African villager, it was usually through the agency of the district commissioner. For the average African, the district administrator was a new chief working alongside or through indigenous dignitaries. The district officer thus became a 'white chief' exercising his rule directly or indirectly according to the rules of the colonial power which he served.

The white chiefs

The vast majority of the administrators of the four colonial powers under consideration were drawn from the middle classes of their respective mother countries. The British at first did not insist on any specific educational qualifications for the colonial service, and recruitment was made by selection under the direction of one man, Sir Ralph Furse, not by competitive examination. After World War I many army officers, without university degrees and some very poorly suited to their task, entered the British colonial service. By the 1930s a university degree was becoming increasingly necessary for entry; but recruits were usually, though not exclusively, drawn from the older and more prestigious universities and from élite 'public schools'. Cadets in the 1930s received one year's training at Oxford and were required to pass examinations in law and African languages. The French and Belgians, by contrast with the British, recruited on a competitive basis; and entry into their colonial services was dependent, with certain exceptions, on passing through special colonial schools established to train colonial administrators. The French administrator had to pass through the Ecole Coloniale, established in 1889, reorganized in 1927 and renamed in 1934 Ecole Nationale de la France d'Outre-Mer (ENFOM). The Belgian administrator trained at the Université Coloniale at Antwerp or at the Ecole Coloniale. Belgium and France recruited staff without these qualifications who, after serving a certain time in a separate grade, could be considered for promotion into the administrative grade proper.

A few brilliant and distinguished people managed to reach high office in the early Portuguese Empire, but by and large the quality of the average Portuguese administrator remained low until the reforms introduced by Salazar in the 1930s under the régime of the 'New State'. Low pay and bad conditions of service all too often meant the recruitment of men who were prone to corruption and to neglect of duty. Though the Escola Colonial Superior had been founded in the first years of the twentieth century, it was not until 1926 that it was integrated with the colonial administration. And only with the improved conditions of service under the New State did a better class of administrator, who had graduated from the school, begin to dominate the service.

Except in the case of many Portuguese officials, the average colonial administrator was a man of solid character; he had a university degree or its equivalent in experience or training, though he was usually rather unimaginative. Perhaps the best service was that of the Belgian Congo, where the reaction to the Free State scandals led to insistence on high standards under Belgian parliamentary as distinct from royal control. In their approach to the problems of African administration, the French and Portuguese officials represented powers with distinctly assimilationist and centralizing tendencies. The British and Belgians, on the other hand, believed in a more decentralized system. They were preoccupied also with the problem of implementing indirect rule by using streamlined forms of traditional society. The British, however, did not apply this policy in Kenya, where the local white settlers enjoyed great political influence, or in Southern Rhodesia, where white immigrants dominated the state. In Kenya and Southern Rhodesia Africans were governed on a pattern closer to that of French West Africa than to that of Nigeria, Uganda or neighbouring Tanganyika.

The colonial administrative services of both Belgium and Britain, whether in Nigeria or in Kenya, were exclusively white. Until 1959, juridically no African could enter the higher grades of the civil service of the Belgian Congo, though some were in fact admitted after 1953. There were a few exceptions. In the Gold Coast, for instance, an African Solicitor General held office during the 1930s. In Nigeria, which was somewhat more backward, the first African Assistant District Officers were not appointed until 1951, though, unlike Kenya, a few Nigerians were employed in senior service posts in technical branches of the civil service, such as the medical and legal departments. The French and Portuguese made no discrimination as to colour, and a substantial number of French West Indians, Goanese and Portuguese mulattoes worked in the local administration. Very few Africans were employed. Though provision was made for their assimilation as French or Portuguese citizens, the educational facilities available to them were such that few became assimilated, let alone qualified to enter the colonial service.

The systems of grading and promotion of officers within the four services were in all cases competitive. For the most part, the standards of the administration were thus kept reasonably high, though in the case of the Portuguese colonies this was not achieved until the 1930s because the officers recruited in the early days were usually of such poor quality. The administrative services of all five colonies under consideration rarely contained representatives of the cream of the metropolitan generation, since Africa was not a popular choice for a career. Nigeria and French West Africa both had difficulties in recruiting, and frequently had large numbers of vacancies.

One of the main problems of all administrations was that of stability. In colonies of widely diverse populations, where few of the African subjects initially spoke English, it was of course desirable for the administrators to learn the local language and to study the culture of 'their' peoples. Yet the central secretariats of Nigeria and Kenya rarely kept a man for long in one station. Indeed in Kenya a study made in the 1930s showed a marked instability of administration, with one official being posted to eleven different stations in six years.[1] The British, as a matter of policy, rarely transferred administrators from one territory to another. In Southern Rhodesia native commissioners formed part of a locally-based service; Southern Rhodesian officials were not seconded to other British possessions, and native commissioners tended to stay in the same district for long periods of time. The Belgians, since they had no possessions other than the Belgian Congo and the mandated territory of Ruanda-Urundi, could not shift their colonial civil servants to other parts of the world. The French in West Africa, Equatorial Africa and Madagascar, on the other hand, systematically posted officials from one part of the empire to another, as well as from one *circonscription* to another within the same colony. For some time the French in West Africa indeed did so as part of a deliberate policy known as *rouage*, which was aimed at preventing officials from becoming corrupt by involving themselves too closely with local affairs. The Portuguese kept their administrators in the colony to which they were first appointed, except where a man secured promotion to the most senior posts within the colonial hierarchy.

The higher the rate of transferability from post to post, the less the administrator was apt to know about local institutions. This did not matter so much where the government aimed at a uniform administrative system, as in Angola or in French West Africa. But frequent postings did prevent that proper understanding of African social structures which was vital to a sympathetic local administration. Frequent postings were particularly serious where a policy of indirect rule was pursued, for indirect rule required that administrators should acquire a high degree of comprehension of the complexities of African society.

Despite the fact that the high rate of transferability tended to impede a good understanding of African society, promotion in the British system depended to some extent on progress made in an African language. Many British officials thus became fluent in African tongues, especially in linguae francae such as Swahili or Hausa. They also learnt and wrote much about the culture of the people whose tongue they spoke. In Nigeria, in particular, the British government not only directly encouraged its officers to make studies of the language and anthropology of its peoples, but financed the publication of such studies. While French cadets at the ENFOM studied African languages, the fact that they rarely stayed long in one colony meant that they had

[1] Hailey, *An African survey* (1938), p. 231.

little chance to pursue them. Whereas the British officer was encouraged to converse with his chief in the latter's language, the French tried to make fluency in French a prerequisite of chieftaincy. The Portuguese, too, insisted on their own language as the medium of instruction and education. However, administrative officers of these colonies have made some outstanding, if amateur, contributions to the anthropology of their African subjects. The tiny colony of Portuguese Guinea, for instance, is served by a Research Centre which has published studies by administrators of nearly every one of the many ethnic groups within its borders.

The administrators in each of the five colonies under consideration all shared the common function of 'political officer', that is, responsibility for the supervision of the maintenance of law and order in their areas of jurisdiction, and responsibility for implementation of central government orders. But their functions differed widely in other respects. As a rule, in Nigeria the British administrator governed, as did the Belgian administrator, through traditional authorities. The aim in both cases was to encourage local self-government by Africans through their traditional institutions. On the other hand, the French and Portuguese and the British in Kenya, whilst administering through 'chiefs', did not look on these chiefs as traditional African authorities (which in very many cases they were not) but as agents of the administration, who had in theory no initiative of their own.

In administration, the British and Belgians regarded their role as executive and advisory, while the French and Portuguese conceived of theirs as exclusively executive. This distinction will become apparent in the next section. Another major difference between the British officials on the one hand, and the French, Belgians and Portuguese on the other concerned the administrator's general role. Both in Nigeria and Kenya, the British administrator exercised no control over the technical services operating in his area of jurisdiction. Agricultural officers, public works officials and medical officers all worked independently of him, being responsible directly to their departmental heads. Since the administrator was meant to encourage local self-government by Africans, in which technical services were supposed to play an increasing role, this policy considerably hampered smooth development. Further, each department often worked independently of the others, in cases where co-ordinated planning would not only have been desirable but was actually necessary.

By contrast, under the French administrator all services were centralized; he was responsible also for economic development. He had under him *agents*, many of them Africans, of the technical services, whose work he co-ordinated. Similarly in the Congo, administrators at the various levels had overall co-ordinating authority. The main function of the territorial administrator (the equivalent of the British Resident) was to make twice-yearly inspections and to report on various services operating in his *territoire*. The Portuguese administrator was not only responsible for all services operating in his area of jurisdiction, but very often had to undertake their operation himself. As Duffy has remarked:

untrained in colonial affairs, sent to dwell in an unhealthy region in which they had no interest, [they were] burdened with assorted responsibilities—legal, financial, technical—which would have tested the capacities of the most dedicated civil servant.[1]

The third major distinction between the various systems was to be found in the interchangeability of local administrator and central secretariat. While French, British and Portuguese administrators were expected to spend some of their tours working in the central secretariats in order to examine the problems of local administration in the context of the administration of the colony as a whole, such interchange was very rare in the Congo.

The last major difference was in the amount of time spent by administrators away from their desks. Belgian administrators, who were expected to be on tour twenty days of the month, appear not to have been overburdened with paper-work. Ideally, British district officers were supposed to undertake regular tours, but paper-work increased so much that they became more and more desk-bound. The official's responsibility for accounts, and, in Nigeria, the lack of qualified assistants for accounting, played a major part in bringing about this situation. The French administrator, in co-ordinating and responsibility for so many services, managed very often by relatively junior staff, was in the same predicament. The Portuguese administrator had multifarious duties; he was the sole legal authority in his *circonscrição*, and hence he remained very much tied down to headquarters.

All junior administrators in these colonies enjoyed one tremendous advantage: this was the fact that up to the end of the 1930s communi-

[1] James Duffy, *Portuguese Africa* (Cambridge, Harvard University Press, 1959), p. 252.

Table 4. *Distribution of administrators*

	Population	Number of administrators	Ratio of administrators to population
Nigeria and Cameroun	20,000,000	386 (Late 1930s[a]—includes those in the secretariat)	1:54,000
Kenya	3,100,000	164 (Late 1930s[a]—includes those in the secretariat and locally recruited staff)	1:18,900
French West Africa	14,500,000	526 (1921—includes those in the secretariat)	1:27,500
Belgian Congo	11,000,000	316 (1936)	1:34,800

[a] See Lord Hailey, *An African survey* (1938), Table III, p. 226, where figures but no dates are given.

cations were generally so poor that officials in out-of-the-way bush stations generally experienced little interference from their superiors. They were very much their own masters. They could conveniently fail to obey an instruction by being away when it arrived, and no one would be any the wiser. No colony was ever closely administered. The British in Nigeria were the most thinly spread; the Portuguese employed a relatively much larger number of civil servants. The distribution of administrators in each colony in proportion to the population is shown in Table 4.

White chiefs and native chiefs

The administrative officers of all four colonial powers used African chiefs in one form or another to rule their African subjects. The relationship between the white chief and the African chief in each case reveals much not only about the character of the various systems of local administration of the colonial powers, but also about the nature of the task set to the colonial administrator.

Of the four administrations in question, that of the Portuguese in Angola was the most direct, that of the British in Nigeria the most indirect. On a spectrum ranging from direct to indirect rule, one would therefore place the Portuguese at the 'direct' extreme, moving through the French in West Africa, the British in Kenya and the Belgians in the Congo to the 'indirect' extreme of the British in Nigeria. The structure is illustrated in Table 5.

THE PORTUGUESE IN ANGOLA. The long-term goal of the Portuguese in Angola was the 'civilization' of the 'native' and his integration into the Portuguese community. Hence any use of, let alone systematic preservation of, tribal institutions as a means of local government was inimical to this ultimate goal. The Portuguese favoured direct administration of their African population. They also employed many Europeans in lowly positions. (No published statistics are available concerning the total number of all Portuguese civil servants employed in the 1930s. Comparisons between, say, the Portuguese and the British colonies are in any case hard to make because of structural differences in their respective bureaucracies.) But even the Portuguese, in order to rule effectively, had to use African auxiliaries. The Portuguese, like all other European powers, were thus forced to rely on chiefs. These chiefs, however, were used not to preserve or develop traditional powers, but rather to bring home to their people the new authority represented by the Portuguese administrators.

The chiefs were called *regulos* and wore para-military uniform. Many of them carried traditional authority in that they came from ruling families, or because they would in any case have become chiefs according to traditional rules of succession. But in the 1930s old soldiers, loyal clerks and policemen without any claim to traditional authority were increasingly appointed to the position of *regulo*. These *regulos* had no authority of their own: they had no judicial functions, no right to raise traditional dues or taxes, nor did they maintain treasuries. They were mere extensions of the arm of the *chefes do posto* with clearly defined functions: to transmit government orders, to maintain peace in their areas, to report crimes, to prevent illicit sales of liquor, to report any suspicious persons, to register births, deaths and marriages, to furnish recruits for the army and for labour, to help conduct censuses, to put down 'witchcraft' and to help spread the Portuguese language. Under them the *regulos* had village heads for each of the villages in their respective areas. These village heads were responsible for collecting taxes, and their salary was derived from a percentage of taxes collected. Significantly, in order to minimize possibilities of corruption at this level, the *regulo* was not himself allowed to

Table 5. *Structure of administration*

	Angola	French West Africa	Kenya	Belgian Congo	Nigeria
European hierarchy					
Central	Governor-General	Governor-General	Governor	Governor-General	Governor
(1)	*District* Governor	*Colony* Lt. Governor	—	*Province* Commissaire de Province	*Group of provinces* Chief Commissioner
(2)	*Circonscrição* Administrator	*Cercle* Commandant de Cercle	*Province* Provincial Commissioner	*District* Commissaire de District	*Province* Resident
(3)	*Posto* Chefe do Posto	*Subdivision* Chef de Subdivision	*District* District Commissioner	*Territoire* Administrateur de Territoire	*Division* District Officer
African hierarchy	*Regulo* Village Chief	Chef Supérieur de Province Chef de Canton Chef de Village	Headman	*Circonscription* (Chief of *Chefferie/Secteur* Chief)	(N. Nigeria Example) Paramount: Emir District Head Village Chief

331

collect taxes. Village chiefs were responsible also for maintenance of roads in their areas.

The real chief was, of course, the Portuguese administrator. He alone administered the law, maintained a police force, controlled the movement of Africans. No African could leave his area without the authority of the administrator, nor indeed could a village move its site. Tax collection was under his direct supervision. He was an agent for the recruitment of forced labour, a commodity desired in the past by many entrepreneurs (though not by the more highly skilled and sophisticated employers, who had no use for unwilling draftees). There were few aspects of native life in which the district officer's presence was not felt through *regulos*, through his subalterns and village chiefs. Though the Portuguese administrator bore a basic resemblance to his colleagues in the British, French and Belgian possessions, the Portuguese administration, however, did show a marked difference from that of other colonial powers in its excessive formalism, expressed in its ritualistic regard for *papel selado* (official documents with the proper seals), in its curious mixture of chauvinism and a highly selective paternalism, and in its marked *étatiste* tendencies that often forced even the most law-abiding foreign entrepreneurs to operate in a curious twilight of legality that forced even the best-intentioned to become wholly dependent on 'right' official contacts.

The African revolution that has struck parts of Angola, Guinea and northern Moçambique brought about further changes which lie beyond the scope of this essay. The 'psycho-social' counterinsurgency programme run by the army has brought the military forces back into government, though perhaps on a different level. Suffice it to say that Portuguese counter-guerrillas in Angola have tried to stem the tide of war, and to gain the confidence of the discontented people by providing a whole range of administrative services, including medical, educational and other forms of assistance. Whether these experiments will be more successful than similar attempts made by the French in Algeria is highly doubtful. All we can say is that they may introduce major, and perhaps irreversible, changes in the colonial Portuguese ethos.

THE FRENCH IN WEST AFRICA. The French were assimilationist in spirit, and believed deeply that French culture represented the ultimate goal towards which their African subjects should aspire. But the problems experienced in applying a policy of assimilation in Senegal in the nineteenth and early twentieth centuries led the French to abandon this goal as a general governing principle. Instead, Africans were to be selectively assimilated; the administration of the vast bulk of the African population was to ensure the development of West Africa for the mutual advantage of ruler and subject. While never dismissing the values of traditional African society as forthrightly as the Portuguese, the French nevertheless believed in a system of rule that would be as direct and as uniform as possible.

But the French had fewer administrators in proportion to the population than did the Portuguese. Because they had to rule huge areas, the French had not only to use chiefs as auxiliaries, but often to accept, if not recognize, chiefs with traditional authority. Like the Portuguese *regulos*, the chiefs under the French were primarily agents of the French administration. They exercised no judicial powers and they were not legally permitted to exact traditional revenues from their subjects. As far as the French were concerned, the chiefs' authority derived not from their traditional position, but from their role as agents of the French administration. The powers of cantonal and village chiefs were uniform throughout French West Africa and did not, in theory at least, vary according to the traditional structure of the society over which they ruled. Wherever possible, the French broke down the powers of the great chiefs, sharing them among their immediate subordinates, though paying honour to the traditional influence of the paramount by recognizing him as a *Chef Supérieur de Province*. Like the Portuguese, they frequently appointed old soldiers and loyal functionaries to chieftaincies, and even imposed as chief over one particular ethnic group a man from another. One of the principal qualifications which the French set up for an African to be recognized as a chief was his ability to speak French.

The chiefs collected taxes, recruited men for the army or for forced labour, maintained the roads, and were held responsible for keeping the peace. The fact that there were fewer French supervisors than in Portuguese territories often allowed chiefs to wield considerable unofficial authority, in particular through illegal collection of taxes. The frequency with which the French appointed chiefs without traditional claims to the office was reflected in the emergence of 'straw chiefs' or unrecognized chiefs, who had traditional authority, covertly settled customary disputes and carried out traditional religious functions for their peoples. The French-appointed chiefs were treated with scant respect by the French themselves. They were subject to the *indigénat* or summary system of administrative justice whereby the administrator could imprison without trial a *sujet* (i.e., a non-French citizen) for up to fourteen days or fine him. Chiefs, in particular village chiefs, were frequently fined, imprisoned or deposed for failing to carry out their duties properly.

The relationship between the French administrator and the chief was that of officer to NCO. Indeed the chiefs became the sergeants and corporals of the empire, while the French administrators, with their judicial powers, their right to impose immediate punishment without trial, their para-military force of *gardes de cercles*, and their functions as agent of economic development, became '*les vrais chefs de l'Empire*'. If their power was less than that of their Portuguese equivalents, it was that they were spread more thinly on the ground. In many cases they also had to deal with chiefs who, in the era immediately preceding the imposition of colonial rule, had wielded greater powers than the majority of Angolan chiefs.

THE BRITISH IN KENYA. For the British, Kenya presented a special problem because of the presence of a vocal and prosperous white settler minority which had gained some power in the local legislative process, in particular with regard to the passing of estimates. There were two administrative systems in operation. One, which applied to the White Highlands, will not be discussed here. The other functioned in the native reserves, which were much larger in extent—though much less prosperous—than the Highlands.

The British government laid down clearly that African interests should be paramount in Kenya. But the administration did not govern the African through his traditional institutions, even though this policy was pursued generally throughout British tropical Africa. Instead a much more direct system of administration was devised. As in French West Africa and Angola, chiefs, known as headmen, were used as agents of government. Some of them exercised traditional authority, but many were appointed because of their educational background or experience in administration. They in no sense carried out traditional functions, and there was no such institution as a Nigerian-type Native Authority in Kenya. It has been suggested by some scholars that the Native Authority system was rejected in Kenya because the presence of a vocal European minority forced the administration to look with a more critical eye at traditional institutions as the basis of native administration.[1] Be that as it may, there were few chiefs in Kenya with wide areas of jurisdiction. Hence the British faced problems similar to those in eastern Nigeria, where tribal society was generally decentralized and where traditional institutions could not easily be used as the basis of local self-government.

While the district commissioners ruled through the headmen directly, they did not wield as much power as their Portuguese and French counterparts. In the first place, they did not have the latters' wide responsibilities for the technical aspects of local administration. In the second place, the British shared judicial authority with native tribunals, appointed by government but presided over by an African. This African was not, however, the 'chief', though headmen officially designated or with traditional authority could be nominated as members of these tribunals. The tribunals were supposed to be constituted in accordance with customary law, but this was not always done. They tried only petty cases, but Africans did exercise some responsibility for their own judicial administration.

As I have already pointed out, the French and Portuguese conceived of their role as purely executive, while the British and Belgians regarded theirs as both executive and consultative in nature. This held true even in Kenya, where British rule was more direct than anywhere else in British Africa except for Southern Rhodesia. In the first place, the native tribunals may be seen as an instance of this; their decisions, including the right to imprison offenders for up to six months, were made by Africans, though subject to the 'advisory' confirmation of the district commissioner. In the second place, district councils with African representation were established from 1924 onward. Though the district commissioner was the president and executive of these councils, he accepted and sought advice from the African members recruited from the modern rather than traditional ranks of African society. African members of the councils in the more advanced areas of Kikuyuland and Kavirondo were often very vocal. Though limited in functions to matters concerning roads, local schools, dispensaries, markets and cattle-dips, they did exert legal authority in that they were empowered to make resolutions, which, if approved by the Governor in Council, had the sanction of law. Many of them commanded only limited resources, but they raised their own revenues and administered their

[1] Hailey, *An African survey* (1938), p. 387.

own budgets. The Machakos District Council in 1926 employed two European officials full-time, one as a forestry officer, another as a road overseer. While local self-government was encouraged neither in Angola nor in French Africa outside the urban areas, the British did foster local self-government in Kenya, though it was based on an English rather than on an African pattern. As Ingham notes, these councils were so modern that

frequently indigenous councils existed side by side with the authorities established by the Central Government although their existence was unknown to the Government. These traditional authorities regulated much of the day-to-day life of certain of the tribes whose members would refer their disputes to the jurisdiction of the recognised elders rather than to the councils or tribunals created by the Europeans.[1]

Here we have a parallel to the 'straw chiefs' of French West Africa.

Though the district commissioner in Kenya was much more limited in his functions than his French and Portuguese counterparts, the district commissioner's powers surpassed by far any possessed by Africans either of a traditional or a modern nature .The district commissioner was effectively the African's new 'chief'. He was magistrate for all serious crimes. He controlled the movement of Africans in his area, since all had to carry certificates and seek permission to move from one area to another. He alone exercised executive powers on behalf of the Native Councils. In areas where there were no such councils, the headmen formed what was described in the twenties as 'a native administrative service'.[2] Only the gravest crimes were sent to High Court judges for a hearing.

THE BELGIANS IN THE CONGO. In their administration outside the urban areas or the concessions (these formed a special case and will not be considered in this essay), the Belgians showed little interest in assimilating the Africans. Indeed, the Belgians tried as far as possible to follow a policy of indirect rule similar to that pursued by the British. Africans should be ruled by their own chiefs according to tradition, shorn of those aspects repugnant to 'civilized man'. At the same time these chiefs would be the principal agents for transmitting to their subjects the orders of the central government. Thus, as far as local self-

[1] Kenneth Ingham, *A history of East Africa* (London, 1962), p. 309.
[2] Address of Acting Governor to the Kenya Legislative Council, 1925, p. 15, cited in Hailey, *An African survey* (1938), p. 388.

government was concerned, the chief determined policy but was subject to advice from the Belgian administrator, who could, where necessary, exercise a veto. But in his role as agent of the central government, the chief was in very much the same position as his counterpart in Angola, French West Africa or Kenya. The Belgian chief was to become 'une autorité qui, d'une part, participe à l'administration européenne, et est intégrée dans son cadre, et d'une autre part, continue à appartenir à l'organisation indigène. Cette autorité constitue le chaînon entre les deux organisations.'[1]

In their efforts to pursue their policy of building up 'an autonomous self-ruling system of local government', the Belgians had by 1919 recognized 6,095 *chefferies*, many of which administered very small areas. While there were some chiefs who ruled over large areas, the majority governed only minute populations. Furthermore, the Belgians recognized also subordinate chiefs of paramounts along with the paramounts themselves. The problems arising from the existence of a plethora of small chieftaincies led the Belgians to reduce their number. This they did by withdrawing recognition from chiefs subordinate to paramounts and by grouping series of small chieftaincies into *secteurs* under the presidency of one of the constituent chiefs who alone was recognized as chief. Such chiefs thus exercised traditional authority (which was not formally recognized by the Belgians) only in the constituent chiefdom from which they came. Their authority as sector chief was Belgian-derived, though as sector chiefs they were expected to organize their sector government as though they were traditional chiefs.

In exercising local self-government, the traditional and sector chiefs had a fair degree of autonomy. They governed according to custom and administered customary law. Native treasuries were established to administer funds derived from court fees and fines, as well as so-called voluntary contributions collected at the same time as the central government tax. After 1933 the central government subsidized these chieftaincy treasuries. The official salaries paid to the chiefs were based on the number of taxpayers in their respective chieftaincies or sectors.

While chiefs had a certain degree of autonomy at the local level, the demands made on them by the central government as represented by the local Belgian administrator meant that much of their time was spent in the role of agent of the administration: as collector of taxes, as

---

[1] Belgian Congo, *Bulletin officiel*, 1933, p. 951, cited in Hailey, *An African survey* (1938), pp. 492–3.

recruiter of labour for public works and for the concessions and as agent for the compulsory cultivation of crops. Thus, while a chief in the Congo exercised an autonomy never enjoyed by his counterpart in Kenya, Angola and French West Africa, the requirements of the Belgian administration too often emphasized his position 'as the lowest grade in the civil service'[1] at the expense of his position as head of a unit of local self-government. Though in theory he was a chief with a certain degree of independent initiative working both alongside and under a European chief, in practice it was the subordinate role of the chief rather than the dual role that was emphasized.

THE BRITISH IN NIGERIA, Nigeria was so vast and contained so many different ethnic groups of such widely differing structure that no one system of native administration emerged. Indeed, parallels may be found in Nigeria for all the systems described above, other than for the Portuguese in Angola. However, the system of indirect rule as formulated by Lord Lugard and his immediate successors in the north did become the goal for the administration of Nigerians even if it was never fully realized even in the north itself. Because of the limitations of space we will here consider only the ideal of indirect rule in northern Nigeria, the Hausa–Fulani emirate, followed by reference to the difficulties experienced in the application of this policy to non-Hausa–Fulani peoples. These difficulties demonstrate parallels between British rule in Nigeria and systems of Native Administration in the other territories under consideration.

Ideally, as Lugard saw it, local administration should be exercised through the traditional political institutions of the African, shorn of such aspects as were repugnant to Western concepts of civilization. The Native Authority, as the traditional political organization was termed, should be as far as possible autonomous in the management of its affairs. Its main obligation to the central administration should be the collection of taxes, the amount of which was determined by the central administration. Of these taxes, a certain proportion would revert to the native treasury. The essential feature of indirect rule in Nigeria was the regularization of expenditure by these Native Authorities through treasuries, revenues of which would be spent only in accordance with a budget subject to scrutiny by the central administration. Chiefs and, where appropriate, councillors would become salaried officials not of

[1] See Lucy P. Mair, *Native policies in Africa* (London, 1936), p. 244.

the central government but of the Native Authority, and their salaries would form part of this budget. Native Authorities had their own courts, where customary law was applied; and only at certain levels were sentences and fines subject to administrative confirmation. The great emirs had powers even to impose the death sentence. The Native Authorities maintained their own police forces and prisons, which were subject to administrative inspection. In function, though not structure, the Native Authorities were similar to units of local self-government in Britain, responsible for roads, hospitals, education, water supplies, sanitation, etc. Some, like Kano, had budgets larger than some British colonies and employed European technical officers. Most important of all, they were the legislative authorities for local government.

The British administrator had no formal executive function in these Native Authorities. His role was designated merely as that of an adviser. His primary function was that of watchdog for the central administration: to see that the Native Authorities were running smoothly, that there were no abuses of the system and to give advice either where it was sought or when he considered it necessary. Lugard conceived of the role of the 'political officer' as one in which he would frequently advise even if his counsel was not sought. In practice, in the 1920s and 1930s the British administrators in the larger emirates left their chiefs very much alone, pursuing a policy of minimal interference.

Such a policy worked in the great emirates, where the emirs remained very much chiefs despite reduction in certain of their powers. The relationship of the emir to the white chief was very much that of a head boy of a British public school to his headmaster. Provided there were no patent abuses, the headmaster left the head boy and his prefects to their own devices. Even when it was necessary to give the emir direct orders, every effort was made to ensure that further transmission of such orders appeared to emanate from the emir himself and not from the British administrator. This policy ran into difficulty only in societies where regular direct taxation was unknown, as in Yorubaland, in small chieftaincies where the British confronted the same administrative problems as the Belgians did in the Congo, or in societies where authority was decentralized or was shared among several groups.

In southern Nigeria the introduction of the Native Authority system and direct taxation provoked riots among both Ibo and Yoruba groups, to whom the idea was alien. The centralization of powers in a single chief worked in the emirates of northern Nigeria. But it had a rough passage in Yorubaland because, though the Oba appeared to be the chief executive of state, decisions were in fact arrived at only after negotiation between a large number of policy-making groups in the state. In parts of northern Nigeria there were many small chieftaincies which the British federated into more manageable units, as the Belgians did in the Congo. In eastern Nigeria, particularly among the Ibo, the British, for want of actual chiefs, appointed as Warrant Chiefs those with some apparent authority among their people. These chiefs, whose claim to some form of traditional authority was sometimes questionable, were much closer in character to the appointed chiefs of the Portuguese and French administrations, or to the headmen of Kenya, than to the chiefs of Native Authorities in northern Nigeria. Even so, they enjoyed much more autonomy than any of these; and their abuse of this power, coupled with their lack of traditional authority, led to the 1929 revolt against them and the British who had appointed them. Finally, the British abandoned the Warrant Chiefs and, after anthropological inquiries, substituted as the Native Authority wherever possible the traditional political authorities, however diffuse.

In ruling Africans through their own political institutions, the British not only modified but in certain cases radically altered them. Nevertheless, the relationship of the British political officer to the Native Authority remained substantially the same: he was above all an adviser to the Native Authority. His role in the affairs of Native Authorities took on an executive aspect only in so far as Native Authorities were not fully capable of administering themselves. Thus, among the economically backward Plateau tribes, the district officer played an executive role inconceivable in large emirates like Kano and Zaria.

While the political officer was adviser on local government affairs, he had to carry out certain functions for central government such as recruiting soldiers and labour, as well as supervising tax collection. These, as far as possible, he performed through the agency of the Native Authorities. His other main functions were to co-ordinate the administration of the various Native Authorities under his control and to act as magistrate in cases which could not be considered within the jurisdiction of Native Authority courts. The British district officer in the emirates of northern Nigeria was a distant chief, a high god, to be appealed to in the last resort rather than to be consulted and negotiated with daily.

The white chief as magistrate

From a judicial point of view, by far the most powerful of the administrators in the colonies under consideration were the Portuguese. Since
in most African societies there was no separation between the judicial
and the executive functions of the chief, his status vis-à-vis his African
subjects was extremely important. In Angola, however, no African,
whether chief or *notable*, exercised judicial authority. All cases, civil as
well as criminal, came before the *chefe do posto* in the first instance. In
criminal cases the non-assimilated African was subject to the Portuguese
penal code, though the administrator was required to place the
offence in the context of customary law wherever appropriate. In civil
matters the administrator was advised by two Africans, either *regulos*
or those who were conversant with customary law. In any matter
concerning an African and a non-African, only Portuguese law applied.

The African was permitted no legal representation, even though he
was judged by Portuguese law. Punishments were severe: whipping
with the *chicote* (hide whip) or the *palmetaria* (hand-bat) were common
forms of corporal punishment. Imprisonment usually took the form of
'correctional labour' on public works projects. Political offences,
though they were rare in the 1930s, were dealt with summarily.

In French West Africa the judicial powers of the administrators
were somewhat more limited than those of the Portuguese. In the first
place, civil cases were judged by *tribunaux de premier degré* presided over
by an African *notable*, but significantly not a chief. Indeed, a feature of
justice indigène in French West Africa was the elimination of the judicial
functions of the chiefs. In criminal cases the *chef de subdivision* presided
over the *tribunal de premier degré*, assisted by two African *notables* as
assessors. Appeal from these tribunals was heard by the *tribunal criminel*
presided over by the *Commandant de Cercle* assisted by two European
and two African assessors.

The most important judicial weapon possessed by the French administrator was his power of summary imprisonment of African *sujets* under
the *indigénat*. This allowed him to imprison any *sujet* without trial for
up to fourteen days (later reduced to five days). He could also impose
fines without trial. Until 1924 all chiefs were subject to the *indigénat*,
but in that year a decree excluded all but village chiefs from its application. Africans committing 'political offences' could by terms of the
indigénat be imprisoned for up to ten years; but it was required that the

Minister for the Colonies be informed of the sentence. The French administrator thus had immense authority over his subjects.

The Belgian system, while allowing for native courts in which chiefs exercised authority in all civil cases and in some criminal cases, nevertheless gave its administrators summary judicial powers similar to those of their French counterparts. An African could be imprisoned by an administrator for up to seven days for *infractions aux mesures d'ordre général*. The only difference between these powers and those possessed by the French administrator was that they were subject to judicial process. However, in such instances the administrator, as police magistrate, was judge in his own case. But since the *Parquet*, or central judicial supervisory body, scrutinized all cases appearing in police magistrates' courts, there was some small check to his summary powers.

While civil cases were tried by African *tribunaux de chefferies* and *tribunaux de secteurs*, there was appeal from these courts to the *tribunaux de territoire*, composed of African chiefs as judges, but presided over by the Belgian *administrateur de territoire*. As police magistrate the *administrateur de territoire* could try all cases for which the maximum penalty was not more than two months' imprisonment. All offences of a more serious nature committed by Africans came before the District Commissioner's court, which served also as the court of appeal for the territorial courts. From the District Courts there was appeal to the professionally staffed Tribunals of First Instance. While allowing chiefs some function in the administration of civil law and some related criminal offences, the administrator had much greater legal powers than did the chief.

In British Africa the legal powers of administrators varied widely from territory to territory. Kenya and northern Nigeria present two extremes. In both systems the administrator was a magistrate and had supervisory powers over the administration of 'native' justice. In Kenya, however, native courts, which as we have seen were not chiefs' courts, could try only cases not involving sentences of more than six months, with the right of appeal in all cases, whereas in northern Nigeria the emirs' courts were empowered to try some cases for which there was no right of appeal. The emirs' courts themselves acted as courts of appeal from the subordinate Alkali courts. In Kenya the district commissioner acted as magistrate for preliminary inquiry into serious charges such as murder, rape and arson, and as judge in all other cases not dealt with by native courts. As far as the native courts were concerned, he had to confirm sentences of six months and acted as a court of appeal for all judgements made in them. He inspected their records; and even where no appeal was made to him, could on his own initiative order a retrial in his own court.

In the larger Nigerian emirates, as already noted, grave offences, including those involving the death sentence, came before the emirs' courts and were tried in accordance with the *sharia*. Death sentences had to be confirmed by the Chief Commissioner. Indeed, such was the confidence placed by the British in the judicial processes of the large emirates that it was seriously mooted in the 1920s that Europeans and Lebanese be subject to the Alkali's, rather than to British courts.

Up until 1933 the residents of the northern provinces presided as judges of the provincial courts, which had powers in cases not scheduled as coming within the province of the customary courts. In the northern emirates nearly all cases concerning 'natives', whether indigenous to the emirate or immigrants, came under the purview of the Alkali courts. Control of these courts was indirect: the colonial administration confirmed appointments, inspected the courts and reviewed cases. Where they were dissatisfied, they could transfer a case to the provincial court, or suspend sentences. They had no right to reverse a decision, only to order a retrial, in the provincial courts, of the case concerned. After the abolition of the provincial courts in 1933, the administrators retained their right to review cases, but were divested of their judicial role, since magistrates' courts now replaced the provincial courts, which had come in for considerable criticism on the grounds that their judges combined executive with judicial functions. Under the new system there was usually appeal from the customary to the British courts. However, in certain instances the final court of appeal for the African was still the emir's court. Thus an African arraigned before the district court could appeal against conviction to the Chief Alkali's court. From there he could appeal to the emir's court, which in this instance was designated a final court of appeal.[1] Thus in the emirates of Northern Nigeria the emirs enjoyed judicial powers unparalleled in any other African colony. Correspondingly, the British administrators there, after the abolition of the provincial courts, enjoyed more limited judicial powers than any of their counterparts in other colonies.

[1] See B. O. Nwabueze, *The machinery of justice in Nigeria* (London, 1968); and Elliot A. Keay and S. S. Richardson, *The native and customary courts in Nigeria* (London and Lagos, 1966).

Socio-economic roles of the bush administrator

By far the most important role played by the administrators of the four colonial powers was that of the tax-collector. In all five territories under consideration Africans were taxed directly by the colonial administration through the intermediary of the chiefs. However, in parts of Nigeria Africans were not taxed until the late 1920s; and in the neighbouring British colony of the Gold Coast direct tax was not generally introduced until after the Second World War.

Taxation was vital to the colonial economy not only in raising revenue to pay for the cost of the colonial administration, but also for raising funds for development projects such as roads, railways and ports which would contribute directly to the expansion of trade. In those days the mother country gave very little financial assistance to the colonies. Individual British territories did, in fact, sometimes receive small grants-in-aid of local revenue, loans-in-aid, or interest-free loans. The British also gave a little help under the provisions of the Colonial Development Act of 1929. In addition, the British Treasury accepted a contingent liability by guaranteeing colonial loans, thus enabling the colonies to borrow on conditions more favourable than they might otherwise have secured on the London money market. The British also subsidized some colonial research.

But the modern concept of aid by the mother country to its dependencies was not accepted. Development was largely financed in one of two ways: by revenues raised either from direct or from indirect taxation, or by loans subscribed to by investors overseas. Direct taxation was never as important a source of revenue as indirect taxation on exports and imports. Direct taxation nevertheless forced Africans to grow crops for sale so that they could earn cash with which to pay their taxes. This was also a means of forcing Africans to seek work on the farms of white settlers or in mining industries. Thus, as a supervisor of the collection of taxes from the Africans, the white administrator not only contributed significantly to the expansion of the economy, but also had considerable impact on the taxpayers themselves. In French West Africa, for example, taxation compelled peoples from densely populated, non-cash-crop growing areas of French Sudan and Upper Volta to seek work on the ground-nut fields of Senegal and on the cocoa farms of the Ivory Coast. Many Mossi from Upper Volta preferred to earn their tax-money in the mines and cocoa farms of the

Gold Coast, where remuneration was higher than in the Ivory Coast. Because most colonial administrators believed that all men had a moral obligation to work, direct taxation was one way of forcing them to do so.

A second method of gaining the same end was compulsory labour. In all five territories maintenance of local roads was effected through obligatory work enforced by the chiefs and supervised by the administrative officers. In Nigeria, after 1933, with the passage of the Forced Labour Ordinance the use of compulsory labour outside the Native Authorities was forbidden, except in special circumstances; such a case apparently arose only once—during the Second World War (see below, p. 347). However, before the passage of this act administrative officers had conscripted labour for use on railway construction and other public works projects. In Kenya, when voluntary labour was not available, administrative officers could, with the authorization of the governor, conscript labour for public works projects or porterage, though a limit of sixty days per man per annum was imposed.

In the Belgian Congo, with its legacy of excessive use of forced labour in the Free State, the question of compulsory labour was a sensitive one. As in Nigeria, inasmuch as the bulk of forced labour for public works projects was conscripted by the Native Authorities, the administrator was relieved of the necessity to intervene directly in its recruitment or use. Native Authorities maintained roads, built schools and rest-houses with such labour. Belgian administrators limited their demands largely to compulsory recruitment of porters and canoe-paddlers. There was no law permitting the use of forced labour on public works projects.

In Angola, compulsory labour was required of any African who had no apparent occupation. The moral obligation to work was written into law. Administrators could conscript labour for public works projects, in particular roads, within the areas administered by their *regulos*. In addition, they could use such labour on public works projects outside the area from which it was drawn. The Portuguese administrator thus was responsible for the miserable situation of the African in Angola, which outside visitors called variously a 'modern slavery' or 'serfdom'. It happened often that because of the demands of the Portuguese for compulsory labour, villagers were unable to cultivate adequate crops to feed themselves.

In French West Africa all non-assimilated Africans had to undertake twelve days' labour for the administration, which they could redeem at one to three francs per day. In addition, administrative officers could recruit workmen for public works projects in return for payment. The most common use of such labour was on the construction and maintenance of roads and on large projects in areas where hands were scarce, as on certain stages of the construction of railways. In addition, Africans were conscripted into the army. The most massive 'compulsory recruitment' took place during World War I when France hoped, but was quite unable, to raise a black army of a million men.

In addition to drafting labour for government undertakings, administrators in some of the colonies acted as recruiting agents for white farmers, for European commercial companies and for mining industries. This practice was most flagrant in Portuguese territories. Until 1921 it was carried on openly and quite legally. But in that year a decree was issued abolishing forced labour by private firms or individuals. Actually, however, the practice continued, if not always with the assistance of administrators, at least with a blind eye turned towards the activities of the recruiters. In French West Africa, as distinct from Equatorial Africa, where there were large concession companies, the French administration undertook little recruiting of labour for private enterprise. The main example of compulsory recruitment of this kind was in the Ivory Coast on the European cocoa and coffee farms. Significantly, however, a number of rich African cocoa-farmers had access to this labour supply. These African growers complained bitterly at the discriminatory practices of the Free French administration during the Second World War in cutting off their supply of such labour and not that of the European farmers.[1]

In the Belgian Congo one of the legacies of the Free State was the administration's policy of supplying labour for European commercial enterprises. However, in 1926 administrators were forbidden to assist in the recruitment of labour for European companies. They were directed also to ensure that chiefs did not force their subjects to serve these companies. However, they were permitted to use every legal means to persuade Africans to work for them. In practice, they continued to assist in such recruitment, which continued in many instances to be forced, though the responsibility lay with the chief rather than

[1] Michael Crowder, *West Africa under colonial rule* (London, 1968), p. 497; F. J. Amon d'Aby, *La Côte d'Ivoire dans la cité africaine* (Paris, 1951); and Edward Mortimer, *France and the Africans* (New York, 1969).

with the administrator himself. In 1931 the Colonial Minister announced that 'members of the territorial service had been forbidden to accompany the recruiting agents of private employers on their rounds'.[1]

In Nigeria, with one notable exception, British administrators never recruited labour for private enterprise. However, in the Second World War, when Britain was cut off from her Far Eastern tin supplies by the Japanese occupation of Malaya, increased production of tin in the Jos plateau became an imperative. To achieve this, forced labour for the private tin-mining companies was recruited by the administration.[2]

In Kenya, by contrast, European officials did assist in recruitment of labour, and by the notorious Labour Circular No. 1 of 1919 were instructed to use 'every possible lawful influence' to assist European farmers in obtaining African manpower. This policy was reversed in the early 1920s, when the British laid down that the administration had no formal obligation to recruit for European farmers and that as private entrepreneurs the settlers should take their chance on the labour market without public assistance. This was, however, provided indirectly, in that taxation of Africans in unproductive parts of the reserves forced them to seek labour on the European farms. Through compulsory labour, whether for public works projects or in private enterprise, European administrators were responsible not only for redistributing large numbers of African workers, but for causing much hardship and suffering in many instances both to those conscripted and to their families. This was particularly true of Angola.

In French West Africa and the Belgian Congo the administrator had the duty of forcing the African, where necessary, to cultivate certain crops. In French West Africa administrators in certain regions had *champs administratifs* on which the African peasant had to work without pay. In the Belgian Congo the administrator could compel Africans to produce crops for internal consumption or for export where he considered this necessary. In Kenya, however, the administrator found himself for a time in the reverse role. He had to prevent Africans in the reserves from cultivating coffee in competition with the white farmers on the grounds that African plantations would spread disease.[3]

Such were the principal economic functions of the local administrator, and each of them affected the social pattern of the local popu-

---

[1] Cited in Mair, *Native policies in Africa*, p. 235.
[2] *The Times* (London), 18 June 1942.
[3] Hailey, *An African survey* (1938), p. 386.

lation in its own way. These functions increased, of course, as technical services were co-ordinated by the administrator, as in French and Portuguese Africa, where there were no African 'native authorities' or local government councils responsible for local development.

Conclusion

The bush administrators formed one of the few groups of Europeans who really knew anything about Africans. Sir Charles Temple draws a vivid picture of the ignorance of African life that existed in northern Nigeria among the departmental officers of 'the Secretariat, Treasury, or any and all the technical departments':

In the morning he is called and fed by native boys who are nearly always out of touch with their own people. He goes to work, which is done with pens, ink, and paper, or possibly with various tools: in the course of work he may come into contact with a few native clerks in European clothes or with skilled native artisans, a special class entirely out of touch with the natives generally. He is fed at midday and returns to his work. In the evenings he takes his exercise for the sake of his health with other Europeans. He is fed again and goes to bed. This he does for 365 days and then gets on a steamer and goes home. He spends his leave recruiting his health, occupying his mind on matter as little connected with official duties as possible. This goes on for eighteen years. He retires.

Temple concluded:

It is a point not to be lost sight of that few Europeans working in a native Protectorate are in a position to learn anything about the native population, even though they may spend a lifetime there.[1]

Temple's picture, drawn in 1918, was substantially true for all five colonies under consideration in the inter-war years. Even though the bush administrator could claim to know more about his subjects than any other European except the missionary, whose understanding was nevertheless usually distorted by the special optic with which he regarded Africans, he never had that intimate knowledge which gave African chiefs such great control over their subjects. Administrators relied for their information, especially where they did not understand the local language, on interpreters, on court messengers, on sepoys, on

[1] C. L. Temple, *Native races and their rulers: sketches and studies of official life and administrative problems in Nigeria*, 2nd ed. (London, 1968), p. 189.

gardes de cercles. But these invariably exploited the administrator's ignorance, each to his own advantage, accepting bribes from Africans who wished them to intercede with the administrator on their behalf or threatening with exposure chiefs who had something to hide if they did not pay them what they requested. It was in the interest of this group of intermediaries to keep the truth from their employers. The stock-in-trade joke of the white administrator telling the people one thing, and the interpreter deliberately translating it to mean something different, was not far from everyday reality. Given these obstacles, it is surprising how much some of the white chiefs did manage to find out about their subjects, as evidenced by their notebooks, the records and 'anthropological' studies.

From the imperial point of view, the bush administrators were the key officials of the colonial régime. In many cases the European district officers and their wives also served as models or as a reference group in matters of dress, etiquette and behaviour to aspiring middle-class Africans, often with sad results. In French West Africa, the Belgian Congo, Kenya and Nigeria they were the last group of officials to be replaced by Africans. Yet with independence they were swept away. Their posts were either filled by Africans or neutralized or abolished altogether. While Europeans continued after independence as permanent secretaries of ministries or as senior officials in the central administration and technical services of government, African governments would not permit the survival of those Europeans—the bush administrators—who most clearly represented the colonial days. Yet in the final analysis these administrators, despite their intimate relationship with the Africans, left a far weaker imprint on the local population than that of the representatives of commercial companies and technical departments of government, whose demands and development schemes substantially changed African life.

Nor did the white administrator exert the personal impact on the individual African equal to that of even the missionary or the teacher. The primary concern of the European chief was with the traditional Africa of the bush; the Africans who were to take over control of the bush from him represented the forces of westernization and modernization generated in the schools, the churches and the new urban agglomerations. The administrators tried to defend themselves and their role by dismissing such Africans, as did Sir Charles Temple, as being divorced from the peasants and therefore unfit to govern them. What surprised these administrators was not that these Africans took over power from them, but that they did in fact summon mass support from the peasants from whom they were supposed to be divorced. The white chiefs were replaced by a new class of African chiefs who had the advantage over them that despite all their apparent alienation from traditional Africa, they generally, though not always, knew their subjects. The new rulers were able to exploit this knowledge to form the mass parties that characterized the period of decolonization and the years immediately following independence.

BIBLIOGRAPHY

Amon d'Aby, F. J. *La Côte d'Ivoire dans la cité africaine*. Paris, 1951.

Brausch, Georges. *Belgian administration in the Congo*. London, Oxford University Press, 1961.

Buell, Raymond L. *The native problem in Africa*. 2nd ed. 2 vols. London, 1965.

Crowder, Michael. *West Africa under colonial rule*. London, 1968.

Crowder, Michael, and Obaro Ikime, eds. *West African chiefs: their changing status under colonial rule and independence*. Ife and New York, 1970.

Duffy, James. *Portuguese Africa*. Cambridge, Harvard University Press, 1959.

Hailey, William Malcolm, 1st baron. *An African survey: a study of the problems arising in Africa south of the Sahara*. London, Oxford University Press, 1938.

An African survey: revised 1956. London, 1957.

Ingham, Kenneth. *A history of East Africa*. London, 1962.

Keay, Elliot Alexander, and S. S. Richardson. *The native and customary courts in Nigeria*. London and Lagos, 1966.

Mair, Lucy P. *Native policies in Africa*. London, 1936.

Mortimer, Edward. *France and the Africans, 1944–1960: a political history*. London, 1969.

Mumford, William Bryant, and G. St. J. Orde-Brown. *Africans learn to be French: a review of educational activities in the seven federated colonies of French West Africa based on a tour of French West Africa and Algiers undertaken in 1935*. London, 1937.

Nwabueze, B. O. *The machinery of justice in Nigeria*. London, 1968.

Perham, Margery. *Native administration in Nigeria*. London, Oxford University Press, 1936.

Temple, C. L. *Native races and their rulers: sketches and studies of official life and administrative problems in Nigeria*. 2nd ed. London, 1968.

CHAPTER 10

THE EMERGENT ELITES OF BLACK
AFRICA, 1900 TO 1960

by MARTIN KILSON

When European empire-builders began to hoist their flags in Africa, they were inspired by the most diverse of motives. Some sought profits, power or prestige. Others hoped to alter the old ways of Africa by bringing 'the plough and the Gospel', 'Commerce and Christianity' to the 'benighted heathen'. But whatever their intentions, the colonizers brought about profound changes, if only as the indirect and unintended result of pursuing capitalist interests. The European powers, for instance, gradually began to support missionary activities, to promote education and to subsidize some health services. They also set up modern administrations of a bureaucratic kind, and all these new institutions significantly affected the traditional social systems. Missions and government bureaucracies, because they played a major part in shaping a new kind of African, merit special attention.

Sources of élite formation

The history of the Gold Coast (now Ghana) provides an excellent instance of the important role played by the Christian evangelist in forming the new élites. Long before the British had established their power in the country, Christian missionaries had already laid the basis of Western education in the Gold Coast. The missionaries began their work in earnest in the middle of the last century. By 1881 they had set up some 139 primary schools, staffed by 200 teachers, with about 5,000 pupils. By World War I the number of mission schools had grown to 200, several of them secondary schools; others provided a professional training to teachers and clergymen. The country's expenditure for education, largely derived from mission sources, amounted to some £52,000 a year.

The missions also gave jobs to their more talented students. Mission-trained men likewise assumed new responsibilities; for instance, they created voluntary associations that often centred on existing missionary establishments. These included such bodies as the Young People's Society of Christ, the Young People's Guild, the Women's Fellowship and the Presbyterian Teachers' Union—all founded at Larteh in the Eastern Province of Ghana.

In addition to these activities, many former mission pupils took up part-time employment in commerce and in the Native Administration while continuing to work for missionary bodies. They thereby broadened their experience, acquired new habits and began to play new roles in society. They also took good care that their offspring should get on in life. Sons of mission-trained men were sent to college wherever their fathers could afford the required expense. By the time of World War II, for instance, no fewer than thirty students had left Larteh for overseas in order to study law, medicine, engineering, nursing, accounting or public administration.

Africans in other British West African colonies like Gambia, Nigeria and Sierra Leone also benefited from missionary education. So did indigenous people from British East and Central Africa, where the majority of successful mission students obtained jobs as clergymen, catechists and teachers in mission institutions. The pattern in Uganda resembled that prevailing in the Gold Coast. In the white settler colonies of Kenya, Northern and Southern Rhodesia, on the other hand, few high-level positions were available to Africans. (One should add, however, that large-scale economic development in Southern Rhodesia only started after the Boer War. In Northern Rhodesia, it was only in the late 1920s that mining began to play a major role, whereas many West African regions had been linked to the capitalist world economy through 'legitimate' trade in ground-nuts, palm-oil or similar produce since the second half of the nineteenth century.) Educated Africans nevertheless laboured under grave disadvantages. Thus, Kenya's first African lawyer did not begin to practise his profession until 1956, whereas by the late 1920s the Gold Coast could already boast of sixty African lawyers. (One of these, E. C. Quist, who was later knighted, was named Crown Counsel as early as 1914. Nigeria and Sierra Leone likewise had at any rate a handful of African legal men by the 1920s.)

In French West Africa, missionaries played a much smaller role in education than in the British colonies. France was split by long-standing disputes between Catholics and anti-clericals; hence there were numerous restrictions on Christian evangelical work in the French

African possessions. By the 1920s, for instance, only 5,000 pupils were attending Catholic or Protestant mission schools in French West Africa, whereas in the Gold Coast alone there were over 20,000 students in mission schools. Yet even in the French colonies, the Christian missions played a significant role in education; they likewise made a major contribution in the Belgian Congo. The rise of the new African élites thus owes a great deal to missionary inspiration.

The colonial governments, too, played an important part in fashioning the new African élites. This is not surprising, for colonial society necessarily bore an authoritarian character, not necessarily in a repressive, but always in an administrative sense. In order to regulate their subjects, the colonial rulers required an effective state machinery; in order to govern, they soon needed indigenous as well as expatriate civil servants. The colonial rulers were thus forced to educate some of their subjects, and the trained African official in turn became a member of a new élite.

All the colonial governments contributed to African education in a greater or lesser degree. From the early days of colonial rule, the British began to subsidize mission schools in a small way. Gradually the governments increased their subvention, and government expenditure on education became steadily more important. In addition, British educationists set up state schools in various parts of colonial Africa. The British also established more advanced institutions, such as Achimota on the Gold Coast and Katsina College in Nigeria.[1] Mission institutions provided higher education for an even larger number of Africans than the government schools. By the late 1940s, as shown in Table 6, a considerable number of British-trained Africans thus held positions of some consequence in society.

In French Africa, the government played an even greater part. Before World War II, some eight government schools had a virtual monopoly in training Africans to be doctors (medical assistants), teachers, pharmacists, middle-level administrators and lawyers. These institutions included the Dakar Medical School, Lycée Faidherbe, the

[1] In Ghana, for example, the colonial government, between 1900 and World War I, gave financial assistance to five private secondary schools—several of which were established on African initiative—and in 1909 the government opened a Teacher Training College and a Technical Institute. In 1927-8, the government went one step farther towards the provision of élite-type education: it opened the Prince of Wales (Achimota) College. Some £600,800 was invested in this institution, with annual costs approaching £80,000. Within a decade the secondary division at Achimota College had enrolled 180 pupils, the teacher-training division 1,952, and the university college 32.

Table 6. *Estimated number of Africans engaged in élite occupations in Ghana, 1940s*

Occupation	Total number
Civil servants	3,295
Lawyers	114
Doctors	38
Dentists	7
Journalists and newspaper owners	32
Surveyors and engineers	210
Merchants	1,443
Teachers	3,123
Clergymen	435
Bank tellers	61
Book-keepers	103
Druggists	231
Cocoa brokers and buyers	1,313

Source: Gold Coast, *Census of population, 1948* (Accra, 1950), p. 392.

William Ponty Normal School—all of them founded between 1910 and 1920—as well as the Lycée Van Vollenhoven. Despite all French theories concerning cultural assimilation, however, the French did not train as many Africans for élite roles as did the British, for élite education was restricted to a handful of government schools. Between 1918 and 1939, for instance, the William Ponty School in Senegal graduated no more than 1,500 pupils for the whole of French West Africa, which then comprised a population of some 22,000,000.

French African graduates also engaged in a more limited number of occupations than did their British-trained counterparts. For example, before World War II perhaps a third of the graduates of Ponty Normal School were medical assistants. Furthermore, it seems that secondary-school graduates in French Africa were less inclined than their British African counterparts to diversify their occupational experiences by holding two or more jobs. The reason for this may be found perhaps in the attitudes of their instructors. In British Africa, mission teachers not only gave lessons, but engaged in such diverse activities as constructing their own buildings, cultivating their own crops, experimenting in agriculture and building roads. Thus, students at mission schools in British Africa learned how to try their hand at many different jobs. No comparable experience was available to African students at élite institutions in French Africa.

The colonial governments played an important role, too, in providing the new African upper-echelon élite with a new style of life and with financial rewards far superior to those received by Africans in other occupations. During the 1930s, for example, two Gold Coast lawyers employed as police magistrates received an annual income of £600 to £840. Another African lawyer, a Crown Counsel, made between £720 to £1,060 per annum. There were eight medical doctors within the £520–£570 income range. Well-educated Gold Coast civil servants were able to earn between £300 and £500 or more. Generally speaking, well-educated Africans could not easily get equivalent salaries in private employment. Only lawyers and doctors in practice on their own, a few journalists, some clerks and merchants were able to secure comparable or better incomes. Hence, members of the African upper-echelon élite tended to gravitate towards government positions throughout the length and breadth of colonial Africa.[1]

The subordinate strata of the new African élites (which I shall call 'sub-élites') also depended largely on the government for their position in colonial society. From World War I onward, the colonial governments gave increasing financial support to primary schools in Africa. Primary-school leavers who were unable to continue their education in secondary schools (that is to say, the overwhelming majority of former elementary-school students) began to fill the ranks of the sub-élites. These included such occupations as clerks, foremen, mechanics, transport owners, bricklayers, tailors, cash-crop farmers and agricultural demonstrators. The number of Africans engaged in these sub-élite occupations in Ghana is shown in Table 7. Like the upper-echelon élites, the sub-élites were often concentrated in the coastal cities. But unlike the upper-echelon élites, members of the sub-élites also took up many jobs in the hinterland towns and in the countryside.

In a certain sense, the hinterland towns were the natural habitat of the sub-élites. The town of Bekwai (situated in the Bekwai District of Ashanti, Gold Coast) stands out as a good example. Bekwai experienced a considerable degree of economic development between the two world wars. Cash-crop farmers made a good living from oil palms

---

[1] In Sierra Leone, for example, nearly 60 per cent of the medical doctors were in government jobs in the late 1930s and the 1940s; by the middle 1950s the proportion so employed was 80 per cent. In Ghana in the 1930s nearly 50 per cent of medical doctors were in government jobs. For lawyers, perhaps 20 per cent of Sierra Leonean lawyers were in government jobs in the 1930s and the 1940s, and in the middle 1950s the proportion so employed was 40 per cent.

Table 7. *Africans engaged in selected sub-élite*
occupations in Cape Coast, Ghana, 1920s

Occupation	Total number
Clerk	8,240
Carpenter	566
Bricklayer	300
Cooper	64
Mechanic	50
Painter	30
Tailor	94
Storekeeper	182
Shoemaker	100
Policeman	119
Dresser	4
Contractor	8
Telegraphist	9

Source: Gold Coast, Census Office, *Census report, 1921, for the Gold Coast Colony, Ashanti,*
the northern territorities and the mandated area of Togoland (Accra, 1923).

and especially from cocoa. (Between 1927 and 1928 local cultivators produced something like 11,800 tons of cocoa, valued at £55,000). A European firm mined gold on a considerable scale. Local branches of government departments concerned with mining problems, agricultural extension and public works provided jobs for many members of the sub-élite. Something like twenty European commercial firms were operating in the area during this period. In addition, the Bekwai District Book reported that already in the 1920s 'petty traders are numerous and many of the firms have branches in villages and sub-districts'.[1] Farming and mercantile enterprise combined with government and missionary activity to provide this hinterland area with a very substantial modern infrastructure. By the 1940s, as shown in Table 8, Bekwai contained a considerable number of artisans as well as Africans employed in white-collar jobs.

African cash-crop producers also owed a considerable debt to government backing. Throughout many parts of colonial Africa officials connected with agricultural departments (and sometimes also public works departments or treasuries) gave support to indigenous cash-crop producers. From the 1920s onward, various colonial govern-

[1] *Bekwai district record book, 1925–33,* Ghana National Archives, Acc. No. 150/53, p. 334.

Table 8. *Africans engaged in selected sub-élite occupations in Bekwai, Ghana, 1948*

Occupation	Total number[a]
Artisans and skilled workmen	4,989
Clerks	268
Teachers (primary school)	111
Policemen	116
Civil servants (technicians)	70

[a] Except for figures on artisans and skilled workmen which apply to the whole Bekwai District (population 15 years and over was 49,000), the figures refer only to towns of Bekwai, Tarkwa and Obuasi (population 15 years and over was 10,800 for these towns).

Source: Gold Coast, *Census of population, 1948* (Accra, 1950), pp. 370, 381.

ments, for instance, organized cash-crop producers into co-operative and mutual-aid or credit societies. In French West Africa, such producers' organizations were known as Sociétés de Prévoyance, which were empowered to undertake a variety of agricultural extension services. Agricultural credit institutions, financed by central government, were also organized in French areas. Together with the Sociétés de Prévoyance they facilitated the rise of an indigenous peasantry producing for the market. This peasantry was as yet relatively small in numbers, but it was capable of functioning in a modern economy. Successful cash-crop producers, too, gained political experience through co-operatives and agricultural credit agencies. Some of these people, for example, were chosen by colonial officials to constitute the executive committees of the Sociétés de Prévoyance. In this way they learned administrative methods and exercised some executive authority, inasmuch as the Sociétés de Prévoyance had the power to tax their members (in 1926 there were 1,010,572 members in Senegal alone) and to allocate for agricultural purposes the revenues so gained.

Assistance for cash-crop production came as well from the various British colonial governments. This was true not only in countries such as Ghana, Nigeria and Tanganyika, but even in Southern Rhodesia, where, in order to increase local food production, the authorities promoted African 'master farmer' schemes and landownership on individual tenure in segregated 'native purchase areas'. The British also played an important part in organizing rural co-operatives. In the

Gold Coast, for instance, the local agricultural department instituted in 1925 the first producers' co-operatives. Agricultural technicians put their skills and knowledge at the service of the African peasants, with the result that the movement expanded rapidly. Having begun with only 30 co-operatives comprising about 1,000 members, the Gold Coast co-operative movement, by the late 1930s, embraced over 400 societies with some 9,000 members. Membership in these co-operative societies was generally smaller than in French Africa, where the peasants had no option but to join the Sociétés de Prévoyance. (Thus, in Senegal in 1926, there were over 1,000,000 members who belonged to 15 different Sociétés de Prévoyance, divided into 138 sub-societies.) In British Africa, the co-operative societies tended to include largely the more successful or adaptable cash-crop producers, whereas membership in these organizations in French Africa was more varied.

By the 1940s, the co-operative societies in Ghana had developed a corps of committed African leaders. Cognizant of the economic and political power of their institution, these men reorganized the local co-operatives at the national level. Their labours resulted in the Gold Coast Co-operative Marketing Association, which, among other functions, co-ordinated the marketing of crops of member societies, rationalized the procedure of local societies, and bargained with the government Cocoa Marketing Board for fair prices. By 1953 the Co-operative Marketing Association marketed more than 20 per cent of Ghana's cocoa crop, valued at £7,000,000 in terms of government prices. In French Africa, the agricultural co-operatives were not nearly so successful. For example, in 1953 the marketing co-operatives in Senegal, known as Sociétés Mutuelles de Production Rurale, sold only about 6 per cent of Senegal's major cash-crop peanuts.

In addition, a certain number of African chiefs made their way into the new élites. Some chiefs acquired a Western education, a new way of life, new economic interests and new administrative functions. These attributes sharply distinguished these men from their more tradition-bound brethren. I shall describe the new-style chiefs as a 'neo-traditional élite'. They cannot, however, be easily divided into an upper-echelon élite and a sub-élite. For some purposes, the neo-traditional élite is most conveniently ranked with the former group; for others it fits in more readily into the sub-élites. Sometimes this stratum seems to possess a status all of its own among the new élites.

Mission education again made a major contribution to the formation of the neo-traditional élite. Some mission schools made special provision for the education of the chiefs. So did the various colonial governments. Civil servants had a natural interest in seeing to it that the chiefs employed as auxiliaries of the colonial authorities should be better educated than their subjects. Some colonizers, the British especially, also had an ideological preference for sending sons of chiefs to the supposed African equivalent of British 'Public Schools'. In 1906, for instance, the Sierra Leone government opened Bo School 'solely for the sons and nominees of chiefs'. At the inauguration of the Eumpe School in Sierra Leone in 1915, the local District Commissioner similarly remarked:

It should not be open to all and sundry, but only to selected pupils chosen from a strata slightly, but not much beneath those eligible for Bo School. The upper and leading classes must be educated before the lower or working classes.[1]

The French too encouraged schooling for the sons of chiefs. Indeed one of the first schools opened in Senegal during the first decade of the present century was designed specifically to teach French and the rudiments of civil administration to the sons of tribal chiefs.

The majority of the students educated in such schools preferred to make their living in the modern sector of the economy. They often became the first African doctors, lawyers, engineers and civil servants in any given colony. But some of them also took up posts in what the British called Native Administration. In many instances they began their careers as minor salaried functionaries in the central services before being promoted to tribal chiefs. In Senegal, for example, the early graduates of the schools for the sons of chiefs served as government or military interpreters until tribal Stools (thrones) became vacant; alternatively, they contented themselves with such minor posts as *chefs de canton*. In Sierra Leone in 1922, some 32 per cent of the graduates of Bo School took up posts in Native Administration; by 1934 about 15 per cent were filling such positions.[2]

Education was an important asset for the neo-traditional élite. For this group, however, education could never rival the importance of wealth and of politico-administrative status. But all these attributes

---

[1] Sierra Leone, *Annual report of the railway district, 1915* (Freetown, 1917), p. 8.
[2] Great Britain, Colonial Office, *Sierra Leone report for 1922* (London, 1923), p. 24; Sierra Leone, Education Department, *Annual report, 1934* (Freetown, 1935), p. 19.

were closely related. Educated chiefs often managed to rise higher in the official hierarchy than their unlettered brethren. Powerful chiefs in turn could use their strategic position within the colonial administration to make money. In Sierra Leone, for instance, an official inquiry in 1956 gave details concerning a certain chief who had built himself a three-storey house valued at £5,000 from taxes extorted from the peasants. Another was making £1,666 from royalty payments (out of a total income of £4,000). A third was earning £375 a year through the sale of crops acquired as a customary tribute. Yet another tribal dignitary had manipulated his customary powers in such a way as to gain a foothold in the transport (trucking) business; he had also gone in for produce marketing, and he had opened a mineral water factory.[1]

Such practices were neither new nor confined solely to Sierra Leone. In 1920, for instance, the Chief Native Commissioner of Ashanti had reported:

An important case was decided in the Chief Commissioner's Court in connection with the cocoa tribute. A Chief claimed the 1d. per tree tribute from a community of Ashantis who had been settled on his land for about 200 years, and who originally paid tribute of 12 yams, two pots of palm oil, and eight loads of snails...The Chief alleged that the settlers were 'strangers' and he was entitled to 1d. per tree which would have amounted to £2,000... It was held that the settlers could not be regarded as 'strangers'. The cocoa industry is the result of individual toil, individual enterprise, individual energy. Cocoa is not found wild in the bush like rubber, timber, and game... All the work is done by the farmer himself and his family, or at his own sole expense. It is neither natural justice nor good faith that they should now be called upon to pay a heavy tax merely on the ground that by their own energy and enterprise they are making valuable use of land which has been in their occupation for all these years.[2]

The typical chief, however, obtained most of his regular income from his official salary. He did not always fare well in comparison with his subjects. Already during the early period of British South Africa Company government in the two Rhodesias, Native Commissioners noted that many chiefs were earning less than the more fortunate labour migrants, those men who returned from the mines with relatively

[1] Sierra Leone, Commission of Enquiry into the Conduct of Certain Chiefs, *Report* (Freetown, 1957), pp. 38–9, 51, 68; Sierra Leone, Commission of Inquiry into Disturbances in the Provinces (November 1955–March 1956), *Report* (Freetown, 1957), pp. 153, 160–1.

[2] C. M. Harper, *Report for Ashanti for 1920* (Accra, 1921), p. 23.

Table 9. *Salaries of chiefs in selected Native Authorities in Uganda, 1948, and in Sierra Leone, 1960*

Uganda Native Authorities 1948	Salary (£)	Sierra Leone Native Authorities 1960	Salary (£)
Bunyore	200–300	Yoni	579
Toro	120–350	Bonkolenken	600
Ankele	150–350	Kholifa	822
Kigezi	180–350	Kholifa-Mabang	360
		Sambaia	700

Sources: William Malcolm Hailey, 1st baron, *Native administration in the British African territories* (London, 1950), I, 51; and Sierra Leone, *Tonkolili chiefdom estimates, 1960* (Tonkolili, 1960).

Table 10. *Salaries of chiefs in the Ivory Coast, 1950*

Class of chief	Salary[a] (in francs)
Chefs supérieurs (6)[b]	560,000
Chefs de province (2)	320,000
Chefs de canton	
de 1ʳᵉ classe (21)	2,055,000
de 2ᵉ classe (15)	1,370,000
de 3ᵉ classe (18)	1,530,000
de 4ᵉ classe (22)	1,760,000
de 5ᵉ classe (18)	1,350,000
de 6ᵉ classe (29)	2,117,000
de 7ᵉ classe (39)	2,730,000
de 8ᵉ classe (74)	4,810,000

[a] In 1950, the franc exchanged at 175 francs to one U.S. dollar.
[b] Figures in parentheses denote number of chiefs in each class.
Source: Ivory Coast, *Budget du service local, 1950* (Abidjan, 1950), p. 82.

large amounts of money in their pockets. By and large, however, salaries paid to chiefs compared favourably with the money income available to the typical peasant or to the wage labourer in the towns. For example, in one small Gold Coast 'Native Authority' (Akim Boseme), the Paramount Chief (Omanhene) in 1940 drew an annual salary of £400. The chief next below him in authority (Krontihene) earned £100. On the other hand, in the large Native Authorities of

Northern Nigeria like Kano Native Authority, the Emir had a salary of £7,700 in 1960; in Western Nigeria many Yoruba obas earned £2,000 salary in the 1950s. Tables 9 and 10 provide a reasonable representation of the salary range among chiefs in British and French Africa in the post-World War II era. In general, the salaries of upper-level chiefs were larger in British than in French Africa. Furthermore, in French as well as in British Africa, chiefs were granted allowances in addition to their salaries. They also put in claims for money ostensibly spent for public services, but actually used for private purposes. The extent of this peculation is hard to substantiate, and expert opinion differed widely in this regard. In Barotseland in Northern Rhodesia, for instance, British district officers frequently censured the Lozi ruling strata for corruption, whereas an experienced anthropologist such as Max Gluckman came to very different conclusions. But whether honest or dishonest, chiefs were a force to be reckoned with in colonial Africa. Many traditional rulers managed to work their way up into the neo-traditional élite, a stratum that attained considerable importance. So strong, in fact, was its position that few African nationalist parties led by members of the upper-echelon élite could afford to overlook the influence of the modernizing chiefs.

The political structure of the African sub-élites

In colonial Africa, the emergent élites generally felt the need to reinforce their positions through political action of some kind. This was especially true because the colonizers were ambivalent in their attitude concerning indigenous politics. Only the Portuguese and the Belgians, in their respective territories, more or less prohibited political activities to the emergent African élites. In French West Africa, there were various restrictions on political participation, but French Africans were considerably better off in this respect than Africans in the Belgian Congo. In British Africa, the authorities officially recognized that Africans had certain political rights, though in practice the position of the indigenous people was more favourable in West than in East of South Central Africa.

In exercising their formal political rights, the upper-echelon élite possessed many advantages over the other strata of the population. The upper-echelon Africans were in this respect somewhat more like the European residents in Kenya or Northern Rhodesia: they had greater knowledge of the government structure than the villagers; they understood the functions and the composition of the various governmental authorities; they maintained personal contacts with senior colonial officials; they were better educated than ordinary folk and they had commonly had experience overseas. The upper-echelon élite, moreover, often lived in or near the colonial capital, and they could therefore get in touch with highly placed colonial administrators much more easily than could the backwoodsmen. The sub-élites lacked these social advantages. Its members commonly lived in provincial towns, in small urban centres or in the more advanced villages. They had not much practical knowledge or theoretical understanding of the way in which the colonial government operated at the higher levels. Their capacity for political action was at first much inferior to that of the upper-echelon élite.

There was, however, a wide range of differences in this regard among the various sub-élites. The most powerful people, relatively speaking, were the white-collar workers—above all the clerks and, to a lesser extent, the school-teachers. These two groups, for one thing, always outnumbered the other members of the sub-élites, as shown in Tables 11 and 12.

Clerks and school-teachers were relatively well educated; they read books and newspapers; they were accustomed also to exercising a certain amount of personal authority either in the office or in the class-room. Hence, they were often called upon to provide leadership to the lower ranks of the sub-élite in religious, tribal, trade union or political organizations. Teachers, for instance, played an important role in pioneering African political organizations in Northern Rhodesia; old-fashioned British officials in Northern Rhodesia thus sometimes referred to the African National Congress as a 'schoolmasters' ramp'!

From the economic point of view, clerks performed perhaps an even more important function than the school-teachers, though the line between the two groups is not always easy to draw. In the Rhodesias, for instance, many ill-paid school-teachers used to turn to office work when times were hard, and when mission salaries no longer sufficed to feed a growing family. In the early days of European colonization, moreover, clerks and schoolmasters were not always wholly divorced from the soil. In the pioneering period of Northern Rhodesia, for example, mission teachers and evangelists on lonely outstations would continue to till their plots, in addition to drawing salaries.

Table 11. *Nigerians engaged in selected élite occupations, 1920s and 1950s*

Occupation	Early 1920s	Early 1950s
Lawyer	15	150
Doctor	12	160
Civil servant	25[a]	786
Clergyman	136[b]	226
Manager	—	100[d]
Teacher	10,000[c]	35,000
Clerk	12,000	27,000
Artisan	5,000	32,000

[a] This figure refers to Nigerians earning over £100. There were in the 1920s nearly 6,000 other Africans in government employment earning under £100, and this category numbered 80,000 in the early 1950s.
[b] This figure refers to Church Missionary Society only.
[c] This figure is for the 1930s.
[d] This figure refers to Nigerian managers employed by United Africa Co.

Source: James S. Coleman, *Nigeria: background to nationalism* (Berkeley and Los Angeles, University of California Press, 1958), pp. 70, 142.

Table 12. *Elite occupations in the Ivory Coast, 1962*

Occupation	Total number
Professional and technical	632
Supervisory	1,077
Managers	284
Clerks	
Skilled	3,770
Unskilled	11,000

Source: Ivory Coast. Inspection du Travail, *Rapport annuel, 1962* (Abidjan, 1962).

Clerks employed by the Northern Rhodesian Native Authorities would likewise often supplement their scanty wages by cultivating crops. Gradually, however, clerks turned into full-time office workers and became entirely dependent on cash wages.

In the towns, of course, the clerks had always had to live on their salaries alone. Because wages here were higher than in the countryside, urban centres became magnets attracting educated Africans from the backwoods. Teachers and clerks thus were apt to move around a good deal. Many migrated to the cities in order to find jobs with European commercial firms, mining companies or government offices. The clerks, in the process, became well acquainted with the workings of a modern economy and administration—to a greater extent than teachers, and to a much higher degree certainly than village artisans and cash-crop farmers. Clerks had more personal dealings, too, with European officials and entrepreneurs; they saw more of the Europeans' way of life, their manner of professional operation and techniques of organization and government. Clerks were therefore in a position to acquire a certain *savoir faire*, perhaps a certain urbanity, however fitful.[1] Clerks were unique also in that they had more contacts with both the upper-echelon African élite and the sub-élites than any other occupational stratum. Clerks in European retail firms, for example, had contact with carpenters, tailors and other artisans who came to purchase tools and wares. Clerks had dealings with cash-crop producers, too. (Clerks, for instance, often had to grade and buy cash-crops like cotton and cocoa for European produce-buying firms such as Cadbury Ltd. and the Swiss Trading Company.) The African upper-echelon élite likewise depended on the services of clerks. An African lawyer or doctor invariably had a clerk in his employ; clerks would serve African lawyers and doctors who purchased luxury goods at European or Asian retail stores. A clerk would initially attend the upper-echelon élite who sought service from a government office. Wage labourers had more to do with clerks than with any other élite group. Clerks often served as foremen, as 'boss boys', as paymasters or book-keepers; and when a workman wanted advice on the job, he commonly went to see a clerk.

African clerks, moveover, were apt to acquire experience in many walks of life. For instance, a clerk might work successively in a European retail firm, in a produce-buying corporation, in a government department, for a Native Authority, or in a mission station. Clerks might also gain promotion to quasi-managerial positions or to more senior administrative posts. They might apply their experience to make their way in independent occupations as leaders of a separatist church, as contractors or as proprietors of private schools. They might obtain additional training at technical institutes or at teacher-training schools; they might take correspondence courses and move into the upper-

---

[1] Clerks have yet to receive from social scientists the special attention they deserve as a unique element among the African new élites. A few novelists, however, have offered insight into their role and status. See Joyce Cary, *Mister Johnson* (London, 1952).

echelons as secondary-school teachers, accountants, surveyors, and even as lawyers. Thus, of the 80 members of the House of Assembly in Western Nigeria in 1951, some 18 (or 22 per cent) began their occupational careers as clerks. Of this number, 2 became lawyers, 8 attained managerial rank in European firms, 10 became businessmen and 1 a professional organizer.[1]

The mobility of clerks within colonial society gave them a unique political position. Clerks were able to render political service to other groups among the sub-élites, the upper-echelon élite and the ordinary workers. Nationalist parties led by the upper-echelon élite in the post-World War II period depended heavily upon clerks as organizers; and the more intelligent or ambitious clerks quickly found their way into top political leadership as party officers, legislators, and politically appointed administrators. Moreover, in the Belgian Congo and in East and Central Africa, clerks constituted from the start a major segment of political party leadership, largely because an upper-echelon élite, like doctors, lawyers and senior civil servants, was virtually non-existent.

The vital role played by clerks may be illustrated by a case study of the Ashanti Motor Transport Union in the Gold Coast. The Union was organized at Kumasi in 1932, with branches in three other Ashanti towns—Bekwai, Sunyani and Mampong. The secretary of the Union, its operative head, was a clerk. As was often the case with sub-élite associations or interest groups run by former clerks, the titular head (president) of the Ashanti Motor Transport Union was an illiterate transport owner who signed official documents with his 'mark'.[2] The Union, however, required a literate secretary, for the Union's statutes laid down that:

It shall be the duty of the Secretary to attend at the Office of the Union, and also at every meeting of the Union, and of the Council and Committees, to record the minutes of such meetings and have them duly confirmed and signed by the Chairman of the next subsequent meeting. He shall prepare,

[1] For detailed biographical sketches see, for instance, Ronald Segal, *Political Africa: who's who of personalities and parties* (London, 1961). See also *Annuaire parlementaire des états d'Afrique noire* (Paris, 1962). This volume contains 1,100 biographical sketches of the political élites in French-speaking Africa.

[2] Another instance of this in Ghana was the Gold Coast Farmers' Committee founded in the 1930s under the titular headship of J. K. Ayew, a semi-literate but successful cocoa-farmer and cocoa-broker; but the operative head was a clerk who had had some commercial training in Britain.

and cause to be issued, all notices to be sent to members. He shall maintain correctly and up to date, the prescribed books, letters and registers. He shall sign on behalf of the Union and conduct its correspondence, and to perform such other duties as the Council shall assign to him. He shall demand all payments and subscriptions as they become due. He shall keep, or cause to be kept a proper account of the receipts and expenditure of the Union.[1]

Only a trained clerk could do this kind of work. Clerks also ran other organizations such as the Nigerian Mechanics' Union (founded 1921), the Lagos Wholesale Butchers' Union (1939), the Lagos Taxi Drivers' Association (1938), the Sierra Leone Young People's Progressive Union (1929), the Sierra Leone Protectorate Education Progressive Union (1929), the Uganda African Motor Drivers' Association (1930), the Labour Trade Union of East Africa in Kenya (1937), and the Association des Anciens Elèves des Pères de Scheut in the Belgian Congo (1925).

Clerks likewise formed organizations to represent their own special interests, including civil servants' and welfare societies. The former were usually the first political bodies founded by clerks, and commonly served political as well as professional functions. Thus the Southern Nigeria Civil Service Union, established in 1921, aimed at securing more government clerkships and higher wages for its members. This was true also of other clerical civil servants' associations, like the African Civil Servants' Association in Nyasaland (1930) and the Sierra Leone Civil Servants' Association (1909). The latter described its purpose as:

A medium whereby representations can be made to government on all matters affecting the interests of the African staff...To make collective representations constitutionally to the Head of the Executive and...the Secretary of State for the Colonies when necessary...and to ensure that mutual improvement and support of its members are maintained.[2]

As the colonial powers became increasingly susceptible to African pressure for change, the African welfare associations gradually became more important than the civil servants' unions. The welfare associations were often run by clerks in private employment, by people who were not so dependent on the favours of white civil servants. The welfare associations included also members of other sub-élites, among them

---

[1] Gold Coast, *Motor Transport Union Ashanti by-laws rules and regulations* (Kumasi, 1932). Mimeograph.
[2] D. N. K. Browne, 'The African Civil Servants' Association', *The Civil Servant*, Dec. 1948, pp. 2 ff.

semi-literate teachers, catechists, mechanics and foremen. The welfare associations thus concerned themselves not only with matters relevant to clerks, but also with issues of concern to other social groups. This was characteristic of the large number of welfare associations organized in Central Africa during the 1920s through the 1940s.[1] For example, the Livingstone Native Welfare Association, formed in 1929–30 by black Northern Rhodesian clerks in private and government employment, had as its aim to 'help the government to improve the country and to deal with matters and grievances affecting the native people'.[2]

The West African equivalents of these bodies were usually known as 'improvement associations', 'progress unions', 'youth clubs' or 'tribal unions'. Though led by clerks, they also comprised other members of the sub-élite, including mechanics, semi-literate teachers and foremen. They also included illiterate people peripheral to modern society, who were normally recruited on a tribal basis. Typical of these associations were such Gold Coast associations as the Ashanti Youth Club (1930), the Ashanti Truth Society (1930), the Akwapim Improvement Society (1930), the People's Education Association (1940), the Bekwai Youth Movement (1940) and the Bekwai State Improvement Society (1950). Among the original ninety members of the last-named association were represented the following occupations: primary-school teachers, clerks, a Presbyterian catechist, a storekeeper, a goldsmith, a carpenter, a tailor and mechanics.

Welfare associations were a qualitatively new feature of the modern political infrastructure. Many colonial governments soon appreciated their potential value and endeavoured to use them for administrative purposes in local government. For example, the Broken Hill Native Welfare Association in Northern Rhodesia was

treated as a kind of advisory board, and was consulted by the District Commissioner before he made his recommendations about the new tax rates. When the new rate was announced, he again invoked the assistance of the Association to explain the change to the general public.[3]

From the 1940s, colonial governments in British Africa took another step forward. The Native Authorities had generally proved incapable

---

[1] The best study of these associations is found in Robert Rotberg, *The rise of nationalism in Central Africa: the making of Malawi and Zambia, 1873–1964* (Cambridge, Harvard University Press, 1965), pp. 115 ff. See also Arnold Leonard Epstein, *Politics in an urban African community* (Manchester University Press, 1958), pp. 42 ff; Lewis H. Gann, *A history of Northern Rhodesia: early days to 1953* (London, 1964), pp. 303–7.
[2] Rotberg, *The rise of nationalism*, p. 125.   [3] Epstein, *Politics*, p. 45.

of providing adequate social services to the various local communities in their charge. British colonial administrators therefore tried to improve the performance of the Native Authorities by giving leaders of welfare societies a more formal role in local government. In Northern Rhodesia, for instance, heads of welfare associations were appointed to advisory councils, including urban advisory councils, that had hitherto represented only chiefs and tribal elders. The clerks appointed to such bodies had invariably gained experience in other modern organizations. They were therefore more articulate than other sub-élite leaders and came to play an increasingly important role in politics. Table 13 illustrates some characteristic organizational cross-links.

From the late 1930s, the colonial government also appointed ordinary commoners to the Native Authorities of the Gold Coast. By the 1940s, most finance committees of Native Authorities in the southern Gold Coast and Ashanti contained 'plebeian' members, including elementary-school teachers and mechanics. In Ashanti, the British authorities likewise set up advisory bodies known as Area Committees. These were composed both of clerks and their allies, and of senior chiefs. The task of these committees was to allocate local services in a more rational fashion. By 1950, a District Commissioner was able to report of the Area Committee at Kwabre Mponua:

The Area Committee continues to work well. They meet regularly and their Committee procedure is good. They recommended to the Area Chiefs that loans should be granted (against levies to be paid during the forthcoming levy season) to three villages that wish to press on with their school buildings. At first the Area Chiefs refused the loan, but at a later meeting, the Committee pressed the matter again and the Chiefs agreed.[1]

Chiefs, of course, were not always so amenable to 'plebeian' advice. On one occasion, at Agogo in Ashanti, for instance, the non-chiefly members thus decided to ignore the Native Authority, and to use their own welfare society as an instrument for performing much-needed local services. A District Commissioner thus wrote regretfully:

Unfortunately the initiative seems to have passed to the Improvement Society, a body headed by Mr T. E. Kyei [clerk in Department of Education] and including quite a number of natives of Agogo living elsewhere. They are collecting money to build a Post Office and to improve the town streets

---

[1] *Kumasi division district record book, 1926–51*, Ghana National Archives, Acc. No. 798/52, p. 358.

Table 13. *Non-chiefly members of Luanshya Urban Advisory Council in Northern Rhodesia, 1949*

Name	Member's occupation	Member's association
R. Banda	Clerk in contracting firm	Secretary of General Workers' Union
A. Chunga	Clerk in contracting firm	—
L. Ngambi	Primary-school teacher	Secretary of Welfare Association
T. Myumara	Hospital orderly	Member of Welfare Association, Chairman of Roan Mine Workers' Union
G. Musumbulwa	Clerk in mining firm	Secretary of Welfare Association, Committee Member of Roan Co-operative Society
A. Chambeshi	Clerk in mining firm	Member of Welfare Association, Treasurer of Roan Branch of Mine Workers' Union
C. Mhone	Clerk in mining firm	Organizer of Nyasaland African National Congress Branch at Roan

Source: Arnold Leonard Epstein, *Politics in an urban African community* (Manchester University Press, 1958), p. 75.

of Agogo, both very necessary projects, but they show signs of trying to usurp some of the functions of the Native Authority, while making use of its powers.[1]

The process of gradually integrating the sub-élites into the local administration, initiated in the 1930s, began to speed up as local governments were required to perform an increasingly large number of administrative tasks. By the middle of the 1950s, the traditional modes of local government were giving way to representative forms in most parts of colonial Africa. The elected local councils were generally controlled by clerks and other members of the sub-élites, especially cash-crop farmers, crop-brokers and middle-size traders.[2]

[1] *Kumasi division district record book*, p. 167.
[2] A survey made by the author in Ghana during the years 1964–5 concerning the composition of the Agona Local Council, Central Region of Ghana, provided figures that are probably characteristic for many other parts of Africa. The Council then included 10 members, of whom 3 were cocoa-brokers, 6 cocoa-farmers and 1 lorry-owner. The Nsawam–Aburi Local Council, Eastern Region, contained 12 Councillors, including 1 cocoa-broker, 2 cocoa-farmers, 1 contractor, 2 clerks, 2 merchants, 1 ex-civil servant and 3 unidentified. In Amansie Local Council, Ashanti, of 12 Councillors, 4 were cocoa-brokers, and 8 cocoa-farmers who were also middle-size merchants.

After the clerks, cash-crop farmers occupied the second most important place within the sub-élites. Cash-crop producers had an independent
source of income, however small; they did not depend upon salaries
paid by European civil servants, merchants or mine officials. African
peasants gradually learned how to deal with government officials,
including agricultural extension officers, marketing board employees,
and other minor bureaucrats. Cash-crop farmers, because they generally
had greater initiative than the more conservative-minded cultivators,
often acquired some degree of education. In time, the cash-crop
growers started to form quasi-political organizations of a new kind.

The first of these groups for which I have found written evidence
was the Aburi–Nsawam Association of Cocoa Growers. This was set up
in 1914 with the aid of the colonial agricultural department for the
purpose of making better use of local extension services.[1] Another
cocoa-farmers' organization, the Akwapim Farmers' Association, was
set up in Ghana in 1918. It was followed in 1921–2 by the Gold Coast
Farmers' Association, organized along provincial (not tribal, as was the
Akwapim Association) lines, and by several Cocoa Growers' Associations formed in 1922 in three divisions of Ashanti (Mampong, Bompata and Tasamanse). Elsewhere in Africa, associations of cash-crop
producers evolved with regularity in the period 1920–40, such as the
Uganda Cotton Association (later called Buganda Growers' Society)
in 1920, the Ibibio Farmers' Association and the Yoruba Producers'
Union in Nigeria in 1930, the Kilimanjaro Native Cooperative Union
in Tanganyika in 1932, the Producers' Marketing Societies in Northern
Rhodesia in 1940 and the Syndicat Agricole Africain in Ivory Coast in
1940.

In general, the British African cash-crop producers were more inclined than were their French counterparts to set up independent
political organizations. Farmers in Francophone Africa tended rather to
utilize the government-sponsored Sociétés de Prévoyance for political
purposes than to found independent organizations. The French African
cash-crop producers were generally less well educated than their opposite numbers in British Africa.[2] The French authorities, with their

---

[1] Gold Coast, *Report on the Eastern Province for the year 1914* (Accra, 1915), p. 14.

[2] It was not uncommon in British Africa for government to undertake special training
of cash-crop producers. For example, in Ghana the government established in 1922
four Junior Trade Schools in hinterland areas (Kibi, Yondi, Mampong–Ashanti and
Asunantsi), which offered to ex-Standard III boys a four-year course in such fields
as food farming, cash-crop agriculture, carpentry, masonry, etc.

étatiste cast of mind, also insisted on keeping the institutional and political initiative in the modernization process in their own hands. In British Africa, on the other hand, the territorial governments tended to favour African initiative.

From the 1930s onward, British African cash-growers thus began to merge their local associations into more extensive federations. These larger bodies wielded more political influence than local clubs. They also benefited from the economy of scale obtained by larger organizations. Economic difficulties commonly played a major part in spurring farmers to combine in a big way. In the late 1930s, for instance, trouble occasioned by low cotton prices and unsatisfactory ginning arrangements induced some fifteen farmers' associations in Uganda to organize a federated body called the Uganda Growers' Co-operative Union. Having founded the Union, the Baganda farmers also became squarely engaged in politics. In time, the Union also assumed wider economic functions. In 1953, for example, the farmers purchased their own ginning plant.[1]

Between 1930 and 1931, a similar development took place in the Gold Coast, where farmers blamed the European cocoa firms for paying unsatisfactory prices. A large number of cocoa-farmers' association members therefore joined to form the Gold Coast and Ashanti Cocoa Federation, whose initial object was to boycott the European firms until the merchants raised the price. In organizing the boycott, the Federation gained the support of the neo-traditional élite, many of whom were themselves involved in cocoa production. No small part of the limited success of the boycott was due to the support of chiefs. For example, in the Bompata division of Ashanti the Omanhene (paramount chief) 'swore oath against the sale of cocoa';[2] and in the Central Province, southern Ghana, the chiefs' role in the cocoa boycott was described as follows by the Provincial Commissioner:

At the suggestion of a person who was not one of the Natural Rulers, a meeting of the Head Chiefs was convened to investigate the causes of the

---

[1] Figures on the precise number of primary associations belonging to the Cocoa Federation are not available; but there were at this time some 415 cocoa co-operatives in Ghana with 9,000 members. Inasmuch as membership of government-backed co-operatives overlapped with independent farmers' associations, these figures give some indication of the following of the Federation. See Gold Coast, Department of Agriculture, *Report for the year 1933–4* (Accra, 1934), p. 9.

[2] Gold Coast, *Annual report on the Eastern Province of Ashanti for the year 1930–1* (Accra, 1931), p. 12.

sharp fall in price of cocoa. At this meeting, a federation was formed and a resolution was passed which placed the sale of cacao under embargo until a certain fixed price should be offered for its purchase. Certain of the Chiefs accepted this resolution and in their endeavours to compel a complete observance of the spirit of this resolution, swore oaths prohibiting the sale of cacao and boycotting the purchase of European manufactures.[1]

As it turned out, the cocoa boycott 'was rigidly observed by most of the farmers in the Colony [southern Ghana] during November and December, but in January 1931 some farmers began to place their cacao on the market, and in February selling became general'.[2] In Ashanti, the boycott was less successful. In the Western Province, for example, it was reported that

there was very little interest evidenced in the activities of the Gold Coast and Ashanti Cacao Federation, with the exception of, perhaps, the Dormaa division in the Sunyani District, where owing to propaganda, the farmers failed to market part of their crops.[3]

The cocoa boycott of 1930 to 1931 marked a new stage in the country's history. Many new federations were set up—for instance, the Ashanti Farmers' Association (later Union) and the Gold Coast Farmers' Committee (located in the southern part of the colony). The Gold Coast farmers organized further boycotts in 1934 and 1937, both of which achieved a wide measure of success. From the 1930s onward, the cocoa-growers formed a powerful lobby. They also played a major part in post-war party politics. To this day, the main lines of political cleavage owe perhaps more to the special interests of the cocoa farmers than to those of any other élite group.

[1] Gold Coast, *Report on the Central Province for the year 1930–31* (Accra, 1931), p. 10. Another rather interesting form of support for the boycott emanating from the traditional sector of society was provided by semi-literate 'youngmen' who turned an indigenous male association called Asafe (historically a military body) into a weapon for backing the boycott. For example, in the Akim Kotoku Native Authority, Central Province, the Asafe clashed with the Omanhene over his failure to support the boycott: 'In January 1931 there was an agitation against the Omanhene in connexion with the cocoa "war"—the young men, worked up by agitators, tried to form themselves into an Asafe with a view to charging the Omanhene with being in league with the trading firms and so weakening the Cacao Federation. The movement did not receive serious backing; the Omanhene dealt with the situation diplomatically and it failed.'

[2] Gold Coast, Department of Agriculture, *Report for the period 1 April 1930 to 31 March 1931* (Accra, 1931), pp. 6–7.

[3] Gold Coast, *Annual report on the Western Province of Ashanti for the year 1930–31* (Accra, 1931), p. 28.

In addition to the cash-crop farmers, other members of the sub-élite as well played some part in politics. These included artisans, money-lenders, transport owners, small and middle-size traders. The market women on the Gold Coast, for instance, often acted as a vocal pressure group. By and large, however, these strata could not compare in importance with the white-collar workers or the cash-crop farmers. Generally speaking, they could only influence politics when acting in alliance with more powerful groups.

The neo-traditional élites

All the colonial powers employed African chiefs in one way or another in local government. The British, however, went much farther in this respect than any other European nation; it was they alone who developed the theory of 'indirect rule' into an accepted feature of colonial orthodoxy. In the British African colonies, chiefs had acknowledged judicial and police functions. They were able to raise local revenues; they controlled their own treasuries; they could issue local administrative regulations. Chiefs and their councillors were of course subject to the supervision of British officials; nevertheless the 'Native Authorities' usually ran local affairs very much according to their own wishes. The neo-traditional élite, unlike the sub-élites and the upper-echelon élites, thus controlled an effective political infrastructure.

The chiefs enjoyed other advantages, too. They acquired a sound working knowledge concerning the colonial government, at any rate on the local level. They sometimes acquired a stake in farming, in trade or in related economic activities. They often strengthened their position by appointing kinsmen to important local jobs. From the 1920s, moreover, some leading members of the neo-traditional as well as of the upper-echelon élites began to be represented in various Legislative Councils of British Africa. In the French colonies, chiefs were also appointed to the Conseils d'Administration, to local advisory councils. By and large, however, the chiefs in Francophone Africa had only a weak institutionalized role in local administration, a role that could not compare in political influence with its British counterpart.

When, after the end of World War II, African nationalist organizations started to play a major part in politics, the British African chiefs were thus in a much stronger position to make their voices heard than their *confrères* in French Africa.[1] During the 1950s the British in West Africa made a deliberate effort to accommodate the neo-traditional élite to the new political systems. In some instances the modernized chiefs were given an entrenched position in the central legislature. (In Sierra Leone, for example, the neo-traditional élite has held 25 per cent of the seats in the legislature, a position enshrined in the constitution since 1951. In Nigeria, the modernized chiefs obtained a foothold in the legislatures, though at the regional level, through Regional Houses of Chiefs rather than in the federal legislature.) Chiefs secured a strong position in two of Nigeria's major parties, the Action Group in Western Nigeria and the Northern People's Congress in Northern Nigeria. Chiefs gained a major position in the main opposition party in the Gold Coast (in the National Liberation Movement), in Uganda (the Kabaka Yekka) and elsewhere.

In French Africa, the neo-traditional élite gained a good deal of political influence during the post-war period. During the 1950s, chiefs won many local elections. Between 1947 and 1952, they won 29 per cent of the seats in the territorial assembly of Mali, 15 per cent in Upper Volta, 30 per cent in Niger and 23 per cent in Guinea. The neo-traditional élite, as shown in Table 14, likewise benefited from kinship ties with other politicians. Between 1947 and 1952, for instance, about 33 per cent of the new élite legislators in the Ivory Coast were related to traditional ruling families. (By 1959, the proportion had increased to 43 per cent.) In Mali, 35 per cent of the legislators were kinsmen of chiefs, 45 per cent in Upper Volta, 70 per cent in Niger and about 50 per cent in Guinea.

The neo-traditional élite gained a comparable position for itself in British Africa. For example, in 1957, 84 per cent of the politicians in the Sierra Leone legislature had chiefly kinship ties. (In Uganda, between 1955 and 1961, the corresponding figure was 30 per cent.) In the long

[1] Chiefs in British Africa benefited immensely from the colonial policy of regrouping the more efficient Native Authorities into more viable administrations at the provincial or regional level. This occurred in the first instance in Ghana in 1927, when three Provincial Councils were organized, and later in 1935, when the Ashanti Confederacy Council was instituted. District and Provincial Councils of chiefs were also organized in the 1930s and 1940s in East and Central Africa, and like those in British West Africa, they had the effect of strengthening the institutionalized position of chiefs in colonial society. Some effort in this direction occurred also in French Africa in the 1930s, when so-called Conseils de Notables were organized to enhance the institutional role of chiefs in colonial policy. But this development lagged significantly behind what was taking place in this regard in British Africa.

Table 14. *Chiefly influence in Territorial Assemblies in French West Africa, 1947–52*

Country	Total Territorial Assembly	Chiefs in Territorial Assembly	Members related to chiefs
Ivory Coast	27	—	9
Mali	28	8	10
Upper Volta	40	6	18
Niger	20	6	14
Guinea	16[a]	4	12

[a] This figure represents those legislators for whom data were available; total member-ship in Guinea Territorial Assembly was twenty-four.

Source: Ruth Schachter Morgenthau, *Political parties in French-speaking West Africa* (Oxford, Clarendon Press, 1964), pp. 401–11.

run, this source of chiefly influence may well prove to be the most important. For the ascriptive attributes of neo-traditional élites give them a more certain legitimacy in modern politics than merit or achievement. For the foreseeable future, the persistence of traditional values, norms and relationships in the life of the ordinary African city and country dwellers will probably reinforce the weight of the ascriptive aspects in the political influence of the neo-traditional élite.

The upper-echelon élites

Many scholars believe that political modernization in Africa was brought about largely by the efforts of the upper-echelon élite. But this was not always the case. Actually, the sub-élites played a rather important part in the development of modern African politics. The political evolution of the upper-echelon élites is nevertheless of considerable interest, especially since it differed in several respects from that of the sub-élites.

The political career of the upper-echelon élite commonly began at a fairly early stage in the history of colonial Africa (especially on the West Coast). Upper-echelon institutions gradually acquired a measure of legitimacy, simply by virtue of having been in existence for many years. Upper-echelon organizations were usually more politically articulate than those of the sub-élites. The upper-echelon élites had a more intimate and sophisticated knowledge of modern political institutions. They were also strategically better placed in relation to the colonial government. Whereas the majority of the sub-élite usually made their living in provincial towns and in the countryside, upper-echelon people tended to congregate in the capitals. Moreover, whenever the colonizers made political concessions to Africans, the upper-echelon élites were usually the first to benefit. This in turn strengthened the political infrastructure of the upper-echelon élite, giving to its members a decided advantage over the sub-élites. In much of West Africa, moreover, though less so in East and Central Africa (save for some regions like Uganda and Barotseland), the early upper-echelon élite was recruited in no small part from high-ranking traditional families. This gave a special legitimacy to the political activities of the upper-echelon élite and strengthened their position.

The first political organizations of the African upper-echelon élite were formed in Sierra Leone. In the late eighteenth century, Sierra Leone, a British colony, became a haven of refuge for slaves who had been repatriated or liberated under British humanitarian or missionary auspices. English-speaking missionaries began to open schools; and it was in Sierra Leone that the first group of well-educated, anglicized Africans made its appearance in Africa. The new élite, for the most part, found employment as merchants and middle-rank traders.

The Gold Coast experienced a similar development. By the middle of the nineteenth century, a number of educated Africans, including merchants and modernizing chiefs, had already accumulated sizeable fortunes by acting as brokers for European firms. The indigenous élite was anxious to secure more government posts for its members and hoped that the colony would ultimately attain self-government through the gradual Africanization of the colonial government. The British, however, disappointed African expectations. From the 1890s onward the proportion of senior African officials in the colonial government began to decline, and the higher ranks of the administration became overwhelmingly European. This process was speeded up by the contemporary development of the British Colonial Service into a body of men available for duty anywhere within the empire.

The coastal élite found a new issue in the land question. Many European firms began to seek forest land for mining and timber concessions. The Gold Coast government, anxious to provide more security for the investment of European capital, and determined also to avoid the underlying conflict between individual and communal notions of land ownership, decided to turn all unoccupied land in the colony into Crown land. This led to a storm of protest in which coastal lawyers, who stood to lose much legal business, joined with traditional chiefs in asserting that all the land in the colony—occupied or not—belonged to some group or individual. The British eventually dropped the Lands Bill. But well-to-do Africans, including coastal businessmen, lawyers and modernizing chiefs, resolved to defend their interests by founding the Aborigines' Rights Protection Society. This body aimed at obtaining an elected African majority on the Legislative Council (a local legislature, first instituted in 1850). The formation of the Society was thus a milestone in African politics.[1]

By the time of World War I, professional people, including lawyers, doctors, journalists, administrators and teachers, were taking a much more important part in politics than the merchants. This change was facilitated by the colonial government, which, from the early twentieth century, tended more and more to select professionally trained Africans to represent Africans in government. For example, between 1863 and 1903 nearly all (9 out of 12) of the educated Africans nominated to the Sierra Leone Legislative Council were merchants. The first lawyer, Sir Samuel Lewis, was appointed to the Council in 1882; but by 1911 lawyers and doctors were pre-eminent among the African representatives in the Council. A similar policy was pursued in Ghana: whereas merchants were chosen as African representatives in the Legislative Council from 1850 to 1900, after that time the government turned towards professional men as legislative representatives. By 1916 three lawyers (J. E. Casely Hayford, E. J. P. Brown and T. Hutton Mills) had been chosen as unofficial representatives in the Legislative Council. Several educated chiefs, one of whom had been a school-teacher before enthronement, had been selected also. Another had worked as an accountant and civil servant before becoming a chief.

In shifting support from the mercantile to the professional elements, the colonial government was responding to some extent to pressure from the big imperialist firms which disliked the political spokesmen of African mercantile interests. But the role of government was only one of several factors that contributed to weakening the merchants. African traders suffered from competition from Lebanese firms. Many

[1] John D. Fage, *Ghana: a historical interpretation* (Madison, University of Wisconsin Press, 1961), pp. 76–8.

378

more were pushed to the wall by the highly restrictive practices of the great firms and by government acquiescence in such methods. The traders thus had less and less time for politics. African lawyers, doctors, journalists and teachers, on the other hand, commonly had more leisure. Because they were better educated, they were more likely to possess the intellectual equipment required to formulate the Africans' political and economic demands in ideological terms. By the 1920s this function was becoming an important factor in linking the politics of the upper-echelon élite to those of the sub-élites. The sub-élites were unable to describe their own status within colonial society in ideological terms. Nor did they know how to set forth wider national goals towards which they themselves might strive as a group. In addition, the professional group alone had both the leisure and the resources to run newspapers. This was a factor of overriding importance, for by the 1920s the press was becoming a major force in shaping a new ideology.

Thus in Ghana, Sierra Leone, Nigeria, and the Gambia the leading members of the first important nationalist organization, the National Congress of British West Africa (NCBWA), conceived in Ghana in 1918 and organized in the other territories in the 1920s, were drawn overwhelmingly from the liberal professions. For example, occupational data on thirty-two active members, including officers, of the Ghana branch of the NCBWA show that 70 per cent were professionals, 8 per cent educated chiefs, and 22 per cent merchants. Table 15 illustrates the point.

NCBWA leaders edited a great many of the leading newspapers, for instance, the *Gold Coast Leader*, *Gold Coast Independent*, *Eastern Star and Akuapem Chronicle*, the *Voice of the People* on the Cold Coast; the *Lagos Weekly Record* in Nigeria and the *Sierra Leone Weekly News*. Other members were active in literary pursuits, especially J. E. Casely Hayford, a lawyer and main organizer of the Ghana branch of the NCBWA, who published several books and pamphlets, including *Gold Coast Native Institutions* (1903), *Ethiopia unbound* (1911), *The truth about the West African land question* (1913), and *United West Africa* (1919).[1]

The leading members of the NCBWA also joined professional associations like the bar, medical, druggists' and teachers' associations and

[1] The upper-echelon élite in French Africa also used its leisure time in editing newspapers, especially in Senegal and Ivory Coast. An African-owned paper, *L'Indépendant*, appeared in Ivory Coast in 1910, and the leading black politician in Senegal in the 1920s produced a newspaper called *La Démocratie du Sénégal*.

Table 15. *Occupations of active members of the NCBWA in the 1920s*

Name	Place educated	Occupation
T. Hutton-Mills	Freetown, England	Lawyer
C. J. Bannerman	England	Lawyer
A. B. Quartey-Papafio	Freetown, England	Lawyer
Kwatei Quartey-Papafio	Freetown, England	Lawyer
J. Jenley Coussey	England	Lawyer
E. C. Quist	England	Lawyer
Akilagpa Sawyerr	Freetown, England	Lawyer
J. Glover-Addo	Freetown, Scotland	Lawyer
R. Sam Sackey	England	Lawyer
K. Ata Amonu	England	Lawyer
W. Ward Brew	England	Lawyer
P. E. Sampson	England	Lawyer
I. B. Nelson	Lagos, England	Lawyer
J. E. Casely Hayford	Freetown, England	Lawyer
J. E. Eminsang	England	Lawyer
J. Kitson-Mills	—	Teacher
J. T. Addy	—	Teacher
J. C. Mensah	—	Clergyman (Wesleyan)
Mark Hayford	England	Clergyman (National Baptist)
Sam Pinanko	America	Clergyman (African Methodist Episcopal Zion)
F. V. Nanka-Bruce	Lagos, Scotland	Medical doctor
C. E. Reindorf	Freetown, England	Medical doctor
Timothy Laing	England	Journalist
J. J. Arkrong	Ghana	Journalist
C. J. Reindorf	England	Merchant
J. A. Vanderpuye	Ghana	Merchant
J. M. de Santana	Ghana	Merchant
H. Van Hein	Ghana	Merchant
S. R. Wood	Ghana	Merchant
S. O. Akiwumi	Lagos	Merchant
E. Ofori	Ghana	Merchant
A. J. Ocansey	Ghana	Merchant

Source: LaRay E. Denzer, 'The National Congress of British West Africa—Gold Coast Section' (M.A. thesis, University of Ghana, 1965), pp. 89–90.

social clubs. In Ghana a whole network of social clubs like the Sekondi Clubs Union, the Cape Coast Literary Club and the Accra Native Club provided members and financial support for the NCBWA. Furthermore, leaders of professional associations and social clubs often overlapped with leadership of the NCBWA. For example, in Sierra Leone the vice-president of that territory's branch of NCBWA in 1920 was head of the Sierra Leone Bar Association and Secretary of the Public Welfare Association, a pressure group composed of leading citizens.[1]

During the 1920s and the 1930s, the upper-echelon élite widely though not universally advocated anti-colonial and nationalist policies. For instance, they called for 'Unity of Purpose and Action among the people' and for 'equal opportunity for all'. This propaganda helped to spread the politics of the upper-echelon élite to wider segments of the population, particularly to the sub-élites who, by the 1920s, were in need of more articulate political leadership than they could get from their own ranks. The upper-echelon élite also made political contacts with the villagers through the modernizing chiefs associated with the NCBWA. There were disagreements between some educated chiefs and the upper-echelon élite over the question of ultimate local control. But the two segments of the élite were sufficiently dependent upon each other to effect agreement concerning their mutual differences. The union between the two groups was strengthened by kinship bonds. Leaders of the Ghana branch of the NCBWA, for instance, belonged to chiefly families or were linked to such families by marriage.[2]

Before the upper-echelon élite could become a prominent political class, they had to build a more extensive political structure. They entrenched themselves in two ways: by participating in the work of government institutions and by establishing new ties with the sub-élites. The two methods were not mutually exclusive; success achieved in one sphere was apt to spill over into the other. In French Africa, government institutions usually played a larger role in the process of linking the sub-élites with their social inferiors than did those of British Africa. This was caused in some measure by the centralizing policy of the French colonial government, especially in regard to promoting political progress, for the French always were fiercely insistent on controlling the mechanism of change. In the 1920s, the 1930s and even later, the French selected members of the sub-élites to sit on the executive committees of the Societés de Prévoyance on the local level, and on the Conseils de Notables at the regional level. Occasionally, members of the sub-élite were also called to the central Conseils d'Administration where they came into contact with upper-élite mem-

---

[1] National Congress of British West Africa, *Constitution*, Secs. 18–19. Text in *Sierra Leone Weekly News*, 4 Oct. 1930, p. 5.

[2] LaRay E. Denzer, 'National Congress of British West Africa—Gold Coast Section' (M.A. thesis, University of Ghana, 1965), p. 91.

bers such as African civil servants, teachers, modernizing chiefs and businessmen. The French, of course, did not expect these bodies to serve political functions. The various councils were intended to assist the French administration.

Nevertheless, political associations and proto-nationalist groups such as the Parti Socialiste Sénégalais, the Amicale Gabonaise, the Cercle Amicale de Port Gentil and the Association des Fonctionnaires (all founded in the 1930s) participated in choosing African representatives to these bodies, and thereby played a semi-political role. In British West Africa, the colonial authorities also facilitated contact between the upper-echelon élite and the sub-élites. But in British Africa there was no pretence that this was anything but a political expedient. For example, communications sent to the government by the NCBWA on the Gold Coast during the 1930s on behalf of cocoa-farmers and others were treated as political documents. The government likewise had a political purpose in appointing members of the NCBWA to commissions of inquiry into education and wages, matters of interest alike to the sub-élites and the upper élite.[1]

The British and the French, though not the Belgians or Portuguese, also made some provision to place elected African representatives on the various legislatures. The French, with their centralizing tradition, gave token representation to Africans in the Chamber of Deputies at Paris (and also in the Consultative Council for the colonies, an advisory body likewise situated in the French capital). The British approach, on the other hand, was very different. No African colony was ever represented at Westminster. The British colonies, however, did have their own legislative councils, and black people gradually obtained representation on these bodies, first of all through nominated, and later through elected, members. In the beginning the franchise was limited to a small minority. In Nigeria, for instance, the suffrage granted in 1922 allowed only for 3,000 voters, who were entitled to choose four representatives. Nevertheless, the effects of granting the franchise to Africans were both immediate and far-reaching, for in order to capture votes, African politicians had to form political associations and to learn the arts of electoral campaigning. Moreover, once the British

---

[1] See, for example, Sierra Leone Committee to Consider the Education Bill, *Report*, Sessional Paper No. 3 of 1938 (Freetown, 1938). See also Sierra Leone, Committee Appointed to Consider Workmen's Compensation Legislation in this Colony, *Report*, Sessional Paper No. 9 of 1938 (Freetown, 1938).

had granted the franchise, no matter on how restrictive a basis, they found that subsequent demands for a widening of the suffrage were hard to resist.

In the same way, the modern political history of Sierra Leone begins with the institution of a limited suffrage. The franchise established in 1924 created an electorate of 1,866 people (all members of the upper-echelon élite, as in Nigeria), who were empowered to vote for three representatives. Sierra Leone politics hinged on two kinds of organization. The first included the Rate Payers' Associations, which had originally been founded to participate in the election of Africans to the Freetown City Council. (By 1924, these Rate Payers' Associations had merged with the Sierra Leone Branch of the NCBWA. and had thus broadened its socio-political base.) The second type of 'proto-party' was exemplified by the West African Youth League, Sierra Leone Branch, which had been set up in 1936 to contest elections to the Legislative Council.

While the Rate Payers' Associations comprised people of the middle-ranking, upper élite, the Youth League included members of the sub-élites, though it was led by I. T. A. Wallace-Johnson, an accountant who later became a journalist and a newspaper owner. The Youth League was backed by teachers, clerks, letter-writers, middle-size traders, and the like, and was formed on 'the principles of Collective Security for the oppressed section of the inhabitants of the country'.[1] This body soon became a model of the kind of nationalist political structure that was to merge the politics of the sub-élites and upper-echelon élite in much of Africa. A perceptive observer recognized this feature of the Youth League rather early:

It is a new phenomenon that Freetown for a year or more has been greatly stirred by the activities of a so-called Youth League. Night after night the Wilberforce Hall has been crowded to the doors and windows by those assembled to consider and foment grievances...though the subjects of protests and demonstrations have by no means always been well chosen or well founded...[Marginal élite] leaders, in short...are coming into their own as the natural leaders of discontent wherever it may happen to show itself.[2]

---

[1] *Sierra Leone Weekly News*, 13 Aug. 1938, pp. 8–9.

[2] William Miller Macmillan, 'African development', in *Europe and West Africa: some problems and adjustments*, Charles Kingsley, et al. (London, Oxford University Press, 1940), p. 76.

Thus throughout the 1920s and 1930s government action concerning African representation and the franchise stimulated a political process whereby the upper-echelon élite became increasingly linked with sub-élites and other popular segments of society. In many colonies, particularly in French Equatorial Africa, and to some extent in Nigeria and Sierra Leone, it was often middle-school teachers, higher ranking clerks, and book-keepers rather than lawyers and doctors who initiated the new proto-parties. Yet the political role of the upper élite should not be underestimated. For an interesting case study, we might consider the history of the Gold Coast Youth Conference, the most articulate and sophisticated proto-nationalist organization which emerged in the 1930s.[1]

The Youth Conference was originally founded in 1929 and re-organized in 1934. It was what Thomas Hodgkin calls a 'congress movement'.[2] That is to say, it loosely joined together a wide variety of groups which all aimed at ultimately seizing political power from the colonial oligarchy. At the policy-making level, however, the Youth Conference was dominated by the upper-echelon élite. Many of the upper élite office-holders were already second-generation members of this stratum. For example, the General President was Dr. I. D. Asafu-Adjaye, son of a wealthy Ashanti merchant, and his brother, E. O. Asafu-Adjaye, a lawyer, was one of the Youth Conference's six Vice-Presidents. The Deputy President, A. M. Akiwumi, a lawyer, was the son of a wealthy merchant; and the General Secretary and operative head of the Youth Conference, J. B. Danquah, a lawyer and holder of a doctorate in anthropology from the University of London, was the son of an influential clergyman in the Basel Mission Society. These and other men of the upper élite controlled the Youth Conference's General Council and the Continuing Executive Committee; the five urban branches of the Conference (Cape Coast, Accra, Saltpond,

---

[1] The case study that follows is based upon materials in the Ghana National Archives (e.g., Acc. No. 913/56) and on Joseph B. Danquah, *Self-help and expansion: a review of the work and aims of the Youth Conference* (Accra, 1943).

[2] Thomas Lionel Hodgkin, *African political parties: an introductory guide* (London and Baltimore, 1961), p. 51. Hodgkin observes that 'By a "congress" I mean a political organization of a specific type, whose principal characteristics are (*a*) a broad nationalist objective, the elimination of the existing colonial system; (*b*) looseness of structure—taking the form, often, of local and functional associations, grouped around a central junta which has entire control over policy; (*c*) emphasis on the idea of representing "all the people".'

Swedru and Kumasi) were also in the hands of lawyers, doctors, accountants, civil servants and wealthy businessmen.

The function of the Youth Conference's branches was twofold: to represent the upper élite interests and to maintain contact with the 'Societies' and 'Clubs' associated with the Conference through delegates to its General Council. This latter function was by far the more significant, for it was through the societies and clubs that the dominant upper élite interacted politically with the sub-élites. Though some of the societies and clubs served members of the upper élite (for example, the Optimists' Literary Club, the Moonlit Literary and Social Club, the Reformers' Club, the Nationalist Literary Club and the Cape Coast Literary and Social Club),[1] most of them were formed by clerks, primary-school teachers, mechanics and other sub-élite groups. Prominent among these societies and clubs were the Peki Improvement and Protection Society, the Anum Improvement Society, the Ewe Union, the Anlo Union, among others. Some twenty associations were linked to the Youth Conference through delegates (two each) to its General Council, and their membership provided the Youth Conference its 'mass' support.

But this was a special form of popular following. The individual members of welfare associations and social clubs belonged to the Conference only through membership in their associations. The Youth Conference was, then, a caucus-type political structure: leaders of special roles and attributes joined together for political purposes on behalf of wider interests. Each association retained its identity and sovereignty, submitting such to the wider goals of the Youth Conference only after caucus discussion within the Council of the Conference. Functionally, this was a rather cumbersome political structure, typical of so-called 'congress' movements. Action was hardly its best attribute, for the consensus required for action was seldom forthcoming. Hence, issues were, so to speak, talked to death and discipline was hard to achieve.

The sub-élite members thus became prone to criticize their upper-élite leaders. As J. B. Danquah, the General Secretary, put the matter:

We of the Youth Conference are accused of talking too much and doing nought. 'Why does not the Youth Conference do something', is a frequent

---

[1] See materials in Ghana National Archives, Acc. No. 151/59.

query. To this I often retort: 'Why does not the Gold Coast do something?'
...Are we sufficiently prepared to do something? Are we conscious of a
common need, of a common platform?...Sometimes I am driven to despera-
tion by those [sub-élites] who ask for action without knowing just what
sort of action they want, or whether the sort of action they want is worth-
while at all. Sometime ago, someone, who was pressing that I should do
something, was asked: 'What do you think is the best thing I can do?'
'Oh!' he said, 'you must be prepared to go to prison for your country.
You must be prepared to do something that will send you to prison.' Is
that so? That man wants me to rush to the next policeman I meet, knock
him down, and then go to prison for it. Then he will call me his hero, a
Gold Coast hero! Or, probably, he wants me to collect two or three hundred
people, rush to the [Christianborg] Castle, climb up to the governor's private
office and tell His Excellency to clear out of the Gold Coast, and, says this
man, I should be damned glad to go to prison for doing such a 'noble' and
'patriotic' act.[1]

The weaknesses referred to by Danquah were multiplied by the
prominent role of the so-called 'patrons' within the Conference caucus.
Pre-eminent among these patrons of the Youth Conference were twelve
leading members of Ghana's neo-traditional élite, including the two
most influential Paramount Chiefs in the country—Otumfo Sir Osei
Agyeman Prempeh II, the Asantehene, and Nana Sir Ofori Atta, Omanhene of Akim Abuakwa. Between them, these rulers could boast of such
honours from the British crown as two knighthoods, one C.B.E., one
M.B.E. and one O.B.E.; and one Paramount Chief was also a Fellow
of the Royal Society of Arts. Furthermore, five of the chiefs were
nominated members of the Legislative Council and three were members
of the Joint Provincial Council of chiefs. These institutional positions
constituted a major source of influence within the Youth Conference.
Patrons with modern professional qualifications included two medical
doctors, a clergyman (who held a doctorate in divinity), and five lawyers
(two of whom were members of the Legislative Council, four holders of
the O.B.E., one M.B.E. and one Crown Counsel). There were also two
senior administrators, a wealthy businessman and a rich cocoa-farmer,
who was also a leader of the Gold Coast Farmers' Committee. (The

[1] Danquah, *Self-help and expansion*, p. 6. Ironically, what Danquah refused to accept
as a legitimate and useful political technique or style in 1943 was taken up a decade
later by a nationalist politician of sub-élite origins, Kwame Nkrumah, who turned
it into an instrument of political success. See Dennis Austin, *Politics in Ghana, 1946–1960*
(London, Oxford University Press, 1964).

last-named, J. Kwame Ayew, was the main link between the Youth Conference and that influential segment of the sub-élites represented by the middle cocoa-farmers.)

For a variety of reasons, among which was the rather tradition-bound view of politics held by its leader, J. B. Danquah, the Youth Conference persisted to the end of World War II as a caucus-type political structure. In 1946, the conference assumed a new form and a new name, the United Gold Coast Convention. But the upper-élite leaders remained unable to find a political style conducive to the needs of the sub-élites and the more popular elements in Gold Coast society. As a result, there was a split in 1949 between the upper élite and the sub-élites, who had since 1946 been in an uneasy alliance in the United Gold Coast Convention. The sub-élites, always larger in number than the upper élite, turned to a new kind of leadership, represented by the Convention People's Party (CPP) headed by Kwame Nkrumah. This leadership took on a ritualistic political style,[1] partly because the leaders themselves derived from the sub-élites and, like their followers, delighted in political ritual.[2]

The discovery of political ritualism by a new, better educated group of sub-élite personalities had profound consequences for the politics of the Gold Coast. A major portion of the sub-élites abandoned the 'congress' alliance with the upper élite and launched their own party, the Convention People's Party (CPP). The political success attained by the CPP during the 1950s was occasioned partly by the political rigidity that distinguished the United Gold Coast Convention and partly by the skill with which the articulate members of the sub-élites exploited this situation and turned their party into an effective machine for securing votes.

The ritualistic style of the CPP leaders helped them to gain the support of the poorer people, the wage labourers, the small traders and the cash-crop farmers. For the leaders had now generally learnt how

---

[1] By 'ritualistic political style' I mean the adornment of the leadership role with extraneous motifs, ideological and personal, that have no intrinsically functional relation to that role. This results in a tendency to treat the ritualistic or 'acting-out' aspects of the leadership role as if they were substantive.

[2] There would appear to be a widespread proclivity towards exaggerated self-praise on the part of such African sub-élites as clerks, primary-school teachers, mechanics, foremen or 'boss boys'. This has been quite marked among the upwardly mobile sub-élites and among those who move out of secular sub-élite roles into religious-type roles, such as leaders of apostolic or separatist churches. (Cf. C. G. Baëta, *Prophetism in Ghana: a study of some 'spiritual' churches* [London, 1962], pp. 76 ff., *passim*.)

Table 16. *Social rank of officers of eight NCNC branches, 1957–8*

Branch	Number of officers	Percentage of sub-élite	Percentage of upper-echelon élite	Other[a] (%)
Enugu NCNC	31[b]	25	51	—
Onitsha NCNC	42	44	54	2
Port Harcourt NCNC	44	50	46	4
Aba NCNC	22	50	45	5
Benin NCNC	25	21	79	—
Ilesha NCNC	8	37	63	—
Oyo NCNC	18	73	27	—
Ibadan NCNC	38	50	36	14

[a] Persons in this category were wage labourers, unemployed, or chiefs: the 14% portion of Ibadan NCNC was made up of chiefs.
[b] Data unknown for seven members of Enugu NCNC Branch Executive.

Source: Richard L. Sklar, *Nigerian political parties* (Princeton University Press, 1963), p. 260.

to speechify in a glib fashion. They seemed to know all about the problems of the modern world, and thereby appealed to the sub-élites whose members had a high opinion of their own group as a viable modernizing force. The sub-élites therefore embarked on a drive for power that might not have gained momentum but for the CPP's leadership. The lower classes too, were inclined to listen to the CPP's rhetorical appeal. The common people were still close to the ways of traditional or preliterate society. They were thus accustomed to leaders who treated the ritualistic or 'acting-out' aspects of rule as essential to the exercise of authority.

In most of the remaining parts of Africa, the sub-élites did not achieve the same degree of success as in Ghana. In most African countries, the sub-élites worked in alliance with the upper-echelon élites; and during the 1950s, during the decolonization period, this alliance played a crucial role in African politics. Nevertheless, the sub-élites acquired solid influence both in the cities and in the country. In Nigeria, for instance, something like 40 per cent of the officials serving the National Council of Nigeria and the Cameroons (NCNC) between the years 1957 and 1958 were drawn from the ranks of the sub-élites, as shown in Table 16.

In the new African states the sub-élites gained a significant share of

Table 17. *Proportion of clerks in selected legislatures*

Year		Number of legislators	Percentage of clerks
1966	Ghana	104	22
1959	Eastern Nigeria	84	19[a]
1956	Western Nigeria	80	2[b]
1952	Ivory Coast	27	33
1946–52	Senegal	50	24
1947–52	Mali	28	40
1948–52	Upper Volta	40	42
1947–52	Niger	20	40
1947–52	Guinea	24[c]	28
1961	ex-Belgian Congo	23[d]	80
1961	Kenya	33[e]	7
1961	Tanzania	48[f]	20
1961	Sierra Leone	52	10

[a] This refers to dominant party only, the NCNC. Opposition parties had 18% legislators who were clerks.

[b] This refers to dominant party only, the Action Group.

[c] Data not available for eight legislators.

[d] Figure for members of Cabinet only.

[e] Figure for African members only; twenty other Asian and European members.

[f] There were fifty-one Africans in Tanzanian legislature in 1961.

Sources: Guy Hunter, *The new societies of tropical Africa* (London, Oxford University Press, 1962), p. 285; James S. Coleman, *Nigeria: background to nationalism* (Berkeley and Los Angeles, University of California Press, 1958), pp. 382–3; James S. Coleman and Carl G. Rosberg, eds., *Political parties and national integration in tropical Africa* (Berkeley, University of California Press, 1964), p. 99; Dennis Austin, *Politics in Ghana, 1946–1960* (London, Oxford University Press, 1964), p. 253; George Bennett and Carl G. Rosberg, *The Kenyatta election: Kenya, 1960–1961* (London, Oxford University Press, 1961), p. 142; Crawford Young, *Politics in the Congo: decolonization and independence* (Princeton University Press, 1965), p. 198.

power at the national level also. This was particularly true in French West Africa, where clerks were a particularly influential group. Clerks also dominated the first cabinet in the former Belgian Congo—they formed the great majority of the local élite. Table 17 shows the percentage of clerks within the legislatures of various important African countries.

The alliance between the upper élite and the sub-élites did not, however, prevent cleavages from arising within the nationalist parties. Even the sub-élites themselves suffered from many internal divisions; and there were further cross-pressures deriving from tribal, religious and regional disputes. Indeed, at the time when independence was attained (mostly between the years 1960 and 1963), these cross-pressures were beginning to alter the terms of the earlier alliance between the upper élite and the sub-élites, and thereby contributed to a new political power system—the one-party state.[1]

Black power and the aftermath of independence

By the early 1960s black élites had taken over from the colonial oligarchies in most parts of sub-Saharan Africa north of the Zambezi. But there were still many differences between the new rulers. Upper-echelon élites were more powerful and had been much longer established in West than in East or Central Africa. In Kenya, Tanzania, Zambia, Malawi and the former Belgian Congo, there was only a handful of African lawyers, doctors, engineers and economists at the time of independence. The upper-echelon élite in these countries consisted mostly of clergymen, primary-school and middle-school teachers, middle-ranking civil servants (including medical assistants, agricultural technicians, sanitation technicians and upper-level clerks).[2]

The new power-holders in East and Central Africa suffered also from other weaknesses. In West Africa, the great majority of élite members belonged to numerous civic and welfare associations, political

[1] Seymour M. Lipset, *Political man: the social bases of politics* (New York, 1960), pp. 86–7. Lipset's comments on response of parties to cross-pressures on their supporters have much relevance to the demise of competitive party politics and rise of one-party régimes in most African states soon after independence. He observes that 'Efforts, even by democratic parties, to isolate their social bases from cross-pressures clearly undermine stable democracy, which requires shifts from one election to another and the resolving of issues between parties over long periods of time...The necessary rules of democratic politics assume that conversion both ways, into and out of a party, is possible and proper...'

[2] According to a source quoted by Crawford Young, *Politics in the Congo: decolonization and independence* (Princeton University Press, 1965), p. 199, there were by 1954 some 11,572 Africans of 'relatively advanced education in the Congo'. By 1960 the highly educated comprised some thirty holders of college degrees, as well as several thousand *diplomés* whose academic qualifications were roughly equal to those of American graduates. The statistics are set forth in greater detail in Bernard B. Fall, 'Education in the Republic of the Congo', *Journal of Negro Education*, Summer 1961, **30**, no. 3, pp. 266–76. Something like 3,000 Africans had been trained to be clergymen up to seminary level. There were over 400 middle-ranking civil service technicians (but virtually no higher civil servants) and some 44,000 teachers. (Of these, 43,000 were poorly educated primary-school teachers, 84 secondary and post-secondary teachers, as well as 734 technical and agricultural teachers.)

Table 18. *Associational ties of élites in East Africa*, 1963–4[a]

Type of association	Percentage in Kenya (N = 457)	Percentage in Uganda (N = 409)	Percentage in Tanganyika (N = 444)
Tribal association	21	8	3
Religious society	6	16	6
Business association	5	8	6
Professional society	9	15	4
Academic association	12	20	7
Charitable society	5	13	12
Social club	23	36	25
Sports club	6	16	11
Cultural society	6	16	11
Trade union	20	5	12
Political party	34	21	22
None	18	17	33

[a] Some persons reported more than one associational tie; hence, the percentages total more than 100. Persons chosen for this survey held important posts in government and other institutions and for the most part earned not less than £1,000 per annum.

Source: Gordon M. Wilson, 'The African elite', in Stanley Diamond and Fred Burke, eds., *The transformation of East Africa* (New York, 1966), p. 442.

parties, trade unions, business associations, professional bodies and the like. In Tanzania, Kenya and Uganda, on the other hand, as shown in Table 18, a substantial proportion of élite members had no such ties.

Yet even when all the differences between the various new élites in the various parts of Africa are taken into account, the new power-holders have more in common than is generally realized. Their skills are primarily of an administrative and manipulative, of an intellectual or political kind. Entrepreneurial, managerial and technical ability remains in scarce supply. The Ivory Coast, for example, is one of the most economically advanced countries in West Africa. Yet few political office-holders in the Ivory Coast, as shown in Table 19, have much experience in commerce, agriculture or management.

But the great majority of the élite remained dependent for their livelihood on government employment or on government patronage. They were what Georges Balandier, a French sociologist, rightly calls an administrative bourgeoisie. Table 20 will help to clarify the position for the Ivory Coast, one of the most economically advanced countries in Francophone Africa.

Table 19. *Category of skills of Ivory Coast office-holders
in 1957, 1959, 1960*[a]

Type of skill	Percentage in 1957 (N = 54)	Percentage in 1959 (N = 84)	Percentage in 1960 (N = 83)
Clerical	22	19	16
Educational	24	24	24
Health-medical	11	13	18
Technical	6	8	12
Legal	9	8	7
Agriculture and commerce	19	19	16
Managerial	9	8	7

[a] 'Office-holders' means members of National Assembly and of the Cabinet.

Source: Aristide R. Zolberg, *One-party government in the Ivory Coast*
(Princeton University Press, 1964), p. 275.

Not only politicians, civil servants and party functionaries depend
on the state. A great many people in private enterprise (including
bankers, insurance agents, merchants, contractors, small manufacturers,
transport owners, and other entrepreneurs with only a small amount
of capital and limited skills) stand to benefit immensely from government favours. In the new state, government is a major industry;
government accounts for the major African-controlled source of capital. Ambitious African businessmen know that success in politics is a
way to wealth.[1] The middle-size cash-crop producers also recognize
the primacy of politics. They need credits and development services of
a kind that only government can offer. They must try to influence the
regulatory powers acquired over the wealth generated by the cash-crop
producers. (Agriculture, after all, remains the major industry in the
new countries. In Ghana, for instance, from 1951 to 1966, farming
accounted for something like 70 per cent of the country's foreign
earnings, nearly 50 per cent of the government revenues and 63 per
cent of the gross national product.)[2]

[1] For example, Kenya, Maize Commission of Inquiry, *Report* (Nairobi, 1966); Ghana,
Commission to Inquire into the Affairs of Nadeco Ltd., *Report* (Accra, 1966); Nigeria,
Coker Commission of Inquiry into the Affairs of Certain Statutory Corporations in
Western Nigeria, *Report* (Lagos, 1962).

[2] See Walter B. Birmingham, ed., *A study of contemporary Ghana* (London, 1962), I, 60,
passim.

Table 20. *Occupation of Ivory Coast office-holders
by economic sectors in 1957, 1959, 1960*[a]

Economic sectors	Percentage in 1957 (N = 54)	Percentage in 1959 (N = 84)	Percentage in 1960 (N = 83)
Government	63	67	66
Private (salaried)	2	5	5
Private (self-employed)	35	29	29

[a] 'Office-holders' means members of National Assembly and of the Cabinet.

Source: Aristide R. Zolberg, *One-party government in the Ivory Coast* (Princeton University Press, 1964).

Since the new African élites look mainly to the government, it is not surprising that they commonly seek to make their position more secure by giving up competitive politics and by establishing a one-party state. By doing so, they are able to restrict the political influence of the poor. The franchise ceases to have its former value, for the electors can no longer freely choose for opposing candidates. Trade unions, tribal associations and similar bodies lose their political independence, and the poor thus lose an important means of making their voice heard in politics. But it remains to be seen whether the one-party system state can really solve the problems facing the new states. The one-party state, moreover, does not necessarily do away with the tensions of diversity. The new African states still have to face a great many tribal, religious, social and regional cross-pressures.

The politicians also have to cope with the 'Man on Horseback'. The entry of armies into politics is not easy to resist, for soldiers, after all, have arms and discipline. Army officers, moreover, often have some training in logistics and other aspects of staffwork that may stand them in good stead for general administrative purposes. But the intervention of soldiers into politics frequently carries ethnic or religious overtones. All too often the military leaders only introduce an additional source of dissension into the unstable alliances between the different African élites. Hence, internecine struggles may become even more frequent and even fiercer than before, and may ultimately have to be resolved by brute force. In the end, one segment or another of the new élites (including some army officers) may well be forced to reorganize the entire system by means of a revolutionary dictatorship. But for the time being, competition between the élites continues according to a well-established pattern, and a realist may well conclude: *plus ça change, plus c'est la même chose.*

BIBLIOGRAPHY

African Education Commission. *Education in Africa: a study of west, south and equatorial Africa.* Conducted by the African Education Commision under the auspices of the Phelps–Stokes Fund and Foreign Mission Societies of North America and Europe; report prepared by Thomas Jesse Jones, chairman. New York, 1922.

Amon d'Aby, F. J. *La Côte d'Ivoire dans la cité africaine.* Paris, 1951.

Annuaire parlementaire des états d'Afrique noire. Paris, 1962.

Ansah, J. K. *The centenary history of the Larteh Presbyterian church 1853–1953.* Larteh, 1955.

Apter, David E. *The political kingdom in Uganda: a study in bureaucratic nationalism.* Princeton University Press, 1961.

Austin, Dennis. *Politics in Ghana, 1946–1960.* London, Oxford University Press, 1964.

Azikiwe, Nnamdi. *The development of political parties in Nigeria.* London, 1957.

Baëta, C. G. *Prophetism in Ghana: a study of some 'spiritual' churches.* London, 1962.

Balandier, Georges. *Sociologie des Brazzavilles noires.* Paris, 1955.

Bekwai district record book, 1925–33. Ghana National Archives, Acc. No. 150/53.

Bennett, George, and Carl G. Rosberg. *The Kenyatta election: Kenya, 1960–1961.* London, Oxford University Press, 1961.

Birmingham, Walter B., ed. *A study of contemporary Ghana.* 2 vols. London, 1966.

Bourret, F. M. *Ghana: the road to independence, 1919–1957.* 3rd ed. Stanford University Press, 1960.

Brokensha, David W. *Social change at Larteh, Ghana.* Oxford, Clarendon Press, 1966.

Browne, D. N. K. 'The African civil servants' association', *The Civil Servant.* Dec. 1948.

Buell, Raymond L. *The native problem in Africa.* 2nd ed. London, 1965.

Cary, Joyce. *Mister Johnson.* London, 1952.

Coleman, James S. *Nigeria: background to nationalism.* Berkeley and Los Angeles, University of California Press, 1958.

'The role of tribal associations in Nigeria', *Proceedings of the First Annual Conference of the West African Institute of Social and Economic Research.* Ibadan, University College, 1952.

Coleman, James S., and Carl G. Rosberg, eds. *Political parties and national integration in tropical Africa.* Berkeley, University of California Press, 1964.

Committee on Inter-African Relations. *Report on the press in West Africa.* Dakar, 1960.

Danquah, Joseph B. *Self-help and expansion: a review of the work and aims of the Youth Conference.* Accra, 1943.

Delavignette, Robert L. *Freedom and authority in French West Africa.* London and New York, Oxford University Press, 1950.

Denzer, LaRay E. 'The National Congress of British West Africa—Gold Coast section'. M.A. thesis, University of Ghana, 1965.

Diamond, Stanley, and Fred G. Burke, eds. *The transformation of East Africa.* New York, 1966.

Epstein, Arnold Leonard. *Politics in an urban African community.* Manchester University Press, 1958.

Fage, John D. *Ghana: a historical interpretation.* Madison, University of Wisconsin Press, 1961.

Fall, Bernard B. 'Education in the Republic of the Congo', *Journal of Negro Education*, Summer 1961, 30, no. 3.

Fyfe, Christopher A. *A history of Sierra Leone.* London, Oxford University Press, 1962.

Gann, Lewis H. *A history of Northern Rhodesia: early days to 1953.* London, 1964.

Ghana. Commision to Inquire into the Affairs of Nadeco Ltd. *Report.* Accra, 1966.

Gold Coast. *Annual report on the Eastern Province of Ashanti for the year 1930–1.* Accra, 1931.

Annual report on the Western Province of Ashanti for the year 1930–31. Accra, 1931.

Census of population, 1948. Accra, 1950.

The Gold Coast handbook, 1937. London, 1937.

Motor Transport Union Ashanti by-laws rules and regulations. Kumasi, 1932. Mimeograph.

Report on the Central Province for the year 1930–31. Accra, 1931.

Report on the Eastern Province for the year 1914. Accra, 1915.

Census Office. *Census report, 1921, for the Gold Coast Colony, Ashanti, the Northern Territories and the mandated area of Togoland.* Accra, 1923.

Gold Coast. Department of Agriculture. *Report for the period 1 April 1930 to 31 March 1931.* Accra, 1931.

Report for the year 1933–4. Accra, 1934.

Great Britain. Colonial Office. *Sierra Leone report for 1922.* London, 1923.

Hailey, William Malcolm, 1st baron. *An African survey: a study of the problems arising in Africa south of the Sahara.* London, Oxford University Press, 1938.

Native administration and political development in British tropical Africa. London, 1941.

Native administration in the British African territories. 5 vols. London, 1950–3.

Harper, C. M. *Report on Ashanti for 1920.* Accra, 1921.

'He buys £7M of cocoa', *West Africa*, 16 Jan. 1954.

Hodgkin, Thomas Lionel. *African political parties: an introductory guide.* London and Baltimore, 1961.

Hunter, Guy. *The new societies of tropical Africa.* London, Oxford University Press, 1962.

Ingham, Kenneth. *The making of modern Uganda.* London, 1958.

Ivory Coast. *Budget du service local, 1950.* Abidjan, 1950.

Inspection du Travail. *Rapport annuel, 1962.* Abidjan, 1962.

John, J. L. 'Memorandum on the evolution of the Legislative Council of Sierra Leone', in Sierra Leone, Legislative Council, *Debates*, 1924–5 Sess. Freetown, 1926.

July, Robert W. *The origins of modern African thought.* New York, 1967.

Kenya. Maize Commission of Inquiry. *Report.* Nairobi, 1966.

Kilson, Martin. *Political change in a West African state: a study of the modernization process in Sierra Leone.* Cambridge, Harvard University Press, 1966.

'Sierra Leone', in *The educated African*, Helen Kitchen, ed. New York, 1962.

Kimble, David. *A political history of Ghana: the rise of Gold Coast nationalism, 1850–1928.* Oxford, Clarendon Press, 1963.

Kumasi division district record book, 1926–51. Ghana National Archives, Acc. No. 798/52.

Lipset, Seymour M. *Political man: the social bases of politics.* New York, 1960.

Macmillan, William Miller. 'African development', in *Europe and West Africa: some problems and adjustments*, Charles Kingsley Meek, *et al.* London, Oxford University Press, 1940.

Marx, Karl, and Friedrich Engels. *On Britain.* Moscow, 1953.

Maxwell, John, ed. *The Gold Coast handbook, 1928.* London, 1929.

Meek, Charles Kingsley, *et al. Europe and West Africa: some problems and adjustments.* London, Oxford University Press, 1940.

'Modernisers in Africa', *Tarikh*, 1967, I, no. 4.

Morgenthau, Ruth Schachter. *Political parties in French-speaking West Africa.* Oxford, Clarendon Press, 1964.

National Congress of British West Africa. *Constitution*, in *Sierra Leone Weekly News*, 4 Oct. 1930.

Neres, Philip. *French-speaking West Africa: from colonial status to independence.* London, Oxford University Press, 1962.

Nigeria. Coker Commission of Inquiry into the Affairs of Certain Statutory Corporations in Western Nigeria. *Report.* 4 vols. Lagos, 1962.

Pye, Lucian W., and Sidney Verba, eds. *Political culture and political development*. Princeton University Press, 1965.

Robinson, Kenneth. 'The public law of overseas France since the war', *Journal of Comparative Legislation and International Law*, 1950, 3rd Ser., **32**, Pts. 3–4.

'The *Sociétés de Prévoyance* in French West Africa', *Journal of African Administration*, Oct. 1950, **11**, no. 4.

Rotberg, Robert I. 'The emergence of Northern Rhodesia: the missionary contribution, 1885–1924', in *African affairs, No. two* (Oxford University, St Antony's College, *St Antony's papers, No. 15*), Kenneth Kirkwood, ed. Carbondale, Southern Illinois University Press, 1963.

The rise of nationalism in Central Africa: the making of Malawi and Zambia, 1873–1964. Cambridge, Harvard University Press, 1965.

Segal, Ronald. *Political Africa: a who's who of personalities and parties*. London, 1961.

'Senegal', in *The Educated African*, Helen Kitchen, ed. New York, 1962.

Séré de Rivières, Edmond. *Le Sénégal, Dakar*. Paris, 1953.

Shephard, C. Y. *Report on the economics of peasant agriculture in the Gold Coast*. Sessional Paper No. 1 of 1936. Accra, 1936.

Sierra Leone. *Annual report of the railway district, 1915*. Freetown, 1917.

Tonkolili chiefdom estimates, 1960. Tonkolili, 1960.

Commission of Enquiry into the Conduct of Certain Chiefs. *Report*. Freetown, 1957.

Commission of Inquiry into Disturbances in the Provinces (November 1955–March 1956). *Report*. Freetown, 1957.

Committee Appointed to Consider Workmen's Compensation Legislation in This Colony. *Report*. Sessional Paper No. 9 of 1938. Freetown, 1938.

Committee to Consider the Education Bill. *Report*. Sessional Paper No. 3 of 1938. Freetown, 1938.

Education Department. *Annual Report, 1934*. Freetown, 1935.

Skinner, Elliott P. *The Mossi of the Upper Volta: the political development of a Sudanese people*. Stanford University Press, 1964.

Sklar, Richard L. *Nigerian political parties*. Princeton University Press, 1963.

Smythe, Hugh H., and Mabel Smythe. *The new Nigerian elite*. Stanford University Press, 1960.

Spiro, Herbert J., ed. *Africa: the primacy of politics*. New York, 1966.

'Summary of deliberations and decisions taken at the Conference of Chiefs and Farmers on 30 November–6 December, 1937'. Ghana National Archives, Acc. No. 765/56.

Thompson, Virginia, and Richard Adloff. *French West Africa*. Stanford University Press, 1957.

Tordoff, William. *Ashanti under the Prempehs, 1888–1935.* London, Oxford University Press, 1965.

Wheare, Joan. *The Nigerian Legislative Council.* London, 1950.

Wight, Martin. *The Gold Coast Legislative Council.* London, 1947.

Wilson, Gordon M. 'The African elite', in *The transformation of East Africa,* Stanley Diamond and Fred Burke, eds. New York, 1966.

Young, Crawford. *Politics in the Congo: decolonization and independence.* Princeton University Press, 1965.

Zolberg, Aristide R. *One-party government in the Ivory Coast.* Princeton University Press, 1964.

CHAPTER 11

THE COLONIAL ERA
IN AFRICA: CHANGES IN THE
SOCIAL STRUCTURE[1]

by IMMANUEL WALLERSTEIN

In any long-term view of African history, European rule becomes just another episode. In relation to wars and conflicts of people, the rise and fall of empires, linguistic, cultural and religious change and the cultivation of new ideas and new ways of life, new economic orientations...in relation to all these, colonialism must be seen not as a complete departure from the African past, but as one episode in the continuous flow of African history. J. F. A. Ajayi.[2]

The colonial episode, as has been pointed out by many of the contributors to this volume, affected profoundly every aspect of African life. The extent of the influence varied, of course, from colony to colony, depending upon circumstances. One effect, however, appears to have been more or less general. This is the change which colonial rule brought about in the essential frameworks within which social action in Africa occurred. In the process, the relative importance of various social groups shifted considerably. The present essay examines the stresses and strains caused by these changes and the way in which the resulting problems have been resolved.

For our purposes, we shall consider the period of colonial rule in Africa as roughly 1885 to 1960. It is true that a few coastal areas of Africa were under European colonial rule before 1885 (sometimes as early as the sixteenth century), and that about one-quarter of the continent remained under colonial rule after 1960 (or even as late as 1968). Nonetheless, the years between 1885 and 1960 represent the one period during which most of the land area and most of the people of

---

[1] I am indebted to G. Arrighi, P. Duignan, L. H. Gann, T. K. Hopkins and T. O. Ranger for their critical comments.

[2] 'The continuity of African institutions under colonialism', in *Emerging themes of African history*, T. O. Ranger, ed. (Nairobi, 1968), p. 194.

the African continent were under the legal and administrative juris-diction of one or another of the European powers.

In order to discuss the overall change that occurred between 1885 and 1960, it is useful to make a summary sketch of the general situation in the earlier period, 1500 to 1885. Three features of this period have an important bearing on the subsequent discussion.

First, in various parts of Africa during the sixteenth to the nineteenth centuries, a number of states bearing all the marks of the process we currently call modernization either came into existence or expanded. For instance, we see examples of the consolidation of a reasonably large territory under a centralized, bureaucratic system that encompassed a population far larger than any defined by visible kinship groups. We find specialized production and the production of goods for long-distance trade and for distribution within the state. In addition, this period bore witness to the emergence of a professional trading class, sometimes a distinct branch of the state bureaucracy, sometimes an alien trading class given permission to operate within the boundaries of the state. Important strides were made also in the area of technologi-cal development, both by invention and by borrowing.[1]

Secondly, the major relationship between Europe and Africa from 1500 to 1800 revolved around the slave-trade. One consequence of this association was the strengthening of states who served in one way or another as procurers of this export commodity, and the development of a coastal trading class who served as middlemen between the inland procurers and the European purchasers arriving with their boats. A second and perhaps equally important consequence, however, was a delay in the emergence of cash-crop agriculture in slave-trading areas as a result of European interference. Boahen cites the instance in 1751 when the British Board of Trade ordered the Governor of Cape Castle to stop cotton cultivation among the Fante, giving as a reason:

The introduction of culture and industry among the Negroes is contrary to the known established policy of this country, there is no saying where this might stop, and that it might extend to tobacco, sugar and every other commodity which we now take from our colonies; and thereby the Africans,

---

[1] Evidence for this can be found in the following volumes, *passim*: Daryll Forde and P. M. Kaberry, eds., *West African kingdoms in the nineteenth century* (London, Oxford University Press, 1967); T. O. Ranger, *Aspects of Central African history* (London, 1968); Jan Vansina, *Kingdoms of the savanna* (Madison, University of Wisconsin Press, 1966); Roland Oliver and Gervase Mathew, eds., *History of East Africa*, Vol. 1 (Oxford, Clarendon Press, 1963).

who now support themselves by wars, would become planters and their slaves be employed in the culture of these articles in Africa, which they are employed in in America.[1]

In the third place, during the late eighteenth and the nineteenth centuries, the slave-trade was gradually abolished. Great Britain in particular took it upon herself to try to enforce this abolition on all parties, affirming a doctrine of support for free, 'legitimate' trade in Africa. The immediate impact of the drive to end the slave-trade was that trade and profits declined, and many European administrative operations in Africa had to be cut back or abruptly halted. The weaker European powers simply dropped out. Denmark withdrew completely;[2] and the Netherlands, which tried for a time to stay on by maintaining the slave-trade, was eventually forced to transfer her forts to Great Britain.[3] Even the British withdrew from Ouidah (Whydah), and several times contemplated abandoning all their West African forts.[4] That they never actually took this step, however, was due solely to the protests of the merchants, who realized—if some British civil servants did not—that it was Britain, as the dominant world commer-

[1] Cited in A. Adu Boahen, *Topics in West African history* (London, 1966), p. 113. Boahen adds: 'After the abolition of the slave trade, West Africa was allowed and indeed assisted to produce these very cash-crops but again forbidden, as it were, to produce manufactured goods which she was to continue to receive from Europe.'

[2] 'After the publication of the decree of 1792 prohibiting the slave-trade [the Danish governor was], the first to suggest that, since they were no longer useful as suppliers of slaves to the Danish islands in the West Indies, it might be better to sell the Danish settlements' (Georg Nørregaard, *Danish settlements in West Africa*, Boston University Press, 1966, p. 218).

[3] [The government of the Netherlands] 'despairing of the prospects of legitimate trade, wrote off [its West African] settlements as an expensive nuisance and set about cutting its losses to a minimum' (Douglas Coombs, *The Gold Coast, Britain and the Netherlands, 1850–1874*, London, Oxford University Press, 1963, p. 1). Cf. A. W. Lawrence, *Trade, castles and forts of West Africa* (London, 1963), pp. 168–9. The fort was abandoned in 1807, the very year of the Abolition Act. Cf. Colin W. Newbury, *The western Slave Coast and its rulers* (Oxford, Clarendon Press, 1961).

[4] 'In 1827 the British government instructed Sir Neil Campbell, the governor of Sierra Leone, that British territory should not be extended...and ordered him to withdraw the British officials and garrisons from the Gold Coast forts' (J. D. Fage, *An introduction to the history of West Africa*, 3rd ed., Cambridge University Press, 1962, p. 126). See also Coombs: 'Only the pressures of interested merchants, a determination to keep down the slave trade, and a sense of moral obligation to the natives kept Britain [in West Africa]. In the [eighteen] thirties she came as close as was possible, short of complete withdrawal, to leaving the settlements altogether...In 1853 a Colonial Secretary looked forward to abandoning West Africa once the slave trade was completely suppressed...' (*The Gold Coast, Britain and the Netherlands*, pp. 4–5).

cial and industrial power, which stood to reap the greatest benefit from the new situation. The abolition of the slave-trade facilitated the reconversion of production to cash-cropping, which occurred notably in West Africa with the rise of the palm-oil and peanut-oil export trade in the nineteenth century. The abolition of the slave-trade released African energies[1] at the same time that the developing European economy now desired the very cash-crops they had previously sought to suppress.[2]

In short, many parts of sub-Saharan Africa, especially West Africa, were engaged in a process of relatively autonomous development, tied to the European world in a limited but important manner through the intermediary of merchants or state trading agents on each side, who were in turn linked, in some cases ambivalently, to political authorities on each side—in the African case, to inland hierarchical chiefs;[3] on the European side, to their respective governments.

[1] Rodney observes: 'It is obvious that because of the Atlantic slave-trade people could not lead their ordinary lives. The majority of the population of West Africa lived by farming, and agriculture must have suffered during that period. In the first place, the loss of so many people represented a loss of labour in the fields. In the second place, those who were left behind had little reason to plant crops which they might never be around to reap. At the end of the eighteenth century, one of the arguments used by Europeans who wanted to abolish the Atlantic slave-trade was that abolition would allow the Africans to work and produce other commodities which Europeans could not. They pointed out that as long as the Atlantic slave-trade continued people found it extremely difficult to carry on worth while activities' (Walter Rodney, *West Africa and the Atlantic slave-trade*, Historical Association of Tanzania Paper No. 2, Nairobi, 1967, p. 16).

[2] Boahen reminds us that the idea of a palm-oil export trade was encouraged by the British Royal African Company in the first two decades of the eighteenth century, but 'this attempt was...abandoned mainly because of the trade in slaves. From the abolition of the inhuman trade, more determined efforts were made and the Africans were now encouraged to obtain oil as well as kernel from the nuts for export' (*Topics in West African history*, p. 123).

[3] A variation on this formula could be seen on the East African coast, where the Sultanate of Zanzibar was a political incarnation of this merchant group, and the merchants were hence in a far stronger position vis-à-vis the inland chiefs. Gray describes the situation thus: 'Sayyid Said's ambition was not to create a territorial, but an economic empire in East Africa. His position was that of a great middleman, controlling the intercourse between East Africa and Europe, Arabia, India, and America' (J. M. Gray, 'Zanzibar and the coastal belt, 1840–1884', in *History of East Africa*, Oliver and Mathew, eds., I, 223).

It can be argued that the role of the Khedive of Egypt vis-à-vis the Sudan trade was basically similar. See J. E. Flint's discussion of British hesitation as to whether they would do better using the Sultan or the Khedive in opening up the Lakes region: 'The wider background to partition and colonial occupation', in *History of East Africa*, Oliver and Mathew, eds., I, 352–90.

Yet, in 1879 this whole structure began to crumble, and by 1900 it had ceased to exist. No doubt this was not what Great Britain desired. John E. Flint has stated it succinctly:

[Before 1879, Britain's] commerce was supremely competitive...did not need the protection of colonial tariff preferences, and...it seemed that the other powers were in no position to retaliate by establishing colonies of their own as protected areas for their exports...The free traders could dream of the day when Africa would be completely dominated by Britain, but this would not be through colonies, but by gradual penetration, decade by decade, of British trade and British missionaries.[1]

The major difficulty was that while this grand design suited Britain admirably, it suited other European powers such as France and Germany far less well. To challenge effectively the British economic hegemony in the world, the other industrializing powers needed, or felt they needed, larger markets for their industries and access to raw materials. Thus started the scramble for Africa; and once it had been started, Britain had no choice but to join in or be the loser.[2] From the Berlin Conference of 1884 to 1900, Africa was partitioned and 'pacified'.

The primary objective of this sudden imposition of colonial administration on most of Africa, in contrast with the earlier, long-developing commercial penetration, was to establish political control of the territory, which thereby made it possible to establish primacy in its econo-

---

[1] 'Chartered companies and the scramble for Africa', in *Africa in the nineteenth and twentieth centuries*, Joseph C. Anene and Godfrey N. Brown, eds. (Ibadan University Press, 1966), pp. 111–12. This was reinforced by the fact that France, Britain's only serious rival in African trade, was seriously embarrassed by its defeat in the Franco-Prussian War of 1870. Flint analyses the history of this rivalry and the impact of France's defeat in 'The growth of European influence in West Africa in the nineteenth century', in *A thousand years of West African history*, J. F. A. Ajayi and Ian Espie, eds. (Ibadan University Press, 1965), pp. 359–79. For France's conversion to a protectionist colonial trade policy from 1873 on, see Colin W. Newbury, 'The protectionist revival in French colonial trade: the case of Senegal', *Economic History Review*, Aug. 1968, 21, no. 2, pp. 337–48.

[2] See Flint: 'The Berlin West African Conference which began in November 1884 thus had its origins in an attempt to destroy British informal influence on the Niger and Congo, the two most important avenues of access to the interior of *Tropical Africa*' ('chartered companies', p. 121). Similarly, see Hargreaves: 'At last [1884] it seemed agreed that *some* governmental initiative was needed to protect Britain's future commerce in the Niger and the other Oil Rivers—including the Cameroons...' (John D. Hargreaves, *Prelude to the partition of West Africa*, London, 1963, p. 314).

mic transactions.[1] The ideal was monopolistic rights, although not every colonial power was strong enough to enforce such a policy; and Britain, as we have said, did not need to use extensively the weapon of exclusion. She merely wished to keep from being excluded herself. With these motivations, it became imperative that if possible no area be left in limbo, that European annexation or protection[2] be as extensive as possible.

Colonial conquest, rapidly achieved albeit often with considerable difficulty, involved in its very essence two fundamental changes of the boundaries of social action in Africa, one political, the other economic. Virtually all peoples became subject to a central administration, one of the fifty or so colonies. Each of these colonies absorbed politically a far larger number of entities of varying structures that we have come to call traditional political authorities. Thus, by and large, the scale of political administration became larger, the number of entities in Africa fewer, and above all the boundary lines were altered.

With regard to the second of the fundamental changes—the economic—each colony became part of an international economic network. The basic political decisions that determined the structure of that network were taken centrally and outside of Africa. Economic enterprise within the colony was dependent upon these decisions. The structures were different from those of the earlier, looser networks of which some African states had been a part.

The political boundaries were drawn primarily to include as much territory as could be conquered or negotiated diplomatically. Since the lines were established by each European power essentially out of fear of a claim of sovereignty by another European power, they were frequently arbitrary in terms of the previous lines drawn by the African states now enclosed or divided.[3] The important point, how-

---

[1] Newbury speaks of the 'fear of exclusion from regional markets as a motive for territorial expansion'. He also demonstrates that the result of colonial occupation was 'some polarization of national trade in the respective colonies of France and Britain' (see Colin W. Newbury, 'The tariff factor in Anglo-French West African partition', paper presented at Yale University Conference on France and Britain in Africa, Imperial Rivalry and Colonial Rule, 25–9 March 1968 (mimeograph), pp. 29, 33.

[2] 'Protection' was simply a formula whereby the British in particular sought to emphasize that their only objective was to keep from being excluded themselves. In theory, a protectorate was limited to control over foreign policy. In practice, it soon became extremely difficult to distinguish a 'colony' from a 'protectorate'.

[3] Arbitrary does not mean deliberately capricious. Hargreaves notes: 'Since European claims were often based upon treaties with African rulers, there were many cases

ever, is not that pre-colonial political and cultural units were sometimes divided among European hegemonies but that they were included within, and eventually subordinated to, a new juridical entity, the colonial territory and its administrative and legal systems.

The characteristic link between Africans and Europeans was no longer that between trading partners, each more or less backed up by his separate government. The relationship now was one between European administrators and African subordinates (primarily, as we shall see, chiefs and civil servants). And the trading operation was now carried on within a single political economy rather than between two political economies. If Africans did not play the game according to European rules, they were subject to political sanctions, certainly *de jure* and to a great extent *de facto*. They could be removed from their posts by the Europeans, and removed they were, often with great dispatch.

The consequences of the exercise of colonial authority—an authority administered within the framework of a new (and usually, for the African, larger) political unit than before—were several. One was the revamping, often the undermining, of previously existing systems. Whether, as in many hierarchical systems, the 'chief' was weakened[1] or, as in some systems, his powers were increased, in all cases the form and operation of the authority system were altered to suit the needs and desires of the colonial power. Moreover, the consequences of these changes were often felt not only in the particular (rural) area where they occurred but throughout the new unit, the colony.[2] In the next place, movements of labour tended to take place within the imperial colonial boundaries, if only because both transportation and currency

where the new frontiers coincided with traditional ones; other things being equal, the colonial powers preferred to follow chiefdom boundaries, where these were known. But even these boundaries might still divide Africans of the same language and culture, and once they came under effective European occupation they became harder to cross than would have been the case in the past' (*Prelude to partition*, pp. 348–9).

[1] A classic study of how this occurred, even where the colonial authorities intended otherwise, is K. A. Busia, *The position of the chief in the modern political system of the Ashanti* (London, Oxford University Press, 1951).

[2] A careful, detailed study of this process may be found in the article by A. G. Hopkins, 'The Lagos strike of 1897', *Past and Present*, Dec. 1966, no. 35, pp. 133–55. Hopkins describes how the intrusion of British authority into the hinterland of what was later the Western Region of Nigeria undermined the control of African farmer-chiefs over slave labour, who transformed themselves into independent cocoa-farmers. The rural transformation, combined with a European commitment to low urban wages, led to both an urban labour shortage and to a refusal to raise wages to attract these rural ex-slaves. The result was the Lagos strike, and its suppression.

systems made it the easiest path of the migrant. Where migration patterns crossed international lines, as in the case of Moçambique labour moving to South Africa, such a pattern was often followed with the express encouragement of the colonial authorities. Thirdly, the new political boundaries became in time the logical unit within which associational and political activities took place. Each colony began to acquire a personality, one recognized by its inhabitants. It became, in short, a social reality.

Membership in a specific international economic network led also to major social change in the individual colonies. We have already suggested that the prime objective of establishing colonial administration was the creation of a pre-emptive monopoly.[1] Quite aside from formal political limitations that could now be placed on traders outside the imperial network, the indirect effects of participating in a given currency zone were considerable.

[1] It is true that Germany, for instance, never seemed quite to establish such a monopoly. But as Henderson has noted, the prevention of counter-monopolies was clearly part of the original intent. 'In the early eighties German expansionists could point to renewed colonial activity by foreign countries... Clearly if Germany did not act promptly the few remaining regions of the world suitable for exploitation would be appropriated by other powers' (W. O. Henderson, *Studies in German colonial history*, London, 1962, p. 4). Similarly, Henry Ashby Turner, Jr.: 'As long as large parts of the non-European world were free of colonial rule, German commerce could get access to the markets and resources of Africa and Asia regardless of the discriminatory policies of the imperialist powers. But if those powers were to carve up all the non-European world, German overseas merchants would be at their mercy' ('Bismarck's imperialist venture: anti-British in origin?' in *Britain and Germany in Africa*, Prosser Gifford and Wm. Roger Louis, eds., New Haven, Yale University Press, 1967, p. 51).

Germany, which started late, and had a poor selection of colonies, thought she would gain more from pressing for free trade than from advocating protectionism as did France. See Louis: 'The Franco-German colonial entente began to collapse during the Berlin Congo Conference of November 1884–February 1885. From Bismarck's point of view, one of the main purposes of the conference was to secure equal commercial opportunities for German traders. Germany's natural ally on this question was free-trading Britain and not protectionist France' (Wm. Roger Louis, 'Great Britain and German expansion in Africa, 1884–1919', in *Britain and Germany in Africa*, p. 9).

Nonetheless, despite a free-trade policy, obligatory in any case for German East Africa under the terms of the Congo Act of 1885, Germany imposed some protectionist tariffs in her colonies, subsidized shipping and sometimes drew material for railway construction exclusively from Germany (cf. Henderson, *Studies in German colonial history*, pp. 37, 61). The effect of more political control on trade patterns was in any case significant. One has but to compare the trade statistics of colonies like Tanganyika or Togo over the period 1890–1960. Up to World War I Germany's role both as importer and exporter rose sharply, and then declined just as sharply as she lost political control.

The most immediate effect of colonial rule was its impact on the African traders, whose ability to play their traditional late nineteenth-century 'monopolistic role as middlemen' was drastically curtailed.[1] The merging of European trading firms into large-scale enterprises capable of mobilizing vast amounts of working capital, commanding superior or exclusive credits with European colonial banks, and having direct access to a European commercial network, put the African traders at a great disadvantage from the outset. These giant firms were in a much better position to take advantage of the expanding economic opportunities brought about by the establishment of colonial rule than were their African counterparts (or Arab traders in East Africa). The change took some thirty or forty years to accomplish completely, but by the end of World War I the radical decline of the relative importance of the African, as well as of the Arab, trading class had become an accomplished fact.[2]

A standard feature of the colonial economy was the development or expansion of an export commodity. Many minerals were extremely profitable, and were developed wherever possible under the aegis of a European firm. Of the total gross output in all of Africa, during the colonial period over two thirds was produced in South Africa, the Belgian Congo and Northern Rhodesia. But agricultural products (notably cocoa, coffee, tea, palm products, ground-nuts [peanuts], cotton, tobacco, wine) were in steady expansion throughout the continent. Although in West and North Africa the colonial authorities

[1] Peter C. Lloyd, *Africa in social change* (Harmondsworth, Middlesex, 1967), p. 52.
[2] See A. G. Hopkins, 'Economic aspects of political movements in Nigeria and the Gold Coast, 1918–1939', *Journal of African History*, 1966, **7**, no. 1, pp. 133–52 (esp. pp. 134–5). See also Lloyd, *Africa in social change*, pp. 77–8. For East Africa, the pattern is made clear in various articles in *History of East Africa*, Vol. II, Vincent Harlow and E. M. Chilver, eds., assisted by Alison Smith (Oxford, Clarendon Press, 1965). The effect of French firms on Senegalese traders in French West Africa was the same. See A. Villard, 'Comment travaille Faidherbe', *Bulletin d'informations et de renseignements de l'A.O.F.*, Oct. 1938, no. 204, cited in Jean Suret-Canale, *Afrique noire occidentale et centrale*, Vol. II: *L'ère coloniale, 1900–1945* (Paris, 1964), pp. 15–16. Suret-Canale describes the process of formal concessions to European firms in French Equatorial Africa, pp. 29–58.

See also the following account by Vansina of the fate of Ovimbundu traders in Central Africa. [Ovimbundu] 'trade went on uninterrupted throughout the [nineteenth] century...When the [colonial] wars were over [in 1902], the price of rubber had dropped, the colonial governments began to bar access in their territories to traders from Angola, and a great famine in 1911 killed many traders in eastern Angola. In Ovimbundu tradition, this date marked the end of the long-distance trade' (Vansina, *Kingdom of the savanna*, p. 201).

could partially build on an already established cash economy, the introduction of cash-crops was in most communities the consequence of
either colonial administrative pressure on African farmers[1] or of expropriation of the land by white settlers (as in Kenya, Algeria, Southern
Rhodesia). Of course, in many instances, despite opposition by the
colonial administration or the settlers—who in certain cases preferred
to encourage Africans to offer themselves as wage-workers—African
farmers proceeded to develop cash-crops because they found them
profitable.[2] Whatever the motive for entering the world agricultural
market and whatever the social organization of export production,
each colonial administration, as the political arm of the metropole,
sought to tie a segment of the African population into the larger
imperial economy either as independent producers or as wage-workers,
and in all cases as consumers. As a consequence, the economic well-
being of the African population was continually and increasingly
subject to the fluctuations endemic to these systems. Furthermore,
once colonial administration had been established, this shift in the basic
orientation of the colonial economy often occurred quite early and
rapidly.[3]

Both the mines and the cash-crop areas, as well as the commercial-
administrative urban centres, needed labour; and they all obtained it
largely through circulatory migration, partially forced, partially induced, initially by means of taxation.[4] The need for clerical labour was

[1] A typical instance was the role of the British administration in fostering cotton production in Uganda. See Cyril Ehrlich, 'The Uganda Economy, 1903–1945', in *History
of East Africa*, pp. 399–402. These pressures were not always rational, as demonstrated
in detail for the Gold Coast by R. H. Green and S. H. Hymer, 'Cocoa in the Gold
Coast: a study in the relations between African farmers and agricultural experts',
Journal of Economic History, Sept. 1966, **26**, no. 3, pp. 299–319.

[2] For a discussion of wage-employment versus cash-cropping as alternative options for
Africans, and the views of the colonial administration and settlers on these alternatives,
see G. Arrighi, 'Labour supplies in historical perspective: the Rhodesian case' (Dar es
Salaam, mimeograph, 1967).

[3] R. Szereszewski argues that the changes in the structure of the Gold Coast economy
brought about between 1890 and 1910 determined the pattern of economic production
throughout the rest of the colonial period and after independence. See *Structural
changes in the economy of Ghana* (London, 1965). A similar argument for Rhodesia
has been made by G. Arrighi in *The political economy of Rhodesia*, The Hague,
1967.

[4] How this worked is well described in Lewis H. Gann, *A history of Northern Rhodesia:
early days to 1953* (London, 1964), pp. 100–11. Some of the purely economic reasons
why migratory labour has continued to be a key element of African economies are
expounded in Elliot J. Berg, 'The economics of the migrant labor system' in *Urbaniza-*

met through the establishment of Western educational structures. This did not mean, however, that higher administrative posts were open to Africans. On the contrary, at the beginning of this era there were many qualified Africans in the civil service; but soon after the setting up of colonial governments there followed a steady policy of deliberate exclusion, which only ended with the rise of the nationalist movements.[1]

The establishment of firmly-bounded, administered territorial units forming integral elements of a particular imperial economic system, was the main accomplishment of European colonial conquest, one that had been realized by and large throughout most of Africa by the outbreak of World War I. The colonial order was based, as we have said, on a new alliance of Europeans and Africans. On the European side, the key actors were the colonial administrators (joined in some areas in an important secondary role by white settlers). On the African side, the key actors were the chiefs, who were increasingly incorporated into the colonial bureaucracy,[2] and a small urban clerical and professional bourgeoisie, who were largely Christianized. The centre of interaction of European and African shifted from the port of trade, at which representatives of two separate societies met, to the administrative offices, in which governors and governed met.[3]

tion and migration in West Africa, Hilda Kuper, ed. (Berkeley, University of California Press, 1965), pp. 160–81.

[1] 'In 1883, of the forty-three "higher posts" in the Gold Coast, nine were filled by Africans, including seven District Commissioners' (see David Kimble, A political history of Ghana: the rise of Gold Coast nationalism, 1850–1928, Oxford, Clarendon Press, 1963, p. 94). For the exclusion of Africa from the senior civil service about the turn of the century, see pp. 98–105. For resentment of Africans against their formalized subordinacy in the Uganda civil service of 1929, see David E. Apter, The political kingdom in Uganda: a study in bureaucratic nationalism (Princeton University Press, 1961), pp. 196–8. Similarly, one must see that the use of akida in German East Africa meant the use of Africans as medium-level civil servants. When this practice was dispensed with by the British, it involved the use of European personnel at lower levels of the civil service than previously.

[2] J. M. Lonsdale calls them the 'political communicators'. He says that: 'In the ideal case, the political communicator, king or chief, whether traditionally legitimate, traditionally recognizable as usurper, or jumped-up mercenary and buccaneer, remained also a social communicator, in close relationship with his tribesmen or peasants' ('Some origins of nationalism in East Africa', Journal of African History, 1968, 9, no. 1, p. 121).

[3] This is precisely what Georges Balandier meant by 'the colonial situation' (see 'The colonial situation: a theoretical approach', in Social change: the colonial situation, Immanuel Wallerstein, ed., New York, 1966, pp. 34–61; and also in Social change, Max Gluckman, 'Malinowski's "functional" analysis of social change', pp. 25–33).

The colonial order was, however, a misnomer. The colonial period was in many ways, as we become ever more aware, an exceedingly disorderly one. There was not only conquest (euphemistically termed at the time 'pacification'); there was also the deliberate disruption of existing social organization, a practice the Europeans engaged in in order to reorganize the economy.[1] Both these phenomena, plus the resulting social changes, created a series of underlying strains which led, it now seems inevitably, to the rise of a nationalist movement.

There were three strains of some consequence. The first was the channelling of the African urban middle class, old and new, into administrative positions, primarily within the governmental bureaucracies (both national and local), but to some extent also within the bureaucracies of the export–import firms and the missionary churches. The clerk caught between two worlds has become a common object of literary study. To concentrate on his psychological dilemmas, however, is to miss the key factor, the structural bind in which this class found itself.

The school graduate had virtually no option except to choose a career in one of the three European-controlled bureaucratic structures (government, export–import firms, missions). To rise within these bureaucracies he was obliged to conform not merely to the norms of the organization internally but to a wider code of behaviour and manners characteristic of the European (largely middle-class) expatriate in Africa. The more he cut himself off from the customs of his African rural community, the greater was likely to be his reward in the bureaucracy.

At the same time, however, into this same administrative machinery there was introduced another class of people, Europeans who were making their career in the colonies, who not only entered these bureaucracies at a higher level than the African school graduate but who also monopolized the top posts. As the African administrative

[1] The practice is documented for Tanganyika in L. Cliffe, 'Nationalism and the reaction to enforced agricultural improvement in Tanganyika during the colonial period', Kampala, Uganda, Makerere College, East African Institute of Social Research, *Conference Papers*, Jan. 1965. Cliffe also indicates the direct link between the disruptive regulations of the British and the rise of nationalist sentiment. Compulsory cultivation in the Belgian Congo is described both in Roger Anstey, *King Leopold's legacy: the Congo under Belgian rule, 1908–1960* (London, Oxford University Press, 1966), p. 82; and in Michel Merlier, *Le Congo de la colonisation belge à l'indépendance* (Paris, 1962), pp. 79–87. Merlier says: 'Without the intervention of the State, colonial agriculture could never have been established in the Congo' (p. 84).

bourgeoisie grew in numbers, so did the European administrative class, the latter—at least until about the 1950s—at a faster pace than the former. The result of this trend was that the sole career outlet of any significance available to educated Africans not only carried with it an arbitrary (racial) limit of aspiration but a limit that grew tighter and moved *lower* as the years of colonial rule went by. It was inevitable that with every passing year the irritation of this class would increase. However, despite the fact that the proportion of Africans in senior bureaucratic positions declined, their absolute numbers grew because of the steady expansion of the various administrative apparatuses. It thus became more and more plausible to work collectively to change the system, first in various social organizations, later in trade-unions and proto-nationalist political groups.

The second source of tension was less universal, its emergence being in part a consequence of the extent of production for the imperial market in a given territory plus the absence of a significant number of white settlers. As the market grew, so did the number of educated urban Africans; and they then became more differentiated as a class. In the tightly stratified system that characterized the colonial period in Africa—and this became ever more marked with the passage of time—pecking orders rapidly emerged, and each stratum perceived an advantage in maintaining a distance between itself and the next lower stratum. The lower stratum in turn sought to blur the distinction, thereby rising. This effort led to conflict over the expansion of educational facilities (advantages to the lower stratum) and the creation of social exclusiveness or reduction of social contact by means of clubs and class endogamy (advantages to the higher stratum.)

In colonial Africa this issue had already arisen in some territories by the end of World War I, and it became acute after World War II. In the higher stratum were the professionals, medium high civil servants and religious personnel and the more important chiefs in their urban social roles. In the lower stratum were the lower civil servants, the primary-school teachers, the health personnel, and the skilled workers, a stratum which showed a significant jump in size during and as a result of each world war. The conflict between these groups, each fighting essentially for the relatively small share of the pie available to urban Africans, was made acute following each world war not merely by the increase in size of the lower stratum, but by the decline in real incomes brought about by the disruption of trade combined with inflationary trends in the imperial mother country.[1] When such conflicts became acute, the 'lower middle class' elements expressed their views in the form of more militant and often more radical nationalism, calling for expansion of education, for the suffrage, and for diminution of the legal authority of chiefs.[2]

These lower middle-class elements wanted thus to take on simultaneously both the colonial régime and their principal African interlocutors (the administrative and professional bourgeoisie, plus the higher chiefs).[3] To do this, they needed strength beyond their own numbers and resources. They found immediate support in the African merchant class, such as it was, many of whom were simply graduates who tried to break out of the administrative careers for which the colonial administration had destined them.[4] These aspiring middle-class elements began to seek active support for their struggle in the rural areas, where they hoped to channel the latent and irregularly erupting discontent of the peasantry.[5] This discontent was not new; it was rather a continuing phenomenon of the years of colonial rule.

These unresolved discontents of the rural, monetized populations

[1] This is very well documented for West Africa for the period 1939–49. See Elliot J. Berg, 'Real income trends in West Africa, 1939–1960', in *Economic transition in Africa*, M. J. Herskovits and M. Harwitz, eds. (Evanston, Northwestern University Press, 1964), pp. 199–238. Berg speaks of the 'universality and severity of the decline' (p. 203). For evidence of a decline in real wages in Northern and Southern Rhodesia 'during the war and early post-war years', cf. W. J. Barber, *The economy of British Central Africa: a case study of economic development in a dualistic society* (London, Oxford University Press, 1961), pp. 204–8.

[2] To be sure, if for some reason the chiefs, or some chiefs, were at that moment under attack by the colonial administration, the radical nationalists might rally to the support of these chiefs. But in general they were suspicious of the chiefs, even hostile to them, regarding them primarily as agents of the colonial administration.

[3] And sometimes they took on the Asian or Levantine intermediate trading groups as well.

[4] Some of the most unlikely Africans, given the notoriety they later achieved, made such attempts at an early stage in their careers. See, for example, Patrice Lumumba; see also the case of General China (of Mau Mau fame), in his autobiography (Waruhiu Itote, '*Mau Mau*' *general*, Nairobi, 1967). In the case of 'Field Marshal' John Okello (who played a controversial and noteworthy role in the Zanzibar revolution), see his *Revolution in Zanzibar* (Nairobi, 1967), pp. 35–83. Oginga Odinga calls himself, in a letter to Jomo Kenyatta in 1952, 'a nationalist businessman' (see his *Not yet uhuru: the autobiography of Oginga Odinga*, London, 1967, p. 101).

[5] The distinction between tribesmen and peasants has been discussed for Africa by Lloyd A. Fallers, 'Are African cultivators to be called "peasants"?' in *Current Anthropology*, 1961, **2**, no. 2, pp. 108–10. Fallers believes that pre-colonial African cultivators were 'proto-peasants', ready to be made into peasants by contact with Islamic or Christian culture. Cf. Lonsdale, 'Origins of nationalism', pp. 123–4.

led to the third source of tension under colonial rule. The colonial system could not meet the demands of the peasantry without altering the basic economic pattern (and this was especially true in settler territories). On the other hand, with time and increasing education, this discontent threatened to become transformed into a conscious radicalism far more dangerous in the long run than simple, albeit destructive, outbreaks of rebellion.

Of course, except in a few relatively egalitarian groups, rural discontent undoubtedly predated the imposition of colonial rule. But colonial rule, once established, exacerbated these sources of irritation in four ways, as a result of which rural discontent was on the rise through-out the colonial era.[1]

In the first place, colonial rule meant conquest. This rule, once im-posed, was exercised over chiefs as well as over ordinary men. Chiefs were removed, replaced, strengthened or weakened in power. Whatever the specifics, there was widespread change in personnel and often in structure, and as a result some loss of legitimacy, especially as the chiefs were progressively incorporated into the colonial administrative system as agents performing unpleasant tasks. In addition, Christianity spread largely in the mood of opposition to traditional customs and hence rulers. The combination of these two elements meant a general lessening of the effectiveness of traditional constraints on rebellious behaviour.

Secondly, cash-crop production enabled those who controlled ad-ministrative decisions of allocation (the chiefs) to determine owner-ship rights in a system that, in the cash-crop areas, slowly but surely became one of private appropriation. In the course of time, it was largely those with high traditional status who acquired rights to exten-sive tracts, often at the expense of those who emigrated or were made to emigrate to the towns.[2] From the point of view of the average rural

---

[1] The literature on peasant rebellions and rural radicalism is expanding at a rapid rate. See, among others: Martin Kilson, *Political change in a West African state: a study of the modernization process in Sierra Leone* (Cambridge, Harvard University Press, 1966), pp. 60–3, 110–12; T. O. Ranger, 'Revolt in Portuguese East Africa: the Makonde rising of 1917', in *African affairs: Number two*, Kenneth Kirkwood, ed., Oxford University, St Antony's College, St Antony's papers, No. 15 (Carbondale, Southern Illinois University Press, 1963), pp. 54–80; Robert I. Rotberg, *The rise of nationalism in Central Africa* (Cambridge, Harvard University Press, 1965), pp. 55–92; and Herbert F. Weiss, 'Introduction' in Centre de Recherche et d'Information Socio-politiques, *Congo 1964* (Princeton University Press, 1966), pp. xi–xxii.

[2] Iliffe has described this process for Tanganyika. 'Partly because they had a traditional monopoly, and partly because they were supported by the Germans, the Haya chiefs

African, the process began to be regarded as chiefly usurpation of the land. Once it was perceived in that light, the ability of the chief to curb rebellious impulses of his subjects (whether directed against him or against the colonial régime) was bound to diminish.

Thirdly, the great geographical mobility, which was the consequence of a labour force with a solid migratory base, led to the spread of ideas, aspirations, frustrations and boldness. Fourthly, there was the discontent that arose in the neglected areas, where the Africans became aware of the growing disparity between their own standards of living and those of the areas favoured by the colonial administration. This is what Iliffe has called the 'politics of unimprovement'.[1]

Thus, broadly speaking, African nationalism represented an alliance against colonial rule of the middle classes (largely urban) as the vocal leadership, and the rural elements (semi-urban) as the not-too-easy-to-control supporters. Two factors seem most likely to have increased the initial militance (violence) of African nationalism. In countries where the middle class was more developed and hence more differentiated, it was more likely to suffer from internal divisions. In that case the lower middle-class element would assume a more militant stance. If the peasantry was more dislocated, more uprooted from traditional social restraints, the spontaneous outbreaks would often be more frequent, more extreme, and their impact on the overall militance of the movement greater. This did depend in part, however, on the extensiveness of the colonial repressive machinery.

The schema thus baldly outlined shows immediately where the conflicting interests within the nationalist movement lay. The leaders and the supporters started out with differing underlying objectives and expectations. Since each segment brought to the nationalist movement a crucial part of the strength needed, each had to suppress its differences momentarily. But the conflicting aims were there from the beginning, available for exploitation by the colonial régime.

obtained most of the early profits from coffee-growing...Very much the same happened in Kilimanjaro...Again the chiefs and their courtiers had the best opportunities'. Of course, the chiefs were not always the only ones who obtained land. When, as amongst the Chagga, a group of 'new men' also 'acquired' land rights, rural discontent was fanned by the attacks by these men on the privileges of the rural chiefly planters. See J. Iliffe, 'The age of improvement and differentiation (1907–45)', in The history of Tanzania, I. Kimambo, ed. (Nairobi, 1968).

[1] Kimambo, The history of Tanzania. The forthcoming work of I. Kimambo on the Pare tax uprisings in Tanganyika will lend support to this argument.

The leadership of the nationalist movement was very largely rooted in the administrative-clerical bourgeoisie (whether of the higher or the lower stratum). As we have noted, they found colonial limitations frustrating. They wanted the end of these arbitrary career limits, and it was political sovereignty that appeared to promise fulfilment of this desire. But, if anything, they found the individual limitations in the economic arena even more frustrating. Very few Africans still remained as middle-sized merchants, and their rise within the colonial framework to the rank of large-scale commercial or agricultural entrepreneurs—to say nothing of industrial entrepreneurs—was clearly out of the question. This was perfectly obvious not only to those who, despite everything, persisted as merchants, but also to that larger group of clerks and teachers who cherished such aspirations or who made futile attempts to pursue such inclinations.[1] These middle-class elements wanted control of the state machinery, partly for its own sake to be sure, and certainly for the sake of eliminating career discrimination; but also because they wanted to recapture the role of commercial middleman between Europe and the African hinterland, a role they had played in the nineteenth century and earlier, and of which they had been deprived by colonial rule.

The rural (semi-urban) masses had somewhat more diffuse objectives, less clear in their detail, requiring less obviously a control of the national bureaucratic apparatus. They wanted to be 'less oppressed', and saw this being accomplished in one of two ways. One might be designated generically 'romantic nativism', which involved shuffling off the over-

---

[1] On the difficulties of a business career for Africans under colonial rule, see the vivid description by Odinga in *Not yet uhuru*, pp. 76–94. Iliffe describes two pertinent cases in his article cited above. One is of Klemens Kiiza, a coffee-grower who sought to establish a coffee-curing factory, and after fifteen years of difficulty had to admit defeat in 1946. Iliffe comments: 'This story...shows very clearly the problems which faced an energetic improver in this period: lack of capital, Asian business competition, international economic uncertainty, official suspicion, the necessity and danger of organizing the farmers, and governmental paternalism which restricted enterprise. Even those like Kiiza who gained most during the age of improvement found that they could not gain all they wanted. They were too hemmed in by the structure of colonial rule.'

The second case was that of Erica Fiah, a Ganda shopkeeper in Dar es Salaam before the Second World War. Iliffe says of him: [His] 'business interests as a shopkeeper quickly brought to him the lesson that Klemens Kiiza was learning at the same date in Buhaya. The colonial system was itself an obstacle to improvement beyond a certain point...' Fiah's reaction was to organize an urban radical group in 1934 which drew its membership from African traders and shopkeepers who shared his frustrations.

lay of European presence in the rural areas, and hopefully with it the African collaborators, some of the chiefs. Many of the independent neo-Christian cults, many of the messianic movements, some political stirrings were of this nature. They seemed to be heavily 'localist' in orientation.

The other path, for the ordinary uneducated man, more modern in appearance and reality, was to aspire to the status of a member of the middle classes through one or both of the two paths of entry: education and cash-earning jobs. The demands of this group for universal education and an expansion of the employment sector were more strident than their demands even for suffrage, though suffrage was seen as a necessary part of the package. These demands were national rather than local in orientation, and nationalist—because the colonial administration was regarded as the first bulwark to be overcome. In an insufficiently expanding economy, these national demands would later take on local, that is 'tribalist', qualities, but this is largely a post-independence problem.

Decolonization thus took on the form of a struggle, on the one hand, between a nationalist movement composed of two disparate elements with only some convergent goals; and on the other, the colonial administration allied to a small handful of African collaborators. As time went on, the verbal radicalization of the rural, or semi-urban, groups proceeded or threatened to proceed apace.

The response of the Europeans (outside of southern, settler-dominated, Africa), faced with this array and this perspective, was to come to terms with the middle-class leadership by arranging a rapid transfer of power to them in the expectation of ending their verbal radicalism before it became coherent, ideological and national in organization. From the European point of view, this operation was on the whole successful, since the rapid decolonization did largely accomplish these two objectives.

Decolonization has in one sense meant that the relations between Europe and Africa have returned to their pre-colonial status. The main point of contact is once again at the port of trade. The African entre-preneurial class is once more, just as it was before colonial rule, linked closely to, often part of, the state apparatus. The categories of politician and entrepreneur are heavily overlapping, at least for the present.

This new alliance of economic interests within Africa and the Western world was, however, forged at the expense of many groups, which explains why it met with some resistance. On the European end, the losers included many of the white farmer-settlers (and thus areas like Kenya and Algeria were harder to decolonize than some others), as well as the top European administrators (for whom the loss has been eased by the gradualness of their actual removal and the generous pensions that were arranged). In addition, some big European enterprises have lost out in cases where they were not big enough. (This is true *a fortiori* for Asian economic enterprises.) In the process of carving out an area for African enterprise, the weaker among the Europeans have either been eliminated, or replaced by stronger Europeans. This explains in part why Portuguese economic interests, who fear that the loss of political monopoly would lead to their direct replacement by American, British, French and German firms, have been so resistant to decolonization.[1]

On the African end, the price has been largely paid by two groups: the small handful of chiefs and professionals too compromised in the earlier alliance with the colonial administration; and the mass elements who have been curbed or at least disoriented by the transfer of power. These latter groups were for a while given more educational facilities, to be sure, and some social services. But essentially there has been no shift in the basic economic structure of the various territories, now nations. Job-creation has ground almost to a halt, while cash-crop prices continue to decline. Hence the amelioration of the economic lot has been sharply limited. These people are now facing a significant decline in standard of living.

There is no doubt that the 'curbing' of these groups cannot continue indefinitely under such circumstances, and one might argue that post-colonial internal disorder—including the ethnic rivalries, the breakdown of parties and the military coups—reflects this fact. But decolonization nonetheless did blunt the impact of the gathering storm and did afford a considerable breathing space for the existing politico-economic system.

In summary, we have argued that the establishment of colonial rule brought about essentially two types of changes. One occurred in the composition of the groups primarily engaged in the alliance of the Western world and Africa, from merchants with merchants, to administrators with chiefs and clerks. And the second type of change is to be

---

[1] Even the British, French and Belgian groups have had this fear vis-à-vis American, and, to a lesser extent German, firms (and in the case of the Belgians, French firms).

found in the structure of the African social system: the creation of new territorial units and the subsequent involvement of these units in specific imperial economic networks. We have then argued that the process of decolonization and the attainment of independence have reversed the first change while retaining the second. The nationalist revolution thus has been of considerable benefit to the African middle classes, but has had little significance so far as the rural and semi-urban masses are concerned. The new states are being built on the same sands as the old colonial territories, on the sands of mounting social discontent. Ultimately, the present social structures will crumble, but some time may yet elapse before the winds blow and shift sufficiently to bring this about.

BIBLIOGRAPHY

Ajayi, J. F. A. 'The continuity of African institutions under colonialism', in *Emerging themes of African history: proceedings of the International Conference of African Historians held at Dar es Salaam, 1965*, T. O. Ranger, ed. Nairobi, 1968.

Ajayi, J. F. A., and Ian Espie, eds. *A thousand years of West African history*. Ibadan University Press, 1965; reprint 1967.

Anene, Joseph C., and Godfrey N. Brown, eds. *Africa in the nineteenth and twentieth centuries*. Ibadan University Press, 1966; reprint 1967.

Anstey, Roger. *King Leopold's legacy: the Congo under Belgian rule, 1908–1960*. London, Oxford University Press, 1966.

Apter, David E. *The political kingdom in Uganda: a study in bureaucratic nationalism*. Princeton University Press, 1961.

Arrighi, G. *The political economy of Rhodesia*. The Hague, 1967.
'Labour supplies in historical perspective: the Rhodesian case', Dar es Salaam, mimeograph, 1967.

Balandier, Georges. 'The colonial situation: a theoretical approach', in *Social change: the colonial situation*, Immanuel Wallerstein, ed. New York, 1966.

Barber, W. J. *The economy of British Central Africa: a case study of economic development in a dualistic society*. Stanford University Press, 1961.

Berg, Elliot J. 'The economics of the migrant labor system', in *Urbanization and migration in West Africa*, Hilda Kuper, ed. Berkeley, University of California Press, 1965.
'Real income trends in West Africa, 1939–1960', in *Economic transition in Africa*, Melville Herskovits and Mitchell Harwitz, eds. Evanston, Northwestern University Press, 1964.

Boahen, A. Adu. *Topics in West African history*. London, 1966.

Busia, K. A. *The position of the chief in the modern political system of the Ashanti: a study of the influence of contemporary social changes on Ashanti political institutions*. London, Oxford University Press, 1951.

Cliffe, L. 'Nationalism and the reaction to enforced agricultural improvement in Tanganyika during the colonial period', in Kampala, Uganda, Makerere College, East African Institute of Social Research, *Conference Papers*, Jan. 1965.

Coombs, Douglas. *The Gold Coast, Britain and the Netherlands, 1850–1874*. London, Oxford University Press, 1963.

Ehrlich, Cyril. 'The Uganda economy, 1903–1945', in *History of East Africa*, Vol. II, Vincent Harlow and E. M. Chilver, eds., assisted by Alison Smith. Oxford, Clarendon Press, 1965.

Fage, J. D. *An introduction to the history of West Africa*. 3rd ed. Cambridge University Press, 1962.

Fallers, Lloyd A. 'Are African cultivators to be called "peasants"?' *Current Anthropology*, April 1961, **2**, no. 2.

Flint, John E. 'Chartered companies and the scramble for Africa', in *Africa in the nineteenth and twentieth centuries*, Joseph C. Anene and Godfrey N. Brown, eds. Ibadan University Press, 1966; reprint 1967.

'The growth of European influence in West Africa in the nineteenth century', in *A thousand years of West African history*, J. F. A. Ajayi and I. Espie, eds. Ibadan University Press, 1965.

'The wider background to partition and colonial occupation', in *History of East Africa*, Vol. I, Roland Oliver and Gervase Mathew, eds. Oxford, Clarendon Press, 1963.

Forde, Daryll, and P. M. Kaberry, eds. *West African kingdoms in the nineteenth century*. London, Oxford University Press, 1967.

Gann, Lewis H. *A history of Northern Rhodesia: early days to 1953*. London, 1964.

Gifford, Prosser, and William Roger Louis, eds. *Britain and Germany in Africa: imperial rivalry and colonial rule*. New Haven, Yale University Press, 1967.

Gluckman, Max. 'Malinowski's "functional" analysis of social change', in *Social change: the colonial situation*, Immanuel Wallerstein, ed. New York, 1966.

Gray, J. M. 'Zanzibar and the coastal belt, 1840–1884', in *History of East Africa*, Vol. I, Roland Oliver and Gervase Mathew, eds. Oxford, Clarendon Press, 1963.

Green, R. H., and S. H. Hymer. 'Cocoa in the Gold Coast: a study in the relations between African farmers and agricultural experts', *Journal of Economic History*, Sept. 1966, **26**, no. 3.

Hargreaves, John D. *Prelude to the partition of West Africa*. London, 1963.

Harlow, Vincent, and E. M. Chilver, eds., assisted by Alison Smith. *History of East Africa*, Vol. II. Oxford Clarendon Press, 1965.

Henderson, W. O. *Studies in German colonial history*. London, 1962.

Herskovits, Melville, and Mitchell Harwitz, eds. *Economic transition in Africa*. Evanston, Northwestern University Press, 1964.

Hopkins, A. G. 'Economic aspects of political movements in Nigeria and the Gold Coast, 1918–1939', *Journal of African History*, 1966, **7**, no. 1.

'The Lagos strike of 1897: an exploration in Nigerian labour history', *Past and Present*, Dec. 1966, no. 35.

Iliffe, John. 'The age of improvement and differentiation (1907–45)', in *The history of Tanzania*, I. Kimambo, ed. Nairobi, 1968.

Itote, Waruhiu (General China). *'Mau Mau' general*. Nairobi, 1967.

Kilson, Martin. *Political change in a West African state: a study of the modernization process in Sierra Leone*. Cambridge, Harvard University Press, 1966.

Kimambo, I., ed. *The history of Tanzania*. Nairobi, 1968.

Kimble, David. *A political history of Ghana: the rise of Gold Coast nationalism, 1850–1928*. Oxford, Clarendon Press, 1963.

Kirkwood, Kenneth, ed. *African affairs: Number two* (Oxford University, St Antony's College, *St Antony's papers*, No. 15) Carbondale, Southern Illinois University Press, 1961.

Kuper, Hilda, ed. *Urbanization and migration in West Africa*. Berkeley, University of California Press, 1965.

Lawrence, Arnold Walter. *Trade, castles and forts of West Africa*. London, 1963.

Lloyd, Peter C. *Africa in social change*. Harmondsworth, Middlesex, 1967.

Lonsdale, J. M. 'Some origins of nationalism in East Africa', *Journal of African History*, 1968, **9**, no. 1.

Louis, Wm. Roger. 'Great Britain and German expansion in Africa, 1884–1919', in *Britain and Germany in Africa*, Prosser Gifford and Wm. Roger Louis, eds. New Haven, Yale University Press, 1967.

Merlier, Michel. *Le Congo de la colonisation belge à l'indépendance*. Paris, 1962.

Newbury, Colin W. 'The protectionist revival in French colonial trade: the case of Senegal', *Economic History Review*, Aug. 1968, **21**, no. 2.

'The tariff factor in Anglo-French West African partition', paper presented at Yale University Conference on France and Britain in Africa: Imperial Rivalry and Colonial Rule, 25–9 March 1968 (mimeograph).

The western Slave Coast and its rulers: European trade and administration among the Yoruba and Adja-speaking peoples of south-western Nigeria, southern Dahomey and Togo. Oxford, Clarendon Press, 1961.

Nørregaard, Georg. *Danish settlements in West Africa, 1658–1850*. Trans. by Sigurd Mammen. Boston University Press, 1966.

Odinga, Oginga. *Not yet uhuru: the autobiography of Oginga Odinga*. London, 1967.

Okello, John. *Revolution in Zanzibar*. Nairobi, 1967.

Oliver, Roland A., and Anthony Atmore. *Africa since 1800*. London, Cambridge University Press, 1967.

Oliver, Roland A., and Gervase Mathew, eds. *History of East Africa*, Vol. I. Oxford, Clarendon Press, 1963.

Ranger, Terence O. *Aspects of Central African history*. London, 1968.

  'Revolt in Portuguese East Africa: the Makonde rising of 1917', in *African affairs: Number two*, Kenneth Kirkwood, ed. (Oxford University, St Antony's College, *St Antony's papers, No. 15*). Carbondale, Southern Illinois University Press, 1963.

  ed. *Emerging themes of African history*. Nairobi, 1968.

Rodney, Walter. *West Africa and the Atlantic slave-trade*. Historical Association of Tanzania Paper No. 2. Nairobi, 1967.

Rotberg, Robert I. *The rise of nationalism in Central Africa: the making of Malawi and Zambia, 1873–1964*. Cambridge, Harvard University Press, 1965.

Suret-Canale, Jean. *Afrique noire occidentale et centrale*. 2 vols. Paris, 1958–64.

Szereszewski, R. *Structural changes in the economy of Ghana*. London, 1965.

Turner, Henry Ashby, Jr. 'Bismarck's imperialist venture: anti-British in origin?' in *Britain and Germany in Africa*, Prosser Gifford and Wm. Roger Louis, eds. New Haven, Yale University Press, 1967.

United Nations. Economic Commission for Africa. *Economic survey of Africa since 1950*. New York, 1959.

Vansina, Jan. *Kingdoms of the savanna*. Madison, University of Wisconsin Press, 1966.

Villard, A. 'Comment travaille Faidherbe', *Bulletin d'informations et de renseignements de l'A.O.F.*, Oct. 1938, no. 204.

Wallerstein, Immanuel. 'The range of choice: constraints on decisions of contemporary independent African states'. Forthcoming.

  ed. *Social change: the colonial situation*. New York, 1966.

Weiss, Herbert F. 'Introduction', in Centre de Recherche et d'Information Socio-politiques, *Congo 1964*. Princeton University Press, 1966.

CHAPTER 12

MISSIONARY AND HUMANITARIAN
INTERESTS, 1914 TO 1960

by C. G. BAËTA

There is an ancient Hebrew proverb which says, 'Where the sin began, there the retribution set in'. It is not surprising that in World War I serious fighting first flared up in the African colonial territories. Bismarck's Berlin Conference of 1884, called primarily to settle the Congo Basin disputes, had sought to lend international recognition also to other imperialist claims arising from the earlier phase of the scramble. There was need to stem the threatening tide of disorder and possible armed conflict between the European powers involved in the race for African colonies.

But the matter could not rest while a single square foot of African land remained unoccupied. Thus the Berlin Conference, by appearing to accept effective seizure, by whatever means, as the test of the legitimacy of sovereignty claims, in fact provided a ready formula for the uninhibited completion of the grabbing and partitioning of Africa. By the outbreak of the war in 1914 the entire continent, with the exception of the ancient Kingdom of Abyssinia, and of Liberia, regarded as under the special protection of the United States, had been parcelled out among France, Great Britain, Germany, Belgium, Portugal, Italy and Spain.)

However, even this total share-out could only bring a temporary truce. Considerations of prospective economic expansion and of imperial security strategy, particularly on the part of the major powers, made territorial adjustments appear desirable even if they could be effected only at the expense of some other power or powers. Naturally a great upheaval, such as the war, presented a suitable occasion for carrying out such changes of frontiers. Thus, just as before the war European international politics had for the most part meant African politics, so also for both sides a major objective of the war itself, at least at the beginning, had been to capture the African colonial possessions of the enemy.

As early as 13 August 1914 British naval forces raided Dar es Salaam;

by the 26th of that month the Allies had taken Togo and had invaded the Cameroun while the Germans, on their side, had attacked and disrupted the main communication line of Uganda, the Victoria-Nyanza–Mombasa railway. For shorter or longer periods large areas of the continent became battlegrounds, both sides using mainly African troops and labour contingents composed entirely of Africans. Foodstuffs and other commodities of all kinds, as well as services and labour, were freely commandeered; and thousands of Africans were callously and pointlessly interned in camps under conditions of uttermost wretchedness. Whole villages with their surrounding farms were looted, burned, or completely destroyed. An extreme example of the depredation that took place is the case of the Batanga district of the Cameroun, where as much as thirty per cent of the entire population was simply wiped out.

According to many estimates, altogether more than a million Africans saw active military service. Tens of thousands of them were employed in European theatres of the war not only as transport carriers, stretcher corps, drivers, etc., but also as soldiers. In the fighting in German East Africa some missionaries, notably the then Bishop of Zanzibar and Dr Arthur of the Church of Scotland Mission, accompanied to the front Christian youths drawn from their areas as carrier-corps, in order to give them spiritual ministrations and general guidance in strange surroundings and unaccustomed conditions of living.

The war made the first significant dent both in the self-confident ethnocentrism of Europeans engaged in humanitarian enterprises in Africa, and in the high opinion held of them by the Africans whom they were trying to serve. The complete cessation of the flow of money and supplies from Europe brought many missionary families to the verge of want, with Africans quietly observing their reactions. Africans witnessed most painful scenes at the arrest and deportation of Europeans, and saw humiliating treatment meted out to them in internment. Indeed these processes were as a rule carried out by African soldiers under the command of their European officers. An upsurge of warm human sympathy and fellowship from which the usual elements of the normally prevailing master–servant complex were largely absent, developed in many African Christian congregations whose missionaries had been removed. This expressed itself in sustained concern about their welfare, eagerness for news of them and countless prayer meetings organized on their behalf.

Reports of heavy loss of life at sea resulting from torpedo-boat activity visibly affected those constantly living under the prospect of forcible transportation to prisoner-of-war camps in Europe. Unsparing war propaganda, considerable loss of nerve on the part of many Europeans finding themselves in enemy hands, the conduct of some of the military on both sides, and the combination of other circumstances during this time of stress left little substance in claims of superiority of race or of a mission to redeem benighted blacks.

The experience of the war, the return home from distant lands of thousands of African troops, economic unrest in some areas and other adverse consequences of the war, affected African thinking. On the positive side, the Africans' mental horizons broadened. Vastly improved means of communication gave a great impetus to the spread of new ideas all over the continent, particularly in the towns, but also to some extent in the rural areas. Broadly speaking, in the British colonies, the then still quite thin layer of highly educated and even of more modestly educated Africans was affected by nationalist stirrings in India and by Pan-Africanist aspirations emanating from persons of African descent in the United States of America and the West Indies. In the French possessions strong socialist and anti-imperialist propaganda conducted through readable and widely-distributed communist tracts and pamphlets was quietly making its impact. Africans now hoped for a better life than in the past. Political agitation became the means by which the right to higher living standards, wickedly denied to Africans for so long, could be wrenched from the ruling powers.

Reports of the period frequently treat, from various angles, the general theme of changes in 'native' feeling. A typical one cites the following features:

the growth of racial consciousness; the weakening of white supremacy; the breaking down of old customs and restraints through the impact of western culture, especially in its influence upon women and home life; the spread of an industrialism which reproduced, in more aggravated form and without essential safeguards, conditions which are imperilling society in the West; the rapid increase of education, too often on lines offering inadequate preparation for those who are being swept into the uncharted currents of modern life; and, beyond all else, the development of the spirit of nationalism and self-consciousness.[1]

[1] *International Review of Missions*, 1924, **13**, p. 390.

A South African view characteristically presents the picture as follows:

[W]hile the Natives 'have for generations remained quiet, docile, even supine in their trust in the essential goodness of Englishmen, now a remarkable change has come over things...The black man, under the guidance of an ambitious younger generation, has developed intelligence and some feeling of independence that has made him less easy of management.[1]

A more perceptive assessment and forecast for the future is made by Georges Hardy in his appraisal of the speeches delivered at the Pan-African Congress held at Brussels in 1924, at which Africans voiced their aspirations for their continent. He urged that such a gathering should not be regarded as

an exceptional manifestation due to a few denationalized Africans or to external influences: the desire to be admitted into the human family without reserves or compromises, without outbursts of indignation or smiles of derision, will to-morrow fill the heart of the whole of Africa.[2]

In missionary circles widespread and serious heart-searching arose regarding the place, role and objectives of their enterprise within the colonial set-up as a whole. Before the war, the purely secular and gain-motivated aspects of imperialism had as a rule been largely ignored or played down by them. The great majority of missionaries had given full and uncritical credence to the officially declared metropolitan claims of altruistic, humanitarian and idealistic intentions in acquiring and holding colonies. In their contacts with Africans, missionaries had usually sought to bridge the gulf between the administration and the people. They had encouraged Africans to welcome the benefits of European rule, to co-operate with it and to give it full and glad obedience. The revelations attendant on the war and critical voices beginning to make themselves heard soon thereafter, seemed to be casting some doubt not only on their idealism but even on their good faith.

Many missionaries had displayed a narrowly nationalistic spirit, both in their personal attitudes and in the conduct of their work. At the outbreak of war, some of them were immediately called up, or volunteered, to fight with the troops of their respective nations. When it became necessary for the work of one mission to be taken over by

---

[1] H. D. Hooper, *Africa in the making*, pp. 38–9, quoted in *International Review of Missions*, 1924, **13**, 488.

[2] Georges Hardy, *Vue générale de l'histoire d'Afrique*, p. 173, quoted in *International Review of Missions*, 1924, **13**, 488.

another mission of a different nationality in order to preserve the work, great resentment was shown by the retreating mission; and strident protests could be heard that *our* parishes, *our* schools, *our* natives were being taken away. Such attitudes stood in strange contrast to St Paul's satisfaction that Apollos should water what he Paul had planted, since God alone gave the increase. They also accorded ill with the behaviour that should be expected of the professional representatives of Christ's universal rule of peace.

The spirit of divisiveness and competition among missionary agencies and personnel could not fail to raise serious doubts as to whether this enterprise was truly the supranational endeavour for the Kingdom of God that it claimed to be, or merely an arm of imperialism, or knowingly and intentionally a combination of both. Incidentally, after the war, the makers of peace expressed their view of this matter in the interesting decision to regard the property of the missionary agencies as supranational, to be held in trust for educational, religious, cultural and welfare purposes among the Africans of the areas in which the investment had been made. The belongings of the individual agents, on the other hand, were treated as the personal goods of ordinary nationals of their respective countries.

However, the spiritual resources of the Bible, as well as the quite remarkable support shown to them through the loyalty, steadfastness and the generous, often sacrificial gifts by friends of foreign missions at their home bases in practically all the countries concerned, soon enabled missionary societies to rally round with purified purpose and renewed strength for their adopted task. The International Missionary Council, which, under the genial and statesmanlike leadership of its General Secretary Dr J. H. Oldham, had done so much during the war to prevent or halt disruption and to uphold 'orphaned missions', became the focus of greatly increased interdenominational understanding, mutual consultation and international co-operation in mission. The spirit emerging soon after this period of 'disappointments and heart-breaking fears' is well expressed in the following statement by Edward Shillito, one of the mission secretaries:

The war itself comes as a challenge to the disciples of the Kingdom to call into being, by the mercy of God, a work which might never have been but for this tragedy. As all came into the war so into the sweep of the Kingdom also all must be brought.[1]

---

[1] *International Review of Missions*, 1919, **8**, 443.

Thus as early as the 1920s many missions were already getting back on their feet, though in a chastened mood. Gradually some of the missionaries who had been removed from their fields of activity were permitted to return. But their new assignments usually implied less direct control of Africans than had previously been the case. There appeared to be general acceptance of the principle of speedy devolution of authority and leadership responsibility from expatriate to indigenous mission personnel. It had become abundantly evident that continuity and progress in the missionary work which had been started could only be obtained, let alone maintained, if indigenous Africans made the work their own. While some missionaries who had been in the field before the war experienced a certain amount of difficulty in adjusting to the new climate of thought and mode of relationships, the majority of them, and particularly the newly-appointed staffs, willingly co-operated in implementing the new policies. They believed this evolution to be the will of God, and considered it a privilege to have some share in developing more genuinely indigenous African churches than in the past.

Roman Catholic missions, which, owing to the international structure of that church, with its firm central authority, had suffered less disruption and distress than the Protestant ones, were able at the end of the war to report significant advances. The numbers of their African adherents had risen by leaps and bounds. The general trend of missionary strategic thinking of the period, both Catholic and Protestant, is well reflected in Pope Benedict XV's Apostolic Letter 'Maximus illus' of 30 November 1919, which urged all missionary bishops to forward the movement for the building up of a native clergy

by starting seminaries and to train Natives who show signs of a vocation to the priesthood. And this not only to assist the foreign missionaries in humbler offices, but in order that it [i.e., the native clergy] may be equal to the accomplishment of its divine task, and in course of time duly assume the government of its own people. For since the Church of God is Catholic and cannot be a stranger in any nation or tribe, it is proper that out of every people should be drawn sacred ministers to be teachers of the Divine Law and leaders in the way of salvation for their own country to follow.

Obviously these ideas had vital implications going far beyond the confines of ecclesiastical needs and planning. The long-disputed question whether Africans were to be considered as permanently under European tutelage (in its mildest expression, in the elder brother–younger brother relationship) or whether Africans were to take full charge of their own affairs and destiny on a basis of equality with other sovereign peoples, generally came to be decided in favour of the latter view. The former interpretation was rendered antiquated or unprogressive. This conclusion implied that Africans had to be prepared for their role through the process of education, and the period immediately following the war accordingly saw peak activity in educational effort by missionary and humanitarian agencies.

The vastness of the educational task was an important element in bringing various missionary bodies together for mutual consultation and for working out common educational policies. As far back as in 1918 an inter-mission committee was formed in the Congo to co-ordinate school curricula, to plan strategy and policy and to consult with government on educational matters. A further step in the same direction was taken when, a few years later, the Congo Protestant Missionary Conference was established, with a permanent secretary and a central office at Kinshasa, as well as a Union Mission Transit and Rest House in that city for the common use of six societies. In East Africa this movement toward greater co-operation even led to thoughts of unifying all the Christian agencies and their adherents in those parts into one united Church of Christ. The formation of national Christian Councils for interdenominational consultation and co-operation (discussion of matters of doctrine being strictly barred) was launched for the most part in this period of the middle 1920s.

When in 1926 the International Missionary Council held a meeting at Le Zoute, Belgium, the question of African education loomed very large in the discussions.[1] The policy of closer co-operation with governments, and of concentrating especially on village, intermediate and secondary schools and on the training of teachers, was particularly stressed. In several areas, in fact, these policies were immediately put into practice. In the matter of financial support, the Commonwealth Trust seemed to promise substantial assistance for the schemes envisaged. This was a business organization that had been set up by the colonial governments to carry on the missionary commercial enterprises sequestrated during the war on the understanding that part of the profits would be made available for educational, religious and welfare pur-

[1] For a general account see, for instance, Edwin William Smith, *The Christian mission in Africa: a study based on the work of the international conference at Le Zoute, Belgium, September 14th to 21st 1926* (New York, 1926).

428

poses in the relevant lands. However, in the event, the high hopes failed, for the most part, to materialize.

In 1920 the major foreign mission boards of the United States and Britain, after consultation with some boards on the continent of Europe, appointed a commission under the chairmanship of Dr Thomas Jesse Jones to 'make a survey of educational conditions and opportunities' in African countries. The trustees of the Phelps–Stokes Fund generously provided all the money needed for this purpose. Dr J. E. Kwegyir Aggrey, the distinguished American-trained educationalist and public speaker from the Gold Coast, was a member of this commission, as was also, for part of the time, Dr A. W. Wilkie, a Scottish missionary of rich African experience. The commission travelled in West and South Africa in 1920–1, and another commission continued this work in East and South Africa in 1924.[1]

The first report, entitled 'Education in Africa', was considered to be a document of the highest value in the subject, and did much to confirm the rightness of the policy of advancing African education as well as generally strengthening this cause. It 'crystallized conceptions of education which had long lain in solution in many minds, missionary and official' and 'laid great emphasis on character-training as the true objective of education'. Outlining the type of education which should be considered as best adapted to meet the real needs of the inhabitants of the African colonies at the stage then reached in their development, it insisted that the primary end of education should be 'the development of teachers and leaders of the masses', and that 'the education of the masses themselves' should be the second great responsibility.

These studies were very fittingly supplemented on the government side by the publication in 1925 of an official statement on government educational policy. 'Educational policy in British Tropical Africa' was the work of an Advisory Committee on Native Education in Africa appointed by the Secretary of State for the Colonies in 1923. This report also laid 'the strongest emphasis on character training' and recognized 'the importance of religion in the education of Africans'.

All this new thinking led to vigorous fresh thrusts in educational

---

[1] See Thomas Jesse Jones, ed., *Education in Africa: a study of West, South and Equatorial Africa by the Africa Education Commission under the auspices of the Phelps–Stokes Fund and Foreign Missions Societies of North America and Europe* (New York and London, 1921). See also Thomas Jesse Jones, ed., *Education in Africa: a study of East, Central and South Africa by the Second African Education Commission under the auspices of the Phelps–Stokes Fund, in cooperation with the International Education Board* (London, 1925).

experimentation in secondary schooling, usually conducted in boarding institutions, some of them co-educational. Older institutions such as King's College, Budo; Gordon College, Khartoum; and Fort Hare in South Africa (which was able to hold its first graduation of university students in 1924), also received a great new impetus. In the new establishments strenuous efforts were made to relate the training given to the demands of the African situation and the background of African life and culture. The best known of them are Makerere College in Uganda, the Alliance High School in Kenya and Achimota School in the Gold Coast.

The development of central secondary schools fully financed by government though conducted as Christian institutions was matched on the side of the missions and churches by a great effort to establish centres of similar calibre under church auspices, with the intention of building up a highly-educated future membership. With the aid of very generous government grants (always given on the condition that the schools would be equally open to children of non-members of the denomination in question), some of these schools (e.g., Mfantsipim, Adisadel, St Augustine's and Mawuli in Ghana) have practically attained parity with the government schools in size and in quality of staff, of buildings and of equipment as well as in academic attainments as shown by examinations.

However, the involvement of the missions and the churches in education has become a thorny problem in some parts of the continent. On the one hand, as in most countries elsewhere in the world, the state agencies wish to assume complete control of the entire educational system. The proponents of this solution argue that the provision of education is primarily a duty of the state and that it is wrong in principle (whatever the results of actual practice might be) to place large grants for education at the disposal of avowedly partisan religious organizations.

It must also be admitted that with the great expansion in the educational work of church bodies less and less time and attention can be given by them to their own primary evangelistic and pastoral task. According to an estimate made in Ghana, for example, up to three-quarters of a busy pastor's time is absorbed in the work of school management.[1] As a result, the churches' best resources are dissipated on this service; they are financially weakened, spiritually impoverished,

[1] S. G. Williamson, *Akan religion and the Christian faith* (Accra, Ghana Universities Press, 1965), pp. 40 f.

and consequently are rendered insufficiently vital and vigorous to be able to attract or to even hold their own educated younger generation.

Others believe, however, that education is a necessary part of a church, and even independent African churches have not rid themselves of this idea. Furthermore, so firmly established is the churches' prestige in the field of education that large sections of the communities still prefer 'mission education' for their children. Hence, moves for complete secularization of the schools have again and again been defeated. On the whole, it is in East Africa that resistance to state control has been least and that secularization has proceeded farthest and most smoothly.

To illustrate the aspirations of this period it may be noted that Achimota School in the Gold Coast was initially given sufficient staff not only to do its own work properly, but to carry on research— especially on projects concerned with the best means of relating Western knowledge and culture to the African past. Future advance to university status was clearly envisaged. Soon after the establishment of the school a revised constitution removed Achimota from direct government or Education Department control (though the government continued to pay practically all the cost) and placed it entirely in the charge of its own Council or Board of Governors. During the 1930s Yaba College near Lagos, Nigeria, and Buluwasi College in the foothills of Mt. Elgon in Uganda were added, providing similar facilities; and in March 1933 the College of West Africa in Monrovia, Liberia, moved into very attractive new buildings on the occasion of its centenary celebration. Soon afterwards a Booker Washington Institute was also started in Liberia to provide training for rural rehabilitation and advance. The products of these and other key schools established during this period have played very significant roles in the later social and political evolution of their lands.

Still more remarkable, though perhaps less spectacular, has been the great upsurge in the development of teacher-training. In East Africa the 'Jeanes'-type training centre at Kabete in Kenya conducted countless courses for various categories of students of both sexes and different areas of specialization (including tribal chiefs and local authority councillors), and spread out its influence into neighbouring Nyasaland and the Rhodesias, even reaching Portuguese East Africa in the missionary institution at Kambini. The value of these efforts was recognized by the Carnegie Corporation to the extent that it financed an inter-territorial conference on Jeanes methods to enable those involved in their use to exchange experiences and to learn improved techniques. Up to the present moment, in practically all parts of the continent, the clamour for ever more trained teachers and, by implication, for more training centres, continues unabated. Less formal schooling as, for example, in various aspects of domestic life, in midwifery and baby-care, in home crafts and small industries, proceeded at the same time, particularly in the rural areas.

Several centres were opened specifically for the training of women. Examples are the centres at Hope Fountain and Mbereshie in Northern Rhodesia for training women in first aid, midwifery, child nurture and domestic subjects, and the teacher-training colleges for women at Aro Chuku, Port Harcourt, Wusi and elsewhere in Nigeria.

In the territories held by France, educational policy aimed at making it possible for those Africans who fulfilled the necessary requirements (i.e., by attaining certain levels of acculturation and affluence) to become full citizens of France. At its best, the aim of this policy is said to be to regard those under French protection, whatever the colour of their skin or however backward their evolution, as human beings and as souls to be fashioned into a new humanity.[1]

In February 1922 the President of the French Republic issued a decree authorizing the use of Latin, French or any native language of the colonies in public worship. The law, however, also required authorization by the government for establishing any church or other building for public worship and forbade assembly for worship in any un-authorized place. Additional regulations by the Governor-General of French West Africa incorporated all private schools into the government system and forced them to conform to all its requirements.

Belgian policy envisaged an ordered and progressive lower-middle-class, artisan and proletariat African citizenry to undergird a permanent European hegemony.[2] Non-Belgian and non-Roman Catholic missions were viewed by the authorities with the greatest suspicion and had to perform their task under all sorts of restriction and difficulty. 'The ideals which are accepted by the more far-sighted leaders of Belgian opinion find expression in the concluding words of the Belgian Colonial Congress held in Brussels in December 1920: "Let us have faith

[1] *International Review of Missions*, 1923, **12**, 167.
[2] See, for instance, Crawford Young, *Politics in the Congo: decolonization and independence* (Princeton University Press, 1965), pp. 10–105.

and love; faith in the potential perfection of the black race; sincere and disinterested love for the disinherited races of the world. And all the rest will be added unto us".'[1]

As for the Portuguese territories, these have always been officially claimed as part and parcel of the metropolitan area situated overseas. 'Broadly the Portuguese ideal has been that carefully controlled education will in time create an African populace that speaks only Portuguese, embraces Catholicism, and is as intensely Portuguese nationalist as citizens of the metropole. If all Africans in these territories become Portuguese nationalists, *ipso facto* there is no threat of African nationalism. But only 30,089 Africans in Angola and 4,349 in Mozambique had reached the legally recognized state of complete assimilation into Portuguese culture by 1950.'[2] A law was promulgated prohibiting the use of the local languages in any written form and requiring practically impossible educational qualifications of ordinary African preachers. These regulations could be mitigated and permission received for limited extension of Protestant missionary work only after long and tedious negotiations, mainly held in Portugal, between the authorities on the one hand and, on the other, the International Missionary Council, the Missionary Association in Portuguese East Africa and the home boards of the various missions involved. The good offices of the liaison officer of the missions in Lisbon, Senhor Moreira, were of the greatest value to missions of other countries working, or preparing to work, in Portuguese Africa both East and West.

Considerable apprehension was aroused among non-Roman missions by the signing in May 1940 of a concordat between the Vatican and the Portuguese government establishing the Roman Catholic Church and its missions in a position of incomparable privilege over against all the others. Catholic churches were to be subsidized by the state 'in accordance with their needs', and were to receive 'grants of available land for extension and for new undertakings'; their properties would be 'free of all taxes and levies', their personnel would be 'entitled to travel expenses both within and outside the colonies', and 'sufficient stipends and a right to pension on retirement'. They would be 'free to expand

---

[1] *International Review of Missions*, 1924, **13**, 486.

[2] For a general account see, for instance, James Duffy, *Portugal in Africa* (Cambridge, Harvard University Press, 1962); and Helen A. Kitchen, ed., Ruth Sloan Associates, Washington D.C., *The educated African: a country-by-country survey of educational development in Africa* (New York, 1962).

without let or hindrance'. Up to the present time, the Portuguese territories are educationally the least developed in all Africa.[1]

A salient aspect of the general development of education has been the importance attached to the scientific study of African languages and cultures. In 1926, mainly upon missionary initiative, with warm support from several individual scholars in the field and a number of learned societies, an International Institute of African Languages and Cultures was established. The new body soon mounted a vigorous programme of work in linguistic, literary, ethnographical and sociocultural studies. A high-level quarterly, *Africa*, was launched early in 1928 to provide the necessary forum for these discussions 'concerned not only with educating the African but with educating the rest of the world about Africa'. Much scholarly work of great distinction and of the highest value has been done, placing Africa with honour on the map of world learning. On the other hand, such practical matters as the provision of necessary literary tools, the production and revision of bibles, grammars and dictionaries have not been neglected. Notable works in this connexion appearing during our period are the revised Swahili Bible, the *Dictionnaire kikongo-français* (Congo) and the revised Christaller's *Dictionary of the Asante and Fante language called Tshi* (Twi).

Every effort was made to induce Africans to write, and five prizes were awarded annually for books written in African languages. The International Committee on Christian Literature for Africa promoted the publication of books specially written for Africa in simplified and Basic English (the 'Books for Africa' series). Some of these books were translated into French and Portuguese. They included Bible study helps, literature on agriculture, hygiene and various rural and domestic subjects. Grants were made for placing copies in the libraries of several training centres. Missionary and church agencies co-operated vigorously in these efforts. In fact many of them led the way in campaigns for the elimination of illiteracy launched by some colonial governments, notably in the British territories, as part of comprehensive schemes of mass education in African society.

Lord Hailey, the well-known British authority on African affairs, has described the function of education in this continent as being 'to provide the African with better equipment for dealing with his own environment and to prepare him for the changes to which this environment will increasingly be subject'. Elsewhere in the same book he

---

[1] *International Review of Missions*, 1941, **30**, 72–3.

writes: 'In Africa education is, and is intended to be, an instrument of change'.[1] All the major Christian denominations participated in varying degrees in the educational revolution in Africa. A substantial contribution came also from Negro Christians in the United States, mainly through the African Methodist Episcopal and the African Methodist Episcopal Zion Churches, though their full story has yet to be written.

A high-water mark in the history of the growing recognition by colonial powers of their responsibilities towards the peoples under them was reached when, at the close of World War I, the trusteeship principle was worked out as the basis for the mandates system. The enunciation of these principles had the most far-reaching consequences in the entire situation of subject peoples. The peace settlement laid down that the well-being and development of the native inhabitants of the former German colonies then being entrusted, under mandate, to the victor nations, were to be regarded as constituting a 'sacred trust of civilisation'. Securities for the performance of this trust were embodied in the Covenant of the League of Nations. The mandates under which these territories were assigned to the government of various powers provided for the emancipation of all slaves, the suppression of the slave-trade, the prohibition of forced labour (except for essential public works) and the protection of the natives in respect of land, labour and the traffic in arms and spirituous liquors.

These directives promptly received general approbation and recognition as applicable not only with respect to mandated territories but equally to the whole colonial situation everywhere. The missionary and humanitarian agencies at work in Africa generally saw in them the vindication and triumph of the ideas which they themselves had always upheld. When, therefore, certain ordinances were promulgated in Kenya purporting to increase the supply of African labour to European estates, missionaries protested so vigorously that the matter had to be taken up for debate in both Houses of Parliament at Westminster. It was felt to be completely contrary to the principle of protecting Africans and safeguarding their interests that the state apparatus should be invoked to furnish supplies of cheap African labour to European farmers. Eventually a dispatch from the Secretary of State settling the issue stated clearly that it could be no part of the duty of government

---

[1] William Malcolm Hailey, 1st baron, *An African survey: a study of problems arising in Africa south of the Sahara* (London, Oxford University Press, 1938), p. 1207.

officers to assist in recruiting labour for private employers and that compulsory paid labour for public works should be used only when absolutely necessary for essential services, and then only with the previous sanction of the Secretary of State.[1]

Similarly in 1923, as a result of discussions regarding the status of Indians in Kenya, the British Cabinet made an official pronouncement in which the principle of trusteeship was reaffirmed in the most unmistakable and emphatic terms: 'Primarily, Kenya is an African territory, and His Majesty's Government think it necessary to record their considered opinion that the interests of the African natives must be paramount, and that if, and when, those interests and the interests of the immigrant races should conflict, the former should prevail.' This statement goes on to assert that in the administration of the colony His Majesty's Government regard themselves as exercising a trust on behalf of the African population, 'the object of which may be defined as the protection and advancement of the native races'.[2]

It appeared that constant vigilance was necessary to guard against any erosion of these principles. In 1927, therefore, the British government appointed a Commission to East Africa, among whose members was Dr. J. H. Oldham, the wise and energetic Secretary of the International Missionary Council who had usually been the spokesman for missionary interests with the British authorities. 'The terms of reference include the question of closer co-operation between the Central and East African Governments and, what is of great importance, the securing of the position of Africans in relation to future political developments.'[3] In an age of extreme cynicism regarding all protestations of humanitarian principle and high idealism it is important to remember that historically these values were not entirely without their effect on the actual development of affairs. Professor Roland Oliver writes: 'The fact that in a country which was suitable for European settlement economic development nevertheless took a form which encouraged Africans themselves to become producers rather than to be merely the humanely ordered labour supply for European enterprise, was very largely due to missionary representations in the political sphere.'[4]

[1] Great Britain, Command Paper No. Cmd 1509, quoted in *International Review of Missions*, 1924, **13**, 485.
[2] Great Britain, Command Paper No. Cmd 1922, quoted in *International Review of Missions*, 1924, **13**, 484.
[3] *International Review of Missions*, 1928, **17**, 58.
[4] *The missionary factor in East Africa*, 2nd ed. (London, 1967), p. 290.

From the earliest days missionary and other Christian agencies have been very active in combatting the social evils found in their environment. In their time such deeply-rooted and powerful major evils as human sacrifice, slavery, or the killing of twins could be effectively stopped, of course, only by the power of colonial governments. But missionaries and their followers made whatever contribution lay in their power by assisting the authorities. Some missions, as they were able, paid the ransom for men and women put up for sale or pawning, and trained them as free persons to become evangelists and teachers, or artisans in various trades. And in our own period the continuing major struggle against a social evil has been the battle against alcoholism, a great menace to the moral and physical life of all communities, including Christians, sapping their health and vitality, not to speak of their material resources.

In the 1920s Christian agencies sought strenuously but unavailingly to provide effective counter-attractions to the saloons for drinking native beer which had been installed by the municipal authorities in some South African cities and towns. The evil rather spread northward, and was copied in the Rhodesias. In the Congo during the 1930s and 1940s alcoholism became such a serious problem that many temperance workers considered their own efforts to be, at least for the time, even more important than evangelism itself. The first task undertaken by the Gold Coast Christian Council at its foundation in 1930 was to prepare an attack on the liquor traffic in that country. In Nigeria Christian agencies expressed great distress when they found that contrary to legislation providing for the ultimate total exclusion of alcohol by progressive annual diminution of alcoholic imports, the amount of liquor imported in 1940 had unexpectedly trebled since the previous year.

A number of deputations, some of them including very distinguished and influential persons, made representations on this issue for the British territories to successive Secretaries of State for the Colonies. But there was a vicious circle which it proved almost impossible to break. If imports were restricted or too heavily taxed, illicit local distillation promptly increased accordingly. Since the product, owing to the unscientific and usually most unhygienic methods employed, was particularly dangerous to consumers, it had to be suppressed. Apart from the sheer impracticability of doing this at all effectively, it could be charged by emerging nationalism that a local industry was being repressed in the interest of foreign (imperialist) traffickers in liquor. The position was not satisfactorily resolved before independence; and many people, particularly in West Africa, view with considerable disquiet the briskness of the liquor business in post-independence Africa.

The missions played a significant role, too, in the efforts to improve health and sanitation standards. Since health work in some form and on some scale has always been an almost inevitable aspect of humanitarian service in Africa, it is difficult, in a brief review, to make a useful summary of what has been done in this respect during our period. It must suffice to draw attention to the following isolated events and achievements as samples of this great ongoing labour of love. As in the field of education, governments have assumed an ever-increasing responsibility in this area also. But everywhere government is most appreciative of the contribution of voluntary agencies and desires them to be augmented. For even the combined efforts of all fail to cope satisfactorily with the tropical diseases rampant on the continent, both endemic and epidemic, which continue to sap vitality and take heavy tolls.

Sleeping-sickness is a case in point. In the French Cameroun during the 1930s, in an area in which 63 per cent of the entire population had fallen victim to this dreadful disease, the government established at Ayos, 100 miles east of Yaoundé, the capital, a centre for battling with the scourge. The US Presbyterian Mission, to strengthen this enterprise, stationed a specialist in the treatment of this sickness at Abong Mbang to work in close touch with the government doctors. Between the two centres a tremendous job was done to relieve the situation. In the matter of leprosy control in Nigeria, a committee representing British missionary societies, the British Empire Leprosy Relief Association and Toc H, was formed to challenge laymen for leprosy work on missionary salary terms. Out of around 200 Toc H volunteers, six men were recruited and given a nine-month course in elementary medicine and leprosy control work, their expenses being guaranteed by six voluntary sponsors. They travelled around the villages and acted as agents between the doctors and the people. In this connexion the collaborating missions were asked to sign agreements giving assurance that pressure would not be brought to bear upon Muslims to change their faith.

The opening of new hospitals, clinics and health centres proceeded apace, examples being Agogo Basel Mission Hospital in Ghana, St Timothy's Hospital at Cape Mount, Liberia, the new hospital at Pimu in the Congo, the New Native Hospital at Orlando, Johannesburg. The American Baptist training school for medical assistants at Sona Bata in the Congo graduated its first students in 1938. The Princess Christian Mission Hospital under the leadership of the indigenous Sierra Leone Church, in response to obvious need, opened a dispensary on the un-developed Bullom shore opposite Freetown.

A new form of social service in which humanitarian and voluntary agencies have again assumed a leading role is the welfare of refugees. Beginning with Abyssinians who had to flee the Italian onslaught on their country in 1939, countless victims of war, of political upheaval, of ideological intolerance, of tribal conflict and of other forms of strife and commotion have left their homes. So have other migrants who have gone abroad in search of jobs or because they lacked food. These emi-grants, usually without funds or friends, present an acute human problem. The immediate need is the provision of food, shelter and clothing; but then follows the long-range and exacting process of re-settling these people. Fortunately, on the Protestant side, church agencies have been prepared to tackle this new responsibility in the only way that holds any promise of making even a dent in the problem, i.e. co-operatively, through the World Council of Churches' Division of Inter-Church Aid, Refugee and World Service. A recent report by this organization contains the following statement:

In Africa, refugees continued to emerge from South Africa and the Portuguese territories. The need for relief and rehabilitation continued among many Sudanese, Rwandan/Burundi, Angolan, and other refugees from earlier years. The Lutheran World Federation continued to act as the World Council of Churches' agent for work among refugees in Tanzania, and undertook, during the year, a similar responsibility in Zambia. The plight of intellectual refugees and students, especially those from South Africa, was perhaps the most acute of all, although fortunately they were relatively few. They were given relief, educational, and vocational assistance in Ethiopia, Tanzania, Botswana, Zambia, Rhodesia, Lesotho, Swaziland, Kenya, and many other African countries. Funds received by the World Council of Churches for African refugees were channelled through the Ecumenical Programme for Emergency Action in Africa of the All Africa Conference of Churches. These funds, which amounted to $838,000 in 1967, were almost entirely directed to projects for refugees undertaken by national Councils of Churches and their members.[1]

---

[1] *From one to another*, DICARWS (Division of Inter-Church Aid, Refugee and World Service) Report, 1967 (Geneva, World Council of Churches), pp. 19–20.

Before and since general independence, African Christians in most of the countries have, in various ways, expressed their concern and sense of responsibility for public affairs. Vigorous presentations from the pulpit, the press and pamphleteering, public lectures and discussion groups have attacked such social evils as bribery and corruption, nepotism and graft, prostitution, vandalism, tribalism, laziness, drunkenness, absenteeism, untrustworthiness, as well as some of the shadier aspects of political activity. The bid for constructive participation in nation-building on Christian principles has tended on the whole, however, to be almost exclusively verbal and exhortatory, without matching positive action. It is possible, of course, that a more persistent effort might have been made and that Christians in leading positions in active politics might have responded more effectively. However, the battle continues.

It appears that on the African scene there is need for concerted and sustained Christian effort to hold in check some of the excesses usually attendant upon local political strife: victimization of the weak or defeated, intolerance and intimidation, chicanery, a vicious vindictiveness, and similar malpractices. It is also necessary to restrain the tendency towards centralization of political power if democracy, as normally understood in the West, is to be achieved here along with stable, orderly and peaceful national development and social progress.

A subject of perennial interest throughout the period under review was the question of the effect of Christianity upon African culture. Although the mission had proved successful, on the whole, in gathering large numbers of converts wherever it went on the continent, there was much room for dissatisfaction and disquiet. If it had been expected that as a result of this success Christianity would immediately proceed to take the place of indigenous pagan religion in the common life of African peoples, this expectation was not realized. While the converts to Christianity had adopted a Christian confession and Christian rites and practices, their strongly animistic African world-view, with its own native understanding of the structure and functioning of the universe and of human life, remained unshaken. Since in the same communities the practice of pagan religion, far from having been dislodged, has persisted in full vigour side by side with the new faith, there has been constant temptation for the neophytes, particularly in times of stress, to lapse into the more familiar and more congenial thought-forms and religious habits of paganism. In making a plea for more study and a better understanding of the African world, Dr K. A. Busia has fittingly characterized the situation:

For the conversion to the Christian faith to be more than superficial, the Christian Church must come to grips with traditional beliefs and practices, and with the world view that these beliefs and practices imply... [T]he new convert is poised between two worlds: the old traditions and customs of his culture which he is striving to leave behind, and the new beliefs and practices to which he is still a stranger. The Church would help him better, if she understood the former, while she spoke with authority about the latter.[1]

In Ghana, at a Synod of the Presbyterian Church held in 1941, the Honourable Nana Sir Ofori Atta I, Paramount Chief of the Akim Abuakwa State and one of the leading natural rulers of the country, presented a memorandum setting forth his grievances regarding the effects of missionary activities on the life of his people. He stated that he was speaking not only for himself but for all other indigenous rulers as well:

The memorandum condemned the missionary policy which had segregated Christians into a separate community in each town, and complained that converts had not only failed in their responsibilities to the State but had also been led, if not taught, to look down with disgust and contempt on certain aspects of traditional life. The Christian stood aloof from the State festivals such as the Odwira and Adae, and even failed to attend public demonstrations and assemblies whose primary purpose was to show loyalty to the chief and the State. State functionaries, such as drummers, sandal-bearers and linguists, on becoming converts of the Church, all too often abandoned their duties. In other directions, there was complaint that the Mission used education for denomination purposes, and in connexion with marriage the charge that the Church prohibited Christian women from marrying heathen husbands, and was opposed to Native Customary Law marriage. The general impression clearly left upon the chief and the state-elders in Akim-Abuakwa was that in policy and attitude the missionaries had proved antagonistic towards African ways and had not only condemned everything but had also been anxious to substitute for it what was European.[2]

In May 1955, again in Ghana, the Christian Council called a conference on 'Christianity and African Culture'[3] which examined this subject from most of the relevant angles. The topic that aroused

[1] K. A. Busia, *Christianity and African culture* (Accra, n.d.), p. 1.
[2] Williamson, *Akan religion*, pp. 152–3.
[3] A report under this title was published by the Council.

greatest controversy was whether or not the missionary had been right in condemning out of hand and declaring as nonexistent the spirit world of African paganism; whether this rejection was a requirement of Christian faith or of Western science, and whether it was not the reason for the hypocrisy whereby African Christians professed their faith and yet returned to pagan worship in times of real trouble.

The discussion tended to suggest that, since even some Africans who had very successfully undertaken higher academic studies abroad, not to speak of the rank and file of Christians, appeared to continue to interpret their world in terms of 'spirit-powers', the line of wisdom would be for Christian teaching frankly to accept the indigenous African beliefs in this matter. But Christians should proclaim Christ's power to save in the total environment of gods and charms, witches and magic. It may be pointed out, however, that if some of those who had been conditioned to the spirit-world before being exposed to scientific training, did not at a later stage in their lives experience any basic change in world-view, this is not to say that the same is true of those who were never really so conditioned. To anyone having contacts with the recent products of secondary schools in a country like Ghana, it must be quite obvious that beliefs and attitudes in this regard are in transition. Some people apparently are unable to rid themselves of the old views. Others, on the other hand, are greatly puzzled by them and highly sceptical of them.

Whilst the debunking of fetish-priestcraft and spirits is, of course, not the Gospel and may not be the missionary's business, and whilst Christianity can thrive as well in a sacral as in a desacralized environment, the church would place itself in a false position by supporting through its teaching what will most probably prove to be the less tenable viewpoint.

The cleavage between the African world and that introduced by the missionaries has also made itself felt in other ways. For example, missionary educationists could not help observing that what they were trying to build up was hardly at all related to anything in the heritage of their pupils; the new teaching was therefore only superficially learnt and ill-digested. Missionaries thus sought in various ways to give their message some sort of roots in the African past. On the basis of newly available ethnographic studies, some interesting experiments were developed to this end. In Tanganyika, for example, a government officer conceived a plan for starting school-training with the traditional education of the local tribe and then introducing the European skills and learning necessary to fit the pupils for modern life. In the same country the Bishop of Masasi likewise tried out, for several years, Christian initiation schools on the native pattern for both boys and girls. In these institutions the teaching normally imparted by the tribe at this stage, suitably adapted, was imparted to the pupils, with new materials added on Christian ideas of the duties and responsibilities of manhood, womanhood and citizenship. A German missionary to East Africa, Dr Bruno Gutmann, wrote penetrating studies of the Chagga people, advocating as little interference as possible with their aboriginal views and institutions.

However, because the African response was generally lukewarm and sometimes quite negative or even definitely hostile, these efforts did not meet with the success they probably deserved. In view of the events and developments within the political and economic fields, it is doubtless understandable that Africans should view with suspicion any trends towards turning them away from modern advance and guiding them backwards to their own past. Thus these reindigenization movements came to be interpreted as efforts on the part of Europeans to achieve even more complete control of Africans and of their affairs. However, in contexts where government social policies and the opportunities actually open to Africans in public life prevented Africans from entertaining such suspicions—for example, at Achimota in Ghana—similar endeavours to restore features of the African past in the revival of names, dress, the use and cultivation of languages, arts and crafts, were enthusiastically welcomed and eagerly adopted.

The most acute controversy in which church and mission agencies clashed with the people over African customary cultural practices centred on the issue of female circumcision in Kenya. The African membership of the Scottish Mission churches had earlier agreed that the practice should be abolished, and the Mission had made a rule forbidding their African agents to permit it to be done in their families on pain of dismissal. In 1929, however, the Kikuyu Central Association, a new political party formed by nationalist young Kikuyu, extremely suspicious of government, on the whole anti-white (some of them also anti-Christian), raised strong opposition to the prevailing attempts to eliminate female circumcision. These efforts were interpreted as aiming further to de-nationalize Kenyans and to obliterate their heritage, thus making them yet more subject and subservient to

Europeans and acquiescent in their rule. To discredit female circumcision in any way was asserted to be tantamount to gross disloyalty to one's own people and betrayal of one's own ancestors.[1]

Large numbers of Christians thereupon refused to renew their pledge to ban the custom and were suspended from church membership. The Scottish Mission forbade its agents to join the Kikuyu Central Association or to have any dealings with it. But many parents reacted by removing their daughters from the church schools and would not send them back even when the Mission, in some tactical retreat, promised that there would be no more official teaching on the issue during school hours. In a matter of months the number of church members fell ominously. The struggle came to a head when in 1930 a court case taken up on behalf of a girl who had been forcibly subjected to the operation revealed that no legislation in fact existed to protect those who might not wish to submit to it. Of course the state of affairs reached at that stage was such that anyone trying to introduce some such law would have been setting fire to a stack of dry hay.

Many schools, especially those for girls, had to be closed; and even by the end of 1931, when the storm appeared to have blown over, the congregations were still very far from recovering their lost membership, the figures remaining far below those for 1928. Apart from the Scottish Mission, the Africa Inland Mission and the Gospel Mission Society also suffered a significant loss of members. The murder of a lady missionary of the Africa Inland Mission was generally believed to have been perpetrated in this connexion. However, some areas remained unaffected by the conflict, as for example that of the Church Missionary Society (CMS) work among the Kavirondo people.

Another bout with resurgent African paganism in new dress was experienced in the Congo during the middle 1930s in the revival of secret society rites by a politico-religious society called the Kitawala. Eight of their men had to be executed for murders which they had committed under the guise of 'leopard men'. This took place precisely during a period in which the Baptist Mission churches in and around Bolobo were rejoicing over a high-water mark in religious revival, with many and widespread signs of genuine Christian fervour and evangelistic zeal. Possibly the murders were a reaction to this success and an effort at suppressing it through intimidation.

[1] For an analysis see, for instance, Jomo Kenyatta, *Facing Mount Kenya: the tribal life of the Gikuyu* (London, 1953).

The most phenomenal happening within the purview of voluntary agencies in Africa (perhaps the most remarkable in the history of the expansion of Christianity altogether) is the development of African independent churches, religious movements of renewal, protest and dissidence. This began some eighty years ago, and has since spread widely throughout the whole sub-Saharan area. A recent study puts the number of such movements at around 6,000. They are to be found among 250 distinct tribes in more than 33 countries, and altogether involve something like seven or eight million members. The types of religious expression displayed, the often quite startling cults, rites and ceremonies observed, the religious habits practised, the uniforms, vestments and insignia in use, almost comprise the entire range of such phenomena and certainly beggar all general description or classification.

Already a considerable literature is in existence on the subject, consisting of more than 1,500 printed books, articles and other presentations in at least twenty different languages. The intense interest aroused by the manifestations of the movement and its constantly shifting features make it reasonable to predict that many more publications will appear to shed light on this subject.

Since the movements first achieved widespread notice within the context of African reaction to apartheid in South Africa and to white-settler minority rule in Kenya, as well as during the economic crises of the Congo, they were naturally interpreted as having arisen from and being primarily related to politico-economic facts and factors. A notable book on them carries the title: *The religious movements of oppressed peoples.* Indeed these political concerns have played a role; witness the regular religious services held to implore God to throw all the whites into the sea, or to drive out the missionaries and hand over the power in the churches to the black leaders. Also quite a common interpretation envisages 'the gifts of salvation' as a new order in which black people will dispose of ever more wealth and independence. In the Congo the Trinitarian formula was replaced by: 'in the name of the Father of Andre Matswa and of Simon Kimbangu'.[1]

However, that is only one aspect of the matter. For example, Nigeria had a liberal colonial régime, a stable and adequate economy and no white settlers, and yet separatism was first reported there (it may

[1] See, for instance, Efraim Andersson, *Messianic popular movements in the Lower Congo* (Uppsala, 1958); and Jules Chomé, *La passion de Simon Kimbangu, 1921–1951* (Brussels, 1959), which are part of the extensive literature on the subject.

even have been initiated there) as long ago as 1888. The political influence of the independent churches has in fact been much smaller than
might have been expected.

Other significant reasons for the rise and spread of the independent
churches include the breakdown of the old African tribal structure with
the sense of personal security and of belonging which it had given its
members; the dwindling or complete disappearance of the former
authority of the tribal chiefs who had been vital and effective centres of
cohesion. Secessions have occurred in order to create an ethnic church
in response to popular demand, or to honour and cultivate some practice from the African heritage, or again in reaction against white
racialism. The knowledge of European ecclesiastical secession also
offered a stimulus, occasion for which was taken when missionaries
became over-strict in disciplining their converts.

A strong correlation has been shown to exist between the translation
of the Bible into the relevant vernaculars and the rise of independency.
Freedom to secede came with the discovery that Christianity, as actually
presented, failed at many points to accord with the scriptures and that,
for example, in the matter of polygamy missionary policy had over-
stepped biblical authority. There were also personal factors: a religious
experience, a sense of special mission, or a theological concern on the
part of a founder, or less lofty motivations, such as his desire to increase
his personal status and power by administering church property and
monies as well as other reasons.

Two broad streams may be discerned. Dr (now Bishop) Sundkler,
who wrote the earliest notable work on these movements,[1] used the
term 'Ethiopian' to signify those whose main emphasis was independence of white rule or supervision, in church as in state. Their motto
may be said to be their constantly quoted favourite scriptural text in
Psalm 68, verse 31: 'Ethiopia shall soon stretch out her hands unto God'.

The other trend was termed 'Zionistic' by Sundkler, because most
groups representing it originated from the Holy Catholic Apostolic
Church in Zion, Illinois, United States of America. A consultation
under World Council of Churches auspices held at Kitwe in Zambia
a few years ago added the designation 'Aladura' (a Nigerian word sig-
nifying 'Prayer people') to the terminology. The emphasis of the
Zionist–Aladura line, which is laid on the Holy Spirit and possession of
the worshippers by Him, results in extreme religious fervour with

[1] Bengt Gustaf Malcolm Sundkler, *Bantu prophets in South Africa* (London, 1948).

446

appropriate bodily movements, on exorcisms, dreams and visions and their interpretation, fastings and, above all, prayers for healing. Both emphases may sometimes display messianic tendencies.

The independent churches display all degrees of viability. Some of them have become vast and wealthy institutions, highly organized and efficiently run, and seem set to continue to prosper, whilst others are anaemic or on the point of extinction. In recent years the older churches, after a long period of showing complete rejection of the independent ones, are beginning to take a positive interest in them and, through joint efforts, are attempting to assist them at the point where generally they are obviously most deficient, namely, in the matter of some theological education for their agents.

Undaunted by errors committed, major as well as minor, by failures, disappointments and unfavourable criticisms of all kinds, the church and missionary agencies in Africa have continued their humanitarian ministrations throughout the period under review without pause, without flinching or floundering. Ever new and more imaginative responses have been found or are continually being sought in every way to meet the actual challenges of the changing situation. All the resources of skilled and devoted personnel, of money and material goods which could be made available, have been and are being harnessed for the relief of the real needs of the people, spiritual, intellectual, moral and physical.

For a more effective deployment of these resources many projects are now being carried out by a number of churches and missions working together on the principles of what is called 'Joint Action for Mission'. For example, new-look evangelism is not conducted by a lone preacher crying in the wilderness, but by teams of a few persons, each trained in several of the practical skills relevant to rural or urban life as the case may be, as well as in preaching the Gospel. And, as in the present Cameroons project, they may come from different churches, countries, races. Hence the new-style evangelists can communicate their message both by word and by the actual assistance or knowledgeable understanding that they can bring to their hearers.

Almost everywhere African leadership is in control and shoulders as much responsibility as can be carried. Missions have generally been integrated with the African churches, and foreign help now comes on the basis of fraternal assistance from sister churches or fellow-Christians abroad.

The question is often asked what the future prospects of the Christian presence in African might be, given the present and emerging conditions. To this writer the answer is quite simple. Masters good or bad can always be thrown out, and a lot of unceremonious and un-regretted dismissal of bosses has happened recently and continues to happen in Africa. No one ever throws a good servant out. Jesus said, 'I am among you as one who serves'. It appears to me that so long as those who come in His name (be they local churchmen or foreign fraternal workers) remain true to His servant role, they may be sure of rich opportunity to exercise their ministry.

BIBLIOGRAPHY

Andersson, Efraim. *Messianic popular movements in the Lower Congo*. Uppsala, 1958.

Baëta, C. G. *Prophetism in Ghana: a study of some 'spiritual' churches*. London, 1962.

Barrett, D. R. *Schism and renewal in Africa*. Nairobi, Oxford University Press, 1968.

Buell, Raymond Leslie. *The native problem in Africa*. 2 vols. New York, 1928.

Chomé, Jules. *La passion de Simon Kimbangu, 1921–1951*. Brussels, 1959.

Duffy, James Edward. *Portugal in Africa*. Cambridge, Harvard University Press, 1962.

Du Plessis, Johannes. *A history of Christian missions in South Africa*. London, 1911.

  The evangelisation of pagan Africa: a history of Christian missions to the pagan tribes of Central Africa. Cape Town, 1930.

Great Britain. Papers issued by command. Cmd 1509. *Kenya Colony. Despatch to the Officer administering the government of the Kenya Colony and Protectorate relating to native labour*. 1921.

  Papers issued by command. Cmd 1922. *Kenya Memorandum on Indians in Kenya*. 1923.

Groves, Charles Pelham. *The planting of Christianity in Africa*. 4 vols. London, 1948–58.

Hailey, William Malcolm Hailey, 1st baron. *An African survey: a study of the problems arising in Africa south of the Sahara*. London, Oxford University Press, 1938. Rev. and enl. ed. London, Oxford University Press, 1957.

Jones, Thomas Jesse, ed. *Education in Africa: a study of West, South and Equatorial Africa by the African Education Commission under the auspices of the Phelps–Stokes Fund and Foreign Missions Societies of North America and Europe*. New York and London, 1921.

ed. *Education in Africa: a study of East, Central and South Africa by the Second African Education Commission under the auspices of the Phelps–Stokes Fund, in cooperation with the International Education Board.* London, 1925.

Kenyatta, Jomo. *Facing Mount Kenya: the tribal life of the Gikuyu.* London, 1953.

Kitchen, Helen A., ed. Ruth Sloan Associates, Washington D.C. *The educated African: a country-by-country survey of educational development in Africa.* London, 1962.

Lugard, Frederick John Dealtry, 1st baron. *The dual mandate in British tropical Africa.* With a new introduction by Margery Perham. London, 1965.

Macmillan, William Miller. *Bantu, Boer and Briton: the making of the South African native problem.* Rev. and enl. ed. Oxford, 1963.

Mair, Lucy Philip. *Welfare in the British colonies.* London, 1944.

Oldham, Joseph Houldsworth, *Christianity and the race problem.* New York, 1924.

Oliver, Roland. *The missionary factor in East Africa.* London, 1967.

Perham, Dame Margery Freda. *Lugard.* 2 vols. London, 1956–60.

Schlatter, Wilhelm. *Die Geschichte der Basler Mission,* vol. IV. Hermann Witschi, ed. Basel, 1965.

Schlosser, Katesa. *Eingeborenenkirchen in Süd- und Südwest-afrika, ihre Geschichte und Sozialstruktur: Ergebnisse einer völkerkundlichen Studienreise.* Kiel, 1953.

Smith, Edwin William. *The blessed missionaries.* Cape Town, 1950.

The Christian mission in Africa, a study based on the work of the international conference at Le Zoute, Belgium, September 14th to 21st 1926. New York, 1926.

Sundkler, Bengt Gustaf Malcolm. *Bantu prophets in South Africa.* London, 1948.

The Christian ministry in Africa. London, 1960.

Weiler, Hans N. *Koloniale Erziehung und afrikanische Umwelt: zur erziehungspolitischen Diskussion in der britischen Kolonial-verwaltung seit 1920.* Freiburg im Breisgau, 1966.

Welbourn, Frederick Burkewood. *East African Christians.* London, Oxford University Press, 1965.

East African rebels: a study of some independent churches. London, 1961.

Williamson, Sydney George. *Akan religion and the Christian faith: a comparative study of the impact of two religions.* Accra, Ghana Universities Press, 1965.

Young, Crawford. *Politics in the Congo: decolonization and independence.* Princeton University Press, 1965.

CHAPTER 13

DECOLONIZATION IN AFRICA

by CRAWFORD YOUNG

The 1960s began with a spirit of optimism throughout Africa. The 'winds of change' seemed irresistible. The remaining bastions of alien or of minority rule on the continent appeared certain soon to be submerged by the relentless tide of African nationalism. But within a few years a very different mood was to settle over Africa. The liberation of the continent remains far from complete. The irrepressible self-confidence of Africa's leaders at the height of decolonization has often given way to doubts, divisions and insecurity. A depressing sequence of coups has eroded the conviction that the heroes of independence continue to enjoy popular support. The public at large in many African countries has received with apathy, or even with enthusiasm, the fall from power of many leaders belonging to the first generation of the independence struggle. Thus the era of decolonization proper may be considered closed, although the battle for southern Africa will continue.

We shall thus attempt to re-examine the drama of African independence in a mood somewhat different from the enthusiastic spirit the struggle had generated in Africa and elsewhere. These events still remain close to us, and this no doubt may distort our perspective. The relevant files have not yet begun to gather dust in the archives; decolonization has not yet been consigned to the domain of the orthodox historian. We shall explore here the end of empire over the vast African regions that formerly lay under British, French and Belgian sway. The case of the stragglers on the path to decolonization, Spain and Portugal, and of the 'white redoubts' in Rhodesia and South Africa will be left to others.

Decolonization in Africa was not wholly confined to the post-war period. But before 1945 the metropolitan powers had transferred their power in a different environment. South Africa achieved independence in 1910. The power transfer in this case, however, was negotiated essentially between the European leaders of the four states that joined to form the Union. Although Britain did make some efforts to preserve

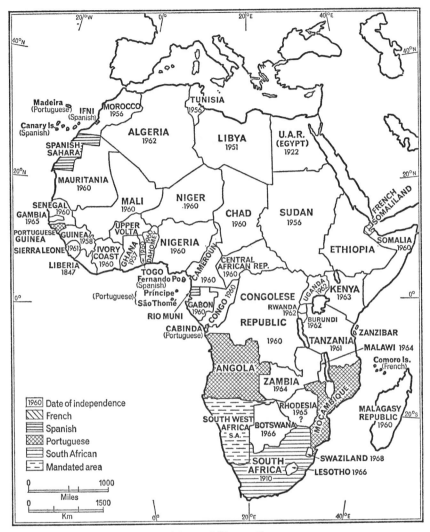

Map 8. Africa, 1968

a voice for the African majority, she did not insist, and was well satisfied with the solution. Egypt regained a restricted sovereignty in 1922. Characteristic of the times was the manner of 'power transfer': Britain simply unilaterally declared Egypt independent of the short-lived 'Protectorate' proclaimed in 1914 after three decades of British rule. There was none of the delicate engineering of constitutional arrangements that accompanied post-war power transfers. Also, Britain retained certain prerogatives and considered herself still empowered to intervene directly in internal affairs. It was not until 1936 that the 1922 declaration of independence was given negotiated substance, and then only under the pressure of fears of Italian expansion. Almost nobody, either in Britain or in Egypt, seriously proposed Egypt's entry into the Commonwealth. Egyptian nationalists would date full independence only from 1954, with agreement on the final withdrawal by 1956 of British troops from the Suez Canal Zone.

Without obtaining a complete transfer of sovereignty, Rhodesia almost joined this group when internal self-government was granted to its European settlers in 1923. But the circumstances and conditions that determined imperial policies in these instances are scarcely recognizable today, and we shall confine our discussion to post-World War II decolonization.

For the rest of Africa, excepting the isolated and weak independent states of Ethiopia and Liberia, colonial rule at the end of World War II seemed destined to continue for an indefinite period. Even Britain, though forced to contemplate early dominion status for India and Ceylon, anticipated no serious challenge in Africa for decades. Margery Perham recounts the remarks of a senior colonial official at a conference in 1939, expressing the comfortable conviction that 'at any rate, in Africa we can be sure that we have unlimited time in which to work'.[1]

The French vision of the future found forthright expression in the famous resolution of the 1944 Brazzaville Conference on the future of French overseas territories: 'The aims of the civilizing labours of France in the colonies exclude all possibilities of development outside the French imperial system; the eventual formation, even in the distant future of self-government in the colonies, must be excluded'. In the case of Belgium, the first mention of a terminal date for colonial rule appeared in a Leopoldville daily in 1946, with 1985 as a possible target. Nearly a decade later, when Professor A. A. J. Van Bilsen proposed a thirty-year plan for emancipation of the Congo, he was greeted with scorn and indignation. The immediate concerns of colonial policy-makers were effective formulas for administering subject populations. Only the claims of settler communities for political participation, primarily in Algeria, Tunisia, Morocco, Kenya and the Rhodesias,

[1] Margery Perham, *The colonial reckoning: the end of imperial rule in Africa in light of the British experience* (London, 1961), p. 114.

seemed to merit serious consideration. Early nationalism was seen in many guises, especially in West and North Africa; but it lacked the unity of purpose and organizational strength to exert significant leverage on the colonial powers.

World War II, however, brought profound changes to Africa. The primary colonial powers, the United Kingdom and France, were no longer dominant on the world scene. An entirely different international alignment resulted from the emergence of the United States and the Soviet Union as hostile superpowers, each the centre of global constellations. Earlier, international rivalries had occurred between colonial powers. Now both major contenders were, in differing degrees, hostile to the perpetuation of the colonial system.

Despite brief Soviet interest in inheriting the Italian colony of Libya as a trust territory, the Soviet Union maintained an intense and vocal opposition to colonialism in Africa. However, closer examination reveals some paradoxes and inconsistencies which in fact diluted the Soviet anti-colonial role until the middle 1950s. Stalin was resolutely hostile to 'national bourgeois' leadership, into which category virtually all African leaders fell. He felt the transfer of power to this group greatly weakened the prospects of communist parties. Also, the French Communist Party, through which links with former French Africa were channelled, was not committed to abolition of empire until the Algerian war was well under way. It was argued that once a proletarian régime had been established in France, the colonial problem would automatically disappear, simultaneous with the end of capitalist exploitation.

Similarly, when the United States first entered the world arena, most Americans were convinced that their country had been born of the first revolt against colonialism, and that America was therefore a natural ally of Afro-Asian anti-colonial nationalism. This analogy was misleading: the American Revolution had been the work of European settlers, not of Amerindians. But President Roosevelt was a fervent anti-colonialist. In 1943, for instance, he had told Moroccan Sultan Mohammed V in Casablanca, to the indignation of the French, that the Four Freedoms proclaimed in the Atlantic Charter applied to the colonies.[1] The legacy of sentimental anti-colonialism had a diminishing impact on American policy. The architects of global strategy became

[1] Roger Le Tourneau, *Evolution politique de l'Afrique du nord musulmane, 1920–1961* (Paris, 1962), p. 206; Jean Lacouture, *Cinq hommes et la France* (Paris, 1961), p. 192. Another sample of President Roosevelt's feelings on the merits of colonialism is the

converted to a new creed combining the old dicta of *Real-politik* with the new science of thermonuclear equilibrium. But anti-colonialism was an important factor in the immediate post-war period, and American policy continued to support cautious decolonization mainly for reasons of cold-war competition.

Not only had World War II diminished the world rank of colonial powers, but the humiliation of France and Belgium had undermined their military prestige. While the metropolitan powers were under enemy occupation, serious rifts had occurred in the colonial establishments in French and Belgian Africa. The struggle between Pétain and De Gaulle as rival claimants to the authority of the French Republic split the overseas French territories into bitter factions; Vichy elements initially predominated in North and West Africa, while the Gaullists launched their eventual seizure of power from Equatorial Africa. In the Congo, the colonial administration became virtually independent. Although Belgium's ablest colonial statesman, Pierre Ryckmans, provided a powerful element of stability as governor-general, the early aftermath of Belgium's swift conquest by Germany led to serious strains. Before fully committing the colony to the Allied cause, Ryckmans had to quell an abortive military coup; he also had to silence potent voices advocating 'neutrality' or even a pro-German stance, especially in church and business circles in Katanga.

World War II all but destroyed colonial rule in Asia with important repercussions in Africa. The Japanese occupation of south-east Asia created conditions where colonial authority could not be fully restored in Indonesia, Burma and Indo-China. The Labour government in Britain was committed to independence for the Indian subcontinent, and the American 1934 pledge to the Philippines was redeemed. Several significant conclusions derived from Asia's independence. First, nationalism appeared to be an irresistible force, which thrived on adversity and grew inexorably. The failure of the Dutch in Indonesia (1945-9) and of the French in Indo-China (1946-54) to suppress nationalist movements by arms lent force to the belief in the inevitability of nationalist triumph. Second, the emergence of an

following comment on French rule in Indo-China: 'France has had the country—thirty million inhabitants—for nearly one hundred years, and the people are worse off than they were in the beginning. France has milked it for one hundred years. The people of Indochina are entitled to something better than that.' Cordell Hull, *Memoirs* (New York, 1948), quoted in Ellen J. Hammer, *The struggle for Indochina* (Stanford University Press, 1954), pp. 42-3.

Asian and Arab group of nations vigorously asserting the rights of oppressed peoples and proclaiming the doctrine of neutralism, created an entirely new factor in international affairs. The new states exerted their influence not so much by traditional diplomacy as by playing on fears of the adversaries in the cold war that the 'Third World' might somehow yield to the solicitations of the other side. In the third place, African nationalist leaders obtained both sanctuaries and material support. Travel facilities, passports, new bases for propagating the cause of independence, all became available. During the 1950s Cairo played a particularly important role; Accra and Conakry likewise turned into havens for African nationalist movements when Ghana and Guinea gained their independence.

The makers of the post-war world also built new international forums where colonial nationalists could plead their case. Of these agencies, the United Nations was the most prominent. In addition, a vast array of non-governmental bodies developed after World War II. Within international movements of labour, youth, women, students and other groups, the cold war produced competing factions, some under communist control, others centring on the non-communist world. Organizations in Africa became the object of intensive solicitation by the competing internationals. Political competitors made their bids in terms of aggressive support for African independence; they offered travel opportunities for leaders, often associated with the nationalist movements, and material backing for the national organizations, which were frequently ancillaries of the nationalist party. Not only did these provide international tribunes; they provided also a means for getting help from member organizations of international bodies within the metropolitan countries.

All of these factors can be associated with the rise of a new, if rather ethereal, vector in international politics, 'world opinion'. Upon close scrutiny, of course, world opinion splinters into a hundred national fragments, each with its own rich diversity. But something referred to and understood as 'world opinion' gained a certain currency as a surrogate for reality; world opinion was perhaps at its most influential between the Bandung Conference in 1955 and the African independence year of 1960. The fabric of world opinion was woven of press declarations, conference resolutions, and similar demonstrations occurring in widely separated capitals, perhaps stimulated through the channels of one of the international organizations. It gained particular force whenever focused upon a single specific dramatic event—the Budapest uprising, the Suez invasion, the Lumumba assassination. The assumption that there was such a phenomenon as world opinion became a significant part of the policy calculus in the terminal colonial period. It was most dramatically present in Belgian forebodings in 1959; the concept of a hostile world opinion irresistible to a small country was a major element in the decision to seek the best terms available with the tumultuous, fragmented Congolese nationalist movement.

President Kennedy's campaign pledge in 1960 to refurbish America's image in Asia and Africa was an implicit tribute to world opinion. The effectiveness of this opinion as a sanction depended greatly, of course, on the general belief in its reality and significance. (It is no accident that the Afrikaners, the Portuguese and the white Rhodesians, militarily weaker than the major colonial powers, held onto power in Africa with the greatest tenacity—geographically situated, as they were, on the periphery of the Western world and least exposed to the intellectual currents generated by World War II and its aftermath.) World opinion as expressed in academic seminars and publications, radio and television broadcasts, leading articles in prestigious journals such as the three Timeses—the London *Times*, the *New York Times*, and the *Times of India*—was nevertheless an important factor during a crucial period of African history. During the scramble for Africa, Western opinion had generally regarded black rule on the 'Dark Continent' as somehow illegitimate by its very nature. Two generations later, it was white rule in Africa that carried the stigma of illegitimacy, and world opinion had a profound impact on this transvaluation in international ethics.

The United Nations as an agency for hastening decolonization deserves special examination. Even at its inception, in San Francisco in 1945, the United Nations had an anti-colonial hue that provoked deep forebodings in delegates representing colonial interests. Two members of the 'Big Five', Nationalist China and the Soviet Union, were bitterly opposed to colonialism. An anti-colonial Australian delegation proposed, to the general consternation of the imperial powers, that all dependent territories be placed under UN trusteeship. The American sense of an anti-colonial history had not yet been eroded by American commitment to global responsibility and Western solidarity. The UN Charter thus established a Trusteeship Council with more extensive powers of supervision and a composition less benevolent toward the colonial powers; the Charter also committed members in Article 73 to recognize that the interests of the inhabitants of these territories are paramount, to develop self-government, to take due account of the political aspirations of the peoples, and to assist them in the progressive development of their free political institutions.

This Trusteeship Council was very different from the earlier Permanent Mandates Commission of the League of Nations. The Permanent Mandates Commission was dominated by experts on colonial administration and sought to enforce minimum standards of imperial decency. Its powers were only advisory and were exercised with considerable discretion and reserve. The Trusteeship Council had representatives of the administering powers, permanent members of the Security Council and elected members, generally drawn from the Afro-Asian and Latin American states. Participants sat as representatives of governments. The Trusteeship Council thus included an important anti-colonial element, and increasingly interpreted its task as enforcing power transfer with all reasonable dispatch.

Oral petitioners representing nationalist organizations were permitted to testify before the Council and were thus able to make their claims widely known. UN Visiting Missions, especially from 1954 on, sharply criticized the sedate pace of political development charted by the trust powers; there was growing pressure for the establishment of firm deadlines for independence. Symbolic of the contrast between League and UN attitudes towards dependent territories, as well as of the generally transformed international environment, was the disposition of former 'enemy territories' in Africa. After World War I, German possessions had been parcelled out to the colonial powers, whereas after World War II, Italian territories were granted independence (Libya in 1951), awarded to an independent African state (Eritrea attached to Ethiopia), or returned to Italy with a firm ten-year deadline for preparation for self-government.

The impact of the trusteeship system was most clearly evidenced in the cases of the French trust territories of Togo and Cameroun. In both instances, the French found themselves locked into a time-table for political advance that was set by the neighbouring British-administered territories. The fact that the British portion of Togo, after absorption into Gold Coast via a UN-supervised referendum, was scheduled for independence in 1957, forced France in 1955 to grant a special status of autonomy for French-administered Togo. Although this statute fell short of the demands of more militant nationalists, it was considerably in advance of the rest of then French

Africa, and increased the pressures for political reform elsewhere. Similarly, in Cameroun, a time-table for full independence was partly forced on France by the announced plans for Nigerian independence, and the imminent prospect of a referendum in British Cameroons to choose between permanent integration into Nigeria, or reunification with Cameroun. The reunification option, which the French supported, was unlikely to have electoral appeal if the choice was between independence and a new form of colonial tutelage.

The General Assembly was still another significant battleground of decolonization. It was first utilized by the Arab group, beginning in 1951, in support of nationalist demands in Morocco and Tunisia. From 1956 on, the annual fall session of the General Assembly was the scene for furious diplomatic warfare between French and Algerian delegations. Even though General Assembly resolutions had no binding force, both sides initially attached great importance to the psychological impact. However, by 1960 the Algerians had probably reaped all the benefits that could be harvested from declaratory UN resolutions condemning France, while De Gaulle had made abundantly clear his profound contempt for 'le grand machin' and his indifference to its exhortations.

These radical changes in the international environment were accompanied and deeply influenced by the new African nationalist challenge to colonial rule. At the close of World War II, nationalism had still to formulate its goals, elaborate its tactics, and fashion its organizational weapon. The central task for nationalist leaders was to enlist the rural mass behind their banners. Before World War II, colonial administrators had tended to dismiss nationalist claims as pretentious and self-interested demands by 'detribalized Africans' who were 'cut off from their own people'. Characteristic was the candid address in 1920 of Sir Hugh Clifford, Governor of Nigeria, to the Nigerian Council:

There has during the last few months been a great deal of loose and gaseous talk...which has for the most part emanated from a self-selected and a self-appointed congregation of educated African gentlemen who collectively style themselves the 'West African National Conference'...It can only be described as farcical to suppose that...continental Nigeria can be represented by a handful of gentlemen drawn from a half-dozen Coast tribes—men born and bred in British administered towns situated on the sea-shore, who in the safety of British protection have peacefully pursued their studies under British teachers.[1]

[1] Quoted in James S. Coleman, *Nigeria: background to nationalism* (Berkeley and Los Angeles, University of California Press, 1958), p. 156.

Deriving from this view was the doctrine enunciated by Lord Lugard the same year: 'It is a cardinal principle of British Colonial policy that the interests of a large native population shall not be subject to the will...of a small minority of educated and Europeanized natives who have nothing in common with them, and whose interests are often opposed to theirs.'[1] In the post-war world these arguments, however, lost their force, as the new leaders visibly obtained wider popular support.

In addition, the tempo of social and economic change began to speed up. The enormous wartime demand for resources of all types continued through the Korean War period, and eventually resulted in unprecedented earnings for mineral and agricultural exports. The new prosperity gave new impetus to light and consumer industries. Modern communications expanded; the modern cash economy penetrated more deeply into the rural areas. Education, especially primary schooling, grew at a rapid pace. Sleepy pre-war towns became major urban conglomerations. A far more suitable social environment for political mobilization thus became available to post-war nationalists.

The first nationalist breakthrough came in the Gold Coast. Here the colonial administration was stunned first by the disorders in 1948 in Accra, and subsequently by the striking success of Nkrumah's Convention People's Party in the 1951 elections. Although there were important pockets of resistance to the new party, Governor Sir Charles Arden-Clarke had no alternative but to invite Nkrumah from prison to form the first responsible government in colonial Africa. The nationalist triumph in the Gold Coast had implications far beyond the modest dimensions of this relatively well-endowed colony. Metropolitan capitals tended to view African policy as a whole, or at least as a series of closely interrelated problems; concessions and reforms offered in one territory could not easily be refused to another. Also, nationalist leaders (excepting the Belgian territories) generally knew one another—especially those in French domains where service in the French National Assembly provided regular occasion for intimate contact. Tactics that proved serviceable in one country would be swiftly adopted in others.

The organizational weapon gradually perfected in the 1950s was the mass single party. In Nkrumah's words:

[1] Great Britain, *Parliamentary papers*, Vol. xxxvi, Cmd. 468, *Report by Sir F. D. Lugard on the amalgamation of Northern and Southern Nigeria, and administration, 1912–1919* (London, 1919), p. 19; quoted in Coleman's *Nigeria*, p. 156.

How is it possible, I asked myself, for a revolution to succeed without arms and ammunition? After months of studying Gandhi's policy and watching the effect it had, I began to see that, when backed by a strong political organization, it could be the solution to the colonial problem.[1]

The CPP thus developed as a model of nationalist organization that profoundly influenced the style of political movements throughout tropical Africa.

The mass party was particularly adapted to the kind of colonial reform that the British and French were prepared to offer. The party created the vital nexus between leadership and mass which generally allowed the new élite to supplant the chiefs, administrative or traditional, hitherto accepted by the administrations as the sole authorized spokesmen for the rural populations. The mass parties grew in size; they steadily enlarged the range of political participation as the franchise was extended from the town to the countryside. They pre-empted the independence platform; they gave expression to the multifold grievances of the colonized, and frequently embodied their aspirations in the militant personality of a charismatic leader. The mass parties thereby methodically laid their claims to succeed the administering powers. Even where the colonizer offered no constitutional channels for change, as in Morocco, Tunisia and Algeria, the weapon of the mass movement proved serviceable as an instrument of liberation.

Mass single parties did not emerge everywhere; indeed, those with an unchallengeable claim to this status during the terminal colonial period, or at least part of it, would probably be limited to Ghana Tunisia, Algeria, Guinea, Soudan (later Mali), Ivory Coast, Nyasaland (later Malawi) and Tanganyika. Senegal, Morocco, Zambia, and Kenya were marginal cases. But many other states, like Nigeria, Chad, Sierra Leone, Congo and Uganda, developed no organizations fully comparable to the CPP–PDG (Convention People's Party of Ghana and Parti Démocratique de Guinée) model. In these cases, the cumulative impact of nationalism was of particular importance. The independence of Ghana and Nigeria necessarily carried Sierra Leone and Gambia in its wake. Similarly, concessions won by Sékou Touré for Guinea or by Modibo Keita for Mali were inevitably extended to Mauritania and Chad. In the Congo, where mass movements were regional in scope, the pace of decolonization was set by the most militant, not by the tranquil and the docile.

[1] Kwame Nkrumah, *Ghana: the autobiography of Kwame Nkrumah* (New York and Edinburgh, 1957), pp. v–vi.

The self-confidence of nationalism grew with its success. When mass parties in 'pacesetter' states succeeded in capturing the people's imagination, leaders elsewhere shared vicariously in the exhilaration. No doubt, Congolese nationalism represented the apogee of this mood of sublime conviction in the capacity of nationalism not only to challenge and dislodge the colonizer but also to fulfil its own promises. Consider, for example, the 1960 campaign platform of the PSA (Parti Solidaire Africain, a regional mass party for Kwilu in the south-western Congo) for immediate implementation:[1]

1. Complete elimination of unemployment, and work for all;
2. Multiplication of schools, especially in rural areas; free primary and secondary education;
3. Wage increases for all;
4. Improvement of housing in rural areas;
5. Free medical care for all non-wage earners.

Fatuous as these pledges appear in retrospect, the extent of unreality at the time was matched only by the fervent conviction they carried both to leaders and led.

The saga of the Algerian revolution further helped to lend an aura of invincibility to the African independence movements. Algeria's Armée de Libération Nationale in a very real sense was fighting for all of Africa. The massive proportions of the struggle—involving at its peak nearly half a million French troops—made it appear a decisive test of the feasibility of suppressing nationalism by force. The other metropolitan powers uneasily eyed this spectacle, following upon the heels of the humiliation of Dien Bien Phu. Despite the fact that violent uprisings—spontaneous or organized—had been suppressed in Madagascar (1947), Kenya (1952–6), Cameroun (1955–8), Ivory Coast (1949–51) and Guinea (1954–6), the confrontation in Algeria was accepted by nationalists and most colonizers alike as the ultimate test. Although the French were by no means defeated—indeed, by 1962 they had militarily contained the nationalist forces—the crucial conclusion drawn from the encounter was the French failure to crush nationalist insurrection even with a massive commitment of resources.

Except for Tunisia and Morocco (and in an earlier day, Egypt),

[1] For this and other specimens, see the invaluable collection of PSA documents, edited by Herbert Weiss and Benoît Verhaegen, *Parti Solidaire Africain (P.S.A.): documents 1959–1960* (Brussels, Centre de Recherche et d'Information Socio-politiques, 1963). See also Weiss's *Political protest in the Congo: the Parti Solidaire Africain during the independence struggle* (Princeton University Press, 1967).

armed force played only a peripheral part in the nationalist campaigns elsewhere. But the implied threat of guerrilla insurgency as the ultimate sanction for a refusal to satisfy the central political demands of the new African leaders lurked in the background. Fear of colonial campaigns weighed specially on the Belgians; the nationalist challenge became acute for Belgium in 1959, at a time when the Algerian example served as a bloody reminder to all colonial powers. Not only had five years of costly and brutal warfare failed to bring victory, but it had in the process destroyed the Fourth Republic, and very nearly French democracy. Congolese nationalists were well aware of this issue, and made regular reference to it. Belgian unwillingness even to contemplate repressive action, once the nationalist genie had slipped out of the bottle, led ineluctably to swift acceptance of the maximum nationalist demand for 'immediate independence'.

Thus nationalism had swiftly grown in post-war Africa from the parlour doctrine of dispersed groups of intellectuals, treated with condescension by the metropolitan powers, to a movement whose ramifications seemed to extend into every village, and whose demands represented an overwhelming consensus. The lament of a senior Belgian observer, who served on a number of delegations to the United Nations to defend the colonial performance of his country, is representative:

Anti-colonialist nationalism has thus become one of the main revolutionary forces of our times. Its virulence has grown in the course of recent years to the point of subjecting the colonial powers, both within and without their non-self-governing territories, to a pressure which—failing recourse to totalitarian methods—tends to become irresistible.[1]

In retrospect, it is clearer today than a few years ago that in sub-Saharan Africa, nationalism in the 1950s and early 1960s was not yet ready for a prolonged trial of physical strength against a ruthless enemy. The success of the Portuguese in postponing their day of reckoning, the ability of 500-odd white mercenaries in routing a large and well-armed, if poorly led, insurgent army in the Congo during 1964–5, the systematic destruction of anti-apartheid movements of all races in South

---

[1] F. van Langenhove, 'Factors of decolonization', *Civilisations*, 1961, **11**, 401–23, reprinted in *Independent black Africa: the politics of freedom*, William John Hanna, ed. (Chicago, 1964), pp. 154–5. Professor van Langenhove, Director of the Institut Royal des Relations Internationales, reflects the view of a large cross-section of Belgian officialdom.

Africa, the striking inability of black Rhodesian nationalists to threaten Ian Smith's unilaterally 'independent' settler régime, all suggest that at least in the 1950s sub-Saharan African nationalists had to win their battles peacefully. But this retrospective conclusion does not dim the nationalists' lustre of irresistibility at the hour of their triumph.

The democratic heritage of Belgium, France and Great Britain was a major asset to the nationalist movements. Hence the political 'ecology' of African nationalism differed sharply in settings where democracy was not a significant value to the colonizer (Spanish and especially Portuguese colonies), or where it had a very restricted racial meaning and took second place to white supremacy, as in Rhodesia and South Africa. But in dealing with Britain, France and Belgium, the nationalist challengers had the inestimable advantage of adversaries who were compelled to rationalize their ultimate ends—to themselves as well as to their overseas subjects—in terms of a democratic ethos. This is not to suggest that democracy was always implemented in African dependencies, or that colonial actions were always measured against this yardstick. The grotesque farce of 'elections' in Algeria under the Fourth Republic or the energetic bureaucratic authoritarianism of Belgian Africa before 1957 were only the most obvious examples of the vast gap between metropolitan democratic theory and colonial practice. But when nationalism and international circumstance forced a clear definition of terminal goals, metropolitan values became important.

As the nationalist movements gathered strength, they found many advantages in appealing to the colonizers for the faithful application to the colonies of the colonizers' own values. Political parties thrive on elections; electoral campaigns provided especially propitious circumstances for extending and strengthening the party apparatus and diffusing its message. In the extreme case of the Congo, the most important party, Patrice Lumumba's wing of the Mouvement National Congolais, achieved its brief moment of success in organizing the masses only during the 1960 general elections. Democracy required the suspension of sundry arbitrary restrictions on nationalist organization that lurked in colonial law books. Democracy implied that self-government could not be refused, once a convincing demonstration had been made that the nationalist party incarnated the popular will.

Thus at the moment of the power transfer the tenets of democracy provided the vital nexus between nationalist and colonizer. The principles of equality, political freedom and majority rule gave the nationalist the means of consolidating his claim to leadership, and placing it within a philosophic frame whereby its legitimacy would be fully accepted by the colonizer. For the metropolitan power, once early power transfer was unavoidable, transplantation of democracy permitted departure with honour. The Belgians, for example, had rigorously excluded political rights for both settler and Congolese during the long period when colonial rule still seemed impregnable. Yet even the Belgians agreed without hesitation with the first official study group, constituted in 1958, that the proper object was the establishment of a democratic state, with full respect for the rights of men, legitimated by universal suffrage.

The ultimate acceptance of democratic values as the standard of terminal colonial statecraft did not come without difficult and devious sophistry. In the British case, there was the heritage of an earlier view of equality that restricted to Englishmen the radius of inalienable rights. From 1917, when Britain conceded in principle that India might eventually become a self-governing dominion, this postulate had been theoretically supplanted. But many years were to go by before it was practically applied in Africa to people who were not European settlers. The older view survived in various forms in settler states, from Cecil Rhodes's famous dictum of 'equal rights for all civilized men' (with Englishmen automatically qualifying, and rigorous standards established for the rest) to the horse-and-rider partnership theories upon which the Federation of Rhodesia and Nyasaland was briefly constructed. Unambiguous commitment to one-man one-vote democracy did not come until the Lancaster House Conference in 1960 in the case of Kenya and the final dismantling of the Federation of Rhodesia and Nyasaland in 1963.

The French long concealed the dilemma within the once-revolutionary doctrine of 'assimilation'. The contradiction between liberty, equality, fraternity and colonialism was apparently transcended by the myth of eventual absorption of colonial subjects as full citizens of an enlarged *république une et indivisible*. Assimilation was of course totally impossible. As Ruth Morgenthau perceptively observed:

Assimilation never applied to the total relationship between France and her colonies. It had meaning in reference only to a tiny, educated African minority. A policy for elites, it was hardly suitable to post-war mass politics. Assimilation originally meant little more than an equal share for all in the administration of law and order. The welfare state changed all that. Assimilation in a unitary state then presumed sharing the resources of rich, industrialized France with poorly developed Africa.[1]

Assimilation was in fact pursued half-heartedly at best.[2] In 1946 it did bring into the National Assembly thirty Algerian deputies and thirty-eight from other French territories in Africa. However, voters were in most territories segregated into two electoral colleges, on a basis that vastly augmented the voting power of overseas Frenchmen and diminished the effective representation of the indigenous populations. Assimilation retained enough vitality during the Algerian War for French propaganda services to stress the theme of liberation of each individual Algerian as the proper goal, in contrast to the nationalist view of liberation as a collective end.

A major determinant for the pace of the final outcome was the web of partisan conflict within the metropolitan community. Britain was set firmly on the path of decolonization by its post-war Labour government. In the post-war context, every major advance was irreversible, and could not be undone by succeeding governments. The most decisive steps, it is true, were taken in Asia, but vital innovations were made in Africa also. The Secretary of State's 1947 circular instructing colonial administrations to institute representative local government was a crucial step away from the outmoded 'native administration' system; it provided the thin edge of the wedge for nationalist leaders to undermine the rural authority of the chief. Nkrumah was imprisoned by a British court of law in 1948 while a Labour government was in power. But it was also during the same Labour government's period of office that Nkrumah was released from prison to form the first responsible government in 1951. New constitutions were introduced in most African dependencies in the immediate post-war period; these increased (or initiated) African representation on legislative councils, and provided more outlet for African political organization. The Trades Union Congress was encouraged to engage its energies in an evangelical task overseas; the Labour government gave its blessing and active assistance also to promotion of co-operatives.

[1] Ruth Schachter Morgenthau, *Political parties in French-speaking West Africa* (Oxford, Clarendon Press, 1964), p. 57.
[2] Indeed, Hubert Deschamps, in a useful epitaph to this debate ('Et maintenant, Lord Lugard?' *Africa*, Oct. 1963, 33, no. 4, pp. 293–306), argues it was never pursued at all. See also Michael Crowder's rejoinder, 'Indirect rule—French and British style', *Africa*, July 1964, 34, no. 3, pp. 197–206.

Above all, Arthur Creech-Jones, Secretary of State for the Colonies, in 1948, in a statement drafted by himself, defined explicitly and irrevocably British colonial aims:

> The central purpose of British colonial policy is simple. It is to guide the colonial territories to responsible government within the Commonwealth in conditions that ensure to the people concerned both a fair standard of living and freedom from oppression from any quarter.[1]

The refurbished Tory party of 1951 was committed not to turn back the clock.

Labour's two Colonial Ministers, Creech-Jones and James Griffiths, both belonged to the party's moderate wing. Doctrinaire socialists, and nonconformist radicals such as Fenner Brockway, were not admitted to the inner councils formulating colonial policy. Although party dogma was visible in the missionary efforts in the trade union and co-operative field, Labour did not try to export socialism to the African colonies. There were probably real limits as to the degree of radicalism in colonial policy that could have been implemented. Colonial administrations— though influenced to some extent by new currents of thought—were not staffed by radical socialists. Administrators had a considerable capacity for thwarting policies believed to be entirely misguided. As it was, although Creech-Jones perhaps pushed faster than many would have liked, Labour policies were not radically unacceptable to colonial officials in the field.

Continuity between Labour and Tory was achieved by the replacement of moderate Labourites by liberal Conservatives in the Colonial Office. Tory imperialists were as carefully excluded from this post as Bevanite socialists had been. Oliver Lyttleton, Alan Lennox-Boyd, and Ian Macleod, who served in the crucial decade of 1951–60, were all cut of the new, post-war Tory cloth. Over strong African opposition the Conservative government did, in its one major African miscalculation, try to impose Federation in Northern Rhodesia and Nyasaland. But even here it was merely implementing a policy that had begun under the Labour government. Conservative governments appointed a series of liberal governors to superintend the delicate final stage of transition to nationalist government. Governors like Sir James Robertson of Nigeria and Sir Richard Turnbull of Tanganyika, caretakers of

[1] Quoted in Sir Charles Joseph Jeffries, *Transfer of power: problems of the passage to self-government* (London, 1960), p. 15.

power transfer, succeeded admirably in gaining the confidence of the new nationalist leadership.

In the 1950s, as decolonization became increasingly a specifically African problem, the Labour left, led particularly by the indefatigable Fenner Brockway, continued to act as a 'ginger-group'. Brockway was in close contact with nationalists throughout English-speaking Africa. At question-time in Parliament, he frequently interrogated colonial secretaries, often on the basis of information supplied from nationalist sources. Through his Movement for Colonial Freedom he organized a small but vocal lobby within the Parliamentary Labour Party to speak for nationalist causes. This caucus of gadflies exercised some influence in cases of specific colonial actions—rustication of a given nationalist, suspension of a particular newspaper. It is doubtful, however, whether much significant influence was exerted over broader policy. Indeed, nationalist leaders had recourse not only to radicals like Brockway, who could be expected to support them in protest actions, but also to the Colonial Office. Ian Macleod in particular was on good personal terms with the more important political leaders, and during the crucial years a great deal of power transfer friction was averted through constant informal bargaining.

Perceptive politicians indeed realized that much more could be accomplished through quiet resort to the men in power than through dedicated but noisy anti-colonial groups. The sincerity of the latter was not matched by their influence with the electorate at large. The 1959 election showed conclusively that an appeal to British public opinion could not achieve the ultimate sanction—altering voting choices. In 1959 the Conservatives sought a new mandate in the face of dramatic revelations of atrocities in Hola camp in Kenya, where Mau Mau detainees were being 'rehabilitated'. The Conservatives were confronted also by the devastating statement in the Devlin Commission report on Nyasaland (1959) that this unwilling appendage to the Central African Federation 'had become, no doubt temporarily, a police state'. Electoral studies (and the results) proved incontrovertibly that the colonial issues had made no perceptible impact on the electorate.

In France and Belgium, metropolitan politics and colonial policy were much more closely intertwined. Unlike Britain, both countries faced the task not simply of attaining goals implicit in past policy but of working out a major reformulation. The Fourth Republic allowed the colonial problem to slowly fester. The question first affected only the periphery; but finally, with the Algerian crisis, it reached the very heart of the French polity. The Lebanese and Syrian mandates were lost after World War II (supposedly through the machinations of 'perfidious Albion'); the coastal establishments on the Indian sub-continent were reluctantly surrendered. After a costly struggle in Indo-China, the three 'associated states' of Laos, Cambodia and Vietnam were abandoned. In its latter stages, Vietnam became a major issue of domestic discord. With the investiture in June 1953 of J. Laniel as Premier of a centre–right coalition, the colonial crisis moved to the centre of the stage in France, where it remained until it destroyed the Fourth Republic. The traumatic disaster at Dien Bien Phu led to the overthrow of the Laniel government, basically on the Indo-China question, in early June 1954. This marked the first time after World War II that a metropolitan government had fallen on a colonial issue.

The crisis catapulted to power the brilliant, unorthodox and bitterly controversial Pierre Mendès-France, a radical pledged to negotiate peace in Indo-China within thirty days and to reach a settlement in North Africa to halt the slow descent into terrorism and violence in Tunisia and Morocco. He was as good as his word on Indo-China, and a week after the Geneva settlement made a sudden visit to Tunisia to pledge full internal autonomy to a nationalist government. But in touching French sovereignty in North Africa, he struck the most sensitive nerves of empire. The strident colonial lobby—rooted in the North African connexion—had powerful resources throughout the centre and right parties of the Fourth Republic. Mendès-France sur-vived the first great debate on North African policy following his return from Tunis, but he had gone as far as he could. No new initiatives were taken in Morocco during his year in office; in Algeria, his response to the outbreak of hostilities on 1 November 1954 was to send more troops. Mendès-France's successor, Edgar Faure, performed the same surgery in Morocco that his radical predecessor had achieved in Tunisia; Faure negotiated the return of the deposed Sultan, Mohammed V, on terms that led to Moroccan independence the following year. But mean-while the situation in Algeria threatened to get totally out of control.

The snap election of January 1956 revealed the spreading malaise that was undermining French democracy. Symptomatic of growing political anomie was the army of fifty-two small-town butchers and grocers who tramped into Parliament behind Pierre Poujade, supported by two and a half million Frenchmen who had cast their votes for his right-wing petty bourgeois protest group. The communists and other far-left groups had increased their representation from 90 to 150; the main losers in the election were the classical right and centre parties that had governed France since the breakdown of Communist–Socialist–MRP (Mouvement Républicain Populaire) 'tripartisme' in 1947. Parliamentary arithmetic, with the calculus of incompatibilities, left the SFIO (Section Française de l'Internationale Ouvrière) as master of the possible combinations. The socialist leader Guy Mollet formed a government somewhat to the left of the 1947–55 coalitions, with ambiguous North African intentions. As a gesture of appeasement to the nationalists, he hesitantly named the ageing General Georges Catroux as Resident Minister in Algiers, and made hints of eventual 'federal' links between a Franco-Muslim Algeria and France. Then, on 6 February 1956, just after the General had arrived in Algiers, Mollet made his fateful visit to Algeria, only to be hooted by a disorderly mob and pelted with tomatoes.

Catroux resigned that night, and Mollet capitulated to the mood of xenophobic nationalism that was sweeping not only French milieux in Algeria but the metropole itself. With the installation of the intransigent Robert Lacoste as Resident Minister in Algiers, the era of National Molletism was inaugurated. Although Mollet retained some ambiguity about his inner thoughts on Algeria's future, Lacoste set about trying to implement the policy set forth one year earlier by his predecessor Jacques Soustelle:

No uncertainty must be allowed to remain as to our inflexible determination to preserve Algeria from the terrible destiny that some are seeking to prepare for it...Algeria and all its inhabitants form an integral part of France, one and indivisible. All must know, here and elsewhere, that France will not leave Algeria any more than she will leave Provence or Brittany. Whatever happens, the destiny of Algeria is French. This means that a choice has been made. The choice is called integration; it is to make Algeria each day more completely a province, different from the others certainly, but fully French.[1]

At this juncture, an inflamed public opinion exerted a pressure on French government policy to a degree never approached in either Britain or Belgium. The intensity of the French nationalist reflex was shown in the near unanimity with which the National Assembly—with the support of the Communist Party deputies—in March 1956 voted

---

[1] Quoted in Michael Clark, *Algeria in turmoil: a history of the rebellion* (New York, 1959), pp. 133–4.

sweeping emergency powers in Algeria to the government. The dreary sequence of defeat and retreat had gone far enough. The imperial footholds in Asia had been abandoned; now Tunisia and Morocco as well were gaining their independence. But Algeria was different; Algeria was 'French'. From the vantage point of 1956, Algeria was the very last line of imperial defence. No subtle juridical exit from the indivisible Republic had been left unguarded. The Indo-China peninsula, it is true, had been only 'associated states'. Lebanon and Syria admittedly were only League of Nations Mandates. Tunisia and Morocco, however cherished, were only protectorates. Togo and Cameroun were UN Trust Territories. But Algeria was France, and had been since 1830. Or so at least every French schoolboy had been taught. Perhaps in recollecting the mood of 1956 one can appreciate the forces that led to the extension of the war in Algeria into a crusade against Arab nationalism and to the Anglo–French–Israeli rendezvous at Suez.

Curiously, so totally did Algeria dominate the scene that major reforms for tropical Africa in 1956 were made with relatively little public attention. The heart of the colonial lobby was in North Africa, not south of the Sahara. Tropical Africa and Madagascar had been affected by the general swing to the right in France in 1946–7; the Madagascar uprising of 1947 was suppressed with brutal energy; tough governors were posted to West and Equatorial Africa, and set about deploying the resources of the administration to thwart the spread of the RDA (Rassemblement Démocratique Africain). However, from 1951 to 1954 an important debate took place within the walls of the senior administration and in the Colonial Ministry. Slowly, the spokesmen for conciliation and partnership with moderate nationalists won out over the advocates of repression. Hard-line governors were gradually withdrawn, and the way was cleared for the introduction of the crucial *Loi-Cadre* of 1956.

The path of reconciliation was smoothed by the willingness of the most important tropical African political leaders to speak in terms of a federal French Union, rather than to insist on independence, like their opposite numbers in North Africa. 'To the mystique of independence', declared the once militant Ivory Coast leader Félix Houphouët-Boigny in 1956, 'we oppose the idea of fraternity'. Socialist Overseas Minister Gaston Deferre, in introducing the reform elaborated by preceding administrations, declared that France was not to repeat in tropical Africa the mistakes of North Africa and Indo-China:

The failure of the federalist policies pursued there was because we sulked, clipped, delayed, dilly-dallied, shilly-shallied, quibbled before we offered conditionally a degree of autonomy which would have had a very different reception, and opposite results, had it been offered in good time and good faith.[1]

Until 1956, despite representation in Paris and the end of the *Indigénat*, the colonial pattern of administration had been little altered in tropical Africa. The French Parliament never voted the necessary organic acts to give real legal status and provide for the internal organization of the territories of AOF and AEF.

The cancer of Algeria progressively infected all French political life during 1956–8. Emergency powers were extended to France itself; journals critical of Algerian policy, such as *Le Monde*, *L'Express*, and *France-Observateur*, were harassed in various ways; and the perversion of information on the government-controlled national radio and television networks became a national scandal. Terrorism, counter-terrorism and running battles between police and Algerian nationalists became part of the daily routine in Paris itself. The degradation of government authority, first visible in unilateral acts by colonial officials such as the exile of Sultan Mohammed V in 1953, was accelerated. The spectacular *coup-de-main* in Algiers, when a plane bearing Ben Bella and four of his top collaborators was diverted en route from Morocco to Tunisia and the FLN leaders were arrested, was decided in Algiers and 'covered' *ex post facto* by the Mollet government. Police and army were both compromised in the increasingly common practice of interrogation by torture.

And within the army there emerged a group of activist officers who developed a new doctrine of 'revolutionary warfare'. The salvation of France—and of French Algeria—lay in a conduct of the war within the guerrilla context chosen by the adversary. These officers, careful students of Mao Tse-tung, became convinced that the war could be won through committing the army to the battle for the hearts of the Muslim population under the slogan of completely integrating Algeria into France. The army was to be charged with a revolutionary social role, as well as with its traditional military mission. Above all, it must not have its task compromised either by recalcitrant settlers who clung to outmoded privileges or, especially, by pusillanimous politicians—

[1] Quoted in Morgenthau, *Political parties*, p. 66.

who, it was believed, had for two decades been humiliating the army by committing it to battles which they denied it the means to win.

In the dying days of the Fourth Republic, the French right, the settlers in Algeria, and large segments of the army became persuaded that the 'politicians' were edging towards a new 'treason'. After the fall of the Mollet government in 1957, the increasingly feeble governments of Bourgès-Manoury and Gaillard fell before the same pressures. The centre–left coalitions pursued a right-wing policy in Algeria, but at the same time quietly sought some way out of the impasse. When Pierre Pflimlin was invested with a government that appeared to favour negotiations, civilian and military plotters were ready. On 13 May a parade in Algiers in honour of three victims of the FLN was converted into a march on Government House. Army Commander Raoul Salan placed the French Army in Algeria behind the insurgents and took the lead in the Committee of Public Safety that was formed the following day. Algeria was in open defiance of Paris. Many units of the metropole were known to be tacitly in support of the insurgents, and rumours circulated of Public Safety Committees being formed in different parts of France. So far had demoralization of the Fourth Republic gone that, despite the labour march of 200,000 to preserve the Republic, in Paris on 28 May, all too few were prepared to raise a hand or even a voice in its defence. The régime could not count on being protected by its armed forces, its police, or even its 'Garde Républicain'. When General de Gaulle announced on 27 May that he had 'begun the process necessary to the establishment of my government', the final nail was driven into the coffin of the Fourth Republic. The following day Pflimlin resigned, and with a final charade of procedural legality 'the system' delivered itself up to Charles de Gaulle. Had the Fourth Republic not gone into voluntary liquidation, it is virtually certain that it would have been destroyed by airborne troops from Algiers.

De Gaulle created a republic that was able to achieve a final solution of the colonial problem. In sub-Saharan Africa, the task was relatively easy. Algeria, however, required all De Gaulle's skill and authority, exercised over a four-year period. The Fifth Republic Constitution vastly expanded the president's executive powers; it sharply trimmed parliamentary prerogatives and provided a new institutional base. The National Assembly was rendered even more docile by the results of the 1958 elections. The new electoral law served to nearly wipe out the communist representation in Parliament. Although on the second round they received more votes than any other party, the anti-communist alliances formed in the second ballot by other parties served to reduce communist strength in the Assembly from 140 to 10. The Poujadists on the right extreme became extinct through lack of public interest, and De Gaulle's own UNR won 188 seats (out of 463). The feeble coalitions of the Fourth Republic had to contend with an Assembly where nearly 40 per cent of the seats were held by irrevocably hostile extremists of the left and right, leaving only the narrowest margin for manoeuvre and a constant threat of defeat through the shift of a few votes. De Gaulle, on the other hand, was entirely independent of parliamentary opposition.

With parliament domesticated, the next obstacle was the army itself. The activists and neo-Maoist evangelists of the revolutionary colonial war had to be removed from positions of decisive influence. This delicate operation was carried out with consummate skill. Keeping his own intentions completely concealed, the General used the scalpel of transfer or retirement to excise gradually the elements whose fidelity to the Republic was suspect. Thus, when the civil population of Algiers took to the barricades again in January 1960, and threats were made to land paratroops in Paris, the army, instead of rallying to insurrection as in May 1958, reluctantly obeyed its orders. The final paroxysm of the army came in April 1961, when military units seized Algiers, and renewed the invasion threat. However, this time the officers actively involved in insubordination could be isolated and disciplined. This left only the colonial irreconcilables, grouped in the Organisation Armée Secrète (OAS). The OAS sought to fight FLN guerrillas through counter-guerrillas, to repress FLN terror by counter-terror, and to impose its will on France through subversion and bloodshed. Although the cause of *Algérie Française* still possessed enough vitality to cause great suffering and damage, this desperate tactic accelerated the psychological rupture with the colonial past. Ultimately the terror campaign brought the OAS into direct conflict with the army, and produced a revulsion in France that enabled the independence agreement with Algerian nationalism in March 1962 to be received with gratitude and relief.

The partial integration of overseas territories in the metropolitan French political framework had created a unique interplay of domestic and colonial politics. René Pleven's Union Démocratique et Sociale de la Résistance (UDSR) occupied a pivotal position in the Fourth

Republic parliamentary spectrum. From 1952 the *apparentement* of Houphouët-Boigny's RDA with the UDSR opened a strategic channel for exertion of African pressure—for example, to secure the transfer of governors deemed obnoxious.

Also, African politicians learned that they could employ the same strategy as the colonial lobby in using parliamentary pressures on the always-fragile Fourth Republic coalitions to outmanoeuvre the administrator on the spot. A striking example was the struggle between Cameroun Premier André-Marie M'Bida and Governor Jean Ramadier (son of the old socialist leader Paul Ramadier) in early 1958. Ramadier had been entrusted with the task of manipulating the removal of M'Bida and his replacement by Ahmadou Ahidjo, judged more suitable on the international scene, and in particular in the UN. In characteristic Fourth Republic style, Ramadier was supposed to execute this plot without involving the government, or without guarantee of government 'cover' if he exposed himself. When M'Bida scented the scheme, he immediately flew to Paris to bring pressure through right-wing deputies and the colonial lobby for the removal of Ramadier. The latter was able to complete the operation, with strong support in the Cameroun assembly, only at the price of his own career, as he had to disobey an order for immediate return to Paris to gain time for a vote of no confidence in M'Bida to take place. M'Bida thus had at least the satisfaction of seeing Ramadier cashiered as governor at the same time he lost his office. Indeed, a substantial part of the post-war history of French colonial policy is a mosaic of petty plots, played out through intricately interlocking political and administrative circuits, with each policy shift leaving in its wake a flotsam of scapegoats.

Although metropolitan politics did not influence Belgian decolonization to the same extent, the nature of the Belgian political system had important repercussions on the character of the power transfer process. During the period in question, Belgium had a relatively stable three-party system. The party divisions related to the three major cleavages within Belgian society—linguistic (Fleming and Walloon), religious (Catholic and anti-clerical) and social (working-class socialists and business–professional–commercial–agricultural non-socialists). The PSB (Socialist) had as its centre of gravity industrial Wallony and was historically anti-clerical. The PSC (Christian Democratic) was Catholic and predominantly Flemish. The Liberals (now PLP) had their greatest strength in Brussels; they were now a conservative party and had only recently shed anti-clericalism. Electoral arithmetic only allowed the PSC a chance of winning an absolute majority—which it enjoyed from 1950 to 1954. The normal solution was a two-party coalition, and all three combinations were tried after World War II.

There was at first a tacit accord among all parties to exclude the Congo from their partisan competition. It is true that continuous subterranean skirmishing along linguistic and religious lines took place within the colonial establishment, but this conflict had been contained within the colonial hierarchy. The socialists in particular played very little part in colonial affairs; on the infrequent occasions when they were included in a government coalition, they fought for portfolios concerned with labour or welfare matters that could bring material benefits to their working-class constituents. Parliament rarely concerned itself with colonial problems unless there was a budget deficit.

The political truce over the Congo broke down in 1954, when the PSC government was replaced by a liberal–socialist coalition. Anti-clericalism was one of the few tenets on which the two ruling parties agreed. Anti-clericalism thus became a major issue for the Van Acker government—leading to the 'schools war' in Belgium and to a bitter conflict with the Catholic missions in the Congo. The new Colonial Minister, Auguste Buisseret, was an aggressively anti-clerical liberal, determined to break what he felt to be the Catholic stranglehold on the Congo. One of his first moves was to appoint a commission of inquiry into the mission-dominated educational system in the Congo, with a view to rapidly building new 'laic' state schools. The commission, as expected, turned in a scathing report—and when the minister tried to reduce the subsidies to Catholic mission schools, the once monolithic colonial alliance between church, state and capital was permanently smashed. In 1956, Catholic bishops made a forthright statement supporting 'emancipation' of the Congo. Although Rome was generally seeking to identify the church with African freedom, there can be little doubt that the timing and wording of the Congo statement were affected by the conflict with Buisseret. This dissolution of the colonial front accompanied a visible nationalist awakening in the Congo—a combination of circumstances of considerable significance in the years that followed.

The colonial administration became badly divided as Buisseret sought to construct a parallel network of persons in key posts who supported his policies. He presided over a ministry whose permanent staff was predominantly Catholic and conservative. The Governor-General, Leon Pétillon, although not a politican, was identified with middle-of-the-road Catholic milieux. Thus Liberal Buisseret was convinced that he would be totally obstructed by his own ministry and the senior administration in Leopoldville, unless he were able to develop his own counter-administration. In Leopoldville and the provincial capitals, certain officials, both liberals and socialists, were known to be 'Buisseret men', with private access to the minister. (Many of the key links on this communication network were Freemasons. The Masonic Lodge has been traditionally an important information channel for anti-clericals of the Belgian commercial and professional community.) Hence, both within the colonial administration and between Brussels and Leopoldville, bitter and paralysing bureaucratic feuds broke out at a time when the colonizers were faced with an entirely new challenge.

In 1956, all three major Belgian parties held special congresses on the Congo—a remarkable sign of changing times. Although their conclusions were not spectacular, and none spoke of independence, the 'solicitude toute nouvelle' of 'la Belgique politicienne' was observed with foreboding in colonial circles.[1] All three parties began to recruit a Congolese clientele. Partisanship in Belgium was sufficiently intense that each party felt an imperative mandate from posterity to save the the Congolese from the perdition which the other parties would inevitably bring. In Leopoldville, the appearance of the first major public nationalist pronouncement, the Manifesto of Conscience Africaine, drafted by Congolese intellectuals identified with liberal Catholic circles in consultation with one or two faculty members at Lovanium University, was viewed by many as a deft manoeuvre to cut the ground from under the forthcoming Socialist Congress on the Congo.

The 1958 elections ended the liberal–socialist alliance; initially, the PSC formed a minority government alone with the help of two liberal votes. Under pressure from the Royal Palace, the new government of Gaston Eyskens tried to 'depolitize' colonial policy by naming as a 'technician minister' the former Governor-General Pétillon. Pétillon then established a 'Working Group' to draw up a plan for the future of the Congo, with representatives from all three parties. Politicians,

---

[1] See the pungent commentaries of Jean Sepulchre, editor of the Elisabethville daily Essor du Congo, in Propos sur le Congo politique de demain: autonomie et fédéralisme (Elisabethville, 1958).

however, do not suffer technicians gladly. Royal protection notwithstanding, Pétillon was quietly dropped when a coalition agreement with the liberals made a cabinet reshuffle necessary in November 1958. He was succeeded by a blunt, outspoken Flemish politician, Maurice Van Hemelrijck.

The beginning of 1959 saw a critical decision forced upon the government. The Working Group presented its report on 24 December, and a full government declaration concerning future Congo policy was promised for 13 January. Then came the shock of the massive and bloody riots in Leopoldville 4–6 January 1959. It is impossible to exaggerate the overwhelming effect of these disorders on Belgium. Public opinion at large for the first time became a factor. The utter impossibility of prolonging previous policies of drift and delay, apparently concealed under a veneer of paternalism and welfare, became clear to all. The riots gave redoubled urgency to the high-level debate as to whether the declaration should include the word 'independence'. The final decision was left to a cabinet committee, three of whose four members were reluctant to see any reference to independence. Van Hemelrijck firmly believed that a clear commitment to eventual independence was the only way to halt the deterioration in the Congolese situation shown by the riots. He finally won agreement after an impassioned all-night argument over an ambiguously worded statement: 'Belgium intends to organize in the Congo a democracy capable of exercising its prerogative of sovereignty, and of deciding on its independence.'

When, only three short years earlier, Professor Van Bilsen had proposed a thirty-year plan for independence, he had encountered a storm of abuse, especially from business milieux and from the colonial administration. But in 1959, hardly a voice was raised to challenge either the government pledge of ultimate independence or the Royal Message that made the same promise in much less ambiguous terms at the same time. The tacit acceptance of the independence pledge by the powerful business interests is at first view particularly surprising. The concentration of capital in Belgium in the hands of a few major financial houses, with massive interests both in the Congo and in metropolitan Belgium, created a fulcrum of economic power that no government—especially no Catholic–liberal coalition—could ignore. In Belgium, far more than in Britain or in France, financial interests in the metropolitan country and in the colonies were indistinguishable. The constant circulation of key personnel between Belgium and the Congo, the vertical integration of much of the economic activity between extraction and production in the Congo through processing and manufacturing in Belgium, meant that the colonial trusts spoke from within the Belgian system, not simply as an overseas lobby. Thus the government had to be assured of at least the benevolent neutrality of the business interests before it could contemplate such a major innovation.

Reticence toward the new policy was most apparent in the colonial administration. What is particularly striking about the final phases of Belgian rule in the Congo was the very small role played by the administration. After the departure of Pétillon, the administration had no voice in the cabinet—the new Colonial Minister, Van Hemelrijck, quickly came into bitter conflict with Leopoldville. In the last months of Belgian rule in the Congo, the once proud and all-powerful administration became increasingly demoralized and ineffectual, discredited in the eyes of both the nationalists and the metropolitan government. Decolonization became strictly an affair to be arranged between Brussels and the nationalists, with Leopoldville a silent, sullen spectator.

The domestic pressures on the Belgian government are of vital import to an understanding of the incredible shortening of the period between the first promise of independence in January 1959 and its final fulfilment in June 1960. Belgium, the first Western European country to recover from the effects of war and to experience a surge of growth and prosperity, had entered a phase of stagnation. Large numbers of in-efficient collieries in Wallony were faced with closure. This painful readjustment produced serious labour unrest; the Socialist Party in opposition was free to give vent to this frustration in bitter attacks upon the Eyskens government. As militant African nationalism spread from Leopoldville into the rural areas in the first half of 1959, the colonial security force, the European-officered Force Publique, could no longer be counted on fully to cope with the growing chaos in the Lower Congo. With the whole-hearted support from the PSB, a violent campaign was launched in Belgium against the utilization of metropolitan troops to quell nationalist disturbances.

The government's dilemma was compounded by the fact that the Belgian Constitution precluded dispatch of conscripts to the Congo without their consent. Since all units had conscripts, this virtually ruled out use of the Belgian Army in the Congo without first amending the Constitution. 'Not one soldier for Union Minière' was a potent slogan; hence the government concluded that it could not afford to brave the public uproar that would have been created by an attempt to alter the Constitution. With force ruled out, the Belgian government could only seek conciliation under conditions where its bargaining power was peculiarly slight.

Although the Eyskens government was not as weak and ineffectual as the final governments of the Fourth Republic, it decidedly lacked the firmness and unquestioned authority of all British governments—or of De Gaulle once the Fifth Republic had been consolidated. The weakness of the Belgian government was reflected most vividly in the astonishing formula chosen for the independence talks in Brussels in January 1960. The fragmented nationalist movements had succeeded in manoeuvring the Belgian government into the position of abdicating responsibility for conduct of these decisive negotiations to a Round Table Conference between the nationalist parties and the three major Belgian parliamentary parties. When the nationalist parties added a totally unexpected new dimension to the talks by achieving by mid-1960 a common front (unhappily shortlived) on the issue of independence, the Belgian government found itself in an impossible situation. The opposition Socialist Party chose for itself the role of arbiter between the Congolese and the two government parties. The Belgian government, through its governing party representatives at the Conference, was thus completely ouflanked. There was no choice but capitulation to the nationalists on the central issue of immediate, total, unfettered independence.

In examining the pattern of power transfer pursued by the three major colonizers in Africa, we must consider briefly a number of variables. These include the theories of colonial administration and imperial ideology that underlay colonial rule, power transfer experiences in other parts of the globe, the nature of post-colonial association, the character of the nationalist movements, the model of government provided by the metropole, the legal status of the dependencies and the presence or absence of settler communities.

The prolonged debate between direct and indirect rule had major implications for the power transfer process. Indirect rule, where it could be successfully applied, as in Buganda and Northern Nigeria, implied a special type of political evolution. This came into sharp conflict with the concept of the modern state that generally prevailed after World War II. C. A. G. Wallis stated the dilemma clearly in a report on the development of local government in Uganda:

479

All the [District Councils] made it plain that they are bent upon reaching the status of a native state. Their object is to achieve a constitution as like that of Buganda as possible. In short they aim at Home Rule...Moreover, it seems to them that this is the logical development of past administrative policy. Clan barriers have been broken down, sections have been amalgamated, a tribal organization has been created and a tribal loyalty has been developed.[1]

The final outcome of indirect rule, carried through to its logical extreme, would be a loosely organized confederation of 'native states'. After World War II, when Britain faced the problem of a greatly fore-shortened time-table, it was clear that such organisms could not compete in the modern world. Thus a unitary state, or at worst a strong federation, had to be created. Special problems arose where modern territorial units were coterminous with 'native states', or over traditional systems that had been ruled indirectly, as in Zanzibar, the three former High Commission Territories, Rwanda and Burundi. In some instances, such as Rwanda, universal suffrage destroyed the traditional structure where this reposed on ethnic stratification. However, in Swaziland, Bechuanaland, and temporarily in Burundi, the traditional hierarchy was able to adapt itself to the rules of Western democracy governing the decolonization process.

Another type of difficulty arose where indirect rule had been particularly successful, in Northern Nigeria and Buganda. Neo-traditional African ruling groups had acquired a modern administrative capability; in Buganda they also wielded economic power. These élites thus became so well entrenched that they could turn the electoral process to their own advantage through parties like the Northern People's Congress and Kabaka Yekka. The British were unwilling to coerce them into the framework of modern independent states unacceptable to the neo-traditional leaders, though the British did not go so far as to accede to Buganda's demands from 1957 to 1961 for separate independence. The neo-traditional political movements that emerged in these areas pre-empted the political field, giving the traditional ruling group not only the sanction of history but of universal suffrage.

The French, although committed to direct rule as an administrative ideology, did not always apply it in practice, especially when wielders of traditional power became pillars of colonial support. In Morocco,

[1] C. A. G. Wallis, *Report of an inquiry into African local government in the Protectorate of Uganda* (Entebbe, 1953), pp. 13–14.

Marshal Lyautey developed a neo-Lugardian philosophy of protectorate, although his successors tended to abandon his theories. The traditional state thus survived the early years of French rule; the sultanate
guaranteed its role as post-colonial successor by taking the lead in
nationalist resistance. In Upper Volta, which largely coincided with the
traditional Mossi Kingdoms, France initially sought to fragment the
Mossi state. But in 1947 the French found the Mogho Naba (paramount ruler) a useful stalking-horse against then radical Houphouët-
Boigny, and for a time backed the resurgent traditional forces. In Chad
there was a radical difference in the administration of the segmentary
Sara-dominated south and of the remote sultanates of the north.
Administration, economic development and modernization were
largely confined to the south, and the Sara were the successor élite. The
northern sultanates remained loosely tied to the modern state, and
sporadically issued secession threats. More generally, however, the
power of traditional authorities was curtailed or ended. Their place
was taken by modern bureaucracies designed to replace, not to
modernize, chieftaincy.

Belgium had embraced a dogma of administration theoretically influenced by Lugard but in practice differing greatly from the dicta of
the dual mandate. With the exception of Rwanda and Burundi, the
large chieftaincies that might have served as instruments for indirect
rule were viewed with distrust and broken into smaller units. The heavy
emphasis on efficiency and productivity led to a degree of intervention
by the Belgian administrators quite incompatible with the postulates
of indirect administration. There was a last-minute revival of interest
in chiefs as a possible counterpoise to the nationalists. But the political
units around which meaningful modern political competition was
centred—first the towns, then the provinces and central institutions—
went far beyond the boundaries of any chieftaincy.

The colonizers' own goals and sense of purpose also influenced the
pattern of decolonization. Britain alone of the colonizers in Africa
entered the era of power transfer with coherent aims. After the unhappy
experience of unsuccessful decolonization in the thirteen American
colonies, the formula slowly evolved of self-governing dominions within the British Empire, later rebaptized British Commonwealth of
Nations after World War II. The Durham Report in 1839 and the
British North American Act of 1867 were major milestones in setting
the framework; the Statute of Westminster in 1931 defined the dominion

concept in its fully developed form. The Ceylon Constitution of 1931, with its grant of universal suffrage and responsible government, established a crucial precedent for the extension of this formula to non-European subjects as well as to Englishmen overseas. The precedent of India was also of vital importance, in clearly demonstrating that power could be transferred to a militant nationalist movement that had proved its popular support.

The existence of the Commonwealth was of immense value in permitting a relatively harmonious power transfer, except in Kenya and Central Africa, where settler groups advanced special claims. The Commonwealth offered an honourable exit, which placed imperial withdrawal within a context of fulfilment rather than liquidation. The vision of the Commonwealth was indeed more important to the colonizer than to the colonized; the British could see a post-colonial future with its former colonies not simply separated but promoted to partnership in the British Commonwealth of Nations. The Commonwealth formula could be acceptable even to militant nationalists like Nkrumah. The India model had proved that after World War II the Commonwealth structure imposed no limitations at all either on domestic sovereignty or on external relations. Commonwealth membership, which smoothed the path to independence, was not therefore incompatible with nationalist self-respect. The fact that the Commonwealth gives indications of declining vitality and significance in the post-colonial world in no way diminishes its historic role in removing psychological impediments to decolonization.

The French had a far more difficult time, particularly in North Africa, because their imperial *Weltanschauung* inherited from the past was peculiarly unsuited to the requirements of the post-war world. Initially, the French chose the enlarged Republic as the ultimate framework for territories legally under full French sovereignty; they saw the French Union as an umbrella for the Protectorates (Tunisia and Morocco) and UN Trust Territories (Togo and Cameroun) which could not, by international law, be simply absorbed. However, the Union was a complete failure. Morocco and Tunisia never participated; the Indo-China states severed their links in 1954. The Assembly of the French Union, a body without power or significance, quickly became bored with its profitless deliberations—and the Supreme Council of the Union, which might be considered a pale replica of the Commonwealth Prime Ministers Conference, met only three times.

Another post-war idea was federalism. This was frequently advanced as a mechanism short of independence for the transformation of empire into a permanent association between France and its overseas territories. Mollet seemed to place some hopes in this formula for Algeria; Léopold Senghor advocated federalism for tropical Africa beginning in 1948. However, federalism was entirely out of keeping with the highly centralized, unitary traditions of the French Republic. Indeed, French writers have generally taken federalism to be synonymous with administrative decentralization. France was always viewed as the senior partner in any such arrangement; the overseas territories would merely enjoy a large degree of internal autonomy. However, both the 1956 *Loi-Cadre* and the concept of the French Community expressed in the Fifth Republic Constitution grew out of the vague notion of 'federalism'. This did concede the creation of separate political institutions in the different territories with freely constituted legislative and executive branches to which the administration was to be responsible; hence federalism was a decisive step towards independence.

The final stage was De Gaulle's 'French Community'. The French Community for a time gave satisfaction to the nationalist forces. But it failed to perpetuate any organic links between France and its African territories, and collapsed only two years after its creation. However, viewed as a means for peacefully terminating outmoded forms of dependence and as a way of by-passing the juridical legacy of 'assimilation' and of the 'indivisible republic', the French Community was an outstanding success.

The Community had an Executive Council composed of the President of France, Ministers concerned with community services, and heads of state of the participating territories. There was also a Senate, drawn from French and other Community legislatures in a number determined according to the population of each state, and the responsibilities it assumes in the Community (Article 83 of the Fifth Republic Constitution). The Community itself (meaning, in fact, primarily France) retained very important powers. Subjects such as foreign policy, defence, monetary system, common economic and financial policy and 'strategic' raw materials were to remain with the Community as long as it existed. A second category (justice, higher education, transport, telecommunications) could be transferred to members by special agreement, under Article 78 of the Constitution.

De Gaulle also introduced for the first time in French colonial history the right of a colonial territory to secede by voting against acceptance of the Constitution in the 1958 referendum, or subsequently through Article 86. However, he made it clear that secession meant immediate termination of all French assistance. The independence option was first mentioned somewhat ambiguously in Madagascar during De Gaulle's spectacular African tour in August 1958 to seek support for his constitution and for his Community. It was at the Brazzaville stop that the epochal, unequivocal offer was made: 'Vous voulez l'indépendance? Prenez-le donc!'—but beware of the consequences.

Alone of the African territories, Guinea seized the occasion for immediate independence in poverty. However, the more militant of the other leaders, and especially Modibo Keita of Mali, accepted the Community only as a temporary stage, leading to independence without economic rupture. The Community had scarcely been launched when Mali began to press for transfer of additional functions, finally using Article 78 to request the transfer of all Community functions to the member states—thereby achieving full independence without risking the costly secession route prescribed by Article 86. When De Gaulle finally accepted this, Houphouët-Boigny, the principal African supporter of the Community in its original form, demanded not only independence in 1960 but withdrawal from the Community as well. With the avalanche of independence demands in 1960, the Community was quietly buried.

The Belgians lacked any historic experience by which they could shape the colonial future; their colonial doctrine could provide no guidance as to ultimate political ends. A Belgo-Congolese Community was pronounced to be the goal in 1952, but this blueprint had major structural flaws. It presupposed partnership at two levels. Within the Congo the European minority would enjoy political parity with the Africans; the Congo as a whole would be the junior member in a Belgo-Congolese partnership. Eurafricanism as a substitute for decolonization could hardly survive the rise of nationalism, and silently disappeared by late 1959. Neither the Belgo-Congolese Community nor a permanent link with the monarchy remained. The Belgians wound up with neither a Commonwealth nor a Community; the only apparent post-colonial formal tie was a hastily negotiated Treaty of Friendship signed three days before independence, but not ratified by either Parliament.

The transition to independence in Rwanda and Burundi was a

relatively peaceful process, although marred by the Bahutu insurrection in Rwanda in 1950 against the Watutsi monarchy. During the long period of colonial torpor there was little serious thought as to the future of these two kingdoms. But once events in the Congo had precipitated local independence movements in Rwanda and Burundi, the two territories—under some UN pressure—were quietly set on their separate paths.[1]

A factor of marginal and diminishing significance was the place of the colonies in the overall global strategies of the metropolitan powers, and indeed of the Western alliance as a whole. In the immediate post-war period, the French and Belgians wanted their colonies to be considered as part of the Western defence system. Algeria was officially defined as part of the NATO area. French willingness to offer the United States air bases in Morocco was in all probability partly motivated by a belief that this would mortgage Washington to support of the French North African position. Part of the unofficial bargain by which Libya became nominally independent in 1951 as an Anglo-American client state was the grant of important military facilities. The two major metropolitan military bases constructed in the Congo in the early 1950s by the Belgians, at Kitona and Kamina, had some ill-defined NATO ties. French and Belgian colonial thinking was coloured for a time by the recollection that their African territories had been residual repositories of national sovereignty during the German occupation of the metropoles and that French Africa had been a platform for the liberation of France. Subsequently the enormous military drain imposed on France by the Algerian War, and the impossibility of modernizing the army in Europe while committing nearly half a million troops to counter-guerrilla action in Algeria, played a part in persuading the French that Algerian independence had to come. Perhaps more important, it was a major argument used by De Gaulle to turn the army's thoughts from the humiliations of the colonial past to the grandeur of its nuclear future.

The differing legal status of various territories had some effect on decolonization patterns. This was particularly true of the UN Trust Territories. The fact that alteration in the legal status of Trust Territories could take place only with the consent of a suspicious UN constituted

<hr>

[1] Professor A. A. J. van Bilsen still spoke of federating Ruanda-Urundi with the Congo in *Vers l'indépendance du Congo et du Ruanda-Urundi: réflexion sur les devoirs et l'avenir de la Belgique en Afrique Centrale* (Brussels, 1958).

a major obstacle to proposals adumbrated to fuse territories. In effect it ruled out Tanganyikan incorporation in a colonial-sponsored East African Federation, or the permanent integration of Rwanda and Burundi into the Congo. As mentioned earlier, Togo was the first sub-Saharan territory under French rule to achieve autonomy in 1955, because its legal status prevented its being placed within the framework of the French Republic.

Other territories were legally protectorates rather than colonies. During the height of the colonial period, this distinction had all but disappeared, but it again became important when the hour of emancipation approached. For example, France could never entice Tunisia and Morocco into the French Union, even when it had full control of their administration. Not only nationalists, committed to untrammelled independence, but also settlers, who feared a dilution of their claims to 'co-sovereignty', were opposed. In the British case, special difficulties arose when one portion of a territory, like Buganda and Barotseland, enjoyed special treaty relationships with the Crown, which it chose to invoke as protection against full absorption into the future independent state.

The character of the tactics and evolution of the various nationalist movements profoundly influenced also the manner in which power was devolved. Where nationalism had no opportunity for utilizing constitutional machinery, and was drawn into violence, as in North Africa, a particularly difficult situation arose. In Tunisia, the relative coherence and effective leadership of the Neo-Destour, cushioned by the two-year autonomy period that preceded full independence, paved the way for independence to arrive under stable conditions. In Morocco the unifying influence of the monarchy perhaps compensated for the latent divisions within Istiqlal. But in Algeria the nationalists took over under conditions of near-chaos. The FLN had employed systematic terrorism on a large scale against both the French and the Algerian rivals of the FLN that left an unhappy legacy. The savagery of the communal confrontation led to the exodus of nearly a million Europeans. An estimated 10,000 Muslim auxiliaries, as well as many other Algerians who had previously supported the French, were liquidated as traitors. The sudden loss of a large European population disorganized industry and agriculture as well as public administration. Moreover, the parallel instruments of authority forged by the insurgents during nearly eight years of struggle had to be merged with the remnants of the former administrative system. At the same time there was a bitter power struggle within the FLN. Independence thus began in highly unfavourable circumstances.

Another problem occurred when—as in the Congo—the pace of development of the nationalist movement outran the ability of the colonizer to give the new leaders a share in the responsibility of government. The colonizers might in such a case be left with the burdens of government without the means, while the nationalists wielded power without responsibility. It is in the nature of nationalism to aggregate grievances. Where it becomes too successful, it can succeed in discrediting and disabling the very mechanisms that will be its own indispensable post-independence armature. The tactic of civil disobedience is peculiarly dangerous, and very difficult to reverse once its initial purposes have been served. The British were particularly alert to this problem, and swiftest to force responsibility upon their successors. Margery Perham has stated the problem succinctly:

power cannot be held in suspense. Once it was known that it would be transferred, the position of the colonial government could become so weak, and that of its still irresponsible successors so strong, that the interim period of uncertainty could become intolerable, if not dangerous.[1]

The presence of a settler community large enough to pretend to a major role in the post-colonial state was a major difficulty for all colonizers. Even where relatively numerous, the settlers were still a small minority, certain to be submerged by universal suffrage. They inevitably demanded a political formula that guaranteed them a veto power in any future institutions. Although after World War II it was too late to claim open white supremacy government on the South African model, they could gain some sympathy in the metropolitan capitals for the argument that representation should be by racial communities, and not simply one-man one-vote, whether the particular slogan be 'partnership' (Rhodesia and Nyasaland), 'parity' (Congo), or 'co-sovereignty' (Tunisia). Settlers urged that the colonizer had a special responsibility to them because of their contribution to the economy, their blood relationship to the mother country, and in some cases active encouragement to settle, which had been given to them or to their forebears by previous governments. In Rhodesia nearly complete self-government had been granted to the settlers in 1923; but elsewhere the settlers could not prevent decolonization, though their

[1] Perham, *The colonial reckoning*, p. 80.

opposition delayed and even embittered its achievement. African nationalists refused to accept anything less than universal suffrage as the basis for representation, perhaps tempered by inclusion of one or two settlers as ministers in the independent government as an earnest of their good faith towards all who genuinely accepted African rule.

In the last analysis, the only security that could be offered to settler communities was the opportunity to return to the metropole with assistance or compensation for their devalued assets, as was claimed by European farmers in Kenya. The metropolitan authorities generally considered that the settlers' future security within the post-colonial states lay in scrupulous abstention from a major political role and in reliance on their economic importance to the country. The home government believed that such a policy would forestall punitive or discriminatory measures by the new governments against European or Asian minorities, a point of view not always shared by the local whites themselves, who felt that they were being made to pay the price of decolonization.

In our opinion, only Great Britain had a clear, coherent strategy and style of decolonization. Power was devolved in an orderly series of steps, by which representative political institutions were built around the bureaucratic core. The embryo of the future legislative and executive branches was created through the Legislative and Executive Councils. Initially both these bodies were little differentiated from the pure bureaucratic state represented by all colonial administrations in their first phases. In the beginning the Legislative Council was composed primarily of official members, with a handful of delegates representing non-official interests, such as the missions of the expatriate commercial community—although in West Africa there had been nominated African members since the nineteenth century (for example, since 1861 in the Gold Coast). The Executive Council was at first composed merely of the heads of the administrative departments. The size of the appointed unofficial membership in the Legislative Council was gradually increased, with a growing number of African members. Finally, an elected element was introduced, perhaps chosen indirectly by District Councils. When the elected African membership became a majority, the stage of 'representative government' had been reached. Meanwhile, a similar devolution was begun on the executive side, with the first African ministers appointed generally dealing in the beginning with social services important to the African community.

We may note in passing that the 'dyarchy' formula, utilized in India, Ceylon and Malta, with a formalized division of functions between colonial functionaries and indigenous ministers responsible to their legislature, was considered a failure and not applied as such in Africa.

During the next phase the British governor chose as prime minister the leader of the African majority party in the elected legislature. All real power now lay with the new prime minister and his cabinet; in general, the colonial governor retained only more or less theoretical veto power. 'Responsible government' finally became independent government.

At the same time, there is a striking difference between the meticulous care with which decolonization was executed in Ghana and Nigeria, and the almost unseemly haste with which Lesotho and Botswana were bundled out the door. As the first post-war British moves towards granting self-government in the African territories, exacting standards were erected as to preparation for independence. Initially, demonstrated capacity to maintain parliamentary democracy on the Western model, proven ability to maintain order and keep public finances tidy, and an adequate reservoir of trained administrative cadres to staff the new state were the preconditions for taking the final step. However, as each successive delegation marched to Lancaster House, the conditions were found to be less rigorous, and the time-table increasingly foreshortened. Had the same standards which were imposed on Ghana been maintained for those at the end of the independence queue, Britain's colonial tutelage would be far from over today. To cite but one example, the phase of 'responsible government' in Ghana lasted nearly six years— while in Uganda it was less than two.

Paradoxically, in sub-Saharan Africa, French policies designed for purposes other than power transfer proved surprisingly serviceable when decolonization suddenly got under way. The doctrine of assimilation perhaps had its strongest impact on the educational system, which did produce a small, but highly trained and competent élite—just barely enough to man the central structures of the new state. The policy of direct rule had for the most part destroyed traditional competitors to the modern state. The abortive efforts to find a permanent place for the overseas territories within the Republic meant that a whole generation of African leaders acquired a decade of experience in one of the toughest political schools in the world—the French National Assembly. The contrast between the outcome of decolonization in the former

French sub-Saharan states and in the Congo suggests that any policy, even a misdirected one, is better than no policy.

The manner in which power was transferred had important consequences for post-independence stability. Except in Algeria, where independence was won by guerrilla war, or in the Congo, where the colonizer lost control over the pace of events, the withdrawing power was able to exert substantial influence on the structure of the post-colonial state and political system. The colonial power based its policy on its own assessment of the requisites for post-colonial stability, on the protection of its investments and other permanent interests, on its perspective as to what constituted 'good government' and on its sense of special responsibility to particular groups—European settlers, minorities of various kinds, its own functionaries. The colonial power's ability to implement its own vision of the future was of course discounted by the degree to which the colonizers' aspirations conflicted with the perspectives of the nationalist élite. But even where the nationalist movement wielded overwhelming political strength during the terminal period of imperial rule, the colonizer possessed one last trump card—the power to fix the date of independence. Skilfully used, this power was of considerable importance.

In the first place, a clear-sighted decolonizer usually exerted some influence over the nature of the successor élite. A crude policy of overtly building an administrative political party, such as the Parti National du Progrès (PNP) in the Congo, or the various movements mounted by the French colonial administration in tropical Africa, was unlikely to succeed. But there were occasions when the colonizers could give discreet assistance to one moderate movement with some popular support to help defeat another party viewed as extremist or otherwise undesirable.

On the British side, Lesotho and Swaziland are probably examples of such a policy. In Sudan, there was a clear preference for leadership that would renounce union with Egypt. In Cameroun the French facilitated the consolidation of power by Ahmadou Ahidjo's Mouvement de l'Union Camerounaise (MUC) and suppressed the Union des Populations Camerounaises of Ruben Um Nyobe and Félix Moumié. In Rwanda, Gregoire Kyabanda's Parmahutu enjoyed the open sympathy of the departing Belgian administration, against the bellicose UNAR (Union Nationale du Ruanda) representing the deposed Tutsi ruling class. In Nigeria, the British, especially those having served in the North, were particularly anxious to overcome the hesitations of the Northern Emir-dominated NPC (Northern People's Congress); they accordingly supported a federal solution assuring the North of regional autonomy, and encouraged the Northern élites to play an important role in the Federal Government. As Western-style democracy subsequently crumbled in much of Africa, and as existing mechanisms for peaceful changes of government began to crack, the issue of which élite was to succeed to power on independence day became even more important than it had seemed at the time.

There was an inevitable tendency for the independence constitutions to be replicas of those of the metropolitan governments. For different reasons, both colonizer and colonized tended to regard the institutions of the mother country as the model of modern democratic government. For one thing, colonial officials felt they could effectively construct only institutions which they themselves knew and understood. The faithful copying of a metropolitan model of doubtful relevance perhaps was carried to its furthest extreme in the Congo. After the key issue of immediate independence had been resolved, nationalists and Belgians set about recopying the Belgian constitution, even down to such unusual features as co-opted senators and division of executive power between a chief of state (modelled on the Belgian king) and a prime minister. In the principal constitutional commentary on the *Loi Fondamentale*, Professor François Perin observed:

The big argument which tipped the scales in favor of the European tradition is the confidence which the functioning of the Belgian regime inspires in the Congolese. The political regime of Belgium has shown itself to be endowed with a rather surprising prestige, even amongst certain Congolese leaders least suspect of indulgence toward the colonizing nation. It is curious to note how often the newly independent nations have yielded to the temptation of trying to adopt the institutions of the erstwhile imperial power. This experiment often proved disappointing, as the historical, economic and sociological conditions of the new nations were profoundly different from those of the former rulers.[1]

In the case of the former French territories, the advent of the Fifth Republic at the hour of decolonization provided a markedly different model. The various measures to reinforce executive powers, to unify the executive, and to prevent chronic executive instability were quickly

---

[1] Quoted in Jules Gérard-Libois and Benoît Verhaegen, *Congo 1960*, 2 vols. (Brussels, Centre de Recherche et d'Information Socio-politiques, 1961), I, 106.

copied overseas. There can be little doubt that the Fifth Republic was a far better model for new nations than the Fourth. In fact, many former British territories rather swiftly rewrote their constitutions to substitute a presidential model for the Westminster original.

Decolonization was greatly influenced by the relative pace with which power was devolved at the centre and at the regional peripheries in the new states. In Uganda and Nigeria, effective power over a significant range of functions, including extensive patronage, was handed over at the regional (or district) level before the new élites had succeeded to power at the centre. In Nigeria, the Southern regions acquired virtual self-government in 1954, while the first federal prime minister was not named until 1957. In Uganda, Buganda became almost completely autonomous by virtue of the 1955 Agreement which brought the Kabaka back from exile. The District Administrations Ordinance of the same year permitted the establishment at the district level of representative governments with important responsibilities. The first Ugandan chief minister was not appointed until 1961. In both these cases, local power centres had become well consolidated before an effective national government could compete with them.

In the Congo, representative institutions were simultaneously created at the centre and in the provinces. After independence, the provincial institutions broke down more slowly than those at the centre. Accordingly, the newly created provincial governments were able to inherit many powers which the central government could not exercise. In the former French territories, by contrast, there were no representative institutions standing between the municipalities or other purely local governments on the one hand and the territorial institutions on the other. Central authority was clearly more secure in these circumstances. However, at an earlier stage the French had implicitly opted for twelve republics rather than two in West and Equatorial Africa; the French made the component territories of Afrique Occidentale Française and Afrique Equatoriale Française the beneficiaries of the 1956 *Loi-Cadre*, and not the two administrative federations. This policy was reinforced in 1958, when membership in the French Community was acquired by the individual territories, not by 'primary federations'. France also unofficially opposed the claim of the Mali Federation to succeed the former AOF.

The French were far from being the only agents of 'balkanization'; devolution to the territories was insistently demanded by important segments of the new leadership, especially by Houphouët-Boigny, and by the territories most remote from the former federation capitals of Dakar and Brazzaville. However, an important part of the nationalist leadership, especially in AOF, was strongly committed to retention of the larger entities. It is at least arguable that if the French had given the same encouragement to the maintenance of these units that the British did to keeping Nigeria one nation, or for that matter the Belgians in the Congo, the outcome could have been different.

For the most part, decolonizers showed a clear preference for a unitary state. At the same time, they were peculiarly susceptible to the appeal of 'minorities' who appeared to be poorly represented in the emergent nationalist political movements, the presumptive heirs of central power. In Ghana, the rise of belligerent regional political movements, especially in Ashanti and the Northern Territories, as well as in Togo, led the British government to force a new general election upon the CPP to obtain a clear mandate on the issue of regionalism and the independence constitution. In Nigeria, a special commission was designated in 1958 to hear the grievances of the 'minorities' in each of the three regions.[1] In Kenya, the Kenya African Democratic Union (KADU) was able to persuade Britain that the smaller ethnic groups in Kenya were in danger of being submerged by the Kikuyu and Luo. The new constitution made significant concessions to regional desires—although after independence the 'majimbo' constitution was swiftly replaced with a unitary basic law. In the case of the Sudan, however, British sympathies for the claims of the non-Arab, non-Muslim populations of the three southern provinces were outweighed by the need to meet the unitary aspiration of the north, as part of the tacit bargain for forestalling union with Egypt.

A particularly delicate and difficult aspect of decolonization was the localization of the public service. In the terminal colonial period, as the output of African universities and secondary schools expanded rapidly, the nationalists everywhere pressed for a swift enlargement of opportunities in the civil service. There was a simultaneous growth of disaffection among many expatriate white functionaries who were out of sympathy with the pace of change. Many officials, for instance, experienced a feeling of personal insecurity or loss of morale. They had

---

[1] Great Britain, *Parliamentary papers*, Vol. IX, Cmnd. 505, *Nigeria, report of the commission appointed to enquire into the fears of minorities and the means of allaying them* (London, 1958).

entered on their careers with the intention of devoting their whole working lives to administration. The British Home Civil Service, however, was not designed to absorb into the metropolitan administration large numbers of former colonial officials. (The French, with their tradition of centralization, enjoyed a considerable advantage in this respect.) Many British colonial civil servants thus faced the prospect of abruptly looking for a new job. The most junior and the most senior British officials were generally least affected by this sense of instability—the former because they had their whole working lives before them; the latter because they looked to drawing their pensions in a few years' time, and therefore often tended to be more 'permissive' in their outlook toward African aspirations than the 'middle rankers' (frequently married men with growing families). In some cases there was a muted conflict also on the African side between the older generation of officials and the new generation of university graduates and holders of advanced technical diplomas as to whether seniority or paper qualifications should count more heavily in assessing a candidate's suitability for promotion.

It was probably the question of Africanizing the public services that revealed most sharply the general miscalculation of all colonizers concerning the time available for a transfer of power after 1945. Despite post-war expansion of secondary and higher education in Africa, planning for the Africanization of the civil service tended to lag behind political reforms. There were no minimum 'standards' for politicians, except perhaps fluency in the official language. But 'Africanization' of the administration was another matter. Formal educational criteria were considered vital, and the manpower shortage could not be quickly remedied. In Nigeria a special commissioner for Africanization was appointed in 1948, and the policy established that no expatriate would be recruited for a post for which a qualified Nigerian was available. In 1939 there had been only twenty-three Nigerians in the senior service; in 1948 the number was still only 182. In Ghana, which had its first African district commissioner as early as 1942, Africans composed only 13·8 per cent of the senior service in 1949, and still only 38·2 per cent in 1954.

Despite the mystique of assimilation, French domination of overseas civil services was, if anything, more complete. The French employed a much larger number of their own nationals even in junior colonial administrative posts than the British. In Morocco, for instance, Frenchmen in 1955 held two-thirds of all civil service posts. There were no fewer than 40,000 French functionaries; another 10,000 manned the public corporations. Even in the economically advanced Ivory Coast, in 1956, at the moment of the *Loi-Cadre*, not a single Ivory Coast African held a decision-making position in the senior administration.

The Congo was again the extreme case. The Belgians assumed that political transition would in effect occur after independence, not before. The only immediate change in 1960 was the pell-mell creation of new representative institutions—a parliament and a council of ministers. The traditional, essential armature of the state, the administration, and its coercive support, the army, remained virtually entirely in European hands. The following figures give the racial breakdown in the civil service by rank in early 1960.[1]

Rank	European	African
1	106	—
2	1,004	1
3	3,532	2
4	5,159	800
5–7	—	11,000

Until 1959, the senior service was in effect purely European, with Congolese subaltern clerks and functionaries in an auxiliary service. There were two legal barriers to Congolese access to the top ranks: the requirement of a university degree (the first class was graduated from Lovanium in 1958) and the stipulation that candidates had to be Belgian (or Luxembourg) nationals. Congolese were considered Belgian subjects, but not Belgian citizens. It was never clear whether they were in fact barred by this clause. The question remained theoretical until graduates began to appear on the horizon. The demand for a complete suppression of these barriers and for equal salaries and perquisites for equal qualifications became a major part of the nationalist programme. Like many other colonial reforms, it was subject to the customary delays and conflicts within the colonial establishment. Perhaps coincidentally, the long-postponed civil service reform was suddenly promulgated on 13 January 1959, a week after the Leopoldville riots. But this came much too late. The Congo became independent with a restless,

[1] Institut International des Civilisations Différentes, *Problèmes des cadres dans les pays tropicaux et subtropicaux, Compte rendu de la 32e session d'études de l'INCIDI, tenue à Munich du 19 au 22 septembre 1960, Staff problems in tropical and subtropical countries, Report of the 32nd INCIDI study session, held in Munich from 19 to 22 September 1960* (Brussels, 1961).

radical nationalist leadership whose policies were to be implemented by a conservative European bureaucracy. Even at best, the conflict potential of this situation was immense—and the Congo was shortly to experience the worst of circumstances.

Localization had to be accelerated; at the same time premature departure of colonial servants had to be forestalled. In the southern regions of Nigeria, the British public servants threatened to leave en masse when regional autonomy was granted in 1953, and when they were to be placed under the orders of African ministers. Eventually arrangements were made for their contracts to be transferred to the United Kingdom, with secondment overseas, rather than for their coming fully under the jurisdiction of the new governments for their terms of service. Opportunities—and inducements—were offered for early termination of services, otherwise known as 'the golden handshake'. British policy was not, however, consistent. In the discussions that preceded the dissolution of the Federation of Rhodesia and Nyasaland, for instance, negotiators from the United Kingdom, Southern Rhodesia, Northern Rhodesia and Nyasaland all apparently agreed that the federal civil servants' handshake should not be too 'golden' lest trained personnel should depart too suddenly and the constituent territories of the defunct federation should be faced with an overly heavy burden of pensions and gratuities. Difficulties arose also over the fact that not all the British dependent territories in Africa were administered by the same service. There were accordingly considerable differences in the terminal conditions offered, say, to former members of the British Colonial Service, of the public service of the Federation of Rhodesia and Nyasaland, and of the Sudan service. These discrepancies led to acid comparisons and occasioned many grievances. Nevertheless the decolonizers enjoyed a tremendous advantage. The world economy was expanding rapidly. Ex-colonial officials quickly found new jobs in Great Britain, Australia, and other countries, so that the British did not have to deal with an embittered lobby of displaced officials and soldiers of the kind that troubled, say, the Austrian Republic in the lean years after World War I.

Among Belgian colonial functionaries, uncertainty and insecurity in the Congo were much more acute. Their feelings were expressed in a letter of 8 May 1960:

On the eve of Congolese independence, the European population of the Congo asks itself anxiously about the nature of the protection that Belgium is prepared to give to its nationals.

The fear expressed by our compatriots is far from being vain and unjustified.

Many Congolese publications contain virulent appeals to racial hatred, and even encouragements to massacre of the Belgians, and rape of our wives and daughters.

Large sections of the native population identify independence with our expulsion, even by bloody means.[1]

Unlike their French counterparts, their pensions and status were entirely linked with the colonial state. To reassure them, on 21 March 1960 the Belgian Parliament guaranteed reintegration of those functionaries unable to continue their careers in Africa. This law had the unintended effect of precipitating the departure of nearly all Belgian functionaries in July 1960. The Belgian Ambassador announced on 12 July that all Belgian civil servants outside Katanga would be considered unable to continue their careers in the Congo—only to have the law retroactively annulled in Belgium in early 1961 because of the total impossibility of absorbing 10,000 ranking functionaries in the metropolitan civil service.

The security forces—as recent history has demonstrated—are a crucial element in the post-colonial state, to which relatively little attention had been paid until the later stages of decolonization. In many cases—Ruanda-Urundi and tropical African territories of France—countries slated for independence had no separate security forces; these had to be created at top speed at the last minute. In a majority of cases the security forces remained under European command at the moment of independence. This at least had the effect of postponing the entry of the army into the political arena, a trend in post-independence politics not clearly foreseen at the hour of decolonization.

What, then, can be said by way of conclusion and interim judgement on a crucial juncture of African history? One is tempted to suggest that post-independence stability and progress provide one empirical test of the success of decolonization—but then it would seem harsh to fault Britain with the failure of Nkrumah's Ghana to fulfil the high hopes of 1957. Still, a well-conceived, smoothly implemented programme for power transfer clearly gives a new state important advantages in weathering the difficult early years of independence.

In the first place, there is no substitute for clarity of purpose nor for realistic goals. Here the British record, despite the many blemishes,

[1] Gérard-Libois and Verhaegen, *Congo 1960*, II, 523–4.

clearly stands out. Although all colonizers miscalculated the pace of decolonization, the British had the inestimable advantage of a framework within which acceleration was possible. In the case of France, on the other hand, Algeria provides the disastrous example of a decolonization forced upon the erstwhile rulers by nationalist guerrilla warfare. The energies of nationalism are drawn into the building up of a revolutionary army, created by the Algerians with signal success. However, there are great difficulties in adapting this mechanism to the needs of effective government and economic development. There is little sign that Algeria has yet made this adjustment. The Belgian case, in contrast with the British, shows the danger of meeting the rendezvous with nationalism empty-handed. The Congo had been well on the road to economic and social modernization. The subsequent social cost of a decolonization gone awry must be counted by years of set-back, intensification of regional disparities, and a chronic gap between public expectation and government capability, with endemic instability and rebellion.

Second, decolonization did not, by and large, provide adequate answers for the problems of securing viable political structures for the post-colonial states. Although one must be cautious in generalizing—some African states, like Tunisia, Tanzania and Zambia, were relatively successful—the wave of coups and instability suggests that many more are in deep trouble. Neither the Westminster model—now largely abandoned—nor the nationalist response of the single-party system can be considered a success. The cherished American formula of federalism seems to have created as many problems as it has solved. In 1966 the three major examples—Nigeria, Uganda and the Congo—all sought to move towards more unitary government.

Third, it becomes even more clear how right Julius Nyerere was in 1961 when he urged that the hour of independence was the time for building larger unities. In retrospect, it would appear that this problem was not assigned sufficient priority. Britain, it is true, did seek to promote federations in East and in Central Africa. But in both these cases British initiatives on federation came to be identified in African eyes with the interests of the local white communities. In any case, political unions are hard to consummate. Senegal and Gambia, for instance, could not be fused despite the compelling geographic logic of Senegambia. For both political and economic reasons the formerly British East African states have drifted apart. Except for a handful of wealthier states like Gabon, Mauritania and Ivory Coast, the former French territories, in particular, are split into small, impoverished independent entities, with dismal economic prospects. Opportunities for constructing larger and more viable entities were clearly lost, and may perhaps never recur. The very existence of separate states creates powerful new vested interests among political leaders, senior civil servants, officers, and even many businessmen, all of whom may have a personal stake in the continued independence of their respective countries.

Finally, the heart of the colonial state was its bureaucracy. Perhaps the most enduring legacy of the colonial era is the modern administrative infrastructure. New nations are committed to rapid modernization and generally rely upon the state as the central agency of development. State administrators thus face a difficult task. If they are fortunate, an effective political party may be available to give them support. But in many African states the civil service tends to become the executive organ of the ruling party. Many ruling parties have unfortunately achieved little success in switching from the pre-independence role of primarily expressing grievances to the harsher task of meeting new administrative and economic challenges. Governments have perhaps an easier time in countries possessed of massive mineral deposits. But the majority must propel themselves forward by peasant agriculture, and for them the quality of the administration becomes perhaps even more crucial. Thus the disabilities of a decolonization that impairs or destroys the administrative infrastructure are prolonged and severe. The supreme achievement of power-transfer statecraft lies in transmitting the bureaucracy intact to the independent government. This implies both a sound strategy of localization and a phasing of devolution of authority to the nationalist successor élite, so that power and responsibility are never dissociated and so that nationalists are never tempted to destroy their most indispensable weapon against underdevelopment.

BIBLIOGRAPHY

Apter, David E. *The Gold Coast in transition.* Princeton University Press, 1955.

Ashford, Douglas E. *Political change in Morocco.* Princeton University Press, 1961.

Austin, Dennis. *Politics in Ghana, 1946–1960.* London, Oxford University Press, 1964.

Belgium. Ministère des Colonies. *La réforme de l'enseignement au Congo belge: mission pédagogique Coulón–Deheyn–Renson; rapport présenté à Monsieur le Ministre Auguste Buisseret.* Brussels, 1954.

Belgium. Parlement. Chambre des Représentants. *Rapport du groupe de travail pour l'étude du problème politique au Congo belge.* 1958–9 Sess. 20 Jan. 1959, No. 108. Brussels, 1959.

Bilsen, A. A. J. van. *Vers l'indépendance du Congo et du Ruanda-Urundi: réflexion sur les devoirs et l'avenir de la Belgique en Afrique centrale.* Brussels, 1958.

Borella, François. *L'évolution politique et juridique de l'Union Française depuis 1946.* Paris, 1958.

Bromberger, Serge, and Merry Bromberger. *Les 13 complots du 13 mai, ou La délivrance de Gulliver.* Paris, 1959.

Brzezinski, Zbigniew. *Africa and the communist world.* Stanford University Press, 1963.

Buchmann, Jean. *L'Afrique noire indépendante.* Paris, 1962.

Butler, David E., and Richard Rose. *The British general election of 1959.* London, 1960.

Centre de Recherche et d'Information Socio-politiques (CRISP). *Morphologie des groupes financiers.* 2nd ed. Brussels, 1966.

Chaffard, Georges. *Les carnets secrets de la décolonisation.* 2 vols. Paris, 1965–7.

Clark, Michael K. *Algeria in turmoil: a history of the rebellion.* New York, 1959.

Coleman, James S. *Nigeria: background to nationalism.* Berkeley and Los Angeles, University of California Press, 1958.

Crowder, Michael. 'Indirect rule, French and British style', *Africa*, 1964, **34**, no. 3.

Dallin, Alexander. 'The Soviet Union: political activity', in *Africa and the communist world*, Zbigniew Brzezinski, ed. Stanford University Press, 1963.

Denuit, Désiré. *Le Congo champion de la Belgique en guerre.* Brussels, 1945.

Deschamps, Hubert. 'Et maintenant, Lord Lugard?', *Africa*, Oct. 1963, **33**, no. 4.

Easton, Stewart C. *The rise and fall of western colonialism: a historical survey from the early nineteenth century to the present.* New York, 1964.

Emerson, Rupert. *From empire to nation: the rise to self-assertion of Asian and African peoples.* Cambridge, Harvard University Press, 1960.

Fauvet, Jacques, and Jean Planchais. *La fronde des généraux.* Paris, 1961.

Foltz, William J. *From French West Africa to the Mali federation.* New Haven, Yale University Press, 1965.

Gérard-Libois, Jules, and Benoît Verhaegen. *Congo 1960.* 2 vols. Brussels, Centre de Recherche et d'Information Socio-politiques, 1961.

Gonidec, P. F. *Constitutions des états de la Communauté.* Paris, 1959.

L'évolution des territoires d'outre-mer depuis 1946. Paris, 1958.

Great Britain. *Parliamentary papers.* Vol. xxxvi. Cmd. 468. *Report by Sir F. D. Lugard on the amalgamation of Northern and Southern Nigeria, and administration, 1912–1919.* London, 1919.

Vol. ix. Cmnd. 505. *Nigeria, report of the commission appointed to enquire into the fears of minorities and the means of allaying them.* London, 1957–8.

Hammer, Ellen J. *The struggle for Indochina.* Stanford University Press, 1954.

Hanna, William John, ed. *Independent black Africa: the politics of freedom.* Chicago, 1964.

Hodgkin, Thomas Lionel. *African political parties: an introductory guide.* London and Baltimore, 1961.

Hull, Cordell. *Memoirs.* New York, 1948.

Institut International des Civilisations Différentes. *Problèmes des cadres dans les pays tropicaux et subtropicaux. Compte rendu de la 32ᵉ session d'études de l'INCIDI, tenue à Munich de 19 au 22 septembre 1960. Staff problems in tropical and subtropical countries. Report of the 32nd INCIDI study session held in Munich from 19 to 22 September 1960.* Brussels, 1961.

Jeffries, Sir Charles Joseph. *Transfer of power: problems of the passage to self-government.* London, 1960.

Jones, Arthur Creech, ed. *New Fabian colonial essays.* New York, 1959.

Joye, Pierre, and Rosine Lewin. *Les trusts au Congo.* Brussels, 1961.

Kelly, George A. *Lost soldiers: the French army and empire in crisis, 1947–1962.* Cambridge, Massachusetts Institute of Technology Press, 1965.

Key, Valdimer Orlando. *Public opinion and American democracy.* New York, 1961.

Lacouture, Jean. *Cinq hommes et la France.* Paris, 1961.

Langenhove, F. van. 'Factors of decolonization', *Civilisations,* 1961, **11**.

Le Cornec, Jacques. *Histoire politique du Tchad de 1900 à 1962.* Paris, 1963.

Le Tourneau, Roger. *Evolution politique de l'Afrique du nord musulmane, 1920–1961.* Paris, 1962.

LeVine, Victor T. 'Insular problems of an inland state', *Africa Report,* Nov. 1965, **10**.

Lewis, William Arthur. *Politics in West Africa.* New York, Oxford University Press, 1965.

Louwers, Octave. *L'article 73 de la charte et l'anticolonialisme de l'Organisation des Nations Unies.* Brussels, Institut Royal Colonial Belge, 1952.

Meynaud, Jean, Jean Ladrière and François Perin, eds. *La décision politique en Belgique.* Paris, 1965.

Morgenthau, Ruth Schachter. *Political parties in French-speaking West Africa.* Oxford, Clarendon Press, 1964.

Nkrumah, Kwame. *Ghana: the autobiography of Kwame Nkrumah*. New York and Edinburgh, 1957.

Oduho, Joseph, and William Deng. *The problem of the Southern Sudan*. London, Oxford University Press, 1963.

Perham, Margery. *The colonial reckoning: the end of imperial rule in Africa in the light of the British experience*. London, 1961.

Planchais, Jean. *Le malaise de l'armée*. Paris, 1958.

Robinson, Kenneth. *The dilemmas of trusteeship: aspects of British colonial policy between the wars*. London, Oxford University Press, 1965.

Schachter, Ruth. 'Single-party systems in West Africa', *American Political Science Review*, June 1961, **55**.

Sepulchre, Jean. *Propos sur le Congo politique de demain: autonomie et fédéralisme*. Elisabethville, 1958.

Skinner, Elliott P. *The Mossi of the Upper Volta: the political development of a Sudanese people*. Stanford University Press, 1964.

Thompson, Leonard M. *The unification of South Africa, 1902–1910*. Oxford, Clarendon Press, 1960.

Thompson, Virginia, and Richard Adloff. *The emerging states of French Equatorial Africa*. Stanford University Press, 1960.

Wallis, C. A. G. *Report of an inquiry into African local government in the Protectorate of Uganda*. Entebbe, 1953.

Weiss, Herbert. *Political protest in the Congo: the Parti Solidaire Africain during the independence struggle*. Princeton University Press, 1967.

Weiss, Herbert, and Benoît Verhaegen, eds. *Parti Solidaire Africain (P.S.A.): documents 1959–1960*. Brussels, Centre de Recherche et d'Information Socio-politiques, 1963.

Werth, Alexander. *The strange history of Pierre Mendès-France and the great conflict over French North Africa*. London, 1957.

Young, Crawford. *Politics in the Congo: decolonization and independence*. Princeton University Press, 1965.

Zolberg, Aristide R. *One-party government in the Ivory Coast*. Princeton University Press, 1964.

CHAPTER 14

CONCLUSION

THE COLONIAL ERA: CONQUEST TO INDEPENDENCE

by A. ADU BOAHEN

Beginning with the year 1920, the colonial episode in Africa falls into two periods, the twenty-five year span from 1920 to 1945 and the post-World War II era from 1945 to 1960. During the first period there occurred the consolidation of colonial rule on the continent. The second period may be described as the classical period of decolonization, or, as Apter prefers to call it, 'political institutional transfer'.[1] The two periods, of course, are not separate, but in more senses than just the temporal may be considered complementary. Indeed, the second is more or less the logical sequel to the first. The earlier period saw the development or introduction by the colonizers, with varying degrees of success, of many political, social and economic reforms. These gave birth to certain classes, and generated a number of grievances and much discontent among the colonized. The impact of the Second World War both on the colonies and on the metropolitan countries, as well as the accelerated pace of economic and social developments that followed the war, intensified African discontent and dissatisfaction. These, in turn, generated radical nationalist movements and political parties whose activities led to the overthrow of the colonial system.

Whether in a fit of absent-mindedness, as Seeley would prefer to term it, or in pursuit of trade, philanthropy, prestige or strategic advantages, during the short span between 1874 and 1902 the European powers of Britain, France, Germany, Belgium, Portugal and Spain recklessly partitioned the continent of Africa among themselves. This period, as well as the two decades that followed, witnessed what some historians have described as the period of pacification. But in reality this was an era of conquest, when African resistance to colonial domination was broken and finally mopped up. It was these same years that

[1] David E. Apter, *Ghana in transition*, rev. ed. (New York, 1963), pp. 3–4.

17-2

saw the beginnings of economic development or exploitation symbolized by the construction of roads and railways, by the introduction
of the cultivation of cash-crops such as cocoa and cotton and by the
increasing appearance on the African commercial scene of European
trading firms and mining companies.

After World War I, which absorbed the energy of the colonial
powers, attention was once more turned to the colonies. The main
preoccupations of the colonial powers were to ensure peace and order
through the working out, in the words of Crawford Young, of 'effective
formulas for administering subject populations', to continue the development or exploitation of the economic potentialities of their
colonies and to introduce some social services. The methods and
formulas adopted for the achievement of these objectives differed from
one metropolitan power to another. They also had differing consequences for the colonial subjects, and variously affected the nature of
the consequent nationalist movements and decolonizing processes.

What, then, were the changes that were introduced during the period
between the First and Second World Wars? What effects did these
changes have on the colonial subjects and what were their reactions?
What was the impact of the Second World War both on the colonies
and on the metropolitan countries? What was the nature of the political,
economic and social reforms that were introduced after the war and
with what effects? What touched off the decolonizing movements, who
was responsible for them, and what determined the nature, pace and
outcome of these movements? Finally, what were the main legacies
that colonialism bequeathed to the independent African states? These
are the questions that are treated in these essays, and the answers help
to shed light on the phenomenon of colonialism and to afford a clear
insight into its impact on Africa during these four eventful decades.

The political changes introduced during the inter-war period were,
to a considerable extent, conditioned either by the attitude of each of
the metropolitan powers towards its colonies, or by the assumptions on
which their policies rested. During this period the British regarded
their colonies as separate entities. The Portuguese and the French, on
the other hand, originally based their administrations on the myth
that their colonies were mere provinces of the metropolitan country
across the seas, or as the French called them, 'territoires d'outre-mer'.
Though the more realistic French later abandoned this attitude in favour
of the theory of association, the Portuguese have held to it tenaciously

up to the present moment, as is evident from Duffy's essay. As late as 1930 Salazar wrote: 'Angola or Mozambique or India are under the single authority of the state. We are a political and juridical unity.' But all of the metropolitan powers may be said to have shared one characteristic in common: none of them was thinking at this time in terms of decolonization. Thus, while the British had set up a central government system in each territory, usually consisting of nominated legislative and executive councils for each colony, the French had established only a single one for the whole of their colonies in West Africa and another one for those in Equatorial Africa. The Belgians had created a single administrative system for the Congo.

As Crowder has brought out, the systems of local government varied too. The British and the Belgians ruled indirectly through the African chiefs and traditional institutions, while the French and the Portuguese governed more directly through either traditional chiefs now turned into civil servants or chiefs appointed by the colonizers. All the colonial powers, however, did divide their colonies for local government purposes into districts or centres, each under an officer, Crowder's 'white chief'. Another change introduced by all the colonial powers during this period was, as Gutteridge has pointed out, the elimination of the military from the administrative field, and the creation of a clear distinction between the army and the police.

In addition, each of the metropolitan powers embarked on economic and social reforms. Indeed, the period was characterized by what has been aptly described as 'the successive advance inland of the traders, miners, the farmers and the manufacturers' frontiers generally from the coast inland'. The only other frontiers which should be included here are the communications, the educational and the medical frontiers. The period was marked not only by trading, mining, farming and industrial activities, but also by the extension of roads, railways, posts and telegraphs and the building of schools and hospitals into the interiors of the colonies. The export figures for 1920 to 1930 covering cocoa from Ghana and Ivory Coast, ground-nuts from Senegal, bananas from Guinea, and gold and other minerals, as well as the increase in the schools and hospitals, make it abundantly clear that considerable success attended the efforts of the colonial authorities.

These advances, however, took diverse paths and occurred under many different agencies. In British West Africa, for example, the extension inland of the farmers' frontier was exclusively the work of the African himself. In southern and eastern Africa, on the other hand, it was accomplished mainly by Europeans; and one of the most striking developments in these areas was the increase in the number of white settlers during the period under discussion. The extension of the trader's frontier, which in fact had been going on for a long time even before the era of partition, was also by and large in the hands of Africans themselves in most of the colonies. On the other hand, the extension of the miners' and the manufacturers' frontiers was throughout the sole responsibility of European firms.

All these developments implied the use of labour, and here again we find striking differences. Whereas forced labour was the exception rather than the rule in the British colonies in West Africa, in their colonies in eastern and southern Africa, as well as in the French, Belgian and Portuguese colonies, forced labour was widespread.

The third main change occurred in the social field. In all the colonies, education was promoted, health services were extended and attempts were made at improvement of housing, especially in the urban areas. As all of our contributors have stressed, education, except in the case of the French, was largely the work of the missionary societies and of the Christian churches. Its main objective was character-training, with the emphasis on primary education and on literary rather than on vocational and technical aspects. It was mainly the British and the French who gave some encouragement to secondary education. In the 1920s the British, for instance, established the Achimota Secondary School in Ghana, the Katsina College in Nigeria, the Alliance High School in Kenya, and Makerere in Uganda, while the French in the inter-war period established about eight schools, including the Dakar Medical School, Lycée Faidherbe and William Ponty Normal School to train medical assistants, teachers, pharmacists and middle-level administrators. The Belgians, too, provided some post-primary courses; but these were almost entirely of a technical character.

The effects of all these changes were very far-reaching and have been treated in detail in these essays. The educated African élite greatly increased in numbers. Their evolution and their political role and the attitude of the colonial officials to them have been emphasized, indeed overemphasized, in this volume. In fact, Anstey, Kilson, Wallerstein and to some extent Post and Young all discuss these themes. Known as the *évolué*, the *assimilado*, and the *immatriculé* and the 'new men' or 'new élite' in the French, the Portuguese, the Belgian and the British colonies respectively, and consisting of lawyers, doctors, senior civil servants, private businessmen and merchants, they played roles of varying importance and effectiveness in the political, economic and social lives of their peoples. Parallel to this phenomenon was the increase in the number of Indians in Kenya and Tanzania and of Syrians and Lebanese in West Africa.

The economic and social changes also gave rise to two other groups of Africans who have received less attention in these essays than I feel they deserve. The first group consists of wage-earners who migrated from the rural areas into the old and new urban centres, the places for the new schools, shops, offices and new mine shafts and the termini of the new roads and railways. Indeed, two of the most typical phenomena of colonialism in the inter-war period were, on the one hand, the partial exodus from rural areas and villages, and on the other hand and indeed as a corollary, the growth of urban centres with their typical divisions into African and European sectors. In many areas there were also the segregation laws, which served to generate among the Africans violent emotions of anger, envy and lust.[1] Most of the wage-earners were elementary-school leavers, while the road and mining labourers were mainly illiterate. It was the wage-earners who formed the professional, tribal, improvement and welfare associations that became such a feature of the new urban centres in the inter-war years. The main objectives of these associations were to fight for better conditions of employment and improved living conditions, and to serve as an antidote against the loneliness, the boredom and the oppressive individualism and impersonality that typified life in the towns.

The second group, to which only Kilson gives some attention, consists of cash-crop producers. The existence of this group was by no means an entirely new phenomenon in Africa. Ever since the slave-trade era in the seventeenth and eighteenth centuries, as is evident from the records of the Dutch and British trading companies, there were Africans who earned their living by producing provisions (especially maize) and also firewood for sale to the slave-ships. During the nineteenth century the production first of palm-oil, ground-nuts and cotton, and later of rubber, became a widespread occupation. The main change here was the stupendous increase in the membership of this group throughout Africa with the introduction of new cash-crops such as

---

[1] Frantz Fanon, *The wretched of the earth*, trans. by Constance Farrington (London, 1967), p. 30.

cocoa and coffee, the adoption of some of the methods and the better seeds used by the whites and above all the deliberate encouragement given by the colonial governments to these peasant farmers.

Owing to the inequality of opportunities, the numerical strength of each of these groups varied from colony to colony. The number of the élite or, as Kilson prefers to call it, 'upper-echelon élite', and the 'sub-élite' in the British and French West African colonies was much higher than those in British eastern Africa or in Portuguese and Belgian Africa. As Kilson has pointed out, while Kenya did not have its first African lawyer until 1956, there were as many as sixty African lawyers practising in Ghana as early as the 1920s.

Now what was the reaction of these new classes to the colonial system which had indeed either generated or aided their rise? In the economic and social fields, Africans clearly welcomed all these new techniques, institutions and machines—schools, hospitals, motor roads and mining machinery. But they generally considered that these facilities were either grossly inadequate, or that they were not being equally distributed among all classes of society or (as in Portuguese and Belgian and British eastern Africa) between the European settlers and the Africans.

Another prime source of conflict was the land question, particularly in territories such as Kenya and the two Rhodesias, where Europeans acquired extensive farms. Certainly land hunger lay at the root of the subsequent Mau Mau rising in Kenya. The colonial governments frequently made over extensive mineral rights to powerful metro-politan companies—a practice that occasioned numerous grievances. In Northern Rhodesia, for instance, both local African leaders and European settlers bitterly criticized the extent of the mineral concessions given to the British South Africa Company. There were similar prob-lems in West Africa. During a debate in the Legislative Council of the Gold Coast in 1939, for example, Nana Ofori Atta I, one of the most powerful kings in the country at the time, drew attention to the ridiculously low annual rents that were being paid by the European mining companies. He said:

One chief gets £66, one chief gets £133; one gets £50; another gets £200; and the last gets £100 per annum. These are the rents payable to chiefs in respect of the Ashanti Goldfields Ltd., and there is nothing that goes to any chiefs in the profits earned.[1]

[1] Legislative Council Debates, Gold Coast, 1939, p. 74.

And this company was paying not less than 70 per cent dividend to its shareholders. When he and the other chiefs wanted to introduce a bill to compel the company to pay them some royalty on its profits, the governor refused his support on the most unconvincing grounds that 'it would be a short-sighted and extremely harmful policy for the Government to interfere in a matter of this sort, because capital is very sensitive and it might have the effect of driving it away to other parts of the world.'

Another source of discontent was forced labour and, in French Africa, conscription and the harshness of the *indigénat*, while in southern and eastern Africa it was the irritating pass-system and segregation laws. The migration of people from the French areas into, say, Ghana and Nigeria resulted partly from a desire to escape from these indignities. But above all, there was dissatisfaction throughout the continent over the neglect of industrialization, the high prices of imported goods and, especially in the 1930s, over the low prices paid for agricultural products. Again, to quote a typical speech in the Legislative Assembly of Ghana in 1939:

Now Your Excellency, as industries are the mainstay of any country, I desire to emphasize the necessity of fostering native industries such as soap, salt, tobacco, sugar, rice, pottery, cloth-weaving, fishing and palm-oil with a view to establishing good internal trade in this country. Why should crafts that have held the people from time immemorial be made to give way for a foreign cargo? Home weaving with all its beauty, for example, make way for Manchester and Japanese goods? Now the Department of Agriculture has often been severely criticised because of the failure of that Department to help the country in creating new industries... are we to understand, Sir, that our Agricultural Department is incapable of helping us to produce locally the articles mentioned in the notice? Surely they are capable, unless, in order to protect the European trade, it is not intended to help us to develop economically. It may be contested that this is a misconception, but I say, Sir, that this is what really exists in the minds of the people of this country.[1]

It is a point often missed by many people that discontent at the social and economic measures introduced by the colonial powers, particularly over land, low prices of agricultural products and forced labour, was by no means confined to the élite; but these measures affected also the farmers and the peasants. Indeed, the period was marked by many rural uprisings and demonstrations. Typical examples were the rebellion that

---

[1] *Ibid.*, p. 153.

broke out in Oubangui in 1929 and the cocoa hold-ups in Ghana in the 1930s.

Even more deeply felt, though rather confined to the upper-echelon élite, were grievances produced by the political changes. As some of our contributors have pointed out, these grievances were more widely and more deeply felt and generated more reaction in the British than in the other European colonies. The main complaint of the élite in British Africa during the inter-war years was based on their exclusion from the running of the affairs of the country, both at the local and central levels, as well as from the civil service. In all the movements organized in the inter-war period, therefore, the cry was not for the overthrow, but rather for the reform of the colonial system; and the main demands were for the Africanization of the civil service and for better African representation in parliament. The National Congress of British West Africa of 1920 called for increased representation on the legislative councils of the various colonies, control over finance by elected members, Africanization of the civil service, and measures to ensure fair competition between African and European businessmen. The Nigerian National Democratic Party launched in Lagos in 1923 also believed that:

Cooperation of the governed with the governing body is the shortest cut to administrative success, provided the administrative policy of the governing body is inspired by sympathetic liberalism or enlightened statesmanship; and provided true regard is paid to the legitimate and reasonable virtues of the governed when constitutionally expressed or interpreted.[1]

And it was partly in response to these demands that the British government introduced new constitutions in their West African colonies in Nigeria, Sierra Leone and Ghana in 1922, 1924 and 1925, respectively, in which the principle of direct election to the Legislative Council was first conceded.

However, the number of seats granted to the élite—four in Nigeria, three in Ghana and three in Sierra Leone—as compared with those given to the traditional authorities, was so grossly inadequate that the struggle for better representation and leadership continued in the 1920s between the élite, on the one hand, and the colonial governors and the chiefs on the other. The struggle became greater in the 1930s with the formation of the youth movements by new and relatively young mem-

[1] *Nigerian Daily Times*, 19 Nov. 1940.

bers of the élite, such as J. B. Danquah, I. T. A. Wallace-Johnson and Azikiwe. Thus, one of the effects of the political changes and the rise of the congress and the youth movements was to cause a rift between the élite and the chiefs—a rift that unfortunately persists even today.

Opportunities for educated Africans differed widely from one colony to another. But all the imperial powers found it necessary, in order to maintain the machinery of government, to employ considerable numbers of such African functionaries as court interpreters, telegraphists, postmasters, clerks, teachers, detectives. In France alone, educated Africans rose to be members of the French legislature in Paris; some were even assigned ministerial portfolios. In the British colonies a handful of Africans were admitted to the local legislative councils and, in a few cases, to the executive councils. In the Belgian Congo, Africans were allowed to carry out a relatively large number of technical jobs, but there was no equivalent for the legislative councils found in British colonies. Neither did Africans attain representation in the Belgian Chamber of Deputies at Brussels. The colonial powers differed also in the way in which they permitted or muzzled public dissent. In British West Africa, for instance, journalists could speak their minds fairly freely in the local newspapers. The Belgians and the Portuguese, on the other hand, imposed a rigid censorship that inhibited the public expression of African grievances.

As might have been expected, the differing policies of the colonial powers produced varying African responses. Belgian Africans during the inter-war period, as Anstey points out, complained mainly at the failure of the Belgian administration to recognize the évolués as 'a separate social class'. The more advanced Congolese Africans also resented the whites' refusal to enter into closer relations with the black élite. So did educated black people in British East and Central Africa, who resented the colour bar in all its aspects. The évolués in French Africa, on the other hand, objected to the indigénat, demanded French citizenship, and also protested against their inferior social status. But French Africans nevertheless felt culturally and intellectually attached to France, and did not therefore think in terms of political independence.

On the whole, then, on the eve of the Second World War the colonial system seemed firmly entrenched and well set for a long run. Though there were demands and protests all over, these were for improvement and reform rather than for the abolition of the colonial system. Moreover, these demands were not well organized, nor did they draw mass support. Little or no *rapprochement* had as yet taken place between the élitist movements and the tribal and welfare and improvement associations of the sub-élite; neither was there much contact between the two former groups and the rural masses. In the metropolitan countries, during the late 1930s there were some discussions concerning reform, especially about integrating the educated élite a little more into the administrative machinery. But there was no talk of decolonization. However, all this was to change after the Second World War. The transformation was brought about by the war itself, as well as by the subsequent activities of the colonial powers and the impact of these activities on the colonial peoples.

The impact of World War II on the colonial system in Africa, which has been fully treated by our contributors, was truly phenomenal. There is no doubt that the war and its aftermath mark a watershed in the history of colonialism in Africa. The ideals of democracy, freedom and self-determination, the principles enunciated in the Atlantic Charter and embodied in the UN Charter, the formation of the United Nations itself, which provided a forum for the attacks on the colonial system and on the colonial powers—all these forces helped in shaping the future. Russia and the United States emerged as the two leading powers and, by a fortunate coincidence, both of them opposed the colonial system, though for very different reasons. These developments all had an incalculable effect on the metropolitan powers themselves. Hence even before the war had ended, there was reappraisal of the future of colonies among these metropolitan powers. The British certainly now conceded that their colonies should become independent. As Arthur Creech Jones put it in 1948:

The central purpose of British Colonial policy is simple. It is to guide the colonial territories to responsible government within the commonwealth in conditions that ensure to the people concerned both a fair standard of living and freedom from oppression from any quarter.[1]

What they were not sure of was the question of when and to whom power should be transferred. And most of them thought in terms of at least another forty years or so. The French, for their part, abandoned the myth of overseas provinces, but also ruled out the idea of autonomy. As it was declared at Brazzaville in 1944:

[1] Sir Charles J. Jeffries, *Transfer of power: the problem of the passage to self-government* (London, 1960), p. 15.

The aim of the civilizational work accomplished by France in her colonies rules out all idea of autonomy and all possibility of development outside the French Empire; the eventual constitution, even in a far-off future, of self-government in the colonies is likewise out of the question.

What finally led to the reversal of this policy in the late 1950s was, as will be discussed below, the military humiliation experienced by the French in Indo-China and Algeria and the consequent reluctance, if not military inability, to start a similar war in Africa south of the Sahara. As for the Belgians, they also embarked on a similar reappraisal. They ruled out the question of independence and instead decided to improve the lot of the *évolués*. In 1952 they introduced the concept of a Belgo-Congolese community. It was not until the end of 1955 that A. A. J. van Bilsen, a Belgian professor, spoke of self-government for the colonies. And even though he thought of an apprenticeship period of not less than thirty years, his views were regarded as impracticable. It was only on the Portuguese that the events of World War II had no impact.

No less profound, as most contributors have emphasized, was the impact of the war on the colonies themselves. In many colonies, the war either brought about the beginnings or accelerated the pace of urbanization as well as industrialization, especially in South Africa and Southern Rhodesia. Secondly, most of the metropolitan countries had been compelled to establish monopolistic control over the sale of primary products to support the war effort. The continuation of this practice, together with the inflationary waves and the consequent high prices of manufactured goods immediately after the war, intensified the unrest and discontent of the inter-war period. Thirdly, the use of African soldiers in Asia brought them into contact with the independence movements of the sub-continent, particularly in India, which left an indelible mark on them. This, together with the disappointments and hardships they experienced after their demobilization, made them active participants in the independence struggles.

Finally, the shortage of European civil servants contributed to appointment of Africans to posts that had hitherto been the exclusive preserves of Europeans. It was, for instance, in the middle of the war, in 1942, that two Ghanaians were appointed for the first time as assistant district commissioners; and it was also in that same year that the governor appointed two other Ghanaians to his executive council.[1] Of course,

---

[1] Florence Mabel Bourret, *Ghana, the road to independence, 1919-1957*, 3rd [rev.] ed. (Stanford University Press, 1960), p. 135.

this trend could not be reversed after the war. In eastern, southern and Portuguese Africa, the end of the war saw also a great increase in the white settler population that blocked most of the channels of economic advancement for Africans. Indeed, according to Bennett, the number of Europeans in Kenya and in Northern and Southern Rhodesia doubled in the years after World War II, while the number in Angola rose from 40,000 in 1940 to 72,000 in 1950, and in Moçambique from 27,500 to 48,000. The psychological impact of the war on Africans, which has been brilliantly summarized by Miss Bourret, merits full quotation here:

To the quickening process brought about by the war in certain phases of economic and political development can also be added the psychological effect which wider contacts with world affairs had upon the West Africans. This influence, of course, made itself felt more in the urban and coastal areas and among the soldiers who served overseas than in the rural districts of the hinterland. The increased opportunities for technical and administrative training gave the Africans powers which resulted in a deeper self-confidence and determination to take a more active part in their country's development. The presence of large groups of allied service personnel in the Gold Coast, the visits of officials from the United Kingdom, the efforts of the information department and the British Council to acquaint people, not only with the facts of the war, but with the idealism which lay behind it, all tended to increase a sense of empire solidarity and to widen the Africans' world out-look as well. The end of the war found the Gold Coast ready and impatient to make great advances in the peace era ahead.[1]

It was not the Gold Coast, now Ghana, alone that was impatient, but the whole of colonial Africa!

All the colonial powers did, in fact, take account of this impatience and effected a number of constitutional, social and economic changes. The British introduced the Burns and Richards constitutions in 1946 and 1947 in the Gold Coast and Nigeria, respectively. They also drew up plans for accelerated educational development, and even for the establishment of universities in their colonies in Africa; and as early as 1940 they set up the Colonial and Welfare Development Fund to finance development in the colonies. (The British thereby extended the scope of the Colonial Development Fund first created in 1929.) The French brought about even more far-reaching changes by the constitution of October 1946. Forced labour was abolished, and all

[1] *Ghana*, pp. 155–6.

inhabitants of the French colonies were made French citizens and therefore able to exercise full civic rights. Above all, the French African colonies, now termed territories, were not only given electoral rights and an elected assembly each, but they could together elect twenty-three deputies to represent them in the French National Assembly in Paris. Like the British, they also set up the Fonds d'Investissement pour le Développement Economique et Social d'Outre-Mer (FIDES) to finance developments in the colonies.

Belgium also introduced changes in the light of the new ferment of ideas generated by the UN Charter. In 1947, for instance, eight people were made members of the Conseil du Gouvernement to represent African interests, and by 1951 all the members were Africans. A year later regulations about the attainment of the status of *évolué* were also relaxed. From then on, even certain distinguished but illiterate Africans, as well as Africans who could read and write and who were not polygamists or had not been convicted for certain stated offences within the previous five years, became eligible for the Assembly. The Belgians also later founded the Catholic University of Louvanium.

Even the Portuguese belatedly drew up an Overseas Development Plan for 1953 to 1958, though their social and political policies, including contract labour, remained unchanged. It was not until after 1953 that attempts were made by the Portuguese to introduce some local government reforms and to correct the abuses in the contract labour system.

But these changes fell far short of the hopes and aspirations generated by the war among both the upper-echelon and sub-élites. An analysis of, say, the Burns constitution of 1946 introduced into Ghana will explain this point. This constitution not only brought about for the first time the legislative union of Asante and the Colony regions; it also for the first time gave the Africans a majority—18 out of 31 members of the Council were to be Africans. Yet the constitution failed to meet the aspirations of either the élite or the wage-earners, for only 5 of the 18 African members were to be elected, and those only by the inhabitants of the four municipalities of Cape Coast, Sekondi-Takoradi, Kumasi and Accra. The remaining 13 were to be chosen by the two Councils of Chiefs of the Colony and Asante.[1] The other

---

[1] Francis Alan Roscoe Bennion, *The constitutional law of Ghana* (London, 1962), pp. 37–9; and Dennis Austin, *Politics in Ghana, 1946–1960* (London and New York, Oxford University Press, 1964), pp. 49–52.

13 members were to be *ex-officio* and nominated members. The constitution therefore meant a return to the heyday of the system of indirect rule, marked by the supremacy of the chiefs and the colonial authorities, to the exclusion of the élite and sub-élites. It therefore stood in sharp contrast to the assemblies in the French African colonies, which were dominated by African civil servants, teachers and commercial employees. This was clearly intolerable in the light of the liberal ideas of the day and of the political aspirations expressed by the educated élite and the ex-servicemen. Not surprisingly, therefore, a constitution which had optimistically been expected to last for ten years endured for only two. Indeed, the Watson Commission set up to investigate affairs in Ghana in 1948 described the constitution as 'outmoded at birth', and went on to point out that 'with the spread of liberal ideas, increasing literacy and a closer contact with political developments in other parts of the world, the star of rule through the chiefs was on the wane'. The Commission further reported that it found 'an intense suspicion that the chiefs are being used by the Government as an instrument for the delay if not for the suppression of the political aspiration of the people'.[1]

In Belgian Africa, progress was even slower. The *évolués* did not attain legal equality with Europeans until 1952. Discrimination in housing and the exclusion of the élite from the higher grades of the civil service only ended in February 1959, after extensive riots had broken out in the preceding month. Discontent among the *évolués* thus increased in intensity with the years. And in all colonial Africa, Africans bitterly complained at such grievances as the inadequate nature of the educational facilities provided, or the high price of imported goods. In many territories, Africans likewise condemned the real or apparent stranglehold exercised by aliens, by white settlers, by Syrians, Lebanese or Indians, over the local economy.

Contrary to the interpretation of some contributors, particularly Crawford Young and Robert Delavignette, the final attack on the colonial system from the late 1940s onward was not precipitated by events in the metropolitan countries or in the United Nations. The process of decolonization was set off rather by the emergence of political parties in colonial Africa and by their multifarious activities. The reaction of the metropolitan powers was admittedly influenced by what Young calls the 'democratic heritage', by partisan conflicts within each metropolitan country and by other factors. These included con-

[1] Report of the Commission of Enquiry into Disturbances in the Gold Coast, 1948.

tradictory pressures on the part of white settlers and other colonial lobbies, world opinion and the activities of the United Nations. These forces, however, merely determined the nature and the pace of decolonization. As 'Matchet' has pointed out in the issue of *West Africa* for 9 November 1968, it was not the activities of anti-colonial movements or of people like Fenner Brockway but rather the actions of African nationalists 'which won independence for the African politicians'.[1]

I find it surprising, therefore, that little consideration has been given in this volume to the formation and activities of the parties that mushroomed in colonial Africa between 1944 and 1960.[2] These parties certainly did not emerge from the blue. They were direct products of years of social, economic and political discontent generated by the colonial system itself and above all by the feeling of frustration, humiliation and indignity among the élite or the middle class. As Anstey has shown, it was, for instance, Lumumba's feeling of frustration and his disillusionment with the Belgians' refusal to practise their professed creed in integration that turned him into such a radical leader.

There were three main reasons why these parties became such effective weapons against the colonial system in the post-war period. The first was that unlike the movements and parties of the inter-war period, these were not upper middle class bourgeoisie movements but mass movements involving the upper and lower middle class (or the higher-echelon and the sub-élites), the peasants and even in some places such as Nigeria and Ivory Coast some traditional rulers and the 'neo-traditional élite'. The leaders of these parties could and did, therefore, speak on behalf of the whole country or of a whole region, and could not thus be written off like those of the inter-war period. Secondly, these parties were much better organized and better disciplined than the earlier parties and associations. Thirdly and most important of all, they were better led. Nearly all of them had been founded or soon came to be led by men usually of lower middle class origin who had been educated abroad either in the United States or in one of the metropolitan countries. The new leaders were also radical in outlook; and unlike the conservative professional élite of the inter-war period, they were ready to use unconstitutional or even violent means or, as one of them called it, 'positive action'.

[1] *West Africa*, No. 2684, Saturday, 9 Nov. 1968, p. 1315.
[2] For a list of these parties, see Thomas L. Hodgkin, *African political parties: an introductory guide* (London, 1961), pp. 179–209.

These political parties were organized differently in British and in French Africa, and this difference in organization had a direct bearing on their effectiveness as instruments of decolonization. The political parties that emerged in British Africa after World War II were territorial parties, whereas those that appeared in French Africa were until after 1957 mainly inter-territorial parties. Typical examples were the Convention People's Party of Ghana and the Rassemblement Démocratique Africain (RDA), which covered the whole of French West and Equatorial Africa. Moreover, until 1954 nearly all the parties in French West Africa were affiliated with or were offshoots of parties in metropolitan France. It was not until after 1954 that the former severed themselves from the latter. Whereas each of the parties in British Africa could thus immediately clamour for independence for its country alone, the French African parties campaigned only on behalf of the whole of French West Africa and could not effectively demand independence. Indeed, as Kenneth Post has pointed out, even as late as June 1956 'the French Union still existed and only students and other radicals spoke seriously of independence'.[1]

Another factor which, even in British Africa, further determined the effectiveness of these parties was whether they were tribalist or regional parties or whether they were national or inter-regional in scope. If Ghana attained independence earlier than Nigeria, it was primarily because the party that spearheaded the attack on the colonial system was a national party with branches in all regions of the country and among all cultural and linguistic groups in the country. In Nigeria, on the other hand, all the parties were regional and nationalistic parties, namely, the National Council of Nigeria and the Cameroons (NCNC), mainly for the Ibo and the Eastern Region; the Action Group (AG), mainly for the Western Region and the Yoruba; and the Northern People's Congress (NPC), mainly for the Hausa-Fulani and the Northern Region. The inter-party rivalry that accompanied decolonization in Nigeria not only delayed independence but it left a legacy of regional and ethnic animosities that have drastically and tragically affected the progress of independent Nigeria. The tribalist structure of these parties in the Congo Republic (Kinshasa) similarly underlay the instability that ensued after independence.

It was the activities of these parties, led by these political leaders from 1944 onward, that won independence for Africa. Such organizations

[1] Quoted in A. Adu Boahen, *Topics in West African history* (London, 1966), p. 152.

comprised groups such as the Convention People's Party (CPP) in Ghana; the NCNC, the AG and NPC in Nigeria; the Sierra Leone People's Party (SLPP); the RDA, the Mouvement Socialiste Africain (MSA), the Parti Démocratique de Guinée (PDG) in former French West Africa; the Mouvement National Congolais (MNC) and the Alliance des Bakongo (ABAKO) in the former Belgian Congo; the Nyasaland African National Congress (NAC), later reorganized as the Malawi Congress Party (MCP); the United National Independence Party (UNIP) of Zambia; the Tanganyika African National Union (TANU); and the Kenya African Democratic Union (KADU) and the Kenya African National Union (KANU). It was not Van Bilsen's speeches and plans but the rise and activities of political parties in the Congo, especially the work of the MNC formed by Lumumba in 1958, that set in motion the events culminating in the precipitate Belgian withdrawal. Independence was not handed to most African countries on a golden platter; it was fought for. Nkrumah, Kenyatta, Banda, Kaunda became detainees or prison graduates before they became Prime Ministers or Presidents.

French decolonization in Black Africa, or, as Delavignette prefers to call it, the secession of French Africa from the French Republic, took place relatively more peacefully and over a shorter period of time than applied for most other parts of Africa. French-speaking Africans gained their independence within the space of two years, between 1958 and 1960. The reason for this was simple: the French had wasted their blood and treasure in Indo-China, where their attempts at repression culminated in the humiliating defeat at Dien Bien Phu. The French likewise suffered heavy losses in Algeria; and by the late 1950s the more intelligent Frenchmen, especially De Gaulle, realized the futility of trying to stem the anti-colonial tide. Fanon has emphasized the effect of Dien Bien Phu on the colonial peoples as well as on the colonizers:

The great victory of the Vietnamese people at Dien Bien Phu is no longer, strictly speaking, a Vietnamese victory. Since July 1954, the question which the colonised peoples have asked themselves has been 'What must be done to bring about another Dien Bien Phu? How can we manage it?' Not a single colonised individual could ever again doubt the possibility of a Dien Bien Phu; the only problem was how best to use the forces at their disposal, how to organise them, and when to bring them into action. This encompassing violence does not work upon the colonised people only; it modifies the attitude of the colonialists who became aware of manifold Dien Bien Phus.

This is why a veritable panic takes hold of the colonialist governments in turn. Their purpose is to capture the vanguard, to turn the movement of liberation towards the right and to disarm the people: quick, quick, let's decolonise. Decolonise the Congo before it turns into another Algeria. Vote the constitutional framework for all Africa, create the French *Communauté*, renovate that same *Communauté*, but for God's sake let's decolonise quick.[1]

The initial wars of independence for French and Equatorial Africa were fought in Africa itself between 1946 and 1951, but the later and decisive battles were fought on the battlefields of Indo-China and Algeria and not in Senegal or Ivory Coast or Chad.

If the struggle is still going on in Portuguese Africa and if it should become more and more bloody in southern Africa, it is because of the reaction of the Portuguese and the white settlers. And in these areas it is quite clear that the ultimate outcome is only a question of time. For however skilled technologically and administratively, however efficient, and however beneficial white minority rule may be even to Africans, settler governance, with its implicit assumption of racial superiority, its overt inequality of opportunity, its two-tiered citizenship and its denial of the dignity of the black man is bound to be overthrown sooner or later. And surely there will always be a place for any European or Indian who is prepared to integrate fully and help the process of replacing ethnic and racial consciousness by national consciousness. The real and ultimate solution to the settler problem in southern and Portuguese Africa is not the Europeanization or Portuguesation of the African, but rather the Africanization of the Boer, the Briton, the Portuguese and the Indian. The earlier this is realized and worked for, the better.

Finally, what are the main legacies that colonialism has bequeathed to independent Africa? Colonialism has indeed left its marks, both positive and negative, on Africa. Some of them will remain forever, while others will be with us for a considerable length of time. The first and most obvious, though destined to be one of the indelible positive marks, is the very physical appearance of the independent states of Africa. Virtually all the states of Africa owe their national boundaries to the activities of the colonial powers in the nineteenth century. These boundaries have not undergone any change with the overthrow of colonialism, nor are they likely to in the foreseeable future. The second positive legacy has been the infrastructure of roads, railways, harbours

[1] Fanon, *Wretched of the earth*, p. 55.

and airports. In many independent African states, a large number of roads have been widened, resurfaced or tarred, or straightened; but not many miles of new roads or railways have been added since independence. A third positive impact is urbanization. There is no doubt that many urban centres in Africa, and even the very capitals of some of the independent African states, owe their foundation or rapid growth to the colonial impact. Fourthly, we have seen the emergence of two classes unknown in traditional African society: a literate middle class and a predominantly illiterate working class. A fifth permanent feature has been the transfer of power within the African society itself. The process of decolonization has meant not only the overthrow of colonial rule, but also the transfer of power from the traditional ruling aristocracy to the new middle and lower classes. As Delavignette has pointed out, independence has not revived the powers of the great kings of pre-colonial and colonial Africa.

Still another significant contribution has been the introduction of cash crops and cash economy, and the consequent entry of African economy into the orbit of world economy. And finally, colonialism has provided the instrument for the creation of a national army. With the exception of the Gambia and a few other small territories, each independent African state inherited from the outgoing colonial power a well-established and disciplined military force.

But these legacies have their debit side as well—a fact that has greatly bedevilled the affairs of independent Africa. The very first and most crucial of these is the artificial nature of the independent states themselves. None of the boundaries drawn by the colonial powers followed ethnic or cultural lines. The result is that each independent African state is made up of a medley of peoples who differ in their history, their social institutions, their language and their culture. And one of the main problems facing leaders of these new states is how to forge loyalty and a nation-state consciousness among these heterogeneous tribes and nations or, to use the words of the late John F. Kennedy, how to make 'a nation out of these nations'. This task has been rendered even more formidable by two additional factors: first, the introduction of party politics, another legacy of colonialism as we have already seen, and the consequent emergence of parties based on ethnic groups, or nations or regions; and second, the retention in most cases of the language of the colonial power as the official language of the new state. Until and unless this problem of developing a nation-state consciousness has been solved and people begin to think of themselves as Ghanaians or Nigerians or Kenyans rather than as Asante, Ibo, Yoruba or Kikuyu, independent African states will remain unstable. A conscious attempt to promote the use of one of the languages of each independent African state as a second national language will be a step in the right direction; and it is a pity that, except for Somalia and Tanzania, none of the new states has so far taken this step.

In the next place, most of these independent African states inherited constitutions that were often mere replicas of those of the metropolitan countries and were consequently wholly unsuitable. Very often they also took over a civil service that was not sufficiently Africanized and that nearly always lacked men with managerial and technical skills. The process of drafting constitutions and of Africanizing the civil service machinery has been a characteristic preoccupation of independent African states. Most of these states were also saddled with mono-culture economies, while a majority of them lacked even the basic secondary industries. The diversification of the economy and in particular of agriculture and industrialization have loomed very large in the programmes of the new states. Then, too, colonialism has burdened Africa with the European settler problem, whose solution is not going to be easy. Even after its solution, it is destined, especially if the whites hold out much longer, to leave behind a legacy of racial animosity and tension which will plague these future multi-racial states for a long time to come.

But the last and probably the bleakest legacy was the nature of the armies that the new states inherited from the colonial powers. As Gutteridge has clearly brought out, most of these armies usually drew their rank and file from relatively backward areas, often from the interior, and sometimes from Muslim populations. The officer corps, on the other hand, was recruited from educated groups. This situation has been one of the primary sources of the tragic events of Nigeria today. Other states inherited armies whose officer corps was at the time of independence wholly European; it was a reaction against this, in fact, that touched off the troubles in the Congo Republic. In French Africa, because of the way the armies had been organized in the colonial days, they remained more loyal to France even at the time of independence than to their own states despite reorganization. This fact alone accounts partly for the way in which French-speaking Africa experienced coups at a relatively earlier stage in its development than did British Africa. Finally—and this is the fundamental cause of the coups in

Africa—soldiers tended on the whole to be better educated, better disciplined, and more efficient than the new crop of politicians. The army therefore often considered civilian mismanagement, corruption and ostentation to be intolerable evils that could be cured only by military intervention. The soldiers had arms and organization; hence military coups became virtually irresistible. It was as simple as that. Indeed, some perceptive observers had already predicted coups in Africa. In his Whidden Lectures delivered at McMaster University in 1965, several months before the Nigerian and Ghanaian coups, Professor Arthur Lewis stated:

In West Africa, as in some parts of the world, the army is likely to be a progressive force, so long as the officers retain control...The officers are better educated than politicians; deeply committed to modernization; and unimpressed by demagoguery. They will intervene only as a last resort, but intervene they will where the pressure of their families and of public discontent reaches bursting point.[1]

Barely a few months later, the army did intervene in Nigeria and about a year later in Ghana. The 'man on horseback', educated, disciplined and armed, is one of the legacies of colonialism, and he is going to breathe down the neck of the African politician for a long time to come.

Viewed in the long, very long span of the history of the African continent, the colonial epoch is one of incredibly short duration. In many parts of the continent there are people still alive who saw the first white missionary or soldier enter their town or village, the first train make its first run on the new railway line, and the first lorry cart away the first load of cocoa, cotton or coffee. But modern colonialism has left a far deeper and far more indelible and far more fundamental imprint on Africa than any of the external forces and phenomena to which the continent had previously been subjected: the Asiatic and Indonesian influence, the Roman and Carthaginian conquests, and the impact of Islam or Mohammedanism. Admittedly, the effect of colonialism has been uneven, varying in space and depth from area to area. Its imprint was more conspicuous, for instance, on the coastal areas than on the inland areas, and on urban regions than on rural regions, where life has been running gaily along following patterns that are centuries old. But by its disruption of the existing political organization and its creation of the present independent states, by its generation of

[1] William Arthur Lewis, *Politics in West Africa* (London, 1965), pp. 87–8.

the new classes of Africans, by its introduction of cash-economy and above all by its spread of education and the Western way of life, colonialism has launched Africa on a course of development that is fundamentally different from its earlier patterns. The future development of our continent depends largely on our own efforts, above all on the co-operation between the independent African states as well as on the world outside.

BIBLIOGRAPHY

Apter, David E. *Ghana in transition*. Rev. ed. New York, 1963.

Austin, Dennis. *Politics in Ghana, 1946–1960*. London and New York, Oxford University Press, 1964.

Bennion, Francis Alan Roscoe. *The constitutional law of Ghana*. London, 1962.

Boahen, A. Adu. *Topics in West African history*. London, 1966.

Bourret, Florence Mabel. *Ghana, the road to independence, 1919–1957*. 3rd [rev.] ed. Stanford University Press, 1960.

Fanon, Frantz. *The wretched of the earth*, trans. by Constance Farrington. New York, 1963.

Gold Coast. Legislative Council Debates. 1939.

Gold Coast (Colony) Commission of Enquiry into Disturbances in the Gold Coast. Report, 1948. London, HMSO, 1948. (Colonial no. 231).

Hodgkin, Thomas L. *African political parties: an introductory guide*. London, 1916.

Jeffries, Sir Charles J. *Transfer of power: the problems of the passage to self-government*. London, 1960.

Lewis, William Arthur. *Politics in West Africa*. London, 1965.

West Africa, No. 2684, Saturday, 9 Nov. 1968.

EPILOGUE

When Macaulay began his great history of England just over a century ago, he vowed to tell a splendid tale. He promised to relate how, through an auspicious welding of order and freedom, there had sprung a prosperity the like of which was not to be found in the annals of human affairs. He said he would undertake to show further how England's opulence and martial glory had grown together; how a gigantic commerce had given birth to a mighty maritime power; how the British colonies in America had become far more formidable than the realms which Cortez and Pizarro had added to the dominions of Charles V; how the British in Asia had founded an empire as splendid as that of Alexander the Great, and far more enduring.[1]

Macaulay's mood reflected the self-congratulatory optimism that characterized a good deal, though by no means all, of mid-Victorian thought. Sentiments of a similar nature later found expression in the traditional historiography concerning white empire-building in Africa. Colonial administrators like Sir Harry Johnston and scholars such as Sir Reginald Coupland wrote of imperial conquest in terms of moral approval—however much they deplored individual abuses. The white man's empires, in their view, had immeasurably added to the wealth and happiness of the entire world.

No present-day English historian writes like Macaulay. No annalist of European colonialism describes white expansion in terms of unqualified praise. Most European intellectuals have rather experienced a prolonged period of cultural self-criticism. African scholars, for their part, wish to reassess their past, to find new pride in their history, and to liberate themselves from the ideological shackles of the colonial age. The present collection of essays reflects the changing climate of opinion; hence the imperial sentiments once expressed by Rhodes or Lyautey do not appear in the foregoing pages.

On the contrary, a good many scholars have become sceptical concerning the value of the record of the European overseas, though they have not resolved the more detailed disputes concerning the history of the white colonialist in Africa. Revolutionary socialists, as well as African nationalists and their white supporters, consider the colonial

[1] Thomas Babington Macaulay, *The history of England from the accession of James II* (Philadelphia, 1879), I, 1–2.

era as an age of plunder, where a favoured few made super-profits at their black subjects' expense. Most reformist liberals, on the other hand, rather tend to argue that colonialism did not really pay, that conquest in Africa was a temporary aberration, that the search for imperial glory only squandered resources which might more profitably have been used in the metropolitan countries. The present study leaves the question undecided; differing conclusions may be drawn from the material presented by the various contributors, though the editors' own findings do not support the Leninist thesis.

Opinions likewise differ sharply with regard to the place of the colonial era within the wider context of African history. Here again, contrasting ideologies make strange bedfellows. Old-fashioned imperialists and Marxist–Leninists alike consider the imperial era as an age of cataclysmic importance—whether for good or for ill. The revisionist, Afrocentric school, on the other hand, remains divided. Boahen's conclusion to the present volume suggests that the last seventy or eighty years of colonial rule have been fraught with profounder consequences for Africa than any previous era of foreign influence or conquests. Scholars such as Ajayi, on the other hand, stress the continuity of African development. They regard the colonial interlude as a brief episode of limited importance. This interpretation we do not share ourselves. On the contrary, we would emphasize the tremendous impact made by Western technology, not only in the field of economic development, but also in the sphere of thought. There was, of course, nothing peculiarly African about this phenomenon. Many of the more thoughtful black people may in some ways have echoed the sentiment expressed by Heine, a sensitive romantic poet and in many ways a pre-industrial man *par excellence*, upon witnessing the opening of two small French railways during the early 1840s:

The opening...has occasioned a tremor here, which everyone must sense who does not remain in a state of complete social isolation...While the mass of the people simply look with amazement and in a state of daze at these great motive forces, the philosopher is gripped by an uncanny sense of awe which we always experience when something incredible, something tremendous happens—an event whose consequences are unforeseeable and incalculable...The most elementary concepts of time and space themselves have begun to tremble in the balance.[1]

[1] Freely translated from Heinrich Heine, 'Lutezia, Berichte über Politik, Kunst und Volksleben' (letter dated 5 May 1843), *Sämtliche Werke* (Leipzig, 1911), IX, 291–2.

We do not know how African thinkers may have looked upon the technological revolution which began to burst upon their countries during the imperial era some two generations later. But we may justifiably assume that more sensitive Africans may have reacted in a manner not wholly dissimilar to Heine's.

The economic revolution led to the creation of new groups. Most of our collaborators have rightly stressed the importance of the new African élites, their rise during the colonial years, and their part in bringing about the end of the imperial system. But the contributors by no means agree on the exact part played by this élite in the struggle for African independence. Boahen emphasizes the political parties formed by the élite and their supporters among the people at large. He looks further afield too, and argues that African liberties were also won abroad, especially on the battlefields of Indo-China, where the French army wasted away its strength. We ourselves would have placed even more emphasis on World War II. The Indo-Chinese and Algerian revolutions themselves owe a great deal to the German break-through at Sedan in 1940, perhaps one of the decisive battles affecting the history of Africa. If the Axis powers had subsequently won the war, or even if Great Britain had concluded a compromise peace, the fate of Africa would presumably have been different. Indigenous parties led by the new élites would have had fewer opportunities for shaping Africa's future. In days to come, the historians of decolonization may lay more stress, too, on the metropolitan 'conscience vote' (one that did not play an equally significant influence in the white settlement colonies on African soil). More emphasis in the future may be placed also on the inability of the colonial powers to pursue a concerted policy in Africa, or indeed to formulate any long-term plans.

Assessments concerning the place of the African élites in internal African politics have varied just as widely as the evaluation of their role in bringing about the end of the colonial system; and the historians of the future are likely to continue to disagree in their interpretation of the record. The majority of the old-fashioned colonial administrators believed that the educated Africans did not speak for the masses. According to the typical British district commissioner writing a letter home in the 1920s, the black élites were at best a small, unrepresentative group of unusual people—at worst 'veranda boys', disputatious barrack room lawyers 'out to make trouble among the natives', and thereby to feather their own nests. In this respect there was no difference between a white settler leader like Sir Charles Coghlan (the first premier of Southern Rhodesia) and a dedicated imperial civil servant such as Lord Lugard. Lugard indeed felt convinced—though with some reservations—that 'it is extremely difficult at present to find educated African youths who are by character and temperament suited to posts in which they may rise to positions of high administrative responsibility'.[1]

During the 1930s, and to an even greater extent during the 1940s and 1950s, such views became unacceptable to most Western academics. The black élite gradually obtained political legitimacy in the anti-colonialists' mind, while the white rulers lost theirs. The future supposedly lay with the detribalized and educated city-dwellers who would build countries like Nigeria into cohesive nations. Tribal traditions and affiliations were considered increasingly less relevant. Tribalism was destined to be swept into the dust-bin of history—together with the tawdry tinsel of empire.

Now the pendulum is once more swinging the other way. Black revolutionaries in Africa talk of 'a second independence' and belabour the 'new tribe, the Wabenze', the profiteers of decolonization, who drive around in Mercedes–Benz cars. Both black and white scholars in the West are likewise reassessing the role played by the 'new men'. Again the language of scholarship uses terms that strangely echo the language used by old-fashioned district officers with regard to their black clerks. Some investigators are currently stressing that the new élite is above all an 'administrative bourgeoisie' that depends on state and party patronage, and that does not really represent the masses. Martin Kilson, an Afro-American scholar, indeed speaks of a pseudo-élite which all too often indulges in 'a ritualistic game' of acting out élite roles that they cannot in fact fulfil.[2] Many deplore the extent of bribery and corruption in the new states. Some deride in bitter terms the growing black 'kleptocracy'. But Africans in fact have nothing to learn in the way of graft from foreigners, be they Tammany Hall politicians of modern fame or British aristocrats who used to manage parliamentary connexions two hundred years ago. Liberia's modern patronage system, for instance, would not have shocked the writer of that mid-eighteenth century English epitaph (recorded in Trevelyan's *English social history*) who proudly wrote:

[1] Lord Lugard, *The dual mandate in tropical Africa* (London, 1965), p. 88.
[2] Martin Kilson, 'African autocracy', *Africa Today*, April 1966, p. 5.

Here rests all that was mortal of Mrs. Elizabeth Bate
Relict of the Reverend Richard Bate,
A woman of unaffected piety
And exemplary virtue.

She was honourably descended
And by means of her Alliance to
The illustrious family of Stanhope
She had the merit to obtain
For her husband and children
Twelve several employments
In Church and State.[1]

Any discussion of the élites in Africa also raises the question of the continent's white, Indian and Lebanese minorities. The European settlers have acquired particular importance, and the great majority of Victorian imperialists would have regarded these European pioneers as the élite *par excellence*. The new historiography, however, has demoted the settler from this proud place. Many scholars, in fact, would refuse to regard the white colonists as an élite at all, but rather as a parasitic remnant. There are indeed some interesting parallels between current reassessments of the settler's role, and the revisionist interpretation of British history current in the 1930s. The critical manner in which scholars like Kitson Clark now reassess the often somewhat emotional and moralistic views expressed by J. L. and Barbara Hammond concerning the Victorian bourgeoisie of England might also be usefully applied to white settlerdom in Africa—a course which the editors have attempted to follow.[2]

The present volume ends with decolonization in the late 1950s and early 1960s. But already an emotional gap separates much of the present-day scholarly world from those earlier years. The short period of decolonization was one of hope for the committed. Many political scientists wrote grandly of 'nation building', of 'mobilization states' in terms that often seem simplistic today. Such disappointments, however, should hardly surprise us. When the old eastern European empires broke up after World War I, when successor states like Czechoslovakia, Poland and Lithuania gained their independence, the new *Staatsvölker*

[1] G. M. Trevelyan, *English social history: a survey of six centuries, Chaucer to Queen Victoria* (London, 1946 ed.), p. 359.
[2] G. Kitson Clark, *The making of Victorian England: being the Ford lectures delivered before the University of Oxford* (Cambridge, Mass., Harvard University Press, 1962).

commonly experienced a brief moment of euphoria. This mood generally gave way to a more sober or a more pessimistic outlook as the years went by. The new African states frequently find themselves in a similar predicament. Many Africans, especially the poor, expected independence to usher in a Messianic age of peace and plenty. But the manifold problems that have beset Africa in the past, and that will continue to plague her in the future, cannot disappear by some sudden magic; hence many hopes necessarily remain unfulfilled.

Again—and this is worth stressing—there was nothing peculiarly African in this predicament. British people in the early 1830s believed that electoral reform would cure all the country's ills. Said Sydney Smith:

All young ladies will imagine, as soon as the [Reform] Bill passed, that they will be instantly married. School-boys believe that gerunds and supines will be abolished, and that currant tarts must come down in price; the corporal and the sergeant are sure of double pay; bad poets will expect a demand for their epics.[1]

In like manner, decolonization raised many unrealistic expectations. The new élites were often unable to carry out their promises. Besides, they used their positions in many cases to enrich themselves at public expense; and they were able to do so because they controlled—if not the means of production—at least those of administration and coercion. Economic development, on the other hand, remains widely dependent on foreign capital and initiative, no matter whether derived from Western or Eastern sources. Economic growth, by force of circumstances, is as uneven in speed and in character as before, and often lags far behind the planners' hopes. Neither Western parliamentary democracy, nor—for that matter—communism of the Russian or Chinese variety, has taken root in African soil, despite the dedication displayed by a new army of secular missionaries who wish to shape that recalcitrant continent in their own image.

Parliamentary régimes have widely given way to one-party states, complete with preventive detention laws, organized adulation for the country's leader, and a new historical mythology. But the one-party states have not developed the cohesion and discipline expected by their makers. Instead, the first-generation leaders have in many cases been

[1] Cited in André Maurois, *Disraeli: a picture of the Victorian age* (New York, 1928), pp. 62–3.

displaced by army coups, and the soldier's power is on the rise in many African countries. Even militant socialists, relying on a populist terminology, men like Kwame Nkrumah in Ghana or (at the time of writing in 1968) Modibo Keita in Mali, have been overthrown by officers. The 'new African', moreover, has by no means been detribalized—indeed the very word has passed from the vocabulary of social anthropologists. On the contrary, ethnic affinities remain strong. Countries like the Congo Republic (Kinshasa), Nigeria and Zanzibar have been shaken by savage inter-ethnic clashes, comparable in certain respects to the bitter outbreaks that once set Croats against Serbs, or Greeks against Turks in eastern Europe. The Muslims of the northern Sudan are engaged in savage warfare against Christian and pagan dissidents in the southern part of the country. The Tuareg of the desert in Mali do not willingly accept the authority of southern Negroes. The Somali of Kenya and those of Ethiopia often wish to throw off the governance exercised by their existing rulers in order to join the Greater Somali Republic. Some African states have arrived at regional working arrangements; but Pan-Africanism, preached at so many international conferences, still remains an ideal for the distant future.

Contrary to many predictions current in the early 1960s, moreover, Western European influence remains powerful in Africa. The former colonial powers, especially France, continue to play their part in many African countries. Above all, the supposedly irresistible tides of history have not swept away the last European bastions in southern Africa. Portugal, the smallest and weakest of the Western colonial powers, continues to pour money and men into its threatened colonies. Despite the assaults of black guerrillas, the bulk of the Portuguese empire remains firmly under Lisbon's control. White Rhodesians have hoisted their own green, white and green flag of independence and have, with their minuscule resources, defied alike the mother country, the United Nations, and what passes for world opinion at large. South Africa remains the industrial giant of the continent. Its military and industrial potential, which has vastly increased over the past twenty years, greatly exceeds the might of all black states combined. One can, in fact, speak of a white counter-revolution by which Portuguese, Rhodesians and South Africans have consolidated their strength, and indeed are trying to gain some influence beyond their borders.

These complex issues cannot be resolved in a brief epilogue. We should, however, like to draw the reader's attention to the fact that

Volumes I and II have been concerned primarily with history and politics. Hence many of our collaborators have had more to say on the leaders than on the followers. The majority of our contributors have dealt with the men who made the empires, with those who maintained them, and with those who sundered them. While the various authors have referred also to the masses, the great illiterate, anonymous majority has generally taken second place in our first two volumes of essays. The general editors thus look forward to the publication of the third volume, to be edited by Victor Turner, a social anthropologist, who, with his team, will deal with additional aspects of imperialism, especially with its social impact on the peoples of Africa. That forthcoming study, as well as a projected volume on economics, will thus fill the gaps which, by force of circumstances, remain in the first two volumes, and will serve to place the preceding essays into a wider social context.

LEWIS H. GANN

PETER DUIGNAN

Editors

BIBLIOGRAPHY

Heine, Heinrich. 'Lutezia, Berichte über Politik, Kunst und Volksleben' (letter dated 5 May 1843), *Sämtliche Werke*, Vol. IX. Leipzig, 1911.

Kilson, Martin. 'African autocracy', *Africa Today*, April 1966.

Kitson Clark, George S. Roberts. *The making of Victorian England: being the Ford lectures delivered before the University of Oxford.* Harvard University Press, 1962.

Lugard, Frederick John Dealtry Lugard, 1st baron. *The dual mandate in tropical Africa.* London, 1965.

Macaulay, Thomas Babington. *The history of England from the accession of James II*, Vol. I. Philadelphia, 1879.

Maurois, André. *Disraeli: a picture of the Victorian age.* New York, 1928.

Trevelyan, G. M. *English social history: a survey of six centuries, Chaucer to Queen Victoria.* London, 1946 ed.

INDEX

ABAKO (Alliance des Bakongo), 519;
counter-manifesto, 218–20
ADAPES (Association des Anciens Elèves
des Pères de Scheut), 199, 367
AEF (Afrique Equatoriale Française), *see*
French Equatorial Africa
AG (Action Group, in Nigeria), 518, 519
AOF (Afrique Occidentale Française), *see*
French West Africa
Abd-el-Krim, 13
Abidjan, 240, 243
Aborigines Rights Protection Society
(Gold Coast, 1897), 39, 378
Abyssinia, *see* Ethiopia
Abyssinian refugees, 439
Accra, 76, 306, 455, 459
Achimota School (Gold Coast, *see also*
Prince of Wales College), 353 and n.,
430, 431, 443, 506
Action Group, *see* AG
Administration, French colonial (after
1946), difficulties of, 226–8
Administration of colonial territories
(1919–39, *see also* Administrators *and*
Colonial services), 282–4, 321–3, 329–42;
middle ranks of, 283–4; structure of,
329–30, 331 (*table*); Portuguese, in
Angola, 330–2, 341; French, in West
Africa, 332–4, 341–2; British, in Kenya
and Nigeria, 334–6, 338–40; Belgian, in
the Congo, 336–8, 342
Administrators, European (*see also* Administration), 323–50; of districts, 323;
qualifications and sources of, 323–4;
training of, 324; grading and promotion
of, 325; 'stability' (continuity of
service) of, 325–7; and anthropology
and local languages, 325, 326–7; and
'law and order', 327; and administration, 327–8; local and central interchange of, 328; time spent 'in the bush',
328–9; and 'paper work', 328; distribution of, 329 (*table*); relations of, with
local chiefs, 327–38 *passim*; as magistrates, 341–3; socio-economic roles of,

344–8; their knowledge (and lack of
knowledge) of Africans, 349–50
Africa Inland Mission, 444
African Affairs Board (Federation of
Rhodesia and Nyasaland), 73, 74, 75
African Languages and Cultures, Inter-
national Institute of, 434
African Methodist Episcopal Churches
(USA), 435
African Morning Post, 50
African National Congresses, 73, 363
African women: importance of, 284;
education and training of, 432
Africanization: 150 and n. 2; in Zambia,
84, 299; present policy of, 164; of
Officer ranks, 295; of public services,
314, 493–7, 510, 513; of legislative coun-
cils, 511; of executive councils, 513, 515
Afrifa, Colonel Akwasi A., 317
Afrikaner Nationalist Party, 125–6, 126, 152
Afrikaners, 104, 105, 118, 119, 121, 141,
152; society, 124; social evolution of,
124–5; in Rhodesia, 126; racial policies
of, 147; attitude to natives modified,
157; linguistic nationalism, 161; and
world opinion, 456
Aggrey, Dr J. E. Kwegyir, 429
Agona Local Council (Ghana), 370n.
Agricultural credit institutions, 357
Agricultural enterprise: early, 103, 104;
Bantu, 100; white and black, 105
Ahidjo, Ahmadou, 474, 490
Ajasa, Sir Kitoyi, 43, 44 and n. 1
Akim Abuakwa (state), 41, 42 n. 1; *see also*
Atta I
Akiwumi, A. M., 384 and n. 2
Algeria, 14, 262, 278, 301, 452, 460, 513,
519; and France in UN, 458; revolutions
in (1954 and 1957–62), 461–2, 468; an
example to other emergent states, 460,
461; elections 'farce' in, 463; deputies
from, in National Assembly, 465;
situation 'out of hand', 468–9; xenophobic nationalism in, 469; Soustelle's
policy for, *quoted*, 469; French public

INDEX

Capital investment (*cont.*)
120, 122; in Tanzania (local), 150; locally controlled sources of, 392

Capitalism *and* capitalists, 101, 144, 351, 352; Indian family, 146–7; exploitation by, 453; Belgian, in the Congo, 477–8

Carnarvon Commission Report (1879, on imperial defence), 307

Carriers (porters), native, 7 n. 2, 10 and n. 1, 16, 18, 228, 307

Carter, Sir Morris, 69

Casablanca, 453

Caseley Hayford, J. E., 39

Cash-crop producers (*see also* Cash crops), 103, 321, 355–8 *passim*, 365, 370–3 *passim*, 387, 392, 507–8; associations and federations of, 371–3, 372 n.; cooperative societies for, 357–8, 370–3 *passim*

Cash crops (*see also* Cash-crop producers), 36, 50, 86, 103, 227–8, 239, 241, 270, 321, 344, 352, 355–8, *passim*, 365, 370–3 *passim*, 392, 402 and n. 2, 413, 417, 504; and political organizations, 371–2; special training for production of, 371 n. 2; delayed, 400–1; during colonial period, 407–8

Caton-Thompson, Gertrude, 27

Catroux, General Georges, 469

Cavendish-Bentinck, Major (*later* Sir) F. W., 69, 70, 82–3, 85, 86

Central African Federation, *see* Federation of Rhodesia and Nyasaland

Central African Republic (*formerly* Oubangui-Chari, q.v.), 273, 296

Centre de Regroupement Africain, *see* CEREA

Cercles des Evolués (in Belgian Congo), 205, 213

Césaire, Aimé, 273

Chad (state), 21, 228, 241, 252, 255, 267, 270, 273, 280 n., 286, 292, 295, 296, 481; and de Gaulle, 247; independence for, 460, 520

Chad, Lake, 270, 305

Chagga, 64, 414 n.

Chamberlain, Joseph, 287

Charte Coloniale (1908, Belgian), 206

Chiefs, the new African (*see also* Elites, neo-traditional), 349–50

Chiefs, Paramount: in Belgian Congo, 337; in French West Africa, 333; in

Gold Coast, 41, 42 n. 1, 361, 372–3, 373 n. 1

Chiefs, 'straw' (of French West Africa), 333, 336

Chiefs, traditional and tribal *and* chieftainship (*see also* Elites, neo-traditional), 35, 36, 40, 42, 54, 272, 276, 283, 341–2, 481, 505; and the 'new men', 35–45, 48, 55; in legislative councils, 41, 42 and n. 1, 48, 378, 510, 511; British attitude to, 46; in Gold Coast Colony, 48; in French colonies, 236–7, 252, 263–4; after 1946, 267; importance of, 267; as recruiting officers, 286, 298; their sovereignty alienated, 320; and the language question, 327; relationships of colonial administrators with, 327, 329–38 *passim*; their knowledge of, and control over, Africans, 348; in new African élites, 358–62 *passim*; and Western education and culture, 358–9; schools for the sons of, 359; educated, 360; wealth, incomes and practices of, 360–2; salaries of, 360–2, 361 (*tables*); peculation by, 362; and 'plebeian' advice, 369; in local government, 374; political influence of, 374–6, 376 (*table*); early hierarchical, 402 and n. 3; their powers modified by colonization, 405 and n. 1; slave-dealers become cocoa-farmers, 405 n. 2; in colonial bureaucracies, 409 and n. 2; as agents of colonial administration, 412 and n. 2, 413, 416; losing their influence, 413–14, 446; supplanted by the new élite, 460, 465; and their mining royalties, 508–9; and the élite and representation on legislative councils, 510, 511; 'no longer suitable as agents of government' (Watson Commission), 516; suspected of being used to suppress popular political aspirations, 516

Chiefs, Warrant, 340

China, 'General' (of Mau Mau), 412 n. 4

Christian Literature for Africa, International Committee on, 434

Church Missionary Society (CMS), 444

Church of Scotland Mission, 423

Churchill, (Sir) Winston S., 247, 248

Circumcision, female 66, 443–4

Civil servants, African, 271–6 *passim*, 282–4, 409 and n. 1; middle ranks of, 283–4

537

Mining (*see also* Copperbelt), 103, 112–20, 352, 356; companies, 107, 108, 114, 115–16; prospectors, 112–13; 'small workers', 113–14; living conditions, 114
Mission schools, Christian, 351–4 *passim*, 358–9
Missionaries *and* missions, Christian (*see also* Mission schools *and* Missionary), 27, 36, 66, 73, 74, 95, 96, 102, 127, 137, 151, 157, 174, 187–8, 203, 208, 233, 243, 244, 322 n. a, 348, 349, 403, 410; and new African élites, 351–3, 354, 356; families in penury, 423; beginning to question their role in Africa, 424
Missionary and humanitarian interests (*see also* Missionaries), 422–48; World War I, and after, 422–6; self-questioning among, 425; inter-mission jealousy, 426; African reaction to, 426; recovery and recuperation, 426–7; and indigenous African participation, 427; Roman Catholic missions and a native clergy, 427; and African sovereign peoples, 428; and educational services, 428–32, 434–5; inter-denominational cooperation, 428; Jesse Jones commission on African education, 429; educational establishments set up, 430; pros and cons of church-organized education, 430–1; in French colonies, 432; in Belgian Congo, 432–3; in Portuguese colonies, 433–4; and African languages and cultures, 434; and books written in African languages and in basic English, 434; and the 'trusteeship principle' applied to all colonies, 435, 436; and social evils generally, 437, 440; especially alcoholism, 437–8; and health and sanitation, 438–9; and refugees, 439; and Christianity and African culture, 440–4; and African independent churches, 445–7; undaunted by errors and failures, 447–8; team-work and present activities, 447; and the future, 448
Missionary Association in Portuguese East Africa, 433
Missionary societies, Christian, 233, 423, 433, 444, 506; educational and medical functions of, 3
Missionary Statute (1941, Portuguese), 188
Mitchell, Sir Philip, 69–70, 71, 85, 86

Mitterand, François, 273
Moçambique (Portuguese East Africa, *see also* Portuguese colonies), 8, 15, 19, 171, 174, 406; Portuguese (urban) population of, 175, 176; during World War II, 176; railway construction, 176; transformed, 176–7; immigrants (1830–1960), 177; a *colonato* in, 178; *assimilados* in, 179; colour discrimination in, 180; Africans in, how governed, 181–2; municipal courts in (1954), 182–3; Portuguese control in, 183; labour law of, 184; scarcity of labour in, 185; migratory labour from, 186; co-operative colonies in, 187; missionaries in (mid-1950s), 188; African Catholics in, 188; education of Africans in, 188–9; health, 189; Portuguese citizenship for Africans, 191; a multiracial colony (?), 191, 192; military forces, 300, 301; African risings in, 301, 332; European settlers increased in, after World War II, 514
Moffat, Howard Unwin, 137
Moffat, John (*later* Sir John), 73–4, 74
Mohammed V, Sultan of Morocco, 453, 468, 471
Mohammedanism, *see* Islam
Mohammedans, *see* Muslims
Mollet, Guy, 469, 471, 472, 483
Mombasa, 4, 85, 313
Monckton Commission and Report (1959/60), 80, 81–2
Mondjeni-Mobe, J., 200 and n. 1
Monrovia (in Liberia), 431
Morel, E. D, 101
Morocco, French, 13, 231, 245, 294, 452, 458, 460, 461, 468, 471, 481, 482, 494–5; independence for, 468, 470, 486
Morocco, Spanish, 13
Moslems, *see* Muslims
Mosmans, Father Guy, 207
Mossi (kingdom and people), 237, 239, 267, 277, 344, 481; Nabas, 252, 267, 481
Moutet, Marius, 232, 255
Mouvement d'Evolution de la Population Africaine, 271
Mouvement National Congolais, *see* MNC
Mouvement National Populaire, *see* MNP
Mouvement Républicain Populaire, *see* MRP
Mouvement Socialiste Africain, *see* MSA

s book is